A L I V E

I N   T H E

S O U N D

REFIGURING AMERICAN MUSIC

A SERIES EDITED BY RONALD RADANO,

JOSH KUN, AND NINA SUN EIDSHEIM

CHARLES McGOVERN, CONTRIBUTING EDITOR

ALIVE IN THE SOUND

BLACK MUSIC AS COUNTERHISTORY

RONALD RADANO

DUKE UNIVERSITY PRESS · DURHAM AND LONDON · 2025

Project Editor: Ihsan Taylor
Designed by Matthew Tauch
Typeset in Alegreya and Retail by
Westchester Publishing Services

Library of Congress Cataloging-in-Publication Data
Names: Radano, Ronald Michael author
Title: Alive in the sound : Black music as
counterhistory / Ronald Radano.
Other titles: Black music as counterhistory |
Refiguring American music
Description: Durham : Duke University Press, 2025. | Series:
Refiguring american music | Includes bibliographical
references and index.
Identifiers: LCCN 2024053635 (print)
LCCN 2024053636 (ebook)
ISBN 9781478032175 paperback
ISBN 9781478028918 hardcover
ISBN 9781478061137 ebook
Subjects: LCSH: African Americans—Music—History and criticism |
Music—United States—History and criticism | Music and race—
United States | Black people—Race identity—United States
Classification: LCC ML3556 .R23 2025 (print) | LCC ML3556 (ebook) |
DDC 780.89/96073—dc23/eng/20250603
LC record available at https://lccn.loc.gov/2024053635
LC ebook record available at https://lccn.loc.gov/2024053636

Cover art: Installation view, *Terry Adkins Recital*, Tang Museum,
2012. Artwork: Terry Adkins, *Off Minor (from Black Beethoven)*,
2004. Wood, steel, brass, 48 × 80 × 48 inches. Courtesy of
Paula Cooper Gallery and the Frances Young Tang Teaching
Museum and Art Gallery at Skidmore College.
Photograph by Arthur Evans.

IN MEMORY OF

TEJUMOLA OLANIYAN

· 1959 — 2019 ·

CONTENTS

Although we might assume life to exist nearly everywhere on earth, it startles the imagination to think something living and breathing could inhabit the realm of sound. Alive in the sound? What could that mean? And yet there it is, or at least there it appears to be.

Not just in any sound, though. For nearly two hundred years, Americans—and through their influence, listeners around the world—have engaged in a kind of magical thinking about US Black music, attributing its tremendous power to qualities thought to extend from the body and spirit of Black being. The multiple discourses describing its expression—the realness of R&B and hip-hop; the sensuous grit of funk; the transcendence of soul; the transfiguring intensities of groove; the unearthly shake, rattle, and roll of a boogie band—are enactments of an interracial agreement about the music's embodied character, an implicit pact on its remarkable ability to reveal the depths of Black experience. Black music's perceived attachments to Black physicality have everything to do with this tacit understanding. Not only do they commonly orient African American listening; they also enable those who are not Black to experience the music's spectacular effect. Despite the widespread awareness of Black music's unique qualities of animated expression, though, most of us have not considered how musical links to the Black body came into being, how the origin of the music's enlivened character traces to an era founded on racial animus and economic struggle: the disposition of modern listening is born of a time when fantastical ideas about a highly valued and subjected Black personhood ruled the land. Sensations of aliveness that seem so uplifting today descend from a long racial past, their endurance fundamental to the history of Black music's value-making.

If Black music's embodied character is now mainly gestured to indirectly through a joyous language of emotion and affect, it is only because the perception contradicts what we already know to be true. Science, after all, has proven that race is not real and that humans are biologically the same. Still, assumptions about Black music's sensible presence persist:

they inspire the apprehension of an ontological peculiarity that, many contend, identifies why Black music is superior to other forms. This same peculiar sensation, moreover, underlies contrasting opinions among those who remain skeptical about the music. If for some Black music's exuberance and drive enable it to reach incredible aesthetic heights, for its detractors the same traits explain why it lacks credibility altogether. What endures as a never-ending tension also indicates a distinctive pattern of growth, with each position in its own way expressive of the belief that there is, indeed, a quality of aliveness animating Black sound.

The enlivened presences heard and felt in Black music are something more than idle fantasy. They are ideological sensations, symptoms of a common sense deeply ingrained in the racial imagination and traceable to Black music's initial conceptualization in the US South. As the book examines, modern-era notions of aliveness have their origin in the 1840s, two decades before the US Civil War, when enslaved workers in their various labors invented a vast musical pageantry, often stunning White listeners who took it to be a sonic outgrowth of "Negro" being. Having been granted this uncanny physical capacity, African and African American slaves invested in it heavily, their sounding practices becoming a critical component of culture-making and a way for them to participate in a nascent entertainment economy. The act of buying and selling Black music—with performances introduced into the market by slave masters and sometimes by slaves themselves—fueled the circulation of enlivened sound across the South. Value rose in proportion to the enslaved person's transactional status as human property.

What made the slaves' music appear so utterly fantastic, though, was how it compromised the laws of property ownership to the point of disturbing the basic principles of southern capitalism. Because the slaves' musical capacities were thought to be racially endowed, the sounds they produced remained formally linked to their "Negro" status. This meant that what was "black" about Black music challenged White possessive claims; its sonic character retained a material dimension of the slaves' physical presence no matter how widely the music circulated, no matter how frequently owners profited from their property's performances. Within the emerging markets of entertainment, racialized Black sound endured as a fleshy resonance, its inalienable nature contradicting capital's exchange mechanisms and compromising the universal authority of White ownership. Through their labor, Black musicians had created something incredible: an expressive form economically constituted as an illicit property that was inextricably attached to the human property that produced it. As Black music gained commercial value, it continued to grow in its primary economy under Black ownership, finding creative sustenance in a rich spirituality and Africanized vernacularity where notions of human sound's livingness were common.

Black music arose as a commodity in contradiction of itself: a cultural practice whose embodied racial essence moved paradoxically within the circuits of capital while simultaneously turning against those circuits to find renewal in the creative and philosophical networks of southern African American culture. After Emancipation, as free Black musicians entered commercial markets and began reshaping popular music, their creative actions supported the same back-and-forth dynamic, which also informed the pattern of musical change. The inalienable possessions of Black sonic being—at once celebrated for their peculiar presence and demeaned as the audible outcome of an abject class of personhood—journeyed into and out of the entertainment economy, their double movements setting into motion an expansive metamorphosis of form. With each outward step into the formal economy, Black music labor turned away, finding restorative inspiration in the wellspring of Black sonic material to forge new enlivened expressions. What structurally revealed a cyclical motion, with Black musicians and their music circulating into and out of commercial markets, mimicked a larger contradiction in the relationship of race to capital: the racially inalienable sounding practices of Black performers participated antagonistically in a system whose efficacy depended on the alienable exchange of commodity forms. The contradiction sustained, and still sustains, a dialectical energy that never resolves. Commerce compels Black music innovation as African American musicians continue to lean back, drawing strength and inspiration from an evolving imaginary of racially conceived animated sound.

To comprehend this dynamic, *Alive in the Sound* closely examines the history of US popular music, giving particular attention to its industrial productions, genre categories, media apparatuses, and means of circulation. The book explores how multiple generations of Black musician-laborers, from George W. Johnson to Scott Joplin, Fletcher Henderson to Muddy Waters, Aretha Franklin to Drake, produced grand bodies of musical creativity while navigating capitalized institutions and negotiating with White competitors who routinely sought to claim ownership of Black music's animated qualities. These expropriative efforts had the effect of amplifying the racial sensation, and hence the value, of enlivened sound. If, over the course of the modern, the unrelenting force of the market spelled multiple losses for Black musicians, it also inspired repeated symbolic gains for African American culture at large: from the onset of the twentieth century, Black music identified the standard by which popular music style would be measured. So successful were Black music's gains that it seemed to take on a life of its own, routinely detaching from the labor that produced it and circulating as a strangely disembodied version of racially embodied sound. As it advanced globally into the commercial arena, Black music grew ever larger, more ontological, its appeal to artists and consumers alike standing in stark contrast to the structures of negation that perpetually challenged Black existence.

Herein lies the informing logic of value production. Over the course of the long modern era, Black music value has developed as an accumulation of economic losses endured by Black labor; these losses, which mark the music's aesthetic and commercial value, have repeatedly inspired African American musicians to produce new innovations advancing popular style. Through these means, losses generated through the expropriation of Black creativity realize symbolic "profits" that compel the invention of new animated forms. *Alive in the Sound* analyzes the complexities of Black music production, demonstrating how its multiple modes of valuation—aesthetic, racial, economic, commercial, symbolic—have worked in relation to magnify its ontological character, historically unfolding as a metamorphosis of multiple profits from loss. The book focuses chiefly on the massive labor force that shaped Black music to show how the creation of new expressions of aliveness sustained the music's back-and-forth evolution. Contradictions orienting Black music's dialectical growth—the positive and negative extremes of its stature, the movements that Black music and musicians have performed within and against the entertainment economy—emerge as critical components in the production of value, underlying the music's ironic positioning both at the center and on the margins of popular culture.

Methodologically, *Alive in the Sound* bears certain resemblances to my earlier book, *Lying up a Nation: Race and Black Music*. Both examine the musical constitution of racial difference: how Black music, as sound and idea, emerged historically out of racially asymmetrical power struggles to realize racially distinctive forms. Yet whereas *Lying up a Nation* focuses largely on the US colonial and antebellum periods, *Alive* concentrates on Black music's participation in the modern commercial economy, mapping patterns of growth from the late antebellum era to the turn of the twenty-first century. And while *Lying up a Nation* directs its attention to the discursive regimes and notational practices that constrained the production of music knowledge, *Alive* approaches its subject through the lens of political economy, examining the guiding mechanisms of popular entertainment, where the contradiction of race to capital mobilizes the invention of peculiarly inalienable alienable forms.

In pursuing this method, *Alive in the Sound* pushes back on studies of Black music that locate expressivity exclusively within the racial containments of African American culture, arguing that attention to social forces, commercial institutions, and professional performers external to Black domains is critical to comprehending the formation of value. The book interprets racial antagonism not as a transhistorical structuring principle hermetically sealed within Black existence but as something that develops materially out of the conditions of exploited Black labor. From this, Black music's racial distinctiveness takes shape: aliveness is inherent to its cultural form, enacted by musicians performing their putative states of audibility within commercial forums. In fulfilling the expectation of capital's progression through the invention and reinvention of enlivened sound, Black music reaffirms its status as a racialized cultural property. The double movements symptomatic of its contradictory character drive a cyclical motion that directs the progression of popular style while repeatedly tracing back to Black sonic and philosophical pasts. The cycles amount to the creation of a semiotically open performative enactment—a storyless historical structure—bound to the legacies of race and labor. *Alive in the Sound*, then, is less an alternative history of Black music than it is a charting of how the music's distinctively double life-in-the-making presents itself antagonistically as counterhistory.

This is all to say that Black music's distinctiveness is the offspring of an illicit origin, a racial-economic anomaly that perpetuates ongoing struggles of ownership. Structured in the contradiction of race to capital, Black music has flourished, arising as a cultural practice unlike anything heard or experienced before it. As it circulates, the music spreads its sensations of aliveness, its propertied conditions participating in an enduring tug-of-war between Black musician-labor and the legions of consumers who, through their purchase power, claim Black music as their own. Black music's antagonistic relationship to capital is what makes it seem so different, so enduringly enlivened, so valued: it is vital to its emotional intensity and expressions of aesthetic truth. Yet it is also why anachronistic racial beliefs, otherwise dismissed over the course of multiple decades of civil struggle and progress, have continued to inform its understanding. *Alive in the Sound* analyzes the complex conditions that have made Black music this way, a form and practice at once cherished and enduringly bound to race and racism's ideational life.

ACKNOWLEDGMENTS

The idea for this book first began to emerge in 2008, when I was asked by Barbara Weinstein to present a paper on the study of music for a Presidential Panel of the American Historical Association. That paper (subsequently published under the title "On Ownership and Value"), which received incisive responses from Jerma Jackson, Ingrid Monson, and Shane White, set me on a journey to explore what I felt to be the crucial topic in Black music studies—namely, how value is generated. Working for a while in fits and starts, I was ultimately able to give the subject due attention after receiving in 2013 an appointment as a senior fellow at the University of Wisconsin's Institute for Research in the Humanities (IRH) on the Madison campus. Benefiting from a reduction in teaching and service responsibilities during those four years, I set the groundwork of this book. I'm deeply indebted to the IRH's late director, Susan Stanford Friedman, whose unflagging support enabled me to move the project forward, and to the community of IRH fellows with whom I had so many enriching conversations.

I'm also grateful to several other Madison colleagues/friends and students who've helped me to think hard about Black music, culture, and musicality more generally. In the School of Music, Lee Blasius and Brian Hyer, my neighbors down the hall, were endlessly provocative and engaging during our many conversations; I have learned so much from them. Same goes for my casual exchanges with Nadia Chana, Pam Potter, and particularly Charlie Dill, who could effortlessly move across a circuit of ideas from Deleuze to Muddy Waters. I am chagrined to think how I took for granted my frequent banter with the late Richard Davis and am dismayed I did not learn enough from him about his extraordinary performance and recording career. Steve Paulson at Wisconsin Public Radio gave me the chance to explore some of the details of this study on the nationally syndicated NPR program "To the Best of Our Knowledge." To other Madison faculty and friends I owe similar thanks: Jerome Camal, Thulani Davis, Suzanne Desan, Nan Enstad, Barbara Forrest, Sara Guyer, Darien Lamen, Toma Longinović, Morgan Luker, Guido Podestá, and Viren

Murthy. Several graduate advisees, together with students from other departments enrolled in my Music and Culture workshop, were helpful to me in numerous ways. They include Christina Baker, Andrew Bottomley, Scott Carter, Dave Gilbert, Katie Graber, Blackhawk Hancock, Ellen Hebden, Marc Hertzman, Charles Hughes, Julian Lynch, Molly McGlone, Melissa Reiser, Griff Rollefson, Fritz Schenker, and Matt Sumera.

In 2014, I accepted an invitation from Aliko Songolo and Tejumola Olaniyan to join a newly established initiative to widen attention on campus to global Black cultural studies. What became a year later the Department of African Cultural Studies (ACS) remained my principal home until my retirement. It was in that context that I developed for the department new curriculum in cultural theory and assisted in forging courses of study in music and sound. Working with ACS graduate students was a great reward. I'm particularly grateful to Tolu Akinwole, Unifier Tshimangadzo Dyer, Harry Kiiru, Kimberly Rooney, and Omotola Okunlola for our work together.

Of all my Madison friends, though, I owe my deepest intellectual debt to Tejumola Olaniyan, with whom I had the pleasure of collaborating in multiple ways over the course of thirteen years. I first met Teju when he served as a reader on the dissertation committee of Wayne Marshall, whose PhD I supervised. Thanks to Wayne, Teju and I became fast friends. We codirected a research circle, staged a major conference, coedited a volume on music and empire, and laid plans for new research initiatives dedicated to Black cultural studies and sound recording. As I was drafting this book, moreover, Teju served as a sounding board, engaging and challenging me—publicly, at UW lectures, at a workshop I organized at the American Academy in Berlin, and privately, over tea at Madison cafés—as I shaped the theoretical underpinnings of *Alive in the Sound*. I dedicate this book to his memory, saddened that we could not carry forward together a new project we were planning.

When thinking of colleagues and friends beyond the Madison campus, it is somewhat overwhelming to recognize the scores of individuals to whom I also feel indebted. Because I presented multiple iterations of this book in the form of talks and essays on multiple occasions over a decade, I cannot possibly give due credit to the many hosts and audiences who have informed my thinking. And so, I am left with this opportunity to express my gratitude to a few publications/institutions, naming parenthetically the people behind those invitations. Jairo Moreno and Gavin Steingo gave me the chance to present research on the early formation of Black music value as part of an essay prepared for "Econophonia: Music, Value, and Forms of Life," their guest-edited issue of *boundary 2*. Other versions or parts of this study were presented at the 2016 Rhythm Changes conference, Amsterdam (Nick Gebhardt, Walter van de Leur, and Tony Whyton; Krin Gabbard provided a thoughtful response); Northwestern (Inna Naroditskaya and E. Patrick Johnson); Columbia University (Ana Ochoa, George Lewis, Harald Kisiedu); University of Michigan (Paul Anderson, Mark Clague, and the late Charles Hiroshi Garrett); University of California, Berkeley (Jocelyne Guilbault, Bonnie Wade, Griff Rollefson); University of Pennsylvania (Jairo Moreno, Guy Ramsey); the Jazz Worlds/World Jazz Conference and the Center for the Study of Race, Politics, and Culture, both at the University of Chicago (Phil Bohlman, and Travis Jackson and Kenneth Warren, respectively); Duke University (Louise Meintjes, Deonte Harris; thanks to Tsitsi Jaji for her penetrating response); and the aesthetics and popular music workshop, "Network Americana," held at the Institut für Musik und Vermittlung, Technische Universität Braunschweig (Dietmar Elflein, Knut Holtsträter, Sascha Pöhlmann). The Berlin Prize/Mellon Fellowship that brought me to the American Academy in Berlin in 2019 provided the means to present portions of this book while pursuing new research. Berit Ebert, Johana Gallup, and Michael Steinberg were key to making that stay so enriching. The Berlin forums included the Centre for the History of Emotions, Max-Planck Institut für Bildungsforschung and the Institut für Musikwissenschaft und Medienwissenschaft, Humboldt Universität. Thanks go, respectively, to Stephanie Lämmert, Sydney Hutchinson, and Stefanie Alisch for those invitations.

And then there are those friends and mentors from whom I've benefited over the years in various ways, through casual conversation, exchanging drafts, and sharing sources. For their many acts of friendship and collegiality, I thank Kofi Agawu, Paul Anderson, Paul Berliner, Tom Brothers, Pat Burke, Eric Drott, Steve Feld, Nick Gebhardt, John Gennari, Ken George, Dave Gilbert, Linda Gordon, Fabian Holt, Allen Hunter, Andrew Jones, Harry Liebersohn, Eric Lott, Jeff Magee, Wayne Marshall, Louise Meintjes, Richard Middleton, Kirin Narayan, Shana Redmond, Anthony Reed, Tim Rommen, Barry Shank, Murray Smith, and Gavin Steingo. Rich Crawford and Jim Dapogny, both now passed, together with Judith Becker encouraged me during my graduate school training to pursue a path that pushed against the conventions of musical scholarship at the time. Finally, special thanks go to Florence Bernault, Phil Bohlman, Jairo Moreno, Rob Nixon, and Tim Taylor, whose intellectual generosity and enduring friendship have been important to me.

To the many librarians, curators, and archivists who have supported this project, I want to thank especially Tom Caw (Mills Music Library, University of Wisconsin), James E. Wintle (Music Division, Library of Congress), John Fenn (Head, Research and Programs, American Folklife Center, Library of Congress), and Scott W. Schwartz (Sousa Archives, University of Illinois).

Among the staff and affiliates of Duke University Press, I am indebted to Nina Eidsheim and Josh Kun, collaborators in the series Refiguring American Music, who welcomed this book to the list; to Senior Project Editor Ihsan Taylor and copyeditor Christopher Hellwig for their expertise and careful attention to the many aspects of production; and to Ken Wissoker, a visionary editor, who steered the preparation of the manuscript with matchless skill. I'm particularly appreciative of his ability to find a remarkably insightful group of anonymous readers who reviewed the manuscript in two rounds. Reports from the first round inspired me to undertake a massive revision of the manuscript. Those from the second—which included a new report from one of the original readers—were as illuminating as they were affirming. Kate Mullen, an assistant editor at the press, patiently guided me through the labyrinth of production details.

Finally, I am forever grateful to my wife, Colleen Dunlavy. Mere words expressed in this rather staid public form cannot do justice to the wonderfully enriching effect she's had on my life and work. Her emotional support, her subtle way of boosting my intellectual courage and confidence at just the right moments, enabled me to see this book through to completion. And her powerful intellectual capacities—particularly her casual fluency in the arcane matters of political economy and the history of capitalism—have contributed profoundly to my thinking about Black music value. Yet above all, it is her quieter nature, her patience, her expressions of love and kindness, that have mattered most to me. To her I owe my greatest debt.

BLACK LABOR, VALUE,

AND THE ANOMALIES

OF ENLIVENED SOUND

SPECTACULAR AURALITIES

About a hundred pages into his monumental study of Black labor during the time of slavery and Reconstruction, W. E. B. Du Bois takes a sudden turn. He abruptly departs from the sober language of social history that had previously informed his analysis and adopts the intonation of religious prophecy to evoke the experience of liberation. The closing paragraphs of "The Coming of the Lord," the fifth chapter in his 1935 publication, *Black Reconstruction in America*, are where things change, as Du Bois engages the rhapsodic tone of revelation in portraying the hour of the enslaved people's freedom. This moment, Du Bois writes, was nothing less than the heralding of the Apocalypse, when "to most of the four million Black folk emancipated by the civil war, God was real."[1]

What is striking about Du Bois's rhetorical strategy is how it makes use of auditory imagery, describing the many sites of freedom to be, more than anything else, a glorious pageantry of sound. "A great human sob shrieked in the wind, and tossed its tears upon the sea—free, free, free." All that was "Truth" (and "Love" and "Beauty," too) "sang with the stars." "Trumpet tones" blared. Black folk of all ages, shapes, and sizes "raised great voices and shouted to God," and in their collective passion they created something profound, "the loveliest thing born this side the seas." Throughout this dramatic commentary—little more than a brief swerve that interrupts the narrative flow for just a few pages—sonic imagery brims with reveries of a lustrous aurality that "swelled and blossomed like incense" and whose "great cadences . . . throbbed and thundered on the world's ears." Here arises a sound-filled humanity that was of the moment, "improvised and born anew," but that was also evocative of another place and time. The celebratory call to freedom wells up "out of an age long past, and weaving into its texture the old and new melodies in word and in thought."[2]

The use of musical imagery to convey what is otherwise difficult to express in conventional prose was not new to Du Bois. He employed a similar technique over thirty years earlier in his celebrated work *The Souls of Black Folk*, the "singing book" in which extravagant claims about the power of the spirituals, or "sorrow songs"—where he introduces the phrase "born this side the seas"—assume their place alongside dramatic prophecy and staid social criticism.[3] But *Black Reconstruction* is a different kind of text, a massive, seven-hundred-page revisionist study of a newly conceived Black proletariat, whose politics of struggle were brought into form through historical analysis performed at a granular level. Du Bois's aim, as David Levering Lewis describes it, was to produce nothing short of "a tour de force of legitimate propaganda for his people," by which he would show, as Du Bois himself put it, "the Black worker as founding stone of a new economic system in the nineteenth century and for the modern world, who brought civil war in America." Given the depth of his materialist commitments, it may seem strange that what otherwise proceeds as a tale of a fateful, asymmetrical battle against the pernicious forces sustaining White-majority rule—forces enabled by the commanding influence of monopolistic capital consumed in "an orgy of theft"—locates a source of hope in the seemingly superfluous sound of the "Negro" worker class. Despite Du Bois's professed love of the sorrow songs, one would think that he might have stayed within the stylistic bounds of scholarly scientific discourse.[4]

For Du Bois, though, Black music and labor were of a piece. In the clamor of "wild orgy and religious frenzy," the "howling and dancing" among "gangs of dirty Negroes," one could hear the living qualities of a working people, an economic class for whom the very act of unpaid labor—the labor on which a nation was built—was deeply and profoundly audible.[5] Music among the enslaved was at once a common, orienting practice and a byproduct of labor, an expression of humanly organized sound constituted within the activity of work, just as its creation beyond the fields and shop floors entered into circulation as a form of entertainment, sold to paying customers by slave owners and sometimes by the slaves themselves.[6] "Negro" sound and labor moved together as a resonance of duty-bound flesh, the auditory outpouring of emancipatory aspiration never fully separating from the body as such. Unlike the common portrayal of Euro-Western "Music" as an objectified, autonomous form, the reports by White people who experienced Black sounding practices suggested a different kind of aural sensation in which the strange clamoring of slaves seemed to arise directly from their physicality; slave music put on display the inherently audible character of the Black body.[7] Racialized Black sound was a recognizable sign of the slaves' inferiority, a negative indication of a person-thing that was, from the outset, heard. Nonetheless, this same peculiar phenomenon of embodied sound—consistent with the naming of slavery the "peculiar institution"—routinely drew the attention of White populations who commonly thought of themselves as being less endowed with sonic presence. As a result of an anomaly in the economy of racialized labor, what had been born from the flesh and bones of a reboant people disseminated outwardly via the nascent markets of exchange, introducing listeners to the newly conceived, audible child of southern Black consciousness. Du Bois was keenly aware of Black music's enlivened character and its basis in the productive relations of enslaved labor. The "noise" of voluble Black workers, he writes, betrayed Black sound's animated character: it "lived and grew, always it grew and swelled and lived," as if it were a sentient autonomous form. What it grew from defined its basis in the negative: the beauty of "Negro music" was "distilled from the dross of its dung"—from the living shit of slavery's bare life.[8]

Du Bois's alignment of Black music and the negative conditions of slave labor speaks to economic processes that trace to the heart of value production.[9] In just a few pages, tucked away in an otherwise conventionally crafted political history, he locates the critical aesthetic triumph of the slave era in the invention of a powerful sounding practice developing from the activity of unfree Black workers. This sound-producing labor, enacted within the inherently unjust economic structures of slavery, provided the material ground of a strange and fascinating aurality, the setting from which the racialized auditory expressions named "Negro music," and later "Black music," would be constituted, assembled, and cast. Brought into social understanding as a novel performance for purchase, this racialized sound introduced into everyday exchange practices an aberrant form whose qualities of inalienable humanity proved disruptive of capitalist processes and the norms of ownership. Constituted as a recognizable, socioeconomic invention under the rule of White mastery—under the legal claim of Black bodies as forms of human property—Black music came into public knowledge as a contradiction in the process of ownership; it would be conceived as a property claimed by another property, a property-in-slaves, that for all practical purposes had no business owning a property of their own. The emergence of African American sounding practices as an audible property-of-property seemingly animated by the bodies of its owned producers shows how different Negro music was. And because the contradictions of race underlying the production of value have never resolved, so would it continue to be.

The sound of Black folk identified a condition of aurality unlike any before it. Entering public knowledge as a cultural phenomenon in the 1840s and 1850s, it marked the nation's first open recognition of the slaves' ability to produce coherent sonic form. Conceived as an audible externalization of the slave body, of a being that was widely assumed to be less than human, the fleshy sounding practices of Black music would always remain, in one sense, something less than Music, forever inferior to the exalted aesthetic expressions of Europe: the singular and unqualified object form, *Music*, with a capital *M*. Then again, in its extraordinary range of sonorous beauty and diversity of creative invention, Black music also appeared at times not entirely unlike Music. By the middle decades of the nineteenth century, it had been informing the genres of American popular music and folk song, as it drew the praise of northern and European visitors to the South, who often spoke admiringly of its strange, exotic qualities. And as it pushed the limits of what Music could be—in all its likenesses and unlikenesses, in all its accumulated identifications and misidentifications by a White majority—Black music gained a peculiarly heightened positivity, its animated qualities, if not fully inalienable, remaining nonetheless under the racial authority and possession of those thought to be an inherently audible species of personhood. Emerging from the negative, thingly resonance of the racialized body, this new cultural phenomenon, Negro music, being less than Music, would gain a magnified hyperpositive value. Through its qualities of embodiment, it would also become something greater than Music, imbued with enlivened character. Such was the social process informing Du Bois's proclamation of Black music as a remarkable invention and which I will identify in this study as the music's double character. Conceived in the negative, "distilled from the dross of its dung," Black music had arisen in the aftermath of civil struggle as "slavery's one redemption," revealing in its animated properties a magnified, hyperpositive presence. This negative/hyperpositive relation inherent to the production of value—observable in its concrete manifestations but also as a logic with its own temporality operating at an abstract level—would endure as an unresolvable tension consistent with the racialized, psychic twoness of a racially preoccupied nation.[10]

To be "distilled" conjures the ethers, which, by turns, suggests a physical process of separation and transformation. In its becoming, a Negro music is revealed as a distillation of spirit. The metaphor of distilling appears in "The Coming of the Lord," where Du Bois depicts the music's ascent as an auditory incarnation of Jesus, an apocalyptic, musical rendering that exceeds the limits of the ordinary and "sits today at the right hand of God."[11] In this usage, it might seem as if Du Bois were suggesting that Black music had ultimately extracted itself from the mundane suffering of slave society, its spiritual character having detached from the struggles of the world. Yet Du Bois never loses sight of the importance of the music's constitution within a subjugated class of African American labor; he remains committed to the view that Black music developed dialectically, realizing value as a negative relation to capital. Born from the contradiction of slaves acquiring their own property—a partially inalienable property that would never be fully accessible to its owners—this racially "Negro" music comes into being, its fleshy sensation relationally connected to the status of the slave as an audible property. Out of this strange dynamic, Black music acquires its animated, spectral character, being a distillative demonstration of the forces of injustice producing enlivened sound.

Du Bois is scrupulous in drawing out the process. The ground from which the enslaved bear witness to a sonic miracle in chapter 5, "The Coming of the Lord," is introduced in the preceding chapter, "The General Strike," through a detailed analysis of the slaves' political campaign against their owners, which he portrays as a mass movement of labor activism. "Can we imagine this spectacular revolution?" Du Bois asks, for one might find such active participation dubious, given the desperate attempts by White masters to keep their human property unaware of the impending civil conflict. Yet despite the enormity of their challenge, the slaves persisted, joining the Union's armed forces in their own campaign for freedom, and "the wild truth, the bitter truth, the magic truth, came surging through."[12] Out of the materiality of struggle emerged a new truth, announced in the rapturous "howling and dancing" of Black performance. Du Bois evokes this spectacular incarnation at the conclusion of "The Coming" in his quotation of Friedrich von Schiller's "An die Freude" ("To the Joy"). By aligning the animated "howl" of the freed slaves' exclamations with Schiller's poetry, Du Bois alludes to a climactic moment of another masterwork, the "Hymn to Joy" (a.k.a. "Ode to Joy") chorus in Beethoven's Symphony no. 9 in D Minor, op. 125, where the "acoustical shock" of Schiller's very same words disrupting the instrumental norms of symphonic composition are famously featured in the fourth movement. The "miracle, of its production," which had given birth to slave sounding practices, by which the freed people, as Du Bois's described it, "howled the hymn of joy," now stood in comparison with the transcendent character of what many at the time believed to be Europe's greatest musical masterwork. What had been "distilled from the dross of its dung" materialized out of subjugated labor as an equivalent of humanity's greatest beauty. Black music would give to those who could discern it an audible indication of truth cast in the negative.[13]

The miraculous production of "howled" sonic mastery would not have come about had it not been for the tragedy of slave labor and the racism that justified it. Tragedy was the circumstance in which a people could be imagined as things, and living things could seem to resonate sound. Tragedy was the social condition that enabled an enslaving population to perceive their living property as audible bodies rendering a strangely alienable and inalienable "music"; it was the product of a racial economy in which those same person-things were believed to possess sonic properties embedded in their very flesh. Tragedy as an abstract concept would live on within the productive processes of value-making, playing out repetitively as a materialization of asymmetric racial struggle: Black music's contradictory form would be structured as a repetition of unsuccessful attempts on the part of White mastery, and then a broad consumer culture, to claim and control the sounding practices of a subjugated class. The music's entrance into exchange as an alienable commodity meant that its performances would be available for purchase by anyone with the financial means to possess them.

Significantly, however, the tragic conditions that made Black music so easily obtainable and led White southerners to conclude that they were entitled to own the sounds themselves also made it impossible for full expropriation to be realized. The process by which the music entered exchange for the pleasure of White folk and was subjected to a southern version of primitive accumulation would be undone by the nation's own ideological commitment to racism and White supremacy, which precluded the music's complete incorporation into the greater body politic: White populations could not fully claim Black music as their own without also giving up their privilege and status as "White." And so, the qualities of an inalienable fleshy sound linked to the racialized "Negroid" body paradoxically increased in proportion to Black music's dissemination into commercial economies. Tragedy-in-the-abstract identified the congealed materiality of slavery's racial contradiction, informing the making of Black music's double character. It structured the negative/hyperpositive form of a racialized music that appeared phenomenally alive.

How precisely did the tragic order of slave labor set in motion the creation of such remarkable forms of enlivened sound? Tellingly, this order was by no means merely a reproduction of the labor typically found in capitalist production. In *The Gift of Black Folk*, a study published eleven years before *Black Reconstruction*, Du Bois suggests that the expressive power of Black music ultimately derived not from labor as such but from an unruliness developing out of its relation to labor, from its incorrigible reluctance to accommodate and be at the service of US industry and commerce. Black music provided something beyond mere economic and material gain, giving back to Black folk a precious cultural property as it actively participated in economic production. For that reason, slave populations, as they endured their tragic condition, worked to protect the human essence of their labor from complete exploitation and subsumption. While seated at the very foundation of this late form of US slavery—marking the emergence of a modern global capitalism in which slavery stood at the center, named by recent scholars the "second slavery"—the laboring of unfree people was not simply an abstract force or labor power; it identified a reconfiguring of labor.[14] Although far from unexploited (theoretically, slaves could own nothing, including their ability to work), slave laboring for Du Bois linked to qualities of "Truth" and "Negro spirit," identifying "a tropical product with a sensuous receptivity to the beauty of the world," from which Black music arose. The reluctance on the part of Black workers, judged by many masters and, after slavery, industrial capitalists to be a symptom of torpor and laziness, proposed in actuality an additional inspiration for Black people and the nation: "laziness" marked a refusal by the slave "when he did not find the spiritual returns adequate," offering an orientation to labor and labor time that would enable the United States to grow "economically and spiritually at a rate previously unparalleled anywhere in history." Driving this reluctance to labor's routine exploitation was what typically organized laboring acts themselves. The peculiarly embodied sound of workers' actions gave audible form to a realm of cryptic being resistant to the orders of capitalist production.[15]

The recognition that Black people had introduced another kind of sound-induced labor, an aesthetically informed and performative version of Marx's "living labor"—something not, in Du Bois's phrasing, "as easily reduced to be the mechanical draft-horse which the northern European labor became"—is critical to the comprehension of Black music value as it emerges in the slaves' performances and carries forward into the post–Civil War United States.[16] Du Bois's insight proposes a readjustment of the universalist equalization of labor as labor power, as a commodity form that is quantifiable, exchangeable, and knowable, as it gestures toward a newly imagined quality and condition, that of being-in-labor: a being whose very existence was tragically defined by and conceived as labor—as "total labor" existing in "racial time," as Michael Hanchard names it—but who, out of this state of abjection, realized a new world responsive to its own time.[17] For Du Bois, one of the great ironies of US slavery was how Black laboring brought about the possibility of a healthier embodied form of living that exceeded capitalist production, a way of being produced by those who had been denied by the heinous power of racism the status of human. In the same way, the emergence of animated Black labor introduced a series of enlivened sounding practices that were constituted within and thus inextricably attached to the slaves' laboring acts, as those practices, by expressing outwardly the sonorousness of the slaves' bodies, also inspired the imagining of new cultural intensities. In the spectacle of animated Black sound, listeners began to embrace a view that runs the gamut of Black music history: they would hear in this strange, recondite music aestheticized expressions of life's certainties, an order of valuation frequently described in terms of a temporally expansive truth.

As we will observe over the course of this analysis, truth, as a reference to the ideological power of music's phenomenal experience, would typically remain partial, an incomplete figurative gesture to an absolute ideal that would then be brought into language and made meaningful.[18] Some versions of truth affirmed the certainty of White supremacy, locating in Black music the unthinking "noise" of Negro inferiority. These are the discourses of ridicule and contempt featured in nineteenth-century minstrelsy that would inform popular characterizations of Black forms. Other truths turned in the opposite direction, seeking to extract Black music from its history of subjugation, anointing the music as the representative, positive "voice of the nation." And still others proposed another kind of positivity, claiming that Black music expressed a singular racial coherence that, depending on interpretation, may or may not be shared across racial lines. "Are you getting the spirit?" Aretha Franklin would ask her audiences, leaving it to each listener to ponder. These multiple depictions of truth shared a common conviction—namely, that Black music mattered in profound ways, its importance driving the creation of a veritable lexicon of metaphysical associations mapping extremes of reification and fetishism: if Black music were a ghostly "dead" form, its enlivened character could also quicken the emotions and lift the soul.

These common articulations of truth were true enough for those making and embracing them, their disparate signatures a ready indication of Black music's contested character. As interpretations of value, however, they remain inadequate because they do not explain where Black music's qualities of aliveness come from, nor do they identify the productive processes from which Black music's less-than/greater-than double character developed. As Du Bois shows, what Black music presents most revealingly is not just a set of meanings attached to its phenomenal sonic surface, but a material basis of inspired living arising dialectically from the economic anomalies of sound production. Truth in its primary, negative form—a "truth-content" according to Theodor W. Adorno's negative dialectics—identifies the effect of the racial-economic contradiction orienting the production of value: the paradox of a human property owning an alienable property of sound, whose audible character gains social significance by remaining inalienably connected to Black being.

This primary, structuring truth would typically remain mute while its superficial auditions of aliveness succumbed to the vagaries of representation. As Black music evolved, however, discerning musicians and critics began to echo Du Bois as they too gained a sense of the material processes by which Black music's phenomenal power was made. Across the long modern period, a rich and elaborate commentary developed that variously sought to reproduce in language the music's audible flashes of revelation—as Max Pensky suggests in his elaboration on Adornian truth content, a "nonconceptual mode of aesthetic expression . . . [that] remains off-limits as an option for cognition in a totally administered world"—exposing the singular cultural logic behind the making of Black music's fleshy retentions of animated substance. They help us now to map the various imaginations of truth written over the racial-economic contradictions of valuation.[19]

The sensation of Black music's primary truth, then, begins with the audible recognition of the structural conditions generating value. What is truthful materially is the contradiction immanent in the music's form: the racial-economic relation enabling sounding practices of African American performers to leave the body and enter exchange, only to return after having been enriched by musical reinvention and the accumulation of social meaning. In this way, racialized sounding practices intensify Black music's qualities of aliveness, by which listening communities bring sound into meaning, with many perceiving its uncanny animatedness as a profound affective force. Those identifying the productive basis of its enlivening of the sensory array come closest to comprehending the primary basis of truth's structuring: they recognize music's social power developing within and beyond its common mystification. And out of the cycle of production, dissemination, and return—it is a cycle because it never resolves and thus endlessly repeats—Black music's auditory expressions become the focus of a racial struggle of ownership as the dissemination and retention of animated sounding practices inspire the creation of a complex web of claimed meaning. The sound forms of Black music bring into being, as in Fumi Okiji's Adornian formulation (her focus being on jazz), an extension of "black life . . . as critical reflection," the music itself being "capable of reflecting critically on the contradictions from which it arises."[20]

Beneath the audible surfaces of Black enlivened sound has resided a productive process relating to the enduring legacy of White supremacy. According to this process, the music's structural anomalies endlessly repeat the tragedy of slavery as an unfolding of its unresolvable contradictory character. Cast in the negative relations of production, this primary structuring truth, inspiring so many aspirational truths, is why Black music would always remain Black. What Du Bois—in an effort to convey the freed people's own conception of truth "in word and in thought"—called "the wild truth" of emancipated voices spoke to a larger reality, to the ability of an unruly class of labor to create enlivened sound out of "the dross of its dung." The invention of Black music materializes not as a truth solely shaped in meaning but as a truth built on the contradiction of its double character, as an outward manifestation of value. What accumulates in value as part of Black music's nearly two-hundred-year history reveals a truth proceeding doubly, moving forward progressively and backward in contrary motion, having been constituted in the enduring reality of racial injustice.

Over the course of Black music's history, America would be repeatedly confronted with the music's truth as a contradiction in form, its anomalies typically translated into positive resolutions that masked what was partial, ambiguous, unresolved. The production of Black music value resides not in positivity but in the paradox of a negative relation by which what seems less becomes ever more. Created from the tragedy of loss, Black music's sounding practices introduced a new kind of profit, a new kind of value, its outward and inward cycling within commercial markets accumulating over time as a series of *coalescences* of enlivened sound. Truth's endurance in the negative would drive a cascade of styles, whose perpetual decoupling from the productive processes situated in labor advanced the sensation of a fetishized spectral aurality. If the secondary truths listeners perceived in Black music's aliveness were inevitably partial, commonly playing to the order of the color line and wholly responsive to surface phenomena, so would they reaffirm the underlying generative force of value production: the peculiarity of enlivened sound developed as an enduring symptom of the formal contradictions of race that sustained Black music's back-and-forth circulation and expansion. What was partially true indicated in its falsehood the negative basis of value production, to be discerned beneath the surface appearances of what seemed to be sonorously living.

By the time that Du Bois published *The Gift of Black Folk* and *Black Reconstruction in America*, such claims of truth were being widely celebrated throughout the world. So influential had US Black music become that it inspired Du Bois to describe it as a generous "gift, . . . one of the greatest that the Negro has made to American nationality." This audible gift, given the name "Negro music," was not merely a bestowal of aesthetic pleasure but a reciprocally minded offering carrying the expectation of something in return. It sought back from America a social transformation, an enduring "spectacular revolution" that might someday realize a just and equal world.[21] Brought into being from the tragedy of exploited labor, the gift of Black music proposed, in its material attachment to the superfluity of audible Black bodies, the existence of a different version of productive economy and a different conception of everyday temporal order. It would be a revision of what Marx called "socially necessary labor-time" that consistently challenged the seminal forces of modern capital outlined in *Black Reconstruction*: the South's "organized monarchy of finance" and the "triumphant industry in the North." A lowly worker marked thingly and "lazy" by White property owners had introduced into the United States a productive process whose unresolvable contradictions in form generated phenomenal anomalies of sound: a counterhistory that instigated imaginings of what in life was possible, of what would be right and true.[22] In the reproduction of these anomalies, Black music has continually replayed America's racial contest, the conflicting world perspectives of Black and White cast as a struggle to claim an elusive property according to the symbols and stories that people have attached to it. What appears alive in the sound brings to the surface an evolving manifestation of the generative processes of value-making, whose spectral character issues forth into the world as the audible "ghost of modernity."[23]

PECULIAR ANATOMIES

I've lingered over Du Bois's elaboration on the African American worker at the outset because it calls attention to a vital relation in Black music operating at the deepest logical and structural levels. His observations help us to recognize how the contradiction inherent to Black music's constitution as a contested property was fundamental to its development of value and how that same contradiction continues to play a critical role in the making of American racial identification. Although contemporary scholars routinely acknowledge Black music's significance as a powerful aesthetic expression, and public figures and political leaders champion its national and racial significance, there has been nonetheless a widespread misapprehension of how Black music actually participates in economic processes and how that participation has generated value-based constraints producing the uncanny sensation of aliveness—"uncanny" in the sense of an "intellectual uncertainty whether an object is alive or not."[24] Despite the impassioned claims about Black music's importance in American life, together with the vigorous assertions that it embodies qualities of authenticity and realness—an audible truth depicted as spirit, feeling, soul—the material conditions underlying the source and persistence of its peculiarly enlivened character have remained remarkably underanalyzed. In fact, it seems fair to say that we are still in a kind of guessing game regarding the music's character of aliveness and the many peculiar presences it engenders. Although there is no paucity of claims about why Black music is profoundly important within particular communities—whether they be defined racially, as the "Black community," socially, as listening cultures dedicated to jazz, blues, rhythm and blues, hip-hop, etc., or nationally, according to the broad, deracinated category of (a majority-White) "American society"—these claims rarely seek to consider in an overarching way how the various interpretations of its uncanny qualities relate to each other. By and large, scholars either ignore or fail to recognize the many entangled involvements of valuation operating on multiple levels, which, I will contend, all participate within a dynamic that is at once racial and capitalist, what Cedric Robinson has described as a world economic system of "racial capitalism." And because we do not understand how value is generated, we still do not, in a certain way, know what Black music is.[25]

At the heart of the problem is the mistaken assumption, reaching across the ideological spectrum of scholarship and popular criticism, that Black music is simply another version of Music. My own historical research suggests that it is not. By making this assertion, I do not mean to deny Black music's many commonalities with other kinds of music or to downplay its extraordinary importance among diverse populations, both in the United States and worldwide. Rather, I aim to do exactly the opposite: to bring to attention how Black music's affective qualities of aliveness indicate a fundamental difference in its constitution as a cultural practice, which traces to its growth of a double character across wide stretches of time and place. The historical denigration of Black music as an abject, negative form appearing alongside its extravagant celebration as "the most beautiful expression of human experience born this side the seas" gives a pretty good indication that we are dealing with something different from the common, auditory object form named "Music." For what is Music, after all, if not a creation arising from a particular historical moment and set of social circumstances, its prolific articulations cast provincially in the fourteenth and fifteenth centuries according to an assembly of ideas consistent with what would become Modern Europe's own "enlightened" self-understanding and then transposed outwardly across the hemispheres and into territories of the variously visited, colonized, and conquered?[26] In its exalted status as an art form in the twentieth and twenty-first centuries—a status fueled by the heightened capitalization of the arts—Music came to inhabit multiple arenas of public life, its principal identification with the cultural elite extending into the worlds of the popular and the vernacular. During this time, Music has been frequently associated with social and political movements, commonly portrayed in the context of pop as an aesthetic expression antagonistic to institutional forces of domination, particularly those controlling the ownership and distribution of art. Yet the enduring perception of Music as an aestheticized object form has also made it appear to be largely decontextualized from the material conditions of the political-economic. It is indeed in its perceived qualities of absoluteness, as an ineffable entity that does not refer to anything outside itself, that Music is thought to locate its transformative powers of expression.[27]

Black music, by contrast, emerges out of a wholly different social and material environment, having been first constituted within an economic matrix specific to the time and place of US slavery and to the slaves' principal status as beings-in-labor. (Despite the prior existence of African sound forms, Black music as Negro music becomes a recognizable social practice—is socially constituted—in the late antebellum South.) It is a unique cultural phenomenon in its own right, a form that, despite its bountiful celebration over the course of its history, consistently assumes the position of the negative; in comparison with Music, it is diminished by its racial qualification as "Black." Yet, as we have seen already with the sorrow songs, it is from its status as a negative outgrowth of an inferior species of humanity that Black music acquired its hyperpositive qualities of aliveness. This ironic double tendency of a negative turning into a hyperpositive, of something less than Music transforming into something greater, developed out of the racial contests of ownership that enabled slave music to acquire economically generated value. In its accumulation, value in Black music became perpetually enriched, the contradictions within its institutional associations and social conception as a doubled aesthetic presence (as a legal property, a racial property, a commodity, a carrier of cultural and aesthetic meaning) linking materially to its anomalies of en-livened form. For this reason, arguments seeking to redirect critical atten-tion in celebration of Black music's putative likeness to European musical inventions—a position commonplace in jazz studies but also pervasive across criticism of nearly all twentieth- and twenty-first-century Black genres—inadvertently undermine the understanding of how Black music's exceptional cultural presence accrues from the anomaly of a slave owning an audible property of its own. Above all, they leave unattended the funda-mental matter of how Black music's evolution as a peculiar form of labor is itself indicative of a foundational economic struggle consistent with wider conflicts in the racial production of knowledge in the United States.[28]

Consider, for example, the conventional view of Black music's origins during the antebellum era. While it is not uncommon for historians in various disciplines to acknowledge the music's emergence as an impor-tant force of resistance under slavery, they have by and large assumed those qualities to operate principally at the level of the aesthetic, as in the frequently romanticized portrayal of the slave songs as spiritual "songs of protest." Having been granted the elevated status of Music, the songs cor-respondingly diminish in significance, being denied a purposeful role in political and economic development.[29] Indeed, such evening out of sound-based phenomenological orders—narrating Black music as a purely musi-cal form, whose semiotic potential could only reflect, and thus be contained within, a common, southern experience—has tended to co-opt Black musical particularity, narrowly representing it as a minoritarian cultural practice existing largely outside of capitalized processes while also staying comfortably situated within an otherwise stable and coherent social reality. A similar tendency has informed historical studies of Black music as it developed across the twentieth century. When music scholars celebrate Black music's soulful qualities according to the exclusive terms of Music, they sacrifice comprehension of its strange capacities as a value form. While giving important attention to African American musicians and musical achievements, their presumption that Black music is just another kind of Music tends to leave unanswered fundamental questions about how its uncanny sensations of aliveness came into being. Black music accordingly remains burdened by the claims of its equivalence to the unqualified form, Music, even as its qualifying markers, "popular" and "Black," betray enduring public skepticism across the White majority about its status as a wholly legitimate, artistic expression.[30]

Literary and cultural critics, meanwhile, have generally done a better job of analyzing the disruptive performativity of Black music, both as a practice of the enslaved and as a postemancipation cultural expression. Their means of interpretation have opened up new ways of comprehending Black music's processes of creation and its relationship to the precariousness of modern, Black subject formation.[31] And yet there has also been a tendency across Black literary and cultural studies—its influence extending into musicological criticism—to interpret Black music performance from the time of slavery to the present as a kind of static, musical indigeneity, a radical alterity whose aesthetic value, while perhaps arising from the economic conditions of the nation-state, also purportedly remains qualitatively distinguished from the complex social history that brought Black music into public knowledge. Here, at times, too, Black music conforms to an aesthetic object form, even if matters of labor and social context are highlighted. Despite frequently acknowledging its deep connection to the relations of production, and particularly to the struggle of labor against capital, Black music expression in these depictions seems always to abide by the norms of conventional musical understanding. Accordingly, as Black music proceeded to develop, it would appear to endure in its separability, in the consistency of an affirmative sonic blackness. Value, in the end, would seem to arise not because of, but in spite of, Black music's basis in the anomalies of labor. Even in its more precise critical depictions, where, for example, Black music is perceived as a radical performance practice unobservant of conventional fixities in form—the aesthetic phenomenon that Fred Moten locates "in the break"—the idea that the accumulation of value could somehow precede the material conditions of racial economy verges on mystification, implying an inviolable alternative that is ironically suggestive of the ineffable qualities associated with the European category of Absolute Music.[32]

The common opinion that Black music is categorically equivalent to Music has given rise to a public understanding that affirms its routine situatedness within the realm of art and encourages explanations of value deriving directly from its phenomenal qualities and character. This returns us once again to the relation of value to listeners' and musicians' deeply held views about what one can actually hear in it, to what may be characterized as a distinction between value and meaning. The comprehension of Black music as a type of Music has created the impression that the affective meanings and indexes that listeners discern (what a music "sounds like") correspond directly to its valuation, despite the lack of an explanation about how these two orders, meaning and value, are formally related. A public-radio guide for broadcasters, for example, suggests that the "qualities of craft" in jazz join with "qualities of heart/spirit" in identifying the music's "core values." The late composer, Olly Wilson, goes further, arguing that "the empirical evidence overwhelmingly supports the notion that there is indeed a distinct set of musical qualities which are an expression of the cultural values of peoples of African descent."[33] It stands to reason that what music is thought to *sound like*, to mean, should be somehow connected to its value. In fact, the idea of locating a macro-level valuative basis for cultural expression operating at the micro-level has been a central aspiration in the study of value across the social sciences for over a hundred years.[34] But a casual consideration of value's relation to meaning may falsely suggest that they are basically the same thing: what is valuable seems meaningful, what is meaningful, valued. Such a posture does not help if, say, we want to unpack the value-meaning complexity that orients Duke Ellington's defiant challenge to the critical category of jazz, "I am not playing jazz, I am trying to play the natural feelings of a people."[35]

If we are to explore potential linkages between the concepts of meaning and value in their relation to Black music, then it seems critical, as a first step, to distinguish the larger valuative claims from the words that listeners put to the musical sounds they hear. For it is, after all (and despite Wilson's claims otherwise), something of a leap of faith to suggest that the way Black music sounds is directly connected to the way value accrues. To address this problem, I'll be making a basic distinction, designating, on one hand, what Wilson names the "expression" that listeners recognize as a category of meaning. Value, on the other hand, is a racial-economic structuring built on the unresolvable contests of music ownership that, in involving a complex of auditory and nonauditory dimensions, produces over time an accumulation of seemingly enlivened sounding practices. Grounded in fundamental, social asymmetries underlying racial hierarchy, value in Black music is structured doubly, its negative and hyperpositive axes being consistent with its generative basis in racial contradiction. And in this way, it sets constraints for the making of meaningful musical experiences. Let's look at this distinction more closely, elaborating on the observations introduced earlier.

"Meaning," as I employ it here, is the assembly of discourses, broadly construed as metaphorical, that propose a particular signifying capacity attendant in aestheticized, musical expression.[36] Depictions of meaning often imply direct communication and precise symbolism, asserting that Black music possesses the ability to express tangible ideas and qualities of understanding. Commonly, such interpretations respond to surface appearances, to the phenomenal qualities of Black sound, which inspire among the music's listeners a host of associations and emotional responses—stories about themselves or, among those outside the African American community, about Black people. In the 1870s and 1880s, for example, White journalists, in their characterizations of various Black professional performances, noted hearing a gleeful insouciance and effortless virtuosity that was thought to reflect the unthinking natural ability among those of African descent. Reporters writing about jazz in the 1920s frequently employed metaphors conjuring the sensation of chaos as a way of encouraging White consumers to associate Black sound with a debased racial character. As African American observers became more involved in shaping Black music's public discourse, moreover, depictions changed, with new attention paid to how slavery's tragic afterlife affected the perception of "Negro" sound. Thematic references to sorrow and tragedy noted by, among others, Frederick Douglass ("the songs of the slave represent the sorrows of his heart") and W. E. B. Du Bois ("the soul beauty of a race which [the black artist's] larger audience despised") joined an assembly of conceits, from the lowly (protest, resistance, struggle) to the uplifting (spirit and soul, but also joy, ecstasy, pleasure, freedom), as part of a grand mapping of affect and emotion.[37] The condition of tragedy materialized in Black music's contradictory, double character became the basis for imagining meaning and discerning in its sound qualities of positive truth.

"Value," in contrast, describes the accumulation of economic, aesthetic, and cultural profit that accrues from abstract, social processes—that is, being largely unrecognized, as a structural causality—and drives the production of anomalous forms. Accumulation begins in economic exchange, when sounding practices performed by Black music laborers enter commercial markets, as those same practices, thought to be racially inalienable, remain inextricably attached to and under the possession of the musicians themselves.[38] This fundamental paradox underlies the racialized sensation of aliveness, driving efforts by White performers, consumers, and institutions to obtain it. The struggle for ownership becomes ideologically bound to the assertion and maintenance of Whiteness: White actors seek to reclaim a cultural and economic property conceived in the national imagination to be legally theirs. Essential, racialized sound inspired efforts to reclaim rather than claim Negro music because Black people never held the legitimate right to own property or to define the culture of a White nation. As a result, the perpetual failure on the part of White musicians, consumers, and institutions to completely incorporate and embody Black sounding practices—perpetual, because for it to succeed would require the end of racial distinction—repeatedly intensified the music's inalienable qualities, driving the production of more value.

The accumulation of value, then, begins with the creation of racially animated sound arising from the forces of injustice, its makers' monetary losses converting into profits measured in the form of an animatedness that would grow as multiple profits-from-loss. This is what realizes "profit" in the negative and inspires positive affirmations of Black music; it is an outcome of Du Bois's "spectacular revolution" appearing against the tragedy of slavery and what he calls the rapaciousness of White society's "orgy of theft." Among its failed possessors and creators alike, profit-from-loss becomes an invitation to explore what may be meaningfully imagined in Black musical sound. Across the music's history, this primary relation would serve as an abstraction of perpetual conflict, a way of conceiving profit from the expropriation of Black music's cumulative body of creation, or "sonic material." In the contradictory process producing value, Black music reveals its racial becoming.[39]

In this sense, Black music value carries materially a moral compass as a form built on the asymmetries of injustice as it also exceeds them. And to this extent, it becomes an orientation for the making of meaning; the structural anomalies of contested ownership producing perceptible qualities of enlivened sound set the constraints of interpretation, even as the actualities of meaningful musical experience appear potentially limitless. Analytically, we can separate them this way: in the constitution of Black music, value comes first. Whereas one might think of meaning as a kind of discursive surface or parole consistent with commodity fetishism, Black music value is a labor-generated quality, a material-based langue operating underneath, even as its force as a structure shows up solely in Black music's many concrete appearances. If this underlying "structuring structure" carries in its disjunctive and contradictory form the conditions for aurally imagining tragedy and injustice, it is not in itself a directive on how one listens or an indication of what Black music ultimately signifies. Meaning may articulate to the aspects of form that carry and sustain it, but the phenomenal experience of Black music remains open. In itself, Black music says nothing, being akin to what Nicholas Cook calls in his discussion of meaning in musical works, "unstable aggregates of potential significance."[40]

Making an analytical distinction between meaning and value is not meant to suggest that meaning is unimportant. On the contrary, as it is derived from musical experience, meaning is dialectically involved in value's formation; it would be a mistake to frame meaning outside of value's production or to reduce value to a conventional Marxian understanding of economic base. In fact, the most influential metaphors are what inspire meaningful interpretation across the musical landscape, from spirit communication in Kaluli gisalo singing (the act of "lift-up-over-sounding") to the congregational experience of "sounding sacramentality" in contemporary Black gospel.[41] Meaning and value develop relationally, particularly at the point when Black music enters national markets, the accelerated exchanges reorganizing popular music's stylistic development. For example, around the turn of the twentieth century, a cluster of popular meanings associated with fantasies about the primitive began to articulate to those qualities of Black sound that seemed most peculiar and distinctive: improvisation, deviations from tempered pitch, timbral effects, and above all, consistent use of syncopation propelled by a propulsive beat. The coalescence of sound and idea redirected Black music's commercial production, which in turn fundamentally transformed the larger character of American pop, just as Black music's sonic material also underwent a qualitative change. Music formations coalescing at that moment became associated with fantastic notions about Black people and their thingly appearances on recordings, informing the making of a vast rhythmic-meaning complex, a veritable *beat knowledge*—a way of knowing and responding to new notions of "beat."[42] This knowledge would inform musical performance across the racial divide, setting up a meaning-to-value relation generating experiences of multiple, positive truths.

As important as meanings are in comprehending the formation of value, however, they alone cannot determine the character of musical experience, nor can they substitute for the primary material truth that value reveals. Interpretations of meaning typically develop as a response to Black music's enlivened character rather than as an explanation of it. Accordingly, they tend to conflate meaning with value, as Wilson did; they are not adequate analytics in themselves. Meanings alone, for example, do not reveal why Black music, while consistently marginalized from the popular mainstream, has supplied for well over a century the primary aesthetic impulse in the development of American popular style. Nor can meaning tell us why Black forms acquire greater and greater racial coherence as they become more and more available in commercial markets—why they appear progressively *Blacker* over the course of Black music's history. Meanings remain limited in the analysis of Black music value because they are not directly bound to the productive process generating forms that are paradoxically fungible and inalienable. Critics content to focus on meaning in itself often seem to assume that Black music's qualities of aliveness have always existed, naturally and mysteriously animating a music in ways akin to the commodity's fetishized relation to labor-based production. If we are to understand how these uncanny appearances were first constituted and then developed over time, it will require stepping away from the claims about precise signification and becoming attentive to value as an economically driven cultural logic.

There is, ultimately, a bottom-line reason why we can't locate value solely in the meanings attached to musical experience. This has to do with music's limitations as a signifying practice. As a vast body of musicological, philosophical, and linguistic-anthropological scholarship has shown, it is beyond the ability of any kind of music, Black music or otherwise, to sustain precise meaning across a listening community.[43] "Music," Susanne Langer famously writes, "*is an unconsummated symbol.* Articulation is its life, but not assertion; expressiveness, not expression." Musical signs, the music theorist Naomi Cumming explains in her important book *The Sonic Self*, "belong to a class of interpreted relationships, which present an object of signification, without either pointing to a definite state of affairs [i.e., a specifiable meaning], or making a statement about it." As Jairo Moreno puts it succinctly in his illuminating assessment of Cumming's work, "Musical signs require verbal mediation." They are, as Adorno calls them, "second hand semiotic objects" from which a kaleidoscope of meaningful experience accrues.[44]

These theoretical insights are instructive. They reveal that listeners do not uniformly share a common aural experience, even if they happen to agree on the same language to describe what they hear. Nor, for that matter, will any single listener consistently discern a set of musical signs in precisely the same way, time after time. Musical experience cannot be rendered consistently; it is not as if listeners can expect to have exactly the same engagement with music, on repeat. The same might be said about any aesthetic experience, but it is doubly so for music. This is because music is not a coherent and reliable semiotic system beyond the workings of its own nonlinguistic grammar; it is not possible to interpret musical meaning as one would read a text. (Herein lies the reason why analyses of lyrics in pop songs routinely fail to convey music's affective power.) On the contrary, it is ironically from music's limitations as a system of signification that its aesthetic and social importance develop. In its nebulous relationship to spoken language, music achieves great communicative effect, its density of ambiguous signs inviting a complex cohering of imagining and feeling. Steven Feld, in a now classic essay, describes musical experience as a "special kind of 'feelingful' activity and engagement" that comes forth for listeners during a performance out of the "generality and multiplicity of possible messages and interpretations." From its phenomenal condensation of affective symbolism, music produces a "form of pleasure that unites the material and mental dimensions of musical experience as fully embodied."[45]

Black music shares with other kinds of music these same capacities and limitations of signification, just as its affective power derives from a condensation of symbolism, producing forms of pleasure. If it conjures imaginations of sorrow, pain, and jubilation, if it inspires the spectacular sensations of ecstasy, belonging, and positive truth, it does so according to the semiotic limitations of music; it can only communicate fleetingly as listeners will their ideas upon its phenomenal surface. What distinguishes Black music from the greater corpus of musical expression, however, is also what enables such extremes of meaning to articulate to sound. Having been constituted under slave capitalism, it brought into the world a contradiction in form, its peculiarly animated sensations setting constraints in the formation of meaning. Over time, as Black music began showing up in popular entertainment markets, listening publics imposed onto its fleshy sounds the norms of conventional Music in an attempt to tame it and make it resemble other kinds of popular musical diversion. In the process, Black music assumed its incongruous position as a popular form simultaneously at the center and on the margins of public life.

If Black music had not entered the commercial economy, it would never have developed its vast complex of value; it would never have become available for listeners to imagine it as part of a collective experience. At the same time, the public dissemination of Black music also invited consumers to overwrite its valuative production according to a set of emerging tropes that were thought to explain its racial authenticity and uncanny animated character. These attempts to retrofit Black music into Music's conventional understanding—as part of what Eric Lott has called "a profound White investment in Black culture"—could only bring greater attention to its economically and racially conceived qualities of inalienable labor, which further compromised attempts of incorporation.[46] Distance inspired appeal, driving a broad, ideological commitment in majority-White public contexts to possess the enlivened properties of Black music, while African American communities, newly motivated to embrace an increasingly valuable cultural property, found its embrace publicly affirmed. And so, as Black music would be "condemned to meaning," the underlying productive processes generating value were obscured beyond the surface qualities of aliveness.[47] These surfaces seemed to speak like the commodities to which they were attached, even as Black music itself had nothing directly to say. "Since time immemorial," Adorno writes, "human reactions to artworks have been mediated to their utmost and do not refer immediately to the [art] object. . . . Interest in the social decipherment of art must [therefore] orient itself to production rather than being content with the study and classification of its effects."[48]

Sorting out how Black music sets constraints for the making of meaning begins by becoming attentive to its productive basis as an anomalous labor form. Appearances of aliveness first occur with Black music's constitution as a property-of-property, by which it introduced across public culture sonic substantiations of animated presence: sensations of animatedness were part and parcel of its double character as something less than and greater than Music. And as Black music proceeded to develop over the course of the decades, its peculiar conditions of valuation ultimately revealed its basis in not one, but two, incongruent economies, each with its own temporal orientation. In the first, an economy bound by race, Black music's exchange moved inwardly, intensively, the development of style driven by free music laborers and unpaid musicians performing within a diversity of African American lifeworlds. If intensive exchange would always be racially porous because of the many occasions in which Black musicians performed for White people, so would it be perceived as racially specific, as affirmatively Black. In the second, an economy defined by capital, music exchange was transacted extensively, developing according to the function of commercial enterprise and the clock-time efficiencies of the working day. In this circumstance, Black music actively participated in majority-White entertainment markets, circulating freely as it was presented by a new labor force of African American musicians.[49]

The dynamic of race to capital (identified henceforth as race-capital) would set the parameters of Black music's unique progression as a value form. What was learned by Black musicians performing within capitalist exchange subsequently informed the internal, aesthetic workings of Black entertainment economies, as style practices and forms were reconceived and refashioned. These changed dynamics would then cycle back once more into popular markets, where they would undergo further revision. The cyclical pattern regulated the expansion of Black music's sonic material, giving shape to an aurally centered "counterhistory that is born of the story of race. . . . speak[ing] from the side that is in darkness, from within the shadows."[50] It is a storyless story arising from the material truth of value's production. Black music's double economy of race-capital functioned as an incongruent structure involving two profoundly different measures of transaction, two separate spheres of value-making, the music's evolution as a binary relation mirroring not only the fundamental, racial dichotomy of Black and White but also the dual character of the commodity form. In their entanglement—an interplay of use and exchange different from the classical Marxian position that advocates their complete separation—Black music's twin spheres moved ahead as they repeatedly traced back in contrary motion to the music's origin as an anomalous creation of "lazy" slave labor.[51]

In his influential theory of the "changing same," initially formulated as part of his groundbreaking history *Blues People*, Amiri Baraka described a similar kind of double-sided cyclicity by which value emerged. For Baraka, Black music value developed out of an unresolvable struggle for ownership between capital and labor, between White-controlled institutions and the creative lives of Black working poor: those free people of color who forever carried the enslaved's burden as an unsovereign subject, as "Non-American." The history of Black music, Baraka contended, followed the logic of this struggle, progressing as a series of "definite stages" whose stylistic "transmutation" represented "in microcosm . . . the Negro's transmutation from Africa" to the "Negro American."[52]

Unlike the status of race in the relation of race-capital, however, sameness in Baraka's conception—which for him established the basis of the music's value—was neither consistently dialectical nor racial. Despite its presence in the ongoing struggle between Black and White, what was the "same"—congruent with the intellectual currency of the moment—remained monolithically African in spirit, having undergone initial transformations in early slave culture. In musical terms, even as the "same" evolved stylistically, or "formally," as Baraka described it, it stayed fixed in substance, being an essential, African "vitality, . . . [a] nonmaterial . . . value . . . the one vector out of African culture impossible to eradicate."[53] In working from this position, Baraka paid little attention to how the intensive economy within African American communities continually remade Black music practices as part of its dialectical relation to capital. He disregarded how the sameness of Black-generated stylistic practices representing the purportedly stable portion of the "changing same" was itself a product of a prior relational development. In retaining their putative sameness, stylistic practices repeatedly cycled outward into the world, where they gained new social and economic value. From there, they traveled inward, bringing back home a style enriched with new value, the back-and-forth movements reaffirming racial intensity while also reshaping Black music and the greater character of US popular music.[54]

The perpetual returns of Black music practices into Black-centered intensive economies were critical to the formation of value. What returned reinforced the music's racialized appearance as an inalienable possession, which enabled African Americans to assert and reassert their claims of ownership.[55] To this extent, rather than entirely compromising Black music value, as Baraka assumed, the unresolvable, dialectical interplay of race-capital paradoxically intensified the music's enlivened appearance, even as its sonic material routinely evolved, drawing from the language and forms of White-majority popular and vernacular musics.[56] Yet at the same time, public valuation of Black sound also had an economically devaluing effect, its increased availability making it subject to claim by White musicians and consumers who sought to possess—to make alienable—what was thought to be Black music's inalienable qualities of enlivened spirit. The repeated efforts on the part of White musicians and White-dominated entertainment institutions to control Black music, to shift monetary value away from Black-owned capital, would compromise Black people's own assertions of exclusive ownership, affirming the tragic tendency of profit-from-loss running across the history of Black music's valuation.

For Black musicians and communities, value has accrued from the repetition of botched attempts by White-controlled institutions to claim from Black music that which is never fully claimable. Such attempts, which must always fail, nonetheless create for White capital an accumulation of commercial profit, which heightens Black music's tragic status in exchange markets. What Black musicians ultimately gain is a profit in the negative: the continual losses of economic and aesthetic control and capital-driven profit generate another kind of profit in the intensification of what in Black music is deemed inalienable, alive, true. The repetition of profit-from-loss reveals a primary tendency in Black music's productive growth, which drives a process of unfolding and infolding of sonic material as part of the relational interplay of race-capital. In the asymmetrical involvements of Black to White, a property-in-difference is obtained. If the conflict were somehow to resolve, the music's unique cultural status would collapse.

It is not, then, in an exclusive ontological separability where Black music's value develops but in its anomalous constitution as the original cultural property of a property-in-slaves. Here, Black music reveals its epistemic radicalism based in the racial-economic: it produces a qualitatively different kind of auditory knowledge and temporal experience arising contestably out of the structures of capitalism itself. This inner radicalism developed directly out of the contradictory relation of race-capital, whereby Black music acquired its strange public presence. As a result of the unresolved social and economic contradictions originally introduced into exchange under slavery, Black music repeatedly realized its exceptional qualities of embodied aliveness, its fetishized appearances motivating White consumers' incessant attempts to claim what was inalienable and racially bound to Black ownership. Aliveness in Black sound would emerge as African America's dialectically generated, creative engine, a contradictory, negative center consistent with Du Bois's portrayal of Black labor. In its accumulation of contradictory properties, Black music proposed a contentless shadow story, a "mute music" of contest and becoming, its primary truth materialized in forms cast in the negative. The centrality of music performance in the affirmation and assertion of African American culture would become so powerful, so everlasting, that it would rewrite the conventions of US history, bringing into public knowledge proletarian-centered sensibilities informed by the double character of Black music.[57]

Celebrating the political force of Black sound at the moment of slavery's defeat, Du Bois draws our attention to the social and aesthetic implications of an insider culture dubiously interacting with a greater world economy. He shows us how the seminal conflict between White capital and Black labor brought about new aesthetic forms conceived in the contradiction of a double relation, "distilled from the dross of its dung." If Du Bois, in upholding a nineteenth-century understanding of art and aesthetics, believed music to directly express meaning, he was also the first to identify how value accrued, recognizing how the qualities of "Negro spirit" that were thought to be alive in the sound of Black music developed from the material conditions of economic struggle, producing an unresolvable form to which meanings adhered.[58] Steadfast in his critique of Black popular entertainment, Du Bois remained nonetheless committed to modern social thought, the virtuosity of his dialectical materialism (above all, his conception of a Black proletariat and famous theory of "double consciousness") inspiring later critics—Baraka, Ralph Ellison, Houston A. Baker Jr., and Paul Gilroy, among them—to fashion their own views of Black music's evolution.[59]

But Du Bois also helps us to recognize another dimension that is critical to the generation of Black music value. For this, recall from the opening of this introduction his discussion of the unruly character of southern Black work life, where slave sounding practices evolved as part of a labor form "not as easily reduced to be the mechanical draft-horse which the northern European labor became." This is the point at which he locates the inspiration for Black labor not only in the work relations among slaves, but also arising from somewhere external to US slave society, "out of an age long past." For Du Bois, for whom "a sense of history informs nearly everything [he] wrote," the slaves' inspiration derived from another place, from where they inherited a "tropical, . . . sensuous receptivity to the beauty of the world" that sustained them in finding "spiritual returns adequate."[60] Du Bois's words are suggestive of a different locus of value accumulating in the production of "Negro" sound that, while participating and changing in the dueling economies of race-capital, did not require full interaction with that economic relation to sustain an informing presence. Instead, it enriched the sensation of enlivened sound by imparting qualities tracing from a recessive knowledge, from what may be thought of as an affective way of knowing that reaches back before and outside the time of capitalism, which, in its dialectically bound participation within the economy of slavery, frequently coupled with metaphysical beliefs in the spirit world or in Christianity. Conspicuous in southern Black life at the end of the slave era, this back-leaning affective relation assumed a presence in Du Bois's vivid metaphorical display in which he sought to capture the sensation of the Apocalypse heard in "the loveliest thing born this side the seas."

As it emerged from the depths of slavery as a supplemental energy attached to Black music, this third valuative relation born in the past would intensify the temporal and spatial energies sustaining the music's enlivened character. It enabled Black southerners to claim possession of Black music's fleshy qualities by which they conceived connections between racialized sound and a broadly imagined realm, otherworldly and "long past." Into the modern, this same quality would be subjected to economically driven fetishisms, as Black music entered the universe of racialized symbolism and participated in interpretations sustaining institutional efforts to incorporate Black music into a mythic national whole. Yet, this sensation also articulated to another kind of fetishism drawn from the first European encounters with Africa, which upheld Black music's incongruent character. These latter fetishisms inspired listeners to recognize how aliveness was not part of a common whole but rather structured negatively in contradiction to capitalism's incorporating tendencies. It is these mediated attachments to the past that affirmed Black music's enlivened character and enabled means of contemplating a variety of imaginings in line with the structural contradictions underlying valuation. We may think of this temporally disruptive sensation as past-time and its fetishized renderings and misreadings as diverting pastimes to which past-time remained dialectically connected.[61]

Past-time, as a sensation, comes about from a backward turn, an about-face imagining of an order of cultural knowledge antecedent to capitalism—"imagining," because its access is changing, dynamic, depending necessarily on its mediation and fetishization—that was first constituted under capitalism as part of the slaves' reinvention of labor. In its refusal of what Marx called "real subsumption" by capital, past-time identified within the field of the enslaved people's sounding practices a conceptualizing territory, a means of calling beyond to prior worlds that became influential in the affective complexities of Black secular and Christian musical performance.[62] Past-time afforded a way of comprehending what many performers and listeners during the time of slavery and into the modern era believed to be historically, socially, and metaphysically expansive in the sonic substance of Black music. The sounds aligning with Black pasts, while participating in commercial markets, introduced a disjunctively heightened feeling, seemingly anterior to and beyond the present day and connecting to a realm of knowledge that exceeded economic constraints otherwise generating audible property. As a phenomenological terrain, moreover, past-time aligns with Baraka's conception of Black music as something conceptually "Non-American": it is at once epistemically external to the norms of American Music and critical to Black music's racial character.[63] Musically evocative of an incongruous temporality, past-time brought forward "the form of a figure from the past now activated in the present that confers historical status on it but also announces the 'presence' of the past in the present." Its historical disjunctiveness would be available for African Americans to claim and possess and for all listeners across racial category to discern. Past-time proposed during slavery and, in its continual metamorphoses, still proposes today an understanding of Black music as an accumulation of affective knowledge residing in the material production of enlivened sound. It interlinks contested pasts and presents as part of the music's counterhistory, consistent with Harry Harootunian's sense of "the present [as] the crowding of differing historical times, which marks the modern from the presents of prior pasts."[64]

Past-time accordingly identifies an affective orientation first existing within the auditory cultures of the enslaved that proceeded to develop incongruently in relation to White power. Phenomenologically, it is consistent with what Theodor Adorno and Hanns Eisler characterized as the "archaic" nature of listening in the way that "the human ear has not adapted itself to the bourgeois rational and, ultimately highly industrialized order as readily as the eye, which has become accustomed to conceiving reality as made up of separate things, commodities."[65] As an analytical tool, moreover, past-time offers a way of comprehending the sonically induced sensation of divergent pasts and temporal realms in excess of everyday experience, all cohering, unfolding, and infolding as part of a dynamic, audible present. In this respect it participates in the formation of value and meaning by intensifying qualities of aliveness. Evoking prior sensory realms, past-time imparts an affect that is at once distensible and disjunctive: it invites uncanny experiences constituted under capitalism that carry power to simultaneously expand and disrupt conventional sensations of time and place. In its accumulation, it magnifies the spectral immediacy of Black sound, revealing multiple, embodied past presences.[66]

Past-time is not a literal transposition from one time to another, nor is it a directive on how to read meaning in Black music. Rather it provides analytical specification of a socially contrary condition evolving over the course of Black music's development, having first emerged as part of a grand ideological refiguring in late-antebellum slave culture. In this way, past-time aligns with a Black Atlantic temporality that "specifies the boundaries not of community but of sameness by introducing a syncopated temporality—a different rhythm of living and being."[67] Recorded reminiscences by former slaves indicate that they routinely recognized the role of sound-making in the imagination of a shared heritage, suggesting that pastness was part and parcel of Black music's racial coalescence. Although the actual practice of music was specific to the locations of southern culture they inhabited, many slaves acknowledged the conceptual presence of "Africa" in its performance. The works of Lawrence Levine, Roger Abrahams, Sterling Stuckey, and Michael A. Gomez, moreover, have shown that slaves' conceptualizations of the African past fostered metaphysical linkages that impacted the temporal character of everyday experience. These imagined pasts, in turn, routinely aligned with the sounding practices that slaves performed during labor, ritual, and leisure, the correspondences contributing to the making of a greater sonic ontology. In this circumstance, Black music acquired material qualities of embodied *history* that subsequently evolved across the eras of Reconstruction and Jim Crow.[68]

Although sensations of past-time developed as part of the economic transactions producing slave music, its coherences did not exist apart from slave music's formal qualities and was not initially commodified. Instead, a sense of pastness was available conceptually to those slaves who recognized and claimed it as part of their own meaningful experience. Among those for whom the past was important to their understanding of a shared sensory knowledge, past-time enabled the perception of performance as an intensity populating the auditory world with a sensuous accumulation of older affects drawn into new imaginings and memories.[69] These intensities of the past in the present gave to Black music greater intersocial complexity and ontological depth, its expression of "posthumous" temporal qualities—a laying out of the time of labor against the intrusions of capital time—being Black-owned and Black-purposed. Together, the concept of past-time and the enslaved peoples' economically driven properties of enlivened sound joined in the situation of performance, enabling them to aurally take possession of imagined pasts, and in doing so, to bring those pasts into their own sound ecology.

Past-time as a phenomenal condition first develops as part of the oblique, backdoor engagements with African systems of thought that were common on the African continent before the time of European colonization and were brought by enslaved people to the Americas. This was a world where, as Achille Mbembe succinctly puts it, "humans did not entertain a competitive relationship with objects . . . [and where] objects were part of us, and we were part of objects." Spirit and being, person and thing, temporalities of past and present routinely inhabited inanimate forms, as part of a greater "network of knowledge" tracing back centuries, the many versions of this deep relationality carrying forward well into the African colonial era, when they became the subject of Euro-Western scholarship.[70] Translated into anthropological theory as "animism," this African order of relation, though not exclusively auditory, frequently involved sound as one of the objective materialities participating in animated world-making, particularly in the multiple regions on the African continent where sound-producing instruments and even sounding practices themselves could be inhabited as "spirited things."[71] Whether in ritual, healing practices, or everyday life, the broad variety of African performed sound, together with the voices and instruments generating it, played a critical role in shaping a larger ecology of self in collaboration with exterior forms and realms: among people, animals, plants, and inanimate objects; between the living and the "voices of the dead"; between the greater present and the ancestral past. Humanly organized sound brought forward and condensed worlds in ways consistent with Wole Soyinka's comprehension of Yoruba temporality, where "life, present life, contains within it manifestations of the ancestral, the living and the unborn. All are vitally within the intimations and affectiveness of life, beyond mere abstract conceptualization." Performed sound cohered and condensed these multiple past, present, and future presences, moving them forward as they became connected to collective imaginings of a relational ecology—a vast cultural biome populated with the living, the undead, and animated things, all active in the making of new, aesthetically energized socialities.[72]

As African philosophical systems were introduced into colonial North America and the slave communities of the US South, similar coalescences of ontologically heightened sound routinely developed. In a diverse assembly of otherworldly references—spells, charms, spirits, ghosts, haints, witches, magic, goofer, toby, mojo, hoodoers, conjurers, zombis, superstition, second sight—writers across the nineteenth century documented the presence within everyday slave experiences of a temporally nebulous aliveness inhabiting Negro music.[73] The representations, typically written by White observers, were in most cases meant to demonstrate the primitive character of the African disposition. What they revealed instead—confirmed in the suggestive writings and recorded reflections of former slaves—was the presence of a powerful, sensory Africanity supplementing the economic production of the slaves' new properties of sound, their wraith-like peculiarities cohering, at times tenuously, at others tenaciously, to a temporally expansive ecology of Black living. This broad sphere of affect enjoining slaves to their present, past, and future worlds was a relational interface that established profound intimacies and wide ecological imagining, linking person to person, person to thing, and person and thing to other, temporally diffuse, metaphysical realms. What eventually coalesced as Negro music in the 1840s and 1850s introduced into the new economies of southern entertainment a temporal intensity, a racially animated gravitas that held the capacity to draw slaves into close relation to a sense of the past. As the enlivened presences of an "undead," ancestral world congealed retrospectively, posthumously as part of Black music's conceptualization, the music's qualities of past-time sustained the intersocial, person-to-object ecology of a distinctively African sentience. Out of the archive of slavery's history, sonically motivated sensations of pastness and otherworldliness would become common to evolving self-identifications as "slave," "Negro," "Black," "African," "Christian."

Past-time is neither an appeal to unsubstantiated claims of an essential Black nature nor a reaffirmation of formalist arguments regarding African retentions. It is, rather, a critical extrapolation from the historical record that helps us to comprehend the phenomenal effect of Black music's aliveness as it played out over the course of two hundred years. First observable as part of the slave era, it identifies in the twentieth and twenty-first centuries—after continuous, dialectically generated transformations—slavery's insistent place as a philosophical and audible "founding stone," the source base and afterlife of an affective order crucial in the making of Black music. As an interpretive strategy, moreover, the concept of past-time develops from the premise that what were perceived as Black music's "peculiar" qualities of aliveness could not have materialized as they did had it not been for the full-frontal presence of Africa in the American South—as a realm of knowledge, as an ontologically expansive ecology, as a tradition of sounding practices and performance learning.[74] A force associated with Africa's legacy of animism, it locates the existence of a fetish character different from commodity fetishism, one developing from African systems of thought, being aligned with what William Pietz, in a classic set of essays, called the "irreducible materiality" of animated things.[75] What is conveyed in Black music as past would always seem to exceed the compass of the alienable, being suggestive of a multidimensional new-world ancestry participating within the grand historicality of US slavery. Yet past-time is not pure form; it imparts no essential African sensibility. Indeed, the audible sensation of an African pastness would appear increasingly oblique as Black music carried forward, becoming refashioned within the productive and affective orders of popular entertainment. Past-time does not, then, prescribe meaning, nor does it disarm the dual interplay of race-capital as a structuring force. Rather it introduces an additional analytical concept to explain the temporal and affective incongruities associated with aliveness as a call to something beyond the here and now. As such, sensations of past-time would ultimately participate in the processes of commodification as part of the racial contest of ownership.

The enduring struggle over music ownership sets the contours of the past itself. What coheres as a seminal claim of Black music under slavery is then subjected to further challenge as sounding practices proliferate and expand as a new sonic knowledge during the interregnum commencing at the end of the Civil War. At this point, free Black musicians were actively participating in a wide variety of performance situations in which disruptive temporalities contoured the character of musical experience. These ranged from Christian communities seeking spiritual truth in Jesus to Pentecostal worshippers involving practices clearly linked to Africa; from "colored minstrels" engaging in parodies of White people in blackface to secular gatherings of Black people enjoying the pleasure of new commercial styles. As Black music penetrated national markets, however, its expressive capacities inspired a series of reimaginings of it as a historical form. The dynamic relation of race-capital accelerated the growth of White-driven sentimental portraits of African American music's past, proliferating tales of happy "darkies" singing and playing on the plantation, maudlin stories of mournful slaves suffering in labored chant, sensationalistic reports of clamorous Africans alternatively expressive of nature's utopia and dystopic horror. As a result, a new sense of the audible past aligned with, as it informed, the increasingly controversial, stylistic features coalescing as Negro music. If these new articulations, generated chiefly in markets controlled by White institutions, were ideologically invested in incorporating Black music into a singular conception of American popular expression—conceived in this study as diverting "pastimes"—they nonetheless brought into racially specified affective orders new disruptive intensities of past-time, affirming the peculiarity of Black-generated sound's ontological character.

By the first three decades of the twentieth century, the continuing fascination with Black music heightened the sense of wonder among White consumers about where these strange sounds were coming from. Commentaries grew ever more frequent and sensational, affirming the view of the music's origin in the primal pasts of Africa and the plantation South. The depictions typically served to demean and ridicule, to encourage once more the negative perception of African Americans as a "repetitious" people. But these same narratives had the unintentional effect of supplying the perceptible character of Black music with greater temporal coherence, inspiring among African American musicians and their audiences new attention to peculiarities in sounding practices that were thought to trace back to realms prior to the music's entry into popular entertainment markets. Into the twentieth century, as Black music underwent public translation—its odd-sounding commercial labels, "blues," "ragtime," and "jazz," evocative of the southern past—so did the music's pastness confront the forces of exchange to influence the production of style. Commonly bound to practices centering around propulsive, asymmetrical rhythm—the aforementioned assembly of performance practices expressing a greater *beat knowledge*— the disruptive sonic material conjuring sensations of past-time reaffirmed Black music's double character. It would become in the arena of pop an alienable commodity form, consumed as a playfully animated and diverting *pastime*, and a racially inalienable possession, an inspirited *past-time*, caught fleetingly in its discursive translations as something incongruently alive.

Across the late nineteenth century and into the time of popular music's commercial institutionalization—identifying in this study Black music's long modern era—listening communities would typically be aware of how Black music's formal anomalies gestured backward in time. The music's qualities of aliveness frequently sounded old in their strange newness, as popular discourses gave stress to bygone places and eras: to plantation slavery and songs of frivolity and sorrow; to New Orleans's Storyville, the putative birthplace of jazz; to the Mississippi Delta, the mythic place of origin of the blues; to a monolithic, primal Africa. What was alive in the sound would remain temporally out of joint; it is what made Black music sound uncanny—different from Music. Over the course, Black music would be once more "condemned to meaning," as listeners across the color line sought to capture in words what they heard as a recessive knowledge conveyed in aesthetic qualities of truth.

As explored earlier, truth as a positive condition would always remain partial, being caught up in the idealizations of people and powers, the aspirational and the imagined. According to the ideology sustaining White power, Black music's truth commonly depended on failed attempts to possess an unpossessable, racialized property; among African Americans, inversely, the experience of truth frequently involved the music's paradoxical growth of value through the botched attempts by White capital to expropriate it. And hidden away in the structuring processes generating enlivened sound, Black music tenaciously revealed an enduring, unspoken truth arising out of racial contradiction: a truth residing materially in forms that remained open to reception and meaning. The structures that brought forward audible qualities of aliveness provided ways of listening critically beyond fetishism to comprehend fetishism's powers and discovering why Black music appeared so enchanting—they enabled one to discern the interplay of pastimes and past-times in the making of spectacular sound. This version of truth suggests one most in line with Black music's productive processes and the temporal incongruities they fostered. Recognizing this version of truth requires confronting the fetishisms of meaning that Black music enabled.

Past-time thus turns always to the present, to a repetition of new relations, to the witnessing of Black music's emergence out of conditions of alienation. As a disjunctive possibility it corresponds to what Nathaniel Mackey, in his glorious critical portrait of Black sound, poses as "an otherwise unavailable Heaven . . . [a] utopic insinuation of an accretional 'yes' which annexes the trace of its historical loss."[76] Past-time's complex expression within the greater economies of race-capital would play out as part of the contrapuntal cultural production of Black music as an impure pure form composed in the negative. The conceptual sum of its double-sided productive processes—property-of-property, being-in-labor, meaning and value, profit-from-loss, race-capital, past-time and pastime—would collectively bring into view a sense of Black music as a dynamic, accretional complex continually in the making: a seemingly enlivened sonic entity that grew and regressed, at once structured in and incongruently related to the greater productive tendencies of American entertainment capitalism. Black music's intricate relations to race, the economic, and the African past show it to be something more than an aesthetic form in the conventional sense, something different from Music. It stands as a catalyst of African American culture's becoming as it assumes a principal position in the production of a greater American social knowledge. In its double-sided interplay, Black music would arise across the twentieth and twenty-first centuries as the critical shadow force in the evolution of pop, identifying the nation's principal aesthetic means of difference-making and the primary cultural influence sustaining Blackness and Whiteness as social categories.

Here, then, in this never-ending contest of economized, racial struggle, developed the fundamental dynamic structures at work in the making of Black music's value. To employ Du Bois's own Hegelian language, it revealed a negatively rendered "spirit" consistent with its place in the expansion of capital, arising as an ontological sonic entity seated at the right hand of "God." Listeners would come to hear in its audible sentience charges of profound meaning, brought into understanding by the many narrations accompanying the music's rise to power. If, in the end, Black music directly communicates no consistent assembly of signs, it nonetheless achieved what Adorno called music's cognitive character: a nonsentient complexity suggestive of being, which in this instance would be structured as part of a long slave era that has repeatedly spoken and still speaks today.[77] Black music reveals in its double form a contrary manifestation of America, a counterhistory materialized in sound that repeats as a primary truth the nation's unresolved conditions of race.

BLACK MUSIC AS COUNTERHISTORY: METAMORPHOSES OF A VALUE FORM

Thinking about Black music as counterhistory develops directly from its initial form as a property-of-property and the outward-inward, forward-backward movements of its historical progression. What is counter in the music's pattern of growth maps on a grand scale the contradictions orienting performances of enlivened sound. These structural parallels between the abstract movements in Black music's cyclical progression and the concrete musical qualities of aliveness not only call for a different approach to chronicling the development of style but also prompt a rethinking of the way that race in America is musically felt and imagined.

Just as Black music has openly participated in the world of capitalized entertainment, so have its incongruities of form repeatedly troubled that participation. Ascending as an afterlife of slavery, it has in its historical accretions lived up to its tragic character: protected as an inalienable property Black music is perpetually beset by the relentless forces of commodification. What sustains the music's accumulation of value are its tenacious embodiments, which insist on the primacy of blackness in American life. In this way, Black music asserts the negative dimension of its double character. Demeaned by fetishization, it gains value in its formal refusal of its complete absorption into capital. The music's spectral qualities are aesthetic indications of an insistent "Negro" past guiding its contrapuntal development and informing its temporal feeling.

Black music's counterhistory begins with slavery because slavery is its founding stone, the tragic beginning of an ongoing, asymmetrical struggle that initiates and then perpetuates the invention of form. Because this struggle never resolves, the contradiction inherent to the music's production repeats, recovering multiple pasts into newly performed presents: the contradiction of race persists in the anomaly of the music's double character. Black music's refusal to conform to consensus, moreover, is consistent with the way it gestures backward as it evolves; gesturing backward is a fundamental part of its forward progression. What disseminates outwardly cycles back, intensifying and expanding to bring into public listening an aesthetic immediacy—the racial particularism of enlivened blackness, which casts its ghostly presence over the entirety of pop.

In many histories of American music, Black music's various expressions organize into genres that trace a steady progression of style. They are the components of a development rendering Black music as a category of Music. Having been imposed from above, however, genres have tended to be reluctantly acknowledged by musicians, some of whom have equated them with slave names.[78] Although genre categories are essential to the greater understanding of how value developed, they can tell only part of the story, for they disregard the give-and-take of Black music's distinctive evolution. Thinking about Black music as counterhistory, in contrast, redirects attention to the ironic tendencies of the music's productive processes, seeing its key transformations as part of a struggle to define Black worlds. Black music evolves neither as a singular, coherent Music nor as a neat sequence of styles, but as something more akin to a species in metamorphosis. As it advances and retreats and advances again, it changes in quality and character, with each stage carrying forward aspects of the past as it enacts transformations into something new: new coalescences that affirm the paradox of economically generated inalienable form.[79]

Alive in the Sound proceeds as an ontological mapping, a charting of the music's growth as a series of coalescences that bring forth multiple versions of sensational, animated presences. Although the coalescences of a given moment are what identify historical periods, all coalescences share as their basis the racial contests of ownership central to popular musical innovation. The book examines how Black music's various coalescences participated in the making of four larger transformations, or metamorphoses: the anomalies of enlivened sound arising from slave labor; the scabrous inventions of free Black performers working after the Civil War; new formations given the commercial names ragtime and jazz that developed as part of the first networks of modern popular entertainment; the innovations of swing, modern jazz, boogie, rhythm and blues, and free that oriented the greater musical and affective design of mid-to-late twentieth-century American pop. Each metamorphosis identifies a particular aesthetic organization emerging out of transactions between Black music labor and the constraining forces of commerce: at every phase, performative *sounding practices* give way to more stable coherences (*sound formations*) that contribute to the growth of a historically evolving body of *sonic material*. The market's tendency to incorporate innovation inspires variation, with subsequent music incorporations motivating advances yet again. Through the process, Black music continually transforms, becoming more and more expansive, as its orientations to the past also deepen.

Transactions commenced with the entry of the slaves' sound world into public forums, marking Black music's first metamorphosis. This is the point when enslaved people began to present their audible labor before White audiences, triggering the conceptualization of the cultural phenomenon, Negro music. A tracing of the second metamorphosis turns to the world of free-Black music labor that organized directly after the Civil War as part of what Thulani Davis powerfully describes as the Black South's "Emancipation Circuit."[80] From the 1870s to the first decade of the 1900s, a population of itinerant Black musicians living and working on the edge of southern society—many performing in blackface as "colored minstrels"—introduced into commercial markets forms of enlivened sound that accelerated the exchange of a racially inalienable property. This second metamorphosis was less the result of rebellion than a manifestation of a powerful auditory dissensus: a vagrant proletariat engaging in the production of socially irritable, "scabrous" sound.

"Contests of Ownership in Early National Markets" charts the expansion of Black music's third metamorphosis as it enters national entertainment markets during the first three decades of the twentieth century. It begins in chapter 4 with an analysis of the commercial transactions giving rise to seminal versions of Black popular music. The entrance of these embodied forms into the circuits of capital resulted in massive economic and psychic losses among a new urban-professional labor class. But they also generated a substantial symbolic profit, taking the form of a transformative beat knowledge that led to a qualitative shift in the magnitude of Black music's temporal complexities and historical depth; these manifold changes fueled the growth of value. As it reared on its hind legs—in Zora Neale Hurston's evocative rendering at the conclusion of chapter 6—Black music assumed the posture of an occupying force that overwhelmed modern musical culture with its peculiar spectral presences.[81]

The three chapters that compose the final section examine Black music's fourth metamorphosis. They focus on the fifty-year period (ca. 1930–1980) when a late-modern manifestation of musical aliveness comes into being. The move begins when a community of savvy musician-professionals bring their ongoing struggle of ownership into public view. The continuous interplay of Black innovation and its translation into the procrustean categories of a White-controlled music industry—as swing, rhythm and blues, bop, urban blues, commercial gospel, cool, etc.—drives Black music's ontological expansion as a spectacularly enlivened expressivity. Its dual stand as a hyperpositive and negative form establishes it as both the primary influence and a shadow presence in popular music. An afterword considers the consequences of these developments as Black music moves into a new phase of development.

Through the many stagings of profit-from-loss, Black music has ascended, harnessing the past to move forward, evolving according to its now familiar two-step motion. Through these means, it has realized an expressive capacity that defies the subsumptive power of capital: overtaking American sonic culture, Black music—a music widely acknowledged as the production of Black people—has disseminated into the world, reorganizing popular sensibilities on a global scale. Rhythmic revolutions led by swing and boogie set the stage for a cumulative advancement that carried forward across the decades and into the twenty-first century. With the coalescence of what Amiri Baraka named New Black Music, it organized as a late-modern apotheosis, its animatedness reaching outwardly to form a musical version of Du Bois's "color line [that] belts the world."[82] Out of the complex evolutionary biology of enlivened sound, New Black Music extends its global reach, its late-stage metamorphosis realizing illicit truths-in-form that repeat the tragic, racial struggle at its core. *Alive in the Sound* examines this process, showing how through multiple unfoldings Black music has endured as the phantom center of American musical expressivity.

FIRST METAMORPHOSIS

PROPERTY'S PROPERTIES OF

RECONSTRUCTIVE POSSIBILITY

· O N E ·

S L A V E   L A B O R   A N D

T H E   E M E R G E N C E   O F

A   P E C U L I A R   M U S I C

PROPERTIES OF EMBODIED SOUND

When the free Black musician Solomon Northup was put up for sale after being abducted by slave traders in Washington, DC, his subjective status, no matter his own sense of himself, changed abruptly. Northup's seizure brought about a profound shift in his social position, transforming him from a free citizen of the republic into a form of alienable property, his sentience as a person-thing obtaining a value measured by traits both human and chattel. A gifted violinist, Northup acquired his newfound economic significance with the help of musical skills he had developed through years of practice, perfecting the technical intricacies of what was known at the time as "string music." What made his playing so diverting—appealing enough for him to be captured and sold into the southern slave market—had everything to do with that learning as a free citizen and laborer in the North.[1] When Northup made his fateful journey to Washington from his home in Albany, New York, he was attempting to put those skills to use, to bring his artisanal labor into the entertainment market. Upon his abduction, however, those same skills and labor would be reconceived as expressions of natural ability, which were thought to be inextricably connected to his racialized body. Northup-the-slave would take a loss of his own humanity; he who was once a musician-laborer now occupied the category of a living thing—a being-in-labor whose very existence was defined by and conceived as unpaid labor and whose newly acquired, "natural" musicality informed the character and perception of his work.

It may verge on the obvious to suggest that Northup's kidnapping and new life, famously narrated in his autobiography, *Twelve Years a Slave* (1853), marked a beginning that would forever affect his own conception of himself. After all, being a slave, being labor in a literal sense, was a tragic if commonplace experience for millions of Africans and African Americans who suffered the sorry fate of chattel slavery. Yet in its relation to musicality, the transformation is nonetheless startling. For what was formerly conceived as a kind of skilled labor-for-hire had collapsed into the body, integrating as a quality of the enslaved subject itself. If musical performance among free people represented a form of alienable labor that could be exchanged in the market, it had been recast under slavery into a condition of the living person-thing. What was once understood as a commodifiable activity based on learning now appeared as an audible extension of the slave; it was not "labor" per se but a naturally embodied sound inherent to the flesh and signifying the inferior character of "the Negro." Like that of most slaves, Northup's musicianship would have been deemed equivalent to his physical attributes, being inextricably linked to his inferiority as a racialized person-thing, even if his consummate playing skills must have made such certainties seem dubious. If musicality were naturally a part of his body, then so, inversely, would his sound productions retain qualities of that body, the various portrayals of "lively," "energetic," and "soulful" sound being among the many indications of slave music's fleshy resonance.

We can then, by turns, already understand how the racist assumption of natural musicality produced powerful anomalies as the enslaved's sounding practices entered the structuring field of the economic. The belief that this "Negro music" brought into audible form the substance of the slave body introduced an epistemic shift consistent with a greater transformation of the Black subject from human to thing. Sound-based qualities of fleshiness, which would be represented discursively as the many "peculiarities" of Negro music, were not Music as such but rather sonic extensions of a being-in-labor—the strange living resonances of an abject Black body.[2] So it follows that the sounds produced by Northup's own performing self were not only audible portrayals of his being but also truthful in that they always remained partially owned by him, even as they openly participated in an exchange economy.

Northup's performances were part of a special kind of laboring not equivalent to that of the field hand, the house slave, or the artisan who produced goods and services essential to the southern economy. He was of the class of "Negro musicians," a fiddler who was routinely put to service for the pleasure of White people. The sounds he played, named "slave" or "Negro" music, had arisen as a centerpiece of plantation leisure, providing entertainment for slaveholding families and their visitors, together with townspeople who listened and danced to slave musicians hired out for various occasions.[3] Although the most conspicuous forms of sounding-making activity among enslaved people took place in fields and other work contexts relying on collective labor, it was these special creations of music appearing at the interracial contact points of White musical diversion where a distinctive category of audibility emerged. The slaves' public performances brought into being a sound world under the containments of White mastery that was simultaneously retained by slaves, who claimed ownership of that same sound world as part of their very bodies. And the more that slave musicality circulated within the southern exchange economy, the greater would be the sense of the enslaved people's ownership of it. What was socially constituted as the property of the master now appeared under the possession of a slave body generating sound. It was this structural anomaly, brought about in the contradiction of an inalienable racial form entering markets exchanging alienable commodities, that set the parameters for the making of the slaves' sonic property: a property-of-property whose audibility gave the appearance of having something alive in its sound.[4] Slave sounding practices were inhabited by the embodied presences of the slaves themselves.

The racist perception of the slave as an audible being became the impetus for the invention of a new music value: an animated property-in-sound whose accumulation of varied meanings would grow according to its disruptive involvement in commercial markets. The valuation of Negro music as a troublesome property arises at a historical moment when US slaves, having been deemed less than human, could now be imagined as a kind of peculiarly magical person-thing emitting a strange kind of music all the while they participated in the routines of everyday labor. In their capacity to resonate sound, they mapped sonic extremes consistent with Black music's uniquely double character: born of the laboring body, it disseminated the irreducibly fleshy essence of the Black racial self as it also decoupled from its embodied source to become a point of contest in the struggle of ownership. This "Negro music," as a production of the late antebellum racial economy, would overtake the cultures of the South and eventually the metropoles to the North and around the world, its value rising in step with its strange relation to capital production. In its qualities of enlivened sound, listeners could now discern the kernel of Black being, suggesting an audible X-ray of the character of race.

In this chapter, I want to expand on the analysis laid out in the introduction to set the groundwork for the book's overall argument, plotting out a thesis that seeks to explain the historical development of Black music as an enlivened form. I will show how the slaves' uncanny qualities of embodied sound took hold as part of the confrontation of the slaves' musicality with their own classification as exchangeable properties of labor, the anomalies generating qualities of animatedness that identified the basis of the music's valuation. In their performances, slaves brought into being a most peculiar entity consistent with the "peculiar institution" as a whole: a racialized sonic possession whose power and significance arose out of the contested interplay of relations distinguishing social and ontological categories of slave and free. The emergence of Negro music in the 1840s and 1850s—at a time of growing civil and political unrest over the matter of slavery—signaled a seminal coalescence developing out of the structural dislocation of slave subjection and White mastery, whereby a sonic manifestation of Black labor marked the invention of a property form and economic value existing within and at odds with exchange relations. Although slave performances remained fundamentally linked to everyday field labor, their sounding practices soon began to challenge the integrity of Music as a social category, precisely because they always appeared to exceed the White population's ability to claim and possess them. In the greater context of US antebellum slavery, African America had brought into being its foundational cultural property, a racially embodied sonic surplus, its strangely inalienable and alienable double character consistent with the structures of racism organizing a greater colonizing logic across the Americas.[5]

PROPERTIED LABOR

An analysis of Black music as an anomalous form of labor begins with the peculiar quality of the producer itself, with the enslaved individual as a "species of property." Unlike the Enlightenment conception of "Man," whose subjectivity and sovereignty related to an inalienable condition of liberty as property—in the famous words of John Locke, "Every Man has a Property in his own Person. This no Body has any Right to but himself"—the slave's humanity had been forcibly reconstituted as something akin to the products and productive means of southern agrarian economy: to the workhorses, hogs, and fowl with which they were routinely compared. Negro slaves, as beings-in-labor, endured a precarious existence in late antebellum contexts, commonly perceived as literal versions of work. Slaves epitomized reified living forms; less than human, they were laboring machines "attached to the soil" that had undergone "a recoordination of nerves, muscles, eyes, and hands."[6] Purchase of slaves in southern slave markets accordingly involved an assessment of the quality and condition of these means. The slave body was rendered an assembly of components requiring close examination before purchase. A prospective buyer might size up the condition of the slave by checking skin quality and color, strength of limbs, coordination, demeanor, and disposition. As Daina Ramey Berry shows, the health of the slave body could even influence transactions beyond the slave's life, affecting what an owner might receive from the sale of a corpse for scientific study—what she evocatively calls "the price of their pound of flesh."[7] Buyers could approach purchase this way because they understood slaves as beings beneath the category of the civilized. In fact, their inferiority had grown into a fundamental concept in the structuring of the superior, White subject, effecting a critical common sense: the social irrelevancy or "death" of the slave, in its "natal alienation," was what registered the willful humanity of White mastery. This same fundamental condition of degenerative alienation was what catalyzed the production of inspirited musical value.[8]

By the 1840s, the category "slave" had been established in the context of the antebellum South as a determining measure of social and economic value, representing a critical component of the White majority's supremacist understanding of itself: masters in possession of individualism and reason. As propertied labor, enslaved people gave material form to the presubjective, disharmonious condition that conceptualized White humanity and society as a "harmoniously organized whole."[9] Representing the most valuable form of property in the land, slaves identified the principal means by which White people measured their rank. The greater the number of slaves owned, the higher one's social position and power, and in the act of ownership, the slave master realized freedom. "To own, to possess, to understand the *meum et tuum* [mine and yours]," wrote the proslavery political theorist Louisa McCord, "is one of the first distinguishing characteristics of reason, and in proportion as man becomes enlightened on this point, he rises above the beast." In this passage, McCord is propagating a view on the dialectical advancement of history first articulated by G. W. F. Hegel, who famously argued that Africans were a backward, inferior race—a people without history or historical knowledge.[10] Unlike the slave owners of antiquity, however, whose possessions attended to life's necessities so that they could enter the polis and exercise their rights of freedom, the antebellum slave owners of the US South with whom McCord was aligned aimed above all to put their freedom to action in order to accumulate money and capital. That slaves were a measure of material wealth meant they could serve in the same way as other forms of capital in the market economy. Not only could slaves be bought and sold; they could also stand up as collateral for borrowing, bringing into play a variety of practices of mortgaging and trading between living and inanimate property forms.[11] All of this suggests why virtually all White southerners were so deeply committed to slavery even though only a minority of them owned slaves. Notions of capital accumulation and ownership were inextricably linked to racial category and to its claim as the economic basis of production. As Edward Baptist has summarized, "The entire structure [of the southern economy] was bottomed on, founded on, funded by the bodies of enslaved people."[12]

The embeddedness of slavery in the functions of the US economy has inspired many contemporary historians to argue that despite its reliance on unfree labor, the southern economy might best be recognized as a dimension of a greater transatlantic capitalist enterprise, the centerpiece of what Sven Beckert has called, with reference to a particularly significant commodity, an "empire of cotton."[13] Recalling a position taken by Du Bois a century earlier, these scholars have demonstrated how a political structure once thought to have been a kind of in-between, "neither feudal . . . nor capitalist" (what Eugene D. Genovese famously called "seigneurialism"), largely operated as part of a forward-looking capitalist formation.[14] Rather than identifying an entirely different mode of production, a globalized southern slave empire was, in nearly every measure, a modern capitalist economy parallel to that of the North, differing only in its inclusion of person-slaves as commodities that existed both as part of the relations of production (i.e., contributing to the constitution of the economic structure) and as productive forces (objects of labor power; as literal means of production). New recognition of the undeniably capitalist character of the southern economy has accordingly made its inconsistencies with Marxist political economy seem less relevant. As Walter Johnson, one of the leading voices in this conversation, has observed, what emerges as the critical question is not whether or not slave labor fits within the conception of capitalism and its dependency on free, wage labor but rather "What would a theory of political economy that treated the labor, products, and experiences of people of African descent as central to (rather than prior to) the history of Western capital look like?" If US slavery was not fully capitalist because it was labor itself—a body that labors—rather than abstract labor that was being bought and sold, this "comes to seem less a comment on the character of American slavery than a comment on the orthodox definition of the term, 'capitalism.'"[15]

The new history of southern capitalism represents a critical turn in the way that scholars comprehend the political economy of slavery in the United States.[16] It marks a shift from prior notions of a strange seigneurialism or paternalism to an equally strange mode of modern capitalism whose ideological commitment to "freedom" happened to depend on the juridical enforcement of institutionalized slavery. Acknowledging the political force of capitalism in its subsumption of enslavement represents a key change in the understanding of antebellum southern culture. Yet as important as the new history has been in exposing the underlying Eurocentrism of free-labor-based Marxist political economy, it also tends to downplay the critical significance of Marx's observation that capitalism and slavery represented two distinctive perspectives of labor, regardless of whether the category "slave" is comprehended as labor power or not. What matters here is not the conflict of differing modes of production as part of a greater interpretation of historical materialism but rather the way in which slavery and race brought about differing conceptions of labor-based musical performance in its relation to differing subject categories of "Negro slave" and "White mastery." No matter how well inculcated many enslaved people were within the southern slave economy, their status as "slave," officially, a property-without-property, established a fundamentally different order of being, an ontological realm whose sounding practices coalesced within and against the greater order of capitalist exchange. The slaves' dual status as both sound-making laborer and audible labor was fundamental to the coalescence of what would be named Negro music, a coalescence that materialized as a racial logic the constitution of the slave subject, together with structures enabling slave-specific conceptions of freedom. It was, in particular, the social category of audible embodied labor—a noisy means of production named "slave"—that structured this coalescence as something anomalous to capitalism's formation as an economic system.

The point, then, is not to dally over traditional Marxian orthodoxies but rather to consider how Negro music, as a property of and in labor, emerged as a direct result of its constitution under slave capitalism at the same time that its creation as a property-of-property underlay its anomalous character and eventual cultural value. This recognition of the racial-economic basis of Black music is instructive in the consideration of slaves' production of culture and constitution of the subjective self, affirming a line of argument consistent with Afropessimist theories of social death while also identifying ways in which forces of domination established the basis of life-affirming creative acts.[17] For in my reading of the formation of Black music, the tragedy of "social death" is how animated audible "life" emerges. In the incommensurability of a sound-filled social order of slaves, existing within the bounds of southern capitalism's property relations and prohibitions, Negro music is made. We might do well, then, to expand on Johnson's previously stated question about the insertion of slavery into capitalism in order to ask: What happens to the look of US political economy when the full potential of slave sounding practices is placed front and center? The answer suggests the necessity of a critical move beyond the familiar narrative orders of American history and its commitment to a modern Enlightenment slave subject struggling to rise above the shackles to consider different orders of audible being, "ways of being human . . . that do not lend themselves to the reproduction of the logic of capital."[18]

AUDIBLE PROPERTIES

The African and African American slaves who invented the first North American Black music had already been participants in the southern racial economy from the outset, being identified as forms of labor or productive means—commodities in and of themselves.[19] As Graham White and Shane White explore in *The Sounds of Slavery*, the enslaved lived and worked in an environment where sound was among the modalities by which their behavior could be disciplined and conditioned for the fundamental purpose of production and profit. From the perspective of many White citizens in the US South, the sounding practices that so frequently accompanied slave behavior extended predictably from "the Negroes'" status as things. Their production of sound, often cast as a quality of noise—"It is a symbol of their savage degradation," as one observer expressed it; a "horrid dissonance, against which . . . a whole bale of cotton would be required to stop the ears," wrote another—was consistent with their failed humanity. A French nationalist traveling in Florida in the 1830s suggested that "nothing proves better the moral degradation of the negro than the joy and content he expresses in state of slavery. Draw near to a plantation, and [one hears] noisy outbursts of laughter." Frederick Olmsted, moreover (who was also admiring of slave musicality), conflated the sonic world of the human and animal in his portrayal of "two negroes with dogs, barking, yelping, shouting and whistling after 'coons and possums." In yet another instance, noisy sound marked the inferiority of a group of two dozen slaves lounging "lazily enough, chattering, laughing and singing (apparently perfectly happy)."[20] Some slave owners sought to contain the sound of the slaves' bodies by prohibiting singing, preaching, or talking with the threat of a vast array of physical punishment: stocks, gags, paddles, and whips. In one instance, an owner prevented a slave preacher from calling others to nighttime worship by affixing a metal implement to his mouth. Moses Grandy recalled the horrific experience on one of a fleet of slave ships heading to North America, where "the cries and groans were terrible, notwithstanding there was a whipper on each vessel trying to compel the poor creatures to keep silent."[21]

Masters and bosses employed sound to regulate the temporal behavior of their slaves, disciplining them to abide by the rule of the clock as it had organized labor since the beginning of modern capitalism.[22] "About half past four in the morning," the northern novelist Kate Conyngham recounts, "I am regularly awakened by a bell, as loud as a college or chapel bell; which is rung in the belfry of the overseer's house, to call the slaves up." Frequently, they interacted with them not as workers but as property summoned, calling them to order as one might a herd of cattle. Some slave owners went so far as to attach bells to their slaves' collars to discourage them from running away, as discussed by Moses Roper. A former Georgia slave similarly remembered how his owner "Stevens fixed bells and horns on my head. This is not by any means an uncommon punishment. I have seen many slaves wearing them." When transporting slaves in a coffle, moreover, traders might employ fiddlers to mark their step, sometimes assigning the task to one or two slaves, as depicted in the narrative of Amos Dresser.[23] To be sure, audibility was one of the foundational qualities of what Stephen A. Best calls the slaves' "fugitive properties," racially distinguishing the Negro from the White person, its body's outward aurality identifying a fundamental difference. It is for this reason that when they tried to escape ("at every turn advertisements are stuck up for runaway slaves"), masters would attempt to retrieve their property by describing its distinctive sonic features. Among the first representations of African vocal practices in the eighteenth century were characterizations of the audible Black body, bringing into relation the physical qualities of voice with things and creatures in the natural world with which they were commonly associated. "James, about 30 years of age . . . his jaw teeth are out, is remarkable fond of singing." And Cajah, whose "voice sounds as if coming out of a hollow tree."[24]

Into the late antebellum period, characterizations of the slave body as an auditory form increased in pace with the interactions of White and Black southerners. Nearly everywhere they labored, slaves were perceived to be making sound. A team of "half starved" Negroes working along Savannah's wharves performed "a kind of monotonous song, at times breaking out into a yell, and then sinking into the same nasal drawl." Rowers in Georgia "accompanied their labour by a wild sort of song," while others—from a group of porters loading luggage in Philadelphia, to a man pushing a wheelbarrow, to city youths selling potatoes and baked pears—continually brought sound and labor into close relation.[25] The very action of the laboring Black body seemed to possess a fundamental audibility; Negro work itself was inherently audible, suggesting an indexical relation between sound, labor, and the body in motion that had evolved into a mode of iconicity, a naturalized common-sense understanding of the sonic qualities of Negro flesh. Such displacements of sound from the Black body itself introduced a new kind of acousmatic knowledge conceived as racial resonance in the abstract. An early report from Savannah in 1817, for example, verges on a kind of immateriality in which slaves, absent from view, assume a disembodied audible form: "Nothing is heard near the water but the negroes' song while stowing away the cotton." Yet another report from New York from around the same time, eighteen years prior to the statewide abolition of slavery, similarly figures Black street workers metonymically as sound forms among "the cries of New-York" (figure 1.1).[26]

To this extent, sound not only marked slaves but also identified them as audible things whose externalized, sonic properties conjoined with other fleshy expressions of Negro behavior. And because audibility expressed something fundamental and true about the Black people's nature, White owners sought to exercise that nature to control their bodies and improve the character of work. As Mark M. Smith explains in his important accounting of the nineteenth-century US sound world, "Slaveholders . . . stress[ed] the rhythm of industriousness . . . and the sober tones of organic social and economic relations." When effectively harnessed, the slaves' sounding practices could be incorporated into efforts to increase the efficiency of what planters called "Nigger work."[27] Singing, in particular, staved off the condition of sloth. By exciting the Africans' natural qualities of sound-making, White mastery sought to contain another natural quality, the

1.1 "Sweet Potato Vendor" (1830).

propensity toward laziness, and thus help to organize labor in productive ways. In fact, it might even be fair to say that controls of singing functioned materially to isolate and identify slave music as a productive force, particularly in the large stretch of southern territory where planters commonly relied on gang labor.[28] Clearly some owners thought so. "While at work," a southern planter wrote in his report on the "management of Negroes," "they should be brisk. . . . I have no objection to their whistling or singing some lively tune, but no *drawling tunes* are allowed in the field, for their motions are almost certain to keep time with the music."[29] And because these fleshy, working machines were thought to be natural sound producers for reasons attributable to race and physiognomy ("Niggers is allers good singers nat'rally. . . . I reckon they got better lungs than White [folk]"), they could easily be induced to sing, even if their intellectual limitations rendered such singing basically as noise; "his songs are mere sounds."[30]

Singing not only served to discipline slave labor but also reinforced the enslaved's status as a different kind of human, giving form to their social reality as chattel property: their audible nature exposed certain truths about their being. By forcing slaves to make sound, moreover, owners sought for them to reinforce their own subjugation as exchangeable commodity forms. "The horror they feel in moving further to the South," observed Edward Strutt of Jesus College, Cambridge, in the early 1830s, "may be seen even in the ballads they are said to sing before the Whites."[31] Slaves in groups put up for sale would sometimes be made to sing to maintain order, extending the organizing powers of collective song. In other instances, slaves were forced to perform as part of their display on the auction block, where they were expected to demonstrate qualities of physique and temperament attractive to those who might buy them.[32] "Before the slaves were exhibited for sale," William Wells Brown observed, "some were set to dancing. . . . This was done to make them appear cheerful and happy."[33]

Such displays were unconscionably cruel, in an obvious way. But they were also symbolically so. Enforced play intensified the perception of slaves as performative things whose seemingly lighthearted actions affirmed their distance from the realities of southern social and economic life. This sentiment was expressed after slavery in the inane short story "Dinky," where the main character, a free Black boy—in an attempt to earn enough money to rescue his impounded dog—puts himself on the auction block, singing and "jumping juba" to demonstrate his worth. At least a few masters, finally, appeared to ignore the slaves' qualities of audibility altogether. J. Hector St. John de Crévecoeur was astonished by how some owners seemed to "become deaf" to the slaves' misery. "They neither see, hear, nor feel the woes of their poor slaves." The sounding slave, constituted as a kind of noisy audible flesh, could be classified as a commodity that speaks, as in Fred Moten's rendering, except that in these instances there was nothing economically fetishistic about it. Although the slaves' sounding practices had entered exchange and been drawn into the contest of ownership, their exchange value did not mask labor but, on the contrary, heightened awareness that these commodities were about production as such. The slaves' audible nature was merely a quality of their thingly, labor-specific form.[34]

In their efforts to render slaves as propertied labor, many masters directed what they perceived to be the Black person's innately noisy nature— "there is no silent path among them," registered one observer in 1854—in yet other ways that might be construed as productive. Across the slave era, observers recorded how the slaves' proclivities for making sound became a resource available for entertaining White people. Colonial and post-Revolutionary reports, for example, show already that owners sometimes extracted additional value from slave labor for their own pleasure, as in the story of the Virginia slave, Old Dick, whose young master, Tom Sutherland, "made me play the Banjer" while Tom and others danced a "Congo Minuet."[35] Antebellum accounts describe White owners frolicking among their human herds and ordering them to act out their affiliations with livestock and pets. The former slave James Watkins recalled in his narrative how

> Our masters sometimes brought ladies and gentlemen to look at us, but when we saw them coming towards us we ran to our cribs, fearing lest they should be coming to buy some of us; but we were called back, and had then to amuse them by performing various antics. We had to run on our hands and knees like dogs, and jump over each other like horses, to stand on our heads, to butt one another with our heads like sheep, and to dance and sing, some knocking old tin cans together, others jingling bones, and others beating juba [patting], the forestep, the backstep, the middle step, the juba singing.[36]

Northup's narrative from 1853 clearly indicates that some slaves were purchased largely because of their performance skills, just as Harriett Beecher Stowe's portrayal of "Topsy" in *Uncle Tom's Cabin* the year before shows how deeply such a purpose had become impressed upon American thought. "Here, Topsy," Tom's owner, Augustine St. Clare, calls out, "giving a whistle, as a man would to call the attention of a dog, 'give us a song, now, and show us some of your dancing.'" Other accounts appear across the historical record. To name one more, consider the case of Lavinia Bell, a free Black girl stolen from her parents in Washington, DC, and shuttled away to Texas, where she was sold to a White family. On its Texas farm, Bell was, according to a newspaper account from 1861, "brought up a 'show girl,'" whose owners "taught [her] to dance, sing, and cackle like a hen, or crow like a rooster" for the entertainment of crowds. Bell's novel imitations not only reinforced her subhuman stature but also put on display once more how slave sound production was perceived not as Music but as another kind of amusing or pleasing sound, an audible extension of a thingly condition.[37]

The truth of the slave body's inherent audibility typically stood well outside the normative measures of Music, even if the slaves' performances sometimes seemed to resemble it. Ambiguities in interpretation—as incomprehensible noise and as a comprehensible yet troubling difference—reached back to the earliest European encounters with African practices as they would grow increasingly hierarchical according to scientific racist ideology in the late eighteenth century. By the late antebellum period, White observers were advancing similar characterizations of Black musicality as an inherent noise that played the line of Music. Samuel A. Cartwright's 1851 depiction captures this distinction. According to Cartwright, for the slave, "music is a mere sensual pleasure . . . there is nothing in his music addressing the understanding [of form] . . . his songs are mere sounds, without sense or meaning." As evidence, Cartwright stressed slave music's inferior qualities: "It has melody, but no harmony"; the former being associated with the body, voice ("gratified by sound, as his stomach by food"), whereas the latter connecting to "the mind" and to the rules of European tonality. Vocality and melody, together with the percussive expressions of patting, stomping, and the like, were nothing more than bodily enactments: audible extensions of a living property. As a kind of prosthesis not sufficiently externalized to be fully expropriated by Whites, these sounds socially marked the slaves' natural proclivities toward barbarism, heightened sexuality, laziness, and play, suggesting a peculiar evolutionary manifestation somewhere between animal and human.[38] And yet Cartwright's deliberation about what he called the slaves' "music" suggests that Black sounding practices deserved consideration. His efforts to make distinctions between slave music and Music reveal that he recognized certain likenesses.

It is around this time that White perceptions of slave vocalizations and instrumental playing as outward-extending sounds of a living property were increasingly giving way to the opinion that these sounding practices were a kind of music, or perhaps even something akin to normative Music. In large part, the shift in perception arose materially, as a consequence of changes in the ways that slaves performed when entertaining at White gatherings. The copious references to slave instrumental practices indicate that more and more slaves were learning to sing and play in ways informed by European-centered musical rules and that these practices—diatonic and pentatonic scales, strophic song forms, duple and triple meter, tonal grammar, norms of equally tempered intonation—qualitatively reshaped the style of public musical performances that White people commonly encountered.

Racially interactive rituals relating to the harvest and Christian religious worship, together with the everyday occurrences of singing while laboring, became sites of potential relation whereby the inherent noisiness of the Negro would be reoriented in ways drawing similarities to European Music.[39] These interactions were what probably prompted the use of Enlightenment-inspired nature rhetoric in the affirmative depiction of slave singing as akin to "the bird song that goes beyond the bloom" revealing a "subliming spirit." Increasingly, nature becomes a familiar point of reference, a rhetorical strategy that displaced song from context, which in turn reinforced the autonomy and potential exchange value of Black music. Who would not want to bear witness to performances by "a people whom, above all others, the gods themselves have made musical"? These are beings who "hold the mirror up to nature; nay, it is nature's self displayed so fully, and with such graphic power." Reports from across the antebellum era similarly acknowledged the curious quality and character of the slaves' naturalness as sound makers, reinforcing the sense of a musicality that was inherent. "The Negro is as full of music as an egg is full of meat," observed a minister in the 1850s; "none wanted voice; they all had it, and to spare," said yet another.[40] For the White population, such transgressions from labor practice may have been uplifting at the same time their autonomy suggested there might be some trouble afoot.

The widespread activity of entertainment eventually produced a new category of labor, the Negro musician. Versions of Negro musicians were already in place in the Colonial era, being both "well trained as dining room servants and as scientific musicians . . . playing together on various instruments, at balls and parties."[41] As more and more slaves learned to play Euro-Western music, however, their masters turned these newly acquired labor skills into inventive ways of turning a profit. Documentary evidence accounts for numerous references to slave instrumentalists being hired out to perform at plantation parties, resorts, and carnivals, on steamboats, and in southern towns. The performances were part of a general practice of slave hiring that deeply informed the southern economy and complicated easy distinctions between paid and unpaid labor.[42] By hiring out their slaves, owners could extract even more value from their property. Musical skill offered to these owners an additional means of income, and when slaves would otherwise not be at work, their musical party performances realized a kind of surplus accumulating beyond conventional labor and increasing their economic value all the more. As Dena Epstein discovered in her seminal studies of slave musical practices, "In the larger towns [in the South] it was not uncommon to find an advertisement" of a musician's services for hire, inspiring some owners to train their slaves musically with the intention of hiring them out.[43] Others sought to purchase slaves who possessed such talents already, and those with special talent might work exclusively as musicians. George Walker, a fiddler and bandleader from Virginia, was available "for hire, either for the remainder of the year, or by the month, week, or job." And, as we've already seen in the autobiography of Solomon Northup, being hired out as a musician made the course of his twelve years of enslavement more bearable. It is also what led to his enslavement in the first place.[44]

The increased presence of Negro musicians in a variety of public forums marked a critical transformation in the valuation of slave performances as they began to enter exchange markets. By grouping together loosely related sounding behaviors under a single discursive category, "Negro music," the southern social world of White citizenry and Black entertainers elevated the significance of the slaves' sounding practices, which came to assume something akin to material, accessible commodities, their concrete manifestations being purchasable as forms of labor. While the performances of slaves would always remain inalienable to the extent that the slaves controlled the actions of their own bodies, their public presentation encouraged their abstraction and translation into something alienable, to be conceived within the category of Music. This conceptualization was not simply the effect of discursive representation: Negro music's concretization also arose from its new position as an exchangeable item within the money economy. Like money itself, Negro music had taken on the status of a symbol that brought into form the very entity it symbolized: the slave as a creator of a kind of Music, whose properties of signification drew it into comparison with aestheticized art forms. In this way, Negro music's entrance into commercial markets asserted the slaves' own belief in their humanity, a belief aligning with abolitionist efforts.

The coalescence of Negro music as a coherent assembly of embodied sounding practices prompted narrators from both the South and North to give closer scrutiny to these practices, their depictions helping to get a better sense of their audible character. In many instances, they described Black sound as it compared to the normative practices of Music. One witness, for example, marveled over the display of a group of Black firemen on a Mississippi steamboat, "sing[ing] with great life and energy, . . . one of them chanting the burden of the song, and the rest at the end of every two lines, striking in, by way of chorus." In another, Olmsted detailed the extemporaneous performances of a "gang of Negroes . . . rais[ing] such sound as I never heard before, a long, loud musical shout, rising and falling, and breaking into falsetto, . . . the melody was caught by another, and then, another, and then by several in chorus." Colonel James R. Creecy, moreover, wrote admiringly in 1860 about the qualities of Negro beat and repetition, departing from a common tendency to disparage them as

African-derived "temporal vibrations"—those "barbarisms of a uniform rhythm [producing] sluggishness to the point of gloom and depression." "In their movements, gyrations, and attitudinizing exhibitions," Creecy remarked in contrast, "the most perfect time is kept, making the beats with the feet, heads, or hands, or all, as correctly as a well-regulated metronome!" Theodore F. Seward similarly commented, "The first peculiarity that strikes the attention is in the rhythm. This is often complicated, and sometimes strikingly original."[45]

Read together, these and other observations, appearing across a copious body of representation, indicate an emerging discourse of Black musical distinctiveness, in which the details of repetition, responsorial interplay, "improvisatored" practices, and unusual vocal techniques (e.g., "making tubes of their open palms, to give their voices, which, in all conscience, were lou[d] enough, more volume") were now being comprehended in their relation to European musical practices: "Such music . . . is better worth listening to than half the vocal concerts of cities." And in this comparison with and distinction from European Music, Black sounding practices were beginning to resemble creative forms produced by "reasonable men." "Blacks were 'reasonable,' and hence 'men,'" Henry Louis Gates Jr. writes, "if—and only if—they demonstrated mastery in the arts and sciences." After the Civil War, such shifts in perception would drive continuing efforts to elevate Negro music as a form of Music by committing it to writing, as it would become codified in the landmark study *The Slave Songs of the United States*.[46]

Rising awareness of a new Black musicality suggested there was indeed some trouble afoot, raising a palpable concern among White southerners: if the slaves' musical skills implied a form of reason, then they might be human after all. Recognizable musical skill suggested that they also possessed other sentient qualities—qualities of feeling, emotion, thoughtfulness, and intelligence. The coalescence of coherent forms of slave music intensified an already tense social moment: as abolitionists appealed to the belief that Negro music reflected the struggles and suffering of slaves, proslavery commentators, in an effort to suppress the threat, opted for rhetoric accompanying the new blackface minstrelsy, which characterized slaves as noisy, repetitious, and sloth-like. The resulting conflict in views was consistent with the rising debates over slavery that characterized the 1850s and that would precipitate Civil War.

Such trouble over the character of Negro music clearly perplexed observers, making them appear at moments unsure how to represent this most peculiar, social form. Sometimes they even shifted their opinion in the middle of an essay. A journalist reporting in a Charleston newspaper, for example, at first marveled over the talent of "little negro boys. . . . aged six to ten years" whose performance as the Ebony Sax-Horn Band would "try the skills and strength of grown men." Nevertheless, the band's performance did not make sense until it was reduced to a modest, audible form for the pleasure of White people. That the boys "should play difficult music, with all the precision of a practiced band, is, if no new thing, at least a very pleasant species of entertainment." A Georgia physician plainly outlined the paradox: "Despite their kinship with hogs in nature and habit, the Negro has music in his soul." This quality of musicality, which he named a "sixth sense," seemed to be something more than mere sound. While slave musicality served to limit their proclivities toward laziness, it also increasingly complicated the status of slaves themselves, both in their disposition as a kind of labor and as a social agent in possession of a powerful aesthetic form.[47]

ANIMATED PROPERTIES

There is a curious moment in one of the foundational texts on the history of antebellum slavery, a passage that brings into relief the transformative force of the slave sound world. It is the point when the distinguished historian Kenneth M. Stampp states in passing, "rarely did a contemporary write about slaves without mentioning their music."[48] Stampp makes this assertion with considerable authority. *The Peculiar Institution: Slavery in the Ante-Bellum South*, represented a seismic change in the writing of southern history, being the first overarching study of US slavery to give voice and representation to the slaves themselves. Stampp achieved this feat through consultation of a massive body of sources, devoted largely to the thirty-year period before the Civil War. The appendix of his 1956 monograph lists over 150 collections and archives that he consulted in the preparation of his book. Stampp's research involved the perusal of many hundreds if not thousands of documents housed in national collections and archives, and it is remarkable to think that he had discovered within them so much mention of slaves engaging in musical performance, particularly so after a century or more of virtual silence about Black musical invention.[49] Slave society was, of course, a world in which everyday speech was already brimming with references to its most valuable property. As one writer put it in 1828,

"The White conversation is apt to be darkened in its complexion; indeed, three quarters of sociable discourse [in southern states] is often engrossed by the topic of slaves."[50] And yet the conspicuous increase in references to slave sounding practices identified a new attentiveness among mastery to something once given little regard. We might wonder, accordingly, what was all this chatter about? Why the sudden fascination with what would seem to be merely an aural accommodation to the mechanisms of labor and to the recent whims of White seekers of pleasure?

On one level, White southerners' new interest was consistent with the aforementioned rise in European-influenced Negro music entering the forums of leisure. In these instances, slave performances accommodated basic needs of White entertainment, and their appeal amounted to little more than a curiosity or trifle; listeners were fascinated with how those deemed subhuman could perform something akin to Music. While such talents may have also been off-putting, challenging claims that slaves were inferior, many White observers ultimately seemed to overlook the contradiction that some among the vast population of slaves possessed musical talent. Multiple indications show that White people rationalized the slaves' musical abilities by explaining them away as acts of thingly imitation, much in the same way that musical automatons in eighteenth-century Europe reproduced tuneful melodies.[51] As Saidiya Hartman argues, moreover, any sense of humanity that might have been associated with Black cultural practices could serve to reinforce racial hierarchy. The themes of sorrow and "natural Christian" sensibility suffusing representations of the public genre, the "spiritual," for example, affirmed the slaves' subjugation by disassociating them from that which was normative and free. In this way, the putatively sorrowful and natural qualities of Black music provided further evidence of the slaves' limits as human beings.[52]

More fundamental, though, was a second outcome of incorporating European practices—namely, how these new performances, despite their public availability as Negro music, could never be successfully introduced into the logic of market exchange. The slaves' musical performances had coalesced into a new kind of racialized ownership that while openly participating in slave capitalism also exceeded complete possession, even by those White people who owned slaves, precisely because slave sounding practices were thought to be inextricably connected to Black flesh. While the principal object of exchange in these circumstances was the slave laborer who performed at social events, the audible character of the Negro was a kind of sonic truth that racially distinguished slaves from the class of

White folk, who were thought to be comparatively silent. For public slave performers, the condition of audibility would have been fundamental to their subjective makeup, and increasingly slaves were also thinking along these lines. This is precisely what Solomon Northup had insisted on when he recalled the benefits of a skill that had gotten him into life-transforming trouble. But ownership of sound in slave communities was hardly limited to those occupying the social category of "musician." Many if not most slaves routinely participated in social acts of music-making as part of their everyday labor, and in doing so, they claimed those musical sounds as their own. Accordingly, the inalienable character of Black music mattered increasingly as slave performances moved into exchange, not only for musicians but for all people of African descent. Black music identified the coalescence of a form of racialized possession benefiting the entire community, as it was sold and traded by its key purveyors.

The coalescence of slave sounding practices supplied African Americans with a new kind of animated property taking the name "Negro music." These enlivened sounds identified a congealment structured in dominance that conceptualized retrospectively (as an accumulating body of sonic material) qualities believed to have existed outside and prior to dominance and that had become recognized by the 1840s as a property form inextricably linked to the Black body. From the perspective of a White public growing increasingly familiar with slave performances and for whom the humanity of slaves had become a combustible subject of debate, Black music practices possessed an essential character traceable to the slaves' sentience, exteriorized aurally as embodiments of racial flesh and presumed by White observers to link directly to a world stretching far into the racial past. If the slave were a propertyless, propertied thing, it had nonetheless, through a peculiar racial-economic magic, come to possess a lively, animated property of its own, a property that brought into the everyday the audible presence of the past as a locus of belonging. Such temporally capacious qualities of possession, which we will consider across this analysis as a condition of past-time, appeared to assume considerable authority in slave circles, given the extent to which musicality increasingly organized social life.

Efforts to extract from slave sounding practices qualities of aliveness thought to have existed prior to Negro music, as if they were an absolute set of cultural essences—a "metaphysics of Africanity"—belie the evidence at hand.[53] For what was undoubtedly a diverse range of practices developing as part of Black colonial performance remains caught in the figurations of eighteenth-century representation, vaguely appearing on occasion as interruptions in the normative order and depicted as barbaric "noise." Attempts at recovery can only be false because they work from a faulty assumption—namely, that there remains in the historical record retrievable certainties of a pure Black orality existing apart from its representation on the hearable side of an aural/ocular "Great Divide."[54] At the same time, we do possess knowledge about how African auditory practices informed the affective sensibilities of slaves, even if it comes to us as second-level mediations. As Susan Scott Parrish writes in her characterization of colonial Black culture in the British Atlantic, "The colonial perception of Black epistemology was not a mere projection. . . . It was loosely based upon . . . a belief in the manipulability of a spiritualized nature [which was] common to the plantation and even urban cultures of African slaves in the colonies." The hidden signs of nature, which were linked to plant cures, conjure, and supernaturalism, together with ontological ambiguities of people and gods, the animate and the inanimate, the living and the dead, were "readily apparent and audible to Africans" across the Americas. Together they suggest endurances of cultural ecologies of precolonial Africa, particularly in the ways that sound production triggered spirited connections between people and their worlds, a perceptual orientation given the name "animism" by nineteenth-century European scholars, as discussed in the introduction.[55]

Rather than representing this acoustical phenomenology according to the abstract category of "Africanisms," then, we might better comprehend it as an aggregation of practices that variously took shape within the regimes of domination radically transforming Black subjectivity, including those occupying regions of North America. Distinctive, semiotically rich, and suggestive of an order of knowledge constituted within and against European-based imperial epistemologies, these cultural practices could never be separated from the enduring material conditions of terror and social fracture so commonplace as part of the slaves' tragic experience, even if, in their concrete, phenomenal immediacy, they had the likely effect of enabling fleeting imaginations of the past that opened up the possibility of drawing connections to spirit worlds—of creating new relations between humans and things, as past-times. Moreover, these ecological realms of thought among slaves gained value as they developed in contested relation with the views of their masters, the slaves' surreptitious qualities owing not only to African beliefs in the supernatural—"the witch and ghost stories so common among negroes," as Tatler would put it in his 1850 guide,

"Management of Negroes"—but also to their need to guard sacrality and its audible resonance as a precious possession.[56]

Crucially, Black sonic worlds gain even greater significance as part of the slaves' confrontation with tragic existence. Monique Allewaert has suggested that the relationship between diasporic African supernaturalism and the conditions of social death on a mass scale became central to the emergence among slaves (particularly those maroons living in tropical circumstances) of a distinctive ontology distinguished from European Enlightenment conceptions of the autonomous citizen-subject. This "disaggregated and opened . . . parahuman" personhood, she writes, was "not predicated on the understanding of the body as an enclosed and organic form."[57] Allewaert is proposing that the slave ontology was an order possessing qualities of relation to the natural world not entirely subject to, or easily claimable within, a modern Euro-Western-based epistemology. It is, once more, suggestive of an open, temporally fluid, and relationally capacious connection between persons and their environment, consistent with a sonically inflected African cultural biome existing prior to Europe's colonial occupation.

When observed alongside historical and ethnographic studies of indigenous African music traditions, the materialist-oriented ecocriticism of Parrish, Allewaert, and others proposes a suggestive body of accumulated evidence, circumstantial as it may be, of a distinctive order of sound-inflected personhood. Whether or not uniformly "parahuman," these identity formations involved processes of relation and exchange in which sound environments and performance practices—together with their inextricable linkages to animated properties of the natural and supernatural—encouraged among Colonial-era slaves forms of subjectivity that supplanted the "metaphysics of Africanity" still today claimed by some scholars. If, moreover, we accept the premise outlined in a long trajectory of scholarship devoted to the African diaspora that documents the mediating role of sound in enabling exchange and contact between people and their gods, between ancestors and things, and between humans and the livingness of the natural world, then we can begin to discern a sustaining force in the auditory among North American slaves—to understand their modes of engagement as conveying a discernible, enlivened resonance. This is not to buy into stereotypes of natural musicality or even to suggest more subtly that Africans in North America were somehow unusually equipped to produce value due to an innately aural personhood. The kind of value I am focusing on in this study would take form later, with the rise of Negro music within the political economy of the late antebellum South. "Aliveness" as a phenomenal condition of value production ultimately required mediation within the racial-economic, its truthful source base remaining obscure, showing up phenomenally in the surface appearances of uncanny sound.

What is nonetheless important to recognize about this early historical moment in the colonial era is the extent to which a conceptualization of enlivened sound as a temporally and ontologically dynamic cultural force had already occupied slave beliefs, having been introduced from Africa as part of the complex interplay of African people and their lived and imagined worlds. As explored earlier, the expressions of life that Africans commonly discerned as a relationship between people and their phenomenal worlds—of nature, of the inanimate, of ancestries—were consistent with an order of knowledge linked to the idea of the fetish (cf. introduction). As William Pietz explains, fetishes arose as part of the epistemological confrontation between Europe and Africa, from "a breakdown of the adequacy of the [existing] discourse[s] . . . to translate and transvalue objects . . . triangulated among Christian feudal, African lineage, and merchant capitalist social systems." What Pietz calls the "irreducible materiality" or inalienable character of the fetish finds a parallel in the animated properties later identified in Negro music, through which the racialized sound worlds of eighteenth-century slaves gave way to the belief in the inherent audibility of the slave body.[58] Coalescences of Negro music in the late antebellum era brought into recognizable sonic form a version of enlivened sound developing from the US slave economy as it also introduced a perception of the form's unobtainability: a seemingly unknowable possession rich in its Africanity that was circulating within southern public culture.

African-informed sounding practices linking past and present as past-times would be subsequently reconceived in the exchange relations governing US slave society, informing White perceptions of "the Negro" as a person-thing. It is what encouraged White southerners to hear slave performances as audible extensions of the Black body and to perceive the Black subject as a putatively inferior life-form, which, apart from its economic value and productive capacities, had also taken on special importance in the formation of southern culture. White responses to slave sounding practices, in turn, reinforced the slaves' own perceptions of their performances as powerful and special. The phenomenon of sonic "peculiarity" suggested a transformation of the sensory arena for Black and White alike, introducing into southern lifeways an auditory vehicle for exceeding everyday experience and imagining in the human production of the audible a way of accessing greater meaningfulness—what in the modern would be conceived as Black music's multiple truths. If for White southerners what was true about slave sound was its inextricable relation to the slaves' propertied bodies, for the enslaved their sounding practices identified what was true about their humanity beyond the dominance of capital, amid an otherwise tragic existence. Despite their dramatic contrast, these contested truths held in common a recognition of the value of sound in the comprehension of Black being and how its possession would be critical to the way in which slave life was lived.

Truth in Negro music arises as a seminal sonic gesture toward states of transcendence and the unreachable, which over time would evolve in its interplay with European aesthetic knowledge. As a concept, it provides a way to analytically specify how Black sounding practices first coalesced as a force linking the physical and metaphysical: in its possession, truthful sound armed slaves with a powerful force for navigating the world as it brought into White realms certainty about the audible character of an uncanny property. If, as previously discussed, these truths would mostly remain partial (cf. introduction), they nonetheless enable us to explore where the sensation of enlivened sound comes from; they mark a starting point for observing the repeated discussion of Black music's strangely spectral appearances that would trace across modern thought, as they direct our attention to the primary, material basis of truth in the production of Black music value.

Truth, in this respect, is not an audible disclosure of the world as it really is; it "is not what artworks mean." Rather, it is an outcome of the conditions producing the aural phenomenon of aliveness at the heart of the music's valuation. In its primary, material form, truth identifies the structural contradictions within an aestheticized cultural practice to summon an appearance of the illusion of nature while at the same time also materializing the lie of unmediated purity. For Theodor W. Adorno, this truthful "second nature" is a quality of negation or "non-identity . . . that which is left out, discarded, repressed or occluded." In the context of southern slave cultures, a racialized version of truth in Black sound arises from the tragic reality of slavery and the racial contradictions it generates.[59]

Versions of truth congealed among slaves in the accumulation of highly valued sonic material: in the incongruencies of past practices and present inventions that converged in the instances of performance. The slaves' own positive truths came to be heard in what were meaningfully perceived as the time-altered and time-altering expressions evoking otherworldly pasts that were Black-owned. These performances reiterated as they generated new sonic material, driving imaginations of the past occupying the present, which in turn produced new ways of imagining a world beyond those to which the enslaved were physically bound. It was at these moments when Negro music first coalesced in exchange relations. Slave musicality begins a historical process of unfolding and infolding, of outwardly extending as alienable form and drawing that form back in, to produce new inventions of sonic blackness. This extensive/intensive motion immanent to Black music's double character locates its primacy within a greater Black counterhistory.

Scholarly efforts to comprehend the tremendous affective and culture-producing power of antebellum Negro music typically focus on the ritualized settings of performance, most notably the ring shouts and Africanized Christian worship described by Michael A. Gomez, Sterling Stuckey, Samuel A. Floyd Jr., and others. This attention to ritual grows from anthropological research dating back to Émile Durkheim, who theorized ritual as a key generative force in the making of culture, particularly in its ability to congeal past significances and bring them into formal coherence in the present.[60] Multiple studies of Africa and the African diaspora have reinforced this line of inquiry, demonstrating the constitutive effects of sound production in ritual acts.[61] Yet as important as ritual settings were in antebellum slave communities, they were probably no more significant than the more routine, auditory acts that oriented the slaves' lives: those everyday circumstances of quotidian expression—of "drawling tunes" that served to regulate the action of work. It was in these mundane labor circumstances, during which slaves not only fulfilled the role of laborers but also of labor as such, that the "peculiarity" of the enslaved's sounding practices exposed the limits of slave capitalism's domination; amid their endless laboring, slaves were also actively involved in weaving the webs of culture they inhabited together. The multiple representations of slave sonic expression noted throughout this chapter may already be enough to convince readers that the natural musicality so frequently assigned to slaves pointed to the profound importance of sounding practices exterior to capitalism in constituting their worlds. Colonial and antebellum slaves alike inhabited cultures that were acutely auditory, engaging in relations between the worldly and the otherworldly, the past and the present. The power of performed sound revealed above all in its ability to collapse and expand time, drawing in and out the imaginable realms of African and slave humanity.

Amid the tragedy of slavery's catastrophic disruption, slaves acquired from practices passed down over the generations ways of intensifying social and metaphysical relations through sound, just as they continually invented new ones, amassing a dynamic body of sonic material that became codified in their condition of "peculiarity." Routine musical engagements in everyday interaction provided techniques for creating coherences between people and their environments and for producing connections between the here and now and times past, as part of the phenomenology of past-time. Acknowledging that slaves inhabited a fundamentally different order of sound knowledge while living in the same sonic universe as White mastery helps us to reconsider the consequence of Euro-African epistemic incongruities. For despite the difficulty of reading against those incongruities as they have informed Western texts, we can also recognize in a fundamental way how truly different a music based on "bodily motion . . . freed from effort by repetitions" really was. Such recognition, in turn, helps us to comprehend the significance of later scholarly accounts of African music as "the life of a living spirit working within those who dance and sing," by which they in "being possessed (or inspired) [give] their singing and dancing a superhuman character, connecting with the sphere of religion." Here, in the words of the Austrian comparative musicologist Erich Moritz von Hornbostel—the key figure in the creation of the world's first phonographic archive of African music—we confront the beginning of a legacy of "scientific" representations of Black sound that has been at once illuminating and obscuring. In Hornbostel's observation, difference arises from a materialized collision of musical epistemes cast discursively in Western scholarship according to racialized separation.[62]

Reading between the lines of a legacy of Western racialist discourse, we may conclude this: the sonic has played a critical role in early Black ontological constitution, being central to the North American slave experience, as it drew from practices and knowledge reaching back to periods in Africa before slavery. The primacy of sound in colonial-era Black cultures is what rightly inspired Parrish and others to challenge the literary-centeredness of twenty-five years of Black cultural studies in the United States, proposing that African America's foundational trope of the "talking book," originally theorized by Henry Louis Gates Jr., be replaced with what she calls the "talking woods": a world of ontologized sound evoking past and future worlds as inhabiting the present, where resonances of the body connected to other bodies and to the objects of ritual and nature, producing expressions of relationally inclusive life.

This is not, however, to propose that Black music could have taken the forms it did apart from the forces of dominance, as if its essence were to lift up out of endless loss as pure forms of immediacy and presence.[63] Such interpretations still linger today because the perception of Black music in the West has always encouraged its mystification—that Black sound contains secret ways of knowing. The historical record makes clear that by the time of the American Revolution White observers already believed that Africans and their enslaved offspring were, despite their inherent inferiority, in possession of a kind of aural animatedness standing in contrast to the seemingly lifeless, "dead" forms of expression performed by their White counterparts. And these beliefs would grow stronger and more coherent as Black music property coalesced. There is a sense, indeed, that White motivation to acquire Black music was consistent with the processes of capitalism in which music production was beginning to take part, whereby the dead labor of capital performs vampire acts of resuscitation, as Marx describes. This rising curiosity among White folk had an enabling effect of upholding among slaves the social and cultural importance of their own musicality. Such outside interest and desire to possess would, in turn, drive the course of the music's performance, its changes expressive of a struggle to control and maintain new coherences of Black form.[64]

If the animated sounding practices of southern slaves played a generative role in the constitution of Black cultural epistemics across the Americas, they would undergo a fundamental transformation as slave performances began to inhabit new orders of knowledge and value in the capitalist economies of the late antebellum US South. This new valuation took coherent form only when slave sounding practices entered exchange and became racially identified as Negro music—the first coalescence of Black music. At this seminal moment, which began in earnest in the 1840s with the development of distinctive African American slave cultures and the corresponding escalation in public discourses of a Negro musicality, a new concept of slave musical ownership arose out of the primary, racial contradiction at the heart of slave capitalism. Emerging from a wrinkle in the mode of production enabling the creation of an audible property-of-property, a publicly acknowledged slave music confronted exchange processes of the southern marketplace, simultaneously widening and reducing the gap between Black and White worlds. Formulated as something less than and greater than Music, Negro music in its double character seemed strangely familiar in musical terms and yet equally foreign in its expression of

qualities inherent to the propertied bodies of slaves. What appeared unobtainable by White people would be construed as a form in possession of
something more: the qualities of aliveness existing beyond property law's
containments.

PROPERTY'S PROPERTIES

Historians have been acutely aware that US slaves, despite being a
species of property, also owned forms of property in the face of legal sanc-
tions against it.[65] These property forms were mainly material goods variously acquired that could improve the quality of their lives. In the work
of Dylan Penningroth, the long-recognized existence of slave property re-
ceives new attention, and its significance is shown to be more far-reaching
and complex than previously understood. Penningroth's account outlines
the manifold ways in which the accumulation of money and the acquisition of property coursed through slaves' lives. Some of the enslaved took
on additional labors (planting, sewing, carpentry, etc.) for barter or cash;
others hired fellow slaves and even their own children from their masters;
still others succeeded as entrepreneurial middlemen who created complex
labor networks in which hired slaves hired other slaves who, in turn, addi-
tionally hired slaves.[66] The economic impetus at the heart of this development was the task system, the principal relation of production organizing
slave labor across most of the South, particularly in the context of agricultural work. Under the task system, slaves were assigned a set of duties
that they were expected to accomplish over the course of the day. Once
completed, they were often allowed to work for profit on their own. And
because labor under the task system was frequently performed in groups,
slaves could help one another, whether it be a man assisting his wife in
harvesting crops or a woman stepping in for a friend so that she could take
on paying work. As a result of these practices, slaves accumulated money
and goods, which they could barter and trade with other slaves, free Blacks,
and, sometimes, poor Whites.

The task system produced a series of labor relations that were deeply
interdependent, developing from an expanded sense of kinship. Rather
than creating a grand, familial network of clearly identifiable associations,
this kinship lineage, Penningroth explains, suggested a far more precarious set of connections, variously competitive and supportive. He shows
that the micro–labor practices followed the disrupted patterns of social

relations under slavery, being consistent with the fractured quality of the slaves' lives within a regime that questioned their status as subjects in the first place. For this reason, ownership became critical to slaves not only because of the depth of their poverty in the face of subsistence but also because the claims of ownership "were tangled in the same threads that tied slaves to each other." The relational nature of slave property—both in the interdependence of labor and in the frequency of several slaves collectively owning valuable possessions—meant that ownership, if tentative and contingent, was also deeply social. These tangles of relation, moreover, crossed over into other realms of social exchange, informing incentives for slave marriage and for having children (who could assist in familial duties as well as those of the master) and the creation of an extended sense of community. They even affected the social experience of the metaphysical, including African-based sacred practices such as conjure, which could be bought and sold as a commodified form of service. As slave property was brought into existence, it would carry with it differing conceptions of materiality consistent with their experience as slaves and extending back to African orderings of social property among kin.[67]

The rise of Negro music identifies a peculiar kind of possession whose value, in the first instance, was derived from its material tenuousness as a property form. Being something owned and retained as part of the flesh, Negro music always remained in the slaves' possession, even when its principal mode of expression—as part of working in the plantation fields—served economically as a natural lubricant within the greater forces of production, warding off what masters perceived to be their inborn tendencies toward laziness. If singing during the practice of labor was itself an unstable, tentative expression, seemingly incoherent, immaterial, and unreliable as a cultural possession, it was nonetheless a property always retained by and within the slave. As a mode of communication—even when performed in what were likely, at times, halting, stop-start responsorial acts—Negro music continually revealed a potential for reaffirming the concrete nature of social relationships, much in the same way that material property forms reinforced the "threads" of relation making up slave communities. Yet because the properties of Black sound were not only socially constituted but also carried within them the bodily presence of the slave, Negro music was likely to enable a level of emotional and affective involvement that far exceeded material forms. What is more, because musicality among slaves transcended the local circumstance of performance, being abstracted as a state of being according to White claims about the Negroes' natural musicality, the sense of its affective embodiment would continually grow in social value. Negro music brought into the world a new mode of the sensible produced "under the very nose of the overseers."[68]

The profound importance of a sonorous Black possession explains why White people were able to comprehend slaves' singing at work as a kind of pleasure and to witness in their sonic relations expressions of happiness, particularly as the discourse network of southern plantation fantasy became increasingly familiar by the 1840s and 1850s. There was, in fact, some accuracy to the perception: apart from acts of ritualized sorrow, singing in everyday instances would, at times, have been a pleasurable event, even if the slaves' own conditions were otherwise dreadful. And as the slaves' singing continued, lingering conspicuously in performances of labor, inhabiting and frequently overwhelming the auditory place of southern plantation culture, it also identified an abstract, semiautonomous quality of being that was only partially under the control of ownership. This newly conceived possession of slaves accordingly brought into public knowledge the fabrication of White loss, a loss revealed in the animated fleshiness of slave sounding practices. As a materially tenuous property in the first instance, the slaves' possession of Negro music revealed a complex value, a "profit" grounded in their own tremendous losses as racialized subjects and expressing the logical tendency of profit-from-loss. If the enslaved's music performances enabled masters to claim a valuative surplus from their human property, they also offered to slaves something in return—a profit directed back to themselves. The performances reaffirmed the slaves' social relations in ways that no other cultural practice could, marking the creation of a possession or profit whose value was enabled by their subjugation.

Slaves were well aware of this new ironic mode of ownership, having endured systemic economic exploitation their entire lives. "In Tennessee," Jourdon Anderson wrote retrospectively to his former master, "there was never any pay-day for the Negroes any more than for the horses and cows."[69] Taking advantage of Negro music's potential, they exchanged it when they could, performing in southern markets. Such transactions for personal profit were, in fact, fairly common among musically talented slaves living in or near towns, whose performance skills were reported in southern publications: "The negro musician, Hicks" of Columbus, Georgia; "the jolly old negro musician," Ike Fennell, of Memphis, "whose violin has 'many a time and oft' discoursed its bewitching strains for the amusement of almost all our young people." Such reports reach back to the beginning of the century and even earlier, as in the runaway ad for Abram from 1801, a carpenter, who worked as a fiddler without his owner's consent.[70] Reports show that these musicians could be strategic in making sure that they acquired a portion of the transaction's amount. For example, when George Walker's owner hired him out to play his fiddle at parties, he asked those who hired him that they not pay Walker directly, apparently because Walker had a habit of taking a cut for himself. And then there was, of course, the accomplished fiddler whose story began this chapter. When Solomon Northup performed for White customers, he not only sold his talents on behalf of his master but also, as he explained with a seeming sense of satisfaction in his autobiography, "returned with many picayunes jingling in my pockets—the extra contributions of those to whose delight I had administered."[71] Musicians with less training or talent also bartered and bargained their performances for all kinds of benefit and profit, whether it be in the form of a few coins, a sip of whiskey, or the granting of some leniency in their tasks.[72] We can imagine, finally, how Lavinia Bell, James Watkins, and Old Dick all sought to gain from their newly conceived and racially specified ownership of Negro music.

It follows, then, in a most fundamental way, that music ownership among slaves, if not inherently a form of resistance, could be nothing but illicit, identifying a claim on a property legally owned by slaveholders. What slaves had claimed illegally was a part of themselves, a quality of their own flesh, externalized and given form as enlivened sound.[73] This is why, after all, musical performances by slaves in more developed, ritualized settings, away from the fields, were so frequently done in private: in nighttime rituals, in the "talking woods" of Black sociality where slaves would congregate and claim for themselves their own time and social connections according to a secret practice that would be later popularized in folkloric representation as "stealing away."[74] The very nature of these instances and their attention to a kind of ownership of slave-based performativity suggests that slaves were engaging in a different order of relation—in an incipient, intensively regulated economy of race—bringing to bear and reaffirming African-conceived notions of sound's relation to a broad temporal ecology, even if these practices did not convey a uniform sense of "African identity." As group performances, however, it is unimaginable that they did not reinforce among the participants a social relation to each other, increasingly specified and understood racially as Negro, as Black.

The ring shouts, sermons, testimonies, patting practices, and acts of responsorial singing that show up repeatedly across the historical record identify another modality of exchange that largely deflected the production-oriented market structures of southern slave capitalism as it sustained the slaves' dynamic social relations—relations that may have variously mimicked the disaggregated relations of subjects theorized in ecocriticism and that sustained new coherences of sociality deriving from African systems of thought. In the antebellum music performances of the illicit, slaves could come into contact with prior realms and experiences, making imagined pasts audible in the present and creating retrospectively new temporal orders through acts of singing and playing. There is a sense, indeed, that sound production in the slaves' here and now carried the power to elicit truths in direct relation to its antagonism to White dominance—that the invention of Negro music as slaves' property provided a new means of conjuring relations within broad temporal and metaphysical fields of the imagination. What seemed alive in the sound of Negro music developed as a value form in its confrontation with White mastery's possessive claims. Confrontation secured and made present the sound of difference as something under the slaves' possession.

Copious displays of Africanity in the slaves' performances heightened the economic distance of this newfound property from the control of slave owners. Commentaries referencing "shouting Negroes" engaging in bombastic performances that featured "hooting," proclaiming, and (with reference to a drummer at a pinkster) "rolling his eyes and tossing his head with an air of savage wildness" strongly suggest a kind of performativity with precedents in West Africa, newly conceived as an embodied possession under the slaves' control. The "foolish and ridiculous dances peculiar to the negroes" reported by an observer in Florida in the early 1840s, together with Olmsted's 1859 observation—"Negroes are excessively superstitious. They have all sorts of 'experiences,' and enjoy the most wonderful revelations. Visions of the supernatural are a nightly occurrence, and the most absurd circumstances are invested with some marvelous significance"—may be read as part of a grand matrix of slave relation oriented and abiding by the production of sound.[75] In the act of overturning pots, moreover, commonly described in Black music studies as a means of muffling the slaves' singing, we can locate what was far more likely yet another African-based performance technique: a way of disguising the voice in order to assume the presence of a spirit and call to the dead for knowledge. This knowledge would be "spoken" from the earth, fashioning again a new kind of cultural possession. Increasingly, slaves came to understand these acts as their own and owned, their sense of ownership reinforced by White southerners' view of them as manifestations of enlivened peculiarity. What was illicit as sonic property became illicit not simply by itself but according to its conception within the legitimate orders of the US slave economy and under the juridical laws of ownership.[76]

The idle chatter among White southerners that Kenneth M. Stampp observed tells us something important about the significance of Black music in antebellum life. Their incessant conversations about slave music exposed a troubling realization: they identified the moment when White mastery begins to recognize that slaves possessed a fully formed property of their own, a highly valued "spirited thing."[77] For while constituted in the present, Negro music seemed to come from another place: it consistently drew on and developed older sonic material that did not abide by the learning traditions and temporal order of the here and now. And after becoming economically legitimized, this strange sonic inspiration echoing from the past acquired socially productive power, enabling new imaginations of a connection to past worlds, to past-times ironically heightened by Negro sound's entrance into the southern economy. The successes of racially motivated economic contests in the production of music drew slave communities backward, reaffirming in the sensation of past-time the slaves' collective tragedy and loss. This audible past arising from the cyclical push and pull that generated new sonic material is what establishes the nascent ground of Black music as a temporally disjunctive, ontological form.

From here on, Black music advances within and against exchange processes as an evolving cultural entity whose aesthetic power develops within a structure of racial contradiction, being akin to what Paul Gilroy has described as "material . . . [that] does not fit unambiguously into a time-consciousness derived from and punctuated exclusively by changes in the [modern] public." It brings into the social world manifestations of counter-history, the music enacting in its sonic progression a cognitive character, revealing an "unconscious writing of history" (cf. introduction). By the end of the antebellum era, the sounds of the slaves had coalesced as a mode of musical cognition structurally bound to the contradictions inherent to racial capitalism. What seemed inalienable revealed truths arising from the tragedy of abjection, from the fundamental condition of Black music as an illicit property. Stampp's passing comment ultimately points to a growing anxiety among White southerners, who now realized that what slaves had gained in the new economy of exchange also identified what they themselves had lost. And the more they paid attention, the more they realized how far from the White citizenry's access this newly conceived cultural form actually was.[78]

The slaves' extemporaneous sounding practices established a material order of relation operating in the auditory environment, a performative dynamic and mode of sociality whose routine involvement and possession were not limited to the musically gifted and whose inevitably haphazard, spontaneous engagements would nevertheless establish a defining condition for the slaves' everyday relations among themselves. It was in these performance acts where the slaves' sounding practices were continually regenerated, reconceived, and discursively constituted, informing the public and private performances of Negro music heard beyond the plantation fields, as aspects of those performances circled back into labor, where White listeners witnessed a property's properties conspicuously on display. Significantly, the activity of slave sounding in the plantation fields was not only an audible manifestation of the laboring body but also a social relation whose racialized qualities of laziness, suffering, and play reoriented the very understanding of Black labor among master and slave alike. As the sounds of work congealed into the expressions of Black musical play that entertained mastery at their parties and frolics, they also perpetuated the powerful sensation of embodied audibility consistent with the slaves' status as beings-in-labor. This linkage is critical to the understanding of Black music valuation. Value in Negro music accrued as an indelible marking of flesh and blood, producing in sound a fleshy viscosity inextricably linked to the slave as a commodified form of labor, while also exposing indications of a different ontological order altogether: in Negro music, all could hear, if not fully comprehend, the strange new quality of enlivened sound.

For White listeners to have comprehended this new value would have meant that they actually understood how slaves had acquired an anomalous property. The generation of enlivened sound, however, developed more or less in secret, beneath the phenomenal experience of the sound's animated peculiarity. Aliveness had as much to do with the racial-economic structures generating sensations of sonic illicitness as it did with its audible appearance. This secret would begin to coalesce as the first stage of Black music in a series of concrete markers—the various "peculiarities" that consumed White, public attention. Yet as it conformed to exchange processes, so would Black music's excessive corporeality interrupt those same processes. This anomaly—already apparent before exchange in the perception of the Negro as both person and thing—further informed the sensation in slave sound of a pure concreteness consistent with its inalienability, which would carry value and even a quality of agency, not unlike that of the piano player's in Dipesh Chakrabarty's reading of Marx's analysis of productive labor: it supplied a "fleeting glimpse" of a different order of relation existing and participating within capitalism and yet neither subsumed by nor even subsequent to it. "The relations that do not contribute to the reproduction of the logic of capital," Chakrabarty writes, "can actually be intertwined with the relations that do. . . . One does not gain epistemological primacy over the other."[79]

Such fleeting glimpses are what opened up to the enslaved oblique, backdoor engagements with realms temporally distant and outwardly expansive—to past-times enabled by the power of enlivened sound under firm command of their own bodies. Black music, as Negro music, introduced a peculiar kind of political form, developing as a cultural contradiction whose disruptions marked the beginning of a mode of value production unprecedented in the West. And enhancing that racial-economic valuation was Negro music's relation to a third economy of intensively generated involvements that drew backward and forward the connections and dislocations with old-world and new-world Black ancestries and spirit worlds. The fleeting glimpses of illicitly possessed embodiment existing beyond the bounds of capital opened African American cultures to realms of truth shaped within and against the production machinery of race-capital. Because of this relation to a third economy, Negro music, no matter how formally innovative it actually was, would consistently invite a retrospective sensibility conjuring in its forward progression the productive involvements of past-time. As multiple imaginations of pasts congealed in the present as part of the slaves' performances, they would convey a sense of disruptive difference, particularly among African Americans who never relinquished their past for the simple reason that it was repeatedly affirmed by their status as "Negro." The racial signature of Blackness occupying slave sound carried an enduring temporal signature, its experience introducing into slave culture a means of imagining what would be newly possible. In Black sound's embodied aliveness, slaves could begin to discern a form of cultural power: they would hear the beginnings of a counterhistory cast in the negative.

The enlivened presence of slave sounding practices existing within a human property explains why Black music's aesthetic and cultural value never seemed to dissipate once African American performance style entered widespread public circulation, beginning with its parody in blackface minstrelsy during the 1840s. The mark of theft that would come to define the character of minstrelsy also includes in this early period the sign of reclamation, whereby White people, in their incessant appropriations of Black music, sought to reclaim what they saw as a property lost to the sounding bodies of Africans and African Americans. Reclamation of property illicitly possessed by slaves becomes central to the constitution of White racial subjectivity as it reaffirms Black people as "enemy." For White people to reclaim, they "must first become the enemy . . . to apprehend the enemy 'from the inside,'" assuming what Eduardo Viveiros de Castro calls "the enemy's point of view." For Herbert Marcuse, such designations of difference are inherent to the very validity of cultural coherence: there "has always been a 'foreign' universe to which the cultural goals were not applied: the Enemy, the Other, the Alien, the Out-cast."[80] And so it follows that the act of conquering by inhabiting contributed to the instability of Whiteness itself. "Negro melodies" in the United States, observed a bemused English writer in 1851, at the height of blackface minstrelsy's popularity, "are hummed on the streets. Young men, when they meet you and wish to appear comical, imitate the peculiar chuckle of the sable race. This painful state of things has been going on for several years."[81]

Efforts to reclaim lost property through both casual and ritualized acts of performance were repeated again and again because of the consistency of White mastery's commitment to racial difference. What was inalienable and always in the possession of African Americans lived on as enlivened forms as a result of the enduring structures of racism. Animated fleshy sound had assumed the position of a critical negative value, whose perpetual loss to White claims generated new forms of anomalous sound. If abstract labor was for Marx "the secret of the expression of value" (measured as a theoretical aggregate of socially necessary labor time), it was the animated labor of slaves inhabiting an enlivened music property that contradicted its significance and sustained Black music's racially and economically informed aesthetic value well after the point when slavery had ended.[82]

Into the era of Reconstruction and the age of Jim Crow—its very name being derived from the widened spatial presence of Black music in US social life—White Americans continued in their desperate acts of reclamation. These acts seem somehow desperate because they would always be futile from the outset; the White citizenry of the republic could never successfully regain what had been lost, even as Negro music, and then Black music, became established as a public category and commodity form. In fact, over time, the perceived distance between Black forms and their White musical imitations expanded, just as the legitimacy of White claims faltered, even while the fundamental musical similarities between Black and White styles grew stronger. If the performances of blackface decoupled

Negro music from the fleshy qualities of the slave body, these mediations never diminished Negro music's animated properties. On the contrary, its qualities of aliveness seemed only to intensify in direct proportion to the music's circulation; the music's essential value escalated in both economic and symbolic terms as distinctions between what was real and authentic, what was counterfeit and fake, became murkier. An oft-cited essay from 1855 meant to celebrate Negro music did so by conflating slave creations with minstrel parodies; William Francis Allen's Reconstruction-era publication that sought to present the slave spirituals in the most positive terms lapsed into a rhetorical style consistent with "darky tunes."[83]

Value in Black music developed out of this murkiness, being caught up in White fantasies of authenticity deriving from the music's perceived enlivened character. What appeared dually accessible and inaccessible entered commercial markets according to modes of fetishism distinctive of Negro music. If what William Pietz calls the "irreducible materiality" from Europe's early modern era identifies a first order of fetishism underlying musical Blackness, those animated qualities would intensify according to a second order of fetishism, famously outlined by Marx in volume 1 of *Capital*. In his opening discussion of the relation of commodities, Marx describes an uncanny process of inversion, whereby relations between people as workers take on the character of thinglike material relations, while commodities develop humanlike "social" connections, what Marx calls "social relations between things."[84] In this way, commodities obtain a quality resulting from the obscuring of human labor that simultaneously contradicts, as it heightens, the sense of irreducible materiality in the fetish of early European-African contact. Fetishism in this second order, commonly identified by the Marxian term *commodity fetishism*, describes how commodities decoupled from their origin in labor take on an enlivened presence that is actually complementary to the power Europeans perceived in African religious objects: separated from labor, Negro music would eventually overtake the status of Black musician labor, disseminating embodied presences within exchange environments while at the same time retaining in sound audible qualities of racialized flesh. It is this coalescence of two fetishistic orders that lies at the basis of Negro music's aliveness, as a dual character possessing concrete and abstract qualities tracing to the "life" and then "afterlives" that fueled Black music's life story journeying the complex structures of the US racial economy. What is alive in Black sound, then, is neither the first order of fetishism nor the second, but both. Aliveness develops out of the incongruent double relations of the alienable and the inalienable, the negative and the positive, its anomalies constituted within the seminal social form of the slaves' music property.

As Black music proceeded to circulate as a form of commodified free labor performed by Black itinerants and professionals, and then into the twentieth century as a sound formation emitted from piano rolls and phonograph records, listeners attached new aesthetic value to its racialized qualities, claiming to hear a distinctive embodied blackness indelibly marked in the sound itself. No matter how far the music traveled into the emerging global economy, it would always refer retrospectively to embodiments derived from a first order of fetishism, to a past incongruently related to the structures of capitalism. In the end, though, it was its boundedness to the contradiction of race-capital that generated and regenerated its doubly fetishized character, and through these means, Negro music—that peculiar sound form variously standing somewhere between Music and not-Music—advanced the beginning of a "spectacular revolution," generating fleeting glimpses of truths that challenged normative orders of knowledge. In its multiple peculiarities this seemingly magical entity, taking form as Black music, was and would be unlike anything the world had known before.

SECOND METAMORPHOSIS

FREE LABOR AND THE RACIAL-ECONOMIC TRANSACTION OF ANIMATED FORM

TWO

SCABROUS SOUNDS OF A

VAGRANT PROLETARIAT

AUDIBLE DISSENSUS

What do we make of the bare fact of Black music's modern be-ginnings? For in a commercial sense, at least—the social circumstance by which "modern" in this study is understood—it could begin, as much as anywhere, with the drunken murmurings of a "little wooden-headed body" resting upon its master's knee. As Lynn Abbott and Doug Seroff discuss in their invaluable history of southern Black vaudeville, the first published depiction of blues describes the Black ventriloquist John W. F. "Johnnie" Woods, with his doll, Henry, who sings "the 'blues' . . . in this drunken act" to the delight of a group of Black spectators in Jacksonville, Florida. This telling, which was originally published in 1910 in the Indianapolis-based *Freeman*, a prominent, nationally distributed African American newspaper, stands a far cry from the heroic claims and commonplace assertions that in the sound of the blues one can discern a transparent truth, a point in history from which an unambiguously Black musical modern commences.[1] In the *Freeman*'s account, Black music's modern beginning is identified from the outset as a mediated utterance, a human voicing routed through a mimicking object whose "singing" amplifies the thingliness of its own eerily human presence. That this singing thing was funny—"he set the Air-dome wild"—had a lot to do with Henry appearing to be ripe from the fleshy pleasures of booze. But its poignancy also derived from the performance's attachments to the external contexts of structural racism and the funda-mental ambivalence orienting "Negro music"—namely, the ownership of a "residual ontology" extending from slavery as an audible afterlife.[2]

Commodified blues performance begins with a mechanical thing, a mindless laborer whose claim on a cultural practice through a wobbly minstrel-inspired phraseology—"Trans-mag-ni-fi-can-bam-dam-u-ality"—brought into public knowledge a new form of enlivened sound.[3] Henry's exchangeable materiality introduced into twentieth-century culture an excessive human sonority not unlike the animated sounds of slaves, its qualities of thingliness strangely generated from the livingness of its ventriloquizing master. Because the stage character, Johnnie, also presented a different kind of livingness, having descended from a species of property, his creations with and through Henry pushed the limits of what "human" looked and sounded like. And because Henry himself was not completely inanimate but rather a form enlivened by Johnnie's reified humanity, their collaborative routines challenged what might otherwise have seemed like a clear distinction between beings and things. Together, "Negro" and "wooden-headed body" generated an aesthetic practice somewhere between the living and the unliving, giving to their blues a spectral quality, its heightened sensuousness engendered by the material fact of its opposite. For audiences across the races, the animated character of blues and other expressions of Black music were the stuff of thingliness. What appeared alive in the sound was energized in racial contradiction, intensifying as it disseminated in the new markets of commercial entertainment.

What coalesces in the second decade of the twentieth century as "blues" marks the culmination of a forty-year struggle between a new class of free Black labor and the revitalized forces of capital emerging in the aftermath of the US Civil War. The aesthetic result of that struggle—during which two generations of itinerant Black laborers made their way through worlds still actively engaged in a protracted race war—developed into a vast array of vernacular languages establishing a seminal modern Black music. Blues appeared as a late outpouring of sounding practices from rural communities, the variety of expressions materializing in aesthetic form the existential confrontations that oriented Black southern life. These dubious forms of vernacularity were largely the creation of poor laborers who invented practices for the pleasure that music inspires but who also sought out paid opportunities as a means of survival. In their everyday pursuit of work, Black musicians were guided by a tendency to bypass conventional strategies of making a living with hope of earning some money by playing music. Navigating the openly hostile southern environments—being repeatedly confronted by White southerners who, confounded and outraged by the Confederacy's military defeat, refused to conform to emerging national aspirations of racial justice—this seminal class of free labor pursued creative lives in the informal economy, realizing in their day-to-day routines the enrichment of a developing body of sonic material that ultimately made a profound impact on the growth of Black music value. Blues identifies the high point of a grand auditory coalescence that arises out of the sounding practices of the slave era and overwhelms the sonic cultures of the South from the last decades of the nineteenth century. Its pivotal sound formations mark the apex of Black music's second metamorphosis in value, when a contrarian class of reluctant laborers—a vagrant proletariat whose status as labor sets the ground for social behavior working against that status—brings into the world a dissentious audibility administered by a new kind of music property.

The appeal of a singing dummy forty years after the end of slavery offers plain evidence of the predicament that Black people were facing at the moment of the White South's resurgence. Although a fascination with connections between the inanimate and the animate, between things and bodies—what Mark Seltzer has called "a rivalry between technological and biological modes of generation"—had become deeply seated in American consumer society, the ambiguity of that uncanny relation carried powerful consequence in the lives of African Americans.[4] For Black people, thingliness was a brutally familiar subject position that created all kinds of intraracial calamities and jockeying as they contended with the weight of their lowly status. From the time of their enslavement, Black southerners had been treated as living things, a reputation they would endure for decades as a result of heightened segregationist practices and legal implementations—sharecropping, debt peonage, menial work, convict labor camps, vagrancy laws, unjust contracts—that sought to sequester Black populations and deny them basic civil rights. The end of Reconstruction and the rise of systematic forms of suppression reinvigorated acts of racially motivated violence that aimed to affirm the Black population's thingly stature. Although these forces were aggressively challenged by African American resistance initiatives at the grassroots level and as part of the uplift politics of aspiring Black elites, the bald asymmetry of White-over-Black power made gross inequity and injustice a familiar dimension of everyday life.[5]

Black musicians could do no better than other African American southerners in their efforts to escape the burdens of a racist regime. In many ways, they fared even worse. For musicians represented the lowliest of a lowly class, whose seemingly useless acts of performance were widely thought among White southerners to epitomize the superfluity of Black being. Yet in other ways, Black musicians managed to create something beyond conventional Black-southern lifeways by directing their seeming uselessness toward the making of influential aesthetic practices. As we will observe across this chapter and the next, despite their common hardships and traumas, Black musicians in the South who participated in the free economy frequently held a different kind of relationship to labor and the laboring life. This partly had to do with the forums in which their work was conducted, which gave them the chance to avoid the scorching heat of the field, the physical risks and drudgery of the factory, the blood and stench of the killing floor. Black musicians could pursue a working life in entertainment, and although this life carried its own burdens, it also afforded them, when they could find paying jobs, a kind of pleasure not found in other circumstances of labor.

The pleasure of performance gave Black musicians something else: protection from the affronts that typically accompanied interaction with the racial majority. For an increasing number of White southerners, the Black act of making music, despite its practical uselessness and seemingly "natural" occurrence, appeared at times uncommonly moving, mapping extremes of affect, from utter delight to what the essayist James E. Hungerford called the "luxury of woe, . . . to be sad without any personal cause for being so."[6] In comparison with a defeated Confederacy and amid the ruins of a desecrated South, Black musicians seemed to many to have gotten the better end of the bargain, going about their ways, performing and sometimes even profiting from their joyous noise and plaintive acts of "luxury." For other White folk, though, the rising tide of itinerant musicians spreading their dubious pleasure as they marauded through southern towns, playing before Black and White alike, was a matter of growing concern. It was on these grounds that White citizenry sought to contain Black music and to police the limits of its ownership—all to reaffirm the status of "Negro" as the nation's servant class. For it was the case, as Nancy MacLean observes, that "from slavery forward, . . . work has proved a key site for constructing social inequality—and for challenging such inequality."[7] White power's failure to completely succeed in its efforts to claim enlivened form had the unintended effect of intensifying Black music's dissentious character and elevating its value.

White-controlled commercial enterprises did not attempt to erase Black performances so much as to convert them into a diverting form of labor, to establish a grand store of surplus corporeality to service the consuming interests of White citizens. This was the primary aspiration on the part of the White population: to economically devalue and make fully exchangeable a ready form of accessible entertainment, their motives consistent with the larger aim of removing Black people from all facets of ownership and citizenry—to incorporate the Black population into an orderly "picturesque." Under Jim Crow rule, as Leon Litwack has observed, "to be forced to dance or imbibe some alcohol, or to be compelled to fight each other all for the entertainment of White spectators, were familiar acts of public submission."[8] In the same way, professional Black stage acts and random street performances were tolerated by White people when they upheld a White right of claim on Black behavior. Yet if Black performances carried modest value as a kind of purchasable pleasure or even a potential source of exploitation—what Antonín Dvořák called in his famous 1893 observation in the *New York Herald* "the real foundation of any serious and original school of composition in the United States"—full access to that value would be encumbered by Negro inferiority. That is, because Black music was not Music per se, it could never be properly incorporated into the White body politic. What appeared to be a limitless natural resource remained insistently obscure, its expropriation continually deferred.[9]

What this meant in a practical way, particularly during the period prior to the rise of mass-produced distribution mechanisms by which Black music eventually circulated, was that while African Americans attending colored minstrel and vaudeville shows could identify in the live acts a sense of racially determined ownership—could hear and claim possession of sounding practices inextricably connected to their own racialized selves—new generations of White consumers could only access those same performances as exchange values, the use they put them to being largely disconnected from the music's racial origins. As paying customers, White listeners needed to repeat their purchases, returning to their favorite shows again and again, their claims limited to the act of witnessing made possible via commercial transaction. This same distance, moreover, compromised access among White performers of blackface, whose earlier attempts to control Black music were challenged by the appeal of Black-performed plantation acts.[10] No matter how hazy the line between the races may have been, only one perceived to be "Negro" could legitimately claim as one's own cultural property the enlivened character of Black audibility.[11]

The intensification of Black music ownership identifies the basis for the creation of a new expression of intrusive audibility: the scabrous sound of vagrant Black labor, an illicit form antagonistic to economic production in ways akin to an irritation of human skin. *Scabrous* identifies the irritable character of enlivened, fleshy sound "rough to the touch," together with the irritating, dissentious effect of that sound as it enters public circulation. These two qualities of scabrousness produce a dialectically generated sonic-social inflammation newly affecting Black music's qualities of aliveness in the music's relation to the greater body politic. What is phenomenally scabrous as irritable, embodied sound becomes disruptive to the social body, disturbing the economic mechanisms of capitalist exchange. Yet despite its irritability, scabrous sound endures because of its racial trueness and odd pleasurable effect: what appears inalienable inspires the want of possession. Deemed "scandalous" and "indecent," it gains value in the way it exists beyond the orders of White knowledge and claim.[12]

The sensation of scabrous aurality initially attracted audiences mainly among the Black poor, who embraced its bawdy fleshiness and celebrated its embodied qualities. Then it began drawing the attention of White folk, both poor and rich, whose responses proposed a litmus test affecting the sounding practices and patterns of behavior among an aspiring Black labor class that entered the entertainment business. Having been generated by the Black body, scabrous aurality intensified Black music's less-than/greater-than value as it circulated across the late nineteenth-century South, drawing vexed responses of ridicule and fascination from White folk and Black elites. And as it disseminated into the common receiving fields of consumer markets, scabrous sound reaffirmed another side of the double character underlying Black music's production of value: what was alienable and ready for exchange also remained inalienable in its connection to the Black subject's racial status. This paradoxical tendency endured from the time of slavery as a peculiar dimension of aliveness, the racial basis of its ownership increasing value as it circulated.

For these complex reasons, Henry, the singing dummy, provides a more reliable representation of what would emerge as Black music after the Civil War than that typically found in conventional histories of the music's "roots." For the blues, together with the other Black musical expressions to be examined here and in chapter 3, begins not simply from the presence of a pure rural-southern vernacularity but rather from the negative condition of an abject "Negro" subject as audible human-thing existing within capitalist networks of public sociality. Out of this condition, a new material relation between sound and embodiment evolved, which granted to African Americans the basis for producing a creative renaissance amid renewed racial domination. The sound formations of Black music—distinctive coherences of sonic material circulating within Black communities—entered commercial transaction, driving new coalescences of value that broad-ened the social reach of an accumulating Blackness. White refusals to ac-knowledge the legitimacy of Black claims of ownership became a critical impetus to the music's valuative growth: scabrous sounds, incurable irrita-tions of enlivened resonance fused to the body politic, carried into nascent commercial economies, disseminating the uncanny sensation of aliveness, of sound formations seemingly both inanimate and animated. The appeal of irony-inflected performances of blues and other Black vernacular forms would accordingly affirm what Paul Gilroy has identified as the central-ity of death figures in the valuation of Black music: what at one moment appears thingly at another comes alive, its spectrality mirroring the dia-lectical relation of reification to commodity fetishism. Black music grows according to a pattern of advancing returns, its multiple recollections and reaffirmations producing a time-altering imaginary: a counterhistory that ultimately accumulates as modern musical forms.[13]

A DUBIOUS FORM OF FREE LABOR

Given the many challenges that Black southerners confronted with the resurgence of White regimes after the Civil War, it should come as no surprise that the overriding concern for the musicians among them was how their performance abilities might help them get by—how they could make money. However precarious their new place in the formal economy might have been, however dubious their labor was perceived, these play-ers and singers sought to participate within the logical orders of market capitalism—among the "heterogeneous array of paupers, prisoners, 'coo-lies,' peons, servants, contract laborers, sharecroppers and many others who worked the wide borderland between slavery and freedom." Their mo-tivation was simple: they wanted to find a place within the work economy to gain whatever profit their musicality would afford. If musicians were going to make a living on their talents, as many of them attempted to do, they would need to earn enough at least to maintain the most basic level of subsistence.[14] That steady employment was well beyond what most could hope for—census records in themselves cannot determine whether or not a self-identified "musician" earned a regular wage—does not diminish the fact that musicians routinely competed to land paying jobs as often as they could, getting by, when they could not, by finding other kinds of work.[15] The enduring skepticism on the part of White southerners about whether or not Black performances were actually labor or simply a kind of childlike activity had a direct effect on both the limits of the musicians' ability to find employment and the cultural value that would be attached to their diverting performances. As a result of Black music's peculiar social status, audiences across the races increasingly grew attentive to this seemingly playful labor, teasing the line between thingliness and the audibly fantastic, and prompting African Americans to find their way into its public presentation.

The archive of American musical entertainment during the final three decades of the nineteenth century teems with traces of free Black musician-laborers traveling about, appearing and disappearing, arising out of anonymity only to fall back into the forgotten blankness against history's record. Sporadic reports, published chiefly in African American newspapers, together with more detailed coverage in national and regional magazines and occasional mention in private letters, give a scattershot representation of what was most certainly a much larger and more frequent assembly of events. Even then we get at least a sense of the remarkable variety of performers for hire, the "musicianers," "music physicians," and "songsters" (the terms invented by Black players and listeners) who sang, whistled, or played on any number of instruments, from guitars, banjoes, mandolins, and fiddles to trumpets, cornets, bones, drums, and combs.[16] Because many of the representations of Black musicians at work were devoted largely to the strange qualities and curiosities that White writers perceived in their sounding acts, the character of Black performance as a labor form must often be interpreted against the grain, assisted by the limited firsthand records of musicians, together with those of others who discussed various matters, from pay scales and job preferences to working conditions and White violence. Despite the severe limitations of the historical record, enough is known to begin to get a sense of the precarious position of Black laboring musicians in the South's rural economy, as their peculiar audibility entered public knowledge. That the musicians' performance acts would never be understood simply as labor or Music related directly to the way in which *Negro music* was acquiring value as a vital cultural property central to the social imagination of Black America. If free Black sounding practices would sometimes take on qualities of autonomy suggesting a form of Music, they always and inevitably found their way back into the containments of the Black body and the enduring claim that those of African extraction were racially different in their possession of resonant flesh.

Armed with exceptional skills in sound production, African American musicians made their way into the workforce of popular entertainment.

2.1 "Street Music" (*Harper's Weekly*, 1872).

Performing for pay occurred in multiple venues: informal settings such as open-air medicine shows, sex houses, and barbershops; as a break-time diversion for outdoor laborers; for town parades; at places dedicated to stage entertainment such as on riverboats, in local theaters, and in saloons, which, by one count of establishments in eastern Kansas during the 1890s, numbered in the thousands.[17] In these diverse settings, all kinds of groups would assemble. Black musicians moved around in small companies or on their own, appearing as instrumentalists, congregating as string duos and trios, guitar-vocal combinations, or, more formally, as brass bands, singing quartets, jubilee choruses, and "colored minstrels" in blackface. Some musicians, of course, were content to perform occasionally with the many local ensembles, whether for money or not, while making a living some other way. "In nearly all Southern cities," a reporter from Boston observed, "large brass and string bands, conducted entirely by colored performers, . . . are constantly engaged by the Whites on all public and festive occasions requiring music."[18]

In multiple instances, musicians joined the money economy haphazardly, even inadvertently, their endurance within it depending on a combination of ability, ambition, and luck. If a musician were especially talented and had acquired the skillset of a singer, actor, and dancer necessary to work in theater, they might try to find opportunities in one of the well-established touring shows, a direction particularly appealing to the new generation of performers who pursued music work in the 1880s and 1890s. As George Moxley told the *Freeman* in 1907, "There was no avenue for the colored entertainer but *Uncle Tom's Cabin*"—that is, shows dramatizing or parodying Harriet Beecher Stowe's novel, also known as "U.T.C.s" or "'Tom' shows"—"the minstrels, and the jubilee companies." Within these venues, the most gifted would gather; as W.C. Handy put it, "All the best talent of that generation came down the same drain."[19] Some of the ensembles were owned and run by African Americans, most notably Charles "Barney" Hicks, whose early successes enabled him to bring a company to Germany in 1870, his Original Georgia Minstrels subsequently presenting a dramatization of Stowe's novel in Sydney in 1878. Ultimately, however, nearly all would be overtaken by White capital. A few of the most ambitious Black performers, finally, through talent and good fortune, became stars, their stage names often qualifying them by their racial status and physicality: "The Colored Mario," "The Black Swan," "Black Patti," "Blind Tom," "Blind Boone."[20]

Beyond the most successful, though, there was also a surfeit of musicians who roamed among the itinerant population at any given time, stravaging the roads of the rural South where still, in the mid-1880s, an observer could note that "almost every plantation furnishes good banjo and violin players, who execute well on both instruments, without any advantages of instruction or any knowledge of music."[21] They constituted the center of a vagrant class of anonymous figures largely outside the money economy who showed up in passing in various accounts, their numbers suggesting that these players made up the lion's share of southern musicality in public spaces. So conspicuous a presence were these performers that at times Black sound seemed to be audible everywhere. The Black vaudevillian Billy McClain, for example, recalls that in Kansas City during the 1880s the city seemed so overrun by Black musicians that it appeared as if "about every four dark faces you met was a [vocal] quartet."[22]

Busking on street corners, in alleyways, on steamboats, at railroad stations, and on trains, a variety of Black players, dancers, and singers existed on the margins of music's exchange or outside the economy altogether. They were the dubious class of scabrous performers joining the "rogues and vagabonds, idle and dissipated persons, jugglers, or persons practicing unlawful games or plays" who were populating towns and cities across the South and into the North and West.[23] The unavoidable presence of unemployed entertainers reflected the rising appeal of Black music as a form of popular entertainment as well as the uncertain economic conditions they endured. Even if musicians were fortunate enough to secure work with a touring show, they could just as easily find themselves stranded, without pay—a problem that particularly afflicted those working for smaller companies.[24] Such personal calamities were probably not uncommon, with musicians often ending up in the most unlikely places. Left to fend for themselves, they could be subject to charges of vagrancy that might lead to time in a prison work camp or a fate even worse.

The fleeting, occasional references to Black music appearing in and out of labor reinforce the perception that these performances were contributing to the affective experience of southern life and were doing so in an increasingly expansive way, the diversity of expression drawing the attention of a wide listening public. As before, Black musicians continued to bring their audibility into the social, both at work and in the circumstance of everyday living, with many continuing the practice of making music with others and for themselves. What was different, though, was that now their musical skills were frequently the focal point of conventional commercial transactions. The musicians who performed in bars, saloons, or at the large outdoor play parties and barbecues that could draw hundreds of local Black citizens were typically obtaining some sort of wage. At times, this might amount to a simple form of barter; at others, it required hard cash on the barrel. By the turn of the twentieth century, reported Howard W. Odum to the scholarly community of folklorists in 1911, a generational shift had occurred: "The majority of younger Negroes must be well paid for their music." Even the musician on the street, playing for a handout, obtained something of economic value for his or her purposeful acts of performance, and with greater and greater frequency, this exchange was based on money.[25]

Despite the casual informality of many of these transactions, the US dollar, now identifying the primary mode of exchange, established an organizing relation that carried into the broad sensory field. Money formalized relations between performer and listener, its structuring effect tracing to the interiors of rural Black communities. And just as many Black laborers recognized greater profit when trading with Whites, so did many Black musicians prefer working for White-run establishments, which, as Karl Hagstrom Miller highlights, often proved ironically safer than appearing at a Black bar or juke joint.[26] As a result, the buyer-seller work economy of musical exchange would perpetuate a racially asymmetrical economic relation while at the same time establishing a forum involving interracial social and cultural transaction. Despite the gross inequities and injustices that were the norm in these environments, routine engagements induced greater cross-racial awareness of musical practices, tastes, and preferences. These commonalities not only amplified White-majority interest in Black musical performance but also strengthened the view that what Black musicians presented as their own was fugitive, illicit. The exchanges carried a critical potentiality consistent with the radicalized status of a Fanonian lumpenproletariat in their emerging contacts with southern town and city life.[27]

The recollections of two leading performers on the minstrel circuits provide a sense of how early professional ambitions affected the character of Black music expression in these new commercial settings. In his autobiography of life in the Black entertainment business, Tom Fletcher was matter of fact about his accommodation to market forces. Fletcher begins his book by recalling how, as a boy, growing up in Portsmouth, Ohio, a mill town near the Kentucky border, he had already recognized in musical performance a viable way to earn a living. "I was more interested in money than school," Fletcher writes near the outset of his story. This, he explained, was simply a matter of practicality. "The colored people . . . couldn't read or write but they all could count money somehow, and they all knew the value of money." With telling elaboration, Fletcher details a childhood centered strategically on developing his skills in singing, dancing, and musicianship all with a profit motive in mind. What prompted these ambitions ("my chief delight") were the colored minstrel shows—Black performers typically performing in blackface—and the *Uncle Tom's Cabin* stage performances, which had become popular among southerners across the racial divide. After first seeing a live show, Fletcher writes, "I decided then and there that I was going to be a showman." Before he had turned fifteen in 1887, Fletcher was already performing on a tour boat as part of a trio, earning "some assorted stick candy and a little bag filled with pennies, a few nickels, but no dimes." Soon after, he was appearing on stage with Howard's Novelty Colored Minstrels for five dollars a week "and cakes" (room and board), earning enough to send some money home to help his family. Fletcher's early successes would ultimately lead him to run his own "pickanniny" band (a boys' band), which was so popular it gained a formal relationship with the manufacturer C. G. Conn, which supplied the ensemble with musical instruments.[28]

W. C. Handy, meanwhile, in his own oft-cited remembrances, demonstrated an exceedingly acute pecuniary sensitivity to the relationship between musical performance and profit. He must have been a careful bookkeeper with a fastidious money manager's affinity for detail, for Handy, in his narrative, provides a scrupulous accounting of his earnings for a series of performances and employments. His opening pages, which report with due admiration his grandfather's social standing as the "first colored man to own property" in his home town of Florence, Alabama, proposes an important relationship between Black ownership, legitimate labor, and hard currency.[29] It is in the popular idea of Black musical distinctiveness, recounted in his vivid descriptions of makeshift instruments derived from the detritus of dead animals—following a slave practice as it reinforced Black music's ambivalent relationship to the living and nonliving—that Handy recognized early on a variety of ways to earn money playing music. But it was from witnessing the reception of a lowly down-home trio that upstaged his own ten-piece dance orchestra that he learned "the beauty of primitive music: . . . my idea of what constitutes music was changed by the sight of that silver money cascading around the splay feet of a Mississippi string band."[30]

Handy's money calculations may seem crass, suggesting that he perceived in the string trio no inherent aesthetic qualities but saw instead a Black sounding practice from which he too could profit. Value, we might suppose, was wholly determined in financial terms. Yet this seems off the mark: his sentiments about Black music's economic potential arose from a practical ambition to make a living in the music business when few options were otherwise available, and his thinking about what was racially inherent in Black music may well have been evolving at this point. He, for one, had recognized that, whether a bearer or an embodiment of the qualities of aliveness congealed in Negro sound, he might get by selling what White and Black audiences found appealing: "People wanted movement and rhythm for their money."[31]

The pathway in pursuit of those opportunities was most certainly rough. Fletcher's and Handy's portraits of life on the road were undoubtedly sentimental, airbrushed, most likely to cast Black musicianship within the narrative conventions of popular autobiography. Although nominally free, Black musicians endured an intractable position of racially prescribed inequality, being the subjects of a dubious humanity that rarely enabled just pairing with White people and frequently led to acts of White-against-Black violence. To avoid these casually egregious assaults, many musicians chose, sometimes with resentment, to live life on the move at a time when the larger populace of Black southerners was beginning to head northward and westward, migrating from country to city in search of work and better living circumstances. Movement was part and parcel of the fugitive character of the Black musician and Black music alike. Still, finding work playing an illicit sound was difficult, and most jobs, as Fletcher notes, amounted to one-night stands. This is why witnessing unemployed musicians traveling about became a common habit in southern communities, heightening suspicion and prompting White citizens to police their behavior.[32] With little work to be had, musicians persevered nonetheless, roaming the streets and performing for handouts most anywhere. Illustrations and photos from the era document Black performers as part of the street culture, with mandolins, banjos, and guitars in hand, singing or dancing. Vagrancy was also why it was not uncommon for depictions of Black musicians to be set in rail stations, where travelers might encounter them playing, singing, or whistling for pennies, such as, in one instance, when a performer drumming on "tom-toms" attracted the attention of the German-born opera and operetta composer Jacques Offenbach.[33]

Rail stations became a common venue for Black performances because they were often the only places where vagrant Black folk could settle in for a night, being poor and otherwise knowing that most hotels, being White-run, wouldn't have them. Handy recalls one of those moments, describing the time when, while nodding off, he was roused by "a lean, loose-jointed Black [who] had commenced plunking a guitar beside me while I slept. His clothes were in rags, his feet peeped out of his shoes. His face had on it some of the sadness of the ages. . . . [His was] the weirdest music I had ever heard."[34] This well-known passage is typically cited as an early example of the blues. It also gives further demonstration not only of the arduous existence of southern Black entertainers but also how different the work life of those entertainers really was. Because of the restrictions imposed on them, together with the many qualifications attached to the category of Black music in the first place, White listeners developed a similarly strange, even dysfunctional relationship to its performance. Black music labor obtained a kind of extravagance both in its superfluity and in its peculiarity, suggesting an ever-present public property adhering to Black flesh. It remained insistently under Black possession even while it set the tenor and tone of outdoor spaces.

What most fundamentally distinguished the vagrant class of Black musicians from conventional laborers was what they produced: the coalescence of bodily enacted sounding practices and sound formations that were now taking on a new presence in southern life. Despite their common appearance in the markets of buying and selling, Black performances were just as conspicuous outside commercial forums, heard on the streets and sung in workplaces from factories to mines to plantation fields. The "weird" music that Handy overheard offers just a sliver of a much greater body of sonorous activity being increasingly brought before the public, just as it was continually reoriented and remade for that public, its multiple variations putting on display an evolving series of performative actions at once coupled to European-based musical practices as they were distinctive of the auditory worlds of southern Black people. More than ever, White citizens were learning just how *peculiar* Black music was, its strangeness enhanced by its new position in and around market structures.

As Black sounding practices coalesced into new sound formations, they suggested in their vast, proliferating peculiarity a baseness and cheapness consistent with the superfluity of Black labor itself. As Handy recalled, his music teacher, Y. A. Wallace, stressed the low estimation of Black music as it was received in commercial entertainment. In American society generally, he explained, musical skill amounted to little more than a feminized "parlor accomplishment" and Black music could only be something worse. The musician's life, he insisted, would bring Handy into traffic with "idlers, dissipated characters"—the "rogues and vagabonds" who ranged about America's cities.[35] Music labor would always remain a suspicious practice, and in the eyes of the respectable citizens, whether White or Black, the decision to pursue a musical life along the boundaries of the working classes promised a poor and lowly existence.

It is unlikely, in the end, that such opinions mattered much to the vast majority of African American musicians who were finding their way into the musical worlds of the South. They certainly couldn't have been entering the fray for bourgeois respectability and security, even if most of them still hoped to make a little money to get by. Apart from the many challenges and hardships, the proliferation of their numbers suggests that Black musicians, most of them men and women in their teens, twenties, or early thirties, often had different purposes in mind. Most fundamentally, the act of performing music for money was always tempered by its qualities of pleasure and creativity, by the pleasure of creativity, whether that pleasure be found in the artisanal discipline required in learning a craft; in contemplative practice, a version of "the sovereignty of quiet," in Kevin Quashie's evocative rendering; or in public engagements effecting many types of sociality and affective experience.[36] The role of music as a constitutive force in the making of the social is routine to our knowledge of musical engagement more generally. A vast body of musicological research has shown that performing music can locate a powerful affective mode of cohering relations, its practices setting broad yet nonetheless recognizable parameters for the ways in which people engage with one another. We might do well, though, to abide by the proposal of Bill Dietz and Gavin Steingo, who argue that such powers arise *"precisely* [from music's] radically ambiguous nonpartisanship," from a "fundamental ambiguity" of interpreting such heterogeneity in the act of musical engagements. Music excels in semiotic imprecision, opening wide possibilities of aesthetic significance. The flexibility and open possibility of a new kind of thought develops from the invention of forms whose meaningfulness remained unspecified.[37]

For Black musicians, "pleasure" in music did not correspond to a narrow system of signs but rather arose from their own social status as qualified human beings, which paradoxically afforded them a space for inventive, aesthetically centered actions. Through their musicianly efforts, they produced new sound formations growing from an ever-expanding corpus of sonic material, which sometimes entered exchange relations but otherwise became a way of affirming their own intensively oriented racial connections. Working Black musicians represented a reluctant class of labor for whom the act of performance itself carried the greatest significance. Among outsiders, there might even have been a sense of envy about the lives that Black musicians led, however unfortunate and unenviable those lives were. The common appearance of the young entertainer conjured the idea of someone who might cheat the fate of menial jobs and the involuntary servitude that otherwise proved the sorry lot for many millions of southern Black women and men. Commercial success as a musician could afford the possibility of avoiding the riskier forms of agricultural and industrial drudgery typically afflicting the unskilled population of the South. It proposed a way of finding creative satisfaction while also sometimes gaining some cash-in-hand.

It stands to reason, then, that while Black music laborers might have been perceived by White southerners and many among a developing African

American middle class as the embodiment of cheap forms of life whose existence was meant to serve the greater social purpose of labor under a new capitalist regime, these same workers also managed to introduce a distinctive character of being within and against the "repetitive and predictable process" of the hired field hand and factory worker. Black music performance stood in contrast to the challenging routines of repetitive labor that had long been associated with agricultural work and that fueled the new mass-production processes of commercial industry. If Black rural musicians were alienated workers, their actions defied the "taciturn and instrumental character" associated with such capitalized routines.[38] This was the case even as Black folk themselves appeared to embody the qualities of repetition that had long been identified with racial difference—the perpetual, static "Africa" in Hegel's depiction of "that which is without history and resolution"—and that also informed the perception of Black music as directionless noise.[39] Increasingly, "the primitive characteristic of patience under repetition" ascribed to Black manual labor was recasting the dominant perception of Black music practices, conjoining sound-making with bodily motion. And if those same qualities of repetition epitomized a condition of the workers' reification, they didn't seem to have much purpose in an economically productive sense. For they realized no finished product or surplus value beyond the strange affective complex that now openly consumed Black folk engaged in contrasting fits of dolefulness and joy.[40]

What was lacking potential as economic productivity in Black musicians' seemingly senseless repetitive acts realized something beyond the drudgery of routine. Performance reoriented the sensory arena of working practices, crafting restructurations in the time and space of labor consistent with the worlds Black people typically inhabited. These restructurations, from the remaking of the use value of open-air venues to the claim of the late-at-night as the preferred hour of performance, could prove deeply affecting and lasting—they became ripe for a provocative intersection of aesthetics and politics, recalling Du Bois's depiction of the slaves' instrumental strategies of laziness in work situations. It is in these contexts that a vagrant class of Black labor brought into public life an expansion of sonic material expressing a new, though seemingly older, antimodern character "not confined to the usual major and minor forms, as stereotyped in modern music; but . . . constructed in such modes as are naturally used by the human voice in speaking as well as in singing." Newly invented approaches combined with a range of existing sounding practices, giving shape to sonic material at once historical and distinctive to the postemancipation era: responsorial singing and playing (call-response), "barbershop" harmonies, bottleneck-slide techniques, ragging tunes, blue-note inflections, and above all, vivid displays of syncopated improvisation and percussion that propose an overarching conceptual knowledge, a veritable auditory episteme of the beat.[41]

If, as Jacques Rancière argues, "time and space are political because their distributions define forms of subjectivity and political participation, . . . defin[ing] who can be seen and heard," the situating of dubious aesthetic forms within these distributions carried the potential of creating a new set of rules, a way of restructuring the logic of musicality in private and public life.[42] Spontaneous, racially specified performances generated welcoming fields of participation and engagement; these, in turn, produced a joining of performers and listeners into clusters of creative sociality, inviting new orderings of the political as a particular sensory distribution that affected the common sense of public knowledge. They amounted to scabrous intrusions of value-making, truthful challenges to what the respectable classes of White people deemed orderly and right.

We should take care not to glorify the antagonistic relation of reluctant music labor to ordinary work. Even today, any musician who has played professionally knows how hard that life can be. Yet no matter how industrious Black working musicians might have been, what I am describing here is something different from the hardscrabble diligence at the center of the myth of American exceptionalism. There is, in fact, good reason to think long and hard on how southern Black musicians were actively laboring according to another order of inherently illicit "production," realizing something more akin to Marx's own positive conception of labor as, in David Graeber's words, "the way human beings exercise their imaginative powers to create their worlds."[43] Seemingly lazy and lethargic, Black music labor was generating a new kind of expression, coalescing as dynamic forms of possibility. These forms, in turn, inspired affective orders of relation in which congregations of hearers, often inspired into vivid body movement—shouting, swaying, leaping, and displays of exuberant dance—expanded the imagination of what was possible as beings-in-labor.

Put simply, Black musicians were producing surplus value through collaborative acts of unproductivity. Antebellum slaves had already invented a unique kind of surplus in the constitution of a racially claimable, animated property, coalescing publicly according to the dubious category "Negro music." Now, in the context of the Reconstruction era and then more elaborately in the diverse forums of racial contest and conflict characterizing the late nineteenth-century South, the free progeny of the enslaved were following along similar lines in yielding another kind of dubious production. These scabrous acts had introduced an audible racial presence that was transforming public soundscapes as they found their way into commercial markets. Despite their putative inferiority, musicians proposed modes of creativity that could be productive in a formally unproductive sense. What was deemed racially less-than Music had obtained a symbolic surplus, becoming something greater as it inspired imaginations to affective realms beyond the ordinariness of commercial markets. For these creators, their sounding practices and sound formations were likely what they believed to be aesthetically and emotionally true.

The multiple forms of Black music circulating among the new labor class of free Black southerners were not trivial expressions operating on the sidelines, nor were they merely a conventional work practice inhabiting an informal economy. The sound of Black music labor was accumulating a vast and plentiful negative value whose abject character, when brought into exchange, generated its opposite, a hyperpositivity recognized concretely as pleasurable, enlivened sound. In southern Black music, Black and White audiences alike were beginning to recognize a new manifestation of culture, a kind of animated yet reified positivity arising out of a reified yet animated negativity, positioned at once below and above the social category of Music. While the formal expressions developing from this relation did not conform to any fixed practice or style, and while listeners' perceptions of meaning in these performances differed widely according to proclivity, experience, and racial status, the expressions shared a material orientation according to a cultural logic casting Black music as double in character: as it moved into southern social life, it coalesced as scabrous forms expressive of the racial and physical properties attributed to African Americans.

SCABROUS AESTHETICS

Paolo Virno argues that performance as a public act carries the potential for a political praxis in the way that it brings together dynamic groupings of people. Advancing a theoretical position first articulated by Hannah Arendt, he proposes that the performing arts possess a strong affinity with politics because both performance and political action, quoting Arendt, "need an audience to show their virtuosity, . . . need the presence of others before whom they can appear; both need a publicly organized space for their 'work,' and both depend upon others for the performance itself." "Work" appears in quotations because it is a creative labor, unproductive in a classical political-economic sense. But Virno (whose principal concern is the post-Fordist economy) is also underscoring an affirmative sense of concrete labor as creative expression. If, as Marx asserted, the acts of the paid performer as wage laborer do not measure up as a productive economic form of labor, they are, according to Virno, nonetheless productive in another way: "They have a quality that is suggestive of political action. Their nature is essentially amphibian," or ambiguous. Virno is seeking in this instance to bring into relation that which otherwise seems opposed. The gifted artist who wins wide appeal performs "not despite the fact, but because of the fact that his or her activity is closely reminiscent of political praxis." Performance is productive in making anew what might be enacted politically. Or, as Maurizio Lazzarato puts it, "This commodity [of performance] does not produce the physical capacity of labor power; instead, it transforms the person who uses it. Immaterial labor is productive first and foremost of a 'social relationship,'" bringing about what Virno calls "the condition of possibility."[44]

From our present vantage, the creative activities of Black music laborers in the post-Reconstruction era do not readily fit the popular image of the political artist. Their music was neither formally nor meaningfully consistent. It possessed no clear intentionality. Black music at the time did not directly trigger a massive social resistance; one could not hear in it a discernible "sound of protest." Nor did the practitioners adopt postures that might be compared to those of politically minded musician-activists later vitalizing jazz, pop, and folk movements, just as they were at this point far from the category of the organic intellectual at the center of widespread mobilizations with the rise of Black grassroots politics. Saidiya Hartman's depiction of the world view among African Americans in the South at the time befits the outlook of its many young Black musicians. "The first generation after slavery," she writes, "had been so in love with being free that few noticed or minded that they had been released to nothing at all. They didn't yet know that the price of the war was to be extracted from their flesh."[45]

Yet if African American performers entering the music business had no specific political intention in mind, their acts were political nonetheless, if for no other reason than the way they rubbed against the grain of social and working norms, dramatically affecting the sensory orders of public life in the South. The reluctant character of the various actors confirmed their economically unproductive nature. Judging from their haphazard movements and casual assemblies, their very existence seemed contrary to White-held expectations of subjected Black labor. Free Black musicians had introduced a distinctive kind of living, choosing to pursue ways of being that were literal personifications of living labor but through which both their living and their labor became much more. In its seemingly unproductive acts of creative play, a new scabrous class of Black performer enacted an inspirited expressive pleasure, buoyed by the common understanding that what they were creating was something of their own. Such economically unproductive production proposed the conditions for a new kind of performativity akin to what Michael Denning, in his powerful analysis of the politics of global music vernacularity, has called a "noise uprising."[46] In the context of the late nineteenth-century South, Black music's noise uprising registered as a movement broadly conceived to be affirming aspirations of racial equality within common social environments. For this reason, the labor producing this music was inadvertently connected to a greater racial struggle. In their informal involvements in the everyday, Black musicians brought into being sounds materially bound to an abject Black character inconsistent with the economic orders of commerce. They were engaged in the making of politically energized sound formations that materialized a new scabrous aesthetics.

Accelerating the growth of free Black music was the emerging recognition on the part of the White population that a peculiar kind of "colored" expression was disseminating within the markets of southern capital. What appeared scabrous arose as a series of subtle interventions, as Black music made its way into communities beyond the plantation. Already by the 1870s and 1880s, these performances seemed to be nearly as much a product of exchange relations as they were intensively bound to the racial economy of Black people. Negro music's availability, as both a performance and a subject of public discourse, compelled White musicians and listeners to occupy racialized sound—to find their way into its enlivened character. Such efforts not only fueled the reflexive tendency to expropriate a newly conceived form, Negro music, but they also marked the beginning of a hazy awareness about how interlinked Black and White musical practices were.

A case in point comes from folklorist W. Prescott Webb. In 1915, at the close of Black music's second metamorphosis, he described how a White schoolboy in Beeville, Texas, could recite snatches of colored singing. The source of the recitation came from a much larger, multiversed performance he heard performed by Floyd Canada, a vagrant Black musician recently released from jail. Webb proceeded to document the full elaboration, which Canada sang for him at a local depot—"the common meeting-ground of all the races"—his recitation accompanied by a quickly assembled instrumental trio of guitar, banjo, and harmonica. Webb's stated aim was to show how far from the slave era Black music had progressed. This "animated body" of multiversed form, which Webb named "The African Iliad," was not, he argued, an imitation of White-performed minstrelsy; it expressed its own views, its own intentionality, its own aesthetic: a song of "little narrative unity" suffused with "a spirit of restless wandering." "In all this ballad," Webb observed, "the Black has sung nothing about the watermelon-patch; nothing about the forbidden chicken-roost, or the White man's advantage of him. . . . He sings nothing of superstitious fears of ghosts and goblins. . . . He loves, gambles, loafs, bribes the courts, and beats his way on the freight." Above all, Canada's ballad was an expression of his own creativity and ownership, best understood as part of the here and now: "Nothing could be greater than the difference between this song of the modern Black and the songs sung by the ante-bellum darky on the old plantation."[47]

Webb's essay challenged the settled wisdom about Negro abjection as it was portrayed in blackface performances while also showing how a distinctively modern African American musicality had come to inhabit everyday life in the South—a musicality whose qualities appeared so compelling they were entering into the singing bodies of White children. Yet although Webb does not say so, the epic probably seemed modern to him because he had already heard the tune on which it was based. In a passing comment, he remarks that Canada told him his ballad was derived from the melody of "Dallas Blues," a song that Webb apparently did not know by name. This, most likely, was the seminal twelve-bar blues published under the same title in 1912, composed by the White Oklahoma-based musician and businessman Hart Wand and which had been circulating widely as sheet music and in various entertainment settings. (Wand purportedly chose the title because the melody made his family's Black porter homesick for Dallas.)[48]

"The African Iliad" probably appealed to Webb because it fulfilled popular musical conventions. What seemed racially different was in fact musically familiar: a blues melody co-opted and remade by a White bandleader was then remade again by a vagrant Black musician to satisfy the tastes of Black folk, which in turn drew the attention of musically engaged White listeners. The racial confusion about Black music as different and same—bearing associations with the "darky" past and a racially tumultuous present—intensified its scabrous political power. Although it may have appeared comfortably distant, both racially and historically, having descended from the songs of "the old plantation," the oral poetry of Africa, and the ancient epics of the Homeric period (hence, "The African Iliad"), Canada's Negro music also seemed strikingly, assertively modern in ways particular to Black-rural conditions. White confrontations with this scabrous sound broadened awareness of how African American musicians were playing by a different set of rules. If their creative labors were becoming part of a shared universe of musical knowledge, they also suggested another orientation altogether.

Canada's adventitious entrance into the sound field of a small Texas town through the readaptation of an already racially hybrid popular song demonstrates the political charge of scabrous aesthetics: it betrays how an illicit form of music labor could be endowed with the "condition of possibility" that Virno ascribed to political art. Even without evidence of an actual transaction—Webb never mentions paying the musicians for their labor—Canada's performance indicated how music practices were compounding a different kind of value on the borders of the economic. Value developed in the making of a fugitive property that was intruding into the nascent networks of social relation, the exchange with Webb being one of a panoply of similar exchanges taking place in the contact zones between incongruent racial worlds. What Canada had drawn from the repertoire of White-regulated commercial entertainment became part of his creative arsenal as he wandered and labored, his performances enhanced by interracial contacts, feeding back into the entertainment life of rural Black communities as they also disseminated into and confronted White worlds. "The African Iliad" returned to Black southerners a sound formation newly animated by the effects of commodity capitalism, having been recast in the music language of commercial "blues," its valuative energy developing from its back-and-forth, intensive-extensive movements. Value accrued within the vortex of racial struggle over cultural ownership: Canada's creative acts gained disruptive power in their challenge to the character of the sensory arena of rural Jim Crow South. They did so not only by affirming the immediate sensibilities of southern Black folk but also by connecting and expanding those sensibilities in relation to extensive socialities created in commercial markets.

In the language of Jacques Rancière, Canada's musical interventions suggested a "dissensus" of reluctant labor tracing to the heart of Black music's politics of aesthetics. "Dissensus," Rancière argues, is "the very kernel of the aesthetic regime," the mechanism by which art forms catalyze a "re-configuration of the common experience of the sensible." Dissensual artworks produced among those of the "anonymous" classes—"insensible" forms and performances of the marginalized, existing outside normative thought and feeling—carry the potential of disturbing common sensible orders. They realign the grand sensory arena arising from subjective responses to the apparatuses and affective fields of the social. Artworks ironically possess this power, Rancière continues, "because they neither give lessons nor have any destination." Although meanings inevitably adhere to them, they do not stabilize to the point of predetermining reception as a fixed system of signs. And it is this vague, semiotic capaciousness that drives art's transformative potential. By intruding on "the weaving of fabrics of perception," art creates new "plots of temporality," new arrangements of phenomenal responses to the immediacy of lived experience and its time-based relations, past, present, and future. The artwork reveals a capacity to modify sensible orders, changing the feel of place among its inhabitants. In doing so, it introduces a means of restructuring knowledge-making and opening up new imaginings of self in relation to the perceptible world. As it pertains to Black music, the artwork realizes a new "condition of possibility" structured in the antagonistically generated energies of value production.[49]

Dissensus is a useful concept for comprehending more generally the social and cultural impact of southern Black music as it coalesced at the brink of the modern. Drawing on an evolving body of sonic material charged with the historicity of the African American past, Black performers across the South forged sounding practices that intruded on common listening experience as they moved about the interracial contact zones of the region. Their counterhistorical emplotments refigured audible environments, generating a succession of controversies about what public life should sound like. And out of these contests, new value developed. What appeared alive in the sound congealed as a scabrous intensity—a music knowledge not previously thought—whose resonances carried forward temporalities and sensibilities of past worlds that spread across the sonic culture of the present.

The seminal cylinder recording "The Laughing Song" initiated a pivotal technological change in the character of scabrous sound as that sound entered public spaces. It featured George Washington Johnson, an itinerant singer born a slave in Loudon County, Virginia, whose popularity among African Americans in New York's Tenderloin district led to a chance to participate in one of the first recorded sound "experiments."[50] The first of Johnson's two-and-one-half-minute renditions, which was produced in 1890, intro-duced listeners to his strange antics, which combined singing, whistling, and strange vocalizations. A conspicuous feature of "The Laughing Song" is Johnson's laughter, which he performs repeatedly, obsessively, sometimes apoplectically over the course of each chorus, its strangeness contradicted by his unflagging commitment to a steady pulse. Cast between sense and senselessness, the performance is haunting, scary: Johnson's hysterics make him seem like an automaton, which is not far off from how the re-cordings were made. In order to produce multiple versions for sale prior to the mass production of records, Johnson had to sing the song again and again, with each performance captured by about a half dozen phonograph recorders.[51] Over the course of a few years, he purportedly turned out fifty thousand cylinders and 78-RPM discs, his work behavior consistent with racist assumptions about the repetitive character of the Black body.[52]

In his analysis of the recording, Bryan Wagner explores how John-son's lyrics portray his own reification by reducing portions of his body to two inanimate objects of outdoor work: "His ears are like a snowplow; his mouth is like a trap." When performing on stage, Johnson would call atten-tion to his mouth, exaggerating its width by applying white grease paint as was common in blackface and colored minstrelsy. The technique, Wagner writes, had the effect of overwhelming Johnson's entire presence, creating the impression that the singer, in his incessant repetition, was *all mouth*—a veritable repetition machine. As we'll see over the course of this analysis, recording comes to be seen as a fitting medium for representing what was deemed the repetitive character of "the Negro." A century of synchronous labor as field hands had established expectations of music performance: as one music publication put it, Johnson's singing "made for 'good repetition on the phonograph.'" In fact, "The Laughing Song" brought together two sound-making technologies into one: the repeated sounds of a person-thing were inscribed onto a wax cylinder, which together circulated as a commodity, bringing their reiterative sensations of scabrous bodies into the world.[53]

Ultimately, though, Johnson's reification is not enough to explain his remarkable popularity. As Tim Brooks reports, "The Laughing Song" was the best-selling recording of the 1890s, and it seems unlikely that its star performer earned such a following merely because he fulfilled the racist pleasure of a Black man's self-ridicule.[54] For those who embraced the wide-spread belief in the Negro's inherent resonance, Johnson's performances offered access to the sound of animatedness rising forth from a world beyond Western knowledge. His peculiar vocalizations were that of an archaic, timeless species, fundamentally unchanged from its primitive origin. This irreducible quality of fleshy sound indicated an incongruity in Black music's relation to market exchange that exposed the incompletion of its commodification: the qualities appearing audibly alive in Black being remained inalienable, suggesting the resonance of scabrous flesh. In the coming years, awareness of the enlivened quality of Black recorded performances would intensify with the acceleration of commodity production, contributing to the sensation—which Bill Brown explores in his wonderful book, *A Sense of Things*—of a nation overwhelmed by consumable objects. If Americans at this point "lived life peculiarly possessed [by things]," they would find a certain uncanny comfort in the familiar sound of repeating Black bodies heard on record. The ambiguity of personhood that accompanied the invasion of consumer objects reached a high point with "The Laughing Song," its haunting depiction of the reified Black body "disclos[ing] the invisible persistence of the ontological effects of slavery."[55]

All of this helps us to understand why Johnson was so popular among African Americans. It is likely that many were proud of his celebrity, which stood in stark contrast to the dreadful conditions most Black people endured. And those same listeners must have also recognized how his enlivened singing had defeated White claims on it, even as Black music, now literally a sound object, circulated freely as a commodity form. The audible residue of racialized flesh witnessed on record could communicate many meanings. But there is a sense—in the context of marauding scabrous labor, thirty years after the sonic upheavals announcing the "spectacular revolution"— that Black listeners had come to recognize in their performances qualities of the incredible: an otherworldliness that was now occupying the present. By the time of "The Laughing Song," listeners across the public sphere, occupying opposite sides of the racial mountain, were each in their own way becoming newly aware of a racialized sonic possession that, no matter its movements in the newly capitalized entertainment markets, stayed ideologically bound to Black being. These Black sound objects were of the world while also existing beyond it—scabrous commodities refusing complete incorporation into the processes of exchange.

Black listeners embraced Johnson's minstrelized histrionics because they affirmed what many felt themselves to be: a people in possession of forms of sonic life greater than that which White people were creating. Their own incongruity with White worlds supplied the means of innovation, expressing a defiant strangeness that Johnson was now presenting in his bombastic stage acts and on record. At one point in the recording, he widens the gulf between Black and White by staking claim on the African past as he brings it into the Negro present. In the second verse of "The Laughing Song," he professes for his character a royal title:

> They said "his mother was a princess, his father was a prince,
> and he'd been the apple of their eye if he had not been a quince,
> but he'll be the King of Africa in the sweet by and by."
> And when I heard them saying it, why, I laughed until I cried
> and then I laughed.[56]

Despite its satirical play on bountiful fruit and preposterous claims of nobility—about which an incredulous Johnson laughs—the lyric also imagines possibility and promise: not in current life circumstances but in an African homeland existing within the imagination of Black folk.[57] A couple of decades later, James Reese Europe would affirm this sentiment as it was growing among Black performers—a subject to be explored in chapter 4—when he "explained" the Africanized peculiarities of African American creativity to White readers. "The Black loves anything that is peculiar in music," the sensibility stemming from their "innate sense of rhythm" and spirit of spontaneity, often revealed in acts of improvisation, where musicians "had no idea at all of what they were playing." Such fantastical displays, he suggested, are "to us . . . not discordant . . . [but] natural. . . . It is, indeed, a racial musical characteristic [that] springs from the soul."[58]

The peculiarities embodied by Johnson and admired by Europe were, for many, real; indeed, they contributed to the formidable power of Black music's scabrous aesthetics. Yet those same peculiarities were also part of a market strategy, providing ways of taking hold of a Black past under threat of expropriation. If popular representations of Black music reinforced the belief that the Negro was primitive by nature, they supplied African American musicians with an arena of antagonistic creation and a means of organizing musical form: fantasies of racial essence were something they themselves had come to embrace. Sounding practices thought to be inherent to Black people's character—repetition, improvisation, departures from diatonicism and tonality—crystallized within an entertainment industry that had made a bet on the commercial appeal of Negro music. Soon, Black sonic inventions acquired an aesthetic urgency fueled by growing public awareness—after the European colonization of the African continent—of diasporic connections linking Black people everywhere. Although for a time such capacious imaginations of Blackness were particularly popular in Black intellectual circles, there also appeared across African American communities a growing sense that Black music contained a history that made it sound and feel different from the music White people typically enjoyed. This congealing of scabrous politics was ironically enabled by the power of purchase as Black music made its way into the world of popular entertainment.

Sensible intimacies coalescing in Black worlds organized into what Florence Bernault has called, with reference to French-occupied Africa, forms of "colonial transaction": productive collisions of competing knowledges participating in White-controlled commercial markets that brought into being fantastical, animated forms. For Bernault, key to the process that structured the greater imaginary of fantastic beings—witches, vampires, spirits, animated objects, fetishes—was an abrasive relationality operating within and against the trading of goods and the circulation of money.[59] In the United States around this time, similar kinds of tumultuous transactions were taking place between Black musicians and White capital, as money took command as a powerful force in the production of value. Tom Fletcher's statements about the importance of such money-based transactions support one side of the equation. "All of us who were recruited to enter show business went into it with our eyes wide open," he recounted, insisting that what he wanted above all was to make a living.[60] Clearly, however, his accounting of the colored minstrel community shows that he also recognized how economic transaction could produce another kind of value, one by which African Americans could lay claim to a legacy of achievement.

In proposing this argument, Fletcher initially turns not to the familiar territory of colored minstrelsy but rather to the august world of the Fisk Jubilee Singers. Their venerable standing as commercially successful artists provides him with a way of speaking to a higher level of value existing within the world of entertainment, a means of accessing what was honorable and spiritual to edify the play of the low. Through these means, he suggests how amid the crassness and extravagance of colored minstrelsy its musicians were inventing a sensible arena that had been "created from our very souls."[61] Fletcher here is drawing together the disgraced and the celebrated to claim certain underlying likenesses. Money and soul identify an alignment of the boundedness of capital and the unboundedness of the metaphysical, producing a conceptual space made up of an ignoble lot of laboring Black musicians. His own professional life lay between these two intersecting realms, where a new kind of economically unproductive, scabrous aurality developed.

Notice that the possession of what Fletcher names "soul" was not limited to religiously aligned jubilee singers but was distributed widely and equally, having been "created from *our* very souls" (my emphasis). Soul was a stand-in for the conception of racialized cultural property. It referred to a sonically generated sensible order shared by all who labored and whose ancestry was once a form of propertied labor. As illicit subjects moving beyond labor, they shared in the politics of Black music's scabrous pleasure. For Fletcher, "soul" was an orienting truth embraced by the many profane characters in the "colored profession." It identified not only a quality but also a quantity existing within a different order of exchange as it cohered to the money economy. It was a force dynamically practiced and traded among "some highly musical people" working in commercial stage theater. The relationship of soul and money becomes critical to the creative practices of Black music labor and the constitution of value, as it would be to Black music's aesthetics and politics, to the extent that this relationship would be translated and received among African Americans. Rather than resisting the popular market, Black performers and listeners operated in a transactionally connected, parallel economy, a distinctive sensory arena out of which scabrous sound would be generated, "anticipat[ing] what becomes thinkable and possible."[62]

For Fletcher, what becomes thinkable is how capital-fueled sounding practices newly access the past. Although his book is dedicated to African American contributions to colored minstrelsy and later vaudeville, Fletcher actively works to foreground the power of the past intervening in the seemingly innocent portraits of Black stage entertainment. His initial comments, for example, focus not on the figures of the "colored" profession but rather on those among the ancestors, the enslaved populations that, although "help[ing] to build homes for their masters," ultimately became trapped after the war in the drudgery of plantation life.[63] At the center of this heroic ancestry is Fletcher's maternal grandfather, a West African born in the British-occupied Gold Coast (modern-day Ghana), who, after being captured and taken as a slave, continued to practice African customs, which he passed on in stories to Fletcher's mother. The importance of Africa as a cultural bedrock becomes a critical point of departure in the book's chapter 2, where Fletcher engages in a series of freedom tales about cultural life during the slave era. He presents these stories, which describe the slaves' sacred and secular lives, under the title "steal away," suggesting that the two lives were congruent. Whether supporting "religious services" or "good time parties," the various kinds of musical performances that "originated on the plantation" during the act of labor "usually had religion in them." They were each in their own ways sacralized calls for freedom.

If Fletcher and his siblings were obedient to church doctrine, as directed by his mother, a Sunday School teacher, they also inhabited a world where sound and sentiment formed out of a relation to the stories passed on by their African grandparents, who never relinquished an inspirited claim to their past. For them, "their ancestral homes in Africa" were a "dream song" that carried into and contradicted the sensible order of commercial, public culture.[64] Fletcher's narrative presents an engaging display of nostalgic reflection and tall tales that, however apocryphal at times, also describe a sensory field linking music to a dimension of the economy that exceeded the bounds of the market. It is from this posture that he finds the courage to test the limits of his freedom, taking advantage of a "big break" and leaving Portsmouth to become a vaudeville performer.[65]

Fletcher was among the countless number of Black musicians living on the edge who pursued soulful alternatives to the pedestrian drudgery of manual labor. Such welcoming embraces of the faith had been legion throughout the nineteenth century, common even to those for whom Christian orthodoxy was little more than a peripheral inflection within their everyday routines. Although 15–25 percent of adults among the enslaved belonged to a formal congregation, this estimation, Steven Hahn observes, "may simultaneously understate the number whose spiritual sensibilities and activities were influenced by Christianity and exaggerate the social and cultural impact of the denominational faiths." For many slaves and later for free Blacks, the soulful energy coursing through their everyday lives "showed the trappings of Christianity with little of what they regarded as its substance."[66] Their phenomenal orders suggested something akin to an open-ended sensory habitat informed by African perspectives on the relations between people, objects, and spirit forces, the connections giving shape to temporally dynamic phenomenologies. These modes of thought endured well beyond slavery.

"Do I believe in spirits?" a former Alabama slave asked rhetorically during an interview in 1936. "Sure I do," being convinced that Jesus himself said they existed. Another survivor from Georgia gave evidence of spirits by recalling Moses's magic power to turn a rod into a snake. "That happened in Africa, the Bible says. And doesn't that show that Africa was a land of magic since the beginning of history? Well then, the descendants of Africa have the same gift to do unnatural things."[67] Even during conversions to Christianity, Black southerners often played the line between spirit worlds, with "dreams, visions, trances, and voices" accompanying the path to Jesus. These altered states, one minister reported, followed "some form or type which had been handed down for generations."[68] In employing African-derived practices, slaves and free people after them, being less committed to a particular denomination, repeatedly reinvented phenomenal structures that contradicted the perceptible environments of their White and Black Christian brethren. Theirs was a phenomenological realm initiating a scabrous aesthetics that countered the force of White regimes as they also touched on and were affected by them.

Through these means, a dissensual order of belief arose as a structuring truth in the political organization of Black southerners. Churches assumed a central role in this organization, drawing together the faithful and secular alike in their shared commitment to seeking racial justice. During the years directly after the Civil War, Hahn observes, "the community support necessary to conduct electoral politics found its institutional anchors . . . in black religious congregations," with Black churches actively mobilizing and unifying rural Black folk through whatever means they could.[69] Routinely actualizing participation were the varieties of audible display, from the preacher's performative ability of "drawing in" a congregation to "the same story" with the repetitive responses of worshippers. These congregational sounding practices, which were widespread in many churches, acquired a political intensity in their repeated appeals to the spirit. Through this mechanism, Hortense Spillers proposes, the embodied behavior of movement performed by preacher and congregation alike "locates the primary instrument of moral and political change within the community. At crucial times," she continues, the relation "not only catalyzes movement, but *embodies it, is movement.*"[70]

Spillers is here speaking primarily about the sermon in its relation to Black congregations. And judging from accounts from the time, some of these embodied acts appeared connected to African expressive practices. "They have a free flow of language," explained the African American missionary Reverend Henry McNeal Turner, "while they are speaking, their orators are subjected to all kinds of interruptions," and at heightened moments, "the whole house would ring with shouts, and shake with spasmodic motions and peculiar gestures of the audience."[71] As they spoke, exhorted, declared, interjected, and interrupted, meaningful coherences of Black sovereignty congealed with the sounding practices of congregations. Over the course, relationships between embodied performance and grassroots politics were reinforced and aligned, carrying beyond the church into secular life, into the creation of meaningful coalescences of scabrous sound. In their forward-looking aspiration, a vagrant proletariat was participating in the making of modern affects and sensibilities.

Nearly a hundred years before the celebrations of soul that countenanced the civil rights movement, Black people in the rural South were participating in their own mobilizations, their own ways of organizing a sensory ecology animated with enlivened sound. The diversity of expressions proliferating across southern environs shared what Emily J. Lordi describes in her important characterization of soul legacies of the 1960s as a "recuperative logic" whereby "suffering is made to pay off." "What the discourse of soul gave people, then," she writes, "was an assurance that even their most chilling experiences of grief did not isolate them, but rather connected them—with their contemporaries, to be sure, but also with a procession of ancestors whose personal griefs were unknowable but whose historical traumas were rendered increasingly present through national discourse about slavery."[72]

In the late nineteenth century, soul was already paying off, initiating a semiautonomous economy that interrupted monetary transaction with a racially determined means of producing gains. Aligned with the logic of profit-from-loss, soul-inspired sound formations traced across the soundscape, their scabrous qualities intensifying their participation in the market economy. The perpetual tensions between money and soul had a particularly scabrous effect on music performance, as Black performers showcasing their formidable property created tears in the norms of temporal experience, the accumulating sonic energy producing a historicity that accompanied Black southerners' modern self-making. This would be modern not in the image of Europe but in its incongruencies with White public realms. A fundamental difference in the epistemology of rural Black music was its back-leaning tendency, being ordered according to a temporal mode similarly ambivalent in its relation to White public knowledge. This, once again, introduces the complex temporality of past-time, a structurally based refusal of what Michael Hanchard calls the oppressive "racial time" of White power. Past-time confronts the condition of "total labor" regulated by racial time and its constitution of the Negro subject category as a being-in-labor.[73]

Public performances of colored minstrelsy would present a particularly dramatic version of altered temporality, to be explored in chapter 3.

To conclude the present analysis, however, I want to consider the quieter, quotidian incidences of scabrous intervention that occurred routinely and that in their accumulation overwhelmed southern soundscapes at the long turn of the twentieth century. These were the "discreet affects" that were appearing unexpectedly by the thousands in everyday situations animating the scabrous exchanges between Black and White folk. As Rancière argues, dissensual art often produces its effect discreetly, obliquely, as "an affect of indeterminate effect." Understood as part of the aesthetic, it discloses a power to transform through the repetition of subtle gesture. "The images of art do not supply weapons for battles," he observes. "They help sketch new configurations of what can be seen, what can be said and what can be thought and, consequently, a new landscape of the possible." These discreet affects, Joseph Tanke writes, "pursu[e] small openings. . . . Dissensus is not a question of mere perspective; it does not simply allow us to *see* the world differently, it actually *modifies* the sensible world."[74] Such possibility necessarily develops from a semiotically open position. Art forms, Rancière states, have this effect "on condition that their meaning or effect is not anticipated."[75]

Take, for example, Thomas A. Dorsey's childhood recollections about how spontaneous singing in his Georgia community during the first years of the 1900s could qualitatively change the emotional character of the moment for those who were gathered. Dorsey remembers the way his own family and their friends engaged in intimate means of relating through the sounding practice of moaning, by which extemporaneously sung hymns brought a sensation of spirit into the singers' everyday lives. In one instance, he reported how his mother and her visitors would begin improvising as routinely as they would enter into conversation. "I've heard my mother and other folk get together, get around and get to talking and then start moaning," Dorsey explained. Moaning, here, refers not to expressions of sorrow so much as a singing practice involving elongated, sustained tones varied incrementally and performed heterophonically, following the order of a familiar melodic prototype. This act of improvisational maneuvering drew singers together organically and situationally, their vocalizations congealing into a coherent body of sound, with individual voices distinguished in subtle, melismatic variation. Audible alignments of singing produced a shared experience reaching beyond the ordinary, commonly understood in religious terms: realms of spirituality, of ancestry, of soulfulness coalescing in the present.

The occasions were probably not strictly religious, even in religious circumstances, just as moaning could occur in secular settings as part of the cultures of performance common to church groups, social clubs, and secret societies, and at informal gatherings. One could even hear this sounding practice in the private musings of an individual. "He was always humming snatches of some hymn," the South Carolina planter Henry William Ravenel noted about one of the "crazy native Africans" on his family's plantation. "A hum can speak volumes," writes Anthony Heilbut, and above all, "these sounds render the indescribable"—the capacious imagining of temporal and spatial "beyonds."[76] In the practice of moaning, which had evolved into coherent sound formations, congregants created a condition whereby vocalizing gained the capacity to transport singers from the ordinariness of everyday life, as it generated new sonic material based on a legacy of Black performativity. Awareness of how singing drew from "the spirit," moreover, acknowledged past-times in the present. Turning back to the past betrayed the growing significance of the ancestral in the making of modern knowledge and in the production of sound formations that defied the forces of expropriation. Although Dorsey's mother and her friends were probably unconcerned about the immediacies of capital and its encroachment on their everyday lives, they nonetheless endured the interminable pressure of racist domination as part of the time-ordering structures of the economic. Possession of a soulful music practice unconstrained by money and the workday must have carried a powerful significance in their lives, standing in vivid contrast to the conditions of struggle they endured in slavery's aftermath.[77]

Scabrous qualities of discreet affect appeared to have been equally consequential at the interracial contact points of southern life. On the face of it, the routine cultural trespassing by even the most well-meaning White folk disrupted Negro song's ability to decouple from the forces of racial subjugation, the reorganization of sensory environments moving from White to Black. The commercial appeal of jubilee choruses offer one obvious example of how the music's commodification undermined Black aesthetic authority. Time and again, however, Black music's heightened commercial valuation deepened its importance to African Americans living on the fringes of public life. When in the 1880s the circuit rider and congregational preacher William E. Barton undertook as a personal mission the task of painstakingly documenting the "quaint hymns" elderly Tennessee domestic workers hummed while performing chores, he extended a practice of extraction consistent with the folkloric mission—to render "quaint [the] peculiarity of the negro music." By writing down melodies "from some one who would patiently repeat [a hymn] again and again till

I mastered its wonderful syncopations," Barton reinforced their importance within the community. His musical portraits, which he published in three installments, turned ephemeral melodies into a document of a grand tradition, his preservation efforts inspiring elaborate discussions of practice among the women, with one in particular "cudgel[ing] her brains for some of the old ones." An undeniable asymmetry remained, reinforcing the extent of White power's containments of Black music. Yet Barton's involvements also showed how African Americans had acquired an aesthetic authority that turned the tables on mastery: they had become the masters, the experts, who were now instructing an eager White student body who sought to learn the subtleties of "wonderful syncopations" and to acquire a feel for a practice that was decidedly different:

> Negro music . . . can nearly all be swayed to and timed with the patting of the foot. No matter how irregular it appears to be, one who sways backward and forward and pats his foot finds the rhythm perfect. A young lady friend of mine was trying to learn some of the melodies from an old auntie, but found that the time as well as the tune baffled her. At length, when the old woman had turned to her work, the girl got to swaying and humming gently, patting her foot the while. The old woman turned and, patting the girl on the knee, said: "Dat's right, honey! Dat's de berry way! Now you's a-gittin' it, sho nuff! You'll nebbah larn 'em in de wuld till you sings dem in de sperrit!"[78]

Even as Barton sought to reassert his racial authority, casting her words in dialect, the "old auntie" persisted in the role of the expert: she was the one in possession of a valuable cultural property, a sound formation whose peculiarities of time and melodic contour remained within the Black body even as they were generously shared. An aesthetic sensation organized through singing remained under the control of Black folk who allowed White people brief access only after they had put in the proper effort to feel the spirit. These discreet gifts of "patting," "swaying," and "humming gently" would undergo transformation as they entered the structures of exchange, disseminating as qualities of practices subsequently named hot rhythm, syncopated music, jazz, swing, groove. They introduced to the community and then to the world a new order of thought—a knowledge of the beat that would soon overwhelm American popular culture.

Black music's discreet affect carried considerable consequence as musical performances began to proliferate across the time and space of public culture, introducing new thought and new possibility as they carried forward beliefs grounded in the porous interiority of Black rural cultures. The transformative power of scabrous sound multiplied rapidly, its intrusions into the time frames of commerce producing a cascade of interracial contacts. To comprehend these contacts a bit further, we turn, as a final example, to an Alabama planter who in 1885 described with a sense of incredulous wonder his musical encounters with a domestic under his employ. "I have ever before me, in my help, 'Dora,' a striking evidence of the darkies' love of music." Despite being repeatedly turned out of her church "for dancing and singing 'de songs ob old satan," he writes, she seemed to live persistently in a different world among the "dusky wards of our nation." The writer, at once condescending and charmed by Dora's skills, gained a partial view of her world "when I have been playing a spirited racquet or galop I have seen Dora throw aside any work she might be engaged in and rapidly dance from one side of the yard to the other, . . . brandishing in one hand a gridiron and in the other an enormous dish-rag [handkerchiefs being common to religious shouts], presenting a most grotesque appearance."[79]

Dora's "grotesque" behavior was disturbing because it confronted the planter with a sensible order different from his own in which he nonetheless awkwardly participated, her improvised display, probably derived from shouting rituals, imposing a disruption of evenly measured time. We may now, after more than two hundred years of aesthetic contemplation, take all music's time-bent power for granted. But the intrusion of Black-generated orientations involving persistent syncopation and aggressively articulated forms of beat—as likely presented on Dora's gridiron in ways reminiscent of the iron time-keeping instruments of West and Central Africa—had radically reoriented European metric order, its "grotesque" aural quality taking claim of a rhythmic sense once firmly under the planter's control. Such temporal collisions were occurring routinely across the postemancipation South as White observers were confronted with auralities not their own, in which Black folk were consumed in actions that "seemed to absorb [them] with a frenzy of excitement." These "pastimes," as Ravenel dismissively described them, "were probably the lingering shadow of some war dance seen or known [from] native land . . . [and] that had taken possession of his poor brain."[80] Yet Dora's actions, together with countless numbers like them, suggest something more: a powerful temporal alteration or past-time that reached back in reimagining the sonic present. As they began to participate in the new economies of entertainment, the past-times of Black music, like value itself, would intensify and grow.

Dora's actions put on display a tradition of performance that, in the heightened interactions with White folk, had become newly conceived as scabrous. Having developed from a different order of knowledge, her display confronted the planter's perception of musical rightness, the confrontation inspiring a variety of rationalizations that attempted to reduce Black musicality to utter senselessness or remake it into a diverting racial pastime. By the turn of the century, however, African Americans were recognizing how their coalescences of form were gaining value as those same coalescences became wedded to a new politics. Repeated attempts to translate scabrous sound as "a relic of paganism," the "incoherent babblings" of a "superstitious age," would only heighten the perception that "Negroes" were engaging in something beyond the norms of Music.[81]

Black music's metamorphoses in the postemancipation South brought forth a distinctive order of embodied, auditory arrangement, a formal coalescence of the sonorous extending out of a complex, dialectical interplay in the quotidian engagements of everyday life. Scabrous sound formations and performative displays opened up a space where a new kind of thought could emerge, thereby bringing a particular sensory arena into intrusive interplay with White sensibilities. The formalization of Black music practices enabled the expression of a new kind of being-in-labor in which audible properties of the Black body established a distinctive value within the nascent forums of entertainment, its accumulated cultural profit returning as a surplus back into Black southern culture. The conspicuous positioning of reified, Black music labor circulating within the fields of public culture amplified its thingly autonomy and, by turns, its animated, hyperpositive value built on "sway," "moaning," "patting," and beat. As Black musicians advanced their status as labor power, so did Black music continue on its long ascent as an absolute, racial music—an enlivened sound disconnected from the audible bodies of its performers. Neither simply a form of Music nor wholly not-Music, Black music advanced as a new uncanny phenomenon of remarkable intensity, its undecided significance generating a sense of soulful vastness so curiously compelling it seemed nearly to stand on its own two feet.

THREE

MINSTRELSY'S INCREDIBLE CORPOREALITIES

TRANSACTIONS OF RACIST FANTASY

If African American musicians' participation in the money economy made their performances seem familiar to southerners, the nation's
commitment to White supremacy repeatedly contradicted that sentiment, reaffirming how different "Negro" sound was. For however diverting it might have been, Black music, according to prevailing opinion in the
postemancipation South, was still born of a reified subject that, despite
sharing a certain resemblance to common European stock, existed in a
realm all its own. When it came to the act of making music, the bottom
line was one of intention: were the sounds produced by Black bodies an
automatic reflex of animal emotion or consciously and creatively invented?

It appeared remarkably difficult for many White people at the time to
fathom that Black musicians were actually making credible forms of Music.
Hence, the child pianist Blind Tom was "cursed with but little of human nature; he seems to be an unconscious agent acting as he is acted on, and his
mind a vacant receptacle where Nature stores her jewels to recall them at
her pleasure." In a letter from 1885 to the *Philadelphia Times*, moreover, an Alabama writer observed, "The Negroes . . . invent, one might say, their own
music, and manufacture songs which are devoid of all sense, and yet . . .
one is often surprised into the exclamation: 'How well they sing!'" Banjo
players contorted the principles of harmonic progression: "They never have

any set accompaniment: just a succession of indicating chords, connected by the distinctly outlined melody." And in a reflection on the significance of "negro songs," a distinguished Vienna-based scholar submitted that the vocalizations of the freed people were, in the end, "not musical songs at all" but strange vocal utterances, "merely simple poems."[1]

Black music seemed dubious because it came from a being many believed to originate outside of civilization; the "Negro" may have been a natural musician, but its music did not sound natural at all. The mysterious resonances and utterances emanating from its body appeared deformed, *in-credible*—an *unnatural* growth mutating out of control. And yet it was precisely the mystery of this Negro sound's creation that sustained its wide appeal. Indeed, amid the debates, Black musicians continued to move about the South and into the North, performing their peculiar sounding practices that tested the limits of aesthetic credibility. By the time of John W. F. "Johnnie" Woods, W. C. Handy, Floyd Canada, Tom Fletcher, and hundreds if not thousands more, the sound of "Negro music" was transforming the casual listening environments of town and home. A negative value had turned about once again, generating an incredible aurality that exceeded the norms of Music.

The mystery of Negro musicality is what first inspired the infamous parodies of blackface minstrelsy, where White men and women acted out racial fantasies about Black people and the sounds they made. These enactments did not account for the way that Black southerners understood their sound worlds, but rather elaborated on prevailing racist conceits about the audible qualities of the Negro body. Yet over time, the fictions—fetishistic concoctions based on interpretations of surface appearances—gained a certain authority: out of the intellectual fabric of antebellum minstrelsy arose an aesthetic archetype of Blackness that teetered between the abject and the spectacular, creating among White performers and their audiences, as Eric Lott writes in his now classic analysis, "a certain terror as well as great affection"; the effect of blackface "relied precisely on this doubleness." So powerful were the minstrel fantasies of animated Negro sound that they contoured the range of musical understanding, making myths bound to racist projection into social reality, thereby fulfilling myth's potential as truth.[2]

For Lott, terror arose dialectically from affection, from the recognition that what appeared abject was also part of the commonplace: the mystery perceived in the Black subject uncannily betrayed qualities of Whiteness itself. "When the white man steps behind the mask," Ralph Ellison famously observed, "his freedom is circumscribed by the fear that he is not simply miming a personification of his disorder and chaos but that he will become in fact that which he intends only to symbolize."[3] Such disconcerting intimacies appeared at the onset of blackface in the primary character of Jim Crow, the plantation slave whose staged enactments reshaped the affective comprehension of racial being, playing out a fundamental contradiction of White responses to race. If Jim Crow would become the defining marker of racial segregation, serving in 1839 to describe "two colored men" traveling by train who "were compelled to take seats in the 'Jim Crow'" and identifying in 1835 the rioters in a Boston antislavery office who "exultingly . . . jump[ed] Jim Crow," so would it indicate collegial bonds among White men: Martin Van Buren, proclaimed a toastmaster among a group of lawmakers, was "a real Jim Crow of a fellow."[4]

It is one of the fundamental ironies of Black music history that a racist genre seeking to contain the music's animated presence opened new avenues of creative production, ensuring those containment efforts would fail. Through their cruel parodies, White minstrel acts boosted the value of Black music, disseminating beliefs in its enlivened power and inspiring public interest in African American performances. These racial fantasies, in turn, cycled out of public culture to enter rural Black communities, the disparaging figurations turned on their heads to heighten the sensation of Black music's animated character. In this way, minstrel representations of Black social and musical behavior appearing after the war became a creative quarry for the extraction of ideas and sensibilities that raised the cultural value of Black music and strengthened its symbolic linkages to realms thought to exceed White knowledge. What W. C. Handy previously identified as the "drain" that "all the best talent came down" was, in the end, the minstrel stage: "The minstrel shows got them all."[5] The performances steered the process of Black music's commercial expansion, remaking the understanding of what was musically and aesthetically possible among Black and White alike.

By sensationalizing the sensation of aliveness, blackface bestowed on Black music a perverse gift: its racist portrayals confirmed that it possessed special powers extending from the Negro musician's animated flesh. Because these powers were thought to be inalienable, they provided circumstantial evidence of what White people lacked: with each performance, Black music exposed what White America felt it owned but had somehow lost, the efforts to recuperate this value through imitation and consumption being central to minstrelsy's wicked delight. Into the twentieth century, minstrel stage acts led an orchestrated effort to reclaim an ontologized *lost property*, their repeated failure heightening the sensation of racial pleasure under-lying the fantasy of incredibility: containment efforts focusing on the pe-culiar sound of the Negro remained central to the musical construction of Whiteness. What had become highly valued, in turn, accelerated the growth of Black commercial performances in African American communi-ties, as musicians spread the music's ontological energy, exploiting fanta-sies about their music's less-than/greater-than character. At the apex of its second metamorphosis, Black music in its doubled formation would stand as the central value in a nascent entertainment market, its autonomy given to delirious scandal while driving an enduring pattern of innovation and White efforts to consume and possess it.

FLESHY REMAINS

There is no better indication of White America's deepened fasci-nation with Black sound than the bizarre phenomenon of coon song, which gained widespread popularity across the United States during the last decades of the nineteenth century. As it was staged in live performances and circulated via sheet music, the coon song developed from one of the darker sentiments of antebellum blackface—namely, that "the Negro" was a deficient being whose conspicuous presence was putting the nation at risk.[6] Initially, the word *coon* was a term of playful banter: Whigs in the 1840 presidential campaign were known as "coons" after the fashion of the raccoon-skin hat. Within a few decades, however, it had turned into a merciless charge of contempt routinely directed at African Americans. If the slur applied generally to matters of character, it targeted especially a purportedly bestial nature related to the sounds emanating from racial flesh. Robert Toll, James Dormon, and others have shown how the rise of coon songs in the 1880s set the tone for an exceedingly grotesque era of blackface depiction corresponding to aggressive efforts to segregate the races, eventually formalized under the regime of Jim Crow law.[7] The satiric characterizations of coons as depraved and profligate—the figure gaining traction after the international success of a song by the African American composer Ernest Hogan, "All Coons Look Alike to Me" (1896)—were con-sistent with efforts to crush Black aspirations of securing an equal place among the nation's citizenry.[8]

It is for this reason that late nineteenth-century blackface frequently conflated Black music's reputed animatedness with the bodies that White power sought to erase. Coon songs arose as a site of violent display, reenacting in stylized, often cartoonish fashion the decimation of Black bodies that was occurring during a long wave of racial terror, performed with particular brutality in the sordid rituals of lynching. White-composed coon songs and lynching practices arose from the same symbolic universe: both sought to reassert control of African Americans and particularly Black men by defiling them.[9] As a routine, many songs reimagined the Black body in the form of a thing: an animal, a cannibal, a ghostly immaterial presence, a pathetic creature bemoaning its colored condition. Among the genre's more popular characters was the bully, the incredible monstrosity ravaging southern towns whose representation in the song "Dat Cross-Eyed Hoo-doo Coon" as "bandy-legged, snaggle-toothed, and libber-lipped" rationalized his own fate, variously brutalized and decimated; in one lyric, he is burnished in enamel as "Coon Coon Coon" (figure 3.1). Such acts of objectification were, in fact, part and parcel of the earliest incarnations of blackface spectacle. The master texts of minstrelsy, Jim Crow and Zip Coon, found the Negro protagonist in the realm of nature and animals—man as bird and raccoon, in the company of "a ring tail'd monkey, [and] a rib nose baboon." They were indolent, do-nothing characters whose constitution as things commenced their expropriation. At the same time, they never seemed to fully dissipate; there would always be an unobtainable corporeality remaining.[10]

The same refusal to dissipate appears in another antebellum-era prototype, "The Fine Old Colored Gentleman" (1843). In this work, the composer, Dan Emmett, one of the founding figures of blackface minstrelsy, depicts a sad Black person who "drawed himself up in a knot, His knees did touch his chin." Being inextricably linked to the natural world of beasts, this figure "scared the pigs and ghosts" with song and, after his passing ("he guv up his ghost"), "de coons did roar, de possums howled." In their own act of dismemberment, finally, his brethren proceeded to re-create the remains of "dis good old nigger," "Dey went to work and skinned him. . . . And de head of dis here banjo is dat nigger's hide." The lyric was not far from reality. Forty years later, Dr. Thompson Burton, a New York State physician and "prominent republican," turned the tanned skin of a lynching victim—who, before his death, purportedly "gave his body to the attending physicians"— into a pair of shoes. What remained "he cut up in small pieces and gave to his friends as curiosities." One recipient of this "curious relic" reported that the "tanned human skin" of a Black person "resembles sheepskin very closely."[11] In an 1869 adaptation of his song "Ten Little Injuns" as "Ten Little Niggers," moreover, Septimus Winner extrapolated on the routine acts of

3.1 Cover of sheet music for "Coon Coon Coon" (1900), introduced and sung by Lew Dockstader, with words by Gene Jefferson and music by Leo Friedman.

bodily decimation in another fantasy of White-on-Black violence, which described a series of chokings, bee stingings, bear "cuddling," fish swallowing, sun scorchings, and self-mutilations ("one chopp'd himself in halves"), resulting in a trail of unerasable detritus. A residue of flesh persisted, its corporeal refusal to dissipate reaffirming its inalienable character and evoking the imagination of inspirited life: the last of the lot would mate and "soon rais'd a family of ten niggers more." Incomplete erasure of Black audibility gave expression to worry about other kinds of incompletion, of an unsubsumable "Negro problem" that stubbornly persisted.[12]

Late-century White minstrel performance created its own kind of fleshy remain, its own scabrous residue. Its depictions of southern Black culture's scandalous qualities were something more than superficial imaginings of incredible form. The common portrayal of an irreducible materiality had the real-life effect of affirming the species of "Negro" as the "most superstitious of all races."[13] The idea of residue was historically specific and materially grounded, reimagining Black people's purportedly soulful character as an otherworldly and potentially diabolical force. As a signifier of age and duration, the figure of residue supported the understanding of Black performance as an outgrowth of an archaic species, whose fleshy remains—whether in the form of tanned skin or other "relics," such as a man's "toe bone, [which] possesses much of the luck of a rabbit's foot"— were now being brought to life in the colored minstrel and "Tom" shows proliferating across America.[14] Commonly translated by educated classes into a sonorous remnant of the slave era whose racial origin stretched even deeper into the recesses of history, Negro sound had acquired in the popular imagination a quality of profound anteriority, a substantive past-ness occupying a liminal state between living and dying—between "the Ancient and the Modern," as outlined in J. J. Trux's oft-mentioned 1855 essay—whose embodied resonance proposed additional comparisons with the detritus of a lost war: the vestiges of the Confederacy's rebellion, the bullets and weapons commonly referred to as "ruins" or "relics," and to the remains of the body itself.[15]

It is revealing that the very term *relic*—in Roman Catholicism, the re-mains of a saint—identifies an irreducible materiality aligned with the fetish, for the domain of the Black body was certainly seen that way after the Civil War.[16] A relic might refer to a living being, such as a Black man or woman who had survived slavery and was still alive at a very old age. There was, for example, the 103-year-old "King Herod, a Negro of Atchison [Kan-sas]," celebrated as "a relic of olden days" and Mrs. Rebecca Whale, who "remained in bondage to her former master, ignorant of her freedom" until her manumission in 1869, when she was celebrated as one of the "relics of slavery." More frequently, though, the term was associated with acts of violence that had generated inspired bodily remains and with the people who collected them. In Corsicana, Texas, "relic hunters" were those scav-enging the remains of a lynching, "the bones of the victim [being] broken into small bits and passed around as souvenirs." Another group of "relic hunters" in Maysville, Kentucky, were prevented from taking the ashes of a burned victim. Instead, what remained of one thing was placed in another: the disintegrated flesh was "buried in a baking powder can." An inadver-tent method of fetish-making occurred, moreover, when the thumb of an accused thief was shot off by a homeowner and submitted as evidence: "He left a finger," a Columbus, Ohio newspaper reported, and the "relic may convict [the] Negro burglar." Acts of violence in the production of bodily relics were, at times, compared to the object itself: a Black man accused of a crime was subjected to methods of torture so cruel they led to his death; the inhumane act was denounced as "a relic of the Inquisition." Lynching itself, in Arthur Schomburg's formulation, was "a savage relic."[17]

What seemed incredible about the Negro relic was its enduring corporeality, being fetishistic in the original sense of the word: it was thought to carry within it an animated life force, a peculiar truth that inspired White efforts to possess it. As a way of referencing the material culture of a ravaged South, *relic* became a preferred term for describing the authentic intensities of enlivened Black sound. The word showed up consistently in music discussions, including Trux's own confused speculation on the origin of Jim Crow, in which he conflates minstrel performances and the songs of the slaves. If one of those songs was not "first sung upon the banks of the Altamaha, the Alabama, or the Mississippi," then perhaps it was a primitive survival, "a relic of heathen rites in Congo, or in that mysterious heart of Africa." Twelve years later, William Francis Allen proposed that the shouting practices among the freed slaves living on the Carolina sea islands were an audible "relic of some native African dance," while the "incoherent babbling" and enduring "spiritual excitement . . . found in southern Negro camp meetings" was, according to an 1898 account, a "relic of paganism": for "the savage," the spirit remained within the body; there was "no bodily resurrection." The New York critic Henry Edward Krehbiel, moreover, in expressing doubts about Lafcadio Hearn's theory on the relation of Negro vocal cords to blood warmth—"the highest human temperature known. . . . [But] I did not even try to find a colored subject for the dissecting table"—nonetheless acknowledged their shared interest in unearthing the unearthliness of a sound hidden away in the Negro past: "We were looking for unmistakable African relics in [Negro] songs." For Hearn, these audible relics had once been indisputably exchangeable qualities of the Black body. West African griots, he explained to Krehbiel in a correspondence from 1884, were practitioners of "musical prostitution."[18]

Working from this background, Krehbiel proceeded to explore the retention of a hidden essence in the complex of racial psychology and embodiment. In the list of questions outlining the basic premise of his widely read book, *Afro-American Folksongs* (1914), he asks: "Does it follow that because the American Negroes have forgotten the language of their savage ancestors, they have also forgotten all of their music? May relics of that music not remain in a subconscious memory?"[19] Here, once more, the unsubsumable audibility of an enlivened relic persisted. For Krehbiel, as it was for Allen and Hearn, Black music contained something indelible, ancient, even eternal—an incredible condition of animated flesh that endowed it with special value: in its sound, one could discern resonances of racial truth.

But could this truth be intentionally made? For the negative value of a scabrous sound also carried an excessively positive vitality, suggesting that what seemed incredible was consciously produced and exceeded the value of conventional Music. The sense of a hyperpositive emerging out of a negative condition reinforced the perception of Black music's animated character, of its ambiguous ontological aliveness. It is perhaps for this reason that visitors to sideshows at the turn of the twentieth century were enamored of the recorded reenactments of lynchings, which, as Gustav Stadler documents in a fascinating essay, were commercially produced on phonographic cylinders. Through these means, listeners could bear witness to the "MOANS AND GROANS. PRICED ONE CENT!" which were sold to the public as the actual cries of Black men being set on fire. These staged acts proposed a version of the incredible, the purported victims dramatizing confrontations at the borderland between life and death.[20]

The lurid appeal of lynching reenactments provides insight into the auditory power of minstrelsy. Coon songs and other White-performed blackface acts grew so influential not merely because of their sensational depictions but also because these depictions were performed musically within the ritualized settings of the stage. They were cast, as Gage Averill puts it, "in blackvoice, an often crude parody of black southern dialect, diction, timbre, and vocal mannerisms."[21] And it was in ways that parallel the olfactory sensation of lynching victims' scorched flesh that blackface music overwhelmed the imaginations of listening audiences. If the senses of taste and smell, as Orlando Patterson argues in "Feast of Blood," his penetrating analysis of the symbolic orders of lynching, are decidedly superior modalities for recollection—"being 'impervious to time'" and effecting a sense of immediacy with the past—the realm of hearing reproduces that same sensation, prompting a heightened experience of intimacy that can make remembering, whether real or imagined, seem *more real* than the events themselves. In fact, hearing can equal or even exceed the past-gathering capabilities of the olfactory, drawing the listener into an atmosphere of imagined pasts as the past sounds audibly in the present. As scent infects the body, sound overwhelms it; it encompasses the listener, effecting a feeling of closeness, intimacy. In the semiotic language of Charles Peirce, music as "'The Pure Icon' is the mental grasping of a similarity between an object and its referent, a similarity which is not itself represented but simply fills consciousness." "The grasping of an unreflected sense or feeling of a connection or relationship," writes Dean MacConnell, "can overpower subjectivity . . . engulf[ing] an audience with an 'immediate characteristic flavor.'" In the instance of blackface's perverse comic hilarity, this sensation, working from MacConnell's language, would have been "a total tragic feeling."[22]

The capacity of blackface performances to envelop listeners in the tragic sound and feel of the Negro body proposed a means for those audiences to reclaim a possession otherwise lost. Minstrelsy carried the potential of momentarily ascribing meaning: to inspire the imagined sensation of incorporating the audibility of racially embodied form, of repossessing and consuming it, however brutally or lovingly. Most likely in the minds of many White spectators, blackface performance returned the "natural resource" of a thingly being to its rightful ownership. Rather than a direct act of theft, this incorporation represented a partial restoration of that which was, in the first instance, thought to belong to White power. It enabled control of a menacing problem to realize a proper social balance, to restore order to southern culture and to ensure that "Negroes" kept their place. Ultimately, minstrelsy sought to consume the Black body to secure it completely within White structures of knowledge—to make Black music and the Black subject that produced it entirely known. Yet after the performance, the illusion of access would ultimately dissipate as White audiences confronted the fact that African Americans existed in a realm not so easily subsumed through fantastical performances of difference. In its efforts to expropriate and claim ownership, White minstrelsy simultaneously conceived the obstacles to those efforts, heightening the value of inalienable Black forms. And as it constituted racialized imaginations of an audible Black past, minstrelsy also outlined the limits of White cultural authority. In the end, the affective character of a Black past extending from the slave era remained impenetrable, lost without a comprehension of the material basis of what was alive in the sound.

Out of the White performances of blackface, an intensified sensation of Black music's inalienable pastness comes forth as something congruent with otherworldliness and abjection. The sound of the "Negroes" may have been alive in the present, but it also remained linked to other temporal locations, its peculiar character a sonic relic of the unliving. These mounting attachments to oldness and deadness assembling in the racial imagination of White supremacy help to explain why writers from the slave era, and then increasingly from the 1880s—with the rise of the coon song and folkloric representations of African American religious practices—invoked a musically inflected language of spectrality when discussing what seemed newly unsettling about Negro presence. A 1901 commentary by the Atlanta US district judge Emory Speer, for example, ironically relies on spectral allusion in defense of his work to advance legal protections for African Americans. "For nearly a third of a century," he asserted—his words appearing as a caption to an illustration in the *American Economist*—"the white men of the South have surrendered their political convictions for fear of the spook of negro domination. The negro will never dominate the white man" (figure 3.2). Such minstrel-derived references to "spooks" show how the uncanny sensations of fleshy sound were affecting public discourse in a new and powerful way.[23]

Accessing the added value of racial residue, Black music revealed the possibility of a distinctive ontology resistant to commodity fetishism while replicating fetishism's ghostly effect. In its accumulation as a rich body of scabrous expressivity, it would be consistent with African Americans' greater efforts to assert their rights and expectations of racial justice. Significantly, over the remaining years of the nineteenth century and into the next, Black performers embraced the characterizations of spectrality and otherworldliness in their creative expressions. From around 1900, for example, stories of spooks—together with a related figure, the "boogie" (probably from bogeyman; to be discussed in chapter 9)—showed up in the entertainment pages of African American newspapers such as the *Washington Bee* and *Chicago Defender*, suggesting a contemporary analogue to Henry, the animated wooden-headed dummy on John W. F. "Johnnie" Woods's knee. By the 1920s, moreover, the figure of the "spook" had become an empowering force among Black jazz musicians in the creation of a hyperpositive, spectacular music.[24] These changes are important to our own understanding of the counterhistorical dimension of value production: they demonstrate how the imperfect efforts to incorporate Black music into the extensively oriented exchange relations of capital drove new, intensively based valuations that celebrated racialized imaginations of spirit worlds as part of the music's ontological character.

Despite their enabling effects, however, White minstrel depictions of a fleshy, spooky sound rubbing against the grain of southern life remained a part of the apparatuses of domination that sought to contain Black music's ill effects—to sequester an increasingly volatile racial aurality within the

THE SOUTHERN STATES FURNISH A CURIOUS EXAMPLE OF POLITICAL PERVERSITY.

3.2 Illustration in the *American Economist* depicting "the spook of negro domination" (1901). A caption below the illustration reads: "The white men of the South have surrendered their political convictions for fear of the spook of negro domination. The negro will never dominate the white man. —*From the recent address of Judge Emory Speer at Atlanta, Ga.*"

familiar frames of difference. Whereas representations created by elite African American commentators from the same period worked to elevate Black music, presenting it as the common equivalent of European-based artistry, White writers reporting in national magazines, newspapers, and scholarly journals drew portraits of a form that stood transparently outside aesthetic norms.[25] They did so for the simple fact that they were unable to imagine Black music without the qualifying assistance of "Negro" difference. Difference reduced the ambiguities of enlivened sound to something tangible and accessible, committing it to figurations already existing within the White racial imagination. Difference could temper concerns about a sound world that seemed increasingly uncanny and even threatening—the creation of a people who reportedly interacted and were sometimes possessed by invisible forces.

Yet the safety of difference could not accommodate the many intrusions of African symbolic worlds and the time-bending discreet affects explored in the previous chapter. It could not account for someone like "Crazy Will," who, in an apparent reach to ancestry, enacted (according to Henry William Ravenel's recollection from 1876) "a peculiar dance . . . [in which] he used two light rods in his hand, and with these he would make passes at some imaginary person, all the while looking steadily at the sun." Creative practices of this kind could not be successfully reduced to the predictable containment fields of race and degeneracy, nor could their companionable sounds of a surplus corporeality, still common to plantations and routinely heard in the streets and alley ways of southern towns, be conveniently dismissed as abject noise. The rising proportion of the threat may be why White reporters, while acknowledging the peculiarity of Black music's haunting, spectral presence, continued in their representations to rely on figurations of Negro music as a natural occurrence, as anonymous wandering melodies in line with the folkloric. Anonymity supported an aspirational truth—wishful thinking about a docile Negro character.[26]

Such sentimental idealizations ultimately stood in conflict with the widening recognition that Black southerners were creating a profusion of sounding practices, their incredible auditory world—from the percussive assaults of "some dusky warrior" playing a drum to patting practices accompanying boisterous singing and exhorting—demonstrating how "music of any kind," according to the New York *Sun*'s Florida correspondent, Hamilton Jay, "is the negro's passion."[27] Fascination prevailed regarding the tools and instruments with which African American musicians produced sound, their forms suggesting an iconic connection to what resonated from them.

There was, for example, the player of a strange concoction, a "rude mouth organ [made out] of graded canes"; another essay described the construction of a kind of drum that produced animated resonances of the dead, remaking "an empty nail keg with a coon skin stretched over the ends." Other observers, moreover, spoke curiously about the inventive means of singing or playing on conventional European instruments. There was the worker whose "voice as he sang had a timbre resembling a bagpipe [unimaginably] played pianissimo" and the ventriloquists and vocal quartets who mimicked the resonant force of a steam calliope (a technique fashioned after the popularity of P. T. Barnum's steam organ); the fiddler who could imitate the sounds of water, wind, and animals and the guitarist who, by placing a knife to the strings (as in the use of a slide), could make his instrument "'sing,' 'talk,' 'cuss,'" or, from "the rapid running of the fingers along the strings . . . [produce] sound similar to that of a moving train." Jay's essay, finally, described with bemused wonder—and seemingly oblivious to the Brer Rabbit topos—the effect of the Negro's close proximity to nature, naively observing as a scenic picturesque "a colored man [who] had an old battered banjo with only two strings," accompanying a boy whose "song detailed the troubles of an unfortunate rabbit."[28]

The music of children who played for money proposes a particularly intriguing access point into the affective world of Black sound formation, the portrayals projecting an unvarnished innocence revealing mysterious truths. Take, for example, the story of otherworldly child labor, which appears alongside a pictorial rendering of "chin-music," published in *Frank Leslie's Illustrated Newspaper* in 1871 (figure 3.3). Working from field notes and a sketch created on site by Joseph Becker, the anonymous author (possibly Becker himself) details the performance of a "little black Gavroche" (a boy of the Paris streets in Victor Hugo's *Les Misérables*) who, in this instance, played mouth percussion before a small assembly of passersby on a street in Jacksonville, Florida. The author's main purpose, it seemed, was to enlighten the reader about a strange performance practice, whose measure of value rested partly on its access and exchangeability. As a public sound, "chin music" was an openly representative expression under the claim of "this inventive nation." What could be publicly accessed for the purpose of musical enjoyment, though, also supplied a music lesson in its "return to the primitive elements of sound." For "the art of 'chin-music,'" the writer explains—recalling the earlier depiction of Blind Tom—"requires no elaborate cultivation. . . . Nature herself . . . supplies everything that is necessary."[29]

3.3 "Professors of 'Chin-Music'" (1871).

Yet this "little, black Gavroche" had also confronted the writer with a kind of creative ingenuity that was difficult for him to reduce to the sounds of "little half-nude animals of the African race." "Natural instinct" had combined with plenty of talent, which the author closely scrutinizes. Cast in a language mimicking the scientific analysis of racial body type, he cannot pretend to be unaffected by the boy's skills and inventiveness. Perhaps such skills were merely hardwired into the child's body, being an "inheritance" of "the rites and ceremonies of wild barbarians on the Gold Coast"; these exploits, he suggests, "would be difficult for our less supple jaws to imitate." Clearly, though, the boy was not merely emitting sound, as if his body were an involuntary organ. As the writer openly acknowledges, he is making choices, performing with intention and considerable ability. The author's mix of fascination and incredulity are palpable:

> The small performer, after collecting his audience of gaping idlers, will open his mouth, at the same time causing the air to pass vocally over the chords of the larynx, and by striking the cheek and the maxillary joint in a peculiar way, will emit a sound half-explosive and half-resonant. The note given by this natural drum is compared, for quality, to the cracking of a filbert under a hammer. At the same time it partakes of a

vocal character, and has a perfect gamut of expression, so that a skilled professor can play with ease the popular and patriotic airs of the day. Nothing can be more *naïf* than this music of the cheeks, which is as dry and crepitant in quality as the not dissimilarly made cry of the locust or the katy-did. Sometimes two or more performers will travel as a chorus, outraging silence with their rolling fusillade of sputtering sound, in which the ear is half-surprised to catch the likeness of some homely and well-known tune. The young musician generally adds to his choir the "pat-foot" of the plantations, which comes down at every note in the dull stroke of the naked sole, as true to time as the *baton* of Strauss or Pasdeloup.[30]

Evoking a vast soundscape stretching from primal Africa and the plantation past to the timekeeping prowess of the European maestro, then turning course from the environmental order of insects to the "rolling fusillade of sputtering sound" from a machine, the description of "chin-music" introduced readers to qualities of Black aurality now "outraging silence" and occupying the social spaces of southern towns. It did so by depicting a boy's mouth percussion in the stabilizing language of difference; through liberal use of simile and metaphor, the writer sought to bring this "chin-music" into comparison, into the familiarity of "sounds like." If the child's "supple jaws" marked a racial register supplying the raw material of Negro sound production—the "natural drum" of Black flesh—this performance practice, peculiar at least to the magazine writer, was also captivating, suggesting even a kind of Music created through the talents of the "young musician" and driven by the "'pat-foot' of the plantations." Chin-music affirmed the sense of the Black body as born of repetition, as something akin to mechanical labor: expropriable as a thingly natural resource, it would be reflective of an "inventive nation." And yet if this sounding practice was ready for claiming, it came alive only through the ingenuity of a boy no longer under the legal ownership of White people. A free Black body was inventing sounds that White people themselves were supposedly incapable of producing, being that they presumably lacked the "supple jaws" necessary for mouth percussion. The new consumers of Negro music would accordingly have to pay the price: "The musicians may rely upon taking up a collection sufficient to enable them to retire to the market with their black heads buried, according to their favorite sybaritism, in the juicy depths of a huge watermelon."[31]

It might be tempting to dismiss Black music's minstrel fantasies as just that: absurd fabrications that must be distinguished from solid historical fact. But these fantasies were factual nonetheless; they affected perceptions profoundly. For African American musicians, they became an inadvertent gift, providing them with a publicly sanctioned mythic structure, a symbolic order of the incredible that underscored the importance of the past in the practice and comprehension of Negro music. The many comparisons of sensational Black performances to African and African-diasporic practices of African *vodun* and juba, together with the assertions that Negro sound was an otherworldly creation of audible bodies—as in, to give yet another example, the man who supposedly could make "ear music" by emitting sound through his auditory canal—affirmed the importance of the past in comprehending Black music: pastness was critical to the peculiar value form that African Americans were now bringing into commercial markets.[32] Black and White Americans had reached an odd agreement that the depths of the African and slave pasts were still alive in the present, observable in the peculiarity of a newly historicized Negro music. Its peculiar sound was thought to provide an auditory pathway to another order of time and condition, to another world altogether, whose access would become a point of contest in a struggle for cultural ownership. The figurations of this Negro music were double in their intent: by reinforcing the belief in "the Negro" as an otherworldly, audible being, they also suggested that racial difference was a temporal difference inherent to Black being. Within the bodies of Black flesh existed a different time and place, and this temporal incongruity could be sensed in the "archaic" performances of difference. In this way, qualities of time itself threatened to fall under Black control.

It was at this moment that rhythm begins to orient the practice and experience of Black music, its character constraining measures of value, which would soon overwhelm the entirety of popular expression. The new conceptualization of rhythm arose, in part, from the simple fact that White observers were paying closer attention to the details of Black performance. But the belief that rhythm was its essential musical feature developed from the accumulation of connections drawn between Black music, Africa, and the sense that repetition identified both a musical quality and a condition inherent to an inferior species. When a collector of a song from a family house servant recalled how banjo players "nearly always accent the second beat in an accompaniment, and follow with a pause, producing a throbbing effect," she was describing an evolution in the use of non-isochronous beat (syncopation) taking place in the laboratories of postemancipation rural life. But the fact that she spoke of beat in the first place reflected the growing White fascination with that aspect of performance, which, by the 1880s, had reoriented minstrelsy in the heightened rhythmic inventions of coon songs. More than ever, White folk, having been introduced to Black music by a new population of musician-labor, were pondering the real nature of "these syncopated melodies" and the creative ways of propelling music's beat. And in their effort to earn a living, Black musicians accommodated these same expectations. Rhythm itself ascended, animated with racialized aliveness. "The bodies of the saints and mourners swayed in rhythmic measure with the music," in Jay's recounting, to the point where percussive body parts assumed subject positions cast in the passive voice, having been occupied and now obedient to rhythm's power: "Hands were patted as though participating in a break down, and excited feet stamped the dusky floor."[33] Black music had introduced in its evolving displays of repetition a distinctive kind of musical knowledge, a *beat knowledge*, whose ideological attachments to otherworldliness traced to past-times neither objectively African nor as part of the common orders of White-dominant public culture.

If ring shouts, juba dances, corn-shucking ceremonies, and routines of responsorial singing in the fields and churches continued in rural environments—voyeuristically sentimentalized in a crush of illustrations at the turn of the twentieth century—new coalescences of secular performances were emerging rapidly, eventually finding their way into larger commercial settings. And just as musicians sought out the better-paying jobs performing for White listeners and dancers, they also brought back into African American vernacularity the empowering notion that Black music was not only enlivened but incredible, its key valuative qualities deriving from a spontaneous primal intensity—given the name, "hot rhythm"—imagined by Black and White alike to be echoing from the past.[34] So emerges the incredible corporealities of a minstrelsy-inflected Black music out of the racial structures of the scabrous, fostering coalescences of discernibly "Negro" sound. Black music had evolved from an early state of reification into a remarkable, animated form that disrupted aesthetic conventions, disseminating an audible dissensus across the greater South. In its development, this early modern mode of performance proposed a novel and distinctive cultural expression. It would be a new kind of music, one that, at least for some, aligned with the norms of European music at the same time that the encumbrances of race and blackface affirmed its separation.

The "Negro problem" of Negro music accordingly loomed large. Performers were securing greater control of the productive processes organizing and conceptualizing performances; they were the symbolic and practical owners of creative expression and the primary instigators in the making of value. Other Black southerners noticed, for many seemed emboldened by the rising value of African American performance, enjoying its inspirited pleasures, sometimes with total disregard of White presence: "Here by the light of a few smoky oil lamps, and to the soul-harrowing music of a string band, the colored beau and dusky damsels, who rarely speak to a white person, trip the light fantastic toe, not forgetting to refresh themselves at the saloon counter when each dance is ended."[35] In a New Orleans "quarter in which the roustabouts throwaway their earnings," Julian Ralph described how Black partiers indulged in "spectacle of low and almost absent morality," as if returning to "a place in the heart of Africa." So too were Black southerners prone to step away from their obligations during the working day to step into sensible orders of their own making, including religious ones. "The seriousness of African Americans' commitment to [their] religious activities," Tera W. Hunter writes, "was demonstrated by their willingness to sacrifice time from remunerative labor, if necessary, to participate. Household workers [in Atlanta] provoked the ire of employers by abandoning secular toil for what some scorned as 'fetish follies.'" And in other entertainment settings, the class of "colored minstrels" seemed emboldened, taking on their own satiric practices of ethnic and racial stereotype by imitating in speech and song the behavioral characteristics of new immigrant groups. "The Negro" of the postemancipation South had concocted a distinctive, cultural life.[36]

TEMPORAL INCONGRUITIES IN THE WORKING DAY

The most enduring problem was Black music's disruptive relation to temporal experience, whether measured in form or effect. This was particularly the case in the context of labor, where time regulated production and profit. Although sounding practices in work situations typically served to organize the task at hand, they also carried the potential of interrupting work time and introducing time measures of their own. As White folk ventured beyond the common job sites and into venues employing professional Black musicians, moreover, they routinely encountered—as observed across these chapters—aestheticized departures from clock-time precision. For many, the departures were as disconcerting as they were affecting. Negro sound's disorientation of work time suggests why the spectator among those of "light fantastic toe" could speak of a string band as "soul harrowing" and why Fortier described the performances driving the Black workers' debauched behavior in New Orleans as both savage and "not disagreeable." They also help us to understand the motivation behind the many efforts by White southerners to learn how they themselves might enter the peculiar flow of Negro sound.

From the antebellum era, Black music's disturbances of work time vexed southern White power because the sounding practices of African American workers, whether enslaved or free, persistently contradicted the orderly pace of agricultural and industrial labor, reinforcing the ironic view that "the Negro," as a species of labor, was inherently lazy. As discussed at the outset, Du Bois's position that Black workers' "laziness" was part of a different way of racial being—evidence of "a tropical . . . sensuous receptivity" that refused the status of a "mechanical draft-horse which the northern European labor became"—was most fundamentally an argument about a different temporality specific to Black racial sensibilities.[37] Black music, by turns, arose as an outward manifestation of this same temporal disposition, its qualities of aliveness seemingly immune to the time-regulating demands of capitalized labor. Being inextricably connected to a mythologized racial past, it appeared to operate according to its own rules as it entered southern spaces through the vehicle of the audible Black body. What, after all, was most incredible about Black music was its formal temporal expression, which, as it occupied the present, also seemed to be responsive to another temporal realm reaching to the ancestors. Although the perception of incredibility was tempered by the security of White power's position of dominance, there are multiple indications of how Negro sound was disrupting the working day at the economic contact points between White capital and Black labor. The accumulated evidence about the peculiarities of time observed in the previous section suggest that the "Negro Problem" had evolved into—and indeed, may have always been—a problem of sound in its participation in the working day.

Turning our attention to the matter of time itself, we see how changes in temporal order could occur in the most conspicuous of public forums and during the most commonplace of events. James Weldon Johnson, for example, describes how the singing waiters who entertained White patrons at Jacksonville hotels in the 1870s and 1880s unveiled a new language of quartet music that featured innovative means of reordering time in the practice of harmonizing. As a supplement to their table service, these "crack" singing quartets introduced into the well-disciplined orderliness of a public dining room strikingly original vocal practices built on organizing principles still unfamiliar to many White citizens. The performances displayed structuring techniques—including the use of sound clusters to punctuate rhythmic flow according to rules indifferent to tonality—that would have at least distracted the leisurely pace of the meal and in some cases, judging from the popularity of the quartets, brought listeners into a different feel for time altogether. Although most patrons probably understood these seemingly modest entertainments within dominant frames of minstrel hilarity—as part of the natural growth of children's street performances—they also came face-to-face with a new organization of the sensible, as quartet singing put on display approaches to music-making originating in a world apart. The techniques of "chording" and the contrapuntal practices of "basing" that William Francis Allen first documented moments after the end of slavery, together with creative use of "slang chords" that developed improvisationally through "cracking," "snaking," and "swipes," did not abide by the expectations of form that were known to most White people at the time. And as these virtuoso performances "of the colored people, [whose voices] have a peculiar quality that nothing can imitate" entered public awareness as part of the work economy, their audiences gained a lesson in a new musical grammar taught by a Negro waitstaff supplementing their principal dining-room function.[38]

What the quartet singers were creating had already accrued value in a different economy, developing according to the social relations and modes of musical learning of southern Black folk. They were the product of another order of relations that while consistently interacting with commercial markets also retained connections with older sensibilities and approaches to singing as they had been reworked and reimagined over the decades. As the musicians brought these ways of knowing into the realm of White power, they advanced another kind of value into exchange that would be understood as part of the racial and historical conceptualizations of Black music. Temporal incongruities between racial worlds materialized confrontations within the sensible for anyone to hear: they contributed to why Negro music seemed so inimitable, so peculiar. The sense of curiosity and contempt toward Negro music expressed again and again in White discourse paid testament to a transformation occurring in the everyday, as the sensational presence of Black audible bodies challenged listeners with a different quality of pace and feel. Not unlike the "little, black Gavroche" of Jacksonville's streets, the singers whom Johnson witnessed (and eventually joined) were occupants of a strangely new performative orientation, responsive to a past-time experienced as part of the present. And it was the untimeliness of their audible condition that energized performances and inspired Black and White listeners alike.

Sensations of shifting time move to the fore as the primary condition of the Black music experience. It is this condition, arising out of the collision of dueling economies of race and capital (race-capital), that became key to the production of value. Time displacements were at the core of the contradiction between intensive and extensive economies operating at their own rates of speed, their temporal friction identifying the axis point where sensations of otherworldly past-times accumulated. It is therefore not surprising that early students of Black music searched for sonic indications of the Negro past in circumstances where Black people seemed most unaffected by European culture and closest to their racial origin—above all, in the primitive conditions of manual labor. We've already observed several instances where writers described the feeling of a lost time existing in the present. Let's now turn to two additional examples, both occurring about thirty-five years after the time of the Civil War, in which musicians were organizing musical time in ways that set important precedents in the rise of popular music. The first involves manual laborers at work and play; the second shows musicians expressing a purportedly primitive condition in a distinctively new way.

In a brief academic essay frequently cited in histories of the blues, Charles Peabody—great nephew of George Peabody, founder of Harvard's Peabody Museum—details the "peculiarly beautiful" forms of "quasi-music," "weird in interval and strange in rhythm," that he heard among a crew hired from Clarksdale during an archeological dig. As the laborers blasphemed the consecrated ground of a defeated civilization—their task was to excavate the burial mound of Choctaw Indians—they joined in the making of songs of the present: the "syncopated melodies" of coon song and ragtime ("Goo-Goo Eyes" and "The Bully Song"), Christian hymns, together with "distichs" of phrases (couplets, probably sung antiphonally, in call-response) displaying what Peabody, in an oft-cited phrase, described as the "primitive characteristic of patience under repetition." These latter practices purportedly drawing from a world prior to civilization were an insistent reminder of the Negroes' temporally incongruous racial being, their links to a past world bringing to form creative manipulations of time: "Improvisations in rhythm more or less phrased[,] sung to an intoning more or less approaching melody." Songs of struggle, of life and death, Peabody explained—from ragtime and coon song to tales of tragic outcome ("They had me arrested for murder, And I never harmed a man")—"kept up hour after hour a not ineffective rhythm, which we decidedly should have missed had it been absent." Beyond the worksite, moreover, there was an even stranger lot of singing occurring: an "autochthonous music" sung by the local people of Coahoma County. Among them was a worker with his mule, vocalizing not song but "strains of apparently genuine African music . . . long phrases there were without apparent measured rhythm"; a "Negress" putting a child to sleep, "her song was to me quite impossible to copy, weird in interval and strange in rhythm; peculiarly beautiful"; an old man, who "hummed a rhythm of no regularity and notes apparently not more than three of more in number at intervals within a semitone. The effect again was monotonous but weird, not far from Japanese."[39]

Peabody's curiosity about both groups engaging in unusual sounding practices is palpable. He describes with impressive detail the characteristics of performance, turning repeatedly to the matter of musically purposeful deviance: although "their tempo was singularly accurate[,] in their refrains ending on the tonic, they sometimes sang the last note somewhat sharp." Peculiarities within this new order of sound seemed to multiply, ultimately challenging his comprehension of what in music was possible, imaginable. If Peabody sometimes lapsed into the stale comfort of White racial superiority—they were, after all, a "repetitious" people producing "quasi-music"—he also acknowledged that he and the others were fascinated, prompting efforts to reproduce it and copy it down. And when all else failed, he asked the workers to perform for them, to bring their "colored" sonic order into familiar time frames, knowing that by night they continued to sing, often to guitar accompaniment. But "the men were not good on parade," Peabody discovered. "Asked to sing for my wife while she was with us on a visit, they suddenly found it too hot, and as a whole a request performance got no further than very poor 'ragtime.'" The workers protected their possession of song and the discreet affects it created in reordering the sensible. They resisted the expectation of bringing into open view an expression of their own time.[40]

It might have been some of the same musicians who W. C. Handy met up with in Cleveland, Mississippi, forty miles south of Clarksdale, around 1905, when his nine-piece "colored Knights of Pythias band" was upstaged by "a band of just three pieces, a battered guitar, a mandolin and a worn-out bass." This was the same locale where he witnessed "a kind of stuff that has long been associated with cane rows and levee camps"—a scabrous sound, its "little agonizing strain . . . not really annoying or unpleasant. Perhaps 'haunting' is a better word." Despite his initial reaction,

Handy, as is well-known, was humbled by an ironic confrontation of the old and new: his seemingly modern orchestra, he reasoned, seemed weary and out-of-date in comparison to the ancient-modern sound of "primitive music." Much like the sounding practices that Peabody heard at his dig, "they struck up one of those over-and-over strains that seem to have no clear beginning and certainly no end at all," its intense, hot rhythm animating "the thump-thump-thump [of] feet on the floor." Performing for a White audience seeking forms of pleasure measured in time, the trio had taken over the event, altering the very frames of music's temporal order, and soon enough, "the dancers went wild." The string band provided what White southerners, attending a dance at the Bolivar County Courthouse, thought the night should feel and sound like; they satisfied the expectation of a form of pleasure ordered according to the seemingly never-beginning and never-ending sound of an "autochthonous" hot rhythm. And unlike Peabody, they recognized what motivated a transaction, as "a rain of silver dollars began to fall around the outlandish, stomping feet." "The old conventional music was well and good and had its place," Handy concluded, but "they had the stuff the people wanted . . . [and] would pay money for it. Then I saw the beauty of primitive music."[41]

What was truly new, Handy had recognized, was a kind of playing that generated a backward turn: a "colored" music that advanced what was incredible in minstrelsy as it put the pulse of animated sound openly on display. This was, of course, a fantastical revealing, a reiteration of the belief that "Negroes," being a repetitive species, brought their laboring selves into their own music. And yet as we've seen now multiple times, Black musicians willingly participated in this racist fantasy, in part to earn a living but also because many apparently believed that Negro music possessed a superior kind of aesthetic intensity. It was a feeling that drew the past into the present and enabled listeners in dancing motion to imagine a primal temporality extending from and under the command of the musicians' own bodies. It is why, from around 1900, the forms deemed the best and most truthful in Black music, and in popular music more generally, were those that advanced innovation in the feel of beat. It is also why commercial Black music ultimately subordinated song in favor of instrumental practices featuring hot rhythm to satisfy paying customers assembling on dance floors. The feel of the modern would be understood as an expansive temporality that welcomed into it pasts from before and beyond—even ones of a racially exclusive past-time inaccessible to those who were otherwise in charge of the social world. Modern living stood in confrontation with Black music's counterhistory: if its regulating tempo was somehow geared to the motion of industry and labor, it was also echoing traces of archaic temporalities heard in the present as an insistent "thump-thump-thump" of Negro beat.

COLORED MINSTRELSY'S SEDITIOUS PLAY

We'll do well to remember that the confrontations between public time and the time of Black music were occurring within the horrific circumstances of a reinvigorated White supremacy caught up in a spirited frenzy to seek vengeance after the Confederacy's devastating loss. The motivation of White power to perpetuate African American subjugation developed not only from racial hatred—to make Black folk atone for the sin of emancipation—but also from the efforts to stimulate southern capitalism by exploiting labor of the poor. Critical to advancing these ends was the recalibration of labor time to discipline workers and thereby better organize the pace of the working day. Regulating efforts were part of a larger, national struggle over the length of industrial work hours—evidenced in labor-capital battles overwhelming industry—that played out in the contests of time management in agricultural and domestic settings, where "the inveterate prejudices of the freedmen," according to one southern planter, "drove a desire to be masters of their own time."[42]

Whether occurring at the broadest level or as part of incidental everyday interaction, the regulation of work sought to accelerate growth by means of converting *surplus labor*—labor in excess of "necessary labor" claimed by the employer from the exploited worker—into *surplus value*, where the value claimed would be transformed into capitalized labor power to drive the economy. Through this conversion process, concrete labor entered the mechanisms of production, making it no longer possible at the macro level to identify the value of individual laboring acts, which were measured abstractly. As a new component of labor power, this concrete labor became more fully connected to the greater structures of capital. Material actions of workers blurred into the regulating machine of economic production, as concrete labor participated according to the clock-time measures established by industries, businesses, plantation managers, and domestic employers.[43]

As Black music entered the commercial marketplace, its musicians engaged in various performative displays that exploited their labor, with companies and industries accruing profits from their labor surpluses. The music's fantastic reinventions by White minstrels performing in blackface, moreover, produced additional losses, as White stage actors, composers, and entertainment businesses built their wealth on the backs of Black musicians. Yet minstrelsy's sensational representations also had the unanticipated effect of making the new "Negro music" seem more animated than before, which elevated its commercial and social value. What still remained inalienable, attached to the Black body, compromised exchange, disrupting the production of surplus value; or, more to the point, it changed the means by which surpluses were produced. By the twentieth century, as the entertainment industry was growing exponentially, Black music's inalienable sensations of aliveness grew with it, becoming a critical component in exchange and the development of commercial value. It did so by means of a refusal to become completely incorporated into the money economy. Time at the micro (musical) and macro (economic) levels—correlating to the intensive and extensive economies in which Black music operated—set these contests into motion, as Black music made its way irascibly, scabrously, into popular markets.

A seminal moment in this transformation—the third metamorphosis, whose examination begins in chapter 4—comes to us thirty years before John W. F. "Johnnie" Woods and his doll, Henry, performed the first commercial blues. It took the form of a journalistic portrait of the city of Atlanta, written by the naturalist Ernest Ingersoll in 1879, fifteen years after the city's wartime decimation. Ingersoll's essay appeared to be, first and foremost, a celebration of Atlanta's new civil and economic orders, which could be taken as a sign of promise about the South as a whole. In Atlanta, Ingersoll discovered a southern metropolis emerging in the image of the modernizing North; this "Chicago of the South" was a place with "few marks of that tide of war which had surged so destructively across its whole area." The brightness of its future rested on the strength of industry and technology—iron mines, foundries, brick making, and, above all, the circuits of railroads that had brought the metropolis into being. Atlanta, he suggested, was an experiment in the modernization process, a jewel of the former Confederacy, whose lively commerce, stately buildings, and luxurious homes were all indications that the South, too, would display, as another visitor to Atlanta put it a few years earlier, "more of the life and stir of business" driving American progress. In this way, his essay was consistent with the greater tendency at work to suture together broad generalizing narratives through which the memory of slavery performed an act of forgetting and recalibrated the Union under the regime of a rapidly industrializing White supremacy.[44]

No surprise, then, how Ingersoll grew troubled by "certain features that strike the stranger's eye." This was not the promise of W. E. B. Du Bois's "Of the Wings of Atalanta," drawn from the pages of *The Souls of Black Folk*, but rather the copious displays of a pathetic Negro world, a scabrous lot of menial labor that was slowing things down: the routines of the washerwomen carrying bundles of laundry on their heads, "African style"; the clamor of the chair vendors and fruit mongers who otherwise appeared to live a life of leisure. Seeming particularly irritating to Ingersoll was the obsequious attendant in hotels and washrooms: the "brush fiend," a "species of imp." These workers cast misfortune on the city; they were the ones who bridled the pace of progress and menaced social order. Clearly Ingersoll was oblivious to the crucial role that these "pesky" forms of exploited labor were playing in running Atlanta's service economy; without them, the hustle and bustle of clock-time order wouldn't have lasted for long. He seemed more concerned with how conspicuous Black people were and how peculiar their lowly, sloth-like behavior seemed. The worst among them were the shiftless men of Shermantown, who appeared to live in a different order of being altogether. Residing in a settlement named after the famous general of the Union army, these lowly outcasts "devote their time to the lordly occupation of sunning themselves."[45]

Amid his critique of Black southerners' apparent lack of work discipline, Ingersoll turned to their music practices. The author's consideration of musical entertainment as a closing gesture to his essay followed the sequence of events over the course of the day. But its location at the end of the article, after so much celebration of Atlanta's economic life, is also consistent with his negative opinion of a seemingly work-averse population. Capping his grand tour of Atlanta's many indications of the profit motive, Ingersoll took pause after his evening meal for a stroll. As he slowed his pace at nightfall, he appeared to move backward in time and place, entering a "random collection of huts forming a dense negro settlement." "Attracted by music down a dark alley-way," he is introduced to a strange nightlife of boisterous conviviality among the Black citizens of Shermantown who were seemingly uninhibited and unaffected by the dreary routines of daytime work life. In fact, Ingersoll implies, common Negroes did not need to abide by discrete distinctions between work life and play; all time in the world of these "happy people" was diverting.[46]

Proceeding into the settlement, Ingersoll next encountered "five laborers, each black as the deuce of spades," performing as a "'string' band," the scare quotes suggesting that the term was unfamiliar to him. Ingersoll's reference to "laborers" seems curious, particularly after mocking the same class of men for their "lordly occupation." Either he was being ironic or employing the term *labor* as a class or species of personhood—the critical labor power of capitalist America. For soon he would witness these same "laborers" engaged in elaborate, musical play, at which point he realized that "the whole neighborhood is crowded with happy darkies." The diverse nighttime acts of Negro entertainment were the catalyst that brought Black people together, their actions standing in contrast to their lumbering daytime ways, when they endured living and working under the surveillance of a reconstructed White mastery. Like "chin-music," Atlanta's Negro music could be admired because it posed little threat to valuation in the economic enterprise; being something less than Music, it stood far from the productive forces of the economy and the cultural value system of White supremacy. This Negro music suggested a kind of labor dispossessed, rendered a diversion or trifle and vanquished of critical force. But so would these same forms also indicate a greater, more problematic valuation.

If Ingersoll were seeking to trivialize "darkies" at play, he was also giving indication to why Negro music ultimately mattered. Acknowledging that "the music is good," he nonetheless "choose[s] the enchantment of distance." Then again he kept exploring, checking out other venues and eventually coming upon a show featuring "two negroes—genuine negroes, but corked in addition to make themselves blacker!—dressed in the regulation burlesque style familiar to us in the minstrel shows at the North, [who] are dancing jigs, reciting conundrums, and banging banjo, bones, and tambourine to the amusement of two or three hundred delighted darkies."[47] The depiction has the effect of a scenic moment not unlike the picturesque of plantation life or the sentimental characterizations of slavery common to the "Tom" shows. It gives further indication that White northerners, so drawn to the cultural practices of those degraded subjects of civil war, recognized a peculiar value in the "colored" shows, where sound drew audiences closer to the Black body through which they chanced encounters in a time beyond the working day.

Within Atlanta's Black community, performance seemed routinely oriented to economic exchange; the spectators that Ingersoll witnessed probably paid for their pleasure. But what mattered even more was another kind of exchange developing from the deep sociality of the task system, from the connecting "threads" of Black existence that exceeded clock-time regulation and distinctions between work time and leisure time.[48] African Americans in the South were, once again, revealing something of the inner realm of time and culture generated within a different relational economy that drew its audiences beyond the matters of the here and now while still living in the present. The performances concretized a newly conceived mystification of sound constituted in exchange and circulating as and within capital, but that also behaved according to its own rules as the embodied property of Black people. In its scabrous form, this new Negro music presented the ontological properties of audible bodies engaged in performance, their animated qualities and character affirmed by a legacy of performance. Residual afterlives of slavery gave rise to distinctive practices and modes of social relation that operated beyond the disciplining structures of the workday, even as those practices and modes also conformed to the clock-time regularity of industrial capitalism, finding form in the free play of the night.

The street performers themselves were, of course, laborers of a kind. Some were likely to have been working musicians who toured the circuit of entertainment, moving from town to town, taking new jobs as they turned up. Others were probably locals who, when they could find conventional work, also labored in the formal economy by day. And all of these historical actors, as musicians, played with one another beyond the shows when they could. In these situations, their creative practices existed outside the work economy yet always carried the potential to participate within it. We cannot be certain how these players and their audiences responded to and experienced the auditory and visual environments of performance; undoubtedly, they did so in numerous ways. Nor can we be certain about the extent to which each was consciously aware of how socially valued and powerful Negro music was becoming. Yet by playing for money, the performers had to be reinforcing a shared belief that what they were creating was their own. The right to claim access to this contested ownership was accordingly bound to the racial and the economic. Musical creation remained consistent with the two economies of exchange at the center of value production by which symbolic pasts were conjured and cohered as part of the creativity of the present.

The dual economic status of Negro performance advanced a modern phenomenology of aliveness, affirming its status as a powerful auditory form that all African Americans could rightfully call their own. "The right to control inalienable possessions," Annette Weiner argues, "can be used as the means to effect control over others," and in this instance, "control" meant reassembling and redistributing a sensory field, carving out a stretch of the day's temporal order and creating a lively and diverting sound world to inhabit.[49] Despite his misgivings, Ingersoll seemed to be reluctantly acknowledging that Atlanta's Black population was one rich in an auditory culture that was spilling out into the community and rubbing up against the city's evening life. Its incredible resonances, which were drawing in the attention of White people to a peculiarly inviting aurality, introduced to many a symbolic affect of time outside the organization of capital that arose from within it: a post–labor time, when an alluring Negro music overtakes the night.

We might even say that at this particular moment in Atlanta's Shermantown Black musicians and their audiences were engaging in one of many "nights of labor," to recall Jacques Rancière's analysis of creative autonomy, through which new qualities of enlivened sound were taking shape. The repeated practice of musical engagement gave form to a body of performance that registered uneasily yet productively as part of the exchange apparatus, just as the boys who received coins for their "chinmusic" were laboring to fulfill their "favorite sybaritism."[50] In their own version of living labor, as beings-in-labor whose performativity exceeded workday effort, the musicians of Shermantown enacted in extravagant ways a new distribution of how the mood and texture of the night would be ordered. Their performative acts, though enabling any number of individual experiences and encounters, gave rise to structuring forms of sociality that, in their creativity and varieties of pleasure, allowed for the possibility of stretching and expanding temporal modalities, performatively bending them to accommodate those affective aspects of African American life not fully subjected to White dominance. They invited experiences of aesthetic truth.

In its seemingly devalued concreteness, the aural sphere of Black Atlanta effected a distinctively *Negro* form of cultural practice, a mode of racialized performance that was something more than a use value, even as it would be reenacted and ultimately retained as surplus labor within capital production. No matter their instability and dynamism, or the necessity of their constant reiteration as a socializing force, the affective coherences of the Black aural sphere introduced long periods of pleasure that drew striking contrasts to the routines of the working day. In this way, they pointed inward and backward, while at the same time maintaining a consistency in the present; together the performances suggested new frameworks in the order of everyday life, countertemporalities under the claim of Black gatherers engaged in performance events.

Here, once more, we can consider Black musicality and its body of evolving sonic material as enacting forms of past-time: eruptions in the present that evoke and enable social connections to racially coherent prior realms. As a concept, past-time corresponds to the experience of embodied cultural ownership in a scabrous present, going hand in hand with the analytic of abstract value. It traces the production of value to Black music's seminal interruption of capital, its enlivened sound expressive as an afterlife of the musical properties of the enslaved. What is different from the slave era is how the disjunctive character of the Black past intensifies as part of Black music's circulation in commercial entertainment. By entering directly into the productive process, qualities, sensations, and references to pastness enhance Black music's commercial appeal while also remaining connected to a racially exclusive temporal order.

Ingersoll's reference to "genuine negroes, but corked in addition to make themselves blacker!" offers a glimpse into a world of vivid, often extravagant display, produced largely for the entertainment of the South's Black poor. This is the world of colored minstrelsy, which has often been passed over in contemporary music scholarship, valued principally as a springboard for the subsequent development of modern Black genres. The theatricality, absurd antics, and raw comedy of Black entertainers performing in blackface stage acts demonstrated the degree to which the structures of minstrelsy, so deeply indebted to racist stereotype, were driving the creation of a rich symbolic language moving about commercial production at a dizzying rate. Racist imagery endured at the center of an economic process in which colored minstrels eagerly participated in the production of fantastic sensations of enlivened sound. By the time Ingersoll recorded his wanderings through the streets of Shermantown, performers and spectators alike were openly embracing notions of Negro incredibility, probably without being aware of the structures at play in the making of aesthetic pleasure.

The performances of African Americans in blackface still tend to challenge credulity as they inspire feelings of pathos and even pity for those seemingly unfortunate actors performing their own ridicule and exploitation. Seen from the present, there appears to be something very strange going on to motivate so many Black actors to don cork and greasepaint, particularly in circumstances where there was no subjugating power forcing them to do so. What could they have been thinking? Although several

African American leaders and some performers at the time were deeply troubled by the practice and spoke openly against it (notably, the star performer Sam Lucas, who eventually left the business), there were many more who embraced the genre, attended the shows, and, if we believe the scattered reports from the time and after, enjoyed them.[51] What leaves historians today seeming apologetic about even addressing the subject is the lack of clarity about what motivated the phenomenon, and, perhaps, the presumption that these entertainers were performing under duress.

What steers us wrong is, on the one hand, overplaying the significance of early minstrelsy's derogatory depictions as an informing determination of meaning while, on the other, downplaying the constituting effects of southern racism and, more generally, of a national White-supremacist commitment to the devaluation of Black subjectivity and the denigration of anything legitimate coming from "the Negro." These tendencies lead to giving too much credit to the signifying force of early colored minstrelsy and to reading too literally the surface appearance of blacking up as it was practiced among Black performers for African American audiences. It also enables critics to disregard how racist belief had thoroughly organized the sensory array, to the point where Black people themselves sought to uphold the sensational idea that their performances were remarkable in the way they exceeded credibility. While claims of blackface's soul-killing effects may be defensible once African American stage performances became conspicuous in the theaters of twentieth-century popular entertainment— "the public knows me for [only] certain things . . . the shiftless darky," lamented Bert Williams—among southern Black audiences a couple of decades earlier they seemed to occupy a different set of aesthetic possibilities and potentialities, where applying burnt cork or greasepaint had been recoded according to a different grammar. For them, blackface appeared to celebrate a seditious peculiarity that while fashioned within the sign systems of White supremacy also revealed that African Americans were in possession of special qualities of animated utterance that remained under their exclusive control.[52]

This dynamic identifies a turnabout of a different kind, a refocusing of cultural attention inward, into African American communities, and back into the Black past. Its back-leaning turn, however, seemed not so much a regression as a shifting of attention toward an interplay of aesthetic practices that had been widely dispersed and fragmented, never cohering as explicitly "Negro" or "African" but nonetheless marking, in their performance and iteration by African Americans, expressions of racial difference. Colored minstrelsy's turnabout generated coalescences of continually devalued and revalued affects that entered performance as forms of extravagant display. It affirmed those qualities of Blackness cohering in the signifying system of minstrelsy that perpetuated the sensations of animatedness and pastness alive and well in the present, in defiance of the "newness" of capitalism and the commodity form. What appeared outrageously sensational as a world of incredible difference seems likely to have turned difference on its head, drawing African Americans back through minstrelsy's symbolic language to a life-affirming otherworldliness, full of irony, disjunction, and pleasurable play. In its dynamically progressing intensifications, colored minstrelsy brought forward earlier structures of insistent concreteness produced in the slave economy as it disrupted the very processes of exchange, triggering a new intensity of doubly fetishized, animated sound.

For Ingersoll, past-time could only be apprehended superficially as the seemingly childish, self-mocking behavior within the shared phenomenal order of public culture. It registered with the White majority as something akin to a frivolous *pastime* among the many signs of Negro devaluation: of an abject, thingly, and ultimately unproductive tendency at the base of a lowly subject's character. This is the condition of the past that would perpetuate White consumers' fondness of blackface minstrelsy, coon song, and ragtime song. Yet what as pastime seemed coyly irreverent revealed in the qualities of a Black-centered past-time something standing dramatically in contrast to the commitments to industry in US social life. If the valorization process of capital sought to increase rates of production, to synchronize the distribution of means and the circulation of goods, to expand clock-time precision in regional, national, and ultimately world markets—to give shape and constant acceleration to a tendency that Massimiliano Tomba captures in the notion of "just-in-time"—the creative aurality of African American colored performances reaffirmed the aesthetic production of a countertemporality, a time affirming Black music's basis in scabrous labor whose disjunctive character denied as it enhanced the production of surplus value. And it did so while Black music still maintained its relation to the normative time of capital.[53]

In this way, colored minstrelsy marked "the political occasion of an intervention" in disrupting the accommodating role of labor in generating capital-based value. In past-time, what was commonly conceived as the irreversibility of capitalism—what Moishe Postone characterizes as its "treadmill effect"—was interrupted through a catalyzed expression of accumulated, racially based *Black sonic life*. At these moments, from which the affective temporalities specific to Black music would be experienced and sustained, the cycle of loss to gain, gain to loss (why my profit is your loss) became dislodged, further exposing the music's concrete attachments to the creatively working and living body. This disruption exposed what Du Bois called the "ancient" character inherent to Black folk and what Dipesh Chakrabarty, in his powerful critique of the labor concept, named the "archaic." A racially induced, altered temporality would be revealed as slavery's afterlife, the temporal rupture expressed concretely in acts of performance.[54]

"The archaic," Chakrabarty writes, "comes into the modern not as a remnant of another time but as something constitutive of the present."[55] If not fixed essences, Black music's modern constitutions of the archaic were nonetheless brought to form with help from a legacy of sonic material that enhanced the political-economic generation of an enlivened character. In this sense, they derived from logics and performativities enduring from the African and slave pasts while coalescing anew in the historical present. As a condition of the African American "archaic," past-time evolved as part of the racist assumption of Negro audibility and the sensation of an incredible nature deriving from its thingly status. Into the modern, its role of expressing spectral afterlives intensified, becoming critical to the evolving condition of Black music's aliveness and to its emerging stature as a sensational aurality. These emergences occurred in multiple performance venues, and their impact would be all the greater as colored minstrelsy made its way into the fields of public culture.

Past-time's significance to value derives not from its restoration of an African sensibility, even if the legacies of Africa resided in and undoubtedly affected Black-southern and White-southern expressive cultures. For the relational process was so extensive—carrying forward a logic extending back multiple decades—that recovering what had endured as "African" would have been impossible. Even when isolated (as, for example, in the case of the sensation of propulsive beat), these Africanized extractions could not convey the thickly intertwined historicity of their "origins." The African American archaic was an invention in the present through which concrete practices became redistributed and reconceived as part of a greater social abstraction of Black sonic temporality. What matters far more than claims of origins, then, is how these defining markers of race-based temporalities accelerated in their recombination and development as both a condition of capital circulation and as resistances to White supremacy, by which "colored" minstrels heightened the significance and value of their perceived qualities of audibility. The tendency for White writers to remark on Black music's peculiar aliveness developed in relation to the widening availability of African American performances, which upheld the sense of Negro musicality as a symptom of an extravagant aesthetics occupying a liminal place of extremes—between heightened living and reified abjection. Colored minstrelsy, in its orientation toward the pull of a symbolic pastness, performed the art of a surplus corporeality amid socially devalued Negro existence, reaffirming a sensational arena of the spectral, the ghostly, the spook.

Penetrating the hidden realm of colored minstrelsy requires us once more to face the same hermeneutical challenges we've encountered again and again, whereby the repressive force of White supremacy in which modern, Black performativity arose and acquired meaning also sought to deny blackness something more than its own negation. Simply put, there is no reliable historical record of colored minstrelsy beyond the references to shows listed at the time in African American newspapers.[56] Although we know of the existence of a complex circuit of colored shows performing for Black audiences in towns and cities across the South, reaching westward and upward into the Midwest and North, these events rarely gained much attention in the press; even the largest, best-known acts typically received no more than a brief mention. A few scholars, notably Daphne Brooks, have worked to unearth a sense of the quality and dynamic of colored troupes and performances. In one fascinating chapter from her book *Bodies in Dissent*, she explores how the popular figures of the phantasmagoric in minstrelsy, sideshows, and pantomime intersected on public stages. The efforts of Lynn Abbott and Doug Seroff, moreover, have through considerable legwork shaped a valuable narrative of African American performers in blackface; they note how by the 1890s Negro minstrel groups, having already become significant players in commercial entertainment, were welcomed into Black rural communities, the large ensembles featuring star performers feted by locals. Newspaper accounts of troupes, though written for a White readership, are sometimes revealing, such as an 1895 report in the *New York Clipper*, an entertainment weekly, that described elaborate stagings by a large ensemble, The Al. G. Fields Real Negro Minstrels. The troupe featured comic impersonations of ethnic stereotype (featuring Henry Fiddler's "Chinese character") and a spectral olio, "The Phantom Patrol," consisting of thirty performers dressed in black and appearing against black drapes, illuminated with calcium lights. Even a source as valuable as Henry Sampson's *The Ghost Walks*, which chronicles Negro shows during the four decades directly after the Civil War, provides only limited help, for these accounts are again most often of the most celebrated performers who attracted Whites-only or mixed audiences. We have very little firsthand knowledge of what went on at the modest shows produced for Black audiences.[57]

One useful source for cracking the code of colored minstrelsy's inner knowledge is an obscure pamphlet of the "colored profession" written by the performer Ike Simond, the self-professed "Banjo comique," and published around 1891 in Chicago under the title *Old Slack's Reminiscence*.[58] Simond's brief account reveals a dynamic performance world taking shape during the long turn of the twentieth century, as interest in Black entertainment rapidly increased the ranks of professionals and led to the successes of shows by Hicks, Haverly, Calender, John Whiting, and others. Although Simond's text makes repeated reference to the large shows, it is valuable above all in documenting some members of the vagrant population, listing in various accounts and categories over a thousand professionals, most of whom appeared, like Simond himself, in the many minor touring groups, sideshows, circuses, and makeshift assemblies. In several instances, Simond merely records classes of groups and musicians (e.g., banjo players, singing quartets), troupe membership, or the names of performers from a particular location: "Hart's Alabama Minstrels out of Evansville, Ind."; "Little Sykes and the Memphis Students." The locations sometimes include unusual performance settings such as steamboats on the Ohio and Mississippi that featured "colored musical people." From time to time, he makes critical assessments, noting elegant performance attire worn by some groups or passing judgment, calling, for example, John Whiting's Minstrels "the greatest show in the nineteenth century." By and large, though, his chief aim is to create a record of the impressive presence of Black performers in the many circumstances of popular entertainment.[59]

Simond's assiduous archiving is revealing in another way: in its accumulation, it is suggestive of a set of audience expectations highlighting a scabrous aesthetics. It gives the strong impression that colored minstrelsy was a vivid multisensory affair, involving a complex interplay of Black-southern, minstrel-based performance practices and comedic routines, brought together as sensational displays of corporeality common to the circus: "the man alligator," "Old Whistling Charley," "the two-headed girl," "Kee Kee, the hot iron performer," "Jones, the glass eater," "Kerro the Congo Giant." These performers, Simond proudly notes, "are all colored," even "Old Isaac Simmons, who has been turning white for years."[60] In Simmons's case, blackface cork was likely in play—possibly a light-skinned actor, he may have removed it as part of his transformation—as it was for many stage performers. To be sure, such performance strategies stemmed directly from the legacy of White actors in blackface shows. Rather than indicating a form of self-mockery or an accommodation to White preferences, however, they suggested a more fundamental internalization of the qualities of the illicit, of the thingly, in all their scabrous extravagance and ostentatious display. They affirmed the fact of Blackness, of a difference embodied in race that provided access to a broad realm of creativity living on in its own feeling and time. These stagings amounted to textual remnants of a distinctive legacy of production in which playing styles and comedic modes of expression shared value as forms of artistry, cast in a bombastic musical style whose familiarity could be racially claimed: "The 'coon-song' was a relic of the worst minstrel days," writes Alain Locke a few decades later. "But the appeal was not in what they said, but in the rhythm and swing in which they said it."[61]

Among Black people, the "coon" at this time and in this context was a badge of the condition of racism and a marker of an ineluctable Negro being. In its extra-ordinary thingliness, however, it also provided an alternative means of play, a way of making claim on the surplus corporeality of enlivened sonic presence, brought forth in the comic exaggeration of African features in minstrel make-up—white mouth, reddened lips— and, if we extrapolate by drawing from later evidence, the celebration of the erotic, sexualized body: lustful displays and references to asses, orifices, and erogenous zones in blues images and lyrics. In the same way, the "professional language" that Tom Fletcher recalls as being part of minstrel life— what W. C. Handy referred to as a "private" vernacular whose distinctive terms at times probably traced to Africa—did something more than "push against stereotypes."[62] It suggested a form of interiority not preoccupied by polite White-majority measures of value, providing a fleeting glimpse of the untimely world southern Black people typically inhabited. These practices spoke to the present understanding of a past-time defying the "newness" of popular entertainment and the commodity form, as it proposed an animated quality in an ancient, magical phantasmagoria of Negro music's aliveness. In its expression, colored minstrelsy reaffirmed for Black audiences Negro music's status as a shared property connecting to the past: in the apprehension of enlivened sound's progressive accumulation, African Americans would recognize the form and feeling of counterhistory.

Colored minstrelsy, then, employed the Negro's thingly status as a means of crafting an extra-ordinary performativity under the possession of Black southerners. In pushing the limits of the credible, the status exceeded their outward negation, revealing something more: an accumulation of sensational feeling to create distinctive incredible expressions. Colored performers brought into the communities of free Black southerners opportunities for new imaginations of culture while refusing White power's direct efforts to claim enlivened sound. As a symbolic value constituted as part of capitalist exchange, the aliveness of Black music, seemingly divorced from the everyday, remained part of the imaginary for Black and White alike. But unlike White Americans, Black people could, according to their racial status, obtain its mediated, symbolic qualities, to issue claim, if only aspirationally, to a truth value they could recognize as their own. Here we witness quite plainly the politics of dissensus accompanying colored minstrelsy and intensifying in contrary motion to the acceleration of Black music's entrance into the structures of capitalism. Animated in sound and form, colored minstrelsy celebrated its heightened racial "peculiarity" as a convention of Negro living. It marked extremes in bodily form and capability, asserting qualities that African Americans could identify with even as performances of aliveness remained mediated by their expression in commercial markets. In their dynamic aurality, nonetheless, Negro actors gave form to the varieties of inhabited Black being. Colored minstrelsy, as Brooks puts it, locates "the making of a spectacularly incongruous body as a performance strategy unto itself."[63]

In the closing pages of his pamphlet, Simond provides a few examples of his comedic routines. By and large, they are pedestrian, and in some instances, they seem to lack coherence; the dynamism of his performance skills probably didn't translate well onto the written page. A pair of them, however, notably "A Couple of Warm Coons" and "The Educated Coon," prompt us to consider how they would have been received by rural Black southerners at the time. One could imagine, for example, how Simond's copious use of dialect became a basis of seditious play—not so much as a resistance form but rather as a mode of celebrating through exaggerated display the plain fact of Blackness. For it appears that anxiety about White opinion stood far from the minstrel show and its experience. In his yeoman-like documentation of the ostentatious rhetoric of minstrel routines, assuming the role in one instance of a minstrel spelling master and grammarian worthy of William Strunk Jr.'s *The Elements of Style*—"Beware of platitudous ponderousty always; let your statements possess clarified conciseness, compacted comprehensibileness, and avoid excendick conglomerations"—Simond asserts the thingly qualities of a Black living art through which audiences could find pleasure in the diffusion of jokes, grotesque figures, and preposterous modes of singing, speaking, and instrumental playing, all worked out as expressions of a scabrous nature. As a form, colored minstrelsy proposed an organization of time against the working day, affirming a life beyond the "mechanical draft-horse" driving racial exploitation and subjugation.[64]

Simond's "Strunk and White" commentary reveals a deeply ironic knowledge of dialect's extravagance. And it is here, once more, that we witness the incredible corporeality in a Black performance taken to the extreme, whose ironic departures from norms open gateways to imaginings of coherences, animated connection, pastness, and aspirational truths—a past-time contrapuntally related to the clock-time artificialities of the working day. Practices of this kind were routinely racialized, leaving White people convinced, as they would behold them in locations across America, that "such [antics] white minstrels could hardly hope to equal." This, despite the many indications that they could in fact do so, having been participants as minstrels in their formal invention from the 1840s.[65] As a result of a racial contract dedicating to "the Negro" its claim on qualities of audible aliveness, African Americans would bring into being ways of musical knowing that soon confronted in full force entertainment's consuming markets.

THIRD METAMORPHOSIS

CONTESTS OF OWNERSHIP IN

EARLY NATIONAL MARKETS

RAGTIME'S DOUBLE-

TIME ACCUMULATION

LIFE, DEATH, AFTERLIFE

What loss could be greater than the terminating run of existence, that final closure marking the end of life itself? Strangely enough, within the orders of US popular entertainment at the turn of the twentieth century, African American performers seemed to be profiting from such a fateful loss, at least according to the strange, racial-economic logic that ushered Black music into modern commercial markets. It is from this perspective that we'll consider the comments of John Philip Sousa, who, in 1909, proclaimed that ragtime had reached its last, stuttering step.

During a visit in March of that year to The Carolina, a hotel resort in Pinehurst, North Carolina, Sousa made the seemingly innocuous claim that "ragtime has had its funeral; no doubt about it," having suffered from "gout or dyspepsia long before it died." The cause of death, he surmised, was its ceaseless repetition in the consumer marketplace. "Good ragtime," he asserted, "came and then half a million imitators sprang up and as a result the people were sickened by the numerous imitators and their 'stuff.' I have not played a piece of ragtime this season." Sousa did not specify which were the good and bad versions of ragtime; he merely argued that what had once been popular had lost favor and passed on. At this point, he stated, he no longer performed ragtime "simply because the people do not want it." Tellingly, in referencing the first modern genre of US popular music invented by African Americans—that is, a music appealing to a new consumer class and growing as part of the expansive entertainment institutions of the United States and Europe—Sousa remained silent about its racial origins. For him, ragtime drew a proper comparison not with the

Negro spirituals that Antonin Dvořák had condescendingly celebrated but with the less controversial and more distant musical territory of the Czech composer's own heritage. "Some of the best of the old ragtime pieces will bear as clever manipulation as Doviak [sic] bestowed on the old Slavonic dance tunes."[1]

Sousa at the time was among the most distinguished musicians in the nation. Known as "The March King," he first headed the highly lauded military band, the US Marine Band, and then went on to found his own "business" band, known simply as Sousa's Band, winning accolades from European audiences—above all for the ensemble's performances of cakewalks, ragtime, and plantation songs—during a series of international tours. His words mattered, evidenced by the republication of his comments within a few days by newspapers as far away as Los Angeles.[2] One might wonder, though, why Sousa had even bothered to discuss ragtime. Although his band commonly performed arranged versions of popular White inventions of ragtime song as encores for nearly a decade, and he is commonly credited for widening the genre's appeal—his recording of Kerry Mills's "At a Georgia Camp Meeting" contributed to that song's tremendous commercial success—Sousa was not known as a ragtime composer, nor was his assessment particularly new; claims about ragtime's demise had been showing up in press reports since its first appearance on the public stage in the late 1890s.[3] What is more, Sousa's comments amounted to a retraction of an earlier claim that "ragtime . . . will never die," suggesting that he may have been partly motivated by his ongoing commitment to protecting composers' rights and fortunes. As Patrick Warfield and David Suisman have both argued, Sousa's appearances before the US Congress and British Parliament on behalf of sheet-music publishers, who were campaigning against a purported piracy staged by the phonograph industry, showed him to be highly protective of his own intellectual property. Ragtime's endurance could affect the sales of his own compositions. But there also seemed to be something else going on.[4]

A group of professionally active African American composers certainly thought so. In a commentary prepared for his column in the *New York Age*, the critic Lester A. Walton assembled the opinions of a few of the leading figures in New York Black entertainment, giving them an opportunity to assess Sousa's autopsy of ragtime. Walton's article, "Is Ragtime Dead?," which appeared about three weeks after Sousa's published comments, developed from the premise that ragtime, or "syncopated music," was commonly recognized as "being of purely Negro origin." Accordingly,

Walton wanted to know what "some of the young and successful colored composers . . . thought of Sousa's utterances on the subject."[5] A sample of five published replies—from J. Tim Brymn, Will H. Dixon, James Reese Europe, Thomas Lemonier, and J. Chris Smith—unanimously challenged Sousa's claims, offering a sizable body of contrasting opinion that sought to portray the genre as still enjoying a vibrant life.

Smith, for one, attributed ragtime's musical health to its commercial success, noting how he personally profited from his sheet-music sales. The others took bolder stances, claiming for it the status of a national music unmistakably under the direction and ownership of African Americans. Brymn, citing the opinion of an "eminent composer" (probably Dvořák, once again, whose comments about the spirituals inspired Black ragtime composers), argued that "syncopated music" was the "true American music. . . . It is in him and he can't shake it off. . . . The Negro holds a stronger claim to the origin of ragtime than any other race, but, after all, the spirit has been eagerly caught up by all the races."[6] Lemonier went even farther, identifying in Negro music a value higher than that of European art music, an argument he made by invoking a rhetoric of exceptionalist naturalism commonly employed to describe the slave spirituals, as in Du Bois's characterization of the "sorrow songs." "[If] the public is tired of it," Lemonier reflected, "then . . . [it] has tired of nature, the sweet song-birds, the music of the trees, etc. Ragtime music is the only real melody that thrills the heart and moves the feet. . . . It stimulates when the music of the old composers will not."[7] Ragtime, these composers insisted, was too elevated, too racially grounded, too rooted in the traditions of American culture, too aesthetically modern, and too enduringly appealing to succumb to the whimsy of commercial pressures, even if it continued to operate within the frames of popular entertainment. It was, in these ways, greater than, better than Music.

Most direct in this challenge was the composer, bandleader, and labor organizer James Reese Europe, who responded by forcefully arguing that Sousa, in representing the opinion of White composers and songwriters, was speaking from a position of weakness. He wondered if perhaps Sousa, like other White composers, had also succumbed to what he called the "theme-famine" afflicting "so many Anglo-musicians. . . . Mr. Sousa's immunity from [the] Negro rhythmic contagion . . . may be the cause of many of the 'unwhistleable' trios of his latter-day marches." Turning his attention to the politics of entertainment, moreover, Europe argued in a measured tone edged with sarcasm that Sousa's opinion ultimately need not be taken seriously, for he clearly did not understand Black music in the first place. After all, Europe wrote, "there never was any such music as 'ragtime.' 'Ragtime' is merely a nick-name, or rather a fun name given to Negro rhythm by our Caucasian brother musicians many years ago." For Europe, the term itself was evidence of a profound misrecognition among White music enthusiasts who had failed to comprehend modern Black music's racial constancy and enduring connections to the long Negro past. The "nick-name" *ragtime*, he was implying, was but another act of domination, an effort to force Black music into a procrustean genre category. But what particularly irked Europe was that Sousa, perhaps because of his "immunity," was now attempting to extract an undeserved profit from the venerable legacy of African American music. He made the charge with reference to a recent performance at Boston's Mechanics Hall:

> If it was the conservative opinion of Mr. Sousa that "ragtime" music is dead, and the public had tired of it, then why did he . . . at a special Sunday night concert [last February] in Boston, Mass.[,] . . . climax a suite of his own composition ["Three Quotations," 1895] with a descriptive Negro theme, programmed "Nigger In A Wood-pile"? Judging from the tremendous applause following the rendition of this number by such a fastidious audience, had there been any doubt in the mind of Mr. Sousa concerning the popularity of "ragtime" it should have been dispelled immediately.[8]

Walton's staging of the ragtime debate in an African American newspaper probably passed by the notice of most White readers, including those purveyors of entertainment who were less concerned with the opinions of Black musicians than with the consuming interests of their principal clientele. Yet the debate draws our attention nonetheless, being symptomatic of an emerging struggle over the valuation of popular music, as the newly recognized practices associated with ragtime fueled the enduring debate about racial ownership. Sousa's effort to reduce ragtime to a dying, abject form—something less than Music—and Walton's composers' collective ambition to exalt it as the exceptional truth of the modern era—something greater than Music—came from the same impulse: to take command of popular music at a moment when Black expressions were conspicuously entering commercial markets.

Despite Sousa's denials, ragtime by this time had become internationally recognized as a powerful commercial genre whose aesthetic originality awkwardly depended on the vitalizing energy of animated Negro sound. Ragtime's qualities of repetition, which featured practices of "ragging" or syncopating melodies and accompaniments, were what stood out, drawing listeners and dancers into a peculiar sensory organization that seemed undeniably different from what America had heard before. African American musicians such as Europe believed this sound to be their property to protect. He and his colleagues wanted Sousa and the greater institutions of popular culture to acknowledge its vitality and long racial origin—to honor it as a miraculous gift given to the nation by the Negro people. Sousa, however, was hard pressed to do so because White people were generally bound to the ideological position that all Black cultural activity was the alienable property of White America, particularly those actions of labor participating in commercial markets. They thought they had the right to own it all. And besides, what was valuable in Negro music was merely a *potential* for making art. A strong music required White innovation.

Problem was, this same potential was rapidly disseminating as a form unto itself. Having been incorporated into commercial ragtime, Negro music was transforming the overall character of pop. The mass appeal of ragtime extended a nascent developmental pattern that would continue across a century of American music: what was deemed audibly "Negro"—a resonant aliveness emanating from Black being—identified a value that remained structurally impervious to full incorporation by White commerce. What was negative in its "primitive," racial Blackness became the hyperpositive source of pop's creative awakening. As a result of these cumulative losses, Negro music's public value rose, its aesthetic gains also turning back to Black musicians and communities who celebrated its widely acknowledged power. Moving from something declining and abject to what was sensationally ever more, Negro music in its relation to White-produced commercial ragtime would continue to undergo metamorphosis within capitalist processes, accruing value as part of the enduring logic of profit-from-loss. What became valued through its participation in market exchange retreated again and again into the dynamically changing, racial coalescences of Black creativity. These coalescences of performance within Black interiorities, in turn, drove the production of new, intensively oriented modern forms structurally immanent of the tragic inequities of Black historical existence in America.

Ragtime, accordingly, proceeded to evolve not as a singular, unified popular genre but rather as two ragtimes born of the racial divide under Jim Crow, their distinction as "Black" and "White" always qualified by the

dialectical processes by which they both came into being. As a new articulation of music value, ragtime assumed, in its singularity, a Janus-faced
form: a popular genre that developed as part of the apparatuses of commercial markets and an antagonistic, Black-owned creative force perpetuating aesthetically contrapuntal sonic histories temporally incongruent
to the incessant, forward motion of capital accumulation. As a new coalescence of Negro sound, ragtime appeared at once an alienable commodity
consistent with capitalism's amnesic tendency toward growth as well as
a scabrous irritant whose perpetual returns to the past gave new form to
a music-centered counterhistory: Black music's oppositional tendencies
would be assisted by White power's own evolving mythologies about the
Negro's indelible connections to slavery and savagery.

    In its strange social positioning according to two relationally con-
nected yet incommensurable economies—each extending from opposing
sides of the foundational tension of race-capital—ragtime intensified Negro
music's overall qualities of aliveness. As James Reese Europe described
the paradox, the nondevelopmental, "primal Negro rhythmical element—
'ragtime' . . . is undergoing a vast development."[9] The force of contest between what was at once unchangeable and changeable catalyzed the production of racialized peculiarities that cycled into the greater language of
pop, their aesthetic and social value growing at the cost of ragtime's claim
by White consumers. Taken as a loss, ragtime would produce under Black
ownership cumulative gains that accelerated the metamorphosis of a distinctive temporality and supported the evolution of a greater beat knowledge. By the mid-1910s, it had amassed as a concentration of discordant
sound, time, and history: in its appearances as a symbol of the Negro's decline, ragtime identified a new form of enlivened music, its multiplying
profits from loss circulating as enlivened, otherworldly presences.

    The push and pull of ragtime's racial contest—the refusal by White
musicians and consumers to acknowledge Black ownership and the profitable losses that White expropriations produced—proved to be the key generative mechanism by which modern, Negro music arose as a temporally
incongruent double form. Black inventions of ragtime, a modern sound
expressive of a long racial history, introduced into Black and White youth
cultures a new, aesthetic content, coalescing as a kind of opposition to the
oppositionality of popular music itself, whose "modern" one-step departures from the slower, two-step practices of marches, blackface minstrelsy,
and sentimental song also depended on the incorporation of that which
was perceived as Negro music's "ancient," repetitive nature. Increasingly,

commentators drew linkages between the abjectness of repetitive Black labor and the sensation of syncopated, enlivened sound, leaving its more admiring listeners with "blood thumping in tune [and] muscles twitching to the rhythm."[10] In this way, ragtime's development as a historical phenomenon—as a sound formation carrying within its structure a newly crystallizing conception of a contested Negro history—paralleled the forces of capitalist production, its expansion as a forward-oriented aesthetic practice ironically intensifying its back-leaning associations. In its doubled movements, ragtime would open pathways for reclaiming imaginations of the Black past according to the racial measures of its seekers.

RAGGING THE SOCIAL METABOLISM OF POP

The third movement of Sousa's composition, "Three Quotations" (1895), which was the subject of James Reese Europe's critique, provides a useful point of entry for considering how the haunting presence of embodied Blackness in popular markets drove ragtime's development of value (figure 4.1). As is plainly obvious in the full score and in the composer's own recorded performance with his concert band, "In Darkest Africa"—as the last of three "quotations," its subtitle, "Nigger in the Woodpile," has been expurgated in the modern edition—is based on an extraction, by which Sousa, a committed capitalist who openly ridiculed the idea that great art required patronage, realized a form of profit in claiming a seemingly exchangeable resource.[11] His conspicuous use of syncopation and dotted rhythms as a defining feature of the theme's stylistic character draws clear linkages to the melodic conventions of cakewalks and coon songs that had been circulating widely in transatlantic popular music, just as his application of percussion instruments—notably, bones, one of minstrelsy's most common devices—makes a simple and direct gesture to blackface and its parodic re-creations of slave performances.[12] While the work's connection to Black piano ragtime is tenuous, Europe, who questioned the legitimacy of its White popularizations as a category of Negro music, was correct in asserting that Sousa was drawing from forms associated with African American vernacular traditions. Such incorporations had developed not from respect and understanding of Negro music (Sousa never demonstrated such knowledge) but rather from their sentimentalized mediations within a greater popular musical language. For Sousa, music practices performed by Black people, which he probably first encountered during his

4.1 John Philip Sousa, "Three Quotations" (1895), 3rd Movement, "In Darkest Africa," first page. Original manuscript. Courtesy of the Library of Congress, Music Division.

six-week residency at the 1893 Columbia Exposition in Chicago, were free for the taking; they bore no mark of legitimate ownership.[13] Arising from their new, controversial assignments as the nation's folk music, the racialized features of ragtime and other common Negro musical expressions existed as diversions readily available to White citizenry. Being something less than Music, they lacked value beyond their potential as raw material for making musical art.

Sousa's use of ragtime was accordingly consistent with expropriations of Black music common since the rise of blackface minstrelsy, as it mimicked the incorporating tendency of market-driven entertainment culture. Black music's economic value would be measured according to its acquiescence to common formal templates and accommodation to popular taste. Such simple conversions to use value, however, proved difficult to obtain. At least Sousa appeared to think so, having all but acknowledged as much in the third movement's subtitle. In nineteenth-century parlance, the phrase "Nigger in the woodpile," whose earliest documentation appeared in an antebellum minstrel tune, referred to the act of concealing an illicit intention, one typically resulting in an adverse effect. Although the expression did not always explicitly apply to Black-White relations, its racist origin hovered over common usage; that origin was depicted quite literally in a Currier and Ives publication from 1860, reproduced as figure 4.2.[14] The concealed Negro figure identified a blemish on the greater body politic that needed to be contained. But because its inalienable racial qualities were unresolvable, such containment efforts required repetition—having only partially succeeded, they needed to be performed again and again. Sousa's own use of the racist conceit suggested that he too was attempting to claim something irreducibly racial as rightfully his own. Through stylistic allusion, he struggles to conquer the audible Black body once and for all. "Quotation," in this instance, expressed not the intention to borrow, but to deny the legitimacy of Negro ownership: incorporating Negro sound into White composition, Sousa would secure the Negro's status as a form of perpetual loss. And yet the appeal of Sousa's reclamations also suggested that the value of Black ragtime was something more than a natural resource, as loss becomes the basis of the music composition's enlivening effect.

By the time of the performance at Mechanics Hall in 1909, Sousa and other White entertainers seemed intent on reclaiming Black music property as part of an overarching, American sound, and thereby expurgating its racial content. One even begins to wonder if the inclusion of "Nigger in the Woodpile" in the program might have been meant to serve as an

4.2 *The Nigger in the Woodpile,* lithograph (New York: Currier and Ives, 1860).

epitaph to mark the imminent demise of ragtime, to confirm White critics' and musicians' "prophecies of doom": that "ragtime has passed its zenith," the public now "anxious to lay out its corpse." If so, it was wishful thinking, for commercial ragtime's enchanted life seemed to be flourishing. In fact, Sousa's own ragtime repertoire would remain a concert favorite for years, even while writers continued to claim as late as 1918 that ragtime was "gradually losing favor and promising to be eventually overcome."[15] Already by the end of the first decade of the twentieth century, the practices and stylistic attributes publicly coalescing as "ragtime" had begun to meld into the American popular language through the ambitious efforts of a loose network of mostly White performers and songwriters attached to a recently bureaucratized vaudeville circuit that controlled theaters in cities across the nation. As these musicians made names for themselves on stage, they could, in turn, seek the support of an expanding music-publishing industry that was aiming to broaden its commercial markets by bringing sheet music onto performance stages and into American homes.[16] As a

result of this cooperative arrangement between labor and the new entertainment conglomerates, a White-centered ragtime inspired by syncopated Negro rhythm effectively secured a place in everyday public life, the
specificity of its practice taking center stage within the greater abstraction
of the popular.

One might argue that what was perceived as the lingering, racial character of ragtime had been central to US popular music since the 1840s,
when early minstrel tunes such as "Turkey in the Straw" openly combined
Black and Irish-derived rhythmic and melodic orientations. What differed
sixty-odd years later was how racial inflections in commercial ragtime and
more generally in popular song, having been continually reworked and re-
circulated as part of the cyclical give-and-take between Black and White musicians performing in public forums, had become incorporated through the
disseminating power of the entertainment industry into a greater popular
style: what carried the corporeal charge of "Negro" proposed something familiar, timely, so much so that it was now actively participating as a key
value in the making of what "America" sounded like. With the first recordings of African American popular song, moreover, this *American sound* was
commonly represented by White "recorders" (e.g., Arthur Collins, Bob Roberts) who were hired by phonograph companies to perform in a Negro dialect they had mastered after years of imitative practice. "By 1905 or 1906,"
Edward A. Berlin has observed, writing specifically about ragtime, "the
music's racial associations were weakened, and . . . [from then on] ragtime
was the music not just of black Americans, but of all Americans."[17] Significantly, however, the incorporation of African American musical practices
had the ironic effect of making ragtime's racial presence more conspicuous and therefore more controversial: as Negro music was absorbed in the
making of a newly enlivened ragtime sound, public interest in its racial
peculiarities and purported linkages to the slave and African pasts also
increased.

African American musicians were certainly eager to remind listeners
about their central place in ragtime's invention and how race had determined them to be the music's rightful owners. As the appeal of ragtime
opened new opportunities for Black participation, Negro songwriters and
composers sought to defend their claims of ownership by asserting that
the new genre was the progeny of a greater Black Atlantic sound. From
the outset of the ragtime movement—around the time of George W.
Johnson's fame and years before James Reese Europe moved to New York
City—New York–based stage artists were already arguing that the basis of

Negro music's value resided in its inalienable racial nature. Bob Cole and J. Rosamond Johnson, for example, demonstrated the primacy of the spirituals in Negro music's makeup by taking one as a compositional subject, employing "Nobody Knows the Trouble I've Seen" as the basis of their hit tune "Under the Bamboo Tree" (1902). In this rendering, the spiritual's melodic contours gave form to a comic love song, depicting a conflation of imaginary Black Atlantic worlds involving a "maid of dusky shade" and a "Zulu from Matabooloo." Will Marion Cook, in turn, argued that his ragtime music directly descended from the slave songs, as he, in his collaborations with Paul Laurence Dunbar and Jesse A. Shipp, drew more deeply into the music's putative racial origins, portraying a fantastical Africa in the hit Broadway musical *In Dahomey* (1903). Bert Williams and George Walker Jr., moreover, the featured stars and producers of Cook and Dunbar's musical—together with two others, *Abyssinia* (1906) and *Bandanna Land* (1908)—claimed that their own songs were essentially African in nature, suggesting that they connected to an unadulterated, transhistorical vitality carrying forward into their own racial being.[18] As the assertions of Black presence and ownership of ragtime disseminated further into the reaches of the entertainment world, they revealed a problem for White power that wasn't easily going away.

It was not as if the entertainment industry didn't try in its own half-conscious conflicted maneuverings to temper ragtime's associations with "the Negro." The extent of its ability to do so related directly to its own commercial expansion. As White-produced ragtime overwhelmed national markets, it became a platform for a new popular sound, accompanying stage shows and dance routines while also fueling performances by instrumental combos, singing groups, concert ensembles, and marching bands.[19] With the proliferation of music printing and publishing, moreover, popularized ragtime disseminated across the public sphere and into private homes, transforming the listening practices of domestic life. On the covers of sheet music, the egregiously racist depictions of watermelon-loving thieves that were once common in the nineteenth century gave way to innocuous depictions of domesticity and respectable pleasure. The front cover of Percy Wenrich's "Peaches and Cream, A Delectable Rag" (1905), for example, featured a drawing of a comely, young White woman in a high-fashion bonnet.[20]

As ragtime melodies proliferated, becoming fixtures in the repertories of New York vaudeville shows, they insinuated themselves into the sensible texture of a deeply segregated, everyday public life. New songs by African American songwriters such as J. Leubrie Hill and recordings by James Reese Europe sold alongside the works of White composers in shops across the nation, the racial origin of their creation commonly unbeknownst to White customers, while racially derogatory lyrics such as those Charles Peabody heard Black workers singing in Mississippi persisted uneasily as part of a thoroughly minstrelized vernacularity.[21] By the mid-1910s, ragtime could seem at times to have completely exceeded its racial origins, arising as a new kind of leisurely pastime, epitomized in the five *Pastime Rags* (1913–1920) composed by the African American songwriter Artie Matthews, whose Blackness remained largely obscured from public view. Although qualities of the seminal piano ragtime were still often attributed to Negro influence—reaffirmed by the widespread popularity of Scott Joplin's "Maple Leaf Rag" (1899)—the genre's commercial iterations involved the aliveness of Black sound without directly acknowledging its source, being presented openly by a new generation of White performers.[22] White-racial overlays of ragtime were now circulating widely, reaching well beyond the nation's shores, their public display offering to audiences an innocuous form organized around a racially ambiguous beat knowledge.[23] The remaking of ragtime's racial history would encourage the Russian Jewish émigré Irving Berlin to claim ownership of the entirety of the genre, asserting after a string of commercial successes that "such songs of mine as 'Alexander's Ragtime Band' . . . virtually started the ragtime mania in America."[24]

White incorporations of Black stylistics were consistent with a larger move toward rationalization taking place in US commercial markets. Consistently measured in its popular presentations, ragtime had acquired a uniformity in step with the new era of mass production, its obeisance to Euro-Western musical formulae being akin to the commodified unit generated in exchange processes, as in Georg Simmel's characterization of the heightened rationalization of culture that accompanied the rise of consumer society. Quantifiable, specifiable, and empirically knowable, popular expressions of ragtime suggested a structural parallel to "the calculative exactness of practical life" in which an "arithmetic" social perception arose as the outcome of incessant exchange processes, of buying and selling, of acquiring and trading consumer goods whose features frequently fulfilled predictable measures of expectation.[25] In the moments when ragtime appeared to entirely exceed its Black origins, it suggested even a kind of Music, cast within the referential frames of the popular march and having been seemingly extracted from the material forces of its history. Although as late as 1913 socially conservative writers would still insist on occasion that ragtime as a genre was "symbolic of the primitive morality and perceptible moral limitations of the negro type," these charges existed within a heterogeneous dynamic of racial figuration that more commonly sought to repress racial controversies in support of ragtime's claiming by White Americans. Having been reborn the deracinated child of modern capitalism, ragtime would now live on, a benignly invigorating abstract novelty whose affecting syncopated melodies seemed at times only faintly associated with the Black bodies that had originated the style.[26]

Ragtime was not alone in its obedience to the rationalizing tendencies of the entertainment industry. As David Suisman has compellingly argued, the social process of rationalization soon overwhelmed the entirety of popular music to the point where tastes aligned with the symmetries, simplicity, and predictability of mass production. Being economically connected to labor and technology, ragtime also bore resemblances to the other quantifiable and exchangeable products of consumer society. This was obviously the case in its commercially available forms as public performances and published music. But so too did ragtime's enlivened musical components assume fixable, quantifiable materiality. As a unit made ready for consumption, its vitalized conceits conformed to the order of the commodity fetish, dispersing as a flutter of dynamically changing, melodic signs, syncopations, and tonal-formal arrangements increasingly detached from labor—not only from the labor of performance but also from labor necessary for producing sheet music, pressing records, organizing tours, shipping product, and creating mechanized playback devices for the home.[27] With its increasing appearance on piano rolls, moreover, commercial ragtime grew further standardized, its sound fetishized, as the very audibility of its expression became caught up in, as it derived from, means of production not specific to performance. As the *Scientific American* reported in 1915, "In the manufacture of actions for player-pianos there are 20,000 operations from the raw material to the finished product and a total of 4,063 individual parts enters into the making of each action."[28] The sound of ragtime became intimately connected to the commercial processes standardizing everyday life.

Ragtime was controversial, then, not because it identified an absolute form of racial difference but because its associations with Blackness often remained ambiguous. It was this ambiguity that enabled Black sounding practices to be drawn into popular music's metabolism, just as the music's social body sustained those practices' racially antagonistic relation to commercial production. The strange tenacity of ragtime's racial type revealed just how profoundly the phenomenon of Negro music had reordered popular practices and reorganized the production of value: as ragtime's appeal widened, so did the presence of its racial associations, even as the genre succumbed to the incorporating tendencies of commercial markets. However fragmented and caught up in the processes of exchange ragtime was, no matter the degree to which it would be refashioned to conform to the most conventional taste preferences, White listeners seemed never to entirely let go of the idea that a residue of racial embodiment persisted. But of course they did not: it was, after all, this vaguely racial residue that made ragtime so diverting and sustained the belief that there was a fundamental difference between White and Black. At a moment when the character of popular style was transforming in step with Black musicians' growing influence—from stars on stage to a fleet of for-hire laborers playing at fashionable parties and late-night "lobster palaces"—the racial presence in ragtime was not simply familiar. For many listeners, particularly among metropolitan White youth, it was preferred.[29]

Ragtime had reoriented the aesthetic expectations of practically all who paid attention to popular music, prompting a proliferation of practices suggestive of racial embodiment. It was this fleshy, audible mark—not a fixity but an array of features commercially manufactured as "Negro"—that identified something outside of Music; now the outside, having been incorporated into American sound, threatened to overwhelm what was within. Increasingly, listening publics wanted to hear what was outside within their own worlds, even if they did not always directly perceive the flutter of ragtime's conceits to objectively signify "Negro." Nonetheless, some cultural conservatives, fearful that, in the words of James Reese Europe, America's White youths had "become inoculated with that serum—Negro rhythm," tried to disentangle Negro music from ragtime and ragtime from America's Music. In a reflection on the subject, "What Is American Music?," for example, an anonymous writer argued in 1906, at an early moment in the controversy, that "the so-called negro melodies, even if they be original with the colored race, cannot be considered as American, for the negro is a product of Africa, and not of America."[30]

Such efforts, however, only underscored the irony that although this noisy afterlife of Africa was not Music, it had nonetheless become embedded in the sound of America and central to the constitution of an emerging modern value. What was thought to form the negative in Negro music value betrayed its essential role in the making of modern aesthetics: a residue of sound confronted the listening nation with what one writer characterized as the audible character of a "modernized savage."[31]

For this very reason, even the most popular and commercialized forms of ragtime, despite their proliferating diversity and highly mediated representations of Black sounding practices, tended to draw modern listeners back to fantastic imaginations of primitive pasts: back to the woodpile where a "Nigger" lurked underneath, revealing—as depicted in Theodore Morse and Edward Madden's 1908 hit "Down in Jungle Town"—dark recesses in the present.[32] An inspirited liveliness apparent in White ragtime's practice haunted the popular, suggesting an irreducibly racial type imposing repressed pasts onto the present. If the Blackness in ragtime was a collaborative invention of commercial entertainment and the nation's racial imaginary, it nonetheless carried the mark of a surplus corporeality based in Negro labor as it gestured toward something racially unobtainable, lurking in a dark history. Racism's fundamental musical consequence would identify the structural impossibility of Negro music's complete subsumption, despite its conformities to the mechanisms of capitalism and to what James Reese Europe called the "Anglo" musical language of the popular.

Paul Laurence Dunbar's poetic reflections on Negro expressive form speak to how Black music's involvements in popular culture at the time were confronting "Anglo" cultural authority. In his 1903 dialect poem, "The Colored Band," Dunbar reverses the existing White-over-Black aesthetic hierarchy, characterizing the "high-toned music" of the "white ban's serenade" as an inferior form in comparison with what one hears "When de colo'ed ban' comes ma'chin' down de street." While acknowledging that the popular hits of the White marching band are "mighty good to hyeah, An it sometimes leaves a ticklin' in yo' feet," when the colored band "Hit's de walkin', step by step . . . [that] de hea't goes into bus'ness fu' to he'p erlong de eah." By energizing the march with the blood-thumping "hea't" and soul of Negro sound, the ear comes alive. This Negro energy "mek a common ditty soun' divine."

Tellingly, Dunbar singles out among the various "white serenaders" the Sousa Band's expropriations of Negro music—"hit's Sousa played in ragtime"—pairing its performances with "hit's Rastus on Parade." Here, Dunbar is making a direct reference to Kerry Mills's 1895 popular work "Rastus on Parade: Characteristic Two-Step March for Piano," which introduced the cakewalk as a commercial genre. The tune's clever melodic turns and simple uses of syncopated novelty were enough to inspire critics at the time to classify it a work of "rag-time." Dunbar, however, clearly had in mind Mills's 1896 revision and expansion of the composition, which carried the title "Rastus on Parade: A Song of Color."[33] In its revised form, the work received accompanying lyrics by George F. Marion that depicts a bandleader, Rastus—a common derogatory reference to a Black man—whose lusty displays of "hot stuff" excite "the wenches." This "soldier boy," Rastus, one of them says, "you're good enough to eat," as carnal desire links to hot rhythm: "tie loose that music now give us room to shout, . . . just watch them niggers fan de pavement widder feet."[34] By the second verse, what had initially seemed like a story about a colored bandleader turns into a nightmarish depiction of a "black cloud" of "fighting coons" descending on a town, each carrying "a razor by his side." In Dunbar's revision, though, the sordid becomes animated, as Rastus, now the "major man's a-swingin' of his stick," appears as "de lightnin' of de sto'm," and the mob a group of fans, "de little clouds," who encircle him and "look mighty slick." Brimming with charisma, Rastus and his band inspire the "pickaninnies crowdin' roun' him . . . [to] lif yo' feet! . . . Fu' de music dat dey mek'in can't be beat." By revising Mills and Marion's coon song, Dunbar reclaims a cultural property for African Americans, turning what is characterized as illicit into a rhythmically inspired "divine" energy. In doing so, he reasserts the power of the despicable figure lurking beneath the woodpile.

Whether they be "hot stuff" or a musical expression of "divine" intervention, Negro music's rhythmic intensities were drawing the attention of the American listening public, with "syncopation" its controversial center point. By the first decade of the twentieth century, the term had emerged along with "beat" as one of the key signs of what was racial in ragtime, being widely debated among music critics and cultural observers.[35] However trite the act of syncopating or "ragging" a melody may now seem—largely a result of its critical recontextualization as nostalgia music in the wake of modern jazz—it was at this historical moment transformational. It introduced into public knowledge a complex, racially charged aurality that recast the sensible orientation of the popular, proposing a positive version of truth.[36] Syncopation in itself was not a new phenomenon, as writers at the time, seeking to deny Black people's contributions to American culture, sometimes suggested. But for many others, the originality of ragtime's approach to syncopation—and hence, its indebtedness to Black music—was undeniable. For example, in response to cultural conservatives such as Daniel Gregory Mason, who claimed that ragtime's rhythmic practices were a cheap imitation of European musical innovations, the composer Charles Ives wrote, "To examine ragtime rhythms and the syncopations of Schumann and Brahms seems to the writer to show how much alike they are not." "Ragtime is not 'merely syncopation,'" Hiram K.

Moderwell observed at the height of the movement. What mattered was ragtime's "certain sort of syncopation—namely a persistent syncopation in one part conflicting with exact rhythm in another. . . . No one would take the syncopation of a Haydn symphony to be American ragtime."[37]

Moderwell might have added that this persistence had radically altered the stylistic character of popular song melody. Harmonic accompaniment in piano ragtime not only served as a tonal underpinning but now participated in shaping the overall contour of the melodic line. This was particularly the case as ragtime moved toward greater rhythmic complexity after 1900, the relation of melody and accompaniment becoming in many instances nearly contrapuntal. Even in its most basic form, an insistently syncopated melodic figure, such as the common conceit ♪♩♪♩♩, which shows up in dozens of songs (e.g., "Hello, My Baby," 1899), creates in its relation to a march-based duple bass pattern a composite structure that recasts the design of melody as such. As composers and players began to introduce more intricate rhythmic practices—notably, the use of tied-note syncopations that shifted the articulation of pitch away from the fundamental pulse—rhythmic intricacy grew more elaborate, changing the overall feel of the conventional ragtime melody. In these instances, "syncopation" became part of a dense, contrapuntal complexity reminiscent of late-classical and romantic piano repertories as it also responded to the patterned motion of Black-informed ragtime dance.

White pianists such as J. Russel Robinson and Mike Bernard drew wide attention because their playing had effectively incorporated the intricacies of syncopation common to Black piano ragtime and developed them as part of their own distinctive approaches. Robinson's mastery, for example, so impressed the African American musician Spencer Williams that he named him "the white man with colored fingers," while Bernard's virtuosity, which drew from Black innovations to develop his own distinctive approach to piano ragtime, would be heard by some as a pure deracinated creativity emerging as if African presences were never in the picture. When ragtime syncopation subsequently underwent metamorphosis in the context of aggressively virtuosic stride-piano improvisations common in Black quarters, finally, the music's contrapuntal and rhythmic energy correspondingly increased, as sound and body conjoined in the making of an aesthetic power previously unknown to the metropolitan North.[38]

Ragging, then, reoriented the very standards by which popular music would be measured while maintaining the harmonic and formal conventions common to American marches and popular songs. In its grammatical maintenance, the greater corpus of ragtime—even its various Black performances and productions—was in formal terms conservative. It did not restructure the fundamentals of European tonality, which had come to identify in academic musical thought the essence of Music as an art form.[39] Stable forms became the basis for rhythmic alterations, at times so changing the music's phenomenal character that listeners could no longer recognize how consistently tonal order remained in place.

As a force of impending influence, ragtime's contribution to the making of value appeared most assertively in group-instrumental performances where its rhythmic inflections gathered with tonal manipulations to modify the Western scale-form. At a moment when European modernist composers were transforming tonality while maintaining the bedrock of the twelve-note, equally tempered scale, African American string, horn, and woodwind players were introducing dramatically different approaches to pitch articulation, timbre, and inflection while otherwise abiding by the rudiments of tonality. In their manipulations of embouchure, tone color, and fingering—such as when Wilbur Sweatman played three clarinets at once—Black ragtime musicians, together with those in string bands, medicine shows, and vaudeville, produced a sonic antic that was commonly thought to naturally express the racial character of the Negro. These were the techniques that James Reese Europe, in a widely circulated essay from 1919, would "explain" as the "peculiarities" inherent to Negro musicality and the rise of jazz, approaches that had been largely derived from southern vernacular music and hot ragtime. They were also what drove the appeal of the "animal" dances of Vern and Irene Castle accompanied by Europe's orchestra, through which syncopation became internationally known. White players, in turn, emulated these performance techniques and dance rhythms, as "peculiarity" perpetuated the production of value both aesthetically and economically.[40]

Over the course of the 1910s, the sounding practices innovated by African Americans would continue to be incorporated by White musicians and contribute to ragtime's appearance as a popular genre. White translations, most commonly taking the form of piano-based "ragtime song" and the instrumental performances of society dance orchestras, brought into public awareness an aggressively deracinated version of practice affecting musical sensibilities across the races. In this way, ragtime refocused the nature of musical attention altogether, shifting the aperture of perception toward a seemingly superficial rhythmic orientation and its melodic-timbral innovations whose continual reworking changed the character of popular music. As a form, ragtime was far from sheer difference, and this ambiguity of racial position was critical to its valuation. It was simultaneously of the same—claiming the status of Music—but different too: it repeatedly brought into the organization of music audible qualities of dynamically moving Black bodies contradicting the pace of familiar Euro-White forms. This contested, formal-musical relation suggested in microcosm how Black music developed within and against commercial entertainment as part of the logic of profit-from-loss.

BOTCHED ROBBERIES

When James Reese Europe and his cohorts first stepped into New York's music business, they confronted head-on the public claims on ragtime that drew them to the northern metropolis in the first place. Transplanted from small northern localities and various places in the South, they recognized in Manhattan's nightlife the possibility of working as professionals, of making a living in music. At the same time, Black musicians faced the reality that a style that had earned them new attention was routinely appearing in performance and in print under the names of White entertainers—those progenitors of "American music." If new employment for Black musicians had developed because of the widespread appeal of ragtime, the opportunities to make real money performing before White audiences were hard to come by, typically afforded to those better-educated African American musicians who had at least some training in European classical music and some familiarity with the entertainment business. It is likely that these players, ranging from major stage figures to those hired for a single job, were well aware of a striking irony as they pursued their interests: the social forces generating opportunities for Black musicians were the same ones extracting Negro music from Black ownership.[41]

Looking back from the distance of a decade or so, James Weldon Johnson recalled how easily and ineluctably Black musical practices seemed to slip away from musicians' control. "The first of the so-called Ragtime songs to be published were actually Negro secular folk songs that were set down by White men, who affixed their names as the composers," he wrote in 1926. "In fact, before the Negro succeeded fully in establishing his title as creator of his secular music the form was taken away from him and made national instead of racial."[42] Johnson probably would not have thought it relevant that what he had understood to be Negro music was the result of a series of transformations in Black musicians' participation in the public sphere. It did not matter that what was distinctive about this music had not only drawn from the wellsprings of Black musical learning but had also taken shape as part of the formal structures and stylistic expectations of the music business. Such complexities and subtleties did not unseat a more fundamental position to which Black performers displayed deep commitment: the *aesthetic form* that African American musicians brought to the table was better than, greater than, what White musicians had to offer. And what made it better, they reasoned, was not simply the result of greater technique or talent but derived from a different sensibility, an embodied, racial feeling of aliveness extending from qualities inherent to their own laboring selves. The new forms of Negro music were resonant with an uncanny embodied presence, its racial intensities seeming to lift up spectrally as an afterlife of slavery. Bound to an original property, they conveyed for them powerful versions of truth.

The perception among Black musicians and critics that White entertainers were engaging in acts of musical theft developed in step with the common belief across American culture that Negro music was animated with qualities of the flesh. What was different for many Black professionals was how these qualities had become objectified, being directly connected to their own labor and, more specifically, to the losses accrued in their various public transactions. For Black performers at the onset of the twentieth century, musical theft was not simply a social or legal infringement. It carried a deeper, more profound level of effrontery wedded to the enduring condition of injustice that characterized African American existence within the subjugating vastness of White supremacy. The White habit of casually drawing from Negro music and performance techniques was consistent with the perception of Black people as an objectified class of racial property, of person-things whose value could be obtained without concern of remittance at a time when new contentiousness was rising nationally among the poor in their struggles to find decent paid work. White claims upon increasingly monetized musical innovations produced by Black performative labor now took on legal, economic, and moral ramifications in the new big business of entertainment, verging on a kind of sonically oriented body snatching, an attempt to take possession of the value ascribed to resonant racial beings. What Sousa and other White musicians probably saw merely as an attempt to access the natural resources of a national culture was, for many ambitious Black professionals, an effort to rob the sound of their very souls.

It may stretch the imagination to assert that African American entertainers really believed White efforts to copy Negro performances were equivalent to harnessing a portion of the Black body. All musicians, regardless of color or racial status, were troubled by the possibility of losing out in a competitive business. There was, after all, no shortage of incidents in which Black musicians stole from each other. Pianists working Manhattan's Black cabarets and saloons in the 1900s and 1910s, for example, casually copped each other's "tricks," as they called them, the competition firing the pace of style development. "I was getting around town and hearing everybody," James P. Johnson recalled. "If they had anything I didn't have I listened and stole it." Around the same time, trumpeter Freddie Keppard refused to play on the first recording of New Orleans jazz because he objected to not being paid for a sound check and worried that others might steal his style and techniques, the episode now part of jazz lore. Vaudeville performers Willie and Lulu Too Sweet, moreover, having little faith in copyright protections, were similarly concerned about theft, warning that "Miss Too Sweet . . . will prosecute anyone who sings" a recently copyrighted song after another "was stolen from her," implying W. C. Handy to be the culprit. And, of course, anxiety among musicians about other performers taking advantage of their ideas reached beyond the circumstances of modern popular culture. The idea of ownership was deeply seated in European music since the rise of the composer in the early sixteenth century, but similar possessive tendencies have appeared in music cultures throughout the world. When a German ethnologist sought to make a phonographic recording of a group of East African women singers in 1906, one exclaimed after the performance, "Goodbye, my voice!" In postcolonial Zimbabwe, an mbira player told a field researcher, "You have to be very clever about pinching songs, . . . for many musicians will turn their gourd [resonators] away when they see you watching."[43]

White-on-Black acts of thievery carried special meaning, representing something more than a loss of money. Such acts violated something deeper, more symbolic, connecting to an insidious tendency on the part of White power to claim possession of any value arising from Black existence. Musical loss was part of a larger effort of refusal: to deny African Americans the right to vote, to live as legitimate citizens, to own land, to enjoy the entitlements of justice, to claim equal status under the law. Such acts, James Weldon Johnson contended, were "in accord with the old habit of the White race; as soon as anything is recognized as great, they set about to claim credit for it." "The music world is controlled by a trust, and the Negro must submit to its demands," James Europe stated to the *New York Tribune* in 1914, the indignity being in "slight proportion of the price my race must pay in its almost hopeless fight for . . . justice." Some White observers saw the matter of musical sharing in the same way, if from a one-sided, myopic point of view. Why else were so many troubled not by White musicians' attempts of theft but by what was perceived to be ragtime's racialized desecration of White property? The "virulent poison" was contaminating popular style and ruining White youth.[44]

The symbolic power of musical theft as a form of body and soul snatching is why the history of Black music is replete with recurring instances of local deceptions and large-scale fraud. To be sure, shortchanging or stiffing working musicians of their pay has been an enduring practice for as long as African American musicians have been making money, to the point where its occurrence measures as a familiar conceit in the historical narrative. And so we have: Richard Milburn's public whistling taking published form as Septimus Winner's "Listening to the Mockingbird" (1855); Ernest Hogan's "La Pas Ma La" (1895), which became a major hit, sold without rights to royalties for twenty-five dollars; Bert Williams and George Walker's accusation in a correspondence to Booker T. Washington that their managers "have gone so far as to withhold moneys which were legally ours"; W. C. Handy's own lament after misrecognizing the commercial value of his "Memphis Blues" ("While I was getting the praise, another man . . . was getting the money"); Pete LaRocca pilfering Yellow Nuñez and Achille Baquet's "Livery Stable Blues," which he learned while playing in Papa Jack Laine's band; Scott Joplin's shock upon hearing his "Mayflower Rag" as part of the content of Irving Berlin's "Alexander's Ragtime Band," driving him to destroy his unpublished works in fear they might be stolen after he passed away.[45]

Into the twentieth century, these bad deals and poor negotiations set the basis for grand extrapolations, registered at times as charges of thievery of an entire genre, as in Johnson's assertion that Negro secular song "was taken away from him" or William Grant Still's insistence that Handy's title as "Father of the Blues" had been "long usurped by a white man." "All through the years," Tom Fletcher lamented, "the colored people have been imitated, and riches have thus been acquired—by members of other races."[46] The charges of theft were symptomatic of a deeply felt sense of loss perpetuated by White supremacy's routine extractions, justified by specious claims about Negro inferiority or rationalized as a simple practice of cultural "sharing." Over the ensuing decades, the charges would align with a broad refusal by Black artists to accept the genre categories and stylistic labels that White-majority critics imposed on their creativity, which also sheds light on why symbols of money have remained so common in Black music performances up to the present.

The close connection between labor, property, and money served to heighten Black musicians' conviction that their performances and compositions were not mediated reflections but rather an actual dimension of their racial selves. Brymn's claim that syncopated music "is in him and he can't shake it off" and James Reese Europe's characterization of enlivened Negro melodicism as a "contagion" were both part of a complex discourse employed by African American musicians and critics affirming the belief that Black musical practices had developed directly out of their racially audible bodies: ownership of that embodied resonance was a God-given right. George Walker recalled in 1906 that he and his partner, Bert Williams, would "do all we could to get what we felt belonged to us by the laws of nature." In 1913, moreover, Scott Joplin reinforced those assertions, echoing Europe's charge that White people were largely clueless about the essential character of Negro music while implying that its origins resided in a temporal stasis, a past-time tracing back to primal beginnings. "There has been ragtime music in America ever since the Negro has been here," Joplin explained to Lester A. Walton in 1913, "but white people took no notice of it until twenty years ago," presumably, with the entertainment industry's naming of ragtime as a popular genre. In another instance that same year—when discussing his opera, *Treemonisha*—he stated in a matter-of-fact way that what had come to be called "hot rhythm" was inherent to Black being: "I have used syncopations (rhythm) peculiar to my race." And to Walton yet again, "Ragtime is a syncopation original with the colored people, though many of them are ashamed of it." Europe was direct in his assertion that in musical terms, if not in all ways, Black and White live in different worlds. "How could a white man feel in his heart the music that a black man feels? . . . Music breathes the spirit of a race and, strictly speaking, it is a part only of the race which creates it." Later, he would speak the same language in suggesting that jazz derived from "their innate sense of rhythm" and the Negroes' love of what "is peculiar in music. . . . It is natural for us to do this; it is, indeed, a racial, musical characteristic."[47]

In his critical explanations and defenses of Negro music, James Weldon Johnson reinforced these same positions, arguing at the outset of a 1917 interview with the *Literary Digest* that the "only original contributions to the domain of American art have come to us through our negro population," works such as Handy's "Memphis Blues" and the performance practices of ragtime giving to the nation its "vital spark." Seemingly neither a skill nor a talent, the "Negro's contribution," he proposed, was a natural attribute without which "any artistic production. . . . is dead. . . . Like Topsy, [it] jest grew." Negro musicians, Johnson contended in an oft-cited comment from 1915, "put into the music something that can't be put on the paper; a certain abandon which seems to enter in the blood of the dancers. . . . That is the secret, that is why Negro musicians are preferred." This "magic thing" (which probably referred to hot improvising) provided African Americans with a sustaining, centering force: "It is the touchstone; it is that by which the negro can bridge all chasms." Although White musicians could spend long years attempting to reach this same level of mastery, they would only be mimicking what "Negroes do naturally."[48]

Such rhetoric was clearly political. Johnson was aware that Black musicians were initially hired because of the crucial efforts of James Reese Europe and his Clef Club organization, which secured jobs for members at fashionable restaurants and parties attended by the White well-to-do.[49] But it was above all a rhetoric linked to an adamant belief in the inalienable rights of racial ownership informing Black opinion well beyond the arena of musicians. In his introduction to the 1909 edition of Thomas Fenner's collection *Religious Folksongs of the Negro, as Sung on the Plantation*, the Hampton Institute commandant Robert R. Moton affirmed that "the plantation songs [are] a wonderful possession which the Negro should hold onto as a priceless legacy." A year later, when speaking at the 1910 convention of the National Negro Business League, he was even more forthright, declaring that "these melodies belong to us. They are Negro songs. White people cannot sing them." Writing fifty years later, moreover, Sidney Bechet demonstrated the endurance of this line of thought. White musicians might have taken "our style as best they could. . . . But, you understand, it wasn't our music. It wasn't us. . . . . It's awful hard for a man who isn't black to play a melody that's come deep out of black people. It's a question of feeling." Although this racial feeling traced to the flesh, to the very bones of Negro being, it also enticed some progressively minded White listeners who shared the view that Negro music was "a valuable and much-needed gift that will contribute to the future of American democracy." In ragtime, the White advocate Hiram K. Moderwell insisted, citizens would locate "the one, true American music."[50]

Recently, historians have sought to make sense of these racially grounded arguments within the interpretive frameworks of social construction. According to this interpretation, what appears as racial essentialism amounts to premeditated, strategic maneuvers for negotiating careers in a Jim Crow entertainment economy. Karen Sotiropolous and David Krasner, for example, have separately argued that Johnson and his colleagues were calculating when involving racial stereotypes, being able to separate their own actionable self-awareness from the racist assertions and presumptions surrounding them. "The artists played to the white desire for racist stereotypes," Sotiropoulos writes, "in order to participate in the theater. Always conscious that they were performing stage types, however, they manipulated the stage mask in innovative ways." For Sotiropoulous, African American musicians' claims that they possessed a racial naturalness were *nothing but* political: they were simply part of a strategy to reaffirm the racist expectations of a White-majority public. "Natural rhythm" was one of the tools of the trade that supported their collective ambition to find a pathway into the entertainment business. This strategy meant performing in a manner that upheld claims of racial authenticity, as in Williams and Walker's stage persona "Two Real Coons," and what Krasner calls "the real thing."[51]

In taking this position, these authors are seeking to explain why African American artists would embrace such extravagant claims that no longer stand up to scrutiny. They rightly want to lend credibility to stances that today seem demeaning, qualifying them as expressions of strategic essentialism. But this interpretation, however inadvertently, seems to sell the artists short, making the error of assuming that they were merely advocating for equal status to White musicians and stage actors, as if in seeking recognition—and the economic rewards coming with it—they sought the same plane of valuative measure, that above all they wanted the public to recognize that Negro music was just as good as European music—that it too was Music. If, however, we take them at their word, their assertions suggest something more powerful. For it seems far more likely that these Black artists truly believed that Negro music was neither equal to nor the same as, but greater than, the creative expressions of White entertainers. Theirs was a new kind of cultural form that exceeded the value of Music because of its possession of a negatively conceived vitality connecting the modern Black present to its racial past: what was repeatedly described as a dying genre persisted because of something alive in its sound.[52]

Black music's superiority derived from its generative basis as a quality of racial being—from the economic losses routinely inflicted on musicians and African Americans more generally, which, by turns, realized a profit that White mastery relentlessly sought to reclaim. This value, of course, was never fully reclaimable, having extended from Black people's own tragic history, from circumstances that first realized what Johnson would name Black music's "miracle, of . . . production," a process out of which songs and embodied sounds seemingly "jest grew."[53] As a result, White efforts of reclamation would always fail, amounting to a never-ending series of botched robberies.

Despite Johnson's nod here to the language of economic production, it is unlikely that the new generation of Black creative professionals recognized the basis of Negro music's scabrous aliveness in its long history of exchange relations. To this extent, they were consistent with White writers such as Moderwell who judged ragtime according to its fetishized surface appearances and attributed its peculiar qualities to a social condition particular to America, something "you feel in its jerk and rattle a personality different from that of any European capital."[54] But these same professionals were also acutely aware of how difficult it had always been for Black musicians to find legitimate work and how important their own labor was to the creation of a new, aesthetic sensibility—to what Daphne A. Brooks describes as a "constitutive . . . performance practice," an enactment of the modern that also registered as an affirmation or renewal sustaining Blackness in the twentieth century. The entrance of Black performance into entertainment markets had organized a distinctive affect that now distinguished America from European civilization. It introduced a controversial mythic pastness enriched by sensationalistic representations of plantation "darkies" and "dark Africa" that inadvertently disrupted the centrality of Whiteness in American history. In its form, Black music had made America racially hybrid and hence discernibly *modern*. Black artists and critics—and, so argues Karl Hagstrom Miller, Black audiences in the South and North—showed pride about the extent of their music's influence. As Johnson put it in a gesture to ragtime's exceptional nature, "It appeals universally; not only the American, but the English, the French and even the German people, find delight in it."[55]

This brief portrait of Black music's multiple botched robberies helps to explain how loss congealed in the modern as a primary sentiment relating to Negro music value. In the formation of ragtime, loss suggested a condition immanent to the contradictory character of the form itself, meaningfully coalescing in a variety of ways and carrying a powerful symbolism of incompletion. For White listeners, Negro loss often related to the claims of ragtime's imminent demise, which perpetuated recurring attempts to repossess it. For Black people, loss was more frequently bound to the perception of Negro music's enlivened qualities, a sentiment complicated by the reality that aliveness was not actually inherent but rather required the perpetual threat of the music's expropriation. In his own conceptualization of Negro music, Du Bois claimed loss to be its central feature, nominally manifested as the "sorrow songs," those "neglected," "half-despised, and above all . . . persistently mistaken and misunderstood . . . gift[s] of the Negro people." Loss, for Du Bois, was a condition of Black pasts dwelling in the present, which haunted the White majority as it enabled Negro sound to become a balm amid an enduring tragedy: "The Nation," he wrote, "has not yet found peace from its sins."[56]

As a historical condition, loss became inextricably bound to Negro music, identifying a key component in a greater tragedy-in-the-abstract. For some, the music's constant expropriations produced sensations of loss in the whole of Black consciousness—as if the past itself had been purloined and replaced with minstrelized fantasies of plantation sentimentality. Yet for others, and perhaps a majority of Black people, loss could be turned on its head. Judging from the strains of comedy running across fifty-odd years of postemancipation Black performance, loss became a force of empowerment experienced ironically, as a repetitively defiant reclamation of a scabrous intelligence, an aliveness fostering sensations of play and possibility: loss as a spectacular aesthetic affect, as later captured in Ralph Ellison's famous characterization of the "near-comic, near-tragic lyricism" of the blues.[57]

Such creative defamations in Black performance are familiar terrain, tracing back to the early history of blackface minstrelsy, where the Negro body was symbolically subjected to repeated defilement (cf. chapter 3). Into the modern, corporeal loss carried forward into public knowledge to inform perceptions of sound, accumulating in its multiple arithmetic itemizations the resonant thingliness of Black being: Bert Williams's popular, stage song and persona as an empty subject, a spectral "Nobody" (1905); the minstrel-inspired dialect stories of "superstitious Negroes," such as Ellis Parker Butler's "Dey Ain't No Ghosts" (1911).[59] It is, moreover, according to this same pattern of reiterative loss that we can recall the haunting laughter of George W. Johnson's multiple renditions of the "Laughing Song" and the simulated, recorded reenactments of lynchings that provided perverse entertainment at sideshows (cf. chapters 2 and 3). Through the constancy of these negations and reifications, White power structures vainly attempted to reclaim Negro music's unsubsumable residues of enlivened flesh. And in their botched attempts to do so, they reaffirmed a value to the benefit of the music's advancement.[58]

The multiple failures of reclamation inspired the invention of new forms of Black creativity, fueled by White power's yearning to know and gain access to an increasingly mystified Black southern past. These new past-oriented forms sustained the tragic tendencies driving Negro music's peculiar, hyperpositive-out-of-negative formation, their expressions of struggle and subjugation markers of authenticity, truths mediated by the greater sentimentalization of southern culture. Each of these forms in its own way was suggestive of a temporally incongruent past-time: the disaggregated figure of the legendary "Bras-Coupé," whose missing limb and musical prowess underlay the power and potency of Omar in Bechet's depiction of his grandfather's performances on New Orleans's Congo Square; the creative display of "knife songs" conjuring a fantastic world of casual violence, quick death, and afterlife that Howard W. Odum recorded around 1905; the themes of murder and desperation that Adam Gussow, in his book *Seems Like Murder Here*, traced through the symbolic language of an emergent blues genre; the gallows humor of the vaudevillians "Stringbeans and Susie" whose male character (played by Butler May) wore, as Ethel Waters recalls, "a thick chain across his vest with a [jailhouse] padlock . . . hanging in front of his pants fly."[60] Together these creative expressions reaffirmed the mode of tragedy that coursed through African American aesthetic history, working against the perpetually botched efforts of White musicians and institutions to take control of Black sound. No wonder Negro music and its representation often played the line between present and past, the living and the dead, finding value in the sensation of spectrality and calling to mind the figures of the relic, Johnny's dummy, the world of "spooks."

Black music's continuing cycle of devaluation and revaluation invigorated the greater sonic material of African American music practice, informing the invention of inspirited, larger-than-life expressions that would ultimately overtake the popular world. The large-ensemble syncopated works of James Reese Europe; the new, published and recorded versions of blues; the hokum and "screaming comedy" of the Original Creole Band and other vaudeville groups; the dynamic flow of "solid and groovy" virtuosity animating stride piano; the traces of Blackness articulating the rise of a new international music, "jazz": these innovations cumulatively expressed an ironic success, bringing into being a spectacular, sonic substance enriched by contrapuntal affirmations of the tragic past to give rise to Negro music as a modern ontological form.[61] In their assembly— including their mechanical reproductions on piano rolls and phonograph records—the innovations registered publicly as a powerful critical force, the materialization of a musicality that would come to dominate popular culture.

It is in this respect that we should recall James Weldon Johnson's challenge to "the old habit of the white race," whose claims of "credit" also included the expropriation of a range of Black sounding practices and formations. His defiant tone informs our reading of the *Freeman*'s emphatic celebration in 1917 of W. C. Handy, "who ushered into musical composition and popular culture a new FORM. A style to which no man can lay earlier claim—the BLUES style."[62] Modern Black sound formations—coalescences of musical, legal, and social substance possessing a distinctively racial character—made Negro music's inalienable qualities of aliveness jump out, bringing the muteness of its primary truth into the realm of hearing. And just as quickly, those same qualities would disperse into congruency as commodity fetishes circulating in commercial markets, as the ideological tendency of White power drove efforts to reclaim the new "historical" object forms of Black music. Into the new century, Negro music's incredible character continued to carry valuative signs of profitable loss, its repetitions and off-beat asymmetries inspiring alignments with a temporally shifting sense of the spectacular existing within the decidedly unspectacular routines of everyday living.

FIVE

NEW COALESCENCES OF

SPECTACULAR FORM

STRIDE PIANO AND

RAGTIME PIANO ROLLS

NEW TEMPORAL ENERGIES

Spectacular expressions of sonic form could occur in the unlike-liest places and assume the most unusual appearances. After a decade or so of rapid change, while ragtime dominated the popular market, modern Black music in its multiple iterations—from extravagant commercial productions to routine playing by itinerant street performers—underwent a qualitative shift, its sounding practices coalescing in distinctive ways. Two orientations stand out as particularly influential amid the panoply of innovation. In one, startlingly original sound formations developed in the context of live performance featuring highly skilled pianists, some of them classically trained, who entertained residents inhabiting New York's poorest Black districts. In the other, spectacularity materialized as Black music's first major iteration of mechanically reproduced sound, heard occasionally on phonographic cylinder recordings and then more promi-nently on mass-produced player-piano rolls, which, during the 1900s and 1910s, circulated in African American communities while also showing up in the homes of White consumers. Both types of expression responded to the heightened presence of the Black musical past now orienting the social and aesthetic sensibilities of Americans. Both increased the social prominence of Black sounding practices and their congealed formations. And both arose as modern versions of free labor's "miracle, of . . . production," their enlivened presences confronting popular aesthetic sensibilities as they advanced Black music's reputation as a controversial cultural form. Out of the ordinary conditions of loss persistently affecting everyday Black existence, these twin sound formations disturbed the sensible orientation of listening publics in ways that would have a lasting effect across the musical landscape: they reaffirmed the aesthetic significance of what W. E. B. Du Bois named the "spectacular revolution" (cf. introduction), generating sensations of pastness simultaneously incorporating and countering White power's racist fantasies. The power of the experience conjured for many a profundity imagined as a kind of tangible certainty, a truth.[1]

Black music's spectacularity became modern in the way that it altered aesthetic temporalities as musical practices developed and circulated in metropolitan settings, its two primary categories of form aligning with different sides of the contest between racial and capitalized economies (race-capital). The virtuosic innovations of high-velocity piano music developing from around 1910, later given the commercial name "stride," worked intensively, drawing culturally inward as a body-centered racial feeling that condensed the accumulating sonic materials of the past into a musically enlivened "colored people time." Mechanically reproduced Black piano ragtime, in contrast, disseminated extensively, its syncopated patterns appearing as commercially produced piano rolls that entered popular markets in the early 1900s. Although these two primary sound formations emphasized opposing economies, they affirmed what the other embodied, actualizing the dialectical processes that structured the double character of Black music valuation. If stride performance—developing amid partiers working the dance floors of New York's Black neighborhoods—brought new spirited energy to Negro sound, it also factored a loss, its sound affirming prevailing White views about the noise and debasement of an inferior people. If, moreover, the mechanical forms of player pianos mirrored the Black body's condition of reification, they also gained life-affirming effect: the incorrigible aliveness inhabiting a machine-made music extended the haunting power of a sound world existing beneath Sousa's "woodpile" (cf. chapter 4). These vitalized presences of Blackness would grow exponentially as mechanical transcriptions of Black stride performances began to circulate widely.

Together Black music's miracles of production brought into being incredible sonic realms that simultaneously affirmed and refused the conditions of loss. Out of the reifying circumstances of poverty and exploitation, stride arose spectrally, its "distillation," as Du Bois called the spectacular sound of the enslaved people's emancipation, slipping past White power's efforts of incorporation.[2] In their objectification of musicians' labor, moreover, piano-roll technologies circulated disembodied, syncopated melodies to bring about enlivened forms of animated pleasure that interrupted the smooth clock-time processes of capital. Value accrued according to opposing forces, ultimately becoming measurable in the economy of commercial entertainment: in its coalescences of modern form, Black enlivened sound appeared newly illuminated, its spectacularity once again inspiring White efforts to reclaim a property thought to be illicitly controlled by African Americans. As a result, the music's inalienable qualities of aliveness ironically strengthened because of their proliferation, their racial presences circulating across public culture an aesthetic energy that playfully and seditiously disturbed the time-regulated orderliness of the working day. These modern coalescences introduced a new sensibility of temporal disruption, recalibrations of capital-driven time that would carry a distinctive, liberative mood across modern music.

CP TIME IN NEW YORK'S TENDERLOIN DISTRICT

"Breakdown music," James P. Johnson explained when reflecting on his experiences performing in New York's Black saloons and cabarets in the 1910s, "was the best" to get dancers going, "the more solid and groovy the better." Beginning in the summer of 1913, Johnson appeared at multiple locations in the New York area, among them the Jungles Casino on West 62nd Street in Manhattan. As he played for hours into the morning, he kept the pace by inventing variation upon variation of a tune's melodic and harmonic materials. "The dances they did at The Jungles Casino were wild and comical—the more pose and the more breaks, the better," he told Tom Davin, recounting his work there forty years later.[3] Many of the people who frequented the space—named after the Jungle, the informal designation of the Black district on the outskirts of Hell's Kitchen—were recent arrivals from Alabama and Charleston, South Carolina. Being familiar with the exercised playing of string bands and the emotional drama of religious shouting practices, they preferred it when Johnson, a New Jersey native who heard shouts and blues while growing up in New Brunswick and Jersey City, sped up the tempo and set a sturdy, insistent beat.[4] "They were country people and they felt homesick," Johnson explained. And so, at moments, in the midst of dancing at "the Jungles"—in actuality, an empty basement serving as an unlicensed party house and occasional dance studio, frequently subjected to police raids—"they'd yell: 'Let's go back home! . . . Now, put us in the alley!'" Things would take off: "When I got in a hot groove, the piano was walking, [and] . . . they'd dance, hollering and screaming until they were cooked." "The dances," he continued, "ran fifteen to thirty minutes, but they kept up all night long or until their shoes wore out—most of them after a heavy day's work on the docks."[5]

A solid groove—the key feature distinguishing stride from commercial ragtime—intensified by the insistent, propulsive drive characteristic of Carolina shouting, southern string bands, and southwestern piano music: these were the ingredients of a strikingly original sound formation, known in its more exercised forms as the "piano shout," that developed in the mid-1910s and ultimately helped to reorient and expand beat knowledge.[6] The move from ragtime to stride, however, did not simply increase the presence of syncopation and hot playing; it also introduced into the formal prototype of piano ragtime certain innovations specific to the North—notably, a revision of the duple rhythms stemming from the march. In their performances, Johnson and other stride players accelerated tempos while varying the character and intensity of repetition, superimposing ternary rhythmic patterns against duple or common-time meters (e.g., 3:2, 3:4) and employing rubato to stretch out and then condense temporal flow. These innovations, among others, changed the overall rhythmic feel, creating flexibility and elasticity in and around the beat that anticipated what would later be codified as "swing." Rather than reproducing ragtime compositions literally from the written page, moreover, pianists reconceived them as a basis of spontaneous variation, the interpretive act of extemporaneously revising and expanding written forms for lengths of fifteen to thirty minutes being consistent with the paraphrase techniques common to New Orleans jazz improvisation. In some instances, pianists would be joined by other musicians, notably drummers, who commanded the beat and strengthened the groove. Some performers, Johnson recalls, such as "Battle Ax," "worked tempos so fast with his foot that he played rolls on the bass drum." Another drummer, named Eugene Holland, "made a double contact each time the stick hit and it made an echo in the trap-drum rolls." And yet another, Arthur MacIntyre, known as "Traps," "would build a roll for three minutes until it tore the house down."[7]

Players working the saloons and joints of Harlem, the Tenderloin district, Little Africa, the Jungle, and Hell's Kitchen—together with locations reaching into other boroughs as well as over to Newark, Jersey City, and the Jersey shore—developed stride playing by advancing Black sonic materials that had been gestating over the past two decades, often by drawing from and reshaping rhythmic orientations and improvisational approaches of southern migrant musicians who had performed both inside and outside the church. The groove orientation and extemporaneous inventions common to the piano shout—remaining for a time unnotated because, as Johnson put it, "I couldn't write them down and I didn't know anyone who [could]"—made the sound formation a centerpiece of New York's Black dance culture. "When we played shouts, everyone danced," recalled Willie "the Lion" Smith. "I would get a romp-down shout going, that was playing rocky, just like the Baptist people sing." So popular were the shouts that they would name New York's version of rent parties, commonly known as "House Shouts."[8] These, together with other beat-oriented innovations, from reinventions of boogies and stomps to newly fashioned struts, drags, and what Johnson called "the Metropolitan Glide," contributed to the greater coalescence of a practice known for its rhythmic and improvisational power, which, at heightened moments, carried the potential to seemingly bend temporal experience: to inspire the sensation of a time beyond the time of the present.[9]

Many hot ragtime and stride musicians advanced their artistry by looking beyond the sound worlds common to Black entertainment and involving sounding practices and techniques they developed while learning to play the piano. For some—including Smith, Eubie Blake, and Luckey Roberts—this meant making use of the basics of tonal grammar and performance discipline—chord voicings, scale formations, arpeggiation exercises, fingering techniques—they acquired during lessons with relatives or family friends. Another group, however—which included Johnson, Fred Bryant, Ernest Green, and Sam Gordon, the latter having studied in Germany—received formal training in the European keyboard repertories of the eighteenth and nineteenth centuries, during which they were introduced to the rudiments of Western music theory. Johnson, for example, details how, while working under the tutelage of Bruto Giannini from 1913 to 1917, he developed new tools and techniques (notably, writing counterpoint) that would affect his approach as a working composer and musician. Supplementing these studies by "listening to classical piano records and [going to] concerts," Johnson put the new knowledge to productive use. He recalled how "I would learn concert effects and build them into blues and rags. Sometimes I would play basses a little lighter than the melody and change harmonies. When playing a heavy stomp," he continued, "I'd soften it right down—then, I'd make an abrupt change like I heard Beethoven do in a sonata. . . . Another time, I'd use pianissimo effects [playing quietly] in the groove and let the dancers' feet be heard scraping the floor. It was used by dance bands later."[10]

The techniques of classical composition and piano performance, Johnson shows, were instrumental to his creative process. By varying volume and tempo to heighten contrasts, by rephrasing motives and employing harmonic substitutions to develop form, and by tempering his powerful left hand to bring out qualities of the melody in the right, Johnson shaped a new conception of ragtime without sacrificing propulsive energy, which was his hallmark. His incorporation of European compositional and performance practices made his stride playing dramatic, inspiring him to develop his rhythmic approach in intentionally artistic ways. As Gunther Schuller put it, "Johnson focused his attention on the rhythmicization of melodic ideas. . . . Many of his 'melodies' are essentially rhythmic features that happen to have pitches attached to them." "I had gotten power and was building a serious orchestral piano" is the way that Johnson described his approach, borrowing from language employed at the time to characterize the technique of hand editing or "doctoring" piano rolls. This "orchestral piano" orientation became the basis of a new repertoire featuring rhythmically energetic, southern-themed tunes—"Mule Walk," "Gut Stomp," "Charleston," "Carolina Stomp"—that had been reimagined in the context of existing stride practice.[11] The effect was transformative. Instead of repressing the evolution of Black sonic materials, Johnson's approach advanced it. Following in line with the use of tonality in slave string music, the orchestrations of Black show music, and the four-part harmonizing of the Fisk Singers and other progenitors of the spirituals, Johnson's application of techniques gleaned from the classical and romantic repertories increased the intensity of his sound. In this way—by raising the aesthetic value of a discernibly African American innovation—he made his music seem *Blacker*.

A particularly vivid example of Johnson's aestheticizing strategy appears in his abstraction of ring shouts. The technique of lightening his touch so that all could hear "the dancers' feet . . . scraping the floor" recalls an 1867 depiction of a shout from South Carolina in which participants "begin first walking by-and-by shuffling round, . . . the foot is hardly taken from

5.1 James P. Johnson, "Carolina Shout," Third ("C") Strain, opening. Transcribed by Riccardo Scivales.

the floor and the progression is mainly due to a jerking, hitching motion, which agitates the entire shouter, and soon brings out streams of perspiration."[12] In his composition "Carolina Shout," Johnson mimics the vigorous vocal interplay common to shouting practices. In the third strain, he employs forceful, declarative "calls" in the upper register that give way to interlocking "responses" played by both the right and left hands (figure 5.1).[13] In other instances, while honoring the basic design of ragtime composition—noncyclical progression of sixteen-bar (or thirty-two-bar) contrasting sections leading to a key change to the subdominant in the trio section—Johnson, along with other stride composers, mastered the art of combining Black and European-based musical strategies in dramatic, original ways. Those congregating in the Black saloons could claim these innovations as part of their modern world, the music forms themselves having been inspired by their own participating bodies.

Classically minded stride pianists were not merely conforming to the disciplines of European art music; they were employing its techniques to reclaim their own racialized audibility as it had been extending out into the commercial world. Their interpretive strategies made stride versions of Black piano ragtime more virtuosic and formally elaborate. And by artistically abstracting sounding practices originating in southern music, they helped young migrants (together with the locally born) to imagine the past anew: to hear a refashioning and expansion of Black music's embodiment, to discern a modern metamorphosis in the aliveness of Black sound. Especially important was the European technique of development and variation (a version of which was already at play in music-making across the Black and White South), which became a primary means of creating affective intensities reminiscent of shouts and string-band performances. "If he played a tune twenty thousand times," Blake remarked when describing the style of pianist Paul Seminole, "it was twenty thousand times different." The strategy had the effect of producing cumulative power through repetition, creating a sensory orientation inextricably linked to a newly coalescing, modern musical knowledge that also appealed to White voyeurs whose "visits to black saloons," writes Douglas J. Flowe, inspired fantasies of "trips to the old plantation South." For the British travel writer Stephen Graham, such fantasies went over the top, the music calling to mind an idyllic past with "wisps of cotton blowing about."[14] Repeating a formula that reaches back to the era of colored minstrelsy, what by the mid-1910s had grown into a commercially sentimentalized pastime intruded into the sensible environments and past-times of Black folk, simultaneously devaluing a Negro music while also enriching it with racially fantastic symbolism. The seditious play of an imagined Black past as experienced in New York's nighttime entertainment culture was directly colliding with the rationalizing tendencies organizing the working day. This is what America's youth across the color line became newly aware of and was drawn to.

Such a state of affairs puts into perspective Duke Ellington's seemingly fanciful characterization of his first encounter with club life in the Tenderloin district, where "everything and everybody seemed to be doing whatever they were doing in the tempo [Willie] the Lion's group was lying down. . . . The waiters served in that tempo; everybody who had to walk in or out, or around the place, walked with a beat. . . . [It was] one of the strangest and greatest sensations I ever had."[15] What is important here is not the implication of a literal correspondence between musical time and social time, of a singular experience shared and enjoyed by all listeners in exactly the same way; such pronouncements betray Ellington's own fetishization of Black rhythm. Being less attuned to the racial-economic structures driving value production, he could imagine such coherences and find pleasure from experiencing the music this way. Rather, it is how hot music led by a virtuosic stride player produced strikingly original temporal parameters, its rhythmic incongruities inspiring an affective structuring that allowed a diverse community of young Black spectators to listen anew: to hear and feel their own versions of existence arising from the aestheticized play of modern Black music. These innovations invited the creation of a shared sensible order different from ordinary experience and developing in the music's relation to a racially coherent, communal history that reaffirmed the greater shift in hot ragtime and stride. Embodied repetition, drawn from the material foundation of Black labor, had triggered interruptions of normative routines, proposing the possibility of different kinds of negatively rendered aesthetic experience that Black people could claim as their own. The different experiences were indications of how Black music aesthetics were already reshaping the complex of modern musical production.

Aesthetic spectacularity oriented the entry of African Americans into the districts of 1910s Black Manhattan as they otherwise confronted the ordinariness of Black people's precarious conditions. They had moved into the city's most challenging corridors for many reasons, yet with many if not all of them embracing a renewed sense of the possible, of what life could be beyond the pedestrian traumas of southern racism. For African Americans, New York was certainly no paradise, as Flowe recounts in *Uncontrollable Blackness*, his vivid history of Black men's struggles in life and labor during New York's Jim Crow era. Already a grand urban metropolis before the turn of the century, New York could, at moments, afford the chance for decent work or, failing that, at least a way of being that enabled a somewhat easier pace to the everyday. But lasting opportunities were rare. Overcrowded and economically disadvantaged, Black districts, disparagingly referred to as "the Ward, the bottom, the ghetto," writes Saidiya Hartman in her stunning account of Black women facing the harrowing challenges of life there, were "an urban commons where the poor assemble, improvise the forms of life, experiment with freedom, and refuse the menial existence scripted for them. It was a zone of extreme deprivation and scandalous waste, . . . [where] the decent reside peacefully with the dissolute and the immoral." James P. Johnson remembered how frequently mundane tragedies occurred. "Hell's Kitchen," he lamented, "was the toughest part of New York. There were two or three killings a night. Fights broke out over love affairs, gambling, or arguments in general." The banality of Black-on-Black crime was but a residual manifestation of the enduring force of White power, rising unpredictably and at times with incomprehensible hostility. Residents would have found it hard to forget the open attacks by White mobs that ravaged the Tenderloin in 1900 and the role that police corruption played in making harassment routine.[16]

It was nonetheless amid these impecunious zones of desperate poverty that—reaching back to the 1890s and George W. Johnson's fame—aestheticized miracles of production routinely coalesced. The performances of Johnson, Smith, Blake, and Roberts, together with those of Bob Gordon (ironically known as "The March King"), Sam Gordon, Fats Harris, Fred Bryant, Richard McLean (aka the mysterious "Abba Labba," much admired, but never recorded), and others fueled a creative awakening that by the late 1910s had profoundly changed the feel of popular music as it was performed in New York's Black circles.[17] For a time in the early part of the decade, innovative Black piano music resided securely under the claim of its African American followers, representing a cultural property among those for whom substantial ownership could rarely be had. For many, its aliveness seemed personal, familiar—a resonance of their own racialized selves. Yet it was also a new sound affirming a sense of place and rapidly accumulating meaningful signs of possibility under the weight of quotidian hardship. "In the slum," Hartman writes, "everything is in short supply, except sensation. . . . A whole world is jammed into one short block crowded with black folks shut out from almost every opportunity the city affords, but still intoxicated with freedom."[18] And in the after-work playhouses common to the Black districts, young people heard, as Ellington did when initially visiting the Tenderloin, the presence of a distinctive African American artistry commanding the phenomenal order of the night, the music's distinctive temporal character producing a modern restructuring of the sensible. This new spectacular form of Negro music, by turns, invited the experience of something previously unknown, of possibly even catching glimpses of life's certain truths.

The structural contradictions generating value had brought into form a music inspiring episodes of shared meaning: what was heard as enlivened Negro sound catalyzed imaginings of a collective history generating past-time's supplemental energy. In its most evocative and inspiring moments, stride-based playing produced a sensation of release from the otherwise stultifying conditions of the racially common. Although the archive of 1910s Black performance spaces lacks a positive documentation of the diverse experiences had, we can discern from the recollections of Johnson, Ellington, "the Lion," and others a sense that those congregating in the saloons, cabarets, and basement spaces were responsive to a piano-driven intensity so powerful it transformed the perception of everyday temporal experience. The new artistry of modern Black music inspired awareness of another kind of sensible place, a new sonic present where recessive knowledges coalesced as part of an adjustment to the everyday, anticipating "what becomes thinkable and possible."[19] In this altered music time, listeners and dancers fueled by the intensities of performative extremes imagined meanings that pushed the limits of the here and now. A new metamorphosis in the phenomenology of past-time would become central to the evolution of Black music aesthetics.

The sensation of a negative temporality driving aesthetic recalibration is akin to what Alain Locke had in mind when he argued that Will Marion Cook's *Clorindy: The Origin of the Cake-Walk* (1898) had changed conventional ways of listening. With *Clorindy* and a small cluster of other seminal works, "the American ear was just being broken in to the Negro tempo; and its subtleties were missed in the consternation over the new fast pace and swing of "'raggin' tunes."[20] Fifteen years later, this "Negro tempo" had evolved, having been empowered by its cycling forward into the sensational present of modern entertainment and back into a rich and dynamic reservoir of Black southern musicality. The accumulating popular assertions of Negro music's mystified tempo and syncopation were critical to the congealing of stride's assertive, enlivened energy: fetishisms of a historically disconnected "Negro tempo" accompanying the rise of commercial ragtime supplied the illusory conditions necessary for Black music's enlivened character to interrupt its fetishization as a commodity form. Commodity fetishism, that is, sufficiently objectified and positioned Black music within the mystifying structures of capitalism to enable its inalienable character to reveal fetishism's fiction. "The truth of all artworks" under capitalism, Adorno observed, "would . . . not exist without the [commodity] fetishism that now verges on becoming art's untruth. The quality of artworks depends essentially on the degree of their fetishism on the veneration that the process of production pays to what claims to being self-produced." And it is "only through fetishism," he continued, that "the work [can] transcend the spell of the reality principle as something spiritual."[21] Popular fetishisms of Black music temporality and its evocations of sentimentalized pastimes provided opportunities for individually conceived, temporal breaks—encounters of incongruous past-times momentarily revealing the primary truth of Black music as a negatively generated value form.

The inhabitants of New York's emerging African American metropolis gained from modern Black music the possibility of hearing something aesthetically powerful existing beyond the fetishized illusion that had underpinned the music's increased social valuation. By forcefully confronting ordinary temporalities, newly congealing music sensations of the past realized a qualitatively different form of aliveness: past-time would be reaffirmed not as a singular phenomenon but as individual responses to the materiality of history, perceived within Black performances in the present. These weighty coalescences of Negro sound offered pathways to a kind of truth that could be individually sensed in the enlivened forms of musical expression. Although socially conceived as a shared experience, Black music's past-times communicated to listeners differing orders of meaning that carried variously into their daily living; as dimensions of a new art, they, recalling Jacques Rancière, "neither give lessons nor have any destination."[22]

This is why Hartman speaks of Black women's lives in the Tenderloin as "improvisational," occasionally invoking the sounds of public spaces—streets, saloons, dance halls, player pianos, phonograph recordings—to suggest the diversity of sensible feeling present across everyday life. "Improvisation—the aesthetic possibilities that resided in the unforeseen," she writes, a "collaboration in the space of enclosure, the secondary rhythms of social life capable of creating an opening where there was none—exceeded the interpretive grid of the state authorities and the journalists." Although Hartman embraces the view that sound and meaning naturally and directly cohere—"sonic tumult and upheaval[,] it was resistance as music" and "the spare truth of wounded kinship sounded like a blues"—she also effectively conveys how the free flow of Black sound untroubled by the written rules of ragtime sheet music was overwhelming the public space of the slum, where "the streets offered display of talents and ambitions. *An everyday choreography of the possible.*" The cacophony that drew the attention of social observers claiming connections between Black criminality and Black music's "noise," together with the young, White thrill-seekers chasing illicit pleasure, also led Black congregants to reaffirm their claims on the music: it was a spectacular property tenaciously held by African Americans.[23]

Popular culture's mystifications of Black music had enriched its incongruously enlivened and disruptive character. And when its experience was brought into words, it could invoke profound meaning. Stories that Black people told about music's power at the time suggested something akin to a sonic force field antithetical to the bondage that had brought "Negro music" into form. It was at these moments, whether on the dance floor or merely while listening, that participating Black audiences could feel the music's animated presence lifting them up over while still bounded by the burdens of race. It was to hear and to inhabit a phenomenal place differently conceived from the ceaseless impositions of difference—to enter a realm of pleasure momentarily exceeding racism's limits. The vigorous pulse of an assertive, forward-moving stride—generated by what Schuller, like Blake, describes as a "seemingly inexhaustible fertility of imagination . . . [that] produce[d] variation upon variation on the same theme"—brought about a dramatic transformation in sensible experience.[24] And in its evocations of southern styles and introduction of innovative strategies of performance, Black music offered a condensation of available pasts and forward-looking presents, inspiring new ideas about living. Stride performances enlivening metropolitan spaces proposed opportunities not of life as it was thought to have been or should be; they introduced assertive ways of being stepping in contrapuntal motion to normative conceptions of "the Negro character."

INCORRIGIBLE COMMODITY FORMS

If the first iteration of spectacular form imposed a new organization of music time by strengthening sensible connections to an incongruent racial past, the second achieved spectacularity by producing a qualitatively different kind of intervention, one that readjusted the sonic character and temporal orientation of popular music. This latter version developed not from the circumstance of performance but from the vehicle by which musical content was distributed and received: the physical commodities that released purchasable versions of ragtime into entertainment markets. Although not directly related to the act of music-making, early mechanical-reproduction technologies were nonetheless profound in their aesthetic effect. By turning White and Black performances into audible objects, they disseminated a highly mediated, racialized audibility across the US economy, thereby accelerating Negro sound's subsumption by capital processes and fundamentally altering how people experienced it. Black music in its multiple iterations was now more compliant to transaction, and it would also no longer be limited to its concrete enactments. In fact, in its duplication and mediated proliferation, it assumed an encompassing presence within the nation's racial imaginary. Here again we see at work a key contradiction in Black music's valuation: from the abstracting powers of commodification the concrete sensation of aliveness grows.

With gathering force, assisted by the entertainment industry's relentless commitment to the expropriation of racialized economic and aesthetic value, Black sounding practices, as they variously appeared under the umbrella category "ragtime," intruded upon the productive processes and time-space orders of capital, profoundly impacting popular music's design and affective experience.

New forms of mechanically reproduced ragtime were part of a wider cultural initiative to preserve music performances, to make what was audible into something akin to other manufactured goods. The earliest phonographic efforts, Jacques Attali asserts, aimed "to stabilize representation rather than to multiply it." From the outset, however, "this process," James A. Steintrager and Rey Chow argue, had an unintended consequence. As it "wrenches a sound from its source and context . . . the sound *becomes* an object for the listener." The "sound object," as they call it, after Pierre Schaeffer's initial coinage, "was thus neither found nor captured. It was in part machine-made; in part, a construct of iterative perception."[25] Sound objects were an outgrowth of the machinery of capital, their reiterative nature underlying their appeal as exchangeable things. The first commercial recordings of Western music affirmed this aspiration to mechanically turn sound into a thing. As public interest in sound reproduction widened, a nascent recording industry responded by producing inventories of phonographic cylinders and 78-RPM discs for sale at commercial outlets and for playback at arcades and other public venues. The new phenomenon of music *on record* prompted a readjustment in the act of listening: consumers could experience a performance and then experience precisely the same performance again and again. Listening would be reconceived as a repetitive activity taking place in public spaces and in the home, its increasing frequency and familiarity encouraging buyers to perceive recorded music not simply as an entry point into a particular performance but as an item in a collection of audible things.

While opportunities to phonographically reproduce performances by African American musicians were comparatively limited until the 1920s, the objectification of Black music seemed to befit it, affirming audibly what was thought to have been the Negro body's thingly nature. "Negroes take better [to record] than white singers," the *Phonogram*, the record industry's first trade paper, wrote in January 1891, "because their voices have a certain sharpness or harshness about them that a white man's has not. A barking dog, squalling cat, neighing horse, and, in fact, almost any beast or bird's voice is excellent for the good repetition on the phonograph." These comments are consistent with medical observations made three years earlier by Dr. Thomas Frazier Rumbold, who, upon physical examination of a Black street musician, "Charcoal Charley," attributed his powerful singing to the excessive length of his vocal cord. As Scott A. Carter puts it in his study of American vocality, "Charley's vocal organs revealed a physio-anthropological foundation for the nineteenth-century audio-visual logic of African American singers; . . . anatomical excess produced vocal excess." Recording catalyzed a shift in perception of the racialized voice, its technological transfer to material form (akin to the prior commitment of the slave songs to music notation) being the impulse for a new understanding of music's fidelity: the authenticity of Negro sound would be conceptualized in the aftermath of its extraction. What begins in the 1890s with the seminal cylinders of George W. Johnson, presenting, as Bryan Wagner describes the turn, a "voice that is uncommonly suited to replication by the phonograph," develops sporadically over the course of the next twenty-odd years, as major African American stars—George Walker and Bert Williams, James Reese Europe, Ford Dabney, Roland Hayes, the Fisk Jubilees, and others—commit to recording their "Negroness," their racial fidelity to a repetitive and machinic character. Through phonographic reproduction, the reified presence of the Black body as the seminal sound object is formally established, its audible persistence entering the world as a reiterative sonic thing.[26]

Although phonographic recordings would eventually command the process of popular music's dissemination, a different technology was initially responsible for its introduction into public culture, and it was this same technology, more so than phonograph records, that would also drive the proliferation of enlivened Negro sound as it was heard in commercial ragtime. From the onset of the twentieth century to the beginning of the Great Depression, as Timothy D. Taylor explains in his important essay on music commodification, the player piano—first appearing as an attachment to the conventional piano, then as a stand-alone instrument fitted with a reproducing implement or "inner piano" under its lid—dominated consumer music markets, its perforated paper rolls winding their way through a playerless mechanism and bringing to all piano genres a new kind of materiality. For a time, this "automatic piano"—a "piano [that] seemed to play by itself"—became so popular it threatened to overtake manually played instruments. By the early 1920s, at the height of the vogue, its sales dwarfed those of conventional pianos, its commercial success in the performance of ragtime bringing about new opportunities for listeners to imagine Negro presences occupying popular music: to hear racially ambiguous resonances of spectral Blackness inhabiting commodified things.[27] The fact that early ragtime piano rolls—the manufactured media that player pianos played—were produced not by recording artists but by small teams of White industrial labor carried powerful implications in the evolution of ragtime and Black music. The technologies were an early indication of how one sound object challenged the authority of another: recording begins to intrude on the Black musician as racialized music labor confronts its replacement by artifacts and production processes of new capital.

A year after the term "rag" appeared in the publication of a popular hit (Ernest Hogan's "All Coons Look Alike to Me," 1896), newly established piano-roll businesses started manufacturing mechanical reproductions of a burgeoning repertory that was already circulating as sheet music (cf. chapter 4).[28] Most of the compositions and accompanying rolls carried rag in their titles to set them off from conventional songs and instrumental repertories. The word was important. By employing a discreet racial reference to Black musicality, the entertainment industry expanded public knowledge of Black music's animated power while keeping African American musicians at a safe distance. This enabled White listeners to enjoy what was now well-known to be the audible character of Negro being yet avoid actual interracial contact. Commodification serviced a kind of racial extraction that objectified and effectively sanitized Black music's sonic value.

Within just a few years, the American musical landscape seemed overrun with player pianos hammering out mechanized versions of commercial ragtime, the machinic performances' ragged syncopations bringing into form simulations of the Negro body's audibly repetitious character. Through the wonders of a new instrumental technology, works evocative of a racialized affect entered thousands of domestic environments, informing the listening habits of those who otherwise lacked the skills necessary to play ragtime compositions. For many composers, ragtime's associations with African American cultural traditions, and particularly with stereotypes about Black people's love of leisure and play, provided license for them to engage in the sportive and frivolous. Soon the genre was beset with an exhibition of rags given comical or fanciful titles such as "Dish Rag" (1908), "Fly Paper Rag" (1909), "Rubber Plant Rag" (1909), and "Fiddlesticks Rag" (1910). Others verged on the ridiculous, proposing, for example, mock celebrations of condiments served at American barbecues: Charles I. Johnson's "Dill Pickles Rag" (1906), H. A. Fischler's "Chili Sauce Rag" (1910), and Irene M. Giblin's "Ketchup Rag" (1910). Occasionally, rags and accompanying piano rolls were named after southern cities and states associated with African Americans: Memphis, St. Louis, Alabama, Texas, Missouri, Georgia, Florida, Mississippi; Theodore Northrup's "Louisiana Rag" (1897) was the first published ragtime composition for piano, its roll version released shortly after by Universal.[29] Other place-oriented pieces and rolls were more vaguely referential, connoting the foreign and exotic: "Manilla Rag" (1898), "Egypt Rag" (1910), "That Hungarian Rag" (1910), "Pekin Rag" (1910), "Tokio Rag" (1912) (all *sic*). The sense of frivolity and play associated with ragtime, moreover, occasionally inspired titles evoking the animal world. Frequently they were whimsical, as in Harry Cook's "Shovel Fish Rag" (1907), John Oliver Erlan's "Octopus Rag" (1907), and Tom Lyle's "Oyster Rag" (1910). Yet an equal number reinforced ragtime's connection to Black life by naming animals associated with stereotypical depictions of southern Negro behavior: the possums, chickens, and grizzly bears common to African American folklore. And, finally, there were the early piano rolls whose titles joined ragtime to an enduring racism either through veiled imagery—Wenrich's "Cotton Babes Rag" (1909), W. C. Powell's "Dope" (1909), Julius Lenzberg's "Haunting Rag" (1911), and Gus Winkler's "Banana Peel Rag" (1913)—or through explicit use of derogatory language: "The Baboon Bounce," "Jungle Time," "Rastus Rag," "Tar Baby Rag," "Watermelon Trust," "Whittling Remus," "Nigger-Toe Rag."[30]

As part of this broad racialization of the popular soundscape, commercial manufacturers occasionally produced rolls featuring works by African American composers. The extent of their distribution remains unclear. As a rule, White consumers, who by far wielded the greater purchasing power, preferred White-composed translations of Black performances. This suggests that sellers of rolls by African American composers were targeting Black consumer markets, a view affirmed by passing references to player pianos and piano rolls in advertisements and stories published in Black newspapers.[31] Yet many of these same producers were also reaching into White communities. With the commercial success of Scott Joplin's "Maple Leaf Rag" (1899)—after realizing a modest return its first year, it sold a half million copies by 1909—at least eight piano-roll manufacturers produced their own versions of the hit.[32] The popularity of "Maple Leaf" also led to the sale of rolls featuring works by other African American ragtime composers, notably James Scott, Blind Boone, Ford Dabney, Wilbur Sweatman, and Tom Turpin. Joplin, however, continued to receive the greatest attention: at least sixteen of his works were produced on rolls, with several released by multiple companies. Although the productions likely realized a tidy profit for manufacturers, it is unclear how much of it went to the composers themselves. Joplin, for one, famously managed to win royalties on the initial publication of the sheet-music version of "Maple Leaf," earning one cent per copy sold. But there is no indication that he received compensation for his early rolls. Given that US law at the time did not grant publishers copyright protection against recordings of their works, it is unlikely that Joplin or the other composers received anything.[33]

Despite these losses, the broader cultural idea of Negro music saw remarkable gains, particularly in its associations with ragtime. The common appearance of pianos at the center of American households made it easy for consumers to quickly adapt to self-playing instruments, prompting—with greater effect, Taylor argues, than with phonographs—a dramatic shift from family music-making to the new practice of home listening. Whether representing works by White or Black ragtime composers, piano rolls, in their mechanical translation of sheet music into performed sound, redistributed the sonic orders of national and international domestic environments, their iterations and reinterpretations indelibly marked on perforated paper reinforcing the enduring association between the purported repetitive character of Negroes and the repeating action of machines. The player piano's reproductive apparatus introduced a distinctively modern kind of technological magic consistent with what John M. Jordan calls the "machine-age ideology" of American industrial culture, bringing into being something that phonographic recordings could not readily produce: they created the illusion of a pianist of undetermined racial type otherwise absent from the living space, whose presence could nonetheless be acousmatically felt.[34]

There is nothing inherently racial about a performer's absence. But the expectation that, when entertaining White patrons, African American musicians were to remain racially segregated from listeners and dancers established a powerful social convention: while not precisely determining musical experience, it set parameters for how player pianos playing racially inflected ragtime would be heard. As an extrapolation on a fundamental tenet of interracial relations under Jim Crow, absence carried a "colored" value in the context of ragtime, suggesting a musical presence heard but not seen, discernible solely through the instrument's animated sound and the ghostly fingers touching the keyboard. Uninhibited movements of the piano keys offered tactile evidence of a practicing musician in proximity, resulting in the paradoxical sensation of haptic closeness and unavailability: the experience of hearing music without a musician disturbed the intimate relation between performer and audience, together with the proportions of location and time. Listeners' expectations about conventional musical production led them to assume that there was a pianist in the room. But the player's truancy—as if they had abruptly skipped out—implied that the sound was not simply of the moment but was either a kind of echoing remainder or a resonance coming from far away. Absence and distance alike proposed that the piano's articulations were indeed more a recasting of what had been and that the music, after all, was not simply of the here and now but simultaneously present and past, having been reiterated by the "dead" form of a mechanical instrument.

Conditions of perceptual instability—of presence as absence, of the familiar as foreign, of the inanimate as animate—received considerable scrutiny in European thought at the time, framed within discussions of "the uncanny," or in German, *das Unheimliche*. First proposed by the German psychiatrist Ernst Jentsch (1906) to convey the sensation of ontological instability, particularly the sense that an inanimate object might possess animated powers, the uncanny subsequently gained traction after Sigmund Freud's revision of the concept in a 1919 essay. For Freud, the uncanny experience arose from instabilities relating to psychological repression that produced nervous repetitions of double effect, where what appeared certain, such as the character of a person or the sanctity of the home, also seemed uncertain, a source of danger. What both writers had recognized were the conditions of psychic imbalance gathered at the nexus of modern consciousness: a cleavage of the self had formed in relation to the overwhelming forces of urban-industrial life and Western civilization's confrontations with foreignness. For Jentsch, the uncanny was caught up in life amid machines possessing human likenesses: automata. For Freud, who first employed the term in *Totem and Taboo* (1913), the uncanny related to "persons and things . . . charged with a dangerous power" expressing psychological extremes that were understood racially: the subtitle of Freud's book, in its first English translation in 1918, presented a study of "resemblances between the psychic lives of savages and neurotics."[35]

The player piano performing ragtime introduced its own kind of phenomenal instability. What was uncanny about this mechanized instrument developed directly from the experience of hearing sounds linked to the Black body being produced in a new mediated way. An automated music machine generating sound symbolically attached to the racial encouraged listeners to hear within ragtime's syncopated melodies gestures to an older, temporally disjunctive "Negro" realm, to a resonant yet foreign past-time occupying present-day sound worlds. Mechanically reproduced ragtime enjoyed in the comfort of one's home had opened aural pathways to a modern form of listening at once spectacular and troublingly different. What was both familiar and foreign, present and past, invited the musical sensation of a new and strange kind of racial intimacy, an uncomfortable, uncanny joining of the everyday to a disjointed sonic Blackness now plainly heard.

While the uncanniness of the player piano would diminish as it became routine within White domestic life, no amount of time could fully obscure its ability to disrupt the temporality of listening experience, inviting strong associations with the racial past. In the context of Jim Crow America, the piano's iterations of a racially ambiguous ragtime—of two ragtimes conjoined by the suturing powers of the entertainment industry (cf. chapter 4)—bore the mark of a disconcerting kind of auditory miscegenation fostered by mechanical means. Efforts to claim musical Blackness as a possession of White America reinforced ideological linkages between ragtime and cultural traditions of the Black south, as pastimes of racial delight morphed into contrary, incongruent past-times that intruded on the ordinariness of White public culture. Listening took place within a phenomenal order that invited the sensation of a thingly human sensibility arising spectrally from a reproducing mechanism, the apparent singularity of its audible presence but one of multiple repetitions of the same racialized sound resonating in households across the nation. In theory, the manufactured piano rolls could simultaneously reproduce the same sensation of racialized, musical immediacy anywhere people were listening, and in this way, player pianos affirmed the decidedly modern character of the sound object: they held the capacity to create heightened moments of aesthetic certainty by dislocating sound from its source.

Such perceptions of mechanical reproduction's time-altering powers were central to the wider cultural understanding of sound recording in both its phonographic and automatic-instrumental forms when it initially entered American consumers' awareness. The phonograph, as Jonathan Sterne observes, was the first reproducing technology to prompt a fascination with how a machine's remarkable documentary feats could conjure otherworldly auralities, beginning with Thomas Alva Edison's prognostication that cylinder recordings could "preserve religiously the last words of a dying man, the voice of one who has died."[36] Significantly, the notion of recovering sounds from times past was commonly understood in racial terms. We've already observed how initial efforts to record Black voices developed from the assumption that they made audible a condition inherent to a racially static and temporally anterior primitive being. For ethnographers in the United States and Europe, the phonograph similarly offered a means of preserving the sound of "dying cultures," their efforts to document driven by a widespread belief that "primitive music" sustained cultural structures formed at the origins of human time. Within the emerging discipline of comparative musicology (*vergleichende Musikwissenschaft*), the ethnographic recording, as the seminal sound object, would be championed by scholars as a veritable time capsule that preserved sound's fidelity by ironically separating it from its originating context: scientifically produced recordings could capture sonic truths within their crypt-like vessels. Phonographic reproduction seemed readymade for documentation of the racial and ethnic, reaffirming the primitive, the "Negro," as a being still fundamentally linked to a primal past. Sonic substances embedded on wax and shellac endured residually, spectrally, as living echoes of otherwise lost worlds.[37]

Player pianos and their reproducing mechanisms heightened the illusion of fidelity heard on phonograph records by reinforcing the essential place of the body in the making of music. Music creation, these technologies implied, was physical: a human being *should* be present when experiencing the performance of music; it was *natural* to its production. As piano rolls of a racially ambivalent ragtime proliferated, the sensation of a temporally anterior presence materially fixed to recorded music would persist, withstanding the subsuming effects of exchange processes. This tenacious signature of Blackness embedded in the material structure of ragtime's reproduction is particularly important to the structuring of Black music value. It reveals again how an irreducible racial character trumps the power of exchange, challenging the classic Marxian analysis of commodity fetishism. As Bill Brown puts it in his book *A Sense of Things*, if "the phantasmatic social life of things depends on their abstraction"—that is, on the abstracting power of capitalism, which shields from view the necessity of labor in production—that same social life also reveals a contradiction in the way that the commodified thing never fully releases its fundamentally material presence in social relations. "Despite its transformation [into a commodity, it] retains much of its material form and force." When it comes to the materiality of racialized things, retentions are even more persistent. As Brown shows in another study, what he calls the "American uncanny" describes how the amusements depicting Black people circulating widely at the turn of the twentieth century—racist postcards, "Sambo" figurines,

"Nigger" banks—performed a dialectical inversion, as the force of reification gave way to the tenacity of racism's animating powers, the character of Blackness remaining essential as a value.[38]

Spectral sensations of Negro being inhabiting commercial ragtime's material form stood in stark contrast to the businesslike way that piano rolls were made. Rolls were an artifice of the mechanical-production process and White power's aspiration to fully reify the Black body: what gave the impression of a live performance by an absent pianist came about through the collective labor of music editors or "arrangers" and semi-skilled factory workers who collaborated as part of the greater structure of industrial manufacturing. Rolls produced before 1913, as David A. Jasen writes, were "always machine cut without any artist playing the arrangement." Following procedures first established in the mass production of intricate fabric designs on Jacquard looms, music editors, working directly from published sheet music, created a physical translation of the notation, a blueprint of how published ragtime would be committed to paper rolls. Workers, in turn, employing metal punches, performed the actual act of "writing," making perforations on a paper master that corresponded to pitches and rhythms sounded on the player piano. The prototype scroll would then be "orchestrated," typically by the same editor creating the initial blueprint, who instructed the making of additional perforations to produce playing not appearing on the original piano score. These elaborations, which might include arpeggiations, new voicings, daunting rhythmic complexities, and percussion effects—practices stemming from the classical repertory and newly invented techniques mimicking the "excesses" of Negro music—were intended to enrich the overall quality of sound. In many cases, the flourishes and intricate fingerings exceeded the ability of a solo pianist, heightening the sensation of a mysterious virtuosity manifested in the machinic performances of a repeating instrument. The finished master or "stencil" driving the piano's playing established the basis for the composition's mass production. From its material form, apparitions of racialized Blackness were set into motion, disseminating ragtime sound across the international economy.[39]

Commercial manufacture of player pianos and piano rolls was meant to support the clock-time order of the capital-driven workday. On this fundamental economic level, the devices reinforced the organization of Western capitalist societies by entertaining American and European citizenry, providing within the free-time spaces of leisure diverting pastimes that would refresh labor and encourage its return to the main order of business the next day. Yet the piano rolls, as facsimiles of music performance, could not contain the racial incongruencies that otherwise lingered when mechanically driven pianos reproduced ragtime. If these music-making machines sustained the order of work life, they also exposed in their dissemination a crucial interruption of labor that *necessarily* persisted as part of popular music's valuation. Despite the industry's aggressive efforts of expropriation, an animated racial feeling persisted, as roll editors, like their colleagues in music publishing, fashioned repertories that dramatized the modern sound of syncopation, and in so doing, made the audible character of Blackness bolder. Around 1913, moreover, with the introduction of hand-played rolls for "reproducing pianos," which featured the re-creation of the actual playing and touch of skilled ragtime pianists, racial feeling intensified still further. New complexities in ragtime composition—elaborate "classical" harmonies, intricate arrangements, and approaches inspired by blues—raised the genre's artistic merits while also reinforcing the critical importance of Blackness as part of modern musical aesthetics. A "colored" presence coalesces anew at the center of valuation, epitomized in the work of the White ragtime pianist and composer J. Russel Robinson, the aforementioned "White man with colored fingers" (cf. chapter 4).[40] To be "colored" in the ways of the hand identified an aesthetic quality critical not only to piano performances of ragtime but also to the disposition of American popular music. It showed how the haptic character of a musician's presence could be captured, sold, and then brought into the aural environment of a consumer's place of residence, seemingly without technology's mediating effect. This racial "color" formed the basis from which a credible popular invention could be made.

Mechanical reproduction had complicated for all music easy distinctions between what was humanly expressed and what was not. But the ontological presence heard on ragtime piano rolls magnified those ambiguities, reinforcing Black music's ironic relationship to the disseminating forces of capital. Turning racialized Negro sound into a thing in order to extract from it what was special never seemed to exhaust the music's enlivened character: its racially structured refusal to comply with full commodification was key to Black music's never-ending valuative accumulation. Value increased in contrast to the continuing losses that African American culture endured as a rapacious commercial market sought full control and ownership of its prized possession.

As Black music ultimately exceeded the dominance of White ragtime, advancing into the world in the form of piano rolls and then as recordings produced by African American musicians, it realized a racially spectacular stature, unprecedented in the history of US pop. Hand-played rolls featuring performances by James P. Johnson, Eubie Blake, Luckey Roberts, Blind Boone, and Scott Joplin, conjoining with the live performances of stride heard in New York and elsewhere, set into motion a powerful turn in popular music's valuation.[41] The spectacle of virtuosic, racialized sound produced through mechanical means enriched Black music's enlivened presence: what at first seemed less than Music revealed itself to be much more. Once a scabrous irritant circulating in southern locales it had metamorphized into a modern sensation of international proportion, an incorrigible music commodity whose aesthetic power grew in its ambiguous relation to commodification processes. Incorrigibility, as a negative-turned-hyperpositive value, reaffirmed the dominant position of reification at the heart of Black music's aliveness, just as it posed for White America the formidable challenge of containing a seemingly inalienable sonic expression. For as commodified Black music began to actively join commercial markets, it exposed an ordering logic obedient to its enlivened ancestry, challenging the exchange relations on which Negro sound's development had always been based. What mattered here was not simply the physicality of the piano roll, but the inalienable presence of the laboring Negro body that persisted despite Black music's circulation as a commercially produced thing. This newly made, sonic-spectral presence, in its structural connections to the racial past, brought forward an untimeliness into the everyday: Black music's counterhistory coalesced anew, revealing as it reaffirmed "the invisible persistence of the ontological effects of slavery."[42]

BAD BEHAVIOR

How might an incorrigible commodity misbehave? By way of example, let's consider a small cluster of works that appeared with the emergence of recorded Black music during the time of the First World War: Scott Joplin's seven hand-played piano rolls, which were produced under his name by the Connorized Music Company and the Aeolian Company (Metro-Art/Uni-Record Melody) in 1916. The recordings, which document Joplin's performances of "Something Doing," "Weeping Willow," "Magnetic Rag," "Pleasant Moments," "Maple Leaf Rag" (the latter recorded twice), and W. C. Handy's "Ole Miss Rag," were made at the moment when hand-played rolls were gaining popularity. These new offerings heightened consumers' curiosity about the marvels of mechanical reproduction, about how a modern sound technology had seemingly overcome the artificiality and inauthenticity associated with the copy. Now, manufacturers claimed, and many listeners believed, one could hear by way of recording the actual, original performances of well-known musicians and composers. If the early, "machine-cut" roll raised the possibility of experiencing humanly created sound generated by a mechanized "absent" pianist, the hand-played roll attained a higher level of achievement, its "expression," as an Aeolian ad claimed, being "true to the individuality of the respective artists." Joplin's rolls joined other hand-played recordings by African American pianists who were getting attention, such as James P. Johnson, Luckey Roberts, and Eubie Blake, and like theirs, his rolls were anything but transparent. Joplin's sound objects are best understood as products of an asymmetrical relation between a pianist who provided a preliminary draft of inscriptions and a production staff that ultimately determined choices about the precise location of perforations on the finished form.[43]

What one hears on Joplin's rolls frequently and at times radically departs from his actual playing. On some of the Connorized rolls, passages sound an octave higher than written, while on others, notably on "Weeping Willow" and "Something Doing," there are additions of rapid, octave bass lines that do not show up on the score, together with walking bass patterns uncharacteristic of ragtime piano. Many of these editorial revisions would have been challenging for a single pianist, and most certainly for Joplin, who was judged by his peers, including the hot players in St. Louis, to be merely competent. By the time the recordings were made, moreover, Joplin's performance skills had deteriorated after having succumbed to dementia, possibly the result of a syphilitic infection contracted in one of the sex houses that his wife ran. It would have been impossible for him to have achieved the virtuosic feats that occur on some of the rolls. As Francis Bowdery puts it, "The Joplin of the Connorized rolls in a sense probably never existed."[44]

One gains a better understanding of the production processes by comparing Joplin's two versions of "Maple Leaf Rag," the first produced in April, the second in July. The earlier version, which was released on Connorized, underwent extensive revision, the editing process probably supervised by the house arranger and recording pianist, William Axtmann.[45] As an automatic performance on a reproducing piano, the roll creates the illusion of Joplin as a proficient pianist with a light yet powerful touch. It presents playing that is consistent and elegant, the machine frequently turning out rapid octave runs in the lower register, a technique purportedly heard in Axtmann's own playing. Phrasing is clean, precise, the mechanical performance moving along steadily, with clear executions of melodic statements, added slurs, and flourishes not typical of Joplin's approach, together with simulations of deftly played left-hand to right-hand coordination. The Connorized version of "Maple Leaf" would be ironically celebrated as a faithful representation of Joplin as a pianist, canonized in authoritative recording collections produced by the Smithsonian Institution and W. W. Norton.[46]

Three months later, Joplin made a studio recording again, this time for the Aeolian Company's Uni-Record Melody label. In this version, the piano roll demonstrates playing likely to have been closer to Joplin's actual skills at the time, with only subtle additions introduced in the editing process. It shows Joplin as a once proficient pianist having trouble navigating strains that, on the heavily edited roll from three months earlier, had unfolded with ease. Prior simulations of graceful musicianship give way to a rushed and at times frenetic performance, as Joplin, transformed into some kind of infernal machine, stumbles through passages and compresses phrases in a vain attempt to command a challenging piece of music. The version is consistent with Eubie Blake's recollection that when he heard Joplin performing "Maple Leaf" "around 1915 . . . he was so far gone with the dog [syphilis] . . . he sounded like a little child tryin' to pick out a tune." By this point, he was no longer competent as a pianist, his playing eerily suggesting the half-alive subject he had become.[47]

What do we make of these strange creations? Taken together, the two versions of "Maple Leaf" offer mirror images of racism's tragic effects. The more humanlike and "musical" Connorized version is an exercise in technological craftsmanship performed under the direction of an early sound engineer and his team of technicians. The machinic, "unmusical" version produced three months later offers a fair representation of Joplin's actual skills, his wretched state as a victim of Jim Crow America plainly heard. Each in its own way offers a statement on the reification of Black personhood. In the former, the thingly presence of Joplin is brought into coherence as a machine-made simulation of humanly produced sound; in the latter, Joplin's audible fidelity arises from a disease-addled body, the eerie qualities of ghostly aliveness consistent with his destitute condition. In their coupling, the recordings give to Joplin a public countenance, yet one of frightful proportion: a sorry victim living poor and colored whose prior, sage maneuvering as an entrepreneur could not prevent him from succumbing to a premature, pedestrian death so common among African Americans.

In both versions of "Maple Leaf" released under Joplin's name we can recognize material evidence of the surplus corporeality underlying Negro music's valuation. Both play the line between life and death; both expose audible qualities of aliveness; both carry the charge of a sounding practice at once less than and greater than Music. As Joplin's recordings entered the commercial market, they expressed the "fugitive properties" attributable to the newly fungible alienation of Negro anatomy—labor, countenance, voice—in US jurisprudence and legal opinion in the aftermath of slavery. Stephen A. Best locates this turn in the figuration of the "human phonograph," a status bestowed by Willa Cather in 1894 to Blind Tom, the possibly autistic "idiot savant" whose memorized re-creations of the works of Beethoven and other classical composers marveled White audiences. As Best succinctly puts it—underscoring the dialectical relation of reification to commodity fetishism—"Tom's performances placed on display unsettled transformations of sound from forms exchanged between persons (i.e., Beethoven and Tom [as human]) to properties circulated between things (i.e., piano and [Tom as] slave), reproduced on the phonograph." The legacy of slavery congeals as a sonic afterlife in the strangely phonographic thingliness of the free Negro musician: Black sound objects appear on display as documentary evidence of the Black being as abject person and commodified thing.[48]

Joplin's contributions to the making of piano rolls took place within a greater transformation in how Black music participated in American social life during the second decade of the twentieth century. His recordings and others like them were part of a fundamental change in the music's presentation, as recordings, whether appearing as piano rolls or 78-RPM records, began to rival and ultimately surpass live shows in introducing Black music to consumers. Whereas African American musicians remained racially segregated in American society and were still often prohibited from performing before White audiences, their recorded performances—together with versions of their music produced by White ensembles—circulated freely and widely, often exceeding the boundaries of Jim Crow segregation. During the five-year period from 1914 to 1919, 78-RPM recordings featuring performances and compositions by an impressive assembly of artists and groups—among them Noble Sissle, Wilbur Sweatman, Daisy Tapley, Opal D. Cooper, Dan Kildare, James Reese Europe, Ford Dabney, W. C. Handy, Harry T. Burleigh, the Right Quintette, and Will Marion Cook's Afro-American Folk Song Singers—joined with piano rolls by Black ragtime and stride players in disseminating Black music into commercial markets. Many of the productions were made by major firms, notably Victor, Columbia, Pathé, and Aeolian-Vocalion, which boasted powerful distribution networks.[49]

The unprecedented circulation of Black music brought about a qualitative shift—identifying a veritable *phonographic moment*—as the record furthered the advance of Negro sound into the fabric of American culture. What captured White America's imagination, however, also energized its compulsion to dominate: the illusion of the disc's fidelity heightened the aspiration to secure the unmediated truths of Negro sound. Recording became a kind of disciplining device, which, hypothetically at least, resulted in finally making the audibility of the racial body fully accessible, thus realizing in the sonic realm the ultimate ideological ambition of White cultural supremacy: the completion of Negro possession. Symbolic profits gained from Black music's circulation delivered to African American musicians enormous economic losses compounded by the music's increases in value as a commodity form. To be sure, what Black music had achieved in its dissemination it sacrificed in its incorporation by White America, the music's movements in the exchange economy sustaining a tendency consistent with its double character. The new phenomenon jazz, in particular, marked an important step in this pattern of perpetual loss, made tellingly explicit in a claim by the Imperial Player Roll Company, which posted in a trade journal in 1917 a "warning notice" to other manufacturers, asserting its right to wholly claim the new commercial genre: "We originated 'JAZZ.' We were the first to use it in connection with perforated music rolls and the Government has registered the word as our Trade Mark."[50]

Yet such efforts to draw all value away from African American ownership does not explain why modern Black music seemed so appealing. It does not reveal why more and more White listeners wanted to hear what the Connorized Music Company, in an advertisement for Joplin's piano rolls, called "syncopated music as only members of the negro race can [play it]."[51] If this Negro music had fully succumbed to expropriation, its value entirely incorporated into the social body of American music, then why were so many White consumers beginning to purchase not only White musicians' interpretations but also recorded performances by Black artists? What was reified and thingly strengthened the power of Negro audibility, with Black music's embodied character gaining greater primacy as a value marker. *Qualities* of enlivened sound were converted into *quantities* compatible with exchange, the process encouraging the belief that its animatedness was alienable. Yet dispersion of what appeared alienable only magnified the music's ineffability, and in this way, devaluation catalyzed revaluation: the extraction of racial sound advanced the proliferation of inspirited expressions. Despite its many changes as a result of the inexorable expansiveness of capitalist processes—and following what William Sewell has described as capitalism's own seemingly "contradictory [character, being], simultaneously still and hyper-eventful"—Black music in its continuing metamorphosis also remained racially static, setting into motion the modern perception of what Amiri Baraka famously called the "changing same" (cf. introduction). As the music entered deeply into the circuits of the market economy, its qualities interlinking with the broad character of the social, it grew more abstract: the sound of the original person-thing became encompassing, its separation via recording technologies from the laboring body revealing Blackness as a modern phenomenon consistent with living life in an "arithmetic" world.[52]

   This is not simply to repeat the tired claim that Black music's putative authenticity affirmed the taste for otherness in the new age of the modern. Rather, we can recognize how Black music participated in the making of the very sense of modern rationalization; it was instrumental in creating both the racialized character of and an animated alternative to a technology-driven, thing-laden society. As Mark Goble argues, "Race was already so inscribed in the language surrounding new technologies that communicated the immediacy of music like never before, that it was difficult for the musical aesthetic of modernism to register its appeal without recourse to a whole network of racial meanings. . . . Making U.S. modernism itself into a kind of feedback loop between race and technology." In the act of expropriation, of turning the Negro's auditory qualities into quantities, so did the phonographic effect racialize the feel of culture overall, its racially ambiguous expressions of "hot," "syncopated" sound—the hyperpositive values arising out of the negative—mirroring the reified condition of the new industrial experience. And so the player piano's ability to reproduce the human act of musicianship—its "machine-like imitation . . . of notes . . . shot out like bullets"—would reaffirm the absent pianist's relation to the repetitive proclivities of the Negro worker. The fascination of race, as Goble contends, "emerges less as the sign of what remains natural and authentic within the circuitous mechanics of recorded sound, and more as a result of modernism's own commitment to the pleasures of both technology and technique." If Americans at this point, in Bill Brown's words, "lived life peculiarly possessed," inhabiting a topsy-turvy world in which humanity seemed increasingly overwhelmed by things—"we do not possess them; they possess us," as an anonymous magazine writer put it in 1906—they would find both familiarity and release in the mechanized sound of popular music's repeatedly deracinated and reracialized ontology. The American listener succumbs to the diverting commands of a person-thing, as "The Nigger in the Woodpile" in Sousa's rendering (cf. chapter 4) presents itself as a fundamentally modern problem. It reveals to all who are willing to hear it the inaudible structure of Black music's primary truth.[53]

So begins a new contested alignment, a conjoining of two seemingly discrete problems moving in step with the double character of a musically racialized modern. It is a pairing that has shown up previously, if in nascent form, reaching back to the anomalous relation of a property in sound embodied in the audible body of a chattel slave. But with the materialization of Negro sound as a quality contained within the inanimate form of a piano roll or recording, this alignment reemerges as a qualitatively different expression. The enduring "Negro problem" of the nineteenth century—given interpretation in the words of Booker T. Washington and W. E. B. Du Bois—reveals itself to have been from the outset a version of what Georg Lukács called "the problem of commodities . . . the central, structural problem of capitalist society in all its aspects."[54] That "the Negro" could be perceived a "thing" was an unnecessary problem in itself, the result of the nightmarish perversity of White supremacy. Now this unnecessary problem appeared as a modern iteration, its expanse consistent with the escalation of Black music's dissemination: the "Negro problem" joins through the mediating effects of Negro sound the greater problem of commodities that occupied modern industrial societies, as incorrigible things and their productive means overwhelmed social life.

Thinking the "Negro problem" and the "commodity problem" in relation, as part of a larger, sonically inflected social problem, proposes an instructive pathway into examining the accretional evolution of Negro music's value. For the problem beset on Black people was, in the first place, a commodity problem: the problem of being a "Negro," a human classified according to the status of "that," whose surplus corporeality explained the original, common-sense view of the enslaved as audible property. In its afterlife, the sound of the Black body multiplied, exceeding the realm of hearing to inhabit discourse and become part and parcel of the condition of alienation: the sounding Negro body would assume the status of a figure at once symbolic of and alternative to reified life. Being something less than and greater than Music, Black music formally presented its double character, this time in its accumulating expanse: what was illicit and extending from a condition of inferiority revealed, in its fleshy audibility, an integrity linked to enlivened sound. Through these means, modern Black music proposed a solution to the problem of the commodity form, its incorrigible, bad behavior providing an outlet from an existence as reified labor.

In his famous essay on reification, which extends and expands on Marx's analysis of commodity fetishism, Lukács argues that the commodity form identifies, in miniature, the entire logic of modern industrial capitalism. This logic is revealed, he suggests, not simply in the literal thing, the commodity, but in the commodity form, an abstract, analytical category specifying concrete products of capital production, whose qualitative and quantitative double character, as use value and exchange value, gives rise to what he names its "ghostly objectivity." In its concrete immediacy in the present, the commodity form is linked to these larger, abstract forces of production, circulation, and value. And it is because of the form's fetishism that it "can only be understood in its undistorted essence when it becomes the universal category of society as a whole." Because of the necessity of labor in the commodity's mass production, moreover, humanity becomes its victim, suffering "a fragmentation of human life." The commodity form, Lukács famously writes, "stamps its imprint upon the whole consciousness of man; his qualities and abilities are no longer an organic part of his personality, they are things which he can 'own' or 'dispose of.'" The dominance of the commodity form is what metastasizes as a condition of overwhelming, if incomplete, rational calculation—incomplete because it must leave out that which is human yet not rational—across society as a whole. What Lukács once imagined in his early writing as a genuine life, and which he briefly entertains in his "Reification" essay as a potential revivified in forms of "play" (according to theorizations of "living shape" by Friedrich Schiller in his On the Aesthetic Education of Man [1795]), ultimately recedes to the effects of reification. For in play, Lukács concludes, "the world must be aestheticised, which is an evasion of the real problem. . . . Or else the aesthetic principle must be elevated into the principle by which objective reality is shaped: but that would be to mythologise the discovery of intuitive understanding." Reification's overcoming, for Lukács, can take place only in the closed totality of the artwork, which he discusses in his later writings, or in the possibility of proletarian workers themselves acquiring a new consciousness through enduring struggle.[55]

Lukács's outline of the problem of the commodity form leaves inadequate the possibility of a viable solution, a matter that cast doubt on the significance of the aesthetic across twentieth-century critical thought. It would be Theodor Adorno, whose negative dialectics created an opening for imagining a utopian possibility through art, who most successfully advanced Lukács's aesthetic materialism. But we can also recall a work published closer to the time of the "Reification" essay that proposed a way of thinking about labor's potential that pushes back on the commodity form as all-consuming and conquering. In the introduction, we first encountered how, in his book *The Gift of Black Folk* (1924), W. E. B. Du Bois expounded on the significance of African American work life, observing how US industrial strength and material wealth were in large part an outcome of the enslaved people's hardship and involuntary forms of labor. "It was black labor," Du Bois wrote, "that established the modern world commerce, which began first as a commerce in the bodies of the slaves themselves." Particularly important about Black labor for Du Bois was that it provided something beyond mere economic profit, realizing a gain linking to the "Negro spirit." Configured negatively, in the reluctance of audible beings, Black labor offered an alternative orientation: harnessed in song, this audible, *living* labor, so intertwined with acts of singing both under slavery and after, would enable "a renewed valuation of life" that would direct the spiritual advance of the nation.[56]

Du Bois's lasting commitment was to the slave songs, which he had celebrated in *The Souls of Black Folk* (1903) and again in *The Gift of Black Folk*, positioning them to oppose the orderliness of the Protestant work ethic. For Du Bois, the slave songs, or "sorrow songs," having taken knowable public form after their transcription and transformation into concert music, would become the means by which the Black poor realized dialectically a greater self-consciousness, intensified by a "Negro spirit" fashioned in the modern. It is fair to say that when he expanded on these ideas in 1924, he was not thinking of the legacies of ragtime and blues, nor, for that matter, the new developments in jazz. And yet Du Bois was seeking in Black music a response to the same rationalizing tendencies identified by Lukács and other social critics (e.g., Georg Simmel, Max Weber) thought to be overwhelming metropolitan life, and seeking to bring into conception a way of being celebrating the reluctant activities of everyday African American laborers. If we forgive his aesthetic conservatism, and perhaps his tendency to glorify a daily routine under slavery that was, in fact, most often sheer misery, we can recognize how Du Bois's aforementioned statements in

Black Reconstruction in America about a "spectacular revolution" that announced the enslaved people's emancipation also identified the sustaining power of Black music in the modern. And with this, the spectacularity of modern African American forms signaled a new "Hymn to Joy" (to recall Du Bois's allusion to Schiller's poem), the forms' doubly formulated expressions arising against the force of dominance as a "tropical product with a sensuous receptivity to the beauty of the world."[57]

That possibility arose structurally from the incorrigible character of Black music as a commodity form, its "residual ontology" refusing the completion of exchange as it also rode the powers of capitalist circulation, disseminating throughout the commercial world.[58] The enduring qualities of aliveness were understood as an audible extraction from the Negro body, and in this, enlivened sound maintained a durable concreteness, an unrelenting and unsubsumable (if unspecific and dynamic) materiality tracing across modern African American expression. The enlivened sound of Black music would be routinely received as a kind of work-beyond-work, a "lazy" brand of reluctant labor exercised by those who themselves were judged to be not entirely human. In this formulation, Black music's commodification proposes a revision of Adorno's "absolute artwork," whose complete separation from exchange value, as an autonomous "absolute commodity," becomes the sole means of claiming aesthetic value. Here, Negro music, in its thingly, negatively inspired, double character, epitomizes commodification, except that it also repeatedly, repetitiously short-circuits exchange processes.[59] This aesthetic defeat of commodity exchange opens the potential once more for a revealing, for an exposure of a racialized pastness that congeals in Black performances to confront the diverting enchantments of popular pastime: a temporally disjunctive auditory aliveness exposes the mute structures of Black music's truth content, which are grounded in US racial history. The music's "residual ontology" established a material basis for the creation of a double-sided problem, that of "Negro" being and the commodity form. It was a problem at once racial and economic and which, in turn, extended the social dynamic of seditious play first advanced in the slaves' sounding practices and colored minstrelsy.

Schiller's theorization of play in his "Fifteenth Letter," ultimately dismissed by Lukács in his enduring commitment to the possibility of revolution arising out of proletarian labor, would later be reclaimed by Jacques Rancière, whose study of French workers engaging afterhours in "Nights of Labor" (cf. chapter 2) became the basis for his outline of a political promise in a new distribution of the sensory, in a new structuring of life itself. By challenging modernist dismissals of commercial entertainment, Rancière recovers the promise of play's effect—quoting Schiller, "that 'Man is only completely human when he plays'"—in its relation to the formal qualities of the aesthetic, "one that reframes the division of the forms of our experience."[60] What was less becomes more as the grand loss of the "Negro problem" once again interrupts the problem of the commodity form, giving to the passive, "contemplative" worker a new promise in the form of dissensus acts of scabrous aesthetics sounding in the spectacularity of modern Negro music.

What is especially important to recognize here is that in its interruption of exchange processes, the incorrigible form of Black music, being in itself, in William Sewell's formulation, a consequence of capitalism's tendency toward prolific eventfulness, *undermines* capitalism, bringing about a veritable "Hymn to Joy": a new and spectacular social possibility inconsistent with the rational behavior of an arithmetic society. And in doing so, Black music moves further into the social realm of commercial entertainment, as it also coalesces as newly aestheticized expressions of *Black art*. The concretized, fleshy residue of incorrigible Negro sound assumes a level of embodied abstraction, suggesting in its reach a kind of audible "ghostly objectivity" structurally linked to the problem of the commodity form itself. If, once more, abstract labor identified the "secret of the expression of value" in Marxian political economy, it would be the strangely concrete and abstract tendencies of an animated labor form—a form of work that seemed simultaneously always outside of work—that reordered the making of value in entertainment capitalism as Black music's metamorphoses unfolded further into the twentieth century.[61]

SIX

COMMODITY CIRCUITS AND THE MAKING OF A JAZZ COUNTERHISTORY

MEMORY THING

"Jazz," writes Sidney Bechet, "that's a name the white people have given to the music." In a conversation with an admirer at a Paris club, Bechet, the virtuoso soprano saxophonist and clarinetist, sought to challenge the routine depictions of Black music as something merely diverting. The music, he explained, was "more than a memory thing," even as it maintained incontrovertible ties to the past. "Memory thing" was Bechet's way of referring to stale sentimentalism, to journalism's nostalgic portrayals of the music's growth from the proverbial "cradle" of New Orleans. His own relation to Black music proposed a different kind of perception, one characterizing jazz as a sound-induced temporal disruption in which the past was actionably alive in the present. "These people don't seem to know it's more than a memory thing," Bechet insisted. "They don't seem to know it's happening right there where they're listening to it." For these listeners, it seemed, past-time was beyond comprehension, cloaked within the fetishizing forces of diverting pastimes.[1]

What for Bechet was happening suggested the possibility of a sensory realignment, a return, even if a glancing, fleeting one, to a place of imagining where incongruent temporalities assembled as part of the continuing metamorphosis of Black music. With his words, we can begin to consider the coalescence of new sound formations generated according to the logic of double value: value grows as part of popular music's economic expansion, yet its lavish aesthetic profits, taking form as something greater than Music, congeal as the ironic consequence of its tremendous losses to White power's incessant expropriations. This sensational sound "happening right here" and given the commercial name "Negro jazz" produced value by joining while also interrupting the entertainment industry's forward-moving expansiveness, the music's impact on the sensible orders of the everyday intensifying the feeling of multiple pasts crowding in the present. Black jazz performances unfolded as a creative efflorescence in their relation to market forces, enriched by the failed attempts of the entertainment industry to entirely subsume what seemed alive in the sound. Through its active participation in the economy's expansion—to the point of mimicking capital's illusory power "as a social relation which appears in the form of a thing"—Negro jazz grew ontologically capacious, suggestive of a vast network more than a discrete entity.[2] In its double movements, it organized a counterhistorical aurality producing fleeting glimpses of primary truth that defended Black sonic culture from the rapacious forces otherwise accelerating its valuative growth.

For Bechet, sound animated by the Black body represented a gift that could be shared across racial lines, but only if White listeners were first able to span the racial mountain to comprehend its historical grounding and acknowledge it as a property owned by African Americans: "My race, their music . . . it's [the musicians'] way of giving you something, of showing you how to be happy."[3] His tone made clear that this act of generosity didn't mean a willingness to conform to category, as if all Black sounding practices might be included within the commercial genre, jazz. In calling out the label as a creation of the music industry, Bechet sought to expose the disjunction between "memory thing" and the performative reassertion of African America's claims on its own sonic material, which, by the time of Bechet's writing in the 1950s, had thoroughly reoriented the valuative order of the popular. The success of this reorienting largely had to do with the unique behavior of jazz in the market economy, by which it gained heightened critical power.

With the emergence of jazz in the late teens and early 1920s, the Black music commodity assumed a new incorrigible presence. Developing as part of the general activity of exchange within the commercial market—within what Marx called capital's overlapping "circuits" or, as Anthony Giddens describes them, "clearly defined 'tracks' of processes which feed back to the source"—Black performances coursed through the international entertainment economy, their rapid, back-and-forth movements comparable to the positive-to-negative flows of energy in electrical systems.[4] The unrivaled aesthetic importance of Negro jazz was fueled by the unprecedented success of its commodification, from the entertainment industry's ability to translate its racially enlivened sound into palatable representations that moved freely through the circuits structuring popular music. Aliveness as a complex of racial, aesthetic, and monetary value manifested in both sound and idea not only informed the means of production in its relation to musician-labor but also affected the deeper, nonaudible structures of capital growth and accumulation. Marx's interacting circuits of "money capital," "productive capital," and "commodity capital"—each mapping different movements in the creation of profit through surplus value—absorbed all of jazz in its multiple iterations and racial identifications, Black and White, into capital's overarching productive relations. As a result, "jazz," broadly construed, became the focus of what the entire socioeconomic process of popular music was generating. Entertainment capital itself seemed enlivened with an audibly derived, racial presence.[5]

Having coalesced as part of the inner workings of the commercial music industry, Negro jazz assumed an ironic status in the popular imagination. Although socially marginalized, it nonetheless played a central role in the making of musical taste, driving new commercial investments by White-controlled financial power. Entertainment institutions—from performance venues to management companies, publishing houses to advertising agencies, newspapers to manufacturers of phonograph records—coordinated with White-run music ensembles in extracting what appeared primal and unchanging in Black performances, repeating the expropriative maneuvers that traced across the history of African American music. Moving along the circuits of capital, aural sensations of the Black body, having been largely decoupled from Black live performances and recordings, were absorbed into the commercial sphere, their sonic peculiarities in timbre and time inviting sentimentalized imaginations of a racialized past existing beyond capital, as those same peculiarities were gaining value because of it.

What went largely unnoticed was how Negro jazz's direct and indirect involvements in the growth of entertainment capitalism became the impetus for its own coalescence as a modern aesthetic form. As the innovations of African American musicians underwent metamorphosis, moving closer toward the center of popular culture for the first time in the nation's history, they were greeted by White consumers according to the ambivalent social pattern underlying the music's double character. Black expressions assumed a primitive gravitas: seemingly underdeveloped in their linkages to an impoverished South and "savage" African past, they progressed by testing the limits of ordinary listening. What sustained the White nostalgia machine churning out minstrelized fantasies of the southern plantation—epitomized in the celebrated music of the Paul Whiteman Orchestra and then in the ironic performances of Black bands—supplied the economic ground for realizing a new body of racially enlivened music whose startling creativity confronted the conventions of popular musical understanding. As these innovations were fetishized, converted into resources by White performers, they also returned value to the storehouse of Black sonic material, their aural substance having been altered and their aesthetic power heightened by their journeys across the circuits of capital. Through these cyclical movements, the racially embodied qualities of Negro jazz accumulated affective surpluses metamorphizing into a grand and resplendent spectacularity, their seemingly inalienable, animated presences short-circuiting the temporal fields and affective orders of the popular and motivating norm-breaking experiences beyond "memory thing."

The ability of African American musical inventions to short-circuit representations perpetuating White ownership derived from the way a negative sound formation effected hyperpositive gains. The commodity fetish, which elevated jazz to the center of popular culture and brought Black music under the grip of commercial markets, would be repeatedly undone, the circuits of the fetishizing process tripped by the music's scabrous intensities. Such refusals by Black music to succumb to full incorporation produced something that White jazz alone could not: the process actualized the making of a new kind of sensible order, bringing with it a politics of radical contest. The commercial and industrial platforms of entertainment enabled Negro jazz to reorient the broad expanse of music knowledge, its incorrigible sound formations introducing powerful sensations of aliveness that conjured multiple versions of truth.

The perpetual racialization of musical experience made it easy for listeners to enfeeble truthful sensation, to find revelation in fantasies of absolute ownership: the nation's enduring commitment to race encouraged fetishistic illusion without critique, compromising the cultural possibilities of Negro jazz for White and Black alike. Yet the music also provided its own unspoken guidance on matters of aesthetic truth arising from the racial-economic contradictions underlying its ontological appearances. The cyclical pattern bringing forward the music's negative structuring offered clues about why it was that an audible being seemed to be resonating within it. Form itself was instrumental in opening critical paths beyond Negro jazz's fetish character, proposing a way of understanding how the forces of race-capital set the conditions for the invention of spectacular music. While acknowledging the responsibility of capital in fostering Black music's illusory co-optations, listeners began to recognize another kind of fetishism beyond memory thing, its short-circuiting powers derived from the music's origins as an animated property of the enslaved. Negro jazz was, after all, a sonic indication of the primary, structuring truth that accumulated multiple pasts in the present. Under the right conditions and with the proper perspective, it enabled listeners to hear, as Bechet put it, what was "happening right there where they're listening to it."

This chapter maps the conditions from which Black music, as "Negro jazz," arose as a powerful value form confronting the overwhelming dominance of "memory thing" in popular musical understanding. It first focuses on the commercial formulations that created jazz as a genre, whose commodification and expansive circulation fueled massive economic growth. The chapter then turns inward, into the working lives of Black musician-laborers, to explore the movements of Negro jazz in its gestation, emergence, and accumulation as modern ontological sound formations. With this, Black music achieves its efflorescence, initiating the fourth stage of its valuative growth.

THE RISE OF JAZZ AS A CAPITAL FORM

Bechet was certainly aware of how commercial markets affected the performance and development of Black music. Having worked in ragtime and vaudeville groups in the 1910s, he witnessed firsthand the sudden rise in the music's popularity and how what was variously called hot ragtime, syncopated music, blues, freak music, and hokum gathered as part of the overarching rubric of jazz. What fixed the term *jazz* in the vocabulary of pop, though, came from outside Black music: it commenced with the appearance of five White musicians from New Orleans, billed as the Original Dixieland Jass Band (hereafter, ODJB), whose performances in Chicago in 1916 and in New York from January 1917 led to a series of popular phonograph recordings. Within a matter of months, "jass," and soon after, "jazz," was challenging the popularity of all other commercial genres.[6]

For Bechet, the sudden rise in the appeal of jazz meant new opportunities to work, leading him to join Will Marion Cook's New York Syncopated

Orchestra on a tour to England in 1919, where he was famously praised in an essay by the Swiss conductor Ernest Ansermet. But in broad, social terms, the presence of jazz within the commercial apparatuses of the entertainment business also suggested something akin to an occupation even greater in its effect than the expropriations that had given rise to blackface minstrelsy and popular ragtime. For not only had the name *jazz* been imposed on African American performances by "white people," but the entire conception and history of Black music-making coalescing under that name had been dramatically reformulated, in large part at the expense of the musicians who had originated it. "Memory thing" had nearly riven Black music from its racial past.

Jazz as a commercial expression—whether the rapid-tempo contrapuntal arrangements of the ODJB or one of the many versions of instrumentally centered dance music performed by bands and "jazz orchestras"—epitomized the diverting object of consumption in the new domestic marketplace. What made it seem so appealing related directly to the economic and technological processes that brought it into being. The genre arose as the first popular music born of mass production, and it was this origin, distinctive to industrial manufacturing and mass communication, that shaped the music's public comprehension for years to come. Although ragtime had already gained recognition as a mass-produced genre with an international following, its chief, material basis in sheet music and piano rolls qualified the extent of its commercial circulation.[7] Jazz, in contrast, was formally attached to modern capitalism and to the sound-reproduction technology of the phonograph, its vast production and distribution networks crucial to its unparalleled social movements. As Kathy J. Ogren observes in her outline of its early representation, "Jazz was a music of . . . industrial life," being what Gilbert Seldes described in 1924 as a "mechanism which at the moment corresponds so tragically to a mechanical civilization," but which also "may be infused with humanity." In its live performances, moreover, the musical language of jazz, with its rapid tempos and clamorous percussive "noise," suggested to some listeners a temporality and amplitude consistent with modern living. In the words of Irving Berlin, "Its swiftness is interpretive of our verve and speed and ceaseless activity," while others heard in jazz qualities mimicking the chaos of wartime aurality. For the New York *Sun* writer F. T. Vreeland, the jazz ensemble recreated "the humming rattle of a machine gun, only not so musical."[8]

Above all, though, early jazz was a creation of the recording studio, its many versions of mass-produced shellacs driven by a market shift that compelled phonograph companies to move away from the sale of playback devices (notably, Victor Record's "Victrola") and to focus on the production and sale of records. The 78-RPM disc was critical to the music's expansion as an exchangeable commodity, a potential well established with the huge success of the first jazz side, the ODJB's "Livery Stable Blues," which, within a year of its May 1917 release on Victor, purportedly sold over a million copies. Although million-sellers were by no means unprecedented, the sudden, ubiquitous presence of jazz was astonishing to those who marveled about the transformation occurring in American musical consumption, with thousands of households now capable of listening simultaneously to the same peculiar beat.[9] Recognizing the commercial potential of jazz in accommodating new markets for passive listening and social dance, competing record companies—Gennett, OKeh, and notably Columbia, which eventually secured its own contract with the ODJB—hustled to establish relationships with leading ensembles. In the space of three years, jazz would thoroughly revise the way listeners consumed popular music, and in so doing, the genre would begin to acquire a social history, a "memory thing."[10]

Depictions accompanying the emergence of jazz affirmed the music's rightful place in the new markets of mass consumption. Already well known just weeks after the ODJB's first record release in May 1917, jazz quickly assumed a familiar presence on the pages of US newspapers, both in major cities and in hundreds of towns and rural communities throughout the nation. In contrast to the common claim that jazz was from its outset the subject of dispute, articles published during its first two or three years show that it was mostly uncontroversial; in many cases, the reports were approving.[11] By and large, the genre fulfilled common expectations of what a popular musical form should sound like. Newspapers routinely published notices about upcoming events, demonstrating how the live performance of jazz, almost always played by White musicians, had been successfully integrated into everyday social life: the Chamber of Commerce Dance in Olympia, Washington, featuring the Princess Jazz Orchestra; the Rialto Jazz Band's afternoon performances in Anaconda, Montana; the Police picnic "with jazz orchestra," in Portland, Oregon; the saxophone "wizard," R. A. Miller, performing at Salt Lake City's Hippodrome; Harry Slatko's "Rollickers," accompanied by a "Jazz band" in Philadelphia.[12]

Press coverage frequently included advertisements for new record releases. After the initial success of the ODJB, for example, Victor ran dozens of ads in newspapers from Los Angeles to Warren, Pennsylvania, to introduce the band's recordings. These ads sometimes appeared alongside those for other recordings featuring Black or Black-inspired music, such as an "exquisite violin translation" by the Russian-born virtuoso Efrem Zimbalist of Stephen Foster's "Massa's in de Cold, Cold Ground." Columbia likewise publicized the new recordings of W. C. Handy's orchestra, where one could hear "the frenzied swing of a super-syncopation."[13] Occasionally, reporters wrote approvingly about musicians' performance skills, lending greater legitimacy to the genre. A writer for a Salt Lake City newspaper detailed the challenge for classically trained musicians to play jazz, which "really requires good musicians." "To jazz properly," the author explained (employing an epithet that would eventually describe both the practice and the genre), an instrumentalist "must also be endowed with the swing or knack of performing it."[14] Although writers rarely spoke of it, this "knack" did not include skills in improvisation. Early White ensembles, including the ODJB, did not improvise well, their "spontaneity" often the result of rehearsing and memorizing preconceived material.[15]

Now and again, coverage of jazz in its emergence as a commercial genre highlighted its high velocity and reputed noisy harshness, and occasionally, the commentators expressed some irritation with it. Vreeland, we've seen, was not much of a fan of the machine-gun "rattle" that inspired analogies to the battlefield at the height of the First World War. A United Press correspondent writing from wartime London, moreover, reported with dismay the spectacle of a band "jazzing George Cohan's 'Over There,'" the affront to a patriotic song heightened by the sordid displays of "lounge lizards dancing and girls poising elaborate cigarette holders in waxen fingers." Another report was similarly reproving, describing the "wild barbarity" at the core of the genre's "fascination."[16] Still another reinforced the common association of "the Negro" with incarceration in a callous story about how a group of prisoners was forced to pay for the purchase of a jailhouse phonograph to play jazz records at its "prisoners' ball."[17]

Yet in most instances, the recriminations added up to nothing more than rhetorical gestures. The lion's share of journalists and apparently much of their readership found the early forms of jazz engaging—hardly something constituting a serious social threat. This, despite the music's linkages to the African American past, which were routinely acknowledged: illustrations advertising the ODJB's first records depicted it as a Black band.[18] Such indications of miscegenation were apparently an acceptable condition of US popular music as long as "the Negro," under Jim Crow restrictions, remained safely in place. In "What Jazz Music Is," for example, an essay published in September 1917 in the *Dallas Morning News*, the anonymous reporter, relying on a widely referenced essay written a few weeks earlier by the New York reporter Walter Kingsley, stated without a hint of equivocation that the term *jazz* described "when negroes seem infected with the virus that they try to instill as a stimulus in others." Another writer, in an essay published in June of the same year, quoted a local "manager of entertainment" at a Kansas City restaurant who asserted that "no white person has ever produced any Jazz comparable with that of the original Jazz band." Curiously, that Black ensemble went unnamed, although it might have been James Reese Europe's "Hellfighters" band from the 369th Infantry, whose recordings widely circulated and whose return to New York from France in 1919 was featured in national news reports describing how "three thousand negro warriors jazzed their way up Fifth avenue, with a chicken dinner at the end of the trail to lure them on." Finally, Kingsley's own, newsworthy comment that "one touch of jazz makes savages of us all" was, as readers understood from its full iteration, not meant to alarm but rather to entice partiers out for an evening's entertainment. The new Negro-based music, he suggested, would "stir the savage in us with a pleasant tickle. Freiburg's is an institution in Chicago. If you 'go South,' you must visit that resort."[19]

The cartoonish claims about music viruses, savagery, and going South shared a common sentiment: they expressed a general level of comfort with the African American presence in popular music as long as it remained securely under the grip of White power. The enlivened "childlike" sound of the Negro body would not be rendered mute but rather, like Sousa's ragtime—and, indeed, the complex of Black scabrous sound arising since Emancipation—contained for the pleasure of White consumers. Having been reduced once again to the category of a natural resource, Negro sounding practices introduced into the networks of popular aurality seemed at this point only tenuously attached to actual Black bodies in labor, the racially based claims on them having reached a veritable breaking point. As Irving Berlin explained to Vreeland in November 1917, "There are many negro jazz bands in the South, but the best jazz players are white men. It's like everything else they've developed—we've improved on it."[20]

Despite popular music's dependency on Negro sound, performances by Black musicians at White gatherings were few and far between, and when they did occur, the players themselves remained segregated from paying customers.[21] Aliveness in the production of jazz was critical; the presence of colored musicians was not. Accordingly, their marginal standing would remain proportional to the degree of the music's expropriation. At once superfluous and critical to the making of commercial jazz, Black performers gave forth from their audible bodies an animatedness that circulated publicly as part of the "phantom objectivity" of the new jazz commodity form, its scabrous appearances lifting spectrally out of the subsuming mechanisms of capitalism.[22] What seemed alive in African American musical performance would be routinely incorporated into commercial jazz productions as a key value, its participation in the formal logic of commodity exchange driving capital accumulation while its racial coherence was guaranteed by the tenacity of the nation's White supremacist commitments.

Having emerged as the new subject of fascination in popular entertainment, jazz, as ragtime before it, acquired value in two opposing ways that were relationally connected in the music's attachments to the commodity form and the genre category that named it. On one hand, value grew positively as part of the music's compliance with the market's expansive behavior, with performances before paying audiences and on phonograph records compelling the involvement of an intricate network of manufacturing and distribution. To this extent, the enlivened sounds attached to commercial jazz and moving within the circuits of capital were no different from the components of other widely distributed commodities, from tooth powder to cigarettes to playing cards. They openly participated within the greater relations of economic production, their attachments to Black creativity having been loosened and reconceived by White capital and labor.[23] On the other, following a tendency now familiar to popular music's evolution, sounds and modes of playing expropriated from African American musicality into commercial jazz also moved in contrary motion: changed yet not fully subsumed by capital, they folded back into the matrices of Black sonic material. According to this pattern, aliveness grew in relation to Negro music's dialectical movements between exchange and use, the embodied exceptions to exchange value gestating in Black worlds and then returning to public practices to drive new valuation in commercial jazz. What appeared enlivened repeatedly short-circuited the full participation of all that was "jazz" within the processes of circulation, its symbolic alignments with racial Blackness interrupting the smooth distribution of capital.

Such developmental complexities, however, remained far from public awareness. According to virtually all who spoke about it, jazz had simply come out of nowhere. The title of an essay published in June 1917, just a month after the release of the ODJB's first record, captured the sense of its uncanny emergence: "Jazz, the Mysterious Stranger of the Musical World." The *Literary Digest*, in turn, reported in August of the same year that "a strange word has gained wide-spread use in the ranks of our producers of popular music."[24] Two years later, in 1919, it was now, according to the *Digest*, "the latest international word." Despite the wide notice, it somehow remained a mystery, prompting its editors to turn to James Reese Europe for insight. In a guest essay, he reinforced magical thinking as he attempted to "explain . . . its mysterious origins." "'Jazz' is, of course, negro," Europe asserted, "somehow or other all musical originality in America seems to be negro."[25] Apart from its links to the African American past, though, it had ultimately forsaken its roots and exceeded its racial destiny. At least that appeared to be the case where transactions were involved. According to the chorus of the popular tune "Jazzola," which Europe and his Hellfighters recorded in 1919 with Noble Sissle featured as vocalist, the genre was a child of the metropolitan North, a music "the whole world's going crazy about," having seemingly emerged from thin air: "They call it 'Jazzola,' Nobody knows its origination / 'Jazzola,' it's just a dance full of syncopation." Europe himself, together with his cohort, personified this readjustment of the music's history: they were the collective "nobody" of Negro labor giving way to phonographic technology's miracle of "origination."[26]

With jazz, the White nation had invented a modern-day folk form that affirmed America's position of dominance in the world. Wrested from its racial moorings, the newborn creation of popular entertainment was dressed up in an origins tale that serviced its push into commercial markets. Beyond Europe's efforts to reassert the racial authority of African American ownership, most White consumers of popular culture believed that jazz could be owned by no one, which, in effect, meant that it remained a possession of White America. Having acquired the ability to reproduce the techniques of "jazzing" or paraphrasing a musical line, White musicians extended a practice already developed in ragtime, turning the purported "mystery" of Negro sound into a technique that, when learned, could be effectively extracted from its racialized containments. Some African American critics, in turn, saw the music's appropriation in a positive light, claiming it an inadvertent payback that advanced the celebrity of Negro forms and ironically reaffirmed the music's racial origins. In 1925, for example, J. A. Rogers honored the folkloric conceit in support of the critical project of the "New Negro," famously proposing that jazz was "nobody's child of the levee and the city slum." Having been released from the audible Negro body, it carried into the popular as the musical basis of an idealized national mythology. "Jazz," Rogers argued, "is a marvel of paradox. Too fundamentally human, at least as modern humanity goes, to be typically racial, too international to be characteristically national, too much abroad to have a special home."[27]

The residues of racial sound enlivening commercial jazz identified the profitless, losing end of the bargain for African American musicians. The extent of the music's expropriation by White entertainment capital set the tone of the genre's commercial depiction, played out according to a familiar narration about the Black subject's inevitable condition of loss. Jazz in the popular imagination became the music uplifted from the "underworld," the "levee," the defeated and impoverished South. It carried vestiges of repetition inherent to an uncivilized population, the progeny of "jungle parties when the tom-toms throbbed and the sturdy warriors gave their pep an added kick with rich brews." In its attachments to beat-oriented savagery, commercial jazz identified loss as an equivalence of Negro misfortune and weakness. For the "savage," according to Josiah Strong, drawing a contrast to the modern White consumer, in "having nothing, is perfectly contented so long as he wants nothing. The first step in civilizing him is to create a want."[28]

One particularly disturbing tale of loss gained traction after its initial 1919 appearance in the *Literary Digest*, setting into motion the genre's origins narrative. In "Stale Bread's Sadness Gave 'Jazz' to the World"—the protagonist showing up later in Paul Whiteman's memoir, *Jazz*—an unnamed author told the story of a blind, presumably African American "newsboy" and violinist, "Stale Bread," whose personal misery, living on the streets of New Orleans, triggered a chrysalis-like invention: "A shimmying, tickle-toeing, snapping delirium . . . upsetting the equilibrium of the European dance."[29] Loss as the basis of value in the music of Stale Bread established the conditions for valuative growth. Acquirable and transferable via exchange, this mysterious, "snapping delirium" entered the heart of White music capital, its recontextualization realizing its aesthetic potential, as commercial jazz rose within the ranks of the consumer marketplace. Through capital's cheap investments in the sound of superfluous Negro labor, jazz turned a profit. "Ten years ago," a *Kansas City Star* critic reported in 1917, "jazz would not have gained a single admirer, but now, when people carry pet butterflies to cafes with them—as happened one night last week—a thing has to be considerably different to gain even passing attention." Jazz was, the writer acknowledged, of "Negro origin," but that lack was not in itself enough to sustain value. Loss as a racial condition needed to accumulate in order to fulfill "the consistently growing appetite for sensation."[30]

The appeal of jazz developed in step with other sensational things, notably the figures and forms of the exotic that were also appearing in commercial showcases. Jazz as a popular expression had arisen during a moment when tastes were growing receptive to newly available foreign commodities brought into the symbolic order of domestic life. The genre's status as an exotic "sensation" corresponded to what Kristin L. Hoganson calls the "consumers' imperium," being part of a cultural turn reaching back to the late nineteenth century, when the interactive expansions of international markets and military domination inspired public interest in the cosmopolitan. Enlivened qualities in jazz as a commodity may be accordingly compared not only to the components of tooth powder and cigarettes but also to the signs of foreignness projected by an array of exotic novelties, from Indian curries and Orientalist women's fashion to Middle Eastern home decoration and early recordings of "world music." As a "sensation," the genre was part of the entertainment industry's greater, profit-driven effort to conflate the foreign and racially inferior into a singular fantasy of dominance. Commercial jazz provided the excitement of social transgression, a soft version of interracial contact. Capitalizing on this cultural turn, jazz bands, from the ODJB to society orchestras—and later, Black-led jazz ensembles—employed Orientalist allusions to compose a surfeit of fanciful titles: "Burmese Bells," "Cairo," and "Shanghai Lullaby"; "Japanese Sandman," "Oriental Jazz," and "Indian Love Call"; "Song of India" and "Ching-a-Ling's Jazz Bazaar." Whether doing so intentionally or not, the creators of these works reinforced the shared appearance of domestic and international versions of difference, replacing the authenticity of the Negro past with comical racisms of the present. Negro music's life story as a sound born of the enslaved had given way to a newly conceived folklore about a miraculous birth at the service of White diversion. In this sense, jazz drew into alignment with other mass-marketed foreign musics that were becoming commonly heard in public forums and on phonograph records, from "hot" Hawaiian hula to Bohemian polka to circus performances of the "Hottentot."[31]

Jazz, however, was unique in that White listeners could locate the source of its exoticism at home. Unlike other kinds of foreign consumables, its racialized qualities of difference, which commercial capital was eagerly seeking to incorporate, carried an insistent potency: despite its conflation with other exotic forms and the anonymity of its "origination," jazz roamed the circuits of a national sign system that also acknowledged that it was race that made the genre American. Jazz brought together into a single entity the expansionist tendencies of capital's profit motive and the accumulative principle of racialized profit-from-loss: its sudden appearance as a national folk form relied on racial figurations now deeply concentrated in the machinery of commercial music. Its mystery betrayed, after all, White citizens' anxiety about America's racial foundation. Having miraculously undergone a process of translation within the structures of entertainment capitalism, jazz took center stage as a cultural expression whose appeal depended on its recovery of the decoupled fragments of aliveness freely circulating in the public sphere. Symbols of embodiment disaggregated from Black labor amassed in the sound of White jazz bands, whose playing conjured movement-oriented metaphors. Jazz, writers suggested, sounded "dippy," "jerky," "peppy," "peppery," "noisy"; the dance numbers, full of "syncopated" melodies, inspired "snappy," "shimmying" displays. An enduring commitment to an insistent beat as the valuative center of all popular music was captured in a 1918 commentary prefiguring descriptions of jazz common ten or fifteen years later. "Jazz music," the writer observed, "is said to be an attempt to reproduce the marvelous syncopation of the African jungle. . . . The rhythmic aggressiveness . . . its savage gift for progressive retardation and acceleration, guided by the sense of swing, reawakened in the most sophisticated audience instincts that are deep-seated in most of us."[32]

White civilization's quantifiable improvements on the primitive organization of musical time set the standard for jazz music's modern appeal. Jazz musicians, Kingsley reported to Vreeland, "put in anywhere from five to ten extra beats between the notes of a composition," which enables them to recover "an art of rhythm that's been practically lost to all highly civilized persons."[33] Negro-generated rhythm, these critics imagined, would become the musical means of reuniting White civilization with its human origins. Such possessive aspirations were also being championed abroad, celebrated by foreign elites such as Darius Milhaud, who, in 1923, dismissed the ordinariness of symphonic jazz ("mechanized music, rather as precise as a machine") in contrast to "the work of the *nègres* of North America. It is a music that," Milhaud asserted, "though it issued from the same source, has evolved in a completely different manner."[34] Its occupation would begin the aesthetic recovery of a temporally stunted, conquering power.

Projections of temporal profit arising spectrally from Black music's incessant losses oriented the new jazz sensibility. The music's enlivened qualities grew in step with capital growth: what became largely disaggregated from Negro physicality indicated a covertly racial, modern feeling. At times, jazz music's expansion exceeded even the limits of audition, projecting through its wide dissemination a racialized affect into the recesses of American culture. Among the announcements in the evening paper of Klamath Falls, Oregon, on August 14, 1919, for example, was the notice that a "peppery pep artist" known to the community as "Pep," aka George O. Brandenburg, "would be ready to jazz" the Elks. Brandenburg did not play music but rather performed lively jazz stunts at nearby Pelican Bay. In another rendering, closer to the music's metropolitan birthplace, jazz was rationalized into the sonic equivalent of the urban office: the secretarial clatter of the machine age meant that "even typewriters jazz."[35] Into the early 1920s, jazz would become metaphorically attached to the symbolic language of US national media and an increasingly internationalized popular culture, most obviously in F. Scott Fitzgerald's famous coinage of the "jazz age," but also more subtly and arguably more powerfully in the way its racial feeling informed the sensible conditions of the global metropolis. The Irish writer Shaw Desmond's portrayal of the New York subway worker as a reified subject who speaks "as mechanically as a gramophone," having been raised on the "peptonized pap" of "mechanical standardization," demonstrated the extent to which jazz—recalling Joplin's piano rolls—had become embedded in the affective language of a technologized body politic. In the words of German journalist Adolf Halfeld, working at the time as a foreign correspondent in the United States, jazz was the embodiment of the "mechanical life" of a culturally impoverished America now infiltrating European culture.[36]

The depictions were powerful in the way they brought together racialized figurations of repetition and loss and the mechanized condition of modern lifeways. Bound dialectically, their symbolism regenerated in the context of commercial jazz. This alignment is what appeared to drive the comments of another German observer, Oscar Bie, who, in 1925, assessed the modern transformation of popular dance music. Whereas in earlier dance forms, such as the waltz, "only a glimmer of rhythm was apparent, [t]o-day the rhythm has become the essential matter." The music and musicians' commitments to its "spasmodic measures," he continued, wreak havoc on dancers who "throw their limbs out of joint" in their attempts to "reflect the turbulence of the beat." Rhythmic devolution in dance music, Bie surmised, was "a sign of the times": it musically expressed a world inhabited by Negro presence and caught up in "topsy-turvy syncopation." Bie was not simply arguing that jazz was primitive. Rather its primitive essence (akin to Stale Bread's nature as a loss) had been translated via modernizing forces into an enlivening impulse that was reorienting the contemporary social experience: jazz was altering how all music would be heard and understood. Although only "a drop of negro blood is still in evidence," jazz rhythm was racially potent according to the social logic of US racism: "There is a primitive, unspoiled something, a bit of ethnology, in the noise of this music." What Bie called "The New Rhythm" extended Strong's characterization of the "savage": previously "want[ing] nothing," by 1925, it displayed a voracity consistent with capitalism's prolific eventfulness, setting about to ravage, to consume.[37]

IMPERIAL PRESENCES, FOREIGN AND DOMESTIC

As a performance practice, a discourse, an idea, jazz appeared now larger than life in ways consistent with its proliferation as a commodity form. It had become, in no uncertain terms, the cultural and legal property of White America, as it fed the purchasing behavior of consumers, seemingly everywhere. In its expansiveness, commercial jazz mirrored the character of capitalist economic processes, aligning with the influence of the United States as a global power. The breadth of its appeal had the effect of spreading the word and deed of White supremacy, working, in the words of the former Rep. William Langford of Georgia, "for the good of the nation, the happiness of the human race, and the civilization of the world."[38] As part of that effort, the racial qualities underlying value in jazz—its "one-drop" properties, its "savagery," its "bit of ethnology"— spread as well, carrying the symbolism of the Negro as a condition of loss outward into the global marketplace. The continuing inward and outward shifts that long characterized the growth process of Black music in the US economy now seemed located in the temporal cycles of capital, its racial intensities disseminating as spectral abstractions of the Negro body. Jazz, as an expropriation of Black labor by White capital, would not only come to dominate US popular music; it would also restructure the sensible orders of metropolitan entertainment cultures around the world.

Within months of the release of the first ODJB release, jazz commenced its international tour of duty, drawing attention and inspiring debate in European locales—where, reportedly, in Great Britain, a "jazz band parades to King's Palace"—and in the port cities defining the geographic reach of the British empire.[39] So too did jazz follow in the wake of US expeditions as part of an early military-industrial complex, which brought commercial entertainment to those eager to gain knowledge about the recent "sensation" in popular music, most notably, the "latest forms of Ballroom waltz [and] Jazz." Being part of a greater American "quest for new markets," jazz, according to Matthew Frye Jacobson's formulation of "barbarian virtue," followed the nation's "lead down the road of empire," producing a trail of performances by young musicians working their way along coastal cities, from Latin America to Africa, the Middle East to Asia.[40] By and large, the principal targets within these markets were not locals but rather the representatives of the colonizing powers. In 1919 and 1920, for example, the *Ceylon Observer* (Sri Lanka) announced in its society pages a series of "fancy dress balls," whose guests were mainly Western tourists and members of the managerial classes of businesses and government. On a few occasions, for costume parties, some dressed up as "jazz pierrot," presumably a blackface inversion of the stock character from the commedia dell'arte, who donned white face paint. On the dance floor, moreover, visitors to the clubs moved to the "snap" of syncopated music, imitating the Black-based "animal" dances popularized in New York a few years earlier.[41] At other times, they were drawn to performances of commercial favorites heard on record: the "cargoes of jazz," as one reporter described the exportation of American recordings, "carrying the jazziest of song hits."[42]

Soon "jazz"—the term encompassing other kinds of music, from a gramophone record of the 1908 coon-song hit "Down in the Jungle" to a performance of "A Nigger Serenade" (probably a minstrel act) by "a few young men . . . [who] visited several houses" in Ceylon in 1919—became the genre of choice not only for Western clientele but also among a worldly class of metropolitan consumers.[43] In a reconstruction of his "world tour" following the course of jazz along the "jazz latitude," Burnet Hershey, a foreign correspondent for the *New York Times*, surveyed the wide appeal of the genre as it appeared in several cities. At hotel dances in Yokohama, "Japanese men and women outnumber[ed] the Europeans on the floor," the music performed by large Japanese orchestras. Filipino bands and players were for him the standouts: "the Italians of the East." Having played American marches and popular music since the US occupation of the Philippines in 1898, they had developed into a conspicuous labor class that worked the hotel ballrooms and night clubs of Manila and other Asian cities, while also supplying entertainment on transpacific ocean liners. In Jerusalem, finally, Hershey witnessed "bearded patriarchs" attending shows, together with "the credulous Arabs [who] listen in amazement to the new importations

[that] . . . ruffle the ancient complacency of the Biblical city." At the end of the story—seeming at this point a fanciful compilation based on multiple excursions—he returns to New York, skipping over the African continent despite common opinion that jazz originated there.[44]

By the end of the 1910s and with the commencement of its titular claim on an era, jazz had evolved into a popular form materially and symbolically in line with the orders of a globally imagined White supremacy. Secure under the dominance of the US racial majority, it would disseminate an American-based international style, reinforcing in its worldly expression of expropriated Black sound the nation's segregationist commitments. The commercial success of jazz had effectively reduced the audible presence of "the Negro" to a set of disembodied, fetishized conceits that would be reenacted in performance by a new generation of White musicians eager to tour the United States and the world. What we might think of as a seminal expression of global pop—a "new world music"—was at the same time deemed to be inherently different because of its lingering racial alignments, its very *jazziness* signifying a residual aliveness that had developed in dialectical relation to the failure of Black music's complete assimilation. Qualities once claimed "Negro" in origin underwent restructuring within the circuits of capital to emerge as the valuative center of a distinctively modern sound. In its noisy syncopation and snap, the "staccato cacophony" of jazz was heard the world over on "every ship . . . and [at] every stop at a port."[45] Commercial jazz may have been hardly comparable in status to classical music, yet it also possessed something that classical music lacked. In their associations with what was less than Music, White jazz players harnessed the racially enhanced, aesthetic energies of what was greater, and in doing so, ironically civilized jazz to challenge the old-world order.

Into the 1920s, commercial dance bands actively disseminated the imperial language of jazz, reproducing the forms of symphonic jazz that were overwhelming international markets. These spectral inflections of enlivened sound evoking the Negro body supported a new kind of authenticity under White authority; they circulated as symptoms—material evidence of the extent of Black subjugation. At the helm of this insurgency was the bandleader and composer Paul Whiteman, the leading progenitor of "symphonic jazz," who, more than any other White musician, shaped the character of commercial popular music over the next decade. In his widely read memoir, *Jazz* (1926), Whiteman, the self-proclaimed "King of Jazz"—among the book's illustrations is a whimsical photo of the "King" being crowned by the Metropolitan Opera star, contralto Jeanne Gordon—claims the authority once granted to James Reese Europe as the principal interpreter of the genre.[46]

Whiteman's take on jazz history rewrites the narrative according to the theme of US exceptionalism, the music's connections to African American practices effectively repressed. According to Whiteman, jazz—inexplicably—had been "given its start in life by the righteous old Dutch traders" and then "bid[ed] its time among . . . the negroes lounging in the sunshine along the New Orleans levees." And while acknowledging the fable of "Stale Bread," he asserts that jazz was, above all, a modern creation, a "great American noise" erupting from "the premonitory bubblings of the melting pot." In Whiteman's telling, the "primitive African swing" of Negro music morphed into "the broken crashing rhythm of Whitman's poetry, the gigantic steel and stone of the skyscrapers." Jazz was, after all, a White invention "at once barbarous and sophisticated—the wilderness tamed to the ballroom . . . [through which] the whole tempo of the country was speeded up, . . . [its populace] liv[ing] harder and faster than ever before." Jazz embodied White America, revealing "our passionate desire to have it—a desire never satisfied. That is the thing expressed by that wail," he continued, "that longing, that pain, all the surface clamor and rhythm and energy of jazz." Among the consumables was the sound of Blackness itself. For if, as Whiteman put it, jazz owed some of its roots to the formerly enslaved, the connection was merely circumstantial. After all, "the Negroes themselves knew no more of jazz than their masters."[47]

What African Americans did provide to their detriment was an alienable, natural resource derived from Negro labor—"their gift to an alien posterity"—which White musicians transformed into "a racy, idiomatic, flexible American language all our own, suited to expressing the American character." Jazz arose, Whiteman contended, as a modern music with conquering power, expressing a "savage . . . joy in being alive" and bringing forth a liberating sensation from "the soul of America." Recalling Gilbert Seldes, moreover, Whiteman subscribed to the opinion that jazz was a counterforce to the "clanging, banging, terrific rhythm" of American civilization, a "noise" unto itself that would defend against a "machine civilization . . . [which] crush[es] all the normal impulses of human beings." The negative social affliction that is "a particularly jazz darky player, named . . . 'Jas' . . . was the source of the peppy little word that has now gone all over the world," giving rise to a new aesthetic positivity, fashioned in the image of an imperial cosmopolitanism. In its grand stagings, "jazz was beginning a new movement in the world's art of music" that would rival the status of European forms.[48]

Read today, Whiteman's perceptions and prognostications strain credulity, seeming as remarkable in their bombastic self-assuredness as in the joyful ease by which they affirmed White supremacist and imperialist sentiments. The change in how we interpret Whiteman is a consequence of the remarkable turns in the order of music value once the fetishized language of Black vernacularity overtook the organization of popular style. By the early 1930s, with the rise of swing, Negro jazz, together with its celebratory criticism, would remake popular music, its innovations directing style development for the next thirty years. Yet even at the time of the book's publication, in 1926, the views put forward in Jazz were already being questioned by cultural critics and listeners advocating the appeal of African American genres of blues and hot jazz, as sounding practices issued in their names acquired broad notice through live performances, commercial recordings, and national radio broadcasts. Although still mainly occupying the margins of commercial entertainment, newly developing Black sound formations in their diversity were gaining unprecedented attention from audiences across the color line.

There might be a temptation, therefore, to follow a tendency still lingering in jazz studies and set aside Whiteman after first acknowledging his importance in the development of the jazz orchestra. There is no doubt that Whiteman, along with his arranger, Ferde Grofé, introduced approaches that would become central to swing orchestra arrangements, such as the development of melodic material through the interplay of instrumental sections, the back-and-forth movements sometimes mimicking African American call-response singing.[49] But Whiteman's influence far exceeds those technical advances. In fact, the advances themselves were part and parcel of his greater role as the chief catalyst of the new jazz economy. In a perceptive essay, Gerald Early cogently observes that Whiteman's influence is best understood in its success at legitimizing Black-derived practices among White middle-class audiences, inadvertently enabling the eventual embrace of Black music as a true form of American expression. One might take this argument even farther to suggest that Whiteman did not simply broaden popular taste; his musical and commercial pursuits thoroughly reorganized the institutional structures and frameworks of music knowledge supporting the genre's development. If there were a pivotal moment, it was Whiteman's Aeolian Hall concert in 1924, "An Experiment in Modern

Music," which premiered George Gershwin's *Rhapsody in Blue* and presaged in the form of a musical documentary the primitive-to-modern civilizing rhetoric featured in his 1926 book, *Jazz*. With those interventions came the heightened importance of racially enlivened sound in its modern metamorphosis, mediated through the playing of White jazz orchestras. Audible presences of the Black body newly coalesced as a critical component of all popular music directly or vaguely associated with "jazz," whether performed by White or Black musicians.[50]

Whiteman's musical impact, then, was inextricably connected to his presence within the greater entertainment economy. Through his efforts as a bandleader, a recording artist, and an employer of hundreds of workers—from the musicians disseminating the Whiteman brand in multiple, "satellite bands" to the range of nonmusician laborers supporting his concerts and record productions—he played a central role in the broad rationalization of jazz as a business institution, reshaping its mode of production and dissemination, together with its sensible comprehension by musicians and consumers.[51] With the growth of his international stature as the worldly "King of Jazz," moreover—by 1922, his Victor discs were widely available in record shops from Buenos Aires to Nyasaland (Malawi), Manila to Bombay (Mumbai)—Whiteman amplified the range of the jazz genre's effect, which inadvertently extended the global reach of "the Negro" and, by turns, Black music's importance to popular valuation. What seemed vaguely racial and rhythmically enlivened, despite its highly orchestrated appearance, offered in its prolific expanse a blueprint of how Black innovation and consumer expectations would develop. In its global circulation, this phantom presence of Blackness complicated the international image of the United States: "The meaning of the nation itself is both questioned and redefined through the outreach of empire."[52]

Whatever their intention, Whiteman's economic strategies and implementations were profound in the way they recalibrated the social and sonic logics of all that would be named "jazz." By perpetuating disembodied figurations signifying Blackness, his orchestras called attention to what appeared racial in popular music, upholding their translations of Negro sound as a performance model for aspiring musician-professionals. Significantly, Whiteman's musical generation of phantom racial presences so thoroughly incorporated Black sound it established the means for a discernible modern musical Blackness to be constituted and identified. What was "hot" or "commercial," "jazz" or "not-jazz" would later emerge out of the dynamic shifts in music knowledge in the wake of his extraordinary popularity. Rather than introducing White American audiences to qualities of "real jazz"—an anachronistic classification that Early, in his turn to the authority of Gunther Schuller, appears to embrace—Whiteman advanced fabrications of racially enlivened sound as he increased the aesthetic power of their fantastic presence in rationalized metropolitan markets. To recall Mark Goble's formulation (cf. chapter 5), race and reason were dialectically bound in the making of modern aesthetic sensibilities. Through his popularizing efforts—leading to the redesign of the entertainment industry's valuation to favor African American performance—Whiteman's music contributed to the making of a jazz world in which he would no longer be a part. His ambivalent posture explains how in 1936, as Early acknowledges, Duke Ellington, expressing an opinion more common to the prior decade, could still speak admiringly of Whiteman's orchestral sound even when his authority had faded.[53]

With Whiteman, early jazz locates its personification as a capitalized form: the "King" of a racially enlivened music whose imperial reach across the expanse of global entertainment capitalism had the consequence of reorganizing nearly every facet of the jazz economy, from its composition and performance—influencing domestic society bands such as those led by Vincent Lopez and Sam Lanin, together with touring ensembles populated by an international labor force running the circuits of Latin America and Asia—to its circulation via the technologies of mass production.[54] And because these rationalizing processes, in following the expansion of capital, were by nature incorporating and expropriative, they also profoundly affected the commercial production of Negro jazz. By the early 1920s, as Whiteman's business enterprise was already profoundly altering popular music and culture—setting into motion dominating narratives of "memory thing"—the innovations introduced by African American musicians were also entering directly into the commercial economy, fueling sensations of aliveness central to the commercial genre's appeal.

ENLIVENED CAPITAL: COALESCENCES OF NEGRO JAZZ

As jazz was rapidly advancing as the dominant genre in international entertainment, it was also redirecting into Black worlds sonic material and aesthetic attitudes augmented by its passage through the circuits of commercial markets. Jazz, of course, had never really left the sound fields of African American culture, even if many Black musicians were wary of the title given to their instrumental music. The term *jazz*—together with other epithets such as "jazbo," "hokum," "novelty music," and "plantation music," or even the commercialized vernacular labels "blues" and "hot ragtime"—was not about to distract them from the power of a dynamic living legacy that inspired their creativity. Yet no matter how enduring that legacy was, Black relations to the past—along with notions of time and temporality—were also changing in ways consistent with material shifts in the social and economic conditions in popular culture. With the public emergence of Black-performed "Negro jazz" around 1919, these changes would initiate over the course of the ensuing decade a seismic shift in the orders of music knowledge and ownership, the transformations all part of the move toward the music's fourth metamorphosis as part of the world of hypercapitalized pop.[55]

A formative influence affecting the evolution of Negro jazz was the attention it was beginning to get from White youth. As White bands styled after the Original Dixieland Jazz Band and symphonic jazz orchestras overwhelmed the popular music industry, a new generation of White listeners and dancers grew curious about how African Americans played jazz. To some extent, these opportunities were limited to the most economically disadvantaged areas, where Black and White poor intermixed; those of high station tended to remain aloof. Discussing the state of things when he first broke into the New York jazz scene in the 1920s, Benny Carter recalled, "The 'downtown' white world was largely unavailable to us." Yet there were also times when jobs appeared, which many Black musicians welcomed because it typically meant they would earn more. "Better pay for our sort of work," Carter continued, also "provided more opportunities in shows": playing before White audiences was a first step toward finding work in the larger commercial markets. These initial contacts were instrumental in changing the taste parameters of Black musicians as they sought to satisfy new market demands. The changes not only fostered a greater Black presence in jazz but ultimately transformed the overall character of a thoroughly capitalized, popular music.[56]

It is for these reasons that what New York's Black syncopated orchestras typically performed sounded a lot like the music White bands and Broadway ensembles were playing. Black orchestras needed to stay close to the aesthetic norms set by White jazz orchestras, which typically featured popular favorites and show tunes, set within metric orders and rhythmic practices stemming from ragtime and marching bands. Hot playing, if it appeared at all in the early part of the decade, was attenuated, resembling something akin to Henry Busse's "Hot Lips" as it was recorded by White ensembles in 1922. As Mark Tucker and Travis Jackson suggest, "in some ways," the early recordings by James Reese Europe, Ford Dabney, Tim Brymn, Leroy Smith, and other Black syncopated orchestra leaders "seem closer in sound and spirit to the bands of John Philip Sousa and Arthur Pryor or to theater pit orchestras and polite society dance orchestras than to the convention-flouting strain of jazz that characterized the Roaring Twenties." In discussing the Black bands working the circuits of the South, Midwest, and West, moreover, James Lincoln Collier concurs, contending that they were "no different from [those of] the thousands of [White] dance bands that were springing up across the USA in response to the vogue for social dancing."[57]

The syncopated character of ragtime had become so thoroughly incorporated into popular music that it seemed to most White listeners, if not completely deracinated, then inherent to the character of America's sonic makeup. Yet there are indications that Black orchestras attempted to assert their claim on the distinctive features of ragtime by performing in ways associated with the Black South, particularly after the huge commercial success of "Crazy Blues" by Mamie Smith and her Jazz Hounds (1920). With Black consumers purchasing Smith's record by the many thousands—"You couldn't walk down the street in a colored neighborhood and not hear that record," Alberta Hunter recalled—Black orchestras capitalized on its popularity, employing vaudeville-styled blues effects that appealed to listeners across racial category.[58] "Bugle Call Blues," for example, recorded by Ford Dabney's Syncopated Orchestra in 1922, features energetic syncopation, brass growls, and high-register woodwind flourishes (employing pinched reed embouchure and overblowing) presented as a twelve-bar blues—replete with trumpet calls of "Reveille." Another was the Sam Wooding Orchestra's "I've Got to Cool My Puppies Now" (1922), a staid, moderate-tempo instrumental performance accompanying an inspired delivery by the popular blues singer Lucille Hegamin.[59] Perhaps the fifty- and seventy-piece Black Devil orchestras led by Lieut. J. Tim Brymn (known popularly as "Mr. Jazz"), which worked regularly at hotel ballrooms and other New York–area venues from 1919 to 1921, came closest to introducing blues-inspired playing to White dancers. If Black ensembles were celebrating African American presence, though, they also remained quick to conform to standard. Orchestras were responding not only to Mamie Smith's commercial success but also to that of Paul Whiteman, whose 1920 recording

"Wang Wang Blues" featured performance practices common to the early Black ensemble playing.[60]

In pursuit of regular work, Black bands in the early to mid-1920s toured the nation, presenting repertoires that were flexible enough to accommodate racially diverse audiences. Much of the time, they stayed close to the stock arrangements and formulas of popular song, while sometimes, when called on to do so, they expanded their offerings to include other kinds of music for social dancing. In Kansas City, where orchestras performed rough-and-ready, blues-inspired romps for both Black and White audiences, they also presented over the course of an evening styles ranging from waltzes to polkas, fox-trots to schottisches. Buster Smith, who worked as an alto saxophonist and arranger for the Blue Devils, recalled that "we played waltzes and sweet music up in Saginaw [Michigan] for people up there. Had some tunes sounded like Guy Lombardo. Even in South Dakota they liked sweet music and we had to play a lot of that. I had to write a whole repertoire of sweet music to go along with it." In Dallas, meanwhile, despite its rich traditions of boogie-woogie, barrelhouse, and ragtime piano, Alphonso Trent's orchestra, which had a long run at the Adolphus, a fashionable White hotel, performed high-precision society music by hiring the best (and best-paid) musicians in the region. Even in Chicago, with its large population of African American migrants, bands needed to be flexible. King Oliver, for example, while best known for bringing New Orleans–style jazz to the North, had learned to play to White tastes as early as 1917. His Creole Jazz Band could move easily from blues and jazz to popular tunes and the songs of Irish immigrants, and it is likely that he occasionally played these repertoires in Black clubs. Although "colored people," as Clarence Williams remembers, "would form a line twice around the block when the latest record of Bessie or Ma or Clara or Mamie come in," Black listeners were no monolith. As participants in the new commercial market, they commonly enjoyed music that broke from stereotype. As a case in point, Russell Sanjek, the future BMI executive, described how when making his collecting treks to Harlem in the 1930s he was surprised to discover that Black families owned more records by Guy Lombardo than by Fletcher Henderson.[61]

Yet despite these complexities regarding taste preferences, Black orchestras learned to accommodate White Americans' fantastical imaginings about Black people by employing playing techniques that heightened the strangeness associated with the Negro sound. By the middle of the decade, bands typically featured in their performances allusions to the plantation: sounding "modern" meant projecting in the present performance practices evocative of the southern past. If, as Thomas Brothers observes, jazz had been "surrounded by plantation imagery as soon as it left New Orleans," some leading New York establishments wanted to make the association explicit, encouraging the development of fast-action arrangements, hot playing, and solo improvisation. New showcases adopting names suggestive of the plantation myth—the Cotton Club, the Plantation Café, Club Alabam, the Kentucky Club—provided forums for orchestras that brought to life colorful depictions of the folkloric cast in the newness of Negro jazz.[62]

It was around this time, in 1924, that Henderson, while appearing downtown at the Roseland Ballroom, hired Louis Armstrong to modernize his orchestra's sound. Armstrong's relaxed, hot playing spoke to the moment: forwarding-looking in its virtuosity, it was also evocative of New Orleans's already mythical "Storyville." Although Armstrong's skills as an improviser were what got him hired, it was his willingness to perform a minstrel-style stand-up act as the Black preacher "Reverend Satchelmouth" that probably won over many audiences. Ellington pursued a similar approach at the Kentucky Club, hiring, among others, the South Carolina trumpeter Bubber Miley, whose muting techniques—developed after hearing King Oliver in Chicago—gave new character to the band's hot sound in its performance of another vaudevillian-styled preacher skit, where Miley delivered a "sermon" on his horn.[63] Public enthusiasm about hot jazz—affirming racist fantasies captured, for example, in Carl Van Vechten's novel *Nigger Heaven* (1926)—eventually inspired Paul Whiteman to hire White musicians familiar with hot performance practices, bringing into his orchestra, among others, the trumpeter Bix Beiderbecke in 1927.

It might be tempting to uphold hot playing and improvisation as the gold standard of jazz authenticity, to think of the blues and plantation fashions as an inadvertent exposure of real Black music. If so, these features became the standard because of the power of capital, not despite it: racial fantasy enabled Black musicians to remake their sonic past as part of their transactional negotiations in public markets. In all their professional actions, these players were equally motivated by market forces: locating a viable path into the music business was the bottom line. Their turn to hot playing may have offered them an opportunity to embrace and rework what was musically familiar, but it was its commercial appeal that perpetuated the practice. Playing hot—that is, embracing techniques associated with the Black past—had developed as a response to commercial fashion, providing the key means of sounding modern: a commercially conceived "Jazz Age" depended on a back-leaning enlivened sound to complete what seemed missing in a world where Blackness was both fundamental and abject.

In its increasing availability, Negro jazz was a value added, a critical supplement that fulfilled the racial composition of a White-dominant nation. And so, from the mid-1920s, African American ensembles from the most famous to middle liners—among them, the Charlie Johnson Orchestra, the Savoy Bearcats, the Cotton Club Orchestra, the Blue Ribbon Syncopators—produced a bounty of recordings featuring hot sounding practices. Works taking names such as "Hotter Than That," "Hot Bones and Rice," "Hot Notes," "Hot Stuff," and "Hot Strut" grew conspicuous in the White and black-and-tan nightclub scene, their expressions of aliveness—stop time, blues inflections, barrel-house piano, vaudeville effects, a hard-driving groove—becoming regularly featured live and on record.[64]

All this was occurring, interestingly enough, even though many African American musicians preferred playing society music. A sizable number of them were drawn to the orchestral style popularized by Whiteman and, indeed, played an important role in its development. It suited them as it shaped their tastes. Although deeply invested in the relation of aesthetics and racial politics, Will Marion Cook and James Reese Europe, for example, did not equate modern racialized notions of vernacularity with their loftiest aesthetic aspirations. (Hurston's "Characteristics of Negro Expression" would identify a new generation of thought.) Having developed professionally during the era of ragtime and early African American theater—a time before blues vernacularity had impacted popular tastes—they were comfortable leading society orchestras whose principal musical referents to southern music appeared in the form of light syncopation and a steady, solid beat. Similarly, although Elmer Snowden, the first leader of the Washingtonians, moved to New York in order to take work playing on blues recordings, he also struggled with the new fashion for hot playing, thinking it undignified. Ultimately, Snowden's commitment to society music contributed to his expulsion by band members, including Duke Ellington, who, due to aesthetic preference and sensitivity to changing market trends, were willing to exploit racial stereotypes for their own economic gain. Recast as a hot orchestra, the ensemble fashioned a repertoire and performance approach appealing to racial stereotype. In one stage routine, for example—at a time when Black players in New York, otherwise confronted with the challenges of symphonic jazz, were actively developing their reading skills—they performed without sheet music to advance the perception that theirs was a spontaneous outpouring from the natural order. Whether on stage or in the recording studio, playing hot and bluesy became a prerequisite. According to an Ellington band member, the alto saxophonist Otto Hardwick, "The field of recording was quite limited. . . . If you didn't play the blues, there was no room for you."[65]

Put simply, most Black jazz bands crafted approaches that enabled them to stay in business. As Ellington described the situation, "We weren't out to change the world musically. We [just] wanted to make a living and get as much self-satisfaction out of work as we could."[66] Black musicians did not have the luxury to imagine the creation of absolute forms of art: getting work and getting musical satisfaction were one in the same. If they were to claim a stake in the entertainment industry, they would need to play to market demands, and many were willing to do so. As Hsio Wen Shih observed, a significant number of the first Black jazz players were "by birth or by choice, . . . member[s] of the rising Negro middle class," having received formal musical training as adolescents and several—notably, Tim Byrmn, Fletcher Henderson, Don Redman, Joe Steele, Coleman Hawkins, Erskine Tate, Booker Washington, and Johnny Dunn, among others—having gone to college. Acquiring musical knowledge to get ahead was consistent with their aspirations. Like any group of artisans, they honed their skills to work professionally. "The nature of the job," writes Scott DeVeaux, "pushed every band, black or white, in the direction of an eclectic musical policy. Successful black bands performed all kinds of music, hot and square, as well as specialized accompaniments for theatrical productions. Those that didn't had to learn."[67]

The emergence of Negro jazz produced a swell of new bands and with it the rise of a powerful labor force, unprecedented in size and scope, populated by musicians representing diverse regions and backgrounds. The corresponding need for new labor to drive jazz entertainment initiated a remarkable social transformation that mobilized hundreds of performers, many of them making consequential and sometimes dramatic changes in their life paths. Typically, the search for work meant leaving their homes. Black jazz musicians followed the same path as other African American laborers, migrating to major cities, particularly in the North. To this extent, the musicians were partners in the development of a new urban working class, human components within a huge body of labor essential to industrial production. Yet whereas unskilled, manual laborers endured long shifts at steel mills, in stockyards, or on assembly lines, with others bussing tables or working as domestics for White families, Black musicians were responsible for tempering the burden of those challenges, providing sustenance in the form of a night's entertainment in the places where Black people congregated.

Despite these parallels with conventional work patterns, though, Black music labor traced its own trajectory, as musicians followed the movements of orchestras. Typically, this meant the continuing practice of spending long stretches of time on the road. Because the larger economy of jazz "developed in the dances," as Eddie Barefield observed, where "everybody danced [in] every little town and little place," most musicians were nearly always on tour, whether taking short stints or traveling for weeks with bands until jobs ran out. In the Midwest and across the South, territory bands, both White and Black, roamed regions from Texas to North Dakota, Georgia to Arkansas, playing at town halls and ballroom events. Those aspiring to success in the major hubs of urban entertainment were drawn to the larger metropolitan centers, while others fell in with vaudeville troupes, circuses, and colored minstrelsy. If employment in one context collapsed, players moved to another. Count Basie, a New Jersey native who aspired to a career in show business—"[it] was something that I wanted to be a part of ever since I was a little kid"—enjoyed his time in vaudeville, which, until he joined the Bennie Moten Orchestra, included work accompanying the blues singer Gonzelle White. Other players, among them Buster Bailey, Bubber Miley, and Garvin Bushell, together with college-educated musicians (including Johnny Dunn and Coleman Hawkins) also spent time on the blues circuit as members of Mamie Smith's Jazz Hounds. These various displacements of the musician workforce had the effect of further redistributing music knowledge, transforming Black music from an assortment of local styles into a massive network of intersecting practices. For popular musicians of every kind, "the circuits," Nicholas Gebhardt writes, "were inseparable from the way performers were coming to understand the meaning of artistic success." As Bushell put it, "Your social value was set according to your rating in show business."[68]

Black musicians had always known this measure. Playing music for anything other than one's own pleasure was transactional: it involved an exchange of performance for money. To complete the transaction, the performance needed to satisfy those who paid for it. This fundamental economic principle is why the African American instrumentalists assembling loosely as part of the community named "jazz" learned to be flexible about their work choices. No matter their social background or education, they took jobs where they could get them, which sometimes meant spending time on the colored entertainment circuits. "The role of black theatre, tented touring shows, circus sideshows, and vaudeville," Mark Berresford writes, "played a much greater part in the early development of jazz than has been acknowledged." For a time, many jazz historians overlooked these venues because their lowly status contradicted efforts to elevate the music's aesthetic value. It was only with widened attention to the early history of Black popular music that scholars began to recognize how influential the shows were.[69] Touring groups, together with the loose networks of colored showcases (most notably, those organized by the Theatre Owners' Booking Association), not only provided a critical forum for the development of Black musician labor but also enacted a redistribution of another kind: they extended the sensible orientation of southern Black entertainment into the urban North. Vaudeville hilarity and the plantation myth that White jazz lovers coveted moved in step; in their commitment to racial fantasy, they were never far apart.

"When I began my work," Ellington recalled, "jazz was a stunt." One of his first jobs when arriving in New York was to accompany Wilbur Sweatman—a talented vaudeville player known for his ability to play three clarinets at once—for a series of performances at Harlem's Lafayette Theater. In vaudeville, such displays of excess stood as an aesthetic hallmark. In addition to the musical histrionics, spectators might encounter over the course of a show any number of performance acts, from comic routines and acrobatics to jugglers, dramatic sketches, burlesques, and animal stunts. Musicians sometimes took part in the theatrics. When recalling his work with Gonzelle White, for example, Basie described the novel way the drummer Freddy Crump (aka "Rastus the Drummer") took a curtain call. After a showy stage act, "throwing his sticks in the air . . . without losing a beat . . . he used to come dancing back in from the wings and hit the drum as he slid into a split. He used to grab the curtain and ride up with it, bowing and waving at the audience applauding."[70] The mixture of hokum, coarse humor, clownish histrionics, and sexual innuendo taking place over the course of a show was accompanied by what Lawrence Gushee calls "musical hokum—glisses, cackles, slaptongue, and flutter tongue": performance practices featured by the ODJB and early jazz bands. These techniques brought into being a musical language of transgressive play that energized stunts and dance performances and carried blues acts featuring Bessie Smith, Sara Martin, Ma Rainey, and others. As they developed out of colored minstrelsy, the touring vaudeville and circus shows provided the primary place where a league of African American musicians—Ellington, Basie, Cricket Smith, Fats Waller, Joe Smith, J. Paul Wyer, Eddie Durham, and several others—gained formative experience playing professionally. While many musicians eventually moved on to take different musical challenges, others stayed with the tours, knowing what they could expect performing on the chitlin' circuit.[71]

Colored vaudeville and other Black traveling shows represented what Gebhardt describes as "a new form of life," its aliveness developing out of performers' movements within the greater "structure of the circuits" organizing show business. For Gebhardt, the interplay of musicians and economic structures was not only dialectical but also ontological. What constituted the performing subject in the creation of animated sound corresponded to the circuits themselves, whose rapid, incessant flows according to the conditions of capital guided musicians' actions while also establishing a distinctive temporal orientation in their stage shows. Vaudeville performances, as one early producer described them, moved according to an aesthetic of "no waits. Everything must run with unbroken stride. . . . The tempo of the show must be maintained." This sensation of "continuous vaudeville," Gebhardt argues, involving "a highly self-conscious and critical relationship between artist and audience . . . [was] never fixed, . . . but [was] always under review." The new forms of life generated by vaudeville performances were themselves improvised: while adhering to a set of constraints, they came about as the actors and musicians played along. And in their exposure of ontological qualities relating to their own labor practices, they conveyed opportunities for aesthetic experiences suggesting larger truths.[72]

Gebhardt's study considers the whole of vaudeville as it emerged on the American stage. But his insights into the ontological nature of social practices carry particular importance regarding Black touring acts, where enlivened sounding practices brought into being new coalescences of double form. The shows sensationalized the animated properties of Black performances, underlying their value as something both less than and greater than Music. Colored vaudeville's spontaneous presentations seemed to flow from the racialized bodies of Negro players, to be, as one writer put it, "born in the bone."[73] The originality of Black vaudeville lay in the way newly conceived sound formations, rich and abundant in improvisational skill, introduced into the sensible arena forms of Black embodied presence. These formations revealed likenesses to the craft of the colored minstrel Ike Simond and the blues ventriloquist John W. F. "Johnnie"

Woods, yet they were also different in their material relation to the economies driving Black music production in the 1920s. They identify the primary means by which Black pasts, linked to the lives of the enslaved, introduced contrapuntal sensibilities and temporalities into the modern era.

The close relationship between vaudeville and Negro jazz explains why jazz often seemed dubious to the nation's middle classes and cultural elites, including many of those associated with the Harlem Renaissance. Their alignment supplied further evidence of Negro degeneracy, even as it reinforced the belief that the myth of Black people's natural musicality was real. Staged in humble venues often featuring musicians who were unabashed about performing improvised music as part of comedic acts—an example immortalized in the Black Atlantic mashup "King of the Zulus" (1926), where a Jamaican voice interrupts the Hot Five's studio performance to inquire about chitlins—Negro jazz playfully mocked conventions typically associated with respectable entertainment. Regardless of the talent necessary to produce it, a music going by titles such as "Goofer Dust," "Go 'Long Mule," "Heebie Jeebies," and "Georgia Grind" seemed to lack the seriousness expected of art forms. The Black literati was divided: while jazz was featured in Alain Locke's celebrated volume, *The New Negro* (1925), it was also subjected to critique by Du Bois and others. As Sieglinde Lemke shows, moreover, many self-respecting African Americans, including writers for the Black press, kept their distance from jazz because of its association with White slumming. Whatever the reasons, "our worlds were far apart," Benny Carter recalled when describing his relationship with the artists and intellectuals of Black Manhattan. "We sensed that black cultural as well as moral leaders looked down on our music as undignified." As Cab Calloway summarized it, "Those of us in the music and entertainment business were vaguely aware that something exciting was happening, but we weren't directly involved."[74]

ANIMATED ENVIRONMENTS OF DISSENSUS MUSIC

Still working mainly on the borders of the new business of jazz entertainment, most Black musicians found reliable employment in the surfeit of clubs and theaters that opened their doors in African American neighborhoods during the 1920s. While enduring the vexing uncertainties of life in Jim Crow America, they could still count on something unprecedented:

ready audiences drawn from the many thousands of Black residents who clustered in the nation's metropolises, the lion's share of them eager to hear jazz played in city nightspots.[75] We've already considered how in the 1910s the African American migrations inspired the development of Black Manhattan's music culture, providing a multitude of musicians with the chance to perform professionally. Five or ten years later, these same communities had grown and job opportunities with them. New York remained the standout, with its interracial black and tans, venues dedicated to Black audiences, and after-hours musicians' joints supporting late-night sessions.[76] But similar developments in club culture took place in any number of cities and towns across the nation. As Barry Kernfeld demonstrates in his scrupulously prepared overview of jazz nightclubs, Black players and singers in the 1920s were performing nearly everywhere: in Philadelphia and Asbury Park, down in Baltimore and Atlanta, and up in Boston and Buffalo. They commonly appeared in Black clubs in Detroit, Chicago, St. Louis, Kansas City, and Tulsa, and could be heard routinely in New Orleans and Dallas. Performers and singers who traveled to the West Coast often found good work entertaining patrons in nightspots from Los Angeles to San Francisco. Across the United States, the venues offered a familiar forum for new Black urban populations to congregate, to join musicians in experiencing a sound world animated with living presence.[77]

Spirited collaboration and conviviality did not, however, quiet the competition driving innovation among Black jazz players. Getting jobs at the best clubs was challenging, and even when a musician earned a place in a house band or touring orchestra, the situation could end at a moment's notice. Trumpeter Rex Stewart described the hiring process this way: "The usual method of getting a job then," he recalled, "was to descend upon a joint en masse and, one by one, get up on the bandstand and outblow the occupants until you got the crowd with you." The method proved effective. "The boss never failed to ask you if you wanted to work. When the originally employed musicians saw this happening, they knew that was their last night. This was the scene all around town . . . in the days before the musicians' union accepted Negro players." Count Basie similarly recounted his own strategy of securing a spot in a band. Sizing things up at a Harlem club, "I made my move. . . . I was pretty certain I could take the piano player without any trouble at all," his prowess as a performer enhanced by vaudeville stunts: "Throwing my hands up in the air and flashing my fingers . . . without missing a beat." But some players remembered the experience differently. Benny Carter—whose formidable playing skills probably affected his perception—described the Harlem club scene as something akin to a brotherhood of artisans working together to invent a common language. This included inviting the better White players to come to Harlem and sit in after working downtown. "We welcomed them and enjoyed the jamming. . . . We learned from each other."[78]

Clubs proliferated as centers of musical learning, vortexes of knowledge production where players, dancers, and listeners assembled, all participants in the remaking of popular music's sensory environment. Performances could be transformative, the musicians' creative actions, like those of Rancière's nighttime writer-laborers, "alter[ing] the sphere of appearances according to which workers inhabit a specific time and space."[79] As Black musicians responded to the demands of their working situations, so did their playing give the spaces a changed feel. The aesthetic originality of jazz practice captured the imagination of the new communities of migrants, as it impacted the wider sphere of entertainment. These racially affirmative expressions helped to make comprehensible the character of modern life, supplying sound formations so powerful, so compelling, they suggested what Rancière calls "fiction": a social script that rewrites and restructures ways of knowing. "Fiction," he argues, is "not a term that designates the imaginary as opposed to the real; it involves the re-framing of the 'real,' or the framing of a dissensus."[80] The sound formations produced by the constellation of Black bands moving about the greater landscape of US towns and cities supplied a dissensual force, another way of knowing in contrast to the commercialized conventions of public life. These sonic worlds reaffirmed Black music's role as a critical power within popular culture, affecting how the modern would be understood.

The affective coherences of Black jazz performances that reimagined popular sound in the 1920s were not openly defiant acts as one might characterize other strains of modernism. Dissensus moved more subtly, seditiously, operating within market constraints and the field of labor on which musicians depended. By and large, performances were patterned flexibly according to the preferences of clientele, satisfying tastes for orchestral blues and the hot arrangement of pop tunes while supporting the enduring interest in symphonic jazz. Within these basic parameters, Black orchestras advanced their music, revising stock arrangements in ways that brought greater variety and complexity to formal design. The vaudeville-based strategy of "no-wait" drove many of these changes, as arrangers employed a range of techniques—quick sectional shifts, close harmonizations, interplay between instrumental groups, moments featuring striking timbral innovations—that gave performances greater levity and spirit. Developments in ensemble arranging, moreover, accommodated the heightened emphasis on instrumental breaks and extended improvisations, which, by the mid-1920s, had shifted Black jazz away from New Orleans–based melodic paraphrase toward solos displaying the inventiveness of individual instrumentalists. The emergence of "improvisers thinking compositionally," as James Dapogny and Dave Jones put it, changed the conceptualization of form as musicians worked to integrate the personalities of the players into the overall shape of the performance.[81] In New York, which, by this time, had been established as the primary hub of innovation, afterhours sessions were particularly important in forging new directions in solo improvisation. The frequent "chopping" or "cutting contests"—the metaphor ironically evocative of life-and-death struggle—developed into veritable laboratories of competitive experiment where the sonic material of Black music newly coalesced as it challenged the authority of symphonic jazz as the aesthetic center of pop.

Whether working principally as bandleaders, arrangers, ensemble members, or frontline soloists, the professional labor force presenting "Negro jazz" directed its collective attention to new ways of thinking musically. Black musicians joined as partners in the production process, strategizing to create forms that were unlike any previously known. Scholars of early jazz have examined how Black orchestras and instrumentalists expanded the sonic vocabulary of jazz, affirming a developmentalist perspective consistent with conventional musicological histories of style. Yet what motivated these performers was something more than a strictly musical conception of form as it is commonly understood in European-centered musical thought. If the "insatiable search for new sounds" was part of a developing modernist tendency among the music's chief "architect[s]," it was also an expression of a dissensual aesthetic disposition that located value in the possession of racially enlivened music. Although most musicians by this time had adopted a pragmatic view consistent with their roles as laborers working in a competitive market, they also sustained an agonistic relation to their own economic and social containments. These racist constraints by White power motivated the musicians' dissensual posture, inspiring the invention of new Black sonic material that appeared ontologically ambiguous, uncanny, the bodies of their makers seeming alive in the sound.[82]

Sensations of aliveness developed according to the myth of the natural musician, of players who were audible by nature. Such thinking, as we have repeatedly seen, had oriented the experience of Black music since the slave era, the myth subsequently inspiring the scabrous aesthetics of musician itinerants, the extravagances of ragtime and theater players, and the minstrelized acts of vaudeville. Centering musical invention were the perceived peculiarities of Black embodied sound, founded on an ideology that was continually reinforced in everyday conversation and reaffirmed by the performers' strange acts: the hokum of circuses, vaudeville, blues. In the development of the Negro jazz orchestra, enlivened sounding practices amassed as a dynamically changing battery of technique. The accumulation fostered the expansion of sonic material that instrumentalists put to practical advantage in the development of their extraordinary inventions. At the fore was the musical demonstration of racialized presence: of forcefully bringing one's personality into the character of sound. By personalizing one's instrumental approach—featuring playing techniques and improvising skills in the making of ensemble performances—bands brought into being forms that inspired the sensations of grand enlivened presences. The coherences of racialized Black sound introduced into exchange were inextricably bound to the musicians' group sense of ownership as they disturbed common ways of musical knowing. Negro jazz created "a new fabric of common experience . . . a new dramaturgy of the sensible" bound to the myth of the audible Black body.[83] These aural coherences animated by racialized being readjusted the character of listening, performing a kind of Black magic that rewrote fictions of the real, redistributing the mise-en-scène of the musical space. The many *spaces* presenting Negro jazz turned into affectively energized, phenomenal *places*, cast in the sonic "image" of the animated Black performer.[84]

Among the most sought-after venues was the Roseland Ballroom, arguably the top dance floor in midtown Manhattan, drawing Whites-only crowds. Despite its racial code, Roseland provides a particularly useful demonstration of Black music as a counterhistorical force in its relation to capital, where Negro jazz advances as a transformative aesthetic in the commercial marketplace. For seven months a year (October to May), from 1924 to 1931, the ballroom featured one of New York's leading African American orchestras, headed by Fletcher Henderson, the fair-skinned, college-educated pianist whose masterful insights into big band arranging and performance would later set the groundwork for Benny Goodman's commercial coronation as "The King of Swing." For a time, Henderson's orchestra enjoyed great success. Working against the odds, the band leader deftly navigated his way within the White world of musical entertainment, supported by some of the nation's strongest African American musi-cians.[85] With the critical support of his arranger, the West Virginia–born, college-educated clarinetist and saxophonist Don Redman, and featured soloists, trumpeter Louis Armstrong (b. New Orleans) and saxophonist Coleman Hawkins (b. St. Joseph, Missouri), Henderson and his orchestra advanced an utterly spectacular body of sound that entertained wide audi-ences, the live performances reconceived in the studio for the production of a seminal body of race records.

The studio productions—which mark the beginning of Negro jazz as a sound object—give insight into how Henderson and his orchestra enacted form by tapping into the spirit of aliveness driving a legacy of Black sound production. In its sheer volume and intensity, the ensemble effected the sensation of vigorous movement, it being, after all, a jazz dance band. Such commitment to insistent beat was, of course, now characteristic of virtually all Negro jazz orchestras, from the leading New York bands—the Ellington Orchestra, the Savoy Bearcats, Charlie Johnson's Orchestra—to ensembles based in other major cities, from Chicago (Carroll Dickerson) to Detroit (McKinney's Cotton Pickers), to smaller locales such as Kansas City (Bennie Moten) and Buffalo (the Blue Rhythm Syncopators). But it was Henderson and Redman's particular approach to ensemble sound that draws our at-tention here. Although by no means unique in practice, the orchestra's ex-tensive recorded repertoire showcases how Black jazz at the time conveyed life, routinely enacted in nightly performances. As aggregations of sonic pleasure, the recordings impart power, humor, and grace suggestive of a great body in motion, moving prolifically through the world.

One way this is achieved is through the instrumentalists' abilities to mimic sounds of the living, both human and animal. By inventively ma-nipulating embouchure, they offered up rounds of vaudeville-inspired effects: wide, woodwind vibrato and "doo-wacka" horn muting (both on "Chicago Blues" and "Linger Awhile"); brass "wa wa" effects and "sobbing" clarinet motives that enlivened melodies (e.g., "Somebody Stole My Gal"); imitations of a neighing horse ("Forsaken Blues"); the uncanny quality of "talking" with a saxophone mouthpiece ("Go 'Long Mule"). These playful "novelty" effects common to sideshows served as coloring agents that in-troduced sonic caricatures of the living into the ensemble performance. If the assembly of practices playing out in the orchestra's arrangements sug-gested the vernacular act of signifyin', the concept alone fails to capture the affective range overwhelming listeners.[86] The recorded performances conjure a more complex humanity grounded in Black racial existence: they are better understood as audible fictions whose dexterous movements and engaging statements in tone and time effect a colored sense of place that remakes popular orders.

Ontological qualities of sound gathered strength as the ensemble participated in the production of speed and heat. On the recordings, the orchestra's center of gravity shifts from section to section according to rhythmically generated catalysts: stop-time statements; ensemble riffing to accompany solos; forceful, "Western style" back beats; conventional two-beat pulses. In "Copenhagen" (1924) and "The Stampede" (1926), the display of musical personality grows vivid, the complex of moving parts empowered by Redman's advances in arranging—working from a stock arrangement already billed "Red Hot" by its publisher—and the orchestra's greater emphasis on solo improvisation. Together, these approaches anticipated "the Velocity of Celebration" that Albert Murray attributes to 1930s Black swing.[87] The performances established each in their own way an extraordinary sense of driving momentum, suggesting a kind of oversized locomotion years before Ellington's "Daybreak Express" (1933). No wonder the band so often mimicked on its records the technological might of a speeding train, as heard on "31st Street Blues," "I'm Gonna See You," and "Chicago Blues." The titles of the Henderson repertoire tipped its hand: many of them call to mind heightened emotion and exercised bodies: "Shake Your Feet," "Hot and Anxious," "Goose Pimples," "The Stampede," "Blazin'," "Charleston Crazy," "Hop Off," "Raisin' the Roof." And as we listen, we can discern in this concatenation of three-minute fictions boisterous cacophonies of vibrant elegance paired with fleet-footed grooves and precise maneuvers of ensemble rhythm.

For the Henderson orchestra, music form developed as manifestations of the performers' enlivened presence. As Jeffrey Magee puts it in his meticulous study of the band's recorded repertoire, Henderson "composed musicians as well as music": ensemble sound grew from the musicians' ability to realize their expressive potential. In their collaborations, Henderson and Redman organized form to guide the flow of player-driven invention. Whereas arrangers of symphonic jazz tended to adhere to the constraints of popular practice, limiting their orchestrations and arranging to the "arranger's chorus" after the melodic statement, Redman shaped the entirety of works into dynamic complexes of evolving sound, a feat he achieved by swift instrumental shifts in the presentation of melody and kaleidoscopic displays of timbral color.[88] "Charleston Crazy" (1923), for example, is built as a continuing tapestry of exchange between brass and reeds, the melodic structure accentuated as it is interrupted by the stop-time quality of the Charleston rhythm. At one point, over the course of eight bars, one hears "variegated instrumentation that changes in every measure." In "I'm Gonna See You" (1927), moreover, Redman features players' distinctive instrumental voices to make up the broad stretch of form, where "the band plays twenty-three breaks in three-and-a-half choruses." "When You Walked Out Someone Else Walked Right In" presents in the second chorus a halting, staccato statement of the melodic line with brass accompanying banjoist Charlie Dixon's break, his rapid strumming mimicking softshoe, a popular dance technique, which Magee describes as a "soft-shoe stoptime."[89]

A particularly compelling demonstration of musical personality appears in the band's rendition of the popular song "Somebody Stole My Gal" (1924), where the lead players engage in a comic drama, "inserting speech-like exclamations rising to mock anger."[90] In the second chorus, as Hawkins, playing bass saxophone, takes the melody—heightening the sense of playfulness by gracing the line with occasional slap-tongue attacks—he is confronted by Redman's high-register clarinet interjections, their interplay a parody of a man and woman squabbling. And as Redman briefly takes control of the melody, a third actor, playing muted trumpet, cackles in a barnyard raillery to close out the chorus. Over time, Redman and Henderson would give players greater leeway to craft solos that when interspersed with sections of composed material heightened coloristic effect. By the turn of the decade, the orchestra had evolved into an assembly of composer-improvisers, whose virtuosic performances—as featured, for example, in the masterpiece "New King Porter Stomp" (1933)—advanced the role of solo improvisation in the design of swing form.

The innovations of Henderson and other Black orchestras, heard in clubs and playhouses across the land, suggested something akin to a musically ontologized "form of life": a vast, resonant sociality made of the senses and the sensible, which often returned to those who inhabited it profound feeling and, at moments, something suggestive of a higher truth. We first encountered such sensational feats of truth-making in the aftermath of the "spectacular revolution": the colored shows and again in the innovations of Europe and other Black composers, and yet again in the musical interiorities of New York's Tenderloin and Hell's Kitchen districts described by James P. Johnson and Duke Ellington. By the mid-1920s, what was alive in the sound of Black music suffused club environments with a qualitatively different kind of intensity, its dynamically changing feel corresponding to the music's animated character—qualities recognizable, for example, in the timbral complexity of Ellington's "Creole Rhapsody" and "East St. Louis Toodle-oo," and in the rambunctious, New Orleans–style intensity of Bennie Moten's "Goofy Dust" (1924) and "Thick Lip Stomp" (1926).

After nearly a decade accumulating value by circulating in commercial markets, jazz as it was played by African Americans seemed triumphal. For many Black people, it engendered, in the best of circumstances, ideals of what good living might be. Good living played on in the ecstatic forms of enlivened sound, proposing ways of experiencing the Black racial past anew. Through these means, the living character of the club created dissensual zones of awareness where participants could revitalize "spiritual returns" in the form of the aesthetic, reaffirming what Du Bois, in *The Gift of Black Folk*, called Black people's "sensuous receptivity to the beauty of the world."[91] At the Savoy Ballroom, Small's Paradise, and other Harlem locations—together with the complex of establishments entertaining Black and White popular-music enthusiasts across the nation—Negro jazz concretized sensuous power as a means of stimulating past-informed living moving counter to the orders of White dominance. Players and spectators alike gave shape to a culture oriented by a new musical language: a sonic vernacularity without denotative capacity, yet grounded in a people's history, of living and working hard in the cities of America.

If the new coalescences of Negro jazz did not fulfill the aesthetic ideals first imagined by cultural elites such as Du Bois and Dvořák, they ultimately had a greater impact than if they had conformed to European musical standards. Representing a creative intervention in the core principles governing commercial music, Negro jazz altered everyday norms about what music should sound like, its critical effect—as a mode of critique—not only impacting Black circles but also the greater complex of popular entertainment: it fostered the making of distinctive sensible arenas that changed how people engaged musically. Modern aesthetic experience grounded in Black vernacularity begins with the flesh, reaffirming overt feelings of embodied joy. Although Negro jazz encouraged contemplative experience, it did so through the powers of embodiment, its sonic inventions generating behavior that highlighted sexuality, emotional intimacy, and physical pleasure—qualities reaching back to the first enactments of colored minstrelsy. Preposterous embraces of racist stereotype, from vaudevillian-styled slapstick to the sexually lascivious Negro, "Struttin' with Some Barbecue" (1927), exposed, like all transgressive humor, a vulnerability that was best understood by those who shared it. Created in the marketplace amid the fashions of the plantation and, in Ellington's instance—after Josephine Baker's rise to international stardom—"jungle sound," Negro jazz introduced a musicality unlike anything before it. Its originality arose ironically from the tragic sensibility of Black existence, not in the name of sorrow but of spirited play. Over the course of a few years, it motivated a cultural shift that radically changed how being Black felt and urban Blackness sounded to the point of remaking what "popular music" might be and become.[92]

Now vying for the helm of jazz music's making, Black musicians grew ever-more confrontational and proprietary as they moved to protect a valuable property from outsiders and from each other. In contrast to Benny Carter's welcoming attitude, New Orleans performers who had settled in Chicago remained aloof toward the young White musicians who frequented their clubs, calling them "alligators" because, as Buster Bailey put it, "they were guys who came up to swallow everything we had." In New York, Elmer Snowden recalled how Whiteman sent "his spies" to the Kentucky Club to steal arranging techniques and performance practices innovated by the Washingtonians. Recalling his time playing with King Oliver, moreover, the drummer Baby Dodds lamented, "We gave those fellows the time [i.e., rhythm] in music that they have now." The situation could also be challenging when African Americans were running the show. "Playing the colored T.O.B.A. circuit," recalled Claude Hopkins—speaking about the Theater Owners' Booking Association, which, largely White-run, formalized distribution of jobs for Black musicians in the 1920s—"could have been a heck of a thing. . . . [But] Negroes [in business] didn't trust one another then, and everybody wanted to have an executive position." It was at this point that Black musicians began their enduring struggles with record producers and companies that frequently refused to pay royalties. Money tensions could even end the life of a band, or worse. James Reese Europe was murdered by his drummer, reportedly after a dispute over pay.[93]

Music ownership was about something more than money; the many struggles betrayed how value was measured not only financially but existentially. Musicians protected their playing because it was worth more to them, the elevated worth of performance affecting their own sense of self. As a possession connected to being Black, it obtained new properties as a counterhistory. Monetary value and aesthetic value accumulated in relation to the measure of race: Blackness served as a critical determination of the sound's aliveness, reformulating Bushell's yardstick for assessing a player's value in the market. Sounding practices extending from the musician's body took on new importance via economic exchange, making control of one's resources all the more challenging. If Negro jazz were an audible extension of bodies in labor, it forced the contradiction of exchanging inalienable forms to the surface.

The musical performances presented commercially as Negro jazz accumulated economic value according to the same logic of capital affecting the broad circumstance of entertainment. But despite the unprecedented extent of its subsumption, this new metamorphosis of Black music continued to follow the measure of a second economy, involving exchanges of Black-owned properties of enlivened sound. The tension between the two measures of value furthered the sense of incongruity long associated with Black music, its contradictions intensifying its temporal misalignments: what appeared publicly in the present as plantation pastimes faced the challenge of Black claims, fostering incongruent past-times that reached back and reaffirmed a dissensual sonic vernacularity. Misalignments occurred because of the music's precarious position in the market, playing the line as an incorrigible commodity: it participated in circulation while also being bound racially to its audible producers. Such continuing frictions in Negro jazz production of double value intervened in the arc of sound knowledge, driving a "re-configuration of the common experience of the sensible." It inspired listening past "memory thing."[94]

Negro jazz's aesthetic value lay precisely in its disjointed relation to conventional labor, realizing a politics consistent with Rancière's own formulation: politics develops from what people do. African American musicians were the progenitors of an aestheticized kind of labor that was *socially necessary* to a Black-centered moral economy working within and against popular culture, its emancipatory power standing in distinction to workers' daytime obligations in factories, stockyards, and other institutions of industry. Being a musical expression figuratively connected to the machine-based technologies of industrial capitalism, "Negro" versions of jazz cohered as a practice structurally aligned with a symbolically charged, physical place existing beyond work. This racialized sound held the power to short-circuit the abstract tendencies of capital while at the same time drawing from its production and distribution modes to disseminate across America and to reshape the sensible orders of Black laboring classes.

Negro jazz's contradiction of conventional labor set the conditions for what Nathaniel Mackey has called "hear[ing] *into* what has up to now only been *over*heard . . . awaken[ing] resources whereby, for example, *assent* [an accommodation or giving in] can be heard to carry undertones or echoes of a transcending *ascent.*" African American jazz innovations did not automatically specify a resistant world completely apart from the dominance of White-majority racism; they would always be attached to the structures of dominance and "assent." Yet through this same relation Black forms produced dissensual effect. If Negro jazz would "neither give lessons nor have any destination," as Rancière characterizes the undecidability of art works, it nonetheless offered a site enabling such imaginings of ascension, a way of bringing form to temporalities creatively developing from the logic of double value.[95] In the words of Saidiya Hartman, the world of Negro jazz entertainment "fueled the radical hope of living otherwise, and in this way, . . . was just another kind of movement for freedom, another opportunity to escape service, another elaboration of the general strike" that first catalyzed Black people's insistent involvement within US citizenry.[96] While Black venues, from the humblest club to the most lavish cabaret, stood far from the sensational portraits of pleasure-dome fantasy that often represent Black nightlife during the "Jazz Age," they did foster the making of a substantive, labor-based culture for which performances of racially enlivened jazz sound plotted a course of living.

Into the 1920s, Negro jazz as it appeared in Black venues brought into being abstractions of possibility, mapping temporally disjunctive ways of being. Although structured in capitalism—it had developed and had become abstracted *because* of its basis in capitalism—its performances were not obedient to the quotidian, clock-time regularity of industrial, labor-based production. Disavowing the "just-in-time" orientation that Massimiliano Tomba ascribes to market capitalism and industrial production, Negro jazz as it coalesced in Black clubs proposed ways of imagining the possibility of a contrary ethos along the lines of Du Bois's insights into lazy labor—a new version of "colored people time." These performances and performance sites, while relationally connected to normative socioeconomic orders, worked together to interrupt, to short-circuit organizational structures of feeling generated during the working day. In doing so, they inspired the potential for conditions of past-time: glimpses into an otherwise unrecoverable past, as Negro jazz moved listening beyond "memory thing" and the fetishized coherences bound to racism's handiwork.[97]

Black music's structural tendency to redevelop past-oriented sensations of disruption and disconnection generated a flood of accompanying popular discourse that fetishized the freeing effects of hot-inflected rhythmic practices. Yet so did these accumulations produce a countereffect relating to another kind of fetishism in which the aliveness of Black sound was sustained in Negro jazz playing. This cyclical give-and-take of a negative playing to the positive, by which it realizes an exponentially empowered hyperpositive—of "assent" leading to "ascent"—identifies the gestation of something akin to what Brent Hayes Edwards, in his analysis of scat, describes as a "fall" connecting to loss, "an augmentation of expressive potential rather than an evacuation or reduction of signification." This augmentation, which we may now contextualize formally within the contradictory, doubled structures producing Negro jazz—as something less than Music becoming greater—would not have taken place had it not been for the accumulative tendencies bringing forth the music's peculiarly distinctive expansions.[98] The tragedy of ongoing loss—and Black music's further decoupling from Black labor—brought about a liberative potential, a moral profit in the form of a past-inflected capacious sound.

SPECTRAL ACCUMULATION

If by the late 1920s Negro jazz had evolved into a critical force affecting the remaking of modern music aesthetics, it was at the outset of the decade still largely unknown to most White Americans. Although Black bands and orchestras were breaking into national entertainment networks, they had limited direct contact with the White audiences they frequently performed for. Beyond these infrequent encounters, what the majority of White Americans heard was not music played by African Americans but rather a minstrelized antic mirroring the nation itself; "jazz" remained under the institutional control of White power and the cultural authority of young White men. Interracial relations in the North, when they occurred, more commonly took place beyond the musical sphere, particularly in the manufacturing and service industries, where large populations of recent Black migrants worked jobs performing hard labor or menial tasks. It was according to this relationship between jazz as a popular concept and the proliferation of urban Black labor that Negro jazz would obtain a substantial place in music knowledge. As Black musicians asserted themselves into commercial markets, they and their music became caught up in a media-generated sign system that wedded on-the-ground interracial contacts to shifting narratives about a music overwhelming American culture. The tendency for commodified Black music to separate from its makers would grow more acute: jazz as a social idea becomes a catalyst in the production of new racial fantasies and a barometer of changes in race relations, which ultimately proves critical to Black music's expansion and ascension.

Changes in the American public's views about jazz first show up at the outset of the 1920s, when representations in mainstream journalism dramatically shift. What had been formerly characterized as a frivolous form of transgressive fun turned menacing, its sonic attributes symbolically linked to what troubled many White people about the rising numbers of African Americans populating northern cities. Stylistically, reports drawing equivalences between Black degeneracy and the discord of an inferior music recalled the early depictions of ragtime. Yet what was just a few years before relegated to a marginal expression, according to the effectively deracinated qualities of "pep," had now, through the powerful mechanisms of commercial media, spawned a controversy that, no matter Whiteman's efforts to "tame" jazz, seemed to be altering core principles of music and culture.

In an early study of White responses to 1920s jazz, Neil Leonard provides a succinct account of the rhetorical shift, focusing largely on print journalism. As jazz continued to be blithely depicted in the local registers of civic life, sometimes satirically belittled in references to White "nut bands"—Cliquot Club Eskimos, Ipana Troubadours, the A&P Gypsies—it was also subjected to vituperative attacks by social critics who perceived in it "a droning, jerky incoherence" that was inflicting harm on White youth. Jazz threatened to infect America with the moves and postures of dissolute Negroes: to induce "jungle steps" that "excite the basic human instincts . . . [and] are directed by the stronger animal passions."[99] These were not the racist pleasantries previously accompanying the first instances of a "mysterious" music. Now jazz attracted language associating it with conditions of intellectual inferiority. Listening to jazz, the University of Pennsylvania professor J. P. Wickersham argued, triggered senseless and debased thought: "Jazz thinking is the product of the untrained mind, that does not work in any direction." For a growing number of conservative pundits and clergy, moreover, "jazz may be analyzed as a combination of nervousness, lawlessness, primitive and savage animalism and lasciviousness." It was a sound of "evils" and "danger" that led White youth, and particularly young women, into ruin. Having a similar effect to alcohol (which, by this time, was under legal prohibition), jazz became the subject of legislative proposals to ban its propagation. "Jazz music causes drunkenness . . . [by sending] a continuous whirl of impressionable stimulations to the brain . . . which overpower the will," charged a New York physician, Dr. E. Elliot Rawlings. A Kansas City school superintendent speculated, "When it gets into the blood of some of our young folks, and I might add older folks, too, it serves them just about as good as a stiff drink."[100]

Changes in the tenor of discourse about jazz reflected in part the popularity of blues, whose successes on the New York stage and on phonograph records inspired new minstrelizations of Black behavior. A reporter for the *New York Times*, for example, described the clamor of a "noise" strike in a women's reformatory as a "medley of sounds, 'the Reformatory Blues,' [that] may yet make a hit on Broadway, even if the officials appear to disdain jazz."[101] More often, though, writers tried to ignore actual Black subjects, while making vague, derogatory gestures to nameless personae. "Negro" and "jazz" spun a web of racial discourse fueled by the entertainment industry's own dramatic expansion, effectively intensifying the presence of the disembodied, audible Negro according to capitalism's proliferating tendency. Now jazz was powerfully aligned with an abstraction of what Amiri Baraka, in the opening to *Blues People*, called the "Negro as non-American." "Its influence," charged the medical director of a Philadelphia high school for young women, "is as harmful and degrading to civilized races as it always has been among savages from whom we borrowed it." Jazz was part of a widespread social emergency drawn into alignment with the "Negro problem," an association Edmund Wilson made plain in his *New Republic* essay "The Jazz Problem."[102]

It was hardly a coincidence that the dramatic shift in the representation of Negro jazz occurred directly after the eruption of racial violence that overwhelmed the United States during the summer of 1919, when groups of White marauders threatened, attacked, and, in several instances, lynched Black men on the streets of Charleston; Longview, Texas; Washington, DC; Chicago; Knoxville; and twenty-odd other locations. In a foundational historical study of Harlem during the 1920s, David Levering Lewis argues that the chief catalyst for the outbreaks, during what was infamously known as the "Red Summer," was a "classic conflict between labor and capital," as the owners and managers of factories and businesses sought to employ African American migrants to undermine labor-organizing by White workers. The conspicuous presence of Black laborers—even as they routinely assumed the worst jobs in steel mills, in factories, and on the meat industry's killing floors—provided for the many "white victims of postwar economic hardship . . . [an] obvious scapegoat for their woes."[103] As organizing successes mounted, labor conflict metastasized into full-blown racial violence, which, in turn, symbolically translated into the depictions of jazz gaining attention in mainstream media. In its "barbaric" alignments, Negro jazz was no longer just an inferior noise but a formidable, threatening presence. For the music chair of the General Federation of

Women's Clubs, writing in 1921, it was "the expression of protest against law and order, . . . [having] a demoralizing effect on the human brain."[104]

The heightened threat of the Black subject grew in proportion to the increased mediation of jazz in the mass-production apparatuses of the entertainment industry, prompting major record companies such as Victor, in an effort to protect its brand, to reorient "the production of jazz music to align with their identities as producers of [European] symphonic music amid mounting elite anti-jazz pressure." At the same time, after *Victor v. Starr*, the 1922 court ruling that launched the expansion of small "race record" labels, the production and dissemination of jazz recorded by Black musicians also began to increase. While Black consumers remained the small labels' principal consumer target, the phenomenal successes of "Crazy Blues" (1920)—selling seventy-five thousand discs the first month—suggested that White listeners were also buying race records. This pattern of growth in the production of Black sound objects would continue as Negro jazz orchestras led by Henderson and others started recording, prompting, in 1925, the organization of the first jazz studio band, the Hot Five, which produced a series of 78s under the leadership of Louis Armstrong. Among its releases was the 1926 hit "Heebie Jeebies," which, through OKeh's coordinated strategies, "lifted [the recording] into a more lucrative market—that is a white market." Its interracial appeal was confirmed by the trade magazine *Talking Machine World*, which reported the same year that "the recording proved to be a popular one, and was sold to dance lovers throughout the country."[105]

The idea that "Negro jazz" was propagating social menace through its circulation on record developed alongside the continuing production of polite versions of symphonic jazz. Through their capitalization, both forms were gaining wider attention, but it was the appeal of the African American productions that particularly worried many.[106] If Negro jazz was growing into a prized possession of the White nation, it also threatened to become the source of its undoing: Black music's alarming influence developed in relation to the elevation of its value. Alienable features of jazz in its many forms overwhelmed public soundscapes, determining the key value measurement in popular music. What would later be portrayed as an opposition between what was "real" and "commercial" specified at this point, in the early-to-mid 1920s, two interconnected dimensions of a racialized entertainment economy, whose respective identifications as White-equals-alienable and Black-equals-inalienable were materially consistent with the dualism of exchange value and use value inherent to the commodity form. The racially objectionable "Negro problem" projected into the world as something double in character. Irreducible and consistently Black, Negro sound traveled the circuits of the economy, bringing its "problem" into White social experience, its incorrigibility repeatedly short-circuiting White containments and thereby heightening its value.[107]

In this way, Negro jazz developed in opposition to White entertainment capital while at the same time inhabiting the same socioeconomic space. If Whiteman's influence on the social field had the effect of reorienting the habitus of the newly professionalized Negro jazz musician, Black work life produced a counterfield—the y to a dominant x-axis—for African American performers who were bound to the same capitalist structures sustaining the entertainment business but whose aesthetic productions played to a different economic relation where profit accrued from the continuous losses to White expropriations.[108] Given these contrasting orientations, we might want to read differently the lighthearted comments of Walter Kingsley discussed earlier in this chapter: "One touch of 'Jazz' makes savages of us all" presents a different sort of problem when it is viewed in relation to the large numbers of Black laborers descending on northern cities. By the 1920s, that singular "touch" providing an enlivening "pep" to all forms of popular expression boosted the value and status of Black performance. Through its direct participation in commercial markets, Negro jazz gained unprecedented levels of abstraction: soon it was overwhelming national culture, its presence establishing a familiarity, a sameness that firmly implanted race as a steady, irreversible force in the making of popular music. "One touch of 'Jazz' makes savages of us all" identified an unprecedented accumulation of racialized aliveness, an abstract Blackness that readjusted the sound and feel of American music according to the spirited effects of hotness and beat.[109]

Across the decade of the 1920s, threats of audible Blackness, heard yet mostly out of sight, materialized formally as sensations of spectrality tracing across the everyday. Popular references to the superstitious nature of African Americans, common to the comic figure of the "spook," identified the amplification of a familiar conceit, its figurative specificity attempting to stabilize and make claimable the inalienable qualities of enlivened sound. Such figurations showed up, for example, in vaudeville stage comedies that told the tale of "the banjo-plunking, table-lifting spook . . . mouthing *Uncle Tom's Cabin* in Hebrew." In her recovery efforts of folksongs by and about Black southerners, moreover, Dorothy Scarborough juxtaposed the lynching song "Hangman, Slack on the Line"—its melody, she suggested, "recalls the beating of tom-toms in African jungles"—alongside the slave song "Run, Nigger, Run." Other depictions of Black being at the cusp of living and nonliving appeared in the titles of White New Orleans jazz (e.g., the ODJB's "Skeleton Jangle," 1919), and in new-era minstrel lyrics depicting hooded Klansmen scaring the wits out of their victims: "To me dey am a spook, As dey grow stronger, Mah legs grow longer." In a vaudevillian turnabout, the trope of the frightened Negro became the highlight of the Black musical *Runnin' Wild* (1923), where two "colored men" hosting a "'ghost association' meeting" set off on a foot race when things got scary.[110]

If there was a turning point marking the intensification of spectrality in Negro jazz, it was the release in 1926 of Louis Armstrong's hit recording "Heebie Jeebies." The OKeh disc is famous in jazz lore for its popularization of scat vocalizing. According to Thomas Brothers, the term *heebie-jeebies* "had wide currency in the 1920s . . . impl[ying] eccentric movement and vague associations with mental disturbance." As it appeared in the syndicated comic strip *Barney Google* in October 26, 1923, "heebie jeebies" suggested the condition of being spooked. In the cartoon, Google—a character created by the Chicago-based writer-illustrator Billy DeBeck—tells his racehorse, Spark Plug, to "get that stupid look offa your pan—you gimme the Heeby Jeebys!" In a follow-up strip published in December, moreover, the condition, having shifted to the horse under the care of a Black stableboy, draws together a medical illness afflicting an animal and the impoverished speech of an inferior being. He tells Google in Negro dialect, "Yes, Boss, ah got spahky in dis cabin—he's got de heebie jeebies agin—chills an ev'ything else—de doctah wuz heah" (figure 6.1). It is uncertain if DeBeck picked up the expression from Black migrants or invented it himself. Either way, with Armstrong's release it became thoroughly racialized, figuratively aligning Blackness and hot jazz with peculiar, often agitated states of being. Its popularity gave rise to an international dance movement, which, a retired British missionary declared, consisted of "the same dances . . . [I] spent a lifetime teaching the natives of darkest Africa to abandon."[111]

Subsequent references to "the heebies" and "heebie-jeebies" in African American sources aligned agitation and involuntary body movement with otherworldliness, suggesting "haunting; the 'apprehension' that intuits an invasive presence."[112] Although such indications may have already been common in the Black southern vernacular, they gained momentum after Armstrong's comedy began to include spooky encounters and minstrelized caricatures of Africans as part of his mugging antics. In Max Fleischer's film

BARNEY GOOGLE–

By Billey De Beck

6.1 *Barney Google* comic strip (1923).

short "I'll Be Glad When You're Dead You Rascal You" (1932), which presents the cartoon character Betty Boop, an animated image of the disembodied head of an "African savage" turns into a filmed depiction of Armstrong's countenance, then back again to the "savage," as all the while Armstrong sings about a "rascal" after his wife, his various heads chasing Betty Boop's cohorts, Bimbo and Koko. The action takes place against an orchestral accompaniment featuring Armstrong, who quotes solo passages from his 1931 recording "Chinatown, My Chinatown" (figure 6.2). In 1936, moreover, Armstrong appeared in the Hollywood film *Pennies from Heaven*, taking the role of Henry, a nightclub performer, who sings and plays "Skeleton in the Closet" at the "Haunted House Cafe." During the act, he is spooked by an actor in a Halloween-style skeleton costume, whereupon Armstrong's percussionist, Lionel Hampton, mimes playing on its "bones" to the sound of a xylophone.

Rather than disavowing these vaudevillian antics, Armstrong—who, as Brian Harker has persuasively demonstrated, was steeped in vaudevillian dance culture—wholeheartedly embraces them, bringing their sensationalism into the making of spectacular form. He becomes, to quote Edwards once more—this time commenting on the film *A Rhapsody in Black and Blue* (1932), where Armstrong, inhabiting an ethereal, jungle-as-heaven called "Jazzmania," appears as a spirit dressed in a leopard skin—"a spectral presence . . . in the somatic excess of that body." In his capacity as a film performer and actor, Armstrong is the incarnate of "heebie-jeebies." "Bugged eyes" and "satchel mouth," he epitomizes the consummate audible Negro, whose "whole body," an acolyte claimed, "vibrat[es] like one of those electric testing machines."[113] What is different about Negro spectrality in these instances is how its excessive qualities of embodiment seem at once hilarious and unsettling. The films are both racist *and* funny—as when, for example, in "I'll Be Glad," Armstrong sings, "You buy my wife a bottle of Coca-Cola so you could play on her Victrola"—not only because of minstrelsy's impact on American humor but also because Negro jazz had ascended as a valued possession under the always-contested ownership of African Americans.

For many Black consumers at the time, Armstrong's preposterous comedy was part of his creative intelligence: his performances were spectacular in the revolutionary sense of a Black awakening. If the practice of scat heard on "Heebie Jeebies," as Edwards argues, after Nathaniel Mackey, "testifies to an 'unspeakable history' of violence," that quality also appears critical to an assertive, new aesthetics in which insouciant, virtuosic play

6.2 Louis Armstrong in Max Fleischer, *Betty Boop: "I'll Be Glad When You're Dead You Rascal You"* (1932).

takes claim of spectrality's empowering potential. The "unspeakable" reveals what Mackey calls a "telling inarticulacy"—"saying all too much at once."[114] Through this doubled inclusiveness—not a transcendence of the tragic but a dialectical interplay of both sides of Black music's double character—Negro jazz becomes larger-than-life: formed in the negative, it realizes something greater than Music. White spectators were increasingly paying attention. For Mary Austin, in her 1926 assessment of the African American dancer Bill Robinson, such displays of excess assumed a familiar form of primitivism: "The primal freshness" of an emergent swing, revealing, with a nod to Du Bois's *The Gift of Black Folk*, "the chief gift of the Negro, . . . a clean short cut" that restored for White people "their own lost rhythmic powers." Austin's comments were part of the ideological makeup of a cultural elite representing both sides of the racial divide. In his overview of Black artistic productions in *Black Manhattan*, James Weldon Johnson, who, as we've seen, was an early celebrant of racialized rhythmic ownership, approvingly acknowledges Austin's alienable primitivism as a declaration of African American achievement.[115]

The spectrality of Black sounding practices had assumed a mutually agreed-on presence defining a critical feature of a re-Africanized Black music. Having gained a certain authority as a result of continuing academic interest in African rhythmic practices—which, according to an influential Austrian comparative musicologist, Erich von Hornbostel, was part of "the life of a living spirit"—Negro jazz gained metaphysical intensity, its enlivened character symbolically heightened by attention among folklorists to its relationship to "hoodoo," "conjure," "Ghost Talk," and "Hants" (haunts).[116] Having become a familiar reference point in popular depictions of the spirit world, Black enlivened sound seemed readily on display, at least to the extent that its unobtainability had become reified. Among many African Americans, too, Africanized spectrality had grown into a defining aspect of modern aesthetics. The ghostly not only informed musical style but also the character of musicians' evolving insider language.

"Heebie-jeebies" was only part of it. Consider, for example, the many allusions to spectrality in Black musicians' discourse: the "boogie" figure that launched the boogie-woogie fad; the fashion of after-hours dances, known as "spook nights"; the musical work those dances inspired, such as Gerald Wilson's "Hi Spook," recorded by the Jimmie Lunceford Orchestra in 1941. In his *Autobiography*, moreover, Charles Mingus recounts an imagined debate with Fats Waller, whom he credits with giving Louis Armstrong the title "King Spook": the archetypal subject representing the losses accrued by working Black musicians. So pervasive was the relationship between Black sound and the otherworldly it had by midcentury entered American letters. In Ralph Ellison's *Invisible Man*, the jazz-inflected temporalities sounding out of Armstrong's horn become a means of hearing another realm, a ghostly "invisibility . . . where time stands still or from which it leaps ahead." These examples all indicate how spectral accumulation was becoming part and parcel of Black music's commodification, enabling Mary Austin and other White listeners to stake a claim on Negro rhythm—to take possession via "a clean, short cut" of a racial truth bound to Robinson's "African ancestry" and which arose out of "the sincere unconscious of his genius."[117]

But what was, in the end, driving the latest elevation of Black music was not simply an easy accommodation to White fantasy. Negro jazz had also short-circuited "short cuts." In economic terms, it interrupted its own smooth transition into the networks of commercial entertainment. It did so by way of its reluctant participation in the circuits of capital, its inalienable qualities undermining the completion of the circuits' transference of value from Black to White. What was alive in Negro jazz disrupted its fetishization as a commodity, exposing its basis in racialized human labor and effecting a truth in its primary form. Aliveness would be reaffirmed every time a professional African American musician performed.

In its back-and-forth movements, coalescing in Black worlds and dispersing outwardly into the popular, Negro jazz proceeded to create gaps in the orders of commercial music through the mechanisms by which it accumulated value. Turning inward and outward, in two directions at once, it progressively gained profit with each assertion of its fleshy presence. And through its ongoing acquisitions, it evolved into a music moving according to its own exceptional rate, its economic motion seeming to affect listeners' perceptions. "Negro rhythm," J. A. Rogers proclaimed in *The New Negro*, followed the pace of "jazz time . . . faster and more complex than African music," its peculiar temporal pulse being "a joyous revolt from convention," the result of a Black world's pivot on a "nerve-strung, strident, mechanized civilization." Negro jazz had benefited aesthetically as it exceeded commercial gains, drawing on the force of capital to interrupt its absorption into capital processes. Its qualities of spectrality, which depended on its economic abstraction as it made its way through global markets, issued as a negative force, reaffirming the material persistence of the racial body and "causing," in the words of an approving Leopold Stokowski, "new blood to flow in the veins of music." Metaphorically enriched by capital's transfusion, the music grew more voluble, louder, as its spectral presences traveled the circuits of global entertainment, its expansive losses turning profits that increased with each failed attempt by White power to reclaim enlivened sound. Through these means, Negro jazz achieved its peculiar modernism.[118]

It is here that I depart from the otherwise remarkable portrait of 1920s jazz culture crafted by Thomas Brothers in his important study, *Louis Armstrong: Master of Modernism*. Armstrong's "modernism" was not, as Brothers implies, an alternative modernism existing on the same social plane as Euro-Western modernism. It could never have been for the simple fact that Black music could never claim for itself a place as Music.[119] As a racialized form, Negro jazz moved contrapuntally, counterhistorically, within and against the trajectory of Euro-modernism as it created temporal disruptions that drew racialized past-times into the present. These sensations were inspired by forms of Negro jazz that abstracted sounding practices first generated in southern Black music, their modern-day incorporation bringing the sensation of those pasts nearer. Formal designs of hotness and swing that would carry forward as a new sign language advanced the possibility of hearing doubly. Negro jazz proposed a racial return not to an actual, historical past but to a renewal in the present of the fragmented truths of a temporally divergent past-time, suggesting, in the evocative language of Natalie Curtis Burlin (in her portrait of a "Negro Music at Birth"), "a lambent living form," a music now larger, more expansive in its capital-bound short-circuiting.[120]

In her 1928 essay "What It Feels Like to Be Colored Me," Zora Neale Hurston, in her own, inimitable way, perceptively captures this startling double modernism in the form of a negative-bound, extra-ordinary Negro jazz. The essay has been variously celebrated and critiqued according to its place within Black literary modernism. In his book on Harlem, for example, Shane Vogel interprets Hurston's piece from the vantage of Paul Gilroy's "politics of transfiguration." What draws our attention in this instance is not only Gilroy's broad abstraction of the past, which he names "the slave sublime," but also how a scabrous concreteness accumulates within the expansive force of capitalism to produce new versions of enlivened sound. At a climactic moment in the essay, with Hurston seated alongside a White acquaintance at a Harlem club, the fictional New World Cabaret, she witnesses how a jazz orchestra assumes spectral character:

> In the abrupt way that jazz orchestras have, this one plunges into a number. It loses no time in circumlocutions but gets right down to business. It constricts the thorax and splits the heart with its tempo and narcotic harmonies. The orchestra grows rambunctious and rears on its hind legs and attacks the tonal veil with primitive fury, rending it, clawing it until it breaks through to the jungle beyond.[121]

At this point, Hurston makes a gleeful descent as a way of betraying how her "color comes" alongside her pale, clueless friend. Most crucial, however, is neither the story of descent—which, as an aesthetics of presence, carries forward vaudeville's influence while aligning with other primitivisms of "jungle style"—nor her inventive reading of "tempo" and "attacks" on tonality. It is rather her reference to transubstantiation, to the sense that jazz contains an animated quality growing from its basis as an anomalous form. The orchestra, after all, is comprised of a rather ordinary group of working professionals, laborers who, when not playing, simply sit there, "wipe their lips and rest their fingers." But when they play, they are transfigured, rematerializing as a composite audible body. Hurston's comments call to mind the words of one of her contemporaries, the *Chicago Defender's* music critic, Dave Peyton, who, in describing the tight section writing and well-rehearsed performances of the Henderson orchestra, claimed that "each section of his band [seems] molded into one player." It is through such esemplastic power that Negro jazz comes into being, suggesting a resonant incarnation of spectral "life."[122]

The animatedness of hot music did not simply develop from musicians playing. Its ontological qualities grew out of the music's structuring within racial capitalism, out of the foundational contradiction of a former property bringing forth an uncanny progeny. Sensations of aliveness congealed when performers who, in their assembly as a class of worker, became themselves phantom-like while also producing sound formations running counter to their own reification. In their participation within the economic structure of commercial music, the musicians' sound formations circulated as congealed expressions of labor consistent with the greater structure of labor in the abstract. At the same time, the orchestra's performance also denied incorporation, and this reluctance is what generated repetitions of spectacular, living form that overwhelmed those paying attention to its peculiar character. With this, jazz "rears on its hind legs," its pulsating being the result of the concrete labor of a skilled, well-practiced, and musically disciplined band that was, recalling Ellington, not only "mak[ing] a living," not only finding a new level of "self-satisfaction out of work," but also realizing something beyond the powerful discipline of production.

Jazz had achieved as a negative aesthetic form a means of simultaneously enacting and exploring an unrecoverable origin: it brought into the present temporal fractures of a past-time suggestive of historically generated truths. We see at this point past-time itself moving as part of the abstracting principles of capital in the structuring of primary truth, whereby sensations of time before capitalism's assertion on the enslaved grew more resonant in the present day, caught up as they were in the fantasies of representation. Hurston's visit to the "jungle" provides a hint of that which is not claimed. She offers a momentary glimpse at the otherwise unrecoverable form of tragic-comic difference, whose double valuations of loss and affirmation assert a newly Africanized performativity.

What does it mean for a jazz orchestra suddenly to "rear on its hind legs"? Here we are witnessing a kind of initiation: the beginning of Negro music's apotheosis as a superior aesthetic form, secure under the ownership of African Americans. It is the point at which a negatively conceived labor class creates expressions of musical pleasure that, through the resources of capital, metamorphize into new spectacular forms. It marks the moment when the Black past forcefully imposes on the present a contrapuntal history: a past that can only be constituted in the here and now but that shifts perceptions beyond memory thing toward new possibilities of time and experience. Hurston's portrait identifies the point at which a socially expansive Black music, in its symbolic accumulations and repetitive losses, gains more value than it ever had before, conjuring imagery of animallike sonic presences or, in the fashioning of Henry Coward, a British composer and chorus master, of a "gigantic Negro striding over the world with a banjo in one hand and a saxophone in the other."[123] The accumulation of aliveness made Negro jazz seem nearly sentient, evoking the afterlives of slavery that animated its expressive forms. Rearing on its hind legs, it stepped out into the world, claiming aesthetic authority on the backs of a reified Black musician class at once celebrated and subjected.

FOURTH METAMORPHOSIS

RACIALIZED EMBODIMENTS

OF HYPERCAPITALIZED POP

SEVEN

S W I N G

BLACK MUSIC'S NEW

MODERN BECOMING

CAPACIOUS LIFE

During a rehearsal break in 1972 at Philharmonic Hall (now David Geffen Hall) in New York's Lincoln Center, Count Basie and his longtime colleague and band member, guitarist Freddie Green, sat down with the British jazz critic Stanley Dance for a brief interview.[1] Dance was eager to hear their thoughts about swing, the performance practice whose even time, light touch, and seemingly effortless momentum had transformed American popular music in the 1930s. It was Basie, after all, as much as anyone, who established in that decade—first with Bennie Moten's Kansas City Orchestra, then as leader of his own bands—the formal parameters that led to the shift in the music's temporal order and remade jazz in its name. As Dance established at the outset, Basie and Green were among the masters of swing, whose animated energy seemed to rise up from their very bodies. "Swinging," he remarked, "is as natural as breathing to them." And so it was to these two storied figures that he directed the question, "Do you have any working definition of what swing is?" Basie was succinct in his reply: "No, I don't." At the most, the bandleader would make only oblique gestures to swing's "mood," finally offering a seemingly obvious observation, "I just think swing is a matter of some good things put together that you can really pat your foot by. I can't define it beyond that."[2]

In another interview around the same time, in this instance with a group of Basie's contemporaries, Dance raised the question again. Although these players, all members of a quintet led by Jonah Jones, were generally more forthcoming than Basie was, they too were reluctant to reduce swing to a concise definition. They named the great improvisers, reminisced about their favorite bands, and, at one point, considered the opinion that swing as an overarching quality had affected all forms of Black music since ragtime. But they never ventured further. In the end, all of them seemed to agree when the drummer Cozy Cole stated that swing as a coherent performance practice didn't come into being until the mid-1930s, "when Fletcher Henderson and Jimmy Mundy started arranging for Benny Goodman, and Sy Oliver for Tommy Dorsey. And then they began to get colored musicians in the bands."[3]

Basie and the others probably found the inquiries tedious, but they were tolerant of Dance because he respected them and recognized how important they were to the development of swing as the "mainstream" of modern jazz.[4] Given the extraordinary impact of swing, which, by the mid-1930s, had overtaken the full compass of American and European pop, it probably made sense for writers to continue discussing it. Yet the banality of Dance's query also suggests that commentaries like this one grew from an ideological tendency to seek to contain what was ultimately uncontainable. Questions about swing persisted not only because music journalists and their readers sought conclusive answers about it but also because swing was so wrapped up in the anxiety of pleasure that Black music afforded. Perpetuating a conversation about swing's purported mystery sustained the music industry's effort to control jazz practice and perhaps to secure its ownership once and for all. Black musicians were understandably reluctant to participate in such an exercise.

Swing made concrete a fundamental contradiction in the development of modern style: it reaffirmed in the form of a peculiar mode of music repetition the enduring ontological presence of Blackness at the heart of popular music. As a new materialization of racially embodied sound, swing demonstrated how crucial African American sounding practices were to the audible formation of metropolitan cultures and how indebted America had become to a negatively structured music property innovated by Black musicians. Although White listeners were probably not aware of the social and economic structures behind swing's appeal, they could still feel the power and pulse of its enlivened expression. Building on the wealth of sonic material produced before it, swing reconceived for a new era the sensation of animated audible resonances emanating from performers for whom music-making was, as Dance put it, as natural to them as taking a breath.

It is one of the great ironies of Black music that swing's extraordinary advancement also spelled profound losses, measured economically in the profits that the entertainment industry accrued and the fame that White performers achieved at the expense of African American musicians. For no matter how much better things were for Black artists, with a handful of them achieving celebrity, swing's inspirited sound seemed to leave them behind as it took on a life of its own. "Rear[ing] on its hind legs," as Zora Neale Hurston imagined the fury of a hot jazz orchestra (cf. chapter 6), swing gained a level of autonomy inversely related to the losses endured by the unprecedented number of Black musicians entering the entertainment business.

The extent of those losses registered in the escalation of Black music's value. In their public presentation by Black and White musicians, swing's hybrid forms—intensified by a rich racial discourse celebrating Black music's journey out of the time of the southern past—overwhelmed commercial markets, the music's racial-sonic contests driving popular music's economic and aesthetic expansion. Yet as the enlivened qualities of swing traced across national and international media circuits, the visible presence of Black musicians correspondingly receded, even as the necessity of Black labor in the production of value perpetuated repetitions of a cycle where swing's fantastic racial character—its attachments to Black pasts and its dependency on Black musicians producing it—would be successively reasserted and denied. In this way, swing established a new productive relationship between Black music innovation and the structures of entertainment capital, their interplay fostering the evolution of form. In just a few years, popular music—having embraced the paradox of Black forms at the heart of an increasingly deracinated swing—would move away from time sensibilities associated with early jazz in favor of temporalities symbolically aligned with the pace and character of urban society. As swing grew increasingly distant from Black music labor, being incorporated fetishistically into the greater language of pop, it spread its racially animated energies across the greater complex of global metropolitan culture.

We can accordingly observe swing's coalescence as a creation of two temporal orientations, its doubleness akin to the racial-economic motion of ragtime and jazz before it: a concrete music time executed chiefly by African American musicians, measured in the presentation of an orchestra's stylistic character—what would be understood ontologically among Black players as its "personality"—and the abstract time of capital, whereby the production and dissemination of commodified swing favored those innovations that affirmed the entertainment industry's portrayal of it as a sign of modern living.[5] The rise of a racially hybrid brand of swing through the institutional apparatuses of national radio broadcasts, phonograph recordings, and music journalism reinforced its symbolic alignments with modern progress and industry, the music's acceleration within the flow of commodities enhancing its familiarity among consumers and affirming perceptions of it as the sound of the moment.[6]

What was ultimately most distinctive about the swing moment, though, was its racialized temporality, its widely acknowledged "Negro" properties of sound. And however abstract those properties had become amid the music's widespread circulation, what seemed essential to swing always remained linked to its symbolic origin in Black culture. Swing's racial incorrigibility—particularly, its resistance to the protocols of Western music rhythm—reaffirmed its bodily attachments to the legacy of working Black musicians, proposing a musical version of what Moishe Postone has called, after Marx, the "chief contradiction of capital": its structural boundedness to and dependency on human labor. With swing, it was *racialized* labor, whose inalienable concreteness, manifested as sensations of time, persisted as the critical factor in the making of value.[7] Swing's temporality made manifest what "capital posits as its contradictory starting point": a material form of "life," an animated property constituted in the production of "abstract living labor, . . . the excess that capital, for all its disciplinary procedures, always needs but can never quite control or domesticate."[8] Despite the real-life losses that Black musicians and their communities absorbed as part of the economic devastation and racial violence of the 1930s, the sound of swing, as it was performed by Black orchestras and embraced by White bands and listeners, realized a capacious life: newly conceived truths that armed African Americans with tools for creating inspirited cultural worlds.

This chapter examines the pivotal changes taking place in Black music when swing overtakes the listening world, its influence fueled by the disseminating power of the popular marketplace, which intensified relations between its innovative formal qualities and a new public understanding of the Black past. The previous chapter explored a crucial step in Black music's metamorphosis, when the commodity circuits of the entertainment industry brought forward jazz, a powerful, popular genre that nonetheless depended on Black labor for its enlivened character. With swing, Black music transformed qualitatively, its sounding practices further loosened from Black labor while images of the music's symbolic attachments to the Black past paradoxically intensified. The extent of these formal and symbolic alignments—referencing the racial past to call attention to the temporal originality of a music under claim of White America—made swing seem like a wholly new thing. The assembly of relations ultimately set the stage in Black music's continuing metamorphosis for the refabrication of popular music history, with Black music at the helm. In this new narration, swing marks the beginning of pop's advance as it defines the origin of Black music's new modern becoming.

CREATING ENSEMBLE PERSONALITIES

As Basie and other Black jazz musicians made their way into the world of entertainment in the late 1920s, they confronted circumstances dramatically different from those in place just a few years earlier. The massive collapse of the US economy in 1929 devastated commercial markets, forcing closures of hundreds of venues that showcased music performances, stage acts, and vaudeville. In New York alone, 105 dance halls and 45 percent of all Broadway theaters were shuttered, while across the nation, over two-thirds of the unionized musician workforce couldn't find jobs.[9] Players struggled to get by, accepting work where they could, with leaders scaling down their ensembles, changing repertory to feature songs and a singer, and taking their bands on the road to play one-night shows. ("There were a lot of very good bands that couldn't get work in many places outside of New York," Basie recalled.) The record industry was similarly hard hit. Companies witnessed a precipitous decline in profits that crippled business. Sales fell from 105 million units in 1929 to 31 million in 1931; by 1933, totals had dropped to less than 10 million, putting most companies out of commission.[10] The situation was so dire that what was once a diverse line of businesses had been reduced to just two: Victor and Columbia, with a third company, British-based Decca, entering a somewhat improved economy with its American branch in 1934.[11] Because far fewer records were being made, far fewer musicians were working in recording studios, adding further to the numbers of unemployed performers.[12]

Declines in record production enabled another medium, radio broadcasting, to step in. After the success of local programming in the early 1920s, established businesses and entrepreneurs worked to expand radio's potential through the development of powerful regional stations and large broadcasting networks that would ultimately reach across the nation. A complex negotiation involving several companies assisted by the federal government resulted in the founding of the National Broadcasting Company (NBC), the consortium granting its control to the Radio Corporation of America (RCA) in 1926. NBC's promise soon inspired the launching of a competing network with capital support from the Columbia Phonograph Record System. This second entity kept the Columbia name once it gained independence, becoming known as the Columbia Broadcasting System.[13]

Working competitively to build national networks linking key local affiliates, the two corporations fostered a new kind of consumer behavior oriented around home listening. Radio sets playing news, drama, comedy, pop, and classics were common to even the poorest households, with popular music programming attracting the largest listening audiences, particularly among youth and young adults. By the end of the decade, listeners in most regions could tune into broadcasts from network studios and ballrooms featuring live shows (or, from the studios, noncommercial, recorded "transcriptions") of popular hits performed by the leading White bands and star vocalists.[14] By relying on advertisers and their agencies to sponsor programming, moreover, broadcasters erected a business apparatus perpetuating the illusion that radio was the source of pure entertainment: one could seemingly listen to popular music and comedy for free, the references to commercial sponsorships—"the Eveready Hour," "the Clicquot Club Eskimos," "the Chase and Sanborn Hour"—blending into the overall entertainment experience. In this way, the dissemination of popular culture grew further integrated into the capitalized production of mass media, with music performances marketed as a new kind of exalted celebrity immediately accessible through modern advances in broadcast technologies.[15]

The expansion of radio networks amid the downward spiral of the domestic economy solidified the importance of the modern dance orchestra at the hub of mainstream popular culture. By disseminating performances of well-rehearsed ensembles playing stock arrangements, the new technology saturated markets with forms paralleling the overall standardization of the entertainment business. In its style and image, commercial jazz of the late 1920s grew aligned with the technological advancements of its production: it was a "modern sound" upholding high standards of musical proficiency that was even competing with classical music for status and prestige. By and large, performance standards were still being set by White orchestras entertaining White audiences in White-run establishments, and this pattern grew stronger as commercial markets receded. Yet the wide availability of dance music via radio broadcasts also inspired local stations and later networks to showcase performances by the most commercially successful Black orchestras performing in New York, Detroit, Chicago, and elsewhere. Although opportunities were still scarce for Black bands—a problem vigorously critiqued by the *Chicago Defender* columnist Walter Barnes in 1929—stations in major cities opened radio spots for a few of the leading orchestras, notably those headed by Duke Ellington, Fletcher Henderson, Earl Hines, and Claude McKinney, broadcasting their live performances during their residencies at hotels and ballrooms.[16]

Radio performances were critical in helping Black orchestras to break through racial boundaries. To a degree unprecedented in US music history, the broadcasts—first on local stations, then relayed on networks—usurped the oppressive strictures of Jim Crow, making Black music potentially available everywhere to anyone who owned or happened to be near a radio set. While the shows were typically aired late at night, they were nonetheless critical: those playing on major stations with the capability of reaching well beyond city boundaries enabled audiences even in remote areas to hear the distinctive kinds of jazz that Black orchestras were developing. Many radio listeners, in fact, could not discern stylistic differences distinguishing Black orchestras from White ones; the challenge could sometimes be difficult, particularly when comparing, say, Jimmie Lunceford's to Tommy and Jimmy Dorsey's. And in this way broadcasts were effective in pushing against the strictures of racial segregation. Earl Hines recalled how his own orchestra's broadcasts from the Grand Terrace Ballroom in Chicago offered a chance to compete directly with White ensembles: because listeners typically couldn't tell the difference between White and Black bands, "I was in competition with Guy Lombardo, Paul Whiteman, the Dorsey boys."[17]

A radio spot could be beneficial in other ways, particularly if the station tied into a national network. The Ellington Orchestra's broadcasts from the Cotton Club in Harlem where he was in residence from 1927 to 1931 were instrumental in making him a national celebrity, the attention leading to promotional tours (including a European tour in 1933) and new recording contracts. The same was the case for Claude McKinney's Cotton Pickers, whose shows from Graystone Ballroom, broadcast on Detroit's WJR from 1927 to 1931, reached as far south as West Virginia, Arkansas, and Texas.[18] Contrary to the opinion common in critical circles by midcentury that popularity hurt one's reputation ("selling out"), Black musicians had no trouble with commercial success; indeed, they aspired to it. Successful Black orchestras set a standard for other ambitious Black professionals, showing them how they might also make it in the business.[19] Basie recalls, for example, how the achievements of major Black bands motivated the Bennie Moten Orchestra to set their ambitions high. "We felt our chances were [good] of making a big enough hit to get the kind of backing and promotion that would get us into the top clubs and dance halls, especially in New York and Chicago, and get us on the big coast-to-coast radio hookups." After playing with Fletcher Henderson, Rex Stewart followed a similar business strategy. Performing at New York's Empire Ballroom in the early 1930s, "we began broadcasting" and then went out on tour, "hoping that the fan mail resulting from the broadcasts indicated that we had built a name."[20]

The proliferation of radio broadcasts of jazz and other genres triggered a qualitative shift in the pattern of music consumption, as technologically mediated sound reshaped listening, fostering the making of what David Suisman has called "the musical soundscape of modernity."[21] "By the Great Depression," Suisman writes, "the creation of a new musical culture was effectively complete," realizing a transformation that had been developing over thirty years. As radio and other forms of commodified sound became incorporated into the daily experience—with performance venues and recording companies recovering by the mid-1930s—music "was becoming dematerialized at the same time, severed from the tangible realm by the metaphysics of sound recording." Through mechanisms of capitalized distribution, the listening experience widened as it simultaneously contracted: the availability of live and recorded musical performances, whose origins were often separated by great distances, clustered within the singularity of the domestic space. These same sonic resources, moreover, spread nearly instantaneously across public culture, "circulat[ing] as capital that could be used by other industries" to supplement dance halls, department stores, cafés, radio, and movies. Musical experience seemed increasingly to take place secondhand: it was something manufactured and obtained rather than made "by hand." Its effects were seismic. As Suisman argues, "Just as the grand sweep of the Industrial Revolution affected all of society, not just people employed in industrial occupations, the commercial revolution in music ensured that all aspects of music resonated in a new way." As a result, there emerged not only "a *new* musical culture" but also "a new *musical* culture, with more music everywhere, [its omnipresence] . . . signif[ying] the alteration of 'a whole way of life.'"[22]

At the center of this heightened condition of musicality was swing. With its coalescence as a genre in the mid-1930s, popular music would begin again, instigating a veritable flood of Black and White actors into the commercial economy. Together, they effected powerful changes that transformed the music's stylistic character and affirmed its status as a late modern form. The strategies at play were both musical and organizational, as Black and White musician-laborers competed for work in a business remade by radio and a diversified production organization. From the early 1930s, Scott DeVeaux observes, "economic consolidation altered the structure of the dance band business from a loose patchwork of regional music-making to a tightly controlled pyramid." At the top were the leading orchestras in residences at venues in major cities; beneath them were the dozens of territory bands competing for nightly jobs. Increasingly, orchestras resembled small businesses that depended on middle management to book jobs and navigate a bureaucratized market. From the perspective of entertainment organizations, musicians were components within a commercial structure, whose value was measured not only by their musical skills but also by how successfully they complied with the norms of the profession. Some weren't willing. "My brother, James W. Jones," Jonah Jones confided to Dance, "was one of those guys you couldn't hold down. . . . He didn't want anybody to boss him around. . . . I don't think he ever plays any more."[23]

The realignment of the entertainment industry in the early 1930s meant that Black musicians had to compete for what little work was available. Some tried to accommodate market demands, performing music that fulfilled the public's expectations for strong vocal melodies and well-designed arrangements that were in place a decade earlier. Others set out on the road, playing one-nighters on a circuit of dozens of Black venues stretching from Cincinnati to Indianapolis to St. Louis, and downward to Memphis, Little Rock, and Houston. The paucity of good-paying work meant that lesser-known ensembles—Herman Curtis and his Chocolate Vagabonds, Smiling Billy Steward and his Celery City Serenaders, A. Lee Simpkins's Augusta Nighthawks—might occasionally cross paths with the major orchestras (notably, those led by Hines and Lunceford) touring out of big cities.[24] Amid their efforts to meet the needs of their audiences, the more adventurous bands pursued creative directions that challenged familiar performance practices to the point of reordering existing conceptions of music time. Appearing mainly before Black listeners and dancers, they experimented with a new kind of beat orientation, known among jazz musicians by the name "swing," that implied an advance in the rhythmic affect assumed to emanate from Black bodies.

When looking back at the period years later, some African American instrumentalists have suggested that the rhythmic turn was not a natural occurrence but a conscious effort to move jazz progressively away from established conventions of musical entertainment. Jonah Jones (b. 1909), for example, saw swing's emergence as an evolution that betrayed the limitations of earlier practices. The rhythmic feel of ragtime and early jazz, he remarked with some condescension, "wasn't swinging the way we think of swinging today, but it was the best they had." Similarly, the use of march rhythms seemed old and out of date even to players such as the drummer Baby Dodds (b. 1898), who was born in New Orleans, played with King Oliver, and appeared on Armstrong's Hot Five and Hot Seven recordings. He suggested that the banjo and tuba—which were methodically replaced by guitar and double bass in swing ensembles—"always made the [generic, New Orleans] group sound brassy to me. It seemed like it was a brass band or a street band."[25]

Hierarchical views about swing practice—the genre heightened as it would be sensationalized by critics with the rise of bop—represented a jazz version of modernization theory that was embraced by Black musicians themselves, whose ideas about musical value reflected the influence of commercial standards. An aesthetic affirming stylistic growth drove swing innovation, its organization of the beat shifting away from the strongly inflected, duple-time bounce of the march and fox-trot—the latter a southern term alluding to the gait of a horse—toward a steady, common-time flow enabling endless rhythmic variation. "Progress," DeVeaux writes, "involved expanding technical resources within [the swing] context—better (and different) ways to swing, better (and different) ways to get people moving on the dance floor." Changes came about quickly. As Gunther Schuller observed in his classic study *The Swing Era*, "jazz had by 1932 evolved aesthetic, stylistic, technical criteria which were to govern its future for some years without major changes or radical breakthroughs."[26] Swing supplied material evidence of how different Black music and Black people had become.

First emerging in Black entertainment forums in the late 1920s, swing soon dominated the performance style of Black orchestras, and by the mid-1930s, it had been wholeheartedly embraced by White bands, overtaking American dance halls and the greater complex of commercial entertainment. With its sudden rise in popularity—commonly associated with the Benny Goodman Orchestra's dramatic success in 1935—swing developed not only on the ground of entertainment forums but also as part of the transformational effects of modern media: swing's musical growth moved in step with the greater changes in how sound was produced and experienced. And as its dissemination widened through radio broadcasts, nightclub performances, Hollywood film, and a recovering record industry, it garnered a significance consistent with the expansion of capitalized entertainment. Increases in the rate of swing's circulation made an unprecedented range of dynamically changing music almost immediately available, profoundly affecting people's relationship to it. The expansiveness of swing made it seem larger than life: its new orientation to the beat remade the character of pop, to the point of specifying how music in general should sound. Swing reimagined the sensible range of musical culture and did so faster than any form before it, including early jazz, which, through the power of phonograph records in the late 1910s, already seemed everywhere at once. With its commercial rise, swing began to exceed its role as mere entertainment. It now carried a wider relevance as young audiences came to believe that one could better understand the world by listening to swing's many expressions.

It is according to this larger transformation that swing became so troubling in public culture. Not only was it based on African American sonic material but that basis was critical to its valuation. More than any other popular expression before it, swing revealed the impact of Black creative property on the nation's common musical language, even if White audiences in the early 1930s had trouble discerning its influence beyond the most obvious blues and gospel contexts, preferring to listen and dance to versions of racially enlivened swing played by White musicians. Although entertainment institutions (particularly recording studios) perpetuated as they accommodated those preferences by limiting opportunities for African American participation, swing's Black presence haunted popular music, the widespread circulation of Black sonic material complicating the racial stability of American musical life. Swing announced to the world, as DeVeaux put it, "the breaching of the unspoken boundaries that had separated musical repertory along racial lines."[27] Ellington's seemingly innocuous gesture in his 1932 hit recording "It Don't Mean a Thing (If It Ain't Got That Swing)" celebrated the power of the Black body's enlivening effect. According to the lyrics sung by Ivie Anderson (they were written by Irving Mills), "swing" identified a quality suggestive of a living entity: it was a "thing" embodied by a racially animated spirit beyond the power and controls of White entertainment. The enlivened "thing," swing, was a valuable property bound to the Black body; for White musicians to obtain it, they needed to involve or at least learn from those who inherently possessed it. It is why Benny Goodman bought arrangements from Fletcher Henderson after the collapse of his orchestra in 1934 and later hired him to help resuscitate the musical character of the Goodman band.

Swing announced the metamorphosis of a new kind of animated property overtaking the sensible arena. Even as swing became incorporated into the maw of a White-controlled entertainment industry that anointed Benny Goodman "The King of Swing," its embodied energy remained linked to the negative experience of Blackness in America: what was alive in the sound of swing initiated a creative form of politics consistent with prior metamorphoses in Black music. Swing's incorrigibility, its scabrous tenacity as a quality of racialized flesh, set new conditions of cultural ownership, as African American musicians forged a negatively cast, ontologized sound markedly different from popular sonorities existing before it. Their aspiration to create something new in Black orchestral music was motivated as much by the ambition to succeed in the entertainment business as it was to reclaim sonic materials that had become coopted by the White entertainment industry. Indeed, the two aspirations were one in the same: they reclaimed Black sonic materials by setting a new musical direction for pop, which provided the means of gaining commercial success.

Thinking of swing as an expansion of Black music's negative constitution rubs against prevailing views that conceive its rise as the expression of a new, interracial artistry. Swing certainly did change the taste preferences of the larger listening public, the shift enabling, as Lewis A. Erenberg observes in his book *Swingin' the Dream*, a passionate following by White youth, some of whom wholeheartedly embraced swing as an African American musical achievement. What this perspective obscures, though, is how White consumer attention—and the expansion of White-controlled institutions and labor that it catalyzed—suppressed Black participation in commercial markets to the point where many White listeners comfortably ignored the reality that swing originated as an embodied property of African American culture, a structuration underlying Black music's valuation and the conditions of its primary truth. If Black orchestras initially advanced swing innovations, they were soon giving way to a flood of White musicians who overtook the genre. Downplaying the depth of this racial contest allowed Schuller to argue that swing's sudden rush of invention demonstrated how people, when faced with "great financial stress, such as major economic depression, . . . turn inward," enabling the "happy and carefree mood" of swing to emerge. For Schuller, the political is what we distinguish from art.

Politics, he contends, did not "becom[e] a priority for jazz musicians until many decades later."[28]

Given the overwhelming challenges Black people faced from the time of emancipation, it is easy to see why many Black swing musicians thought about the aesthetic character of their music politically, particularly if "politics" is understood, as Rancière characterizes it, as a public negotiation on the right to participate in the making of the sensible world. For Black swing players, politics mattered because their participation in public culture was always checked; they could find no easy pathway to live justly in an unjust society. Those who populated the Black swing orchestras knew racial injustices well, many of whom were reared in the rural South, where African Americans were perpetually disadvantaged, whether seeking employment, looking for a home, or simply trying to live life with some dignity. In these ways, things hadn't changed much since the nineteenth century, with employment scarce everywhere, and when it was available, almost always under the least favorable conditions. Apart from these financial challenges, Black residents endured the challenge of brute existence: the constant threat of violence, which occurred frequently and arbitrarily. The quotidian nature of these assaults, which were most often directed toward young men—with lynching sometimes justified as a way of reducing labor competition— made "politics" for most African Americans just a part of the routine of everyday experience.[29]

Wanting to avoid these capricious injustices, tens of thousands of Black southerners living in rural areas were eager to move away, and Black musicians were no different. Like those before them, they were drawn to cities, which is why so many Black orchestras were populated by musicians originally from the South and Southwest. Cities afforded safety in numbers, making places like Atlanta, Memphis (home for a time of Sy Oliver and Zack Whyte), and Louisville a powerful draw. ("Louisville was really quite a breeding ground for musicians," Jonah Jones recalled.) Many more traveled to the Southwest, Midwest, West, and East, where they looked for work playing music or, failing that, found security amid the dense populations of Black poor clustered in the nation's slums.[30] Fletcher Henderson, who, as we've previously observed, led one of the premier jazz ensembles in the 1920s, was born in Cuthbert, Georgia; his principal arranger, Don Redman, migrated to New York from Piedmont, West Virginia. When Redman left Henderson's orchestra, he joined another headed by Bill McKinney, a native of Cynthiana, Kentucky, whose personnel included arranger John Nesbitt (Norfolk, Virginia) and pianist Todd Rhodes (Hopkinsville,

Kentucky). The Ellington Orchestra featured Jimmy Blanton (Chattanooga, Tennessee), Bubber Miley (Aiken, South Carolina), Barney Bigard (New Orleans, Louisiana), and Cootie Williams (Mobile, Alabama); the Kansas City–based Bennie Moten Orchestra included Lester Young (Woodville, Mississippi), Walter Page (Gallatin, Missouri), Hot Lips Page (Dallas, Texas), and Eddie Durham (San Marcos, Texas). The many all-girl bands running across the territories, moreover, were typically populated by players from the South. Emblematic was the International Sweethearts of Rhythm, whose personnel—including Helen Jones Woods (Meridian, Mississippi), Pauline Braddy (Mendenhall, Mississippi), and Clora Bryant (Denison, Texas)—hailed from southern states.[31]

The draw of the city was its offering of relative sanctuary, of a familiarity of place. In the midst of precarious mobilities and movements, it provided an environment where Black people were more tolerated and Black musicians had won begrudging respect for their peculiar affinity to sound.[32] If White majorities still limited their direct contact with African Americans, they had by then embraced a double-valued sound world delineated by Black expressions, being drawn particularly to what seemed less than and greater than Music as it was discerned in an enlivened beat. Black musicians were well aware of how commercial markets valorized the negative expressions of "Negro" and "hot" rhythm, and White popular composers celebrated its influence in an array of songs: the Gershwin brothers' "Fascinating Rhythm" (1924) and "I Got Rhythm" (1930), Hoagy Carmichael's "Riverboat Shuffle" (1927), and Joseph Meyer and Roger Wolfe Kahn's "Crazy Rhythm" (1928). They capitalized on the enduring preoccupation by inventing repertoires that affirmed myths about Black people's musical nature. The Black swing player was "that rhythm man" who lived by the claim "rhythm is our business" and who, through the powers of swing, made audiences "rhythm crazy."[33] Their commitment to rhythmic practices was thought to have extended from their African origins, which musicians sometimes exploited to turn a profit: Ellington—who declared in 1931 "jazz had its origin in Africa"—created with his orchestra the "jungle sound" featured in Cotton Club shows; Chick Webb formed his "Jungle Band" in 1929, which included a comical "jungle" repertory, notably "Jungle Mama" and a recorded version of "Heebie Jeebies" (1933) arranged by Benny Carter.[34]

Widespread interest in rhythm across Black and White communities was a key driver of swing's progressive development. Departing from the duple feel of 1920s jazz, swing performances advanced a new kind of fleet-footed intensity around which dance movement coalesced. As a commercial genre appealing to Black audiences, swing announced the revitalization of Black music's modern character, providing Black youth with what Cozy Cole called a "password" for entry into the transformative sonic orders of musicians' worlds. It was the secret code that enlivened clubs, bars, and dance halls, making the ordinary seem not ordinary at all.[35] In its many productions, Black swing reaffirmed the hyperpositive character of Black music, contradicting forces seeking to subjugate and oppress Black people in Jim Crow America. For those attuned to the productive relation of its enlivened sound to Black labor, it made discernible once more the qualities of a "mute music" that came alive in the better swing performances (cf. introduction).

We can get a glimpse into this world and the way musical inventions charted its contours through Count Basie's invaluable portrait of the swing era, *Good Morning Blues*. While staying within the conventions of autobiographical writing, Basie, working in collaboration with Albert Murray, artfully captures the mood of the time, offering a vivid portrait of a world inhabited by an engaging cast of characters—Billie Holiday; the singer/bartender Joe Turner; the record producer John Hammond; Negro League pitcher Satchel Paige; the Harlem saloon owner Big John—who were informing influences in his life. In Basie's rendering, swing arises as a creative insurgency of nighttime adventure, where the Black poor in regions far and wide found pleasure in its loud, raucous sound. Describing the scene in Kansas City, Missouri, Basie's transplanted home after his luck ran out touring with the vaudeville performer Gonzelle White, he recalls a place where insouciant young adults bantered, tangled, argued, joked, and played. When not hustling for work, they would shoot pool, play cards, discuss baseball (a favorite sport among Black swing musicians), seek out casual sex—their numbers being overwhelmingly straight men, with queer players (the "sweet" musicians, often pianists, contended saxophonist Budd Johnson) subjected to ridicule—and drink "nips," sometimes to excess, at basement joints "where they used to serve whiskey by the dipper." Basie's is a world familiar to the economically impoverished of the time. It describes a way of living life in the moment, whether in quiet desperation or largely unconcerned about what might come next. For an ambitious group of artisans—the all-boys' networks limiting involvement of the many women players who tended to work in their own bands—it provided the right atmosphere for advancing their craft, which they developed through incessant practice by day, checking out the competition at night. "Kansas City was a musicians' town," Basie writes, "and there were good musicians

7.1 Lindy Hop dancers in a juke joint outside Clarksdale, Mississippi, 1939. Marion Post Wolcott, photographer. Prints and Photographs Online Catalog, Library of Congress.

everywhere you turned. Sometimes you just stayed at one place, and sometimes you might hit maybe two or three or more, but you could never get around to all the jumping places in that town in one night."[36]

What made places jump was the vivid display of musical invention driving new rhythm forms, with swing practices variously coalescing in and around other versions of music time: stomps, shuffles, slow blues, boogie, together with the conventional dance rhythms Black orchestras eventually learned (waltz, tango, fox-trot, one-step, etc.). When a band was jumping, the dancers were too. Ellington determined how well his orchestra was performing according to this chief measure: "Will that musical phrase give 'em a kick? Will they feel like hopping around a bit when they hear that?" One of Henderson's main reasons for hiring Louis Armstrong was to give the orchestra greater energy, and, for a time, as Jonah Jones recalled, "Fletcher had the stompingest band in the country." Bennie Moten also knew well how to get a crowd going. Basie—who worked as pianist and arranger for Moten from 1929 to 1935—remembers how the orchestra, while playing in Ohio, cut the Paul Tremaine Orchestra, the hot solos by Hot Lips Page being especially successful at drawing in White listeners and dancers.[37] Appealing to the dancers was a chief concern: "The ballrooms," Cozy Cole remembered, "were all-important then." The purpose of swing, Barney Bigard stated to Hugues Panassié, was "quite simply to execute phrases that irresistibly drove one to dance." Musicians worked to adapt, whether accompanying those on the floor or the other players on stage. At nearly every performance event, swing instrumentalists interacted with dancers, "feeding" them as they would ensemble members, the energy of their playing developing in response to the dancers' actions.[38]

Sometimes the exchanges got so intense they inspired dramatic changes in the way dancers behaved. For example, when the Moten orchestra had the opportunity to play behind a professional dance act in New York, it triggered a shift in the stage performance as the band introduced hard stomping, Kansas City swing. As Basie put it, "We laid them ensembles on them, [t]hey didn't know what hit them. But they started to move. I'm pretty sure they'd never moved like that before in their lives." In another instance, performing for floor dancers at the Savoy in Harlem: "When we laid that 'Moten Swing' on them, it was shocking. They couldn't understand it, but they knew they could pat their feet and dance to it." Here Basie aligns embodied engagement and sonic knowledge: dancers had not moved the way they did until they heard in a new way, which drove a physical response, if not a conscious understanding, of the band's rhythmic innovation. What was original related directly to temporal flow, to the way a particular swing orientation redistributed the affective environment, altering the sense of place. Recalling his initial appearance at the Savoy, Basie wrote, "The main thing I was concerned about when I went in there that first time with my own band was getting those tempos together. Because no matter what you were playing, the tempo meant everything so far as getting those dancers together."[39]

Basie's remarks recall references by others about how Black musicians worked to audibly reshape the sensible arena, from the time when Ellington, entering a Tenderloin club, thought that "everybody seemed to be doing whatever they were doing in the tempo the Lion's group was lying down" to J. A. Rogers' depiction of "jazz time" as "faster and more complex than African music," "a joyous revolt from convention," to the ways that Louis Armstrong motivated and responded to dancers.[40] "Tempo," for Basie, referred to something more than the music's literal rate of speed; it suggested the qualities of the sensible that a band's playing generated. Tempo was a shorthand for the way the band's performance implied the dynamic motion and flow; it described how a music animated by swing inspired dancers' behavior and restructured the feeling of place. By shifting tempos, the Moten Orchestra performed a kind of time-altering magic: it reoriented the cadence of the performance, the audible complexities encouraging shifts in the affective order. The shifts allowed for the possibility of revelatory moments where the expanse of Black pasts could seem to be rushing into the present. Black swing proposed a new sonic politics, a way of reclaiming past properties, as it instructed dancers on how their bodies should behave in accordance. Against this background, the significance of Basie's remarks about patting feet come into focus. As these engagements played out routinely across the networks of band tours, swing arose as a politically saturated quality of sound indelibly marked with temporalities of the past in the presentation of new performance. Black swing and its patting feet grew collaboratively and truthfully as a form of life.

Thinking of swing as a form of life develops from Gebhardt's earlier portrayal of vaudeville's ontologies of sound, explored in chapter 6. It describes the material conditions from which entertainers produced sound formations arising directly from the audible character of their living selves. Players embraced the mythologies about Black people's natural musicality, which, as Ellington put it in 1933, was "the expression of a people's soul," its qualities of swing being an "indefinable" expression of a musician's character. "Each musician," explained Barney Bigard, "has his own way of producing swing, very different from the musician beside him [in the ensemble]."[41] Although Black swing players were in one way at the losing end, struggling to find work in a depleted economy, they were in another making gains amid the vaunted claims about rhythm's centrality in popular music. While perhaps poor and unemployed, Black musicians were owners of something larger than life: an enlivened audibility that brimmed with seditious energy. Black swing was a transgressive language, political in the way it radically realigned the sensible order. Its radicalism was not pretentious but comedic, on the ground, consistent with the playful spectrality of Armstrong's "Heebie Jeebies." Black swing conjured a comedy of spirits, as in the Lunceford Orchestra's mock church ceremonies, with bass player Moses Allen's preacher routines.[42] Such ironic gestures to the otherworldly were part of what musicians described as a world inhabited by spooks. "Spook was an in jive word among entertainers in those days," Basie explained. "It was something that entertainers used to call themselves. . . . Maybe it had something to do with being mostly nighttime people. So we kept late hours, spooky hours. The hours when the spooks came out."[43] To be a "spook"—harkening back to the world of Black theatrical enter-

tainment and colored minstrelsy—meant inverting the racially derogatory language of White power to realize something hyperpositive. Black
swing's aliveness flourished during these nocturnal hours, being the product of musicians' nearly constant interactions.

Swing's intensities played a powerful role in organizing the musicians'
sensory order: as a product of their collaborative work in honing their
craft, swing sound became a point of orientation in their everyday lives.
Although swing did not directly reflect jazz musicians' social relations, it
could not have developed as it did without the influence of those relations.
Playing music and living the musician's life were bound together, informing one another. After working a show, for example, orchestra members
might reassemble over breakfast and then, after catching some sleep, meet
again later in the day to get back to work. When on the road, they spent
long hours side by side in buses and cars, sometimes living hand-to-mouth
on "sardines and crackers . . . soda pop and bootleg whiskey," sleeping
where they could. Such incessant contact could become exhausting, but it
also produced a form of relation that carried over to their ensemble work,
suggesting a kinship with professional athletes. In fact, Basie's recollections of the band's tours call to mind the kind of banter and play common
to sports teams, particularly those in Negro baseball, which many Black
swing players, including Basie, followed closely. (The Henderson orchestra
played ball competitively; Ellington was himself a serious athlete.) The musicians shared with ballplayers a strong allegiance to collective purpose, to
putting on display one's individual talents while remaining focused on the
larger aim to win. Some musicians, however, strove toward a different and
arguably higher purpose: winning was not only performative but aesthetic.
And if they, like ballplayers, participated in their own gamesmanship, in
those "battle[s] of music," where competing bands tried to outperform or
"chop" the other, their aim was not simply to win but to create expressions
of spectacular being. They sought to bring alive what swing musicians
commonly referred to as an orchestra's "personality."[44]

Black swing orchestras did not simply play "music" or perform "works"
for dancers and listeners. They were in the business of creation, of bringing
into being audible forms that carried forth from the expressive idiosyncrasies of its personnel. Musicians believed that a player's sound revealed
qualities of truth unique to their performing bodies. "Joe [Thomas] had a
lot of personality, and a lot of tricks on the horn," Ed Wilcox, who played
piano and arranged for Lunceford, told Stanley Dance. About Buster "Prof"
Smith, Basie remarked, "there was nobody like him on alto. He had a style

that was different from everybody" and his contributions shaped "the personality of [the] band."[45] Armstrong proposed not only that his playing was an extension of who he was but that "the notes" were animated forms with a life of their own. "That's my livin' and my life. I love them notes. That's why I try to make 'em right, see?" As they worked together, musicians brought into being an orchestra's personality according to the rules of engagement that determined Black musicality over the past sixty-odd years. Sometimes their work drew consciously from the past in playful, life-affirming ways: highlighting Black music's origins in the Black body provided a means of developing a modern Black style. Ellington, for example, explained that the distinctive rhythmic pattern of "East St. Louis Toddle-O" (released on record by Columbia as "Toodle-O") was inspired by "those old Negroes who work the fields for year upon year, and [who] are tired at the end of their day's labour, may be seen walking home at night with a broken, limping step locally known as the 'toddle-O,' with the accent on the last syllable." The Armstrong Orchestra, moreover, employed the languid and luxurious saxophone sound of the Guy Lombardo Orchestra—which was widely admired among Black musicians—as the basis of a sexual parody on its recorded version of "Stardust" (1931). The lunging ensemble protrusions one hears behind Armstrong's paraphrases of the melody were known in jazz circles as the "fucking rhythm." Swing rises ascendant, a bawdy, loud species of life.[46]

By the early 1930s, Black orchestral jazz in its many iterations had grown into an established popular expression, its ensembles populated by skilled musicians who were fluent in the sounding practices they had learned working the entertainment circuits. Despite its challenges, playing jazz offered a pleasurable form of labor, a decent way to make a living. Yet although many musicians were probably practical minded about their place in the business, others shared a higher sense of purpose, seeing their musical creativity more politically as a way of remaking the sound of Black culture. Ellington was a leader among Black musicians in articulating this view, suggesting an evolution in his thinking from the days when he was primarily interested in just getting by. The swing band was now part of a formidable tradition. Employing a common folkloric conceit, he drew a connection between the slave past and the swing present: "What we could not say openly we expressed in music, and what we know as 'jazz' is something more than just dance music. When we dance it is not a mere diversion or social accomplishment. It expresses our personality, and, right down in us, our souls react to the elemental but eternal rhythm."[47]

Ellington's verbosity suggests the influence of a British editor who may have employed such lofty language to convince readers of the band leader's importance. But, as Mark Tucker remarks, the content was likely his. Which is to say that Ellington—whose influence among Black swing players was enormous—saw the swing orchestra as a force moving beyond the pedestrian entertainment ensemble: it was now the producer of Black art. Not art in the European sense of Music with a capital *M*—Ellington openly disavowed his music's associations with the Euro-Western art tradition—but an art cast in the negative that was ultimately greater than Music: swing as spectacular form moving historically counter to the everyday present as it fostered connections to the primacy of Black living, opening doors to truthful encounter.[48] The craft of Black swing was akin to musical alchemy: through the routines of ensemble work, orchestras produced aggregations of sound that were greater than the sum of their parts. A strong performance realized a form of alchemy, transforming individual technique into a coalescence of authentic orchestral sound that was thought to reveal an ensemble's distinctive character.

An orchestra's personality developed according to its relation to time, to the way it was situated in time and made time—how its execution of "getting those tempos together" affected temporal flow. Ensemble time conferred who they were, the key to personality located in the band's approach to swing and the way it made dancers hop around a bit and listeners pat their feet. During their conversation with Stanley Dance, the members of the Jonah Jones group spoke about how approaches to swing defined a band's personality. On the performance style of the Chick Webb Orchestra, which was well-known for its forward-leaning swing, Jones said "it was a different kind of swing again, just as there was a difference between the swing of McKinney's Cotton Pickers and Fletcher Henderson's band. Each had a personality of its own." Turning to a comparison of Lunceford's temporal feel to that of Basie's, moreover, the bassist John Brown observed, "Basie's was a looser type of thing, and Lunceford's swing wasn't as relaxed because the arrangements were more complicated." For Jones, the Lunceford Orchestra "had a different kind of beat. [Its drummer Jimmy] Crawford had his own type of beat." Cozy Cole agreed. Lunceford's arranger, "Sy [Oliver], always had that two-beat feeling" while remaining in a steady, four-beat meter.[49]

The approaches to ensemble time seemed limitless, varying as widely as the breadth of human behavior. Not only would musicians and entire bands play behind or ahead of the beat—an orientation widely attributed to Louis Armstrong's solo style—but also underneath or above. As Schuller observed, "Almost all swing bands, black and white, played very much on the beat, indeed on top of the beat." When underneath, the player or players remained steady to the pulse; when above, they seemed to float lightly yet precisely upon it. These spatial metaphors suggest how musicians understood their position within the time frames of a performance. They also relate to the precision of technique. In fact, swing players may have adapted the figure of speech from baseball: a perfect execution of a pitch or a batter's swing, for example, requires staying "on top of the ball."[50] This means of describing technical subtleties transferred easily to musical performance to inform a comprehension of how stylistic intricacies produced an orchestra's personality. Close attention to the beat was critical to the successful execution of swing and to the expression of who a band was. Beat represented the pivot point, the foundational architecture on which an ensemble moved in time and by which its personality came alive. Orchestras shaped their approaches to convey an attitude, a way of engaging the social world, with the force and character of its swing practice offering a kind of moving portrait of its being. For audiences, an orchestra's swing-based personality expressed what kind of enlivened "thing" this group of players was and how, in particular, the animated qualities of swing appeared as part of its makeup. "Personality" told audiences how much time they wanted to spend time with a band. Did they want to listen to it, to be in its company, to live with it a while and be drawn into its sound? Did they feel compelled to move their bodies according to what it was playing, to what to them it seemed to say?

Steering the expression of an orchestra's personality was the arranger, who rose to prominence during the swing era. For some orchestras, arranging was the work of the leader, who aimed to project their personality into the work. Ellington, Henderson (after Don Redman left in 1927), and later Basie were known for it; Ellington's involvements were distinguished as that of a composer-orchestrator. Other leaders, such as Earl Hines, were content to leave decisions about arrangements to others, such as Hayes Alvis and Cecil Irwin, whom Hines relied on to perform the task. Most often, the arrangers were players in the band who were hired for dual roles. Like Alvis and Irwin, Jimmy Mundy was a recognized instrumentalist (he played tenor saxophone) who set a new course for Hines's orchestra when he became its principal arranger in 1933.[51] Mary Lou Williams was a formidable pianist, but she was perhaps most admired for the dexterity and liveliness she introduced as the arranger of the Andy Kirk Orchestra. Chick Webb's arrangers, Benny Carter and Edgar Sampson, helped to accentuate the orchestra's predilection for a buoyant, full-frontal swing, which Webb directed and urged on in his drumming. Edwin Wilcox, Willie Smith, and particularly Sy Oliver—who innovated formal complexities, chromatic passages, and a strong, back-leaning relation to the beat—gained respect as much for their arrangements for the Lunceford Orchestra as they did for their instrumental playing. Will Hudson, a White player who also arranged for Lunceford, helped to establish the orchestra's trademark fast, riff-based compositions that incited riotous energy. The driving forces of McKinney's Cotton Pickers, Don Redman and John Nesbitt, rehearsed the band almost daily and, during the orchestra's residency at the Graystone Ballroom, ran, as Cuba Austin put it, "a sort of music school in a locker room," helping players with their reading skills and comprehension of the arrangers' strategies for inducing the ensemble's sense of propulsion.[52]

Arrangers often dramatized the singularity of an orchestra's personality by creating designs that inspired the course of players' action. Successful arrangements—the "specials" contrasted to stock arrangements—were ones that made musicians feel comfortable in the performance and made clear their role within it, all toward the greater purpose of maintaining ensemble coherence and a steady sense of swing.[53] A common tactic was to highlight what was distinctive about the instrumental voices of an orchestra's personnel. Trumpet, trombone, and reed sections were typically led by the strongest musicians who guided their section's participation in the arrangement. ("We always had somebody in those sections who was a leader, who could start something and get those ensembles going," Basie recalled.) Some bands worked principally with head arrangements—unwritten plans worked out collectively as an ensemble—relying on leaders in each section to navigate the orchestra through the performance. Others, such as the Lunceford Orchestra, set firm constraints on the players to induce a particular kind of feel. In each, the goal was to produce the sensation that, out of the assembly of players, a single entity was alive, sounding a personality according to a recognizable ensemble beat. This is what Gene Ramey was referring to when he suggested that bands learned "to breathe at the same time," instructing willful young players "to team as well as play solo." Willie Smith recalled how the Lunceford reed section worked assiduously to blend their voices, "so it sounded like one guy playing five saxophones." Through "long associations," Ellington observed in his first published essay, musicians are "able almost to anticipate each other's thoughts so that . . . they should play as one man."[54] When he expanded his orchestra in 1932, he brought together three trombonists, each distinctive in sound and approach, who not only stood out in their own ways when playing singular passages or soloing but could also "when necessary, blend chameleon-like into a single sonority."[55]

The desire to produce a coherent ensemble personality had a profound impact on the development of solo playing, accelerating a shift from melodic paraphrase to extended improvisations. Strong soloists or "get-off men" could enliven a band's performance, the best of improvisers coaxing players into an ensemble groove that created the illusion of a lone voice performing with a singularity of purpose. A hard-driving, swinging band led by a hot soloist also excited audiences and energized dancers. Band leaders were well aware of how Armstrong's addition to the Henderson orchestra in 1924 transformed an adventurous dance orchestra into a new kind of entity capable of moving flawlessly from graceful waltzes to feverish stomps. William McKinney sought to do something similar in 1928 when he took on Prince Robinson as the orchestra's featured reed player, as did Earl Hines when he hired the soloists Jimmy Mundy and Trummy Young in 1932 and 1933. Solo playing, moreover, could become integrated into the fabric of an ensemble arrangement, as arrangers drew on players' innovations and techniques in their scores. In 1931, for example, Bennie Moten instructed his arrangers, Count Basie and Eddie Durham, to "get lips" after they told him about Hot Lips Page's harmonically expansive performances with the Oklahoma City Blue Devils, which they featured in their arrangements. "Staff arrangers," Basie explains, "did not hesitate to use all kinds of little things that other sidemen had been contributing to the overall sound and personality of the band as solo licks, riffs and those wonderful little call and shout things." He later did the same with his own band, hiring Lester Young and Herschel Evans to strengthen his ensemble's solo capacities. As Schuller notes, soloing itself became across the swing repertory "an integral part of the composition," with a particularly successful improvisation often being replayed in subsequent performances.[56]

Strategies for combining solo and section work grew as part of the evolution of Black swing, the various arranging techniques and styles of featured improvisers representing the key means by which orchestras defined themselves and listeners distinguished the disposition of one band from another. Ensemble personalities grew as a discernible aural quality: through the interplay of sections and soloists over the course of a performance, bands were laying out who they were. And like any individual personality, an orchestra's sound, though distinctive, never remained stable. It changed as musicians moved about, playing in one band and then joining another, their own styles developing further from the various informal pickups and jam sessions they played in. The fluidity in the growth of swing practice may be understood as part of a greater temporal energy that came to dominate the listening-scape of American popular culture, as new Black sound redistributed and made its aural character anew. Enlivened Black swing set the conditions for what was right in music and what one wanted to hear, even if Black musicians remained marginal—their peculiarly natural "modern" sounds spooking the sonorities of the present.

SWING-TIME AND THE BODY POLITIC

By the mid-1930s, the personality metaphor that had informed the creative life of Black swing orchestras became aligned with and then largely subsumed by the commercial institutions producing popular music. What was formerly an ontological conception operating within the racially defined networks of African American musicians advanced as another kind of mystification attached to productions sold in the national market. As DeVeaux observes about one institution, "It was axiomatic in radio that if you wanted to stamp your personality unforgettably into the consciousness of listeners, you had to develop a trademark—just like soap or coffee—and hammer it over the airwaves mercilessly." By projecting distinctive personalities through radio and other publicity networks, "commercial" swing (the epithet attributed to John Hammond), performed chiefly by White orchestras, shifted attention away from the racial contradictions underlying the production of popular music to the subtle, disconcerting play of the market. Embodied personalities of ensemble sound took on the fetish character of commodity forms seemingly imbued with a racially nebulous, animated spirit that disseminated across the body politic.[57]

Prior to its widespread emergence, swing existed largely outside the celebrity world of entertainment. A rhythm practice performed for the most part by African American musicians, it participated modestly as part of the sonic clamor of the moment. Yet within a few years, that sensible order changed dramatically, as revisions of Black swing circulated as part of a dynamically changing popular language. Swing's reconceptualization as an active agent in the revitalization of the music industry introduced into the public sphere a dramatically new musical expression, its temporal energy different from what most White Americans had experienced before. Swing's broad appeal as a commercial genre, however, extended an expropriative process that spelled losses for African American musicians: when Black orchestras finally entered the business in large numbers in the late 1930s, they remained in the shadow of White stars and leading bands. Still, the unintended sacrifice was transformative in the reorganization of modern audible life. What was enlivened in swing—a complex and nuanced rhythmic practice unprecedented in the history of Western music—wandered seemingly pell-mell as disembodied, animated auralities across global markets. In its transactional movements, the swing commodity redistributed the sensible organization of musical life: it engendered a veritable swing-time, a normative temporality driven by capitalism that evened out and spatialized the racially ontologized qualities of swing sound. In the process, those same qualities pushed against temporal norms, as enlivened sound persisted in its troubling action.

White interpretations of swing first took shape as part of the panoply of activity in commercial musical production during the late 1920s and the early 1930s. The working musicians who populated live shows, radio programs, and recording studios were expected to perform a diverse repertoire that, while largely centered on stock arrangements of popular melodies ("sweet music"), also included waltzes, tangos, fox-trots, rumbas, blues, and hot jazz. The best players were those who could move with agility across the range of styles; the best of the best—notably, Bunny Berigan, Jimmy Dorsey, Eddie Lang, Wingy Manone, Red Nichols, Jack Teagarden, Joe Venuti, and Benny Goodman—could also perform hot-inflected improvisations. These inventions became featured attractions once swing coalesced as a commercial genre. In New York, where a particularly dense concentration of musical energy flowed within commercial forums, technical proficiency was a must; skills in jazz improvisation meant more opportunities to work. "The big dance-band leaders," Gunther Schuller observes, "always liked to have at least one 'hot' man around for their up-tempo numbers, usually to 'jazz up' the final chorus or two." Still, conventional, commercial forms predominated. "The degree of jazziness was precisely controlled by the leader (or contractor or recording director). . . . Ignoring the melody and just playing on the changes was simply not tolerated."[58]

Schuller characterizes the commercial constraints on White dance music as banalities that inhibited the expression of aesthetically superior swing; only when its makers overcame those liabilities could swing fulfill its destiny as a mature form. It seems far more likely, though, that many if not most White players were perfectly comfortable working within the routines of dance music and Tin Pan Alley. They were, after all, professional musicians in the business of playing the kinds of popular rhythm music that appealed to White people across social classes. Although many aspired to a career playing improvised jazz, they also enjoyed the opportunities their racial status afforded, no matter how much cachet performing hot music as fashioned by the Harlem bands carried. Rhythm music at this time was mutable, dynamic, with no single orientation fully establishing stylistic dominance. Even a player as formidable as Goodman, a clarinetist who was already recognized in the 1920s as a talented improviser, questioned the commercial viability of Black swing as a model.[59] If Goodman joined other leading White musicians (many of whom were, like him, Chicago-born) to play in after-hours sessions or to record minstrel-inflected novelty tunes and hot jazz, the lot of them were probably content playing popular show and Tin Pan Alley tunes, for this was the work they could secure at the depths of the Depression.[60] Although the ability to play "a few bars of 'hot' jazz became virtually mandatory in any respectable dance-band performance," many musicians stayed focused on developing technique and learning a heterogeneous dance-band repertory.[61]

We can get a sense of how early swing emerged in relation to a range of other rhythm practices by turning to the commercial releases of leading orchestras with which Goodman was affiliated as a sideman or leader. The recordings supply important evidence of how Black-based swing entered the language of White popular music, gestating as it inhabited other styles and approaches. "Bag o' Blues" (1929), performed by Jack Pettis and His Orchestra, for example, is an otherwise conventional two-beat fox-trot that gains a kind of racial glamour from intermittent improvised solos and breaks that energize the ensemble. Similarly, on Ben Pollack's "My Kind of Love" (1929), Goodman plays a hot solo, and trombonist Jack Teagarden sings in Negro dialect to enliven the normalcy of an otherwise polite popular song. Toward the end of the recording, the band interrupts the rhythmic symmetry, breaking out into a hot out-chorus featuring aggressive brass playing. Particularly interesting is the strange morphing of style that appears on the 1930 recording "The Whole Darned Thing's for You," which was released under Goodman's name. What begins as a typical version of sweet ballroom dance music turns into a lively jazz performance during the final two choruses. On "One More Time" (1931), moreover, recorded by a studio band and released under the name Roy Carroll and His Sands Point Orchestra, Goodman plays a series of breaks over a strong, 4/4 ensemble swing. Flashes of swing show up once more on "When Your Lover Has Gone" (1931) and "Walkin' My Baby Back Home" (1931), with Goodman again the leader of both sessions. On "When Your Lover," the orchestra first presents a conventional interpretation of the popular tune, sung by Paul Small. Then, after the vocal chorus, it moves into a subtle yet discernible swing feeling. "Walkin'," a popular tune recorded the same year by Maurice Chevalier, features a buoyant 4/4 energy as it anticipates the character of ensemble swing that would flourish in White orchestras a few years later. As Schuller writes, the pair of recordings shows how "the band is consciously trying to play both 'hot jazz' and 'modern.' The result is something well beyond the normal dividing line between commercial dance music and late twenties jazz."[62]

By 1935, swing had overtaken commercial music entertainment. Its aesthetic standards reorganized, the new genre set the course of popular music's style development for years to come. It is routine in jazz history to identify the Goodman Orchestra's August 1935 appearance at the Palomar Ballroom in Los Angeles as the turning point. This is the moment when the band, performing works and arrangements by Fletcher Henderson, captivated young dancers who "surged around the stand to watch and listen."[63] Although Goodman's introduction of Henderson's language and repertoire was critical—marking the moment when, as Cozy Cole put it, White orchestra leaders "began to get colored musicians in the bands"—recordings suggest that the move to swing was neither sudden nor inevitable.[64] Rather, from around 1929, swing practices arose out of a complex of rhythmic approaches, seemingly vying for position amid a contest of diverse temporal orientations.

The question, then, is why did swing come to dominate other forms of commercial rhythm music? Part of the reason had to do with how the temporal feel of Black swing began to influence White musical taste. As we've seen, although many Black bands struggled to find jobs in the depths of the Depression, some managed to keep working, with several hired occasionally to perform in White ballrooms. Also important was the return of Black orchestras to recording studios in late 1932, assisted in part by John Hammond in his work with British Columbia. Typically limited to hot performances that fulfilled racial stereotype, these sessions helped nonetheless to widen public knowledge of the new swing approaches. The commercial availability of recordings, moreover, increased performance opportunities for Black musicians both at home and abroad, driving White interest in hot playing and supporting the growth of an international community of jazz enthusiasts. Principal among them in the United States were college students, who brought Black and White bands to perform at campus dances. As John Gennari observes, some of these enthusiasts—Marshall Stearns, Walter Schaap, Frederic Ramsey Jr., Charles Edward Smith, and Hammond—soon started writing about their musical interests in *Down Beat, Metronome,* and *Melody Maker;* in weekly magazines (e.g., *Saturday Review*); and in politically left publications such as the *New Masses* and *Daily Worker.*[65] In addition to his journalistic contributions, Hammond hosted a show featuring Black performers on the Socialist Party's radio station WEVD. It was against this background that network stations began showcasing dance orchestras playing jazz on their national "11th Hour" broadcasts.[66] From December 1934 to May 1935, NBC featured Goodman's orchestra during the jazz portion of its *Let's Dance* program, during which it introduced Henderson's arrangements to national audiences. Among the listeners were those who later heard the band play at the Palomar.[67]

Yet a change in taste does not in itself explain why the change occurred, nor does it tell us why swing ultimately dominated popular style. Underlying the broad transformation were capital inducements for White orchestras to conform to a standardized swing practice, to even out the diversity of approaches as part of a greater swing-time. This consensus brand of swing was part of the codification of an emerging genre, where swing's heightened access across entertainment networks—assisted by the sonic transformation of public culture that Suisman charted—spread a routinized practice. With the music seemingly everywhere, swing's audible sensation, stretching across the nation and throughout the global metropolitan world, grew increasingly uniform, familiar. In its breadth, swing seemed more spatial than temporal, its immediacy of access and stylistic uniformity suggesting a stasis, as if time, in the case of swing, at least, were standing still. Increasingly, swing's formal temporality appeared to establish the same spatial present, its expressions favoring stereotyped practices in which the nuances of Black performance were codified. Cooptation and dissemination of revised versions of Black creativity were central to swing's modern disposition: their spatialized formulations were part of the subjugation of the primal temporal qualities believed to be at the heart of Black music. If swing's animated energy still derived from "the rhythmic jungle chants of the descendants of Africans," its makers were now taking control of those originating features through the power of capital and disseminating them freely across world markets.[68]

White commercial swing reaffirmed a contradiction fundamental to popular music's development: its expropriation of practices thought to derive from an African-informed "Negro" past became the means of creating a distinctively modern musical temporality. As if to obscure this contradiction, the expropriations seemed ironically to heighten the process of deracination, turning what was before racial and historical into a sound advancing popular music's progress. As it was performed by White ensembles, commercial swing, unlike some other versions of rhythm music, represented a fundamental departure from the feel of ragtime and 1920s jazz, its distinctive temporality articulating to features signifying modern living. Swing's even time and buoyant rhythm moved popular music away from the "spasmodic measures" and "topsy-turvy syncopation" that Oscar Bie had attributed to an earlier dance music, its subtle variances against a steady flow of pulse seeming to many to capture the character of the present day. One writer proposed that swing was "the social outlet of our city"; for another, it was "as if it came from the American ground under these buildings, roads, and motor cars (which it did)." As a popular genre, moreover, the many forms of swing conjured likenesses to its vast listenership: swing revealed "the immortal right of adolescence to assert itself"; "the voice of youth striving to be heard in this fast-moving world of ours." And in its initial accompanying dance form, the Lindy Hop—named after the transatlantic pilot Charles Lindbergh—swing drew analogies to the thrill of flight, its acrobatic "air steps" performed by Savoy Ballroom dancers marking a clear departure from the rural-centered "animal" dances from a generation ago.[69]

A cascade of creative symbolism erupted, its grandiosity growing in proportion to commercial swing's incorporation of Black forms into commercial markets. Swing-time had coalesced as a popular version of aesthetic truth. So powerful was its influence, it appeared to move beyond the auditory, its spatialization across the market economy proposing ties to material culture and the world of ideas. As the reporter Gama Gilbert summarized it in 1938, swing "has been reflected in the nation's literature, and has inspired novels, biographies, mystery stories, scholarly dissertations, countless magazine articles and newspaper features. . . . Ubiquitous in the airwaves, movies, books, and newspapers," he continued, "it has been accepted in the lives of a sufficient portion of the population to have affected its mores and language."[70] The perceived linkages could even exceed the bounds of nation, as swing's metaphorical presence enveloped the world. "American jazz," the magazine magnate Henry Luce suggested, together with "Hollywood movies, American slang . . . [and] American machines . . . are in fact the only things that every community in the world, from Zanzibar to Hamburg, recognizes in common."[71] Global in reach, it proposed a new common language. "Jazz is not white, nor black, nor Jewish, nor Aryan, nor Chinese, nor American," the critic Charles Delaunay wrote defiantly in 1940, at the onset of the Nazi regime's occupation of France. "Jazz is much more than an American music—it is the first universal music . . . [because] it speaks directly to the hearts of men." All encompassing, "swing" was, the *New York Times* declared, "the tempo of our time."[72]

As a concept, *tempo* knows a long history. In music theory, it emerged as a key parameter of the musical work, its direction set by the composer and interpreted by musicians or a conductor, whereas in social criticism, the idea corresponded to human progress in its relation to technological development. In his landmark study, *Technics and Civilization* (1934), Lewis Mumford proclaimed that "the problem of tempo" had become central among the "all-important problems of civilization."[73] But at this juncture in the mid-1930s, when Black bands were laying down their tempos, the word carried an additional charge. Despite the best efforts of the music industry to quiet the source of its newness, swing's intrusive tempos exposed the imprint of a Negro beat: "our time"—a spatialized swing-time—also confronted *their time*, revealing nuances that moved to the embodied pulses of Black rhythm. The disclosure of an influence born of "rhythmic jungle chants" was not in itself surprising. Similar claims about the refusal of Black embodied sound to completely succumb to capital—to fully relinquish its embodied labor to the process of exchange—traced back to the era of enslavement. With the rise of commercial swing, though, the matter of Black music's embodied tempos intensified, impacting thinking about the temporal world White people lived in. Ideas about the relation of race, time, and music were gaining traction as Hollywood film—for example, *Tarzan the Ape Man* (1932), starring Johnny Weissmuller—and activists and scholars—notably, Zora Neale Hurston and Melville Herskovits—contradicted deracinating tendencies, widening beliefs in the persistence of African influence in American culture. For many, everyday living felt different and sounded different from what had gone on before.[74]

The temporal incongruities produced in swing, which circulated through the economy at lightning speed, were now seeming to affect the phenomenal organization of the social world: despite its massive capitalization and incorporation, swing revealed just how deeply a sonically registered "Negro" time was intruding on the time of the everyday. If swing had succumbed to the expropriative force of commercial markets—if it had become normalized and spatialized as a compliant participant in the entertainment industry—it was also bringing forth through the performances of White orchestras racially incorrigible temporalities: disembodied vestiges of a time that regenerated by the tempos of modern Black music. What had been economically fetishized and deflated became substantial, inflated through the commercial dissemination of Black music's primary fetishism: an inalienable energy that pried open norms of temporal experience, congealing as ontologically enlivened sound. Incongruities of music time, economically fetishized and incorporated into commercial swing, were simultaneously revealing sonic breakthroughs of time-shifting performance that created missteps in the temporal regularity of White worlds.

Commercial swing betrayed a trouble of time disturbing the temporal regularity of the social. A distinctively modern aurality, it was enacted through newly invented presences of buoyant aliveness that, through its complex articulations to everyday life, hovered between the unprecedented nowness of the moment and the "savage" intrusions coming forth as temporalities of the Negro past. In its ambivalence, swing materialized the reality of the White nation's uncomfortable yet necessary proximity to its racial other—necessary, that is, to the idea of the United States as what Paul Fritz Laubenstein called "the melting pot of the world." Swing's practice—to summon once more the insights of Harry Harootunian—manifested how "the past leaves imprints in this space" of time under capitalism. Swing had developed necessarily, "perforce," as a genre bringing forward a credit from a reimagined racial past critical to the expression of modern form.[75]

Black swing's intensities were valued because they formally moved popular music toward a distinctively *modern* temporality situated between "our time" and "theirs," neither wholly past nor entirely of the present. What were imagined as archaic qualities of musical feeling were in fact constituted in the present in the ongoing accumulation of Black sonic material that was reorganizing popular music. Swing's time trouble added up to the persistence of a racially distinctive rhythmic intensity that exposed the temporal incongruities of the musical present: Black sonic incorrigibility was "a product now separable from its production, which is never entirely mastered by the forces that have engendered it" and whose expressions "break the spell of routine to introduce different but coexisting temporalities . . . [that] impinge upon the present."[76] Despite its antagonistic position within pop, Black music's impingements were crucial to the valuation of swing because they were what enlivened performances and transfigured the listening experience. As Black swing inspired Black clubgoers to enter a new sensible arena and engage on the dance floor in a new form of disruptive pleasure, it also enabled White followers to begin to imagine how a newly racialized sound might reveal modes of thought not necessarily affirming life as it always seemed. For Black and White youth alike, swing proposed the opportunity of comprehending the past differently from how it was typically known.

The critics who first wrote about swing recognized that its animated energy evoked temporal incongruencies with the public present, even if they were not entirely sure how it did so or what those realms were. These advocates, by and large well-educated young White men, were seminal in their understanding of Black swing as part of a larger creative continuity stretching back to a "pre-historical" southern era in the aftermath of slavery, a concept they introduced as part of their criticism. Inspired by Hugues Panassié's influential book, *Le Jazz Hot* (1934; English translation, 1936), several early jazz writers proposed that the newness of swing had developed out of a long tradition of African American performance that was informing the music's contemporary character. In his fifteen-part series "The History of Swing," published as monthly installments in *Down Beat* in 1936 and 1937, Marshall Stearns portrayed swing's evolution as an inexorable movement from the primitive to the modern, its achievements forged through the shared actions of Black and White musicians. He and other writers pushed hard against the prevailing view that Black contributions were merely a decorative supplement to popular style, highlighting the originality of leading African American innovators. Through the efforts of Stearns and his critical cohort, Basie, Lunceford, Hawkins, Lionel Hampton, and others would join Ellington and Armstrong among the pantheon of the commercial swing movement.[77]

Whatever their intentions, though, White critics, in their steps to situate Black contributions as part of the larger picture of swing, ultimately reinforced White possessive control of the movement. Although their celebrations of Black musicians were undoubtedly sincere, these same writers were above all participants in an industry-wide tendency to expropriate Black value, converting it to conform to the current standards of commercial music. By fostering swing's growth in the consumer marketplace, they expedited a transference of property that resituated Black music time within the temporal coherence of a White-majority history: temporal incongruities produced in the racialized contests of Black and White worlds would be remade and incorporated as a developmentally coherent swing-time. If the commercial swing movement was unprecedented in its embrace of Black influence, its tolerance was part of the continuing aspiration of White power to extract value from African American performances and to turn it into a possession moving to the normative time of capital.

Through these measures, Black music, as swing, would continue to decouple from its makers, repositioned to conform to what Mumford called "the increasing tempo of civilization," whose duration distinguished it from the primitive time of a "savage" past.[78] The spatialization of Black swing as part of a civilized swing-time secured an incongruous Black past in order to erase it, remaking it to conform to the temporal certainty of a "Negro tradition" subsumed within the historical arc of the West.

Key to the process of normalizing swing-time was the critics' reliance on the evolutionary schemes of folklore. In his book *Jazz, Hot and Hybrid* (1938)—the first English-language monograph devoted to analyses of jazz—Winthrop Sargeant stressed Black music's distinction from the conventions of European tonality and meter. The "polyrhythmic peculiarities" from which swing had developed, he contended, identified "a basic ingredient of all jazz." The source of these peculiarities, however, was difficult to establish. Implicit was Sargeant's assumption that jazz innovations were not wholly individual achievements but depended on a kind of natural ferment: forms that welled up organically from the ground of an anonymous folk. Accordingly, the critic's role was to make tangible these reluctant "peculiarities" to reveal what African American musicians could not. "Those who create [jazz] most successfully are the ones who know least about its abstract structure," Sargeant contended, likening the Negro's "natural" musical character to the growth of a plant. "Neither the Negro folk musician nor the plant is consciously attempting to fulfill a geometric destiny" (i.e., apparently, to realize coherent, musical form). By rendering Black music tangible, into what he called "measurable elements," critical language would codify those qualities inaccessible through conventional listening.[79]

For Roger Pryor Dodge, critical judgment fueled the very life of swing's development—it was essential to the music's turn toward serious art. For swing, he surmised, was not merely folkloric but had ascended in its relation to the commercial market, now holding promise as the future art of the modern. As he conceived it in an essay for the Hot Record Society's magazine, HRS *Society Rag*, in 1941, swing in its development manifested the greater evolution of Black being. Yet what ultimately showed real promise was not the Black artist but swing itself. Jazz, in its evolution into a potent, cultural force, had gained qualities of self-possession. Having become fully integrated into the mechanisms of the social, it betrayed a sentience, which Dodge conveyed in his use of third-person declensions of intent (e.g., "Jazz should . . ."). At the time, swing was still in nascent form, having passed through the "process of parturition, childhood, and adolescence." For it to continue to evolve, though, Dodge argued, it would need to pay off its debts and participate more fully in the social world: to "begin to give the future something akin to what it has been given by the past." Its future obligation was neither to Black people nor to the Negro past but to a greater public: in its ascendency as an aesthetic form, jazz assumed an authority above the woeful labor that had created it and now faced the opportunity to enter a new phase of world history.[80]

By giving to History, the musical subject jazz would achieve progress, which was, after all, art's very reason for being. "For jazz to maintain a vital reason for continuing," Dodge surmised, "it must go ahead—not settle back. . . . Jazz should take the next step forward—whatever the consequences. It cannot remain static; that is, whether it progresses or not, it is historically subject to change." To evolve, he continued, jazz should submit to another mastering technology—namely, writing. "Jazz should begin to think in notation terms"; progress would develop through the notation of its recorded masterworks, observed against the background of a greater artistic history. This would make it "more assimilable, more concentrated, more selective."[81] Although the creative direction of jazz might be "a matter for the folk themselves," great art necessitated an intervention from a greater mastery. Style change would accrue from "a *notational* habit of thinking by jazz critics in the interest of greater and continued development." Giving as an example the reproduction of recorded work by boogie-woogie pianist Mead Lux Lewis, Dodge asserted, "Let it not be imagined for a moment that I expect Lewis to worry himself into conscious, compositional activity." Critics, in the end, would do the thinking as part of the ultimate becoming of the jazz subject: they would supply it with an intelligence that performing artists apparently lacked.[82]

Dodge's formulation of swing's development was conspicuously Hegelian. Its fully "assimilable" form would grow from the greater dialectical processes of History—from an unfolding of style leading to art as a worldly subject. With value successfully extracted from the stores of Blackness, jazz, in its latest incarnation as swing, would repay its debt to the world as part of its ascendency in History. For jazz was ultimately under the command of History. And the collaborations of critic and musician would realize its progress, bringing into being aesthetic forms of freedom. It is at this point that the enlivened qualities of Negro sound would come under the claim of swing-time and the greater body politic, its value having been reconceived as "assimilable" and affirming that, in the words of Hegel, "the history of the world is none other than the progress of the consciousness of freedom."[83] Dodge's vision of jazz was that of a music succumbing to the broad structures of the social for the greater good of the White world. His attention to history served not to expose the material conditions of value production but to obscure them. Accordingly, the truths he may have rendered from jazz performances could only be those fulfilling White mastery.

In their celebration of swing, some White writers overlooked the racial contradictions inherent to its production process, perceiving the temporal incongruities at the heart of its enlivened sound as fetishized curiosities that ironically allowed America to lay claim to the aesthetic traditions of Europe. This aspiration enabled them to routinely celebrate Black form while downplaying the individual achievements of African American musicians, reinforcing the view of swing as a vast circuit of sound; the subjugation of Black labor serviced the making of a new and compelling temporal innovation. The composer Virgil Thomson, while acknowledging the "negroid" influence as the catalyst of a twenty-year "dance war" in the United States and Europe—in which "each side . . . had its Negro troops"—suggested that swing became socially comprehensible once it was recontextualized within the legacy of Western art. Swing's formal character, Thomson argued, exceeded the superficialities of historical context, its musical design following the arcane rules of poetic versification: swing's nonaccentual measures or "quantities" mimicked the design of "quantitative verse." Having transcended its origins in primitive and militaristic "beat music"—"the music of the march, the dance, the religious or sexual orgy"—it emerged in the modern as a "quantitative music [that] has no accent," sharing likenesses to the fluid tapestry of J. S. Bach's organ works and the movements of mechanical devices. During a swing performance, Thomson observed, "every voice wiggles around . . . it sort of quivers or oscillates rapidly like a French clock."[84]

Panassié, for his part, while committed to evolutionary folkloric theory to explain swing's "negroid" rhythmic character, ultimately devalued its racial status, arguing that swing lay beyond analytical specification and, in its transcendence, aligned with universal aesthetic form. For despite its ineffability, swing was also empirically observable and therefore accessible to all. "Swing is entirely *objective*," he contended. In any given performance, "there is almost always complete agreement among competent critics" of its presence or lack.[85] The essential, artistic attributes of swing, both subjectively perceived and universally acknowledged, were necessarily undefinable because it was in their indefinability that one located art. For Panassié, as for Dodge and Thomson, swing had escaped from its primitive shackles, realizing in itself the subjectively universal nature of the aesthetic as it had been understood since Kant.

If swing at this moment fulfilled the imaginations of a White consumer republic seeking to bend Black innovation to the will of its social and aesthetic ideals, Black musicians and writers pushed back on the coalescing narrative. Leading voices among them countered popular characterizations of swing, a few publicly questioning White writers' assumed authority. In his 1937 essay "Do Critics Really Know What It's All About?," for example, Benny Carter charged that while critics claim "they are pushing a cause that few people understand," they not only lacked insight but, in some cases—such as when one of the purportedly "very great 'authorities on swing'" couldn't tap his foot in rhythm—demonstrated a fundamental lack of musical competence.[86] Ellington, moreover, chastised Stearns, whose opinions "are often influenced by misinformation or inaccuracy" and famously issued a blistering critique of John Hammond in response to Hammond's essay, "The Tragedy of Duke Ellington," which weighed judgment on Ellington's extended work, *Reminiscing in Tempo* (1935). Frank Marshall Davis, one of the few African American critics writing about jazz, summed up what troubled the Black jazz community in his lone *Down Beat* essay, "No Secret—Best White Bands Copy Negroes."[87]

Yet these challenges amounted to a whisper in comparison to the boisterous celebrations of swing heard live, on record, and on the airwaves. On college campuses, such as the University of Kansas, large crowds of students and faculty "buss[ed] with excitement and pleasure around the 'bright' strains of hot music." Large public events drew many more: at the "Swing Jamboree" staged in 1938 at Soldier Field in Chicago, attendance purportedly exceeded 100,000 spectators.[88] In its ascent, swing took the center of an American success story, winning widespread admiration as a unique cultural achievement: it merged the powers of commerce and performance in the making of a distinctively new, "new world" musical order. There was now in public discourse a certain satisfaction about swing in its affirmation of White America through the successful act of racial expropriation. Its "Negroid" qualities had not been wholly denied—increasingly, Black swing orchestras were gaining attention—but, by perpetuating a practice reaching back to early blackface minstrelsy, were contained and seemingly conquered. Although Ellington won praise for his band's return to the Cotton Club in 1937 and Chick Webb's orchestra could now join Goodman's in broadcasts to England, Black ensembles remained marginally involved in the greater advancement of a "melting pot" ideal. Swing had produced a kind of alchemy of light where racial mixing realized a colorless sound, its white hue moving to a cheerfully buoyant tempo.[89]

A potent depiction of the swing spectrum's colorless ideal appeared in the alignment of two of America's primary expressions of uniqueness: its Negro folkloric heritage and its machinic might. A particularly diverting example appears in the Hollywood movie *Shall We Dance* (1937), starring Fred Astaire and Ginger Rogers.[90] The film, together with several earlier movies, including *Swing Time* (1936), established the duo as the leading commercial performers of swing dance. As Dinerstein observes, the 1937 feature is famous in US film history for a scene taking place in a ship's engine room—the characters are traveling on a transatlantic ocean liner—that centers on Astaire. So full of sonic-technological excitement, the filmic moment, in its involvement of jazz, Hollywood, slang, and machines, seems to come right out of Henry Luce's guidance on universal expression.

At the start of the scene, Astaire remains off camera, presumably watching the action, involving a group of Black workers, all dressed in trousers and white T-shirts, polishing railings and swabbing the deck of a transcontinental ocean liner. At first, the workers' labor follows the repetitive motion of the ship's pistons—represented fancifully on a pristine stage set—and then becomes vaguely coordinated with the entrance of a repeated vocal figure, "zoom zoom," sung by a male quartet positioned off camera. Soon the camera pans to an unlikely sight in a ship's engine room: a makeshift ensemble consisting of a double bass player in a porkpie hat, a drummer sitting atop an abutment whose slatted metal side resembles a washboard, a vocalist using cupped hands to imitate trumpet growls after the Mills Brothers. As the camera moves still further, we see the vocal quartet and three more actors holding instruments—tenor saxophone, trumpet, guitar—who stand in for the burst of diegetic big-band sound performed by the Tommy Dorsey Orchestra. To this, yet another worker, the actor-singer Dudley Dickerson—who in 1936 played the frightened, bug-eyed janitor in the Our Gang film short, *Spooky Hooky*—saunters in and joyously sings against the band's accompaniment a despairing, Depression-era lyric taken from the middle chorus of George and Ira Gershwin's "Slap That Bass":

> Zoom zoom, zoom zoom,
> The world is in a mess,
> With politics and taxes,
> And people grinding axes,
> There's no happiness[91]

With Dickerson's entrance, Astaire appears, seated on a stool, listening approvingly. And after a momentary break of slap bass played by the stage actor, he stands up—as if cued by the unsung song lyric, "Alright, slap that bass, And I'll slap these feet"—and joins the show. He proceeds to sing the opening chorus—a counterpoint of happiness to Dickerson's gloom and doom—and moves into dance, first accompanied by the Dorsey orchestra (still off camera) then by the shadowy movements of the pistons churning out rhythm. By the time he rises from the stool, Astaire has taken ownership of the routine, the Black actors, in their sorrow about the state of affairs ("there's no happiness"), receding and ultimately absent. Swing rhythm is his, which submits to his virtuosic display of dance practices that had originated in the African American tradition. When Astaire sings, "Today, you can see that the happiest men, All got rhythm," he announces White power's command of a value that Black workers in their subjugation have granted to the guardians of civilized society.

What makes the routine so powerful, though, is not the demonstration of White mastery over reified form but rather the uncertainty and instability of its enforcement. Despite Astaire's dominance, laying claim to rhythm's enlivened energy, the entire act runs through the sensory fields of Black aurality and embodied movement. If the Black workers who begin the scene assume the role of repetitive labor servicing machinic technology, they also turn reification's effect on its head, animating the technology through those same repetitive means, bringing life into its perpetual thingliness. Repetition in the negative shifts to the hyperpositive, as the workers' presence aestheticizes the ship's massive pistons, their incessant machine labor inspirited in their association with the rhythm music of Black folk. As Astaire dances, moreover, he moves to the accompaniment of a swing band whose style is modeled after Black innovation (including the boogie-based dance rhythms it plays toward the end), just as his artful stepping to the engine sounds—indebted as it is to the legacy of Black stage performance—celebrates the aesthetic power of racialized rhythm (figure 7.2). If "All got rhythm," that rhythm is a property whose ownership is ultimately contested, the struggle realized through a collision of two temporal orders, two knowledges bound inextricably, dialectically, without resolution. Contest itself is key to the generation of value.

However asymmetrical and staged these contested exchanges are, they reveal an intimacy shared between Astaire and the Black performers. It is a strange intimacy, to be sure, not unlike the kind of "love" amid theft that Eric Lott analyzes in his seminal study of blackface: a sharing strained

7.2 Fred Astaire in *Shall We Dance* (1937).

by the mediating forces of racism, yet which also suggests a kind of mutual respect. Astaire may have been bestowed ownership of this rhythm as a celebrity figure in a nation where the White population reigns supreme, but he too is a servant to the value produced through the creativity of Black folk. He may in its enactment seek to experience racial time, to feel the animated energy of the Tenderloin dancers who shouted to James P. Johnson, "Let's go back home!," to rear on his own "hind legs": for his time as a performer is also a time transformed, different from the normative routine, having been affected by the intrusion of Black musical presences that brought to the White public sphere sensations of incongruent past-time. Yet it is his own Whiteness—that is, a White nation's commitment to racial belief and the superiority it claims—that limits his entry into that domain. His racial privilege determines his exclusion as it undermines White America's full embrace of Black music's offering. This is why the subordinates who open the scene are ultimately the ones passing judgment. After Astaire finishes his dance, he leans over a railing, smiling, seeking approval, which the workers, being representatives of the authority of Black entertainment, grant with a round of applause. Astaire's "rhythm" is confirmed by those compliant Black actors who are paid to share their enlivened wealth.

SOMETHING GREATER THAN MUSIC: ELLINGTON AND BASIE

Shall We Dance celebrated time as a native force of creation: in perpetuating fantasies about the Black body's repetitive nature it also affirmed repetition's necessity in the making of modern value. A begrudging acknowledgment of that necessity contributed to Black music's unprecedented gains, driving a new cycle of profit-from-loss that affirmed the hidden position of racialized form at the center of modern innovation. The film joined in the exuberance of swing as a national, indeed, "universal" fashion, while Black musicians, still on the margins, made their audible presence felt. Panassié's 1938 lineup in *Life* magazine of an all-star swing band featuring several Black performers—Louis Armstrong, Sidney Bechet, Earl Hines, Pops Foster, and Zutty Singleton among them—was indicative of the growing public awareness of Black music's aesthetic value, while other segments of the media apparatus—notably, the jukeboxes making available recordings of African American orchestras—played out the struggle of ownership in the public sphere. These challenges to White power's total conquest supplied the means for Black swing's moment of glory.[92]

With swing now commonly understood as the new beginning of modern popular music's development, White audiences in unprecedented numbers became interested in seeing and hearing Black orchestras and musicians, with many fans eager to learn about their distinctive approaches to rhythm. Despite the casual bigotry affecting White perceptions—by which, for example, Ella Fitzgerald could be applauded by the critic Barry Ulanov in 1936 as "the best cooncrooner I've ever heard"—Black swing expressions were seen by many White enthusiasts as something more than iterations of a static folk prototype: if not yet a true art form, swing proposed a different, peculiar expressivity—something less than and greater than Music—that captured popular attention. Myths about the Negro past could still inspire ridicule, such as when a *Metronome* critic in 1938 derided Zutty Singleton's complex improvisations as expressions of "savage simplicity (typically negroid)."[93] Yet those same myths, fostered by critics as part of the making of a grand racial imaginary, were also contributing to the recognition that African American music had endured over the years, and through its endurance it had gained a legacy, a past, as peculiar and incorrigible as it was.

Ellington continued to serve as chief spokesperson of the Black music community, portraying its music and history in an exalted language consistent with swing's dominance.[94] Having informed readers in 1931 that "jazz had its origin in Africa" and was "the result of our transplantation to American soil," he expanded these ideas to suggest that through struggle against racial hardship Black musicians had gained the authority to express the nation itself. They had done so, he asserted, despite "the tragedy . . . that so few records have been kept of the Negro music of the past." It was they who had kept records, nonetheless, shaping a history of accumulating sonic material that "has to be pieced together so slowly. But it pleases me to have a chance to work at it." Through these efforts, "we as a race have a good deal to pay our way with in a white world."[95] In his 1941 public lecture, "We, too, Sing 'America,'" moreover, which he delivered before a Black church congregation in Los Angeles—the title glossed a line from Langston Hughes's poem *The Weary Blues* (1926)—Ellington elaborated on the significance of the history he and other Black musicians had "pieced together slowly," claiming African Americans to be the nation's real contributors to cultural excellence. "The Negro," he asserted, "is the creative voice of America, is creative America . . . the shot in the arm that has kept America and its forgotten principles alive."[96] Although Black people were still seen as a negative strain on society, their music realized a hyperpositive gain, revealing the secret ingredient, in all its incongruencies, in the creation of a national style.

Ellington was making a dramatic claim for Black music's double value, which he extended to swing and to African America more generally. As far as he was concerned, Black musicians were the ones who had generated the nation's musical excellence; it was they who had advanced America culturally and supplied it with a music capable of heightened aesthetic experience. They had done so not by forgetting the past but by accumulating sounding practices and their sound formations into the accumulating body of sonic material, shaping a knowledge and translating it as part of their own craft. This back-leaning progressivism affirmed the Black centeredness at the core of swing's development. It was an example of why "the history of my people is one of great achievements over fearful odds."[97] Significantly, swing's historicity was enriched by the very forces that sought to expropriate Black form. Through the efforts of critics and concert organizers working for the entertainment industry, the music gained a historical gravitas previously unknown in popular music. The weight of tradition heightened swing's valuation, supplying a credit that encouraged African Americans to recognize and claim it as their own racially affirming art.

Despite these aesthetic advances, however, Black orchestras still depended on White entertainment to stay in business, which required them to balance their aesthetic aspirations against the obligation to satisfy commercial expectations. To some extent, accommodating popular tastes was already aligned with those aspirations, as bands worked strategically, producing music that reinforced swing's place in the common language of popular music. Late 1930s ensembles led by Lunceford, Webb, Hampton, and Hines, for example, advanced their own brands of orchestral swing that won wide interracial appeal and within that context developed compositional strategies and approaches to improvisation that affirmed a primary aesthetic commitment to bring new form to life. Basie, moreover, recalled how John Hammond coached him on how to stage performances at upscale hotels and nightclubs in ways that did not compromise the orchestra's aesthetic commitments. "Hell, we just thought we'd go in there and play our behind off . . . but the people didn't know what the hell we were doing." Hammond got Basie to tone down the intensity and present conventional popular material before "get[ting] down to the nitty-gritty and pick[ing] up the tempo a bit." These accommodations were not only meant for White audiences; they also satisfied the changing expectations and tastes of Black dancers and listeners, as an urbane version of Black swing gained popularity in venues across the nation. Commercial success provided further evidence of Black swing as an evolving form. Rough-and-ready playing and the histrionics of territory bands and roadshows would no longer cut it in the major arenas of popular entertainment.[98]

If Black orchestras in the late 1930s accommodated the professional standards and expectations set forth by the entertainment industry, the most innovative among them also worked within those parameters to drive practices that reconceived Black sonic material and affirmed the ontological capacities at the core of Black music. A new creativity appeared as part of the evolution of swing's aliveness, the players' commitments to advancing individual styles affecting the character of ensemble personalities; new form suggested new takes on the accumulation of Black people's auditory history. Advances in Black swing developed from the key fetishism of Negro rhythm as embodied sound, opening affective pathways beyond typical ways of knowing. Its reconceived tempos invited listeners to consider through the Black swing experience a realignment of the sensible, inspiring once more restructurations of "what becomes thinkable and possible."[99] Working within a racialized swing imaginary perpetuated by the enterprise of popular entertainment, leading voices in Black swing expanded the music's parameters, quietly recalibrating the means of creating swing feeling and the organization of musical time. These creations were successful because they drew from the strength of swing's commercial incorporation—they acknowledged the stature of the entertainment industry and its overwhelming influence over the musical landscape—as they pushed vigorously against it. Through these means, leading orchestras expanded Black swing as a sonic politics, inverting Dodge's claims of history: a European-centered dialectic of jazz growth gave way to forms advancing contrapuntally within the conceptual space of modern public culture, their interruptions of the norms of experience producing opportunities for encompassing counterhistories to rush in, and for the listeners seeking to witness the miracle of swing's live performance to "come in and hear the truth."[100]

Two orchestras stand out among the innovators: those of Ellington and Basie. Their originality grew from a shared aspiration to reorient the temporal character of swing by directly involving musicians in the development of ensemble personality. Ellington's band astonished listeners with spectacular orchestrations featuring vivid timbral colors that evolved kaleidoscopically to frame and support solo improvisations. These complexes of tonal hue realized a temporal feel that, while changing dynamically, created, even within the most complex arrangements, inimitable ensemble swing. The recordings produced over a three-year period (1938–1940)—most notably, the masterworks "Concerto for Cootie," "Ko-Ko," "Congo Brava," and "Cotton Tail," all 1940—provided material evidence of how the orchestra had acquired a veritable group consciousness, where players "almost [come] to anticipate each other's thoughts."[101] Through these means, musicians reimagined the function of the swing ensemble, inventing forms still wedded to bodily movement as they broadened the possibilities of jazz sound and practice. The orchestra's recorded miniatures—commodities circulating for the purpose of public listening on jukeboxes and home listening on record players—offered portraits of a band that set new standards of orchestral arrangement within the swing context, featuring virtuosic improvisations and skilled ensemble performances so precise in their execution that they at times seemed uncannily to speak as a single, living organism, to "play as one man." No matter the extent of virtuosic display, however, the orchestra remained committed to its duty as a dance band, making sure audiences—for example, on the high energy and audaciously complex "Cotton Tail," featuring a fiery solo by tenor saxophonist Ben Webster—would "feel like hopping around a bit."[102]

The Basie band, in contrast, shaped its new sound by reorganizing the temporal concept earlier established by Kansas City orchestras to introduce a spareness and lightness original to the genre. Key was the reorganization of time keeping and harmonic mapping, shifting what were conventionally the roles of drummer and pianist to the other side of the rhythm section. With the double-bass player Walter Page and guitarist Freddie Green guiding the orchestra through the changes while setting the pace—their relaxed propulsion feeding soloists and establishing the ground of the orchestra's swing feel—the others in the section experimented with new ways of playing that reconceived their roles in the band. Jo Jones rethought the practice of set playing, shifting his own time-keeping from the bass drum to the hi-hat, which stretched the duration of his percussion attacks across the ensemble rhythm, the cymbals' light, shimmering resonance fundamentally altering the swing effect. Basie, in turn, abandoned his previous responsibility of laying out the harmonic framework, working instead as a sound colorist and adjudicator of tempo. He became known for his spare, light touch, interjecting crisp, upper-register figurations that sparked ensemble rhythm. As Mark Tucker put it, "The fewer notes Basie played, the more care he took with each one. As the rhythm section's support freed him from time-keeping he could concentrate on the piano's sonority, making its instrumental colour just as distinctive as that of three trombones or Lester Young's saxophone." Together these innovations—heard on the orchestra's Decca recordings from 1937 and 1938 and its version of "Moten Swing" from 1940—transformed the Basie band's ensemble personality, introducing the music world (thanks to a manipulative contract by Decca) to a light, nearly ethereal, yet nonetheless loud and assertive orchestral voice.[103]

The originality of the Ellington and Basie bands derived from performance practices and conceptions unique to African American traditions. At the top of the list was their distinctive approaches to formal invention. Despite their celebrity, both leaders worked against the composer-performer hierarchy typical in Western music, preferring to develop works collaboratively through the interaction of players in the band. Ellington's orchestra gained wide attention from bemused critics who described scenes unfamiliar to rehearsal sessions where "each man has his say," with players consulting and arguing, and, at times, a "particular section hold[ing] a conclave to see if Duke's idea can possibly be carried out on their instrument." These experiments, as one writer characterized them, produced enlivened sonorities previously unheard in Western music: the playing "results in a sound which is not of this world at all."[104] Basie, in his memoir, discussed similar collaborations stretching for long hours of rehearsal, during which players would collectively shape head arrangements and commit them to memory. He recalled how, when developing a head arrangement, leaders of sections "could start something and get those ensembles going," with a soloist in one section inspiring a new accompaniment in another, which, in turn, might become a catalyst for the rest of the orchestra. When they brought these arrangements to the bandstand, they'd do it again. "Those guys knew just where to come in and they came in. . . . Once these guys played something, they could damn near play it exactly the same the next night." These collaborations developed from a casual intimacy among the band members not uncommon to African American performance, reaching back at least to the informal hymn singing that Thomas Dorsey recalled taking place among his mother and her friends (cf. chapter 2). Basie characterized his own group's relationship as something akin to a house party, with friends moving about. "I have my own little ideas about how to get certain guys into certain numbers and how to get them out. I had my own way of opening the door for them to let them come in and sit around awhile. Then I would exit them. And that had really been the formula of the band all down through the years."[105]

The approaches introduced by Ellington and Basie, working collaboratively with their personnel, shaped the personalities of their orchestras anew. By expanding the conception of swing practice in step with its elevated cultural authority, they each produced new qualities of ensemble feeling that reoriented the sensation of temporal movement. Collaborative composition generated aesthetic forms that broadened the scope of musical possibility, inviting listeners to also inhabit the spaces, to "come in and sit around awhile," joining in the shared experience of capacious listening: a way of knowing in sound that welcomed all that once was and would still be sonically available to African Americans. In this way, the new inventions of Black swing affirmed the value of Black sonic material as part of modern living. If Black music's sounding practices still seemed peculiar, dubious, they were nonetheless a fundamental part of the present. Upholding the value of the Black musical past was neither a reclamation of tools of the folkloric nor a "neoclassical" reframing of modern form. Rather, Ellington's and Basie's affirmations were ways of strategizing innovation to effect revised orders of ontological presence. Both orchestras extended in their work an essentially political commitment to creation that positioned Black musical invention at the center of things. Their performances served to bring a reimagined swing back into the fold of Black experience to remake sensible arenas, projecting outwardly a revised popular language that established a new foundation in jazz performance.

Despite the many hurdles they confronted, the Ellington and Basie orchestras managed to stay in business. But most Black orchestras suffered a different fate. By the early 1940s, for a complex of factors at once economic, aesthetic, and racial, the apparatuses of the entertainment industry—from clubs to Hollywood to radio—reaffirmed its grip on the genre, giving favor to White orchestras. While Black swing players were widely recognized by White performers for their musical excellence—the racial relations among them being far more convivial than in other employment sectors—interest in Black music among White audiences, always tentative and unstable, would recede again, motivating the major clubs, ballrooms, radio programs, and filmmakers to give the center of attention to White bands and singers. Facing the huge economic challenges of keeping a large orchestra going, many Black leaders were forced to disband. Musicians sought refuge performing in integrated orchestras when they could. Some leaders, such as Coleman Hawkins, scaled down their ensembles to small groups. Still others ventured South, where they often found humble work performing in Black bands before segregated audiences. This turn of events would soon draw Black instrumentalists to New York, where they assembled anew in Harlem clubs.[106]

Yet if swing as a genre lived on precariously, its influence as a practice would carry across the decades, informing subsequent innovations of jazz and the overarching character of commercial popular music. Swing practices persisted even as new rhythm-oriented fashions—boogie, rock 'n' roll, funk, hip-hop—challenged its authority. Amid the flood of new popular approaches, swing sustained its auratic effect: the buoyancy of swing feel confirmed what the modern sounded like, its animated character setting the sensible tempo of practice across the field of popular culture. What seemed alive in swing was sustained by the extent of its fetishization, its luster as a commodified sound heightened by the productive forces and disseminating power of capital, its intensities in time and feel extending well beyond the limits of the genre itself. And as swing encompassed world listening, its enthusiasts began to imagine for it new communicative powers that rose in proportion with its capacious reach. Swing's practice, that is, many came to believe, expressed elusive truths about race and nation, telling stories about the history of the United States writ large. So power-ful would the music become that it seemed as if one could hear "what's American about America" sounding from its form.[107] These powers at-tributed to swing and jazz at large would orient how jazz players fashioned musical worlds enlivened with animated energy.

EIGHT

LIVING FORMS, IMAGINED TRUTHS

AESTHETIC BREAK-THROUGHS IN JAZZ AT MIDCENTURY

COALESCENCES OF AGONISTIC FORM

Ralph Ellison's essay "The Golden Age, Time Past," in which he famously dismantles the myths and legends of bop's rise at Minton's Playhouse, is itself a kind of mythic treatise in jazz studies. It is one of American music's master texts, a short form celebrated for its stylistic elegance, its provocations of thought, its tonal shifts from the elegiac to the exuberant. This brief missive, first published in *Esquire* in 1959, is typically cited to affirm sentiments about jazz as a resolution of opposites: what is distinctively Black conveys meaningfulness consistent with an encompassing American experience. The paradoxes are what drive the author's various claims that jazz speaks a form of freedom arising from tragedy, epitomizing the democratic aspiration of a more perfect union. For Ellison, what first appeared as a "revolution in culture" spawned by the sorrows of those living on the downside of racial hierarchy ultimately transcended the political, becoming the stuff of art.[1]

If "The Golden Age" has grown weary after all its critical exegesis, it is still useful to think on it for the purpose of gaining insight into the expansion of Black music's value at midcentury, particularly in its expression of what became known as "modern jazz." Central to our concern is Ellison's portrait of bop's relation to time and history in the production of embodied form. The chief purpose of the essay was to call out the sentimentality imposed on bop's emergence, the multiple layers of racialized romance that clouded understanding of its true impulse. Bop, for Ellison, was above all a rite of passage during which players seeking to learn the art of improvisation engaged in an "apprenticeship," its many "ordeals, initiation, ceremonies" providing steps to discovering the sound audible in oneself. For a "jazz man" to "'find himself'" (here, Ellison follows the midcentury custom of masculine referents), one "must be reborn, must find, as it were, his soul."[2] Value developed as performers participated in a musical legacy dedicated to the creation of living form.

Ellison's path to "identity" involved schooling in "tradition" through which musicians, after gaining fluency in the aggregate of the Black music past, realized their creative voice out of "a summation of all the styles." "Tradition" differed from the routine reflections on the emergence of bop that informed popular commentary after Minton's first became a gathering place for young jazz players. The nostalgic reflections on what once was, Ellison asserted, were not accurate depictions, but more akin to what Bechet called "memory thing," a form of historicist thinking that suppressed the disruptive power of Black sound.[3] "Americans," he lamented, "give but a limited attention to history," and as a result, "with jazz we are yet not in the age of history, but linger in that of folklore." The "revolutionary rumpus" of bop was in fact a reaffirmation of a dynamic Black past, conjuring a "suspension of time, . . . [a] time-present." Not the present of an ever-ready commercial world ("the tempo of the motion picture" and the fetishized commodity) but a Black-innovated realm, a counterhistory whereby musicians such as Charlie Parker, whom Ellison quotes in another essay, "could play the thing I'd been hearing"; where, in the midst of a performance, players and listeners alike "were hardly aware of . . . what time it was"; where congregations beholding stunning music creations witnessed metamorphoses of living form, during which virtuosic soloists, as Parker put it, "came alive."[4]

The emerging practice to which musicians gave the name "bop" is important not only because of its dramatic stylistic transformations—the well-known harmonic and rhythmic innovations on swing-based formats—but also for how those transformations organized according to a newly recognized Black aesthetic, whose insurgency drew from a rich reservoir of African American sound. Bop marked the moment when young musicians, many already with secure reputations in the commercial swing industry, embraced the posture of the artist as part of a new conceptualization of Black-centered music-making. From that posture, they advanced sound formations that would remake the sensible arena not just for self-gratification but for the purpose of challenging the existing conceptual parameters in commercial entertainment: remaking their own affective orders meant confronting the world they inhabited. The confrontation drove the expansion of Black sonic material, leading to new sounding practices and new sound formations embodied with the living and buoyed by the gravitas of an expressive tradition that had developed over the past eighty-odd years.

Congregating in the musicians' community of Harlem, bop musicians pursued the invention of an aesthetic language that held music-making as an act of life-making, of creating enlivened sound. At the center of things was the involvement of expression that readjusted the temporal flow of sound otherwise accommodating the swiftly moving sameness of commercial music: small-group improvisation reorganized the music's labor time toward the invention of newly embodied forms. Players harnessed past sound worlds as they remade them, giving priority to the originality of a musician-centered present as it would be heard contrapuntally in relation to a greater music history: the Ellisonian conception of "history"—where "the act of writing requires a constant plunging back into the shadow of the past where time hovers ghostlike"—identified the accumulated property passed on to the progeny by those once propertied themselves, its materializations as modern music acquiring a reinvigorated ontological complexity.[5] Bop players drew strength from the Black cultural past to deliver a sensationally new temporality that redistributed the time of capital against which it had developed. Their projections of sound were revolutionary not merely because modern cultural criticism, in its embrace of a veritable culture of nowness, proclaimed them to be, but because they reimagined the inner radicalism identifying Black music's contradictory relation to exchange: the incongruity of laboring bodies generating enlivened music property as an extension of their audible being.

Bop was a musicians' music whose value derived from its original, embodied displays, from its scabrous forms that pushed against the labor category that otherwise organized their development. As bop was celebrated, its creators found themselves positioned amid a vortex of opposing currents. Granted by commercial media a qualified standing as artists, they witnessed how the possession of their music property shifted from their own performing bodies to entertainment institutions and consumers; no matter the level of their proficiency, they could not transcend their status as "Negro" musicians. The tension between art and commerce, between aesthetic standing and market forces that structured bop's reception, made it difficult to decouple the currents. Ellison himself became caught up in the music's mystification at the same time he critiqued it. After exposing the entertainment industry's fabulism, for example, he exercised his own metaphorical extravagance, proclaiming bop to be a music for everyone, when "the world was swinging with change."[6] Despite his critical acuity, he seemed at times to miss the dual role that the concept of tradition performed: folklorization efforts not only romanticized the jazz past but also raised players' awareness of a past that romance mediated. The mystification of the jazz past heightened musicians' and listeners' attentiveness to jazz as a Black-centered art form that hovered between the symbolic categories of music and Music.

Across a twenty-year period at midcentury (ca. 1940–1960), late-modern jazz extended the metamorphosis begun by swing, drawing temporal energy from the accumulation of sounding bodies from the past heard as "a summation of all the styles." Creative inventions given shape by a new generation of master improvisers performed a collective act of re-orchestrating the audible character of jazz and popular music by building on the expanse of sonic material defining the legacy of Black musicality. The tug-of-war for Black music's ownership—for an ontologized music time that was created within and against the time of capital and the speed of commodity circulation—accelerated stylistic development in relation to the cumulative advancement of commercial markets, leading to the social elevation of the music in the making of "a jazz art world."[7]

Conscious of their place among those before them, Black musicians actively engaged in this world in their contradiction of it. Taking stances unprecedented in American music history, they self-consciously pursued a critical artistry uplifted by the body to spirit the music away from the folkloric gloss of pastime. The process brought into being an expansion of ontologized sound suggestive of an exalted state of cognitive character. This was the "revolution of culture" taking place across a newly coalescing "Black music": the music practices given the commercial names swing, bebop, cool, hard bop, funky jazz, mainstream, and modern jazz—together with a range of new popular forms from urban blues and rhythm and blues to soul and funk, to be discussed in chapter 9—introduced more than simple paradoxes ultimately subsumed into a greater whole. They were the work of artists aspiring toward the creation of agonistic form, whose spectacular expressions enlivened the countenance of popular culture's sensible character.[8]

BREAKTHROUGH

The tenor of jazz performance, the act of "finding oneself" and expressing what Ellison called "an individuality in tone" occupied the center of creative activity, as musicians fashioned ways of speaking to life through the art of jazz improvisation. The metaphor of speech in the production of instrumental music became the primary means of understanding the crafting of style, affirming the common expression among jazz players of "saying something."[9] What these forms revealed in the end were not precise communications of meaning, even if some may have thought so; Black music, like virtually all music, cannot signify directly. Rather, they identified structures bound to a counterhistorical orientation fundamental to the creation of enlivened sound. The aliveness discerned in improvised jazz materialized the conditions of an agonistic property giving rise to spectacular aesthetic experience.

"I had a decision between Frankie Trumbauer and Jimmy Dorsey," the tenor saxophonist Lester Young famously recounted about his early efforts to find his musical voice: "They were the only ones telling a story I liked to hear." Trumpeter Roy Eldridge fashioned his own approach with the aim of developing an original style: "I started to feel that if I could combine speed with melodic development while continuing to build, to tell a story, I could create something musical of my own." Sometimes, musicians' "stories" were thought to signify specific content. DeVeaux, for example, reveals that Coleman Hawkins, as a "purveyor of pleasure," had developed a kind of musical rhetoric messaging male-to-female seduction, the architecture of his tenor solos narrating the act of lovemaking, which, Hawkins apparently believed, straight women could discern from initial caress to climax.[10] Other times, listeners and musicians heard qualities connecting to the musicians' persona or physicality. For Big Nick Nicholas, for example, Hawkins's instrumental timbre, articulation, and sense of rhythmic development called to mind his broad-shouldered girth: "Every note that he played—they were all the same bigness, *all* the notes," whereas other players, diminished by comparison, could create "bigness" only for moments. An improvisation could also suggest a sense of social connection and relation. In discussing two leaders of the swing era, the bop tenor saxophonist Dexter Gordon recognized a kinship despite differences in instrumentation: "I used to get almost the same thing listening to Roy [Eldridge] as I did listening to Lester [Young]—the same 'story' feeling." Yet a perceived relationship or familiarity could pose a threat among competitors in the music marketplace. "Say, man," Keg Johnson warned his brother, Budd, upon hearing Lester Young, "there's a cat out here, he plays a lot of tenor, he sounds something like you."[11]

Telling a story through the act of improvisation is perhaps the most enduring conceit in a copious body of Black music interpretation. What was already a commonplace from the outset of swing would carry across the decades, eventually exceeding the limits of genre to explain the intensive character of popular music writ large. "Stories," as expressions of living form, would drive improvised practices along the dynamic of pop, giving shape to an African American–based aesthetic orientation that set the music's constraints, which were openly shared and reinvented by Black and White musicians. The efficacy of the story metaphor as it appeared in jazz and beyond—in rural and urban blues, rhythm and blues, gospel, etc.—became embedded in performers' knowledge of instrumental practice, as that practice underwent expansion, inspiring new metaphorical conceptions of improvisation: as "journey," "conversation," "dance," "marriage," etc.[12]

The persistence of these figurations suggests that the story metaphor expressed something larger than narrative and conceptually more capacious: a way of being that was organized and advanced in solo improvisation. Creating form anew on the bases of popular song and twelve-bar blues became a means of generating temporal and aesthetic experiences that pushed the limits of conventional listening and enabled a realigning of the qualities of enlivened sound. These new swing-based practices at midcentury stood on the shoulders of a legacy of Black sonic material to forge creations that garnered strength from Black music's history as an agonistic living form. They introduced in a diversity of performances called "jazz" a reawakening of temporal pasts, a phenomenal reckoning with the long range of creative achievement now clustering in the present, inviting experiences among musicians and committed listeners alike of aesthetically generated breakthroughs working within and against the time of capital.

"Breakthrough" is a concept introduced by Theodor W. Adorno to describe the moments when the temporalities of musical works challenge normative time to the point of exceeding the seemingly perpetual flow of rationalized clock time otherwise regulating capitalist societies. In his thoughtful elaboration on the idea, Stephen Decatur Smith explores how Adorno, in formulating the breakthrough concept—particularly with reference to the way the passage of music time reconceives earlier moments in a work—imagined these disruptions as awakenings of "dead time": resurrections of time past that gain in the present an ontologized aliveness comparable to a ghostly "exhalation of breath."[13] The breakthrough concept is consistent with how Adorno more generally understood music time and empirical time in dialectical relation, by which a truth content comes forth. "Only history itself," Adorno argued, "real history with all its suffering and all its contradiction, constitutes the truth of music." Smith suggests that this historical framing of "breakthrough" as an analytical category bears a conceptual relationship to what Adorno's friend and early interlocutor Walter Benjamin named in his philosophy of history "Messianic time"—a simultaneously metaphysical and material temporality residing at once prior to and beyond modern capital: an order of time decidedly akin to this study's conception of past-time. Adorno's breakthrough identified the collision of temporal orders that are subsumed by capital time as they exceed it, opening the possibility of liberating aesthetic experiences.[14]

For Adorno, music's confrontation of capital time becomes the means of identifying breakthrough moments beyond the illusory sensations generated by economic production. In its most radical articulations, music inspires an experience in excess of capital's phantasmagoric conditions, giving way, in a flash, to what he describes metaphorically, after Benjamin, as "constellations" of obscured temporalities: sounds aligned counterhistorically with the quotidian foibles and monumental tragedies left out of the celebratory narratives of history's "victor."[15] The sensation registers as a sudden coalescence in the present of an expansive temporal reach. Breakthrough is the escape route beyond normative temporal orders, reviving historical realms of experience concealed by the rationalizing forces of world economies. It conceptualizes a means of forging musical experiences that confront capitalism's conforming structures that are nonetheless necessary for imagining extraordinary sensory realms. As a component of historical materialism, the concept produces insight not into the past as it was but as it is conceived in its difference in the present, enabling expansive glimpses of a clustering of prior/present durations that, as Smith argues, Adorno and Benjamin both thought to carry an otherworldly truth content.

It is useful to consider Adorno's concept of breakthrough alongside Ellison's depictions of historical time as a way of exploring how ontologically conceived swing-based improvisations introduced their own aesthetic interventions in everyday experience. Both authors recognized how forces of dominance quelled music's potency by blocking its relation to the past, and both acknowledged how Black-centered creative practices necessarily participated in the same commercial worlds that subjugated the labor producing them. For Ellison, most troubling were the illusory spectacles of folklore; for Adorno, it was the full extent of capitalism's blinding power to subsume the diversity of incongruous modes of temporal experience. Yet whereas Ellison ultimately sought to look beyond dominating forces to present early bop as a temporally disruptive musicians' music—to locate a purity of meaning in players' perspectives and performances—Adorno, while largely inattentive to the peculiar consequences of US racism, proposed how the liberative potential of music developed dialectically in relation to subjugating social forces. These largely unresolvable contests between truth and illusion set up the possibility for momentary breakthroughs of the sensible, as music—while conforming to fetishization processes—also exposed their falsity. Music time, Adorno asserted, participated in the economic time of capital as it carried the potential to disclose modes of experience moving against its routinizing force. Value located in aesthetic excesses beyond the artificiality of capital time, illuminating the messy diversity of material history as it was lived and within which art works developed.[16]

Following this line of thought, we can think of breakthrough in Black music as the accumulated effects of a legacy of sonic material on new forms of racially inspirited property, an aurality that incongruously inhabits the common time of capitalized history. Breakthrough identifies a disruptive moment when the weight of Black music's enlivened past animates the present as the present leans back into the past, driving a continuing dialectical relationship between what is alive now and what was then. Benjamin's famous discussion of his concept of Messianic time in *The Arcades Project* suggests a way of comprehending breakthrough according to the logic of Black music's animatedness: "It is not that what is past casts its light on what is present, or what is present its light on what is past; rather an image is that wherein what has been comes together in a flash with the now to form a constellation. In other words: image is dialectics at a standstill." Experientially, it mimics the quality of a dream: "With the intensity of a dream, to pass through what has been [*das Gewesene*] in order to experience the present as the waking world to which the dream refers." Breakthrough, as sonic "image" or aura—as Adorno puts it, "the archetypal image of nature as of what is beyond nature"—brings the opportunity of audibly discerning the source of valuation in the production of Black music's primary truth.[17]

Adorno's insights provide new critical tools for interpreting how the animated character of advanced swing-based practices extending as a "shadow of the past" intensified Black music's metamorphosis as a counterhistorical form. As "a summation of all the styles," it did not produce an affirmation of Black music's Americanness but rather occupied a negative posture within and against it. Building on a rich legacy of sonic material to create new musical sensations seemingly arising from their very bodies, jazz improvisers in their most successful performances exposed the possibility of experiencing a temporal radicalism bound to their playing: the improvisations at their aesthetic height revealed for those able to behold it the structuring depth of Black music's tragic history. These swing-based creations betrayed Black music's advancement as a cultural form whose incongruities of past and present drove agonistic breakthroughs of aesthetic experience. The sensible orders of modern Black music affirmed not the historical time of capital but a racialized version of dialectics at a standstill: what Harry Harootunian describes as the dialectical character of everyday experience, a "crowding of differing historical times, which marks the modern from the presents of prior pasts."[18] As a form of sublation, breakthrough in Black music accordingly exposed the inalienable, living qualities of sound arising from the contradiction of the music's mystification—from the fetishized, spectral qualities that its aliveness publicly registered and overcame.[19]

Comprehending the aesthetic power achieved in swing's ontological expansion requires a turning inward, into the intensive world of Black musicianship that developed at Minton's and carried forward in the making of a broadly conceived jazz community in the 1940s and 1950s. It was at this moment that small groups established the primary musical relation in the production of jazz, their interactions sustaining the flow of group improvisation and the succession of featured soloists. We gain insight into this world by engaging a masterful study of the forms of musical consciousness that emerged as part of Black music's reawakening.

In his illuminating ethnographic portrait of jazz musicians working in New York during the 1980s, Paul Berliner offers a fascinating exploration of how improvisation was organized as a creative exercise that, amid the structures of entertainment culture, produced veritable ontologies of sound. Working from these insights, we can look back to and then move forward from the eras of swing and bop to consider how such ways of knowing took shape across the breadth of modern jazz at midcentury. The practice of "thinking in jazz," Berliner shows, is grounded fundamentally in the relationship between the body and musical performance. This is why ontological language pervades the discourse of jazz players, most of whom were African American: from the claim that musical figures or "licks" possess "lives" of their own, to the observation of the musical work as a sentient communication form that "has [something] to say," to the greater sense, fundamental to jazz thought, that swing itself is an expansive arena in which musicians map out temporally dynamic versions of living form. "That's what makes it come alive," observes Fred Hersch. "People are human, and rhythmic energy has an ebb and flow." A feeling for swing, trumpeter Doc Cheatham insisted, meant having a heightened sensitivity to embodied pulsation. "He's telling a story," Cheatham, whose playing experience reached back to the 1920s, told Berliner about a soloist. If the story is bad, Cheatham observed—evoking an early modernist analogy linking rhythm and human pulse—"he plays like he's got rocks in his blood."[20]

Crafting a good musical story, Berliner offers in his own reflection, requires the possession of a quick and reflexive presence of mind, an ability to spontaneously respond to "unexpected flashes of insight . . . in the heat of performance . . . when the identities of formerly mastered patterns melt away entirely within new recombinant shapes." A successful improvisation goes beyond crafting a good design. Its "story" suggests the revealing of a musical intelligence resonating from the performer's body, as if instrumental sound made the character and personality of the subject audibly present. Kenny Barron's observation that soloists must "save" themselves by introducing musical innovations during the course of an improvisation affirms the idea of an equivalence between players' being and the sounds that they produce. A performance, as a revealing, proposes a sonic translation of a musician's humanity.[21]

References to embodiment appear recurringly across Berliner's study, reinforcing his fundamental insight in instance after instance, from a musician employing a metronome to structure the time of his everyday living space to another's insistence that proper swing must arise from the body's full involvement in the articulation of sound.[22] True mastery, many players assert, is ultimately not a rhetorical but an ontological condition relating to the command of time in performance. Calvin Hill, for example, describes how the bass player Richard Davis projects his self into his sound by manipulating the durational continuum, his personalized shifts of tempo, attack, and placement of pulse opening pathways for others in the ensemble to enter the sound. Hill is suggesting here a quality of breakthrough; it is as if Davis's audible body creates the temporal character of the sonic environment. Hersch, moreover, develops this insight by observing how such embodiments must remain dynamic if they are to avoid becoming routinized and cliché. "A lot of guys in New York will only play with an edge," he argues. "They find their groove and that's their groove. To me, once I do that, there's no point in playing anymore. . . . There are hundreds of ways of playing. I think that a master can play all those different kinds of time."[23]

As linkages between body and time proliferate in musicians' discourse, it becomes clear that for many jazz artists, "storytelling," in the end, speaks to the aspiration of enacting the embodied self by pushing against the weight of conformity. It is the act of "'tapping an emotional reservoir,' whose 'energy' represents a distillation of their experiences with life. . . . It has become an extension of how it is to be alive."[24] According to Berliner's own conception of jazz knowledge, the activity of performance is fundamentally ontological, to the point where the organization of the book itself is a composite map of a collective life story, a way of being that is the social life, jazz. The incipit to the final chapter—marking the end of the life of a genre as presented in a quote by Art Farmer—proposes that music and musician are best understood as a primary intensive relation: "The music is what sustains the player from beginning to end. That's where you get your life from. That's why you play jazz."[25]

Storytelling, as a dominant trope—as Sven Bjerstedt explores in his fascinating study of jazz improvisation—carries such power because it reaches beyond the literal frames of narrative to something larger.[26] The stories that Black music tells are not fanciful yarns of metaphor—DeVeaux's neat distinction between "monologic" and "dialogic" approaches seems too tidy, too committed to an actual narrative parallel—but indefinite renderings of collective embodiment that spark sensations of temporally disruptive aliveness. This more expansive conception of feeling and communication in modern jazz improvisation resets the parameters of interpretation and enables listeners to recognize how animatedness makes possible qualities of breakthrough. "Stories" offer up semiotically nebulous expressions of enlivened intensity that push hard against the norms of conventional music understanding. When Duke Ellington insisted, in refusing the banality and tedium of anodyne journalistic labels, "I'm not playing jazz, I am trying to play the natural feeling of a people," he was showing listeners a way of hearing critically, counterhistorically, of perceiving the luminously ontological realness of Black performance. Among many musicians, writes

Vijay Iyer in a thoughtful essay on jazz and narrative form, "there is a clear connection between 'telling your story' and 'keeping it real.' . . . The story that an improvisor [sic] tells does not unfold merely in the overall form of a 'coherent' solo" but in the micro and macro elaborations of a performance: "In a single note, and equally in an entire lifetime of improvisations." What Iyer calls the "traces of embodiment in African-American music" proposes a truth based in the contradiction of an incommensurable history: on the relationship of race's inalienability to the alienable character of capital.[27]

This is why swing-based sounding practices assumed such outsized proportion in the entertainment economy and why African American musicians in the 1940s and 1950s became increasingly defiant of the music industry's expropriative efforts. Their innovations were meant not for mere diversion but to bring into being forms of audible life—living sound inextricably bound to a racialized people. Black jazz at this point was metamorphizing into a powerful collective property whose value multiplied as it coursed through the expanse of popular culture. Having first emerged from the laboratories of Black ensembles, these animated experiments released an untimely energy that remade modern sound. The seeming limitless range of expression extended the pattern of enriching Black music's sonic material, giving visceral substance to the ontological impulses that guided jazz innovation. Here are some of the multiple ways that improvisers brought themselves into the creation of swing-based practice:

The crafting of a distinctive, timbral "voice" through embouchure, breath control, fingering action, tonguing technique, and attack that advanced a musical orientation beyond European-centered note and scale; the development of personally identifiable figurative patterns and riffs (as Ralph Ellison put it, performing "a certain skill of lips and fingers for the intelligent and artistic structuring of emotion"); the evolution of one's own characteristic swing ("He swung pretty," Trummy Young said of Lester Young; "He's pushing past Prez," Jimmy Rowles commented about Charlie Parker); the transference of performance practices from one instrument to another (Earl Hines's pianistic "trumpet style," Charlie Christian "play[ing] guitar like a horn," Roy Eldridge's feat of "playing fine saxophone on the trumpet," Artie Whetsol's muting techniques which achieved the same effect); virtuosic time-keeping by disaggregating components of drumming (Kenny Clarke's shifting of pulse to the ride cymbal; Art Blakey's playing of out-of-sync patterns on different components of the set); the acquisition of advanced knowledge of harmony and harmonic substitution as a means of creating a recognizable, stylistic character (e.g., Coleman Hawkins's departure from slap tonguing in favor of a harmonically generated style inspired by Art Tatum and other pianists); skillful harmonic transpositions of core repertoire as demonstrations of technical and instrumental command ("a lot of people know a lot but just can't execute it. Bird was able to," observed Buddy Fleet); the invention of vocal practices informed by vocally-inspired instrumental phrasing (Billie Holiday and, among White singers, Frank Sinatra); a new primacy given to twelve-bar blues (in swing, jump, and rhythm and blues) whose simplicity accommodated the making of musical structure in improvisation, marking an emerging retreat from Tin Pan Alley song form.[28]

The sounding practices were all part of the invention of a new temporal energy driving performance, the technical emphasis on repetition and its interruption identifying an overarching aesthetic tendency. In their participation in commercial markets, the new sounds of Blackness accumulated value from their very fetishization, their individual distinctiveness—as commodified markers of life—breaking through norms of White possessive containment. In this way, Black jazz's interruptive capacities of breakthrough were formally linked to the disruptive potential of Black sonic material, a potential grounded in the historical contradiction of a property of property producing incorrigible, animated sound. Together these many dimensions of swing-based music revealed the emergence of a new kind of intelligence heard in jazz performance: a racialized, critical knowledge introduced into public awareness by aesthetically progressive Black artists. Ultimately, the move reaffirmed the politicization of Black music as it furthered its decoupling from the Black subject. Modern jazz increased Black music's reach as an audible expression of fleshy sentience intruding on conventional listening, as it became part of a widening interracial creativity. Within the orders of jazz improvisation, listeners were invited to discern a racially generative, cognitive character—a quality of thought congealing in sound the social dilemmas of Black art and the Black artist.

It is in this sense that midcentury practitioners under the leadership of African American musicians developed the aesthetic concept of groove, which was conceived as an elaboration of swing's embodied character. If sensations of groove were already in play at the turn of the twentieth century (recall, for example, the descriptions offered by W. C. Handy and James P. Johnson), groove emerged as a specified practice in the 1930s among Black swing musicians participating in informal, small-group jam sessions. At nearly the same moment, the term also entered wider public awareness via Andy Kirk's recording "In the Groove" (1937) and subsequently became a common indicator of an ensemble's rhythmic proficiency across multiple genres, from bop to free, rhythm and blues, gospel, and soul to funk and hip-hop.[29] In recent decades, music scholars have discerned qualities of groove in multiple rhythm-based musics—many well outside the African American tradition—putting the concept to scrutiny through disparate modes of interpretation, from formal analysis to phenomenology to political economy.[30]

Among midcentury Black jazz musicians, groove described how improvisers worked collaboratively to produce a dynamic, fluctuating sense of ensemble flow. As a collective effort, groove was an outcome of musicians' individual approaches, the contrast between personal and group sound creating a kind of organized heterogeneity, at once diverse and precise. In this basic way, groove would be identified with the push and pull in swing.[31] Yet in group elaborations on the production of temporal congruency and incongruency—the changes in phrasing, articulation, and attack that move in and around the beat—groove achieved an additional quality. When successful, performances brought about a sense of ensemble personality at the cost of the individual self, as first explored in chapter 7: an aggregation of sound seemingly incorporating the presences of those who were playing. The experience is what Ralph Ellison seemed to be getting at when he characterized the "very life" of jazz as a musician's discovery of self in its loss to an ensemble's improvised "collectivity," whereby the music's swing-induced temporality, as he famously observed in another instance (in his opening to the novel *Invisible Man*), changes character: it "stands still," "leaps ahead," and is "never quite on the beat."[32]

At its most powerful moments, an ensemble's groove engenders a repetition-based intensity that heightens human connection, producing a profound kind of sociality. This is less about "democracy," as Ellison fashioned it, than about intimacy and its limits. Groove creates openings into other kinds of time: distinctive temporalities that are claimed by listeners as they themselves are possessed by them. Musicians and audiences alike own as they are owned by the sonic contours of the moment. On "one night," Roy Eldridge recalled, he was so overcome by the power of his band's groove, he had to take pause: they "swung so much I felt so good I had to stop playing." Identifying groove retrospectively as a swing-era concept, moreover, Jonah Jones (b. 1909) told Stanley Dance, "A melody and swing outswing everything, if everybody gets together. It's like what we used to call 'groove,' where everybody felt the same thing. . . . We'd get into that thing and play an hour, and it was no pressure, no strain. It just flowed, and we didn't get tired, because everyone was swinging."[33]

We can accordingly understand the groove concept as a condition of music time that remakes conventional sociality. Groove produces a temporal defiance within the common that inspires sensations of excess—*breakthroughs* whose critical edge derive from the way qualities of aliveness play within and against the order of the commodity form and its capitalization. This containment by capital is once again crucial because it is in groove's attachments to commercial orders—to the circulation of popular music and the growing abstraction of animated Black music labor—that its incorrigible excesses are revealed. Groove existing hypothetically in an autonomous Black world (hypothetically, because it could not actually exist that way and also be a part of the social) could only produce limited sensation; its outer relations—to capital exchange, to the modern concept of innovation, to the star power of the US jazz musician, to the racial idea of Blackness itself—identify the greater forces energizing the aesthetic intensity of a band's enlivened energy.

If, for Adorno, a musical-temporal breakthrough related to how prior musical moments appeared recontextualized and newly conceived over the course of a music composition, breakthrough as a structural anomaly arising from groove operates at the level of racial contradiction, revealing the sensation of audible bodies exceeding their own reified status. By putting qualities of the scabrous body on display—and at midcentury, jazz musicians were still fully aware of their scabrous status—groove empowered performances, its temporal intensities growing in contrast to the restrictiveness of capital time. It is in this sense that we can recognize in groove sensations of breakthrough: collisions of private and public temporalities bringing forth an awareness of racially embodied excesses—abstractions of Black people's original agonistic condition as beings-in-labor—otherwise obscured by the common time of the public present. Ideologically, groove, in its quality of breaking through, is an intervention in the sensible order of the everyday, which, whether experienced in the circumstance of a club or at home listening to a recording, has the capacity of drawing attention to the embodied acts of musicians' storied performances, to the situatedness of a historically incongruent Blackness as a modern cultural phenomenon.

Breakthrough, then, is an outcome of groove, enabled by the structural incongruencies driving Black music's racial distinctiveness. It arises out of the phenomenal experience of the body as an enlivening force contributing to a performance's affective character. The ontological capacities experienced as breakthrough developed structurally from the contradiction of race-capital, having been brought to the fore via musicians' technical mastery and creative imagination. This is not to say that all listeners would acknowledge "breakthrough" as a radical, temporal act; the very nature of the structuring tensions between Black and White worlds, the very fact of capitalism's power to subsume and render forms exchangeable, meant that for the most part modern Black jazz was otherwise experienced as a diversion, even if its content revealed disruptive qualities of racial inalienability. Yet for those more discerning listeners across the racial divide whose aesthetic sensibilities aligned with the habitus of an expansive musicians' world, midcentury jazz practices carried a power that could unseat ordinary experience. They could hear how Black music continually reasserted its aesthetic presence, drawing on resources from the calamitous vastness of America's racial past in breaking through and intruding on the everyday.

A musical work, Adorno writes, may become capable of truth content only "by being honed to aesthetics"; "the truth-content of an art work requires philosophy." In its coalescences as a midcentury modern form, Black music had become sufficiently incorporated into the structures of the entertainment industry that it could say something in the language of aesthetics about a higher truth. If listeners could never exceed the conditions of capital—the best one could do, as Adorno acknowledged, was to expose the oppressive forces undermining a sustained completion of authentic experience—they could nonetheless glimpse Black music's spectacular aliveness: an ontologically inspired sound formation whose essential physicality repeatedly challenged and interrupted normative historical time. However fleetingly, groove-oriented performances revealed to a growing public audience new imaginations of what in life and living were possible, its temporal ruptures conjuring the truthful qualities of the racial that, to invoke once more the Messianic language of Walter Benjamin, "blast open the continuum of history."[34]

Despite the many-sided challenges to developing jazz mastery, musicians' experiments with time drove aesthetic innovation, their advances marking a progress that moved in opposing directions consistent with Black music's double value. A class of musician judged deviant by the greater public had produced a spectacular sound world now overwhelming commercial entertainment. Rhythmic invention within the swing paradigm expanded Black music's ontological value, its audible aliveness developing as an ongoing give-and-take of stylistic routinization and its interruption. As Martin Williams perceptively observed in his tribute to jazz mastery, *The Jazz Tradition*, the "basis" of the shift from swing to bop "came from the resources of jazz itself. . . . That basis is rhythmic, . . . the rhythmic change is fundamental."[35] Such language betrayed Williams's commitment to crafting a jazz version of new criticism, to a Music-qua-Music approach beholden to a venerable African American legacy existing comfortably within the greater framework of Western civilization. Yet in the name of that "tradition" he also called attention to how rhythm, in the way it condenses and makes audible the tempo of enlivened sound, became a central aesthetic force remaking modern music. Grounded in Africanized sounding practices tracing back to the ontologized "chin-music" of the postslavery South (cf. chapter 3), these enlivened expressions reoriented popular music in a dramatically new way. Rhythmic innovation possessed an incorrigible intensity that established pop as a resistance form, as later theorized in criticism from Amiri Baraka to Richard Middleton.

The evolution of jazz into a practice featuring star performers as participants in a worldwide entertainment industry introduced a distinctively modern, temporal sensibility aligned with musicians' personae, their personal sounds recommitting the place of the laboring body in the invention of Black music. Ontologized, swing-based improvisations heightened the perception of jazz as a form that had developed from what John J. Niles described in 1930 as "twenty odd years of syncopated musical history."[36] Twenty years later, jazz was aggressively confronting the conventions of time and experience. This temporal contest, which revolutionized auditory culture, was particularly powerful because it came about at the very moment when modern aesthetic certainties in European-based artistic genres were otherwise collapsing. It is this fundamental, temporal-rhythmic orientation, a newness whose affirmation of "roots" resurrected as an afterlife qualities of tradition, that Williams recognized as a generative principle in the development of jazz practice.

By the time that Williams had published his book in 1970, swing as a structuring principle had advanced the modern legacy of jazz-based Black music while also setting the ground for the development of a range of boogie-inflected genres, from gospel to blues, soul to funk, and carrying forward in the broad expanse of new-century popular practices coalescing under the rubric of rock 'n' roll. As an orienting affect, swing dispersed across the breadth of modern pop, sustaining the general character of modern beat knowledge. Although many subsequent genres eventually departed from swing's light, four-beat propulsiveness, all remained indebted to its primacy as the orienting temporality of midcentury popular music. In swing, one locates, after Ellington, a foundational "natural feeling" existing within and beyond "a people" that organized the sonic understanding of race and nation.[37]

PHONOGRAPHIC TRUTHS

At a poignant moment in *The Jazz Tradition*, Martin Williams describes a performance at a Philadelphia club in the late 1940s that forever changed his thinking about jazz. During a set led by the soprano saxophonist Sidney Bechet, Williams was awestruck as he suddenly grasped how Bechet's playing seemed to condense multiple temporal and sensory dimensions into a singular, coherent experience. As Williams put it, "I realized in a flash that the man, the instrument, and the sounds, the emotion—all these became by some magic process one thing, one aesthetic whole. . . . It was an epiphany for me. . . . I think it was then that I was first in touch with the essential miracle of the music."[38] This way of linking form to revelation was not unusual among jazz writers at the time. To give one more example, it resembles Panassié's own epiphany at a performance by the Chick Webb Orchestra in Harlem in 1939. As he describes it in his 1947 collection *Cinq mois à New York*, "I suddenly grasped, with an extraordinary acuity, the irremediable imperfection of intellectual knowledge. . . . The love of God, which is the only way of knowing faith . . . is the equivalent of what I had just felt whilst watching Chick Webb play."[39] For both writers, Black sound exceeded rational thought as it inspired perceptions of unities existing beyond ordinary experience. The "flash" that Williams observed and the "sudden grasp" that Panassié witnessed were different from the luminous disruptions of Benjamin's dialectics at a standstill. The jazz writers were imagining coherences: "aesthetic whole" and "knowing faith" described a congealing of the unearthly within earthly patterns of living, where spontaneous creation triggered ways of knowing otherwise absent in everyday life.

Despite their exaltations of the moment, though, Williams and Panassié, together with a host of other writers, had been diligently preparing for the possibility of heightened aesthetic experiences through years of careful study. When not listening to jazz in clubs, they were engaged in learning the history of the music as it had been recorded onto phonographic discs. Williams, who at the time was pursuing a PhD in English literature, would soon leave the academy to embark on a career as a jazz critic. Within a decade, he was widely admired for his encyclopedic knowledge of recorded jazz and for his interpretive approach, which called for an understanding of jazz as a form comparable to great works of literature. Panassié, for his part, had been advocating a similar conception since the early 1930s, when, as a young man living in Paris, he first heard the 78-RPM recordings of Black jazz imported from the United States. In *Le Jazz Hot* (1934), he opens with a brief vignette about an imagined encounter with an owner of "a phonograph record shop," and from there proceeds to outline a grand defense of improvisation against the charge that its dependency on recording made it inferior to notated art music. For Panassié, the "real jazz" was fundamentally an art of the age of reproducibility, whose technology provided the means for jazz musicians to create a repertory of masterworks.[40]

By the middle of the twentieth century, modern jazz had been firmly established as a phonographic medium, standing as the principal means by which most followers in the United States and across the world's metropoles experienced the music. Those particularly taken by its performances could develop their knowledge by building record collections, which enabled them to listen repeatedly to the same performances, turning for guidance to a burgeoning body of commentary that not only appeared in music magazines—including the new, record-centered *Record Changer*, the *Jazz Needle*, the *Jazz Record*, and *Jazz Review*—but also spilled out into well-regarded cultural publications such as the *Saturday Review* and the *New Yorker*. During the fifteen-year period after World War II, the commercial structures supporting jazz transformed common understanding of swing-based practices, giving highlight to an extraordinary range of innovation led chiefly by Black players. Black swing-based jazz on record ascended from the crucible of entertainment capitalism to establish a set of standards of musical practice, its fixity as a recorded object broadening knowledge and inspiring new ways of discussing the specifics of form. Having proliferated in the shape of commercially available 78-RPM discs—and then, in 1949, on long-playing records (LPs)—jazz had grown into a contemplative music whose complexities could be discerned as one would when reading a novel or examining a painting. Recording technology, together with other mass-media apparatuses (network radio, Hollywood film), which had developed on their iterations from the 1930s—the broadcasts on network television adding to the mix by the late 1950s—heightened the attention to form, its experience enhanced by the commercial availability of high-fidelity systems for home listening.

New attention to close listening was enabled by the expansion of a community of critics whose work built on the seminal reflections of writers from the 1930s. The new critics were influential in introducing to growing communities of jazz consumers a vocabulary for describing jazz and understanding its place against the larger development of the music's recorded legacy. As John Gennari examines in his magisterial history of jazz criticism, *Blowin' Hot and Cool*, Williams and other United States–based writers—among them, Nat Hentoff, Leonard Feather, Whitney Balliett, Dan Morgenstern, and Ralph Gleason—were essential to the emergence of an aestheticized way of interpreting jazz performances, their critical attention being guided by their primary research tool, the phonograph record. "An important dimension of the jazz conversion experience," Gennari writes, "was the talismanic power that was thought to inhere in the records *themselves*. The very act of gaining ownership of a valued jazz record became an integral part of the meaning a fan attributed to the music." Although their criticism was also inspired by the vivid spontaneity of live playing, it was the material form of the record, its new releases standing at the center of this "collectors' culture," that commanded their attention, providing the means for developing insights that they could share with readers in their columns and essays.[41]

Gennari's word choice suggests something more than a literary flourish. A "talisman" is a sacred object or fetish, a material form animated with otherworldly powers that brings the force of foreign and ancient pasts into the living present. Critics' fastidious attention to collections suggests that for many of them and for other avid listeners jazz discs were forces of truth supplying a pathway to the spirits. Recordings were sites of excavation supporting acts of expropriation and translation: gaining ownership of them became a way of capturing the sonic surface appearances of structures underlying the formation of Black music value. As attentive listeners, they were responding to the dialectical process by which Black music's aliveness intensified through its circulation as a commodity form: what was inalienable and living in the sound engendered the music's auratic character, its sensations of presence heightened by a modern reproducing technology illuminating the structuring of its hidden characteristics. Exposure of "talismanic power" had reorganized the practice of critical listening. By playing to the two orders of fetishism—to the commodity; to an inalienable-yet-alienable enlivened sound—jazz records inspired the development of elaborate narratives about the music's cultural significance. Criticism celebrated jazz music's animated Blackness by remaking it, investing in the value of an enlivened property extracted from the participating bodies of its leading musicians. By these means, a broad community of listeners widely embraced for the first time the idea of jazz as an elevated aesthetic expression whose distinctive originality communicated profoundly about life as it was lived.

Like the artists they admired did, many influential critics firmly held to the belief that jazz was a conveyor of larger truths. Yet whereas jazz musicians typically located those truths intensively and often negatively within the ontological capacities of improvised sound, their advocates, while espousing versions of that view, also took their cue from the record itself, whose stature as a kind of text drew jazz into knowledge orders previously limited to high art. For many White critics one of the key indications of the jazz record's talismanic power was its connection to an ideologically progressive historicism affirming jazz as an American art form: truth in jazz may have belonged to the victors, but it also grew out of the nation's racial experience. "A land does not take its life and character from those who own its property, or who speak for it," argued Sidney Finkelstein in his 1948 book, *Jazz: A People's History*. "A land is given its real life and character by those who live and labor on it." And so, it followed that "just as American *history* [is] . . . to a considerable extent the creation of the Negro people, so American *culture* is to a considerable extent a creation of the Negro people." What Gennari characterizes as the "jazz crusade" undertaken by critics was dedicated to bringing to the attention of a greater public the "occluded history" hidden away in the grooves of phonographic discs. Countering popular opinion of "the jazzman as a connoisseur of street language, sex, drugs, and existential angst," these writers offered to their readers a "bottom-up" perspective that celebrated jazz as a powerful lens into the character of the nation.[42] Theirs was a shared ambition to show respect for jazz and the Black music tradition by distinguishing it from the barrage of highly commercial rhythm and blues and rock 'n' roll that by the early 1950s was flooding major markets.

Opinions differed about how precisely to bring these purported truths of history into narrative form. Writers such as Nat Hentoff held that interpretation required a critical incisiveness befitting the most formidable intellectual challenge. For Hentoff and "the more intellectually ambitious jazz critics," Gennari writes, "the story of jazz was a metaphor for modern America: its social pluralism, its bursting creative energy, and also, in the music's struggle for cultural legitimacy, its failure to come to terms with the racial underpinnings of its national culture."[43] A proper criticism spoke directly to this problem, demonstrating how jazz practice derived from social and political contest, from the paradox of a subjugated class of citizens creating the nation's highest musical art form.

In a detailed accounting of musicians' views during the late 1950s, Hentoff describes the formidable hurdles that Black performers faced, despite the many gains they had made. In large part, Hentoff showed, the racial tensions among Black and White musicians were largely the result of unfair employment practices imposed from above. White jazz musicians enjoyed better pay, greater publicity, and more widespread attention from the consuming public even though Black players were typically more skillful and inventive. "They tell us we're the best jazz musicians and that we invented the music—so how come they get most of the work?" argued an unnamed bass player. Racial inequity fueled resentment, with some members of the community becoming critical of Black bandleaders who hired White musicians or challenging Black artists who joined White groups; "that [White] combo wouldn't swing at all if you weren't there," argued another anonymous Black musician to a fellow player, their need for confidentiality reflective of the difficulties they were facing. Such talents, Hentoff shows, would be increasingly conceived as objectified possessions of the self—embodied tools of the trade that needed protection and drove the development of style. Mary Lou Williams emphatically stated in a now-familiar explanation of bop's virtuosic origins that bop players "deliberately worked out a music they thought would be hard [for White musicians] to steal."[44]

Martin Williams, in contrast, while openly acknowledging the basis of jazz in the African American tradition and the enduring struggles that Black musicians faced, argued that determinations of the music's greatness transcended the routine disenchantments of modern society: rhythm-based swing practice was a language structure revealing what T. S. Eliot (whom Williams proposed as a model for jazz writers) called the "impersonal" nature of art forms. In his essay "Tradition and the Individual Talent" (1919), Eliot asserted that an art work's "life"—his concern was poetry—does not reside in the biography of its maker; rather, it "has its [own] life in the poem." The job of the poet was to stand out of the way, "surrendering himself wholly to the work." Artists become a vehicle for the flow of history to pass through: they must "live in what is not merely the present, but the present moment of the past." In the same way, Williams asserted that "the primary force acting on the jazz musician was the legacy—the tradition—of jazz *itself*." Recording brought the self of "itself" into the open, where listeners could contemplate how jazz "develop[ed] within the framework of Western music, not as a separate development."[45]

Despite the differences in their practice and implementation, Hentoff and Williams built their critical approaches on a foundation of respect for Black musicians and their creative achievements. They along with other influential writers crafted a language that not only offered direction on musical interpretation but also advocated on the musicians' behalf. Seen as a whole, jazz writing at this historical juncture sought greater recognition and appreciation of the music, its transference to the phonographic medium encouraging perceptions of its relationship to the character of American culture. In its success, though, the same body of jazz criticism also had the effect of changing public conceptions of what they so admired. Despite their commitments to modern liberal politics, critics, in their efforts to elevate jazz into the sphere of art, distanced it from its social and historical bearings. Advocacy heightened the effect of phonography's displacement of modern jazz from the habitus of the music's performance, translating it in ways that conformed to a deep-seated White-dominant understanding of "Negro" culture as a supplier of pleasure and entertainment.

The phonographic revolution of midcentury jazz perpetuated a dialectical tendency at the heart of the production of Black music's double-sided valuation: the inalienable qualities of aliveness celebrated by critics as the essence of a supervalued creativity—the "feeling," "soul," and "groove" identifying something greater than Music—also reinforced the contrasting move to devalue what purportedly revealed the Black body's scabrous nature. It was from this relation of greater-than and less-than value that enlivened sound would be continually generated, frequently at a cost to laboring Black musicians. The double value driving the production of Black music inspired efforts to downplay its negative qualities with the aim of transforming it into something wholly positive. As writers honored the new stars in the industry, the mechanisms that brought jazz into circulation accelerated its decoupling from its basis in labor and increased the rate of its commodification and exchange: Black music as a living body in sound gave way to the making of an animated music living within America's body politic. Having been phonographically excavated from the concrete performance event, the aura of aliveness in recorded jazz intensified, its power looming over the US entertainment industry as a fractal projection of the logic of profit-from-loss. In the process, modern jazz acquired a spectral grandeur recognized on an international scale that compelled the crafting of new narratives celebrating its qualities of liberating, enlivened sound.

A particularly powerful example of this tendency appeared in the symbolic alignment of jazz and the democratic nation-state. Having gained aesthetic legitimacy for its spirit of rebellion and associations with antifascist resistance movements—the *Entartete Kunst* whose recordings were derided by Nazi propagandists—jazz after World War II became bound up with triumphalist claims of democracy as part of the United States' Cold War–era rhetoric: the racially scabrous character of its negative form supplied the basis for the making of an official discourse of freedom. In the British expatriate Leonard Feather—whose *Down Beat* column, "The Blindfold Test," measured musicians' knowledge of recordings by their contemporaries—the State Department, which was now endorsing jazz as part of its propaganda campaign, found a principal advocate. For Feather, jazz was a raucous "resistance" music that, having become unmoored from its racial origins, displayed qualities of transcendence exceeding the limits of human division. In the 1959 edition of *The Book of Jazz*, he asserted that jazz, "originally the music of the American Negro and the American white, now simply the music of the American, will become more than ever a music of the human being." His fervent prognostications—informed by his own early experiences growing up in a Jewish family in wartime London— echoed Charles Delaunay's reflections from the same period (cf. chapter 7). For both, jazz was a musical materialization of a universal ideal, a truth aligned with the very forces that dominated the music's inventors.[46]

Across the middle of the twentieth century, jazz would be celebrated as a spirited, irreverent art of democracy, its growth moving in step with the proliferation of its recorded forms across international markets. Commonly portrayed as a popular art capable of revealing emotional and psychological insight, jazz, for many listeners, both Black and White, had given form to America's achievement in the war's aftermath. If in this narrative jazz would be more openly recognized as the product of African Americans—with recordings by Black artists most commonly featured—it also supported an integrationist cosmopolitanism that reduced Black presences to surface appearances.[47] At times—famously, in *Time* magazine's 1954 cover presentation of Dave Brubeck as the new face of jazz—the music seemed to have shifted away from its racial origins, having become an informing influence in discussions of literature, continental philosophy, and the inner character of the self. The move to integrate jazz reaffirmed a paradoxically disembodied yet ontologically racial Blackness at the service of

White ownership, as a distinctive, swing-inflected practice articulated to narratives of progress within a postwar imperial imagination. "Never before has any branch of music made such rapid progress," Feather declared, stating a position that had become common in jazz criticism.[48] In the victory of democracy over the forces of fascism, modern jazz, through its alignments with the productive capacities of capital, brought into the audible present the sound of boundless potential. Outside musicians' worlds, jazz was saying something too: the ontological structures orienting performance had aligned with narratives perpetuating the myth of consensus, as the occluded history of US racism persisted uncomfortably at its center.

Modern jazz's phonographic turn identified a major transformation in the evolution of Black music value. Its elevation as an art form was part of the greater advancement of the popular industry, which foisted Black music into the realm of aesthetics for the first time in its history. Catapulting into the world, a swing-based practice reorganized modern music's valuative center, its ontological capacities seeming to bring into being an enlivened intelligence, a cognitive character that stood in contrast to the still dubious capacities of the laboring Black musician. It was as if the sound of Zora Neale Hurston's orchestra had not only reared on its hind legs but leapt from the dance floor, exited the club, and turned the corner, its ontological disposition dissolving into the cellular makeup of the social where it cascaded through the bloodstream of the body politic. In its dissemination, jazz music's enlivened qualities ascended, recognized as an informing impulse in the rise of popular music's significance. By the late 1950s, the extent of its global expansion made early declarations of a global "jazz latitude" seem quaint (cf. chapter 6). Not only was modern jazz everywhere; its mediated propagation had transformed the sensible field of public listening. For those who wanted to hear it, the music's spectral intrusions—as a "shadow of the past where time hovers ghostlike"—made the sound of the global modern into something discernibly Black.

As recorded jazz emerged as the new aesthetic truth of the world's metropolitan liberal classes, it also carried forward an early version of audiopolitics among the racially subjugated and poor. In the United States, recordings participated in the making of a "freedom sound" that, as Ingrid Monson shows, produced powerful linkages of jazz and civil rights. Beyond its national origins, moreover, jazz on record was impacting the musical thought of the world proletariat, whose embrace of beat-oriented music in the 1920s had armed a phonographically driven dance revolution with the creative means of political struggle. The art form of an antiestablishment cultural elite linking New York, Paris, and Tokyo became a common reference point within emergent grassroots movements: across the global south, jazz informed an anticolonial cultural project that shared in the glorification of embodied sound. In some instances, such as in African pop, the very term *jazz* supported local imaginations of insurrectionist freedom—for example, the 1950s Congolese bands L'African Jazz and OK Jazz—betraying the influence of United States–based Black music discourses. What provided the soundtrack to the 1956 Conference of Negro-African Writers and Artists (*Congrès des écrivains et artistes noirs*) in Paris affirmed a way of hearing the past against the grain, extending the reach of what Michael Denning has called global vernacular music's "decolonization of the ear and the dancing body." The phonographic revolution giving form to modern jazz moved within and against these forces of entertainment, generating a new kind of international spectacularity that joined in a global vernacular movement, a veritable "noise uprising."[49]

One might be tempted to conclude that the stunning breadth of modern jazz's phonographic reach offered proof of its powers of aesthetic unification—that, unlike more conspicuously commercial forms of popular entertainment, it conveyed an absolute, positive truth. In fact, the many claims on it were more indicative of contest than of coherence, captured in Alexander G. Weheliye's evocative depiction of the phonographic moment as a "sonic Afro-Modernity." Nowhere was the problem made plainer than in the racial politics of the West, where the orders of aesthetic knowledge among Black musicians were overwhelmed by a chorus of high-volume opinion. While commentators in US and European metropoles debated the extent to which jazz had remade the hierarchy of modern music—a position advanced by the American writer and intelligence officer Henry Pleasants in his best-selling books—musicians' conceptions amounted mainly to an insider knowledge poorly represented by even the most well-meaning critics. The tendency to speak for and over Black musicians ultimately compelled artists to question critics' authority and that of the industry at large. Tensions played out publicly in a debate published in *Down Beat* in 1961, where a group of musicians, which included Miles Davis and Cannonball Adderley, challenged the competence of writers to make judgments and to speak on their behalf.[50] While modern jazz was achieving a spectacular moment on a global scale, it occupied more routinely at home the "noisy lostness" of Black existence in the nation's cities. A lofty art of transcendence revealed on its underside the essential struggle by which African American musicians and their followers sought to claim their property once again.[51]

If jazz writers were constrained by their obligation to the entertainment business, musicians weren't much better off: it wasn't as if they held all the answers to the complex question of Black music's negative valuation. Although some seemed to think they possessed the true knowledge of jazz—a sentiment implied in Arthur Taylor's "musician-to-musician" compendium, *Notes and Tones*—they too, as citizens living in modern America, were caught up in the "folklore" that Ellison identified; frequently, they were arguing for a truth value that was merely oppositional rather than critical. Being aware of the ontological capacities of Black sound driving a legacy of racial expropriation did not mean they could also explain the historical forces that generated value. In their efforts to identify aesthetic absolutes, players' claims of truth, despite their sincerity, were commonly personal, idiosyncratic. Some, like Max Roach, embraced spiritualist doctrine—"I am an instrument and being used, and all things are good"—pairing his devotion to Islam with calls for racial justice. Others, notably Art Blakey and Randy Weston, asserted their direct connections to African cultures, which, to artists such as the Ghanaian drummer Guy Warren (aka Kofi Ghanaba), bore a striking resemblance to the imperialist tendencies of the US State Department and intelligence agency (for whom, ironically, he sometimes worked).[52] And still others located unspoken truths in the patterns of musical form, claiming a higher principle discernible in the power of swing- and groove-based performances. At a moment when the phonographic circulation of jazz had made it seem like a public consensus might be realized, the disparity of the music's reach across multiple markets attenuated any hope of establishing universal norms. Having attained unprecedented heights of recognition, jazz and its judgment seemed more contested than ever before.

DISCERNING TRUTHS IN MUTE MUSIC

Jazz took the form of the record in its relation to the global expansion of capital, its antimonies—a celebrated "truth" existing in a sea of conflicting representations—informing the fractured character of its reception. It is in this light that we can consider Adorno's well-known interrogations of popular music as the quintessential expression in the life of the commodity, inhabiting a central position in what he and Max Horkheimer famously named the "culture industry." Jazz—Adorno's term for 1920s- and 1930s-era German and American dance-band music—was among his principal concerns because it had made such a tremendous impact on the condition of modern music knowledge.[53] Across several essays published in the 1930s, he pushed hard against common opinion that championed jazz as modern society's savior, "offered under the trademark of quality goods." Fundamentally, Adorno was dubious about how a putative art generated according to the advancing logic of the commodity form—whose "perpetual repetitions" were consistent with the processes of mass production—could somehow reorganize the alienating forces that generated it. His criticism arose less from elitism than from a profound doubt about any concept of art or culture that did not account for its origins in injustice. He asked, as Simon Jarvis summarizes his work, "Can we imagine a world in which one's joy does not depend upon another's woe . . . in which every pleasure is bought at the cost of someone else's suffering?" Popular music epitomized the contradiction of culture, representing a form of leisure built on the dominance of exploited labor, not the least of which was a massive community of African American musicians.[54]

Jazz was not alone in Adorno's critique: he believed the malignant force of the culture industry was pervasive, affecting virtually all twentieth-century artistic expression.[55] Yet jazz was particularly vexing for him because its regressive influence was so widespread. Having been constituted within and thus subsumed by the entertainment industry, it had lost any vestige of "liberatory potential," its failure supplying evidence that it could not live up to what he termed the social "responsibility of art." Posing as an art form, jazz was a pernicious imposter of truth: what appeared dressed up and sophisticated in commercial contexts sought to seduce listeners with "the truth of an untrue society."[56] Jazz music's truths were untrue because, for Adorno, any art worthy of the claim of truth needed to move—in the image of Benjamin's "angel of history"—against the grain of dominance, exposing the suffering on which all Western art was historically based. The very notion of a viable music with entertainment value amounted to an aesthetic con job: "The critically transformative illusion necessary for art," as James Buhler writes in an important essay on Adorno's jazz writing, had given way to mere illusion.[57]

Given his caustic response to the incessant rush of commodified objects, images, and sounds overwhelming modern society, it is no surprise that Adorno was unwilling to embrace Benjamin's more salutary vision of art in the age of mechanical reproducibility. As is widely known, Adorno's essay "On the Fetish Character of Music and the Regression of Listening"— published in 1938, the same year he began working at the Princeton Radio

Research Project—grew out of a private correspondence in which he challenged Benjamin's argument on mass production's compensatory effects.[58] For Benjamin, mass-produced art (most notably on film) inhibited the repressive dominance of capital: the collapse of art's auratic power under the weight of mass production changed the conditions of sensory experience, carrying the potential to liberate audiences and enable them to reclaim art's significance against the rising tide of fascism. For Adorno, in contrast, commodified art intensified capital's dominance: music repetition conveyed the material character of the commodity as the source of regressive listening. While celebrating music's power—"music represents the immediate manifestation of [human] impulse"—it had become, in its appearances on national radio shows and recording, not the source of mass audiences' freedom but "the locus of its taming." This was a fate met not only by jazz and popular music but by all mediated forms, including European art music: "The diverse spheres of music must be thought of together." Aesthetic value would seem to be largely undone by exchange value. Jazz and popular expressions epitomized the condition, having been generated from the machinery of mass production.[59]

Rather than completely acquiescing to the negative as a fundamental condition, though, Adorno sought across the expanse of his work to contemplate aesthetic possibility dialectically, amid the tragic state of things. His was a negative aesthetics that also suggested a sense of yearning for glimpses of an absent utopia: by revealing the myths and contradictions on which art was based, audiences might apprehend momentary indications of a sensible truth otherwise lost. These were the moments when art seemed paradoxically to interrupt, to break through, the very process by which it had developed under capitalism. They arose not as a transcendence of the tendency of capital—"art can ignore this tendency only at the price of its powerlessness"—but from the development of the artwork's autonomy, and hence, its aesthetic value, as part of the commodification process.[60]

In his late, uncompleted monograph, *Aesthetic Theory* (first published posthumously in German in 1970), Adorno makes a cryptic remark. He suggests, almost in passing, that "the absolute artwork converges with the absolute commodity." Initially, the commentary doesn't make sense. How could two, seemingly opposite realms of the absolute—one existing inalienably as an economically useless art for art's sake, the other alienable and inherent to capitalism—become aligned? If the artwork could indeed exist outside of exchange according to the ideals of an autonomous aesthetic realm, it would remain, as Adorno acknowledges, socially powerless. And if it fully participated in exchange—if a useless, absolute artwork takes the form of a fully alienable commodity—wouldn't it then become subsumed by the forces of capital, its use-value preempted and determined by the needs of the market and the rules of exchange?[61]

For Adorno, it is precisely the economic participation of the artwork in capitalism that generates its value, its status as "art" becoming the basis of social critique. As Stewart Martin puts it in a valuable essay that explores Adorno's comment, "an artwork's affinity to a commodity does not prevent it from contradicting capital, but rather enables it."[62] If the uselessness ascribed to the artwork is after all an illusion—a condition necessary to the artwork's critically transformative power—it nonetheless stands in real contradiction of exchange processes, even as it grows as part of the work's economically determined fetish character. By participating in exchange as a condition of its commodification, the artwork's symbolic value as a useless form increases, drawing the work further away from its concrete origins in labor and use as it aligns with the ideal of pure exchange, of an absolute commodity. What for Adorno ultimately prevents this seemingly inexorable process from happening, though, is an intrusion, not of labor or use value—which already succumbed to the needs of exchange value—but of the artwork's very uselessness, which contradicts the exchange process. "Only what is useless," Adorno writes, "can stand in for the stunted use value. Artworks are plenipotentiaries of things that are no longer distorted by exchange, profit, and the false needs of a degraded humanity."[63]

The limit of the artwork's ascent as a pure exchange value sets the conditions for its power to contradict capital: aestheticized uselessness as an economic category forms the basis of an immanent critique of the self-valorizing capital subject. "The autonomous artwork," Martin argues, "is an emphatically fetishized commodity, which is to say that it is a sensuous fixation of abstraction, of the value-form, and not *immediately* abstract." Seemingly disentangled from concrete, human labor, the absolute artwork, as a form constituted within capitalism, presents its contradiction: it is a material manifestation of capitalism's abstract logic, embodying the accumulated labor necessary to produce it. And so, it follows: "The autonomy of art is derived from its internalization of abstract labour." The absolute artwork, in its uselessness, mirrors an economic realm no longer inhabited by concrete living labor, even as its mediated qualities of humanity, those plenipotentiary substitutions, affirm the existence of an abstracted truth content. This truth content, inherent to the artwork, though fragmentary and mediated by capital, intrudes on the corresponding illusion of capital's self-valorizing powers. As Martin summarizes the process, "The autonomy of the artwork contradicts the autonomy of capital that reduces all singularities to their heteronomous determination."[64]

Adorno's late efforts to claim a semblance of aesthetic experience in a world ravaged by capitalism's "vampire-like" acts—acts that extract the life of living labor toward the goal of absolute commodity exchange—provide insight into his pathbreaking early criticism on the phonographic medium.[65] In "The Form of the Phonograph Record" (1934), he reflects on how an oppressive, reproducing technology might secure qualities of art's livingness toward the promise of an authentic musical experience: to imagine, as he would later ask, "what would art be, as the writing of history, if it shook off the memory of accumulated suffering."[66] At the outset of his essay, Adorno acknowledges the present tyranny embedded in the record itself. The phonograph record "is not primarily humane," he writes, for, as a commodity created in the age of colonial conquest and a world overwhelmed by commercial product, "it already stems from an era that cynically acknowledges the dominance of things over people." Yet through these same means—as a technology that captures and commercializes sound—recording empowers music as it tames it by bringing its sound into the company of writing. To advance this position, Adorno deploys a graceful, poetic language whose form invites imagining the phonograph as a means of supplying a suffocating musical culture with the resonant breath of a literary form. By committing music to a 78-RPM shellac disc, the reproducing technology transforms its sonic properties into text: the records, "fragile like tablets," become negatively rendered defenses against culture's loss, as a "petrified . . . dead art rescues the ephemeral and perishing art as the only one alive."[67]

However emblematic of mass production the recorded medium was, it also produced something remarkable: as a form of writing, it "absorbs into itself . . . the very [musical and social] life that would otherwise vanish." Recording technology's ironic materialization of performed sound discloses an animatedness developing from the disc's falsity as a reification of human expression. For Adorno, it amounted to a distillation of music's cognitive character. "Though the theologian may feel constrained to come to the conclusion that 'life' in the strictest sense—the birth and death of creatures—cannot be ascribed to any art, he may also tend to hold that the truth-content of art only arises to the extent that the appearance of liveliness has abandoned it." Music's truth content would become available only after it had been committed to an inaudible, lifeless materiality. Through this process, "the form of the phonograph record could find its true meaning: the scriptal spiral that disappears in the center, in the opening of the middle [of the disc], but in return survives in time." Where "the curves of the needle" end commences a return, a new beginning, bringing forth a transformed temporality: "*Time* gains a new approach to music. It is not the time in which music happens. . . . It is time as evanescence, enduring in mute music," in the "petrified" knowledge base of a commercial disc. "As a thing," Theodor Levin writes in a penetrating essay on Adorno's phonographic criticism, the record "is a materialization, a reification which transforms an acousto-temporal event into a trace. It is, in short, a writing, but a writing . . . of a special indexical sort."[68]

The record as absolute commodity reveals sensual, aesthetic absolutes enabled by phonographic technology's capture of sound. Translated into material form, these "tablets" preserving the gravitas of music's truth content serve as an archive of potentiality. They will become heard again later, in a better world, interpreted against the grain of the victor's history. For the time being, though, the discs maintain music's truth content in the negative, as an authentic, if soundless, life captured in material form: capital gives birth to an aspiration toward the absolute. This is the "magic" that Adorno thought lost and spoke of longingly in the *Dialectics of Enlightenment*: the nature with which art was endowed, yet which could only be recognized dialectically from a negative posture. And so, the nondurational temporality of "mute music" would persist in the modern era as a back-leaning form of critique—a version of Messianic time—moving counter to the history of dominance. "Mute music" sustained a promise that—beyond its fleeting interruptions as breakthrough—remained for now phenomenally inert, akin to an insect suspended in amber, a substance not unlike the shellac of the recorded disc.[69]

Adorno doesn't directly address the situation of Black music on record, but we can assume he would have argued that it endured the same fate. His disparaging comments about commercialized swing and "hot jazz," and about the relation of jazz to militaristic march music in an era of rising authoritarian power—"jazz can be easily adapted for use by fascism"—show that he saw little "plenipotentiary" potential in the recorded performances of African American musicians.[70] The ascendency of recorded popular hits would have reinforced the sense that Black sound had been expropriated from a now valueless, embodied Negro labor. For Adorno, Black music in its multiple manifestations had become fully subsumed under capital. He could only have reached this conclusion because he did not recognize how

Black music's ontological presences had afforded to recorded swing-based expressions aesthetic possibilities not available to mere Music. If Black music's status as a commodity had compromised its spontaneity and life, the racial contradictions underpinning Black recorded jazz at mid-century brought into being new, enlivened potentialities, affording opportunities to perceive what was, in fact, enduringly sublated: an oblique untimeliness committed to a replayable disc. In place of uselessness was an aestheticized enlivened form that interrupted the seemingly inexorable process of commodification.

Put simply, Black music's truth content was not entirely "mute," the "scriptal spiral" being noisier, more audibly assertive than writing. What was deemed socially "useless" and negative about Black being identified the agonistic origin of its hyperpositive value, an inalienable materiality taking form as enlivened sound. The music's potency lived on in its scabrous ontology, capable of being understood publicly as something incorrigibly less than and greater than Music. This potency was part of the racial-economic logic by which Black music was constituted and progressed into the world: as a structural logic, it too located its primary truth "not [in] the time in which music happens." Yet rather than being rendered lifeless as a script etched onto a disc, it gained life as a mediated voicing of a counterhistorical past-time, which carried into the modern a means of motivating life-affirming performances routinely rendered audible on replayable records. First constituted as the fundamental property of propertied human things, Black music's fleshy qualities entered the temporal sphere of music production, bringing into form a time-distorting *musical life* that moved forward in its dialectical progression as swing- and groove-based practices.

If Adorno missed the primacy of Black music as an enlivened negative art, his challenges are nonetheless important if we are to grasp how to listen for it on record. His critique helps to show how engaged listeners—musicians, critics, audiences—at the emerging apex of Black music's metamorphosis at midcentury, while recognizing a cognitive potential and racial knowledge in its forms, ironically undersold its power by celebrating it, by seeking to make it into a coherent, unified expression. Their desire to possess Black music wholly, whether to claim it as the voice of America or the resonance of African essence, reproduced acts of dominance, shaping Black music into a unity mirroring the rational subject. Even the efforts to locate in sound an occluded history risked the tendency to claim Black music as a property, fixing its meaning for a greater good. These efforts to capture Black music as modern jazz compromised its understanding.

Hearing occluded history as counterhistory requires a different approach, a dialectical listening that works critically against the grain in ways befitting Ellison's conception of "a constant plunging back into the shadow of the past where time hovers ghostlike."[71] It is to begin the practice of what we may call "double listening," consistent with Black music's double value as it coalesces at midcentury in the form of the phonograph record. Double listening commences with a critical attentiveness to the folkloric, working within and against it to hear past-time as it becomes amplified, living on, progressing dialectically, yet incorrigibly, in the commodity form. The metamorphosis of Black music as part of the advancement of capital brings about new heights in its mediation; it is also what enables the rediscovery of its qualities of truth. In this, a truth content emerges neither as an absolute nor a muted trace, but as a noisy, calamitous agon consistent with Black music's negative form. Truth in its primary structural expression repeatedly breaks through, arising doubly: the "flash" Williams heard and the spiritual ecstasy that Panassié witnessed suggest not unities but a dislodging of order, an unbalancing relating to the material fact of humanity's "imperfection," brought forth in the fleshy presences—the "stories"—of modern improvisation. Double listening means to hear the "Negro problem" at the heart of Black music's relation to the United States, from which its value circulates beyond the nation's shores. In its glory, the truth of Black music would remain cast in the negative, perpetually compromised by its dialectical other, with its embodied muteness pushing forward and revealing, growing ever-more alive in the sound.

APOTHEOSIS OF A

NEW BLACK MUSIC

"A PLACE WHERE BLACK PEOPLE LIVE"

Early into his 1966 essay "The Changing Same," an audacious commentary on the aesthetic character of rhythm and blues and free jazz, Amiri Baraka makes a bizarre digression that speaks volumes about his changing views on Black music's significance. After delivering a series of obscure pronouncements about slave ships, "spirit worship," and "bodies responding . . . against you," Baraka asks us to imagine a fantastical situation where money lenders and borrowers congregating in a conventional savings and loan are confronted with a recording of James Brown. "If you play James Brown (say, 'Money Won't Change You . . . but time will take you out') in a bank," he asserts, "the total environment is changed. . . . An energy is released in the bank, a summoning of images that take the bank, and everybody in it, on a trip. That is, they visit another place. A place where Black People live."[1]

Baraka's public embrace of Black popular music was new. Just three years earlier, in his book *Blues People* (1963), he questioned hard bop musicians' embrace of funky and soul jazz, which seemed to him a commercialized debasement of bop's modernist principles. Now, in this new offering, Baraka was overlooking soul jazz's attempt to appeal to a wider audience—driven by record companies' efforts to stay the decline in jazz listenership—and calling for a realignment of the history of style, one that reconceived Black music as an all-encompassing, unifying "energy": the "(total) force" of a historically and temporally conceived "changing same." "The differences between rhythm and blues and the so-called new music or art jazz, the different places, are artificial," he argued, "or they are merely indicative of different placements of the spirit."[2] The seemingly disparate achievements of Ray Charles, John Coltrane, Lightnin' Hopkins, Albert Ayler, and Sam and Dave all grew from a commitment shared with the God-father of Soul to a grand spiritual realignment. By introducing this sound into a public place of financial exchange, Baraka would bring out into the open an otherworldly energy, an audible past-time consistent with what he had described in his book and then again in this essay as a "blues impulse."[3]

On the face of it, Baraka's scenic moment with record and record player in hand seems absurd, being nothing more than a curious play of social incongruities. Displaying the Manichaean commitments for which he would later become well known—his comfort zone, as Gerald Early has put it, lay "between two mutually exclusive sets of ideas"—he relies on hyperbolic characterizations of racial and social difference—sweaty, exercised singing performed within the maw of capital accumulation—in order to make grand claims about a prodigious gulf existing between Black and White people.[4] Just imagine what would happen if, say, Baraka actually brought his portable "hi-fi," as playback systems were called then, into Chase Manhattan in mid-1960s New York. The situation is ludicrous because it would never have been allowed. Amid the bustle of transactional activity, Baraka would likely have been taken down, cuffed, placed under arrest, and, quite conceivably, knelt on, choked, or even worse.

But that's precisely the point. Such an act could never happen because it would disrupt a key mechanism of capital. The music's rhythmic intensity—featuring Brown's assertive vocal punctuations—*would* transform the bank's affective environment, wreaking havoc on the processual efficiency of financial exchange. Through a feat of recording technology, a Black noise would take over, the animated powers of the music filling the room, its accumulating profit as an aesthetic value developing from the confrontation itself. For the bank's customers would have to listen, and by doing so, they would, most likely against their will, be disconnected from the routine practice of deposit and withdrawal, to "visit another place. A place where Black People live." In the same way that Aretha Franklin did around the time, James Brown brought into popular musical practice a power of affect, a palpable sense of audibly enlivened truth that carried across the color line. As Thulani Davis artfully puts it in one of her reflections on Franklin, the greater impact of racialized sound personified by a series of Black stars and groups in the 1960s "threw back the curtain that had been segregation and showed the rest of America how Black America took its joy."[5]

Baraka's digression about James Brown and the modern rituals of consumer lending was, after all, part of a larger debate over the status of Black music in its confrontational participation within the structures of capital. His essay, which closes out a collection made up mostly of previously published articles, may be read as a manifesto on the racial politics of culture: an aesthetic declaration proclaiming victory for Black music in its multiple expressions as part of the struggle for leadership in American musical art. Although Baraka's claims were by no means uniformly embraced, and most likely not by the majority of those who read the magazine, they carried a certain credibility, appearing at a time when Black jazz along with the music's more commercial forms had metamorphosed into a stunning creativity that had once more rearranged the norms of public taste. In fact, Baraka's bombastic proclamations seemed not unimaginable particularly in the context of the mid-1960s, when US Black innovations were for many resonant with civil rights activism and were themselves redefining the wider production of international style. His essay was ultimately a celebration of a global auditory network given the name "Black music," as it was a statement of unambiguous claim: what had won worldwide appeal as a marvel of artistic accomplishment was morally bound to the flesh of Black being, identifying the original property of a once-enslaved, once-African populace.

The continuing struggle over Black music's ownership fueled Baraka's defiance of the greater realm of pop. For he clearly recognized how the music's unprecedented gains came at a great cost. The rarefied artistry of free jazz and the vigorous intensities of "the R&B people" rested on the shoulders of a legacy of creation that had been massively co-opted by an industry driving the consensus tastes of common consumers: "stealing Music . . . stealing energy (lives)." Jazz had paid a high price for its success: "Jazz seeks another place as it weakens, a middle-class place." So did early rhythm and blues, having succumbed losses to "so-called 'pop' which . . . sees to it that . . . dollar-popularity remains white."[6] The bank was a stand-in for the apparatuses of an advanced capitalism that enacted a version of profit-from-loss on a macro scale, where, as William Sewell describes capitalism's brutal logic, "every loss is simultaneously a gain: the bankruptcy of one firm is an opportunity for its rivals; the failure of an investment is a sign to capital to invest itself elsewhere."[7] In financial terms,

Black music often proved to be a bad investment for those who created it. The asymmetry of loss within African American sound worlds—the very necessity of loss for a negatively determined "Black music" to realize aesthetic and symbolic profit—meant that a pattern of racially regulated uneven development would drive creative activity. Black musicians needed to perpetually reinvent their art after each "failure of an investment," their successes a small financial return on the vast commercial expropriation of Black sound. Although a slate of Black stars had achieved a dubious celebrity, their accomplishments could not compare with the extraordinary economic fortunes of the White-controlled entertainment industry, whose dominance further loosened the already tentative grip of Black musicians on their music.

The enduring saga of profit-from-loss illustrates once again the conditions of tragedy that accompany the history of Black music valuation. Yet it also helps us to comprehend, nearly sixty years later, the climax of the music's metamorphosis in ways perhaps more instructive than Baraka's Manichaean view could provide. Black music's evolution within the greater field of postwar popular music revealed processes exceeding the heroic tales of artists overcoming adversity to reach, seemingly untarnished, new aesthetic heights. For the very losses that accumulated were a vital fuel for Black music's ascent: had the sounding practices arising in Black club cultures of the 1940s and 1950s not been first capitalized within an intricate network of racially segregated entertainment economies newly committed to the production of records, Black music would never have achieved its enormous valuative leaps. And had this racialized economy of sound not been so grandly expropriated and reinvented as forms of rock 'n' roll, it would never have revealed on a public scale its agonistic temporal intensities: it would never have become so influential in reshaping the affective orders of contemporary musical life. Expansive losses accrued unprecedented symbolic profits that catapulted Black music to the apex of American musical achievement.

What Baraka had identified was the realization of enlivened sound as an advanced form in its confrontation with the social temporality of capital, where, in Anthony Reed's apt characterization, "the riotous"—the New Black Music—"imprints itself in the fabric of everyday life."[8] Emerging in the postwar moment, it unfolded over the course of the century, giving form to a dynamic "constellation" of previously obscured temporalities and bringing into the range of hearing a paradoxically "mute music" structurally aligned with a tragic past.[9] The qualities defining this constellation congealed as a dramatic face-off at the heart of valuation: out of the contradiction of race-capital, Black music's inalienable qualities of aliveness developed dialectically to reveal a cognitive character materializing within the music itself. This enlivened, if unknowing, subject, born of as it moved to a step beyond the temporal behavior of capital, populated the public sphere with its unruly double character. As Black music evolved across the last half of the twentieth century, it dispersed according to two temporalities: one responsive to the hypereventfulness of capital exchange; the other changing while also leaning backward, moving in contrary motion, incorrigibly expressive of the laboring life of Black being. Through these opposing movements, the music maintained a posture otherwise unknown in American culture: it stood inalienably as the essential racial intensity of Black existence and as an alienable commodity whose aliveness carried into the world repetitive affirmations of the nation's racial myths. Over time, the competing orientations expanded in parallel, the growth of the music's value accelerating within the expanse of capital as that expansion disclosed the stubborn certainty of the Black body enlivening Black sound.

Initiating the process was the creation of new incorrigible forms: "riotous" time bombs of sonic aliveness that moved contrapuntally to swing practices and commercial expressions of jazz. Their contested motion set off a grand metamorphosis where economic losses to African American artists and institutions drove the invention of an adversarial audibility, creating a new source base of capitalized value production. This qualitative reordering of beat knowledge shifted American music's foundation, revising the sonic-temporal field that structured popular music and reaffirming the integral place of the Black music past in the nation's sonic order. Qualities of past-time, which had previously remained oblique, grew more conspicuous, being openly fetishized while also securing greater critical power. The tension fueled a contest of pastimes and past-times that impacted popular culture and ignited Black music's apotheosis of form. By the mid-1960s, Black music had, in the forms of free and R&B—and subsequently with the rise of a corpus of experimental practices and popular outgrowths, from soul to funk to hip-hop—assumed a heightened spectral appearance that listeners, engaging critically and listening doubly, could discern in the flood of recordings. The mass of sonic spectacularity materialized a Negro problem-in-sound formally consistent with the greater conflicts in the global politics of nation and culture.

To do justice to Baraka's seminal insights about "the changing same," we need to reconsider the critical moment in pop that was Black music's remarkable unfolding. The thirty-year period beginning with Black swing's emergence in the late 1930s was marked by accelerated disseminations and sharpened concentrations of enlivened Black sound, guided by new rhythmic inventions that moved counter to a conventional knowledge of the beat. If Black rhythm was aligned with qualities of "Negro" behavioral repetition since the nineteenth century, by the 1950s and 1960s it stood as the principal creative property of African Americans, its ontological capacities intensifying according to its expansion in capitalized entertainment markets. What may be characterized as a quality of "soul" identified a general condition stretching across the last half of the century, where Black music's animatedness became fully expressive as it appeared live and on record. At this moment, mainstream popular form forfeited its leadership: what was alive in the sound took command, perpetuating into the late century and millennial era an audible sensation that revealed multiple, past-time–inflected returns.

RATIONALIZING A NATIONAL BLACK FEELING: CHICAGO'S POSTWAR BLUES MARKET

And so, once again, we can see how the development of Black music value moved perpetually in double time. A racialized child of capital, it morphed as part of its remunerative tendency of giving to the nation while reaffirming its value in Black worlds. Cast symbolically in the negative, Black music continued across the century to amass hyperpositive gains. Locating the impetus of value-making below, it consistently advanced beyond the aesthetic norm: as something greater than Music, it took position as the primary reference point in popular music's stylistic growth. This same dynamic had already fueled the evolution of pop across the long modern, coalescing by the early 1900s as an irreverent beat knowledge known publicly by the names *ragtime*, *blues*, and *jazz*. But the mid-century metamorphosis was different: while still driving mainstream expression, it had also—as a "Black music" performed by Black musicians—assumed a formidable stature within the hierarchy of entertainment. Black music engaged antagonists and enthusiasts alike, heightening the struggle over control of the audible character of the everyday. This final chapter plots out how it came to be.

Stuart Hall observes the transformation of Western postwar culture in relation to the greater evolution of pop and the making of a new music of the people. In a seminal essay—anticipating Habermas's theories of the "public sphere" and more recent conceptions of "publics"—he postulates that popular culture's associations with what he calls the "'underdog'" emerged as a strategy for working classes to invent creative expressions consistent with their own everyday experiences. From the late nineteenth century, capital, taking the form of commercial entertainment and information industries, supplied "the people" with their means of invention, granting them "the power to represent the class to itself." This pattern continued over the decades as part of the greater "containment of popular democracy on which 'our democratic way of life' appears to be so securely based." When mass media and reproduction technologies expanded exponentially in step with the growth of mass markets and the standardization of commodities and consumers, popular culture revealed "a very severe fracture, a deep rupture" formed in the contradiction of dominating forces confronting the commercial power of a people's expressions. The break not only brought about profound changes in the relationship between citizens but also produced new relationships between audiences and an industry marked by "the concentration and expansion of the new cultural apparatuses."[10]

In a follow-up essay, Hall sharpens his focus with contemporary Black culture in mind. Drawing on an influential essay about African American music by Cornel West, he argues that postwar Black popular expressions, particularly in music, consumed world interest because they materialized a crucial tension between US imperial dominance and the assertive rise of once-dominated global populations. Through the power of American communications media, US Black music had gained stature as the voice of the world's multitude, becoming an international sign of struggle. It symbolized "the people" on a grand scale, its value rising at the expense of Euro-Western aesthetic forms: the audible language of Black pop had overwhelmed an elite tradition of Art by means of institutional forces—the entertainment industry and its massive network of business conglomerates—that had also been exploiting Black people. Occupying a "contradictory space" at the center as well as the margins of the popular, Black music—its embodied labor lurking as the abstracted "soul" of the commodity form—performed both linkages and breaks in the fraught relations of race and nation, serving symbolically as a touchstone for dominated groups around the world: it had realized "the grotesque," "vulgar" qualities of a major popular form. "That is why," Hall writes, "the dominant tradition has always been deeply suspicious of [popular culture]," servicing as it has diverse audiences engaged in struggle and steeped in the international language of the underdog.[11]

Hall and West's early insights are valuable to our comprehension of Black music's ascent as a value form, their positions reinforced by a series of subsequent investigations of global Black expression by Paul Gilroy, Veit Erlmann, Penny M. Von Eschen, J. Griffith Rollefson, and others. These studies expand on Baraka's seminal pronouncements that Black music represents the premier world art of the "post" era, as they demonstrate, as Josh Kun puts it succinctly, how "race and popular music have always been experienced not alongside each other, not as complements, supplements, or corollaries of each other, but through each other."[12] Yet if we are to trace Black music's ultimate expansion as an apotheosis of new sonic form, we need first to consider its initial postwar development, when its beat knowledge was remade. With the routinization of swing, a rupture occurred in the audible bounds of Blackness, the music rapidly overtaking American sound worlds and refashioning popular productions of time-based pleasure. Much of this refashioning was initiated not only by African American musicians but also by Black entrepreneurs and Black-run commercial institutions—together with a new generation of Black and White consumers participating in a vast entertainment complex—who sought their claim from the rich well of highly capitalized Black music. The rupture let loose a transformation resonant with the heightened exposure of the "Negro problem" affecting White America's economic and political dominance.

The process begins with the expansion of the postwar commercial marketplace. Rapid economic growth driving an aggressively capitalized industrial state reconceived foundational ideological commitments according to the primacy of consumption: in this postwar, imperial moment, the ability to purchase aligned with visions of the United States as the beacon of the "free world." This is the social movement that Lizabeth Cohen names "a consumers' republic," when an energetic devotion to purchase intensified linkages between consumption and citizenship. Buying the products of US manufacture became integral to a postwar politics of patriotism. "The conviction grew," Cohen asserts, "that consumers held the present and future health of the American capitalist economy in their hands." Accordingly, a consumers' republic would not only deliver "economic prosperity but also loftier social and political ambitions for a more equal, free, and democratic nation." Such ideals, however, contradicted the reality of the massive constraints placed on African Americans as they too sought to participate in the collective pursuit of prosperity. "Every time that blacks were . . . refused service at stores or restaurants," Cohen explains, "both the assumed universality of citizenship and the supposed freedom of the free market were violated." The enduring efforts to subjugate African Americans inspired in Black neighborhoods a series of responsive actions with the aim of advancing consumer citizenship.[13]

Because Cohen is primarily concerned with the development of consumer behavior as part of a greater political economy, she can only provide a sweeping account of the countermeasures launched by Black political organizations and coalitions to foster Black businesses. In *Selling the Race: Culture, Community and Black Chicago, 1940–1955*, Adam Green turns the attention directly to grassroots projects, observing African Americans' fraught relationship to American business culture and consumer society. Green describes how Black involvement in Chicago's local economy worked against racial segregation to realize new, nationally oriented coherences of commercially based self-expression. Countering common narratives of modern urban Black life "as a tale of regress," he details how cultural and entrepreneurial initiatives in Black media, journalism, business, and the arts fueled the formation of racially specific sensibilities of place, which, in turn, encouraged Black people's "enhanced identification with the United States as a national community." "What was transmitted from Black Chicago to the United States and the world," Green argues, was not merely a new conception of racial specificity but rather an "alternate angle of vision" where Blackness as a quality was at once incongruently distinct from and aligned with majority-White America. Through these productive efforts, the United States would be refashioned according to "an evolving premise of national Black feeling," which was itself not singular but expressed multiply.[14]

No expressive production meant more to African Americans and more deeply impacted their feeling of national culture than that which arose from Chicago's diverse Black music scene. From the mid-1930s, the city's Black neighborhoods played host to live performances by a huge array of talent, from swing orchestras and small-ensemble jump bands, to barroom boogie-woogie and singer-piano duos. The bulk of this music labor force arrived in Chicago as part of the enduring flow of African American migrants, who, over the course of three decades, comprised a veritable pastiche of southern Black culture. The musical consequence of the migrations is well-known: it gave rise to swing, gospel, and blues, and established the celebrity of Big Bill Broonzy, Louis Jordan, Mahalia Jackson, Dinah Washington, Muddy Waters, and others. A decade later, though, the flood of talent also produced something more: a new consumer awareness among the Black populations newly employed in the city's burgeoning industries. With many receiving decent pay and attuned to the pleasures of music, they gathered as a huge consumer force with considerable buying power, frequently spending a portion of their earnings within the mass of performance sites that stretched across Black Chicago's South and West Sides.

Clubs abounded, with many of them Black-run or, in the case of the DuSable Lounge and Rhumboogie, among others, Black-owned. Supporting institutions, such as the Groove Record Shop and the Melody Lane Record Shop spun off into larger ventures: Groove gave way to United Record Distributors, supplying records to buyers across the Midwest, while Melody Lane reinvented itself as a record label Hy-Tone Records. The growing interdependency of commercial institutions, in turn, provided important opportunities for musicians. For example, the Bluebird label, under the stewardship of the famed producer Lester Melrose, frequently served as a gateway for artists seeking work in the city's nightclubs.[15] Similarly, the local production of records was supported by radio stations and deejays targeting Black audiences, the programs having the effect of integrating listeners' tastes. On-air personalities, notably Jack L. Cooper, Al Benson, and Daddy-o Daylie—the latter two favoring Black music showing up on independent labels—were critical in driving interest in Chicago's music and shaping public taste.

Through these means, Chicago arose as a principal site in the broad national network of popular music. It did so not simply by providing a place for many artists to congregate but by enabling their creativity to develop within an intricate economy, by which audible aesthetic invention, particularly in the form of the blues, acquired powerful alignments with other social patterns. "Through the 1940s and afterward," Green observes, "musicians and producers revised the meaning of the blues in Chicago— not only through focus on the urban context, but also a more professional understanding of black music, which encouraged artists to view their cultural work in more material terms." This sonic-social coalescence formed the components of a massive infrastructure actively involving copious numbers of Black entertainers and entrepreneurs. It also identified the formation of a new conception of vernacularity, where Black musical creation and a local industry's financial interests became inextricably linked. Vernacularity was no longer the stuff of folklore that Ralph Ellison had critiqued (cf. chapter 8) but a gathering of forces within the structures of commerce and culture that constrained as it enabled the character of urban

Black music—including the making and experiencing of blues. What was "previously [an] itinerant system serving dispersed regional tastes" developed into a veritable "blues industry," producing dramatic coherences of style. Its effects were transformational: "The rationalization of black music encouraged standardization of race culture across the United States, allowing African Americans to share a more simultaneous—a more national—sense of existence."[16]

What Green calls the rationalization of Black music arises out of a larger effort by record companies to find ways to make their products sell. Early producers such as Germany's Deutsche Grammophon and the Victor label produced records that were thought to attain the highest levels of fidelity. The "Red Seal" discs manufactured by Victor were reserved for the European art repertory and set the standard in the United States for what consumer-targeted sound reproduction could achieve. Attempts to produce high-fidelity records worked in concert with manufacturers' desires to create a musical brand, particularly once electrical recording gave them tools for reproducing sound with greater accuracy. By the 1930s, labels actively sought to engineer an economy of style consistent with the standardization of production that oriented US manufacturing from the 1920s, their producers and engineers instrumental in affecting the character of performance. In jazz, there was John Hammond at Decca and, later, Rudy Van Gelder and Alfred Lion at Blue Note. In R&B, Ahmet Ertegun and Jerry Wexler aspired to make the sound of Atlantic Records identifiable. In blues, Bluebird set an early standard, relying on a small studio group led by the guitarist-vocalist Tampa Red, who, with his Chicago Five, performed blues-inflected popular accompaniments. And after the war, the Chicago-based Mercury label featured an impressive lineup of blues and R&B talent, including T-Bone Walker, Dinah Washington, Robert Lockwood, Sunnyland Slim, and Lightnin' Hopkins. These initial efforts ultimately gave way to the innovative productions of Chess Records and the making of a "talismanic" power in the form of phonographic discs, paralleling contemporary developments in modern jazz.[17]

The history of Chess has been well documented, its storied past multiply written, rewritten, and rewritten again. Narratives typically detail the founding of the label by two brothers, Leonard and Phil Chess, and celebrate the remarkable feats of its famous roster of artists, which included Muddy Waters, Little Walter, Howlin' Wolf, Bo Diddley, Chuck Berry, and many others. While the better accounts make mention of the critical role of production in shaping the Chess sound, many more seek to distinguish those techniques from what is claimed to be the music itself, implying that a racial purity lives on in the sound of Chicago blues. In these versions, the integrity of Blackness wins over the rapacious forces of capital, which are sometimes personified in the business concerns of the Chess brothers. And so, with Chess, "the indelible link between the Delta, the breeding ground of southern blues, and Chicago, its northern branch office, was confirmed once more."[18]

What we actually hear on the early Chess releases is not continuity but disruption: a reconceptualization of practice materially consistent with the racial and economic ruptures occurring in Black Chicago and postwar popular culture. Although virtually all of the musicians who recorded on Chess were southern- or Delta-born, their artistry sought not to affirm the musical norms of the Black South but rather to remake them: they forged a modern vernacularity, a new music materially connected to American experience as they knew it. Their achievements represented an agonistic expressivity grounded in commerce, built on an enduring national romance of the rural South—a grand mythology standing in stark contrast to the racial politics of the era. Despite those realities, Chess artists and recording engineers worked together to produce a music seemingly existing beyond the political, its commercial viability made possible by the techniques of the modern studio. The Chess recordings reworked Delta blues in ways consistent with postwar commerce: through the artifice of sound reproduction, they created audible inventions of racial purity, whose aesthetic power decentered pop as it was then known.

The aim to create a distinctive brand was already in place when Muddy Waters made his first recordings for Chess in 1947. As co-owner of Aristocrat (a precursor to his eponymous label), Leonard Chess was eager to produce records that would win the widest appeal, which, for a time, he assumed to be ones perpetuating the familiar sounds of downhome and 1930s-style urban blues. He must have recognized in Waters real potential, despite the commercial failure of his initial attempts: the sides he produced for Lester Melrose on Bluebird went unreleased.[19] Waters, for his part, was imagining something beyond the familiar Delta sound. While still living and working on the Stovall plantation near Clarksdale, Mississippi, he was "drawn to dreams of celebrity by records heard off local jukeboxes," and after a couple of false starts, he ultimately found his way to Chicago in 1943. During a session five years later, Waters, with the help of Chess partner Evelyn Aron, convinced Chess to record some of the material he was experimenting with that moved against the conventions still common among southern musicians performing in Chicago's bars. "I Can't Be Satisfied" proved to be a minor hit among a new generation of African American consumers, helping to set the parameters of an emerging, postwar style.[20]

A good way to appreciate how Waters's approach had evolved is to compare "I Can't Be Satisfied" to an earlier version that he made while still living on the Stovall Plantation.[21] "I Be's Troubled" (1941), which was recorded by Alan Lomax as part of his collecting efforts for the Library of Congress, features Waters singing and playing acoustic slide in open tuning. (He purportedly borrowed Lomax's Martin guitar to make the recording.) Slide playing itself was not new, having become common during the Hawaiian music fad in the 1910s, also being practiced by southern players: Howard Odum refers to a musician playing slide guitar with a knife blade in his 1911 article on Negro folk song. The slide technique then proceeds to flourish across the South in the 1930s, with the commercial release of several popular recordings by Tampa Red.[22] Yet Waters's performance is fascinating in itself, particularly in the way that he brings together vocal and instrumental practices, his guitar playing paraphrasing the melody as he sings it. The interplay produces a striking intimacy, a melding of guitar and voice; at moments, Waters pauses his delivery to finish the phrase on his instrument. Lyrically, moreover, the song's tone is passive. "I Be's Troubled" states a condition consistent with the blues conceit of suffering, the song depicting the limitations on Black life in the South. As the story progresses, the narrator's escape takes a predictable turn: he leaves a woman, moving on without a stated destination and still presumably burdened by his troubles.

With "I Can't Be Satisfied," Waters remakes the song into something qualitatively different. Most obvious is how the lyrical orientation has shifted, as the narrator voices his observations from the perspective of a Northern Black man heading "back down south." Although Waters's lyric makes use of conceits similarly heard on the Stovall recording ("I be troubled, I be all worried in mind . . . I just can't keep from cryin'"), it betrays the conditions and qualities of urban life, where "all in my sleep, Hear my doorbell ring." His declarations are also more assertive, just as the misogyny, however formulaic in blues lyrics, becomes dark with its threat of violence: "Well, I feel like snappin'; a pistol in your face."

But what really turns the song on its head and identifies it as a postwar popular invention is the protean variability of the studio-made performance. On "Satisfied," Waters, playing a dance-band guitar—a Gretsch hollow body with a d'Armond FHC pickup—is clearly playing loud.

At several moments, the amplifier verges on distortion, producing the wobbly thickness and ear-splitting intensity of a live club performance. The sound is arresting, his playing deft and slide work insistent, to the point where it challenges the authority of his own singing. Peter Doyle, in his insightful discussion of the production techniques of the early Chess records, suggests that on "Satisfied," "the instrument is not primarily the voice of that which is other to the singer, but rather is a kind of ventriloquist's dummy."[23] It is as if Waters's guitar comes alive, announcing *"listen to me!"* What had established a vocal-instrumental intimacy on "Troubled" gives way to something of a contest, even as Waters plays as he did in the first version, paraphrasing and finishing the melodic lines of the lyrics. Heightening the guitar's assertiveness, moreover, is the addition of a second instrument played by another musician from the South, the Memphis-born bass player Ernest "Big" Crawford. Crawford's percussive slap-bass accents on the back beat and occasional figurations suggestive of jazz playing empower the performance. They energize Waters's own delivery as the duo moves into a light yet vigorous romp reminiscent of western swing.

This elusive energy, though, would never have been committed to disc had it not been for the innovative ways that Chess and his sound engineer recorded the performance. Despite the multiple references to the company's production techniques—setting up artificial walls and baffles, positioning microphones in discarded toilets, setting loudspeakers and amplifiers inside resonant rooms, directing sound through stretches of cavernous sewer pipe—precise details have never been scrupulously documented.[24] Yet simply by listening, we can begin to discern something about their effect. Across the early Chess repertory, productions often shared qualities of transparency and acoustical depth. On "Satisfied," the sound is resonant, achieved by what was known as a "hot mike," where amplification of the voice reaches just into distortion.[25] It is what makes Waters's performance sound so lurid, so haunting: as Waters's guitar comes alive, his vocalizations grow assertive, nearly percussive. Close positioning of the microphone, moreover, captures the nuances of Waters's vocal delivery, making discernible the personality embodied in his utterance, from the idiosyncrasies of phrasing to his comical recitations of the titular lyric and its variations. The technique brings listeners inside Waters's voice, where they can get close to its resonance and look around, sensing how his sound speaks to his countenance, to the touch of his face. "The microphone," Steven Connor astutely observes, "makes audible and expressive a whole range of organic vocal sounds which are edited out in normal listening; the liquidity of the saliva, the hissings and tiny shudders of the breath."[26] The overall effect encourages the sensation of embodiment, of heightened trueness: a sound that is engineered to sound like life, to seem more real than life actually is. Recording technology's mediating effect ironically amplifies intimacy, exaggerating connections between performer and listener. The version is light years away from the Stovall recording and other records by Delta migrants as it is easily distinguished from the large-ensemble sessions that were common to Chicago blues in the 1930s and 1940s.

While "I Can't Be Satisfied" represents a vigorous step away from the Delta and the jazz-inflected styles appearing on Bluebird, Waters's "Rollin' Stone" introduces a decisive transformation in blues practice. In this performance, recorded in 1950, Waters pushes the blues's formal limits, and in so doing, contributes to the remaking of Black music and the greater character of popular sound. In retrospect, the record might seem a minor achievement in the context of blues and mid-century Black music. It is, after all, one more version of a recognizable Delta tune, "Catfish Blues," performed by a singer accompanying himself on guitar.[27] Yet Waters's interpretation is strikingly original, stepping away from the conventions of narrative-based recitation to produce a distillation of blues performance's key properties.

At the heart of his invention is a simple, repeated riff (example 9.1). It begins with a pickup tone (anacrusis) at the minor third below the tonic, which then settles briefly on the tonic E. The motive then moves into a quick bent-note turn that glides down from the fifth scale-degree, through a blue-note-intoned third, and returns to the tonic. Played without slide in standard tuning, the riff remains at the center of things, orienting the feel and pace of the performance as it is varied and embellished with low-register percussive attacks and upper-register fills, and as Waters changes its metric positioning within the bar. Although riffing is certainly not uncommon in Black music, Waters's forceful execution of it produces a haunting unease that drives musical motion while keeping time unpredictable. The performance's tonal simplicity, working within what is more or less an E minor pentatonic modality, provides a stage for what is above all a display of guitar-driven rhythmic intensity.[28]

Waters's vocalizations, in turn, have an orienting, narrative effect, involving the listener in a male fantasy of sexual attraction and conquest. Musically, though, the vocal component is most important in contributing to the dynamic temporal feel. The song's lyrics and their delivery are bombastic, their assertive charge opening a space for Waters's playing. Snatches of

Example 9.1 Muddy Waters, "Rollin' Stone" (1950) opening.

repeated text ("Sure 'nough, after me"; "Oh Lord"; "Back down the road I'm goin'") rhythmically interact with the guitar work; his playing is less an accompaniment of vocal melody than an actionable involvement of his voice as a second instrument: the playing and singing create a colorful pastiche as Waters's boastful, declarative baritone becomes an equal partner in the execution of the overall texture. At moments—for example, in the recitation, "I got a boy child's comin', he's gonna be . . . a Rollin' Stone"—lyrics and instrument achieve an independence, as words float atop the meter, extending a practice heard earlier in "Satisfied." And although the performance eventually fulfills the harmonic progression of blues form, it is Waters's repetitive guitar figurations and beguiling vocal rendition that define the greater affect of the recording. The work assertively moves away from conventional standards of popular form, whether thirty-two- or twelve-bar.

"Rollin' Stone" would still be a compelling recording even if Waters had performed without the tools of amplification. Yet as a collaboration between artist and sound engineer, it gains a quality just beginning to be heard in Black music around the time.[29] Working with minimal sonic material, Waters and the Chess staff generate a tonality with remarkable coloristic intensity—a dynamic resonance whose aesthetic effect challenges the emotional drama of a hard-driving ensemble. Critical here is the way artist and technician employ amplification to shape timbral complexity. It is clear from the outset of the recording that Waters's amp is turned up even louder than it was on "Troubled," its distortion supplying his guitar sound with a generous timbral density. The sensitivity of the guitar's pickup enables it to capture even the subtlest string intonations, turning the riff's figurative sequence and Waters's subsequent, upper-register fills into an arresting counterpoint, made all the more dramatic by his vivid exploitation of the temporal field. Playing at a slow, leisurely pace, Waters gives each musical gesture room to resonate, to occupy space in the performance. A hint of reverb, probably added late in the production process, heightens the sensation of spatial occupation. When Waters moves into song, moreover, the timbral character changes abruptly. Close miking, with the volume turned up hot, reveals the voice's fleshy idiosyncrasies, once again exaggerating the nuances of Waters's Delta speech patterns. The recording's seeming transparency, as if his singing were placed under some kind of auditory microscope, makes Waters's voice seem massive in ways consistent with the bombast of the lyric: listeners are compelled to enter his fantasy as if it were true. "The persona," Doyle writes about Waters's Chess recordings, seemingly "speaks from the reverberant space" of one "possess[ing] a special charisma . . . [and] hav[ing] special powers."[30] The artifice of amplified sound certifies a racially enlivened music's apparent truth.

The effect of this high-amped, hot-miked, instrumental-vocal interplay is gripping, overwhelming the willing listener. The song's harmonic simplicity as presented enables Waters to explore time through beat-oriented phrases and effects that subtly transform blues performance. Working only with guitar and voice, he introduces a multidimensional percussiveness, where each sonic gesture contributes to the music's propulsion. Amplification not only arouses; it dramatizes and challenges the sensory order. As Robert Palmer put it in reference to Waters's early Chess output, it "can still raise the hairs on the back of your neck."[31] In its movement beyond everyday acoustics, Waters's studio recording makes the routine of performance seem racially fantastic. It enacts a sound greater than Music, revealing an incorrigible audibility resonating from deep inside the Black past as it is recrafted anew. The record advances an enriched sensation of past-time, its temporal incongruencies heightened by phonographic engineering.

Other early Chess recordings employed similar methods of auditory manipulation, rendering through technical artifice a truthful intensity, a sensational, sensationalized Black sound. A particularly important technique was the aforementioned use of reverb and echo, first innovated in the 1940s for Hollywood dramas and horror movies, which soon surfaced as a common feature in popular music recording. As it was brought into Chess recordings, the techniques served symbolically as a way of "compound[ing] the eeriness," innovating a modern racial semiotics conveying the dangers of difference.[32] Because the techniques are at times obviously rigged, they can seem funny, recalling the conspicuous uses of bawdy irony tracing back to colored minstrelsy. On "Juke" (1952), for example—the title chosen by Leonard Chess—the harmonica player, Little Walter, performs with a sense of joyous intensity in a rendering of live club sound. Walter's virtuosity, set against a swing-inflected boogie generated by guitarists Jimmy Rogers and Muddy Waters, and drummer Elga Edmonds, grows more and more furious with each twelve-bar chorus. Over the course, the performance conjures a locomotive of pulsing, seemingly unfiltered urgency, with each musician contributing to its aggressive oscillations, the comedic excesses heightened by hot miking and reverb, both turned up at the climax. "Moanin' at Midnight" (1951), moreover, introduces to record buyers Howlin' Wolf's utterly fantastic contortions of vocal sound, the angularity of his singing similarly exaggerated by hot miking. The record presents Wolf's acrobatic vocal display as he moves from a deep, wide vibrato to an eerie, pinched falsetto, the technical production of distortion so expertly generated it seems to come directly from his mouth. It is what creates, as Eric Lott evocatively suggests, "a voice of gravel and broken glass."[33]

The combination of performance talent and sound engineering was all part of a conscious effort to create in the studio a kind of auditory fantasy world inspired by the emotional aliveness of Black clubs and bars. As Palmer summarizes the Chess productions of the late 1940s and early 1950s, the records represent "one of the earliest examples of a producer, engineer, and musician working together to create the illusion of a cranked-up-to-10 juke joint." It is a spectral illusion enabled by the powers of amplification and sound manipulation, the music's comic supernatural character reinforced through allusions in the lyrics—many of them written by the Mississippi-born producer and studio musician Willie Dixon—to the exotic, the sexual, the psychotropic, the spiritual: haunts, voodoo, heroin, gypsy women, hoochie-coochie. Together, they call to mind a legacy of Black gestures to the otherworldly: the colored minstrels, ventriloquist dummies, heebie-jeebies, spooks. The Chess sound, as Palmer described it, "jumped out at you . . . a new sound so powerful, so vibrant with presence, it was *scary*."[34]

As a body of work, the Chess records were widely embraced by Black consumers in Chicago and other cities and locales north and south, with several of its releases—including "Satisfied," "Juke," "Moanin'," "I'm Your Hootchie Cootchie Man" (1954)—scoring high on *Billboard*'s national R&B charts. The discs identified a critical moment in American music history: moving in tandem with jazz—and extending the seminal film performances of Louis Armstrong—the Chess productions were instrumental in introducing the auditory presence of the southern Black body directly into the public soundscape and a burgeoning field of consumer-listeners. Still operating within African American domains, these sonic presences would eventually be heard on the international stage, inspiring scores of rock performers in the United States, Britain, and beyond. The records set a new standard for what blues could be, just as their uncanny combining of artistry and artifice revealed an intensification of the negative at the heart of Black music's hyperpositive valuation. Through the effects of capital-driven technologies, Black sound formations gained even greater, embodied presence, achieving a spectral luminosity inversely related to their reified character: their aliveness accentuated the "phantom-like objectivity" already inherent to their commodified form. And these residual appearances would be reiterated across listening communities, their dissemination enabled by the vast networks of production—record stores, jukeboxes, radio stations—which by the early 1950s were connecting Black people to one another in the making of a greater conception of Black national publics.[35]

UNTIMELY PLEASURES ON THE SOUTHERN CIRCUIT

For all its importance to the emergence of a New Black Music, Chicago was but a single node in the greater network of activity that reached across the nation, linking not just to other major metropolitan areas—New York, Indianapolis, Detroit, Seattle, and Los Angeles standing out—but to virtually every community inhabited by Black people. Southern locales were particularly vibrant. These were the places where African Americans remained amid decades of migrations, many living on farms or in small rural hamlets. Most towns had a saloon nearby and sometimes a theater, with a juke joint perhaps a little farther out. Larger communities could often claim multiple venues sustaining a vibrant music scene. As before, musicians who performed in local establishments were largely an itinerant lot, working the circuit as jobs came about. There was already a swell of activity by the early 1940s, their numbers increasing to unprecedented levels as more and more clubs opened after the war. Most bands followed the custom of the one-nighter. Work in Oklahoma City could lead to a job in Tyler, Texas, and then others in Hot Springs and Little Rock, Arkansas. They might then venture down to Louisiana, stopping over in Shreveport or Tallulah, or heading to active scenes in Hattiesburg, Jackson, or Yazoo City, Mississippi, then swinging by Gadsden, Alabama. In Georgia, Atlanta, Athens, and Macon were hotspots. There was also work to be had in Florida, from Jacksonville to Tampa to West Palm Beach. "[Bands were] always traveling, working one night stands," the drummer Earl Palmer recalled. "Barely getting by, but [sounding] good. The raggedy bands, we called them."[36]

The role of the South in the making of mid-century Black popular music is well-known, but its evolution as a cultural economy comes alive in Preston Lauterbach's sweeping overview, which focuses primarily on the fifteen-year period from 1940 to 1955. The "chitlin' circuit," as it was commonly known, was an entertainment complex composed of hundreds of evocatively named performance showcases—the Dew Drop Inn, the Keyhole Club, the Black Diamond, Haney's Big House—which, over time, became interlinked as a concatenation of businesses and supporting media.[37] The bulk of the nightspots were Black-run and often Black-owned, their draw among locals making them efficient incubators of evolving practice. "Even small-town and little-city promoters . . . ran complex operations," Lauterbach observes. "They employed bands and the complementary components of a club show, emcees, exotic and interpretive dancers, and comedy-sketch teams. They sent these entertainers out on tour, . . . simply plugging in a name attraction . . . bought from an agent . . . at the top of the bill."[38] Although the competitive energy of Black enterprise produced its share of conflicts—between performers and agents, club owners, and record companies—and restrictions imposed by the law sometimes constrained club dynamics (figure 9.1), in a larger way a collective commitment to the vital importance of musical pleasure helped to forge a profound sense of ownership. This sense of belonging, which remained largely uncontested in southern Black worlds through the 1940s, affirmed the belief, among player and fan alike, that Black music was theirs.[39]

As the chitlin' circuit evolved, the ambitions of its investors grew along with it. Business-savvy club owners from Macon to Memphis and New Orleans to Houston bet their investments on the music's commercial appeal. The most successful investors branched out from their original businesses to create small empires of Black entertainment. The Houston entrepreneur Don Robey and the Memphis-based Sunbeam Mitchell, for example, capitalized on their experience staging shows and chasing money-making opportunities to build a variety of spin-offs that supported musicians. Robey set up a booking agency and a record company, Peacock Records, that serviced his club, the Bronze Peacock, his efforts also launching the careers of a crew of performers that included Clarence "Gatemouth" Brown, Johnny Ace, and Big Mama Thornton. Mitchell's Domino Lounge and Mitchell Hotel began as performance sites that eventually evolved into an informal musicians' employment agency, his showcases nurturing the careers of B. B. King, Little Junior Parker, Little Richard, and others. Shows staged by Robey, Mitchell, and other club owners were routinely promoted by

9.1 Dancers in a juke joint in Macon, Georgia, 1943.

the Black press and on radio stations such as WROX in Clarksdale, WBML in Macon, and WDIA in Memphis, staffed with Black announcers who reached thousands of African American listeners. Those with fewer resources devised more modest strategies. Milton Barnes, owner of the Hi-Hat Club in Hattiesburg, Mississippi, advertised upcoming shows by touring Black neighborhoods on a flatbed with the featured performer, "blaring the attraction's latest recording as they waved to the people."[40]

The chief commodity sold on the circuit was a form of musically generated pleasure that effectively remade the sensory arena of Black southern entertainment. It was an offering to paying customers, mainly Black consumers in their twenties, thirties, and forties, for whom a new, blues-based music invited powerful linkages with other dimensions of their everyday lives. Performances were often over the top, accompanied by raw comedy in the spirit of colored minstrelsy and vaudeville. It involved preposterous acts: guitarists Chuck Berry and T-Bone Walker (see figure 9.2) playing behind their backs and doing splits (acrobatic stunts reminiscent of the circus); Howlin' Wolf climbing stage curtains; the tenor player Leroy "Batman" Rankins playing atop bars and, in at least one instance, swooping down

9.2 T-Bone Walker with the dancer Lottie Claiborne, 1950s.

from stage rafters; superhero band names—Roy Brown and His Mighty-Mighty Men, Little Richard and the Upsetters, Sax Kari's Four Sticks of Dynamite and the Fuse—and provocative song titles—"Crawling King Snake," "Boogie at Midnight," "Atomic Energy"—that expressed the shared belief that Black music was awesome, explosive.[41] The clubs hosting these performances, moreover, were places of casual intimacy, where unabashed behavior was routinely on display: where, for example, women fans showed their affection for Walker in bawdy acts, tossing money and underwear on stage. The clubs of the chitlin' circuit were zones of delight for which the idea of transgression was nothing but an outside label for an indifference to difference. These spaces gave a home to celebrations of life in sound, inspiring a future star to openly proclaim, "This is Little Richard, King of the Blues, . . . and the Queen, too!"[42]

Black clubs on the circuit were fostering something beyond the diversions of conventional entertainment: they provided a meeting ground for exchanges of value that conformed to the circumstance of capital while also exceeding mere purchase or profit. Although compelled by market forces, those who congregated joined together in aestheticized experiences not wholly constrained by commercial boundaries. No doubt performers wanted to get paid for their work. But they were also generating a different kind of value, an enlivened surplus energy fueled by the ascent of a distinctive brand of small-group blues. Club blues was brought to life by extending groove practices also heard at the time in jazz (cf. chapter 8), their distinctive temporalities binding musicians and audiences. Acts advanced via the money apparatus brought into southern Black communities a sound that, for some, was simply entertainment. Yet for many others, it inspired the imagination, suggesting ways of newly conceiving what in life was possible. Although there is little direct accounting of what occurred on stage and the dance floor, passing references show how impactful performances sometimes were. One of T-Bone Walker's fans, for example, told a reporter for the *Houston Informer* that experiencing his music was comparable to religious ecstasy: his "geetar playing 'send my very soul.'" Other "hipped up women," the reporter continued, described how they were "transported 'out of this world' by his down to earth blues."[43]

What was sensational about Walker—about the personality he and his ensemble projected, about the emotional "stories" he was telling by singing and playing—motivated his fans' extravagant acts: their ostentatious displays of giving were gestures in kind to the fleshy aliveness of blues expression. If these currencies revealed the snarl of relations regarding money, spirituality, and sexuality in Black southern life—if, as Julia Simon argues, they communicated calls for justice first fashioned in the humblest rural expressions—they also demonstrated how Black music experience was extravalued, ordered within a symbolic system of embodiment not entirely obedient to capital's limits and temporal measures.[44] As exchanges between musicians and listeners took place in venues sustained by money and profit, consumers came into possession of something greater than mere entertainment. The music's ability to exceed the pace and affect of work life reinforced an association with illicit ownership dating back to the slave era: they laid claim to sonic sensations of embodiment structured in transgression. The frenzy of creative activity animated the circuit, which gave shape to a secondary, shadow economy, where value grew from relations shared within an intensive system of exchange—where a musician's expressivity could determine the success at forging intimate bonds. As Little Jr. Parker put it, "The blues is based on somebody's life," and listeners "expect what you are." In response, they feel it, "it hits 'em in the heart and the love comes out."[45]

These intimate exchanges were particularly powerful because they stood in contrast with the routine obligations that had been ruthlessly imposed on Black southerners since the slave era. Living under an authoritarian regime, African Americans endured the perpetual strain of arduous work, their subjugation serving as a perverse justification of their inferior social status. The new economies of the chitlin' circuit, in contrast, were making critical moves against those racist structures. Although Black musicians had survived as scabrous labor since emancipation (cf. chapter 2), they were now claiming a place in the new markets of southern entertainment, and over a ten-year period, from 1945 to 1955, they would set into motion the transformation of American popular music. Southern Black musicians were driving a wedge into the age-old edifice of work denial—a racialized structure of exclusion that kept Black people out of the best sectors of the economy and imposed on them the most demeaning forms of work. And they were doing so at the very moment when, as Nancy MacLean shows in her powerful history of the American workplace, the structures erected to preserve the most desirable jobs for White people were beginning to weaken. Through grassroots initiatives and activist organizing, a system that "confin[ed] African Americans to the occupational ghetto of manual labor" was put to challenge as a leading edge in the civil rights movement.[46]

A new form of labor organized Black music's critical potential: the very act of playing—and by association, of listening to, dancing to, and purchasing blues performances—was part of a larger struggle in worker and consumer economies. Yet musicians and listeners were less interested in embracing the social conventions associated with those economies than in redefining what "worker" and "consumer" might mean. Recalling Du Bois's conception of a "lazy" living labor—as something not "as easily reduced to be the mechanical draft-horse which the northern European labor became"—the musical productions bore a sense of liberative potential as they were bound to the real-world environments of the Black poor, the irreverent play of the clubs carrying over into their everyday working lives.[47]

Blues performances in their finest fashioning created the illusion of temporal excess, their powerful grooves breaking through the norms of capital time by achieving a relational counterpoint to those norms. These strangely stable and tenuous capital attachments remained critical to the productive process underlying the formation of value.

In the changed environment of the postwar music scene, blues practice arose as a touchstone aligning the sensation of pleasure with the racial politics of the South; together they evolved within the material structures of entertainment commerce. For many occupying the circuit, whether as players or consumers, the music's ebullience established a social coherence seemingly untethered to the social and economic strictures within White domains. "The blues," the trumpeter and composer Leo Smith told Robert Palmer, communicates more than simple pleasure: it "is a literary and musical form and also a basic philosophy." Growing up in Mississippi, where his stepfather played blues professionally, Smith found that by listening to the music, "I feel that I'm in touch with the root of black people." These alignments with the past, which would be celebrated by Baraka as a moral philosophy of "blues people," gestated during the postwar moment, mapping a greater structure of feeling for a new generation of musicians and listeners. They suggest a parallel move to the social coalescences in the formation of Chicago blues and jazz communities taking place around the same time.[48]

As southern blues musicians explored new affective sensibilities, they also maintained the practice of work, finding their way in an economy that had been servicing popular music for the past fifty years. Players navigated familiar pathways, adapting to new challenges as the southern circuit increasingly resembled a version of the national entertainment complex. They contended with scouts and promoters; they negotiated with club owners; they tried to win the admiration of listeners who were not only attending shows but also listening to Black music on records and the radio. The professionalization of the scene also inspired musicians to imagine doing something more than just getting by. Some were eager to grab on to newfound opportunities. It is easy to forget this fundamental material basis of the new southern blues, to get lost in the sensations of irreverent play driving its creation. Yet the chitlin'-circuit sound would not have developed and become as widely admired as it did had it not been for the economic structures compelling musicians to play, listeners to listen, and consumers to buy records. These crucial forces enabled the music to disseminate, interacting with Black styles that were developing beyond the

South. Soon southern blues joined in the unfolding of a greater postwar Black practice, its formidable sound inspiring aesthetic experiences of nearly magical intensity.

A critical step in the process was the push to record. As it was in Chicago and jazz worlds, the more ambitious southern musicians felt compelled to forge a relationship with one of the many emerging independent labels as making records became important to building a reputation and securing new work at clubs. The singer-pianist Roy Brown, for example, advertised his upcoming performance in Galveston by hustling his way onto a local radio show, which eventually led to a record contract with De-Luxe Records. His release, "Good Rockin' Tonight" (1948), was an early hit, ranking third among the records most played on jukeboxes and winning praise in the Black press. In 1949, the *Memphis World* cheered his revved-up performances, reporting that "Roy Brown puts blues singing on a new kick." Louis Jordan, moreover, found early crossover success by modeling his live performances after his recordings. "Many nights we had more whites than colored, because . . . they came to hear me do my records," his success a justification of his stature as a commercial artist, just as his songs, which commonly glorified Black southern culture, offered his Black fans a kind of irreverent celebration of themselves.[49] Mississippi-born singer and guitarist John Lee Hooker, finally, recognized how recording was his ticket to a better life. After the release of "Boogie Chillen," he was overcome by its popularity. "When it come out, every jukebox you went to, every place you went to, . . . they were playin' it in there. It felt good, you know. And I was workin' in Detroit in a factory there for a while. Then I quit my job. I said, 'No, I ain't workin' no more!'" Several other musicians, from Muddy Waters to B. B. King, have recalled how successful records were instrumental to their move away from conventional work.[50]

The many benefits of the work economy moved labor in one direction; the failure to find work, or the familiar experience of exploitation—of earnings unpaid, of opportunities denied—moved it in another. Over time, a scabrous friction developing out of the relation of labor to capital congealed as part of the phenomenal character of blues sound, generating valued resonances otherwise deemed "mute." Committed to language, muteness heard live and on record would gain coherence, registering across the blues community as a spiritually inflected quality of soul. Although sacred and sonic realms had been foundational to Black music since the slave era—a linkage orienting Du Bois's musically inflected *The Souls of Black Folk* (1903)—at this moment, *soul* also took on importance as a secular term, referencing a value system that confronted structures of dominance where capital exploitation and racism aligned. As Paul Gilroy describes it, soul moved within a discrete economy as "a sign that the axiology of the market does not work . . . or applies rather problematically. . . . [It] mark[s] that realm which resists the reach of economic rationality and the commodifying process."[51] Market forces could not claim the collective experiences that had developed among Black southerners as they were fashioned on the stage and dance floor. Nor could they arrest the expressions of musical pleasure as they circulated on record, cycling wildly in the southern marketplace, particularly in the cities where African Americans migrated to.

At the same time, markets remained constitutive: they not only disciplined listening but also enabled the agonistic qualities of a mute music named "soul" to come alive. They disseminated Black music's enlivened presences into the nation as they reaffirmed the affective importance of the past in the listening experience, reinforcing among what was still overwhelmingly an African American audience a comprehension of how the music had ascended out of the tragic. The "recuperative logic" that Emily J. Lordi assigned to soul music in the 1960s—when "suffering is made to pay off" (cf. chapter 2)—congeals in these postwar environments, impacting music knowledge among blues musicians in ways consistent with jazz players. To create music of value, a musician, recalling Ralph Ellison's formula for jazz mastery, "must be reborn, must find, as it were, his soul." For blues and jazz players alike, the word *soul* becomes a term to gesture to the aspiration of breaking through the containments of modern living: successful performances would reach from the bare life of the past to reveal, summoning Adorno once more, "real history with all its suffering" coming forth as "the truth of music."[52]

It is perhaps fitting that a conception of soul's transgressive qualities, seemingly unbounded by the fixities of time and place, enters music knowledge by means of the marketplace. It is first established in popular discourse with the commercialization of gospel: Mahalia Jackson's "Since the Fire Started Burning in My Soul" (1947) was among her first popular recordings. Soon soul becomes a way of comprehending music value as something existing within, yet not limited by, routine transaction, much in the same way that T-Bone Walker performed an unearthly music to the earthly delight of his listeners. Into the 1950s, soul gained currency in pop, giving a new name to the gospel- and blues-inflected music of Ray Charles—notably, his "I Got a Woman" (1954), which was based on the gospel song "It Must Be Jesus," recorded earlier in the year by the Southern

Tones. It was also, as Baraka's opening commentary indicates, widely employed in jazz circles, informing song, instrumental, and album titles of the new "soul jazz": Ray Charles and Milt Jackson's LP, *Soul Brothers* (1957), Mal Waldron's "Soul Eyes" (1958), Charles Mingus's "Better Git It in Your Soul" (1959). The aggressive efforts by the music industry to capitalize on soul as a marketing tool produced notable conflicts with Black musicians. Cannonball Adderley, for one, recalls how "we were pressured quite heavily by Riverside Records when they discovered there was a word called 'soul.' We became, from an image point of view, soul jazz artists. They kept promoting us that way and I kept deliberately fighting it, to the extent that it became a game."[53]

The struggles over the ownership of soul betrayed its ideological significance, following Stuart Hall's recuperation of the concept. For Hall, *ideology* extended from the legacy of Marxian thought to describe the material conditions from which subjectivity is formed; he embraced this view while also rejecting the associations with false consciousness that the term once carried. For Hall, *ideology* not only described the constitution and disciplining of groups but, just as critically, it "has also to do with the processes by which new forms of consciousness, new conceptions of the world, arise, which move the masses of the people into historical action."[54] In his classic study *Urban Blues*, Charles Keil first proposed a union of the concepts in the form of a "soul ideology." Yet whereas Keil portrayed soul as a system of signs according to the symbolic anthropology of Clifford Geertz, we can recognize how soulfulness in its alignment with Hall's definition of ideology identifies a vernacularized politics of aesthetics: in Black music circles, it moved directly within and against the structures of dominance to describe audible enactments of racialized connection.

At its center is its enduring relation to the Black past. To quote Lordi again, soul secured musicians' bonds "with their contemporaries, to be sure, but also with a procession of ancestors whose personal griefs were unknowable but whose historical traumas were rendered increasingly present through national discourse about slavery." Liberative alignments developed out of soul's tenuous relation to market forces and the transgressive music experiences that relation encouraged. In this sense, soul affirmed the connection of art and politics after Arendt, Virno, and Lazzarato (cf. chapter 2), where a seemingly useless labor arises as an expression of political action. Driving that action is the awareness of Black music's negative posture. It is consistent with Ralph Ellison's characterization of a "blues impulse": "To keep the painful details and episodes of brutal experience alive in one's aching consciousness, to finger its jagged grain, and to transcend it."[55]

Soul-inflected blues becomes a vessel for Black southerners to think beyond the conventions of work, to lean back and discern the muteness of a repressed tradition that transgressed the norms otherwise defining "America." The musical and aesthetic transformations taking place on the chitlin' circuit pulled past-time forward: it drew from orientations familiar to Black music's legacy to advance something powerfully new, affirming Ellison's contrapuntal conception of history as "a constant plunging back into the shadow of the past where time hovers ghostlike."[56] Working against the grain of popular conventions that had been established earlier in the century—particularly the standardized song forms of Tin Pan Alley—musicians gave shape to an extraordinary body of sound formations that celebrated the legacy of the Black past, principally relying on twelve-bar blues formats and laying down rhythms that called to mind the force and angularity of hard-driving stomps. These innovations, like many before them, seemed oddly new and old: they pushed the limits of style while drawing from and referring to what had been before. The conviction of syncopation against an assertive pulse perpetuated the energy of shouts while supplying a stylistic platform for the comic extravagances that had sustained Black pleasure in popular music since the nineteenth century.

A time-bending soul aesthetic developed in defiance of the norms of pop and the prevailing expectations about subjugated Black labor. Postwar Black music commonly named "blues" accumulated as a shifting range of practices, a dynamic revelation of sonic material that grew steadily away from the even-time orientation of 1930s orchestras, which, after the broad commercialization of swing, seemed to many plodding, quaint. Although a few southern leaders (notably, Lucky Millinder and T-Bone Walker) emulated northern bands by supporting large orchestras, by mid-decade most had scaled down, giving prominence to a rhythm section joined by a featured singer and a handful of instrumentalists.[57] In these smaller ensembles, horn sections, once fixtures of swing bands, were reduced to two or three instrumentalists, their efficiency consistent with their new role. No longer handling the principal melodic and harmonic material, they focused on shaping timbral color and time, playing punchy, clustered accents as a counterpoint to sung melodies and improvised solos. This turn to an economy of means—as heard, for example, on Roy Brown's "Good Rocking Tonight" (1947)—while partly developing from the need to control personnel costs, ultimately became fundamental to the new practice, which located value in vigorous, hard-driving sensations of beat. Groups played versions of a swing-blues hybrid with just a septet, sextet, or even a quintet, without evident loss in quality. As the vocalist Gatemouth Moore recalled about Louis Jordan's Tympany Five, "He could play just as good and just as loud with five as 17. And it was cheaper."[58]

What mattered above all was making time. More than ever, every musician seemed to be performing with rhythm in mind, working collaboratively toward a leaner, louder, more intense and enlivened blues energy. Singers took a leading role, their evocative portraits of the Black South—Jordan's "Saturday Night Fish Fry" (1949), Wynonie Harris's "Grandma Plays the Numbers" (1949)—bringing listeners into the ensemble's personality to feel its distinctive groove. Others, such as Milburn and Brown, belted out lyrics in saloon fashion, their impressive vocal technique—well-executed articulation and controlled vibrato—giving their performances even greater power. By the early 1950s, moreover, as record companies were encouraging Black singers to reproduce on record the "rock and stomp" excitement of juke joints, artists such as Little Richard and James Brown shifted away from popular conventions, producing fantastic displays of jarringly percussive vocalizations.[59] Piano performance also changed with rhythm in mind. While players still provided harmonic accompaniment, many were more purposeful in laying down tempos, their amply miked pounding creating a counterpoint to the vocals shouted and the horns blaring. By the late 1940s, they had turned into veritable percussion machines, the likes of Brown, Milburn, Ike Turner, and others producing a boisterousness that sometimes rivaled the drumming. Establishing the floor of ensemble sound, finally, were the twin forces of amplified double bass and drum set. Players such as Earl Palmer and, in Chicago, Fred Below replaced the shuffle rhythms of jazz (still prominent in the late 1940s) with a hard-hitting backbeat. Although the backbeat was certainly not new to Black music, by the early 1950s, its distinctive punctuations had redesigned southern practices as it would become a fixture in rock 'n' roll.[60]

The effect of so much percussive beating was a sound inspirited with a temporally expansive sense of life. Chitlin'-circuit clubs were loud, the bands' assertive power animating the spaces, with dancing bodies muscling a sea of sweat, the musk of a hard-working personhood overwhelming the senses. At Haney's Big House in Ferriday, Louisiana, for example, which "seat[ed] about two hundred, . . . Slot machines lined the [interior], . . . the music crackled from the house PA, and the rhythmic bounding on the dance floor shook the walls." Haney's was one of the many venues of high-volume intensity, where instruments played at full force, their amplitude reaching new heights with the help of amplifiers driving instrumental sound. Complex pathways of wires and circuits provided the means of producing the live dramas that animated juke joints, roadhouses, and clubs of the circuit. Amps and PA systems turned up to max, straining their capable output, registered an excess servicing the beat: the merging of "blues and electricity" created a ruckus that excited the extremes, their distorted reverberations literally shaking the rafters.[61] Some recordings from the period captured the spectacular sensation of a live club performance. Roy Brown's "Boogie at Midnight" (1949), for example, is a cascading romp that re-creates the intensity of a band playing live. The mix of bass outlines, clapping, and vocal call-response sets its tempo into motion, the performance reaching its creative apogee with Johnny Fontenette's tenor madness: single-note repetitions that move into a fiery solo, the energy paradoxically heightened by his halting ascent of the blues scale. Amos Milburn's "Chicken Shack" (1948), moreover, describes the setting of a club against a fast-paced boogie, the riffing horns and rhythm section establishing a sturdy groove. Milburn's spoken recitation describes "the chicken shack," a lowdown place of earthly delight "down by the creek": a dive with "no windows no doors, It's just a hole in the wall," where "all you cats" gather in a mix of danger and pleasure: "You'd better be mighty careful, let's have a ball." Jackie Brenston and Ike Turner's "Rocket 88" (1951), finally, is a masterpiece of small-group sound, with Brenston's rich, mellifluous vocals floating over a boogie-woogie ostinato played by guitarist Willie Kizart against Willie Sims's shuffle rhythm. Other players get their moments: the horn section's accompaniments and featured riff choruses; Turner's opening chorus of barrelhouse piano, his use of rapid triplet repetitions creating a bracing energy; Raymond Hill's tenor solo, at times fiery and swingingly relaxed as it passes through three twelve-bar choruses. It is Kizart's guitar sound, though, that sets the ensemble motion and organizes the overall rhythmic affect. If there is truth to the lore that its fuzz-toned distortion was the result of a torn amplifier speaker, the accident not only satisfied the preferences of the record's producer, Sam Phillips, but also contributed to a new aesthetic featuring raucous, percussive drive.[62]

Guitarists like Kizart were by this time at the center of things, the best of them having developed distinctive styles comparable to the master saxophonists of swing. Walker was a clear standout, his fluid virtuosity different from that of his teenage friend Charlie Christian and of Les Paul.[63] Walker's fleet-fingered swing sensibility, clean in execution yet rich in blues inflections, maintained the sure-footed grace of an athlete, staying fixed to the ensemble groove. And in his subtle variations of tone—for example, changing picking action and switching source pickups mid-solo, as heard on "Strollin' with Bones" (1950)—he set a standard for an entire generation of blues guitarists. Gatemouth Brown, though, was a worthy challenger. On his "Gatemouth Boogie" (1947), which looks rhythmically back to swing, together with "Boogie Uproar" (1953) and "Okie Dokie Stomp" (1954)—which heralded the new back-beat—he presented his own Texas-styled guitar action, full of single-note figures, bends, and slides, sounding sharp and nearly shrill from the strong treble and reverb. In contrast, Mississippi-born Guitar Slim, while perhaps not possessing the virtuosity of the others, brought an assertive playing style that made rich use of amp distortion—as heard, for example, on "The Story of My Life" and "Twenty-Five Lies" (both 1954)—to heighten the percussive intensity of his playing. Yet another Houston-based guitarist, Goree Carter, employed similar distortion effects—the sound quality reminiscent of the amplification techniques of Sister Rosetta Tharpe—to turn simple melodic gestures into dramatic, rhythmic articulations. On "Rock Awhile" (1949), a medium-paced boogie in C major, he deftly executes rapid, double-stop (g-c) repetitions—his technique producing a ghost tone of the tonic below—that became a familiar conceit in the playing of Chuck Berry and other rock 'n' roll guitarists.

By the early 1950s, amplified guitar performances dominated southern blues, the proficient skills of an assembly of musicians giving the music a distinctive, electrifying energy. As Robert Palmer describes its sonic character with more than a little hyperbole, "Once a certain volume threshold has been passed, the electric guitar becomes another instrument entirely. Its tuning flexibility can now be used to set up sympathetic resonances between the strings so that techniques such as open tunings and bar chords set the entire instrument humming sonorously, sustained by amplification until it becomes a representation in sound of the wonder of Creation itself— the 'Big Ring.'"[64] If for some it proposed a call to Jesus, for others it suggested a pathway for bringing a decidedly "Negro" sense of pastness into the present. The electric guitar's inimitable sustain inspired the making of magisterial southern dramas fueled by "rockin'" beat: the label's sexual innuendo—calling back to 1920s blues shouters, to the Louis Armstrong Orchestra's "fucking rhythm," and even to the captivating excitement of ring shouts—suggesting a loose semiotics of dissensus. Defying the codes of White southern racism, the full-bore rockin' rhythms of the chitlin' circuit were a pitched call to celebration, reaffirming what Hall earlier described as the critical character of the popular.

Dozens of players emerged over the course. One was the Mississippi-born artist Elmore James, who gained wide attention for his masterful slide playing and distorted guitar sound on a selection of Chess recordings (e.g., "Dust My Broom," "Rollin' and Tumblin'"). Another was John Lee Hooker, who, on migrating to Detroit, brought the blues toward a new level of abstraction. On his aforementioned "Boogie Chillen" (1948), he played and recited against an inventive stop-time beat—the sound of Hooker's foot stomping purportedly run through a makeshift echo chamber to widen its gain and ambiance. "Boogie Chillen" is less a song with instrumental accompaniment than a kind of all-body percussive display. As Ted Gioia describes it, "The song has almost no melody. Even less harmony. In fact, it is hard to call it a song. It's more like a bit of jive stream of consciousness in 4/4 time."[65] The Memphis-based B. B. King, finally, won a huge following after the release of his "3 O'Clock Blues" (1951), which brought to national attention a level of skill and originality previously attributed mainly to jazz improvisers, while the St. Louis–based Chuck Berry emerged as a star attraction for his feverish, rocking boogies, which featured distinctive bent-note repetitions and amp distortions. Together, these and other players widened the range of the guitar as an intoning percussion instrument.

The multiple innovations of postwar southern blues propelled Black music's transformation, quickening and expanding a metamorphosis that had been initiated twenty years earlier. The music's diversity of beat-oriented languages brought about a revolution in time, a critical step advancing the reorganization of feeling and form. It was a stunning achievement, without precedent in the history of American music. The new blues fostered the emergence of multiple expressions of pleasure, its embodied sound generating forms of fleshy property that reinforced racial claims of ownership. For some, this meant nothing more than personal enjoyment. Yet for others, it became the sensible foundation of a new political assertiveness, the music's raucous antagonisms drawing powerful connections to Black liberation movements in the United States and abroad.

In his insightful book *Percussion*, John Mowitt draws out these musical-social linkages, reflecting on how the sound of beating across late-modern Black music gathered semiotic force in its relation to the struggles for racial justice taking shape after the war. For Mowitt, a radical sonic transformation directly paralleled shifts in the politics of culture, and he pinpoints the source of this transformation in the emergence of a rhythmic intensity coalescing at the moment of civil rights action. What he calls "percussing" symbolically connects to the Black body as a subjectivity sourcing a rhythmic sound that was also the object of racism's subjection. As the (musical) producer and (actual) victim of percussive abuse, the Black body materializes symbolically in the modern reinvention of the back beat, which overtakes popular music at mid-century. Although Mowitt's inventive criticism about beating drums and the beating of bodies can be at times overdone—proposing far-flung yet paradoxically rigid interpretations that seem disconnected from the ways in which the music was probably heard—his larger argument is persuasive: namely, that the incidental performances of beat were part of a grand efflorescence of racialized percussive intensity overtaking the nation, its value escalating exponentially in step with the political and economic assertiveness of African American publics.[66] The pronounced shift toward nonharmonic percussing carried a powerful significance: it was a material indication of a Black cultural occupation that found structural parallels in the political moves of activists. These parallels would eventually become coordinated in the ideological complex of soul: the reorganization of beat knowledge catalyzed the reclamation of cultural property to forge new calls to a liberative past, to a sonic counterhistory.

The sensational eruption of mediated forms of time brought Black practices assertively into the mainstream. A welter of rhythmicized sounding practices congealed and disseminated, bringing to bear at mid-century a distinctively new Black sonic presence. Sound formations emerging as purchasable records and live performances established the centerpiece of a new market valuation that simultaneously arrested the power of commodity. Inhabiting the contradiction of the alienable and the inalienable, of labor and soul, these consumer goods generated a new and powerful affect: a sonic life that flourished within a capitalized market as it lived seemingly outside of it. The economic anomalies of Black music's intervention underscore why it posed such a threat to American culture when at the critical moment of 1955 Black and White youth widely embraced it, with the emergence of rock 'n' roll. Although entertainment institutions driving the expropriation of Black music were somewhat successful in quelling its force, the consequence of those losses—the bringing of expropriated form into wide circulation—ultimately empowered its rise to the top of popular culture's value system.

R&B'S PROPERTY RITES

What's in a name? *Billboard* certainly thought there was something to music's naming when the magazine heeded editor Jerry Wexler's advice and changed the title of its Black record sales chart from "Race Music" to "Rhythm and Blues." After the term *rhythm and blues* showed up a few times on its pages earlier in the decade, the trade journal formally adopted it in June 1949—a few months after the commercial release of the first 45-RPM discs—to identify recordings made by African American musicians.[67] The grouping of multiple styles and approaches under a single rubric reflected a common business practice: because recordings were commodities like all other industrial productions, companies and corporations would market them as they saw fit. This included labeling musical styles, which reaffirmed the industry's posture of indifference to the conceptual categories of the music's makers. A brand name, which, after all, is what R&B was, asserted a claim of ownership: marking or "branding" property secured its possession, whether its form be that of a machine-made object, an animal, or a slave. (The practice of branding slaves continued for runaways and criminals until the late antebellum era.)[68] As listening communities grew accustomed to R&B as a label for Black popular music, the new name would set the conditions for a racial tug-of-war over an expression that many felt had been extracted from Black peoples' very souls.

Billboard's decision to replace the race label seemed motivated by changes in consumer behavior accompanying the popularity of small-ensemble blues. The revolution in Black commercial markets that transformed Chicago's blues world and fostered the emergence of the chitlin' circuit was also impacting entertainment at the national level: R&B announced Black music's riotous entrance into the postwar "consumers' republic." If, beyond a few notable celebrities, R&B's performers were still subjected to second-class citizenship in the cultural mainstream, they were enjoying in Black consumer markets opportunities that earlier players could have only dreamed of. Many were working regularly, being featured in Black newspapers and getting heard on radio. Most important, though, were the opportunities afforded by a new Black listenership to record on one of the new, "independent" labels: Atlantic, King, Specialty, Trumpet, Apollo, Jukebox, and Savoy, to name a few.[69] As the genre grew, the taste preferences of these listeners influenced marketing decisions across the industry, as independents and, soon after, major record corporations, expanded production in response to the surge in African Americans' buying power. The switch from "race music" to "R&B"—from phenotype to style—acknowledged how the stature of Black music was changing. It had become a lucrative commodity with considerable commercial value, even as it remained segregated from the popular mainstream: *Billboard's* "Hot 100" list, dedicated to top sales, almost always featured White artists.[70]

The massive capitalization of rhythm and blues was underway, and within just a few years (ca. 1950–1955), it would transform the entertainment industry and ultimately the sonic culture of the nation. As R&B catapulted into the world of Black entertainment, it inspired a legion of southern musicians to venture beyond the chitlin' circuit, just as the circuit itself became intertwined with the greater network of commercial entertainment. Performers representing a diversity of styles and orientations—small-ensemble blues, instrumental trios, jump bands, vocal groups and solo singers backed by studio-style big bands—found opportunities to record. With more and more White teens and young adults following R&B—particularly the studio sound produced by Atlantic—White musicians became actively involved.[71] Perpetuating a tendency reaching back before the dawn of the modern, they took claim of Black-generated material as it entered the common field of experience, reinventing it under the name "rock 'n' roll." While multiple Black singers and instrumentalists initially took center stage at the early rock 'n' roll shows, and several Black players—notably, Berry, Domino, Little Richard, Dinah Washington, and Ray Charles—became rock 'n' roll celebrities drawing a following among White and Black youth (see figure 9.3), White musicians ultimately cornered the market. The new brand introduced into the pop mainstream a spirited form of Music, whose chief inspiration derived from what seemed alive in Black sound.[72]

R&B's racial sequestering in the wake of rock 'n' roll's insurgence was arguably the most consequential aesthetic turn at the outset of "America's half century." It reset the parameters for debates about music and race: the premise of Black innovation inspiring White imitation—a logic that traced the expanse of US commercial entertainment—was reaffirmed, supplying a ready formula to explain the development of popular style.[73] However procrustean and problematic that age-old formula was, it accurately described the economic asymmetries that Black musicians routinely endured. Rock 'n' roll's successes led to a litany of losses. It compromised the opportunities of leading R&B musicians—Roy Brown, Big Mama Thornton, Big Jay McNeely, Ruth Brown, Clyde McPhatter—and it forced lesser-known artists to

9.3 Teens dancing at the radio station WRMA in Montgomery, Alabama, 1957. Alabama Department of Archives and History.

unduly struggle, spelling the end of countless careers. "While the mistreatment of performers was commonplace throughout the pop industry," write Steve Chapple and Reebee Garofalo, "it was particularly widespread among Black artists. R&B artists had trouble getting honest lawyers, managers, fair deals in court, or straight answers to their questions about contract deals. . . . Black musicians were routinely swindled out of their publishing rights, left unpaid for club dates, and denied representation by the American Federation of Musicians."[74]

All of this was taking place amid an ongoing crackdown on the thriving networks of Black entertainment. As George Lipsitz succinctly describes the postwar environment, White power in multiple forms—in local government, commercial institutions, the music business—joined together "to attack rhythm and blues—to censor its sales and radio exposure, to close down night clubs and dance halls where races mingled, and to prosecute entertainers and promoters on 'morals' charges rarely faced by artists in other branches of popular music."[75] The severity of the repressive action was consistent with the wider fear that a racially energized music was ravaging innocent White youth. As Asa E. Carter of the White Citizens

Councils of Alabama saw it, rock 'n' roll was part of an NAACP "plot to mongrelize America." Early coverage highlighted the music's interracial appeal with images of Black and White youth listening and dancing together, the veiled language of the accompanying reporting sensationalizing rock 'n' roll's "insistent brutal notes." Journalists expressed mock fear while going through the motions, relying on racial conceits drawn from the early twentieth century to fulfill their journalistic obligations. Rock 'n' roll, they told their readers, was a form of "madness," expressing "a jungle strain in man," that purportedly incited "riots" among listeners in cities from Newport, Rhode Island, to Oslo. "Going to a rock 'n' roll show is like attending the rites of some obscure tribe whose means of communication are incomprehensible," a *Look!* magazine writer commented, their words juxtaposed alongside images of White teens furiously dancing.[76]

Writers could be glib because they apparently didn't believe there was much going on. Many seemed to assume that rock 'n' roll was a passing fad, its casual expropriations of R&B just another racial novelty act. But at the point of rock 'n' roll's emergence, popular music was depending on a very different kind of racial economy to fuel its development. Because its principal resource was a music publicly recognized as a commercial creation under the ownership of Black musicians, it was far more difficult than it had been in the past for the industry to obscure pop's indebtedness to African American forms. Indeed, at the same time its Black presence was downplayed, so was it exalted when it helped to commercialize the form. R&B, the lifeblood of pop, was a production of commerce, a sound brought into being by a new Black labor force intimately connected to a powerful, if exploitative, institutional complex; this boundedness to entertainment markets and the processes of commodification supplied the music with unprecedented reach. As a result, R&B's financial value soared, which made its aesthetic losses—its extractions from the embodied soul of Black America—increase in proportion. As the tragedy of R&B became seated in the fabric of popular culture's makeup, it would be difficult to miss Black music's presence and "mongrelizing" effects.

Rhythm and blues's inability to realize its commercial promise came about at no fault of its own. It merely represented one of a series of calamities besetting African Americans in the mid-1950s. Black musicians' enormous creative and financial losses were consistent with the widespread efforts of White power to disturb Black social order and quell the initial successes of postwar political activism. In the late 1940s, southern Black organizers were making impressive strides, improving the quality and opportunities of employment, which enabled thousands of African Americans to find jobs in southern cities. As Black incomes rose, White southern conservatives organized in response, setting into motion a powerful backlash—enabled by red-scare hysteria linking left activism with communism—that punished progressive initiatives.[77] It is no coincidence that the cultural uprising named rock 'n' roll took shape at the very same moment that struggles between Black activists and White reactionaries reached a fevered pitch. Appearing in 1955, a year after the *Brown v. Board* decision, rock 'n' roll—a sound animated by the "gift" of Black music's aliveness—was for its detractors a haunted repertoire: its dependency on R&B was evidence that Black sound was overtaking America and threatening to upset the bounds of race.

The linkage between rhythm and blues, rock 'n' roll, and the Black struggle for economic inclusion was critical to the history of Black music value in two ways. First, it newly established a national understanding of Black music as a form of racialized collective property. Because Black performers played such a critical role in popular music's development, White rock 'n' roll could not merely take over; the music's aesthetic legitimacy would ironically depend on extracting value from a scabrous Black music. For their part, White musicians from Elvis Presley to Mick Jagger to Janis Joplin openly acknowledged their debt. And rather than quieting R&B's influence in their performances, they exalted it. Early figures such as Presley and Jerry Lee Lewis—compare his 1957 cover with Big Maybelle's 1955 version of "Whole Lotta Shakin' Goin' On"—together with Black innovators such as Little Richard exaggerated what was thought to be "Black" about Black sound. As Bernard Gendron and Jack Hamilton have each shown, racial stereotype generated the language of rock 'n' roll, as singers gave voice to "caricatures of *singing-black*: . . . accelerat[ing] singing speed, resort[ing] to raspy-voiced shrieks and cries."[78] Second, Black music's insistent presence in rock 'n' roll broadened White public awareness of how it traded according to a different set of rules. Stylistically fluid soul singing pointed directly to this difference: it signaled a public agreement that the embodied sound of Black music commanded greater artistic authority, even as many White listeners still preferred to listen to it played by White musicians. Soul as a sounding practice embodied the paradox of double value: as the critical essence of aliveness, it generated something greater than Music, its selling point being that it was not for sale. The risk that soul in its public conceptualization could be co-opted by a powerful industry amplified its importance in African American communities, particularly among young adults and teens, who represented the music's primary consumer audience.

Guthrie P. Ramsey Jr.'s depiction of family life growing up in 1960s Chicago offers a case in point. At weekend family gatherings, "the musical foreground to these celebrations (and of our everyday lives) comprised a broad selection of Black vernacular music," he remembers. "We paid equal attention to contemporary and 'dusty' artists: Louis Jordan, Sarah Vaughan, Cannonball Adderley, Count Basie, the Supremes, Charlie Parker, Aretha Franklin, Dizzy Gillespie, Otis Redding, Duke Ellington, Dinah Washington, James Brown, Oscar Peterson, the Four Tops, Dakota Staton, Dexter Gordon, Archie Bell and the Drells, and Joe Williams, among many others."[79] The list itself is unremarkable; a similar assembly of recordings could be found in many thousands of African American households. What is important here is the collective sense of ownership, the possession of a racialized cultural property made possible via the form of the recorded disc, whose availability for public purchase was itself symptomatic of the heightened politics of Black music and the conditions of loss and depersonalization imposed on Black musicians. They gave rise to the crafting of distinctive, personalized auditory coherences as well as a group sense of belonging, all of which connected to a capacious, imagined "Black sound." Out of this auditory field, stories and meanings would grow.

In some cases, the phonographic encounters were probably incidental; records could be heard and just as easily forgotten. And for many, their sound amounted to nothing more than a casual diversion. But in its proliferation and repetition, the music emanating from recorded discs also had a cumulative effect, affecting the tenor and feel of the everyday. For those particularly sensitized to the varieties of popular music, recordings helped to contour the inhabited fields of social relation. The perception of Blackness as a quality congealing in sound commanded such power because it accumulated symbolism in relation to similar coalescences of racialized experience: employment, family, dating, sex, street life, friends, sports. Together the music and the circumstances it inhabited were part of an animated life pushing against the pressure of pastime and the oppressive order of White consensus society. When Amiri Baraka, referring to his love of Negro-league baseball, proclaimed, "It was ours," he was paying witness to how the greater extensive properties of the social cohered in and against the making of Black worlds. "It was," as he continued, "Black life that was celebrated by being itself at its most unencumbered." Anchoring those various coalescences for Baraka, Ramsey, and many others was the sense of an inherent, Black audibility, whose perceived aliveness had developed as part of Black music's counterhistorical dissemination. It was in the Black music recording where such coherences of ownership lay, its diverse sound worlds expressive of a relationally constituted "blues people" and "R&B life." Together they assembled as versions of truth: "In me, in us, in the music, in the society," Baraka asserted, "it's all connected."[80]

Appreciating how Black musicians and listeners took to heart their claims of musical ownership helps us to comprehend why the practice of re-creating or "covering" recordings would play such a critical role in popular music aesthetics during the second half of the twentieth century. As Michael Coyle outlines in an important essay, the practice of making cover records derived from an earlier strategy known as "hi-jacking," when record companies routinely produced multiple recorded versions of the same published song, in some cases instigating in-house competitions between their own artists. At any given moment, the same song might be available in two, three, or four different recorded versions. From the mid-1940s to the early 1950s, the practice was largely uncontroversial because productions still gave primacy to the musical work. Acts of hi-jacking served principally to highlight song publications, with performers providing labor to feature the latest hits. Songwriters and publishers welcomed the practice because it advertised their written commercial product, while record companies profited by providing a supplement to a business still chiefly driven by sheet music. The ensuing competition between record companies, who were featuring the hit songs, operated on a relatively even playing field.

Cover records, by contrast, developed at the moment when record companies began to feature singers and performers over the songs themselves. The conflation of records and recording artists was symptomatic of the greater reorientation of entertainment capitalism in the early 1950s, when 78- and 45-RPM records began to claim the largest share of the market. As the nature of competition and profit shifted from songs to artists, the popular music industry turned into an arena of competing performers, with Black musicians' losses mirroring the injustices of racial struggle across the United States. "Why is it," the Black journalist George E. Pitts observed in 1958, "that for every fine Negro interpretation of a true blues or rhythm number there is a version by a White performer, good or bad, that seems to capture the record market?" White consumers' preferences for White musicians singing and performing music enlivened by African American sounding practices would drive the development of a new recorded repertoire favored by the larger record companies. As Coyle puts it simply, "The cover record per se developed only when 'race' records began to have mass appeal on White pop charts."[81]

The record industry's practice of hiring White musicians to cover R&B would result in enormous financial gains for major companies and their emerging stars, together with corresponding losses for scores of African American performers. Black monetary losses to the advantage of White artists—the Clovers' "Fool Fool Fool" (1951) covered by Kay Starr (1952), La-Vern Baker's "Tweedle Dee" (1954) covered by Georgia Gibbs (1955), Little Richard's "Tutti Frutti" (1955) covered by Pat Boone (1956) and Elvis Presley (1956)—gave rise to a powerful narrative that deepened racial tensions and reaffirmed loss as a measure of Black music's value. In the cover, we locate a key articulation of cultural larceny: the theft of a commodity that stands in for the economically determined Black body and that otherwise enables White pop to narrate what it claims as its own. "Rock and roll became white in large part because of the stories people told themselves about it," Jack Hamilton observes, "stories that have come to structure the way we listen to an entire era of sound." It is therefore no surprise that many Black musicians would interpret this experience as a recapitulation of a White sense of entitlement that extended back to the slave era. Louis Jordan, who in the 1940s enjoyed a string of recording successes and at one point, in 1949, tried unsuccessfully to desegregate the seating for his southern shows, later lamented, "As a black artist, I'd like to say one thing. . . . Rock-n-roll was not a marriage of rhythm and blues [to] country and western. That's white publicity. Rock-n-roll was just a white imitation, a white adaptation of Negro rhythm and blues." Amiri Baraka's juxtaposition of James Brown and the institution of banking in "The Changing Same" was motivated by this same transactional injustice—which he later named "the Great Music Robbery"—just as his aesthetic sought to locate an oppositional temporality, seemingly untarnished by grand acts of racial exploitation.[82]

As recording and radio drew Black music further and further away from its makers, the sound acquired a tragic grandeur expressing a higher aesthetic principle: its misfortune had remade music knowledge. After a hundred-year evolution against the forces of exploitation, Black music had organized into a mass of accumulated sonic material, its multiple losses suggestive of an intentionality connecting animated energy to a new generation of Black life. Indeed, Black music seemed *larger* than life: audacious and deeply racial, yet strangely misaligned with actual bodily presences. Through its continuous profits-from-loss, its value climbed as its qualities of aliveness grew more abstract. With Black resonances seemingly everywhere, they heightened sensations of aural spectrality reaching back to the music's formation, its cognitive character, born of capital, exceeding capital's grip. Into the late modern, this disembodied corpus of Black sound ascended, still animated by the enlivened presence of the labor driving it. And as its value increased, it compelled a haunted industry to recommit to making popular expressions from it. This back-and-forth pattern of growth paralleled a greater tendency in US economics across the twentieth century, whereby "property came to be seen not as a tangible thing whose value stemmed from productive labor but rather as an abstract claim whose value stemmed from future revenue flows."[83] Although the celebrities of Black music remained the focus of fans' adoration, its abstraction as a musical intelligence is what powerfully influenced popular sensibilities.

What emerged from all of this was a remarkably dynamic, self-sustaining order of interacting musical, discursive, and economic forces—a vast aesthetic-ideological network grounded in the cultural politics of modern Blackness. In its dynamism and outward expansion, Black music suggested a sonic life unto itself. Into the 1950s and 1960s, it would occupy a central position under the new authority of postwar popular culture, having acquired unparalleled social status via its thematic affiliations with public narratives of racial inequality and injustice. These valuative gains developed in dramatic contrast to the actual struggles of African Americans, whose tales of profit-from-loss informed the negative constitution of soul. Soul continued to orient aesthetic experience, to convey sentiments of racial injustice, tragedy, and uplift, fueled by circumstances set into motion by the cover record and Black people's long history of subjugation. As a late-modern realization of double value, the soulfulness arising from profit-from-loss grew into a critical dynamic perpetuating a race-based conception of Black versus White identities, all the while pop's actual productions exposed the lie of that separation. At the same time it reinforced the growing perception of an essential difference between the races, soulfulness arose from a deep well of shared sound and idea that generated a new temporal morphology oriented around ontologized conceptions of the beat.

AGONISTIC VICTORIES

Amiri Baraka was clearly attuned to this temporal morphology when he led his readers on a trip to "another place": to a realm of heightened sensation where the seemingly disparate energies of R&B and free revealed their fundamental sameness as "different placements of the spirit." By the time he published *Blues People* and *Black Music*, ontologized forms of racial sound were saturating public media, the music's massive expropriations transforming pop into a shadowy soundscape of voluble apparitions and forceful beats. Amid the sonic calamity, Black music's own racial intensities were also gaining attention, yet often at a cost to Black musicians, who watched their market currency rise and fall. Baraka's phonographic fantasy explored at the outset of this chapter proposed an intervention. By playing a record by James Brown in one of the primary institutions of capital accumulation, the sensory arena would be remade, setting off an agonistic energy betraying R&B's compatibility with free. The "different placements of the spirit" traced to a common imaginary—"a place where Black People live."

Baraka had identified a critical transformation that provincial listeners, wedded to their narrow cluster of favorites, overlooked. Black music was once again defending itself against the constraints of the entertainment industry, its wealth of sonic material pushing beyond the style limits imposed by the rubrics of jazz and blues. The formations that had most recently surfaced as free and R&B exceeded those commercial containments, betraying sensible connections that traced to the heart of the music's value-making. Having coalesced within the greater complex of postwar Black culture, these sensational expressions were challenging the expropriative power of the popular industry and reasserting African Americans' claims on their collectively embodied property. For Baraka, Black music was making a declaration, as if its cognitive character could now actually speak. Its message was at once simple and magnificent: we are amid a modern spectacular revolution, at the dawn of the apotheosis of new Black form.

In R&B and free, Baraka recognized likenesses of the spirit that engaged analogically according to Black music's legacy of incorrigible temporalities. As advanced forms, they claimed the power to speak a certain truth tracing back to ancestral practices of making time. "The most apparent survivals of African music in Afro-American music," he argued, "are its rhythms." These identified the "roots" resonant with the primary truth of racism's history. What would otherwise support claims of racial essence at a time when Afrocentric thought was becoming better known also specified formal relationships that the two musical orientations shared. R&B and free jazz were a reaffirmation of rhythm as a generative impulse: together they refashioned sonic material that had long guided popular music. Formally, moreover, both had departed from the standard designs of Tin Pan Alley, Broadway, and Hollywood, moving away from song form while advancing the means of producing sound without regard for Western tonal conventions. R&B evolved as a multilinear ensemble music with loose affiliations to harmonic rules. Free, for its part, pursued the same emphasis on multilinearity while engaging in a massive deharmonization project where tonal center, let alone tonality, was frequently absent.

These "different placements of the spirit" were also transformational in how they altered popular music's temporal affect. In each movement, musicians crafted form through exercised ensemble improvisation. R&B moved in contrary motion to mainstream pop by building on the corpus of blues-based sounding practices that mid-century Black listeners found arresting, the bands' ballistic energy drawing them away from predictable orders of experience. In live performance, especially, they downplayed the qualities of song by enlisting a strategy also common to small-group jazz: groups retooled songs into stagings for extended improvisation, with melodic designs and thirty-two-bar structures giving way to the new priorities of rhythmic intensity, timbral variation, and twelve-bar blues form. In free performances, meanwhile, a common practice of collective improvisation radicalized conceptions of meter, the heterophonic and contrapuntal interaction of ensemble voices creating broad-ranging compressions and expansions of time. Enabled by the polyrhythmic effects of percussionists such as Elvin Jones, Ed Blackwell, Andrew Cyrille, and Sunny Murray, it abstracted the sensation of swing feel. And as in R&B, free's horn players—John Coltrane, Ornette Coleman, Albert Ayler, Archie Shepp, and Pharoah Sanders, among them—tested the extremes of timbral possibility, exploiting their instruments' lower and upper registers to produce rich coloristic effects.

Working in tandem, the two categories of practice, free and R&B, reinvigorated Black music's creative compass and greater beat knowledge, inspiring a stunning reimagining of feeling and form: James Brown's "Papa's Got a Brand New Bag" (1965); John Coltrane's *Ascension* (1965); Sly [Stone] and the Family Stone's "Dynamite!" (1968). Their accomplishments proceeded to recast Black music and the greater field of pop, bringing into being an array of extraordinary creative achievements, from Miles Davis's *Bitches Brew* (1969) to Funkadelic's *Maggot Brain* (1971) to Stevie Wonder's *Talking Book* (1972). No longer just a background sound servicing White pop, the New Black Music stood as a monumental achievement, to be recognized and understood on its own terms. Its untimely energies confronted and ultimately took command of commercial arenas, producing as thoughtful sound a creative intelligence that further complicated the racial segregation of listening experience. At the same time, these commercial successes not only produced a common listening but also drove listeners apart: the celebrity of Black music affirmed for many—Black and White alike—a Black racial exclusivity in performance and experience, supporting and sustaining Black claims of ownership. The music's qualities of spirit betrayed a transgressive soulfulness, its racial coherence reaffirmed by continuing mutations of beat.

Black music's apotheosis developed out of a long history of making time. Rather than a direct descendent of ancestral roots, these coalescences were produced in relation to a heightened abstraction of Black form, its escalating detachments from laboring bodies circulating versions of audible Blackness nearly everywhere. Moving outwardly into the public and pivoting retrospectively toward the past, new Black forms proceeded to turn back into the intensive world of Black sound-making, its resonances growing more animated, invigorated, shimmering with embodied presence. These were the latest incarnations of a music seemingly larger-than-life that had been developing for most of the century. The process progressively elevated the music's ontological character, brought before the public within the commercial frames of jazz and blues. With swing and modern jazz, Black music—music performed for national publics by Black musicians—first took center stage, sensational creations of ensemble personality and improvised life stories that found a home in the dubious arena of "popular art." Blues, in contrast, led listeners into a deep dive of vernacularity, which became the source of its commodification as it grew into a commercial genre. Their pairing established in the social hierarchy of pop a class divide that oriented musical invention and patterned taste. Jazz and blues represent the foundational relation from which free and R&B coalesced.

Chapters 7 and 8 explored in detail the history of swing and mid-century jazz as ontologized values, observing their many renderings within the circuits of commercial entertainment and their many returns to the orbit of Black musicians' activity. These chapters also paid close attention to how swing-based practices evolved in their relation to a variety of musicians' approaches and ensemble interactions. In the present chapter, blues practices have gained greater understanding, yet without a studied consideration of how their ontologized rhythmic orientations coalesced—nor have we sought to explore those formations within the greater complex of double value, how its extraordinary aesthetic appearances arose from its devaluation. It is out of this double relation that what struck listeners as sensually heightened emerged from the figurative ground of difference that depended on Blackness as a negative tendency. The extent of this transformation so fundamentally altered the character of Black music within the greater complex of pop that it successfully challenged the authority of swing. From mid-century, an extraordinary creativity within the blues complex would coalesce into a greater beat knowledge that ultimately joined swing to energize musical productions extending into the present day.

The metamorphosis of modern beat knowledge begins with a rumble, as Black music turns away from swing's even time and embraces the blues-inspired grooves commonly known as boogie. The familiar register of boogie's origins traces to the practices of string bands and barrel-house pianists of the rural South that traveled northward to Chicago and elsewhere in the 1920s. When boogie entered the popular arena a decade later, those same rural practices moved with it. On one hand, boogie was devalued, a thingly, degenerative remnant of the Black South caught up in a frenzy of repetitions. Yet that same frenzy also appeared strange, baffling—a primitive relic in need of resuscitation in the modern present. This is how boogie entered majority-White public culture: as a sonic afterlife, whose quick tempo and strong-beat propulsion seemed like echoes of the past now coalescing as something qualitatively new. At once comical and seditious, boogie's sound formations arose as a formidable agon, a music cast in the negative, its spectral character conjuring the presence of a dominion of ghosts.

The term *boogie* first enters public knowledge as a symbol of racial things past, as White supremacy's call to Africa's ancestors betraying the unsteadiness of racial separation. Sometimes brought into relation with another derogatory epithet, "spook," *boogie* referred historically to the supernatural, to spectral threat, taking form as the "boogie man," "bogeyman," or "bugaboo": fantasy figures who appeared at night to frighten children into obedience and complacence.[84] In the United States, boogie bore a close relationship to the European ghoul, the "Sand-Man," who tears out the eyes of children in Jacques Offenbach's opera *Les contes d'Hoffmann* (*The Tales of Hoffmann*, 1880) and who becomes an orienting figure in Freud's 1919 essay, "The Uncanny" (cf. chapter 5). This American-style boogie was first committed to musical form in Joseph P. Skelly's "The Boogie Man," published in 1880, the same year as Offenbach's work (figure 9.4). The song identifies what is perhaps the first instance of the boogie image in popular music. Its depiction of "the boogie man," a ghost lurking in the

9.4 Cover of sheet music for "The Boogie Man," written and composed by Joseph P. Skelly (Boston: John F. Perry, 1880). Library of Congress, Music Division.

narrator's chimney—its purpose to instill fear in and quiet a misbehaving baby—makes no direct reference to Blackness, but the advertisement of a minstrel song on its inside cover—James A. Bland's "In the Morning by the Bright Light"—encourages an association.

Although nineteenth-century depictions of boogies and bogeys linked only loosely to African Americans, they were often racially suggestive, alluding to a subject's foreignness, darkness, or difference. An 1892 *Milwaukee Sentinel* article, for example, described a local actor's portrayal of Sinbad in the medieval Arabic classic "One Thousand and One Nights" as that of the "Boogie Man," while an 1896 commentary remarked about "the latest boogie man" in international politics, Spain's General Valeriano Weyler. Plainly obvious in referencing a debased Blackness, moreover, was the use of "boogie" to describe the superfluous bodies of Black boys participating in sport for the entertainment of White spectators. "The little 'boogies,' or negroes," who in 1904 and 1905 fought for money in boxing matches, may be taken as a revival of "chin-music" (cf. chapter 3). Here, however, the boys drew contempt from spectators, who ridiculed them for "show[ing] their big White teeth in a comical grin."[85] By the first decades of the twentieth century, "boogie" would become a common, derogatory epithet, referencing the debased and degenerate, applied especially to hard-drinking Black men with swagger: the "boogie" as a defiant character, a scabrous humanity in possession of a strange, unearthly presence.[86]

Out of these racist figurations of the spectral Negro, boogie—in the spirit of Ike Simond's "colored minstrelsy" (cf. chapter 3)—begins to find its way into Black entertainment as a political reclamation of an uncanniness that White America sought to repress. First and foremost, it describes the music of prostitution dens: music of exploited sex workers was "boogie-house music."[87] A connection between rhythmic orientation and sex was nothing new: boogie assembled alongside rag and jazz, musically signifying the "less-than" status of Black folk. Such was the basis from which the blues arrived in the form of "Henry" sitting on his master's knee, introducing the inspiring, dark humor and fleshy beats that opened chapter 2. So too did boogie align with the figures of loss and tragedy, of reified labor and spectrality that flitted across depictions of blackface comedy, transforming sorrow—for example, the mangling of human form in "Ten Little Niggers"—into the exceptional expressivity leading to an emergent form of beat knowledge (cf. chapter 3). In a bizarre coordination with the spook figure, moreover, boogie became an affirmative marker of Black creative production showing up in multiple aesthetic forms. In 1917, Wilbur

Sweatman recorded "Boogie Rag," suggesting that by that time the term had entered the Black vernacular. The disc's release coupled its title with another negative-turned-positive epithet, to which the *Chicago Defender* gave notice in its advertisement of the "Ebony film comedy" "Spooks" in 1918.[88] It would be boogie again that located a little later the distinctive, propulsive locomotion performed by Black string bands and guitar players across southern states.

Even from this quick sketch we can see that strong-beat, intensified rhythmic practices relating to boogie had long informed the character of Black musical vernacularity, just as its ghoulish associations with the world of the dead reaffirmed its basis as a negative value. Boogie rhythms carried a White-supremacist semiotic value of mindless repetition that, in African American communities and then increasingly among a growing number of White listening publics, would become charged with animated power: the boogie of the sex houses was not far from the shouts that James P. Johnson played to accompany Carolina dancers in New York's Tenderloin district in the 1910s (cf. chapter 5). Formally, boogie was probably close to the performances that Johnson heard in Egg Harbor, New Jersey, in 1914, its boogie-woogie rhythm known at the time as "walking Texas bass." The Lone Star state appears to be a key site of boogie's ghostly beginning. Leadbelly, Jelly Roll Morton, and Bunk Johnson all reported hearing it played in Texas joints during the first decade of the century, while W. C. Handy remembers its appearances around the same time in Memphis. The pianists who purportedly brought boogie to Chicago around 1908 affirmed its downward associations, if only by performing where they could: in the poorest sectors of Black neighborhoods. By the late 1910s, "boogies" had become the word of choice to refer to Chicago's rent parties, as a performance style and acts of communal welfare congealed.[89]

Into the 1920s, boogie was one of many approaches to beat-oriented Black performance. It appeared indiscriminately, rising and subsiding according to the movements of itinerant musicians and touring groups passing through rural towns and neighborhoods. Versions of boogie rhythm tended to show up outside the major forums of entertainment that featured ragtime and jazz, remaining conspicuously off the record. It found a more welcome home in juke joints, bars, dance halls, and clubs showcasing small groups and singers. Pete Johnson reports that he heard boogie-woogie in Kansas City, where it was called at the time "western rolling blues" or "fast western." T-Bone Walker (b. 1910), moreover, recalled hearing the distinctive rhythm as a boy, the site of its performance amplifying its otherworldly character. "The first time I ever heard a boogie-woogie piano was the first time I went to church. That was the Holy Ghost Church in Dallas."[90] That Cow Cow Davenport remembered hearing boogie-woogie performed by Pine Top Smith in Pittsburgh in 1924 suggests that even then it was circulating vigorously, if still mainly confined to Black locales. A few years later, though, it gained wider circulation, first with Albert Ammons's "Honky-tonk Train Blues" (1927), then with the release of Smith's highly influential Vocalion disc, "Pine Top's Boogie Woogie" (1928), which, unlike Sweatman's record, features variations on the distinctive boogie rhythm: fast, eighth-note repetitions oriented around ascending and descending major arpeggiations, with players frequently augmenting a particular pattern with blue notes and major 6ths. Smith's verbal instructions on the recording, telling dancers when they should "hold yourself" and then "boogie-woogie" or "mess around," suggest that the record was popular at parties. By this time, he had moved to Chicago, befriending and influencing other pianists, notably Albert Ammons, as boogie practices multiplied and evolved. A year later, Smith was accidentally shot and killed during a brawl in a masonic lodge where he was performing.[91]

If boogie at this time suggested a beloved if errant impulse sounding within the narrower contours of the Black poor, it would soon emerge as a celebrated practice challenging swing for the claim of the "roots" of modern musical aliveness. That moment came with the introduction of a particular version of boogie featured during John Hammond's first "Spirituals to Swing" concert at Carnegie Hall in 1938. Presented to the audiences as a primitive form from which swing's advanced practices had developed, boogie, as "boogie-woogie"—despite its recent invention—joined the spirituals in representing the starting point of Black music's origins tale. Virtuosic boogie-woogie performances by Pete Johnson, Mead Lux Lewis, and Albert Ammons captivated the audience, with Johnson's accompaniment of Joe Turner ("It's All Right, Baby") and Ammons's of Sister Rosetta Tharpe ("Rock Me") being straight-out boogies. The performances were topics of lively discussion, treated with curiosity and condescension in a report published in the *New Yorker*, which—paraphrasing the words of Hammond himself—described Lewis and Ammons as "primitive artists" whose inability to read music "is a good thing, on the theory that if they ever studied technique and harmony, they might lose their natural feeling for their art." The portrait anticipated Roger Pryor Dodge's reassurance to his readers when also discussing Lewis's virtuosity: "Let it not be imagined for a moment that I expect Lewis to worry himself into conscious, compositional activity" (cf. chapter 7).[92] If boogie-woogie was a masterful creation performed by accomplished pianists who had developed improvisation to a high art, it was also a form arising from the negative status of "Negro" inferiority. This Black sound formation's ironic positioning motivated the anonymous, *New Yorker* essayist to decorate the essay with references to bar brawls, police interventions, binge drinking, and unskilled labor (the pianists worked by day as taxi drivers), evocative of a form of life that was itself repetition.

Boogie identifies a pivotal expropriation of Black vernacularity preceding R&B. While swing ascended toward the upper echelon of pop, boogie remained a scabrous property, ready for claiming. Into the 1940s, it circulated widely, moving from bottom up: a primitive form that gained commercial value by means of its reproduction in the entertainment industry. At this moment, boogie arose as a novelty practice in big band performances, its quirky character and strong-beat propulsion adding a diverting quality to swing's even time. The bands embraced boogie as a revivifying rhythmic practice in hopes of sustaining an already flagging swing movement. It was featured in hit tunes by Tommy Dorsey ("Boogie Woogie," 1938), Glenn Miller ("Boog It," 1940), and the Andrews Sisters ("Beat Me Daddy, Eight to the Bar," 1940). In 1941, makers of the film *Ball of Fire* showcased an extended performance by Gene Krupa performing his "Drum Boogie," which he had recorded with singer Irene Daye earlier in the year. The many versions of boogie encouraged the sense of a recovery of the southern past, the primality attached to its rhythm bringing a new, racial signature into the heart of public culture. Figures of spectrality that informed boogie's emergence from the outset were reinvented, as the rhythm practice set the tone for spook shows performed by Spike ("Spook") Jones and the Brian Sisters, the latter whose Halloween film short, *The Boogie Woogie Man* (1942), employed lighting effects to cast the three singers in shadows, mimicking blackface makeup.[93]

Into the 1940s, boogie's incorporations within the entertainment world made it the latest currency of racist fantasy, having disseminated across international networks—to Britain, Japan, and India, where in 1943 Harry Parry and His Radio Rhythm Club Sextet recorded its hit, "Boogi"—as part of the commercialization of swing. As a popular fetish, boogie was the stuff of comical play; but in its revision of beat, it also intruded on popular norms, introducing to a new fan base a different sensible means of organizing music time. In this way, boogie carried forward the homologies aligning metric and social time that by this point had informed the comprehension of swing, while also playing the role of a disruptor of that very alignment. It proposed a new character of style—a critical force within a larger circuit of rhythm—that reshaped beat knowledge in its imagined relationship to the dynamic movements of the spectral, Black body. If boogie had restored the sensation of an inalienable Blackness in motion, it had done so according to a regenerative process by which dissembled figures cast about the auditory universe of popular sound, congealing as newly formulated rhythmic intensities. Over the course, boogie gained huge commercial and symbolic value, having been recombined, regenerated, and newly constituted within the complex of capitalized, popular expression.

Small wonder, then, that Black musicians, recognizing boogie's enormous appeal, worked energetically to take back a precious beat knowledge, reclaiming a property that had been newly valued in the commercial marketplace. In its loss to the expropriative forces of entertainment capitalism, boogie multiplied in value, time and again. A once modest accompaniment to humble blues shows and rent parties had congealed as a popular subgenre of jazz, common in the band books of Black swing orchestras from Count Basie to Sy Oliver. Soon boogie practices already familiar in southern Black music gained prominence in the blues-oriented bands that were altering the character of swing: the Buddy Johnson Orchestra, for example, recorded two boogies in the early 1940s, "Boogie Woogie's Ma-in-Law" (1941) and "I Wonder Who's Boogiein' My Woogie Now" (1942). In the context of small blues and jump bands, though, boogie was less a novelty than an informing rhythmic impulse that grew out of the fundamentals of ensemble practice. To boogie was not only to perform boogie-woogie in a strict sense but also to play hard along the design of fast-paced rhythm, its distinctive grooves keeping dancers moving. Having gained value in national forums, boogie assumed an urgency, its properties congealing Black sensibilities. In Black club circuits across the nation, it gave form to an ontologically charged presence, the starting point of high-energy blues performances.

With the expansion of the chitlin' circuit after the war, boogie emerged as the featured rhythm on dozens of records. And over the decade, it gained prominence, becoming the defining beat of the newly named rhythm and blues, with stellar releases by Louis Jordan ("Choo Choo Ch'Boogie," 1946), Jimmy Liggins and His Drops of Joy ("Cadillac Boogie," 1947), Fats Domino ("The Fat Man," 1950), Ray Charles ("Kissa Me Baby," 1951), and many others. The previous discussions of Chicago blues and the chitlin' circuit alluded to boogie's wide presence. There was "Boogie at Midnight," "Chicken Shack Boogie," and "Boogie Rambler." In some tunes, boogie showed up without reference to it in the title: "Good Rockin' Tonight," "Rocket 88," "Okie Dokie Stomp," "Rockin' Chair Blues." There were also dozens and dozens of other versions performed by musicians who displayed their own distinctive approaches. Madman Taylor's "Mule Train Boogie" (1950) is a haunting concatenation of shouts and narrative sounding against the pianist's rapid figurative outline: a movement between the first and third scale degrees, with occasional blue-note inflections. Bull Moose Jackson's "Cherokee Boogie (Eh-Oh-Aleena)" (1953) is a cartoonish depiction of an indigenous "cry"—the term appearing in the lyric—that provides a platform for Jackson's tenor playing. By the mid-1950s, boogie stood as the signature beat orientation of r&b, producing a grand assembly of animated, often frenzied sounds that moved bodies and inspired the racial imagination.

The reclamation of boogie by "the R&B people" certified its primacy as a key value in Black music.[94] And with that certification, it would spark interest among White youth, launching a tug-of-war that from here on structured popular music's greater development. Boogie represented a critical sensation, the impulse for shaping movements of the body in space, the contours enacted by dancers in turn affecting the way players laid down their enlivened tempos. With the new negotiations of Black and White artists in the making of rock 'n' roll, with Black celebrity confronting the asymmetries of social rank, boogie began its extraordinary journey to the apex of pop. The losses it had earlier amassed seemed diminished in its new accumulation, as its fleshy expressions of bodies-in-sound inspired massive claims by White publics. A playful spectrality rapidly overtook popular listening, as boogie remade popular sound and sensibility, enacting what Richard Middleton has described as an expansive "boogification." With boogie's incorporation, pop would undergo the transformation named "rock 'n' roll."[95]

If boogie haunted pop, it was a welcome specter. Its distinctive rhythm was widely embraced as a figuration inextricably linked to Blackness, although the recognition of its original ownership did not discourage White players from emulating and reinventing it. As Middleton shows, boogie's characteristics, from its eighth-note arpeggiated bass repetitions to the triplet patterns common to its upper-register design, became the means for artists to invent an extraordinary variety of approaches. These innovations extended the practice of racial covering, as in, for example, Bill Haley's aforementioned recreation of Big Maybelle's relaxed, boogie-swing "Whole Lotta Shakin' Goin' On" (1957). Little Richard—performing with the drummer Earl Palmer—produced a series of back-beat-driven shouts that featured boogie. His hit "Tutti Frutti" (1955) not only won him stardom but, as noted earlier, also advanced the careers of Presley and Boone. As boogie's agonistic presence inhabited rock 'n' roll, it inspired a moment of exciting musical interracialism. Little Richard's "Little Richard's Boogie" (1956), "Long Tall Sally" (1956), and "Good Golly, Miss Molly" (1958) joined Chuck Berry's "Roll Over Beethoven" (1956) and "Johnny B. Goode" (1958) among the most celebrated rock 'n' roll achievements, just as Elvis Presley's "Milkcow Blues Boogie" and "Mystery Train" (both 1955) widened the creative palette with inventive extrapolations on boogie's triplet melodic voicing.

Like quicksilver, boogie spread its wealth, its infectious rhythms establishing their hold on the popular vernacular. What had ignited rock 'n' roll would in a few years become a staple in the emerging rock scene, put to creative redesign by British bands—the Rolling Stones, Yardbirds, Led Zeppelin, Cream—American groups—the Mothers of Invention, Johnnie Winter, Canned Heat, the Allman Brothers—and in the revolutionary music of Jimi Hendrix. The stunning achievements of these and many others certified the importance of boogie in the canonical knowledge of rock. Alongside these developments, moreover, boogie continued to guide African American blues performers such as Muddy Waters and Howlin' Wolf, both of whom collaborated with rock's leading musicians, together with hundreds of others who played locally and never recorded. For much of the time it set the rhythmic orientation on which various Black bands invented a distinctive sound heard in Black clubs across the nation. And it would remain a mainstay among Chicago players as they watched its value drift away, a story implied in the closing comments of Robert Palmer's *Deep Blues*: the Chicago sound had morphed into "The World Boogie."[96]

It had, indeed. Boogie's seemingly endless repetitions inspired a panoply of new beat orientations, its assertive linearity extending free and R&B's suppression of harmony and song form in the making of new sonic-sensible designs. With pop's boogification, Black music's temporal feel expanded, taking on multiple elaborations, which were sold under the names of soul, funk, fusion, disco, and house, and orchestrated by a powerhouse of musicians. James Brown would be joined by George Clinton, Nile Rodgers, Frankie Knuckles, and a whole new category of artistry, the DJs, rappers, and producers of hip-hop. New coalescences of form set into motion a grand mosaic of rhythmic invention, with style areas sometimes intersecting: the beats generated by Brown's drummer, Clyde Stubblefield, on "Cold Sweat" (1967) and "Funky Drummer" (1969) were variously sampled, remixed, and remade to stamp the enlivened feeling of seminal funk rhythms on a multitude of hip-hop recordings.[97]

Other offspring of boogie were born beyond US shores. In London in the 1980s, recordings of boogie produced in the United States were resurrected in the form of disco-funk, featured at dance clubs, which in turn inspired the creation of multiracial styles of electronic dance music (EDM), most known under the rubric of drum and bass and its various subgenres, notably jungle and liquid funk. Boogie, moreover, had been ensconced in the tempos of South African jazz since the 1960s: for example, Hugh Masekela's seminal recorded version of "Grazing in the Grass" (1968) and the majestic "Boulevard East" (1965) by Abdullah Ibrahim (Dollar Brand), which gains its personality from the subtle boogie running through it. Into the 1970s, boogie rhythms helped to advance the revolution in sound that overtook Nigeria, from Fela Anikulapo Kuti's Afrobeat to the boogie incarnate, Mixed Grill's "Brand New Wayo" (ca. 1979), while back in the United States and Britain, boogie lived on, its spirited iterations energizing a barrage of late-century and new-century inventions. The flood of boogie rhythms showing up in 1970s rock, pop, fusion, and funk—Fleetwood Mac, "Rockin' Boogie" (1969); Rolling Stones, "Casino Boogie" (1972); Kool and the Gang, "Jungle Boogie" (1973); Weather Report, "Boogie Woogie Waltz" (1973); Parliament, "Aqua Boogie" (1979)—would be redispersed and redirected, its various mutations inhabiting a range of innovations from jazz to disco to EDM and driving another wave of global circulation: Paul Simon's stealth nod to Elvis, *Graceland*; the revved-up intensities of K-pop, J-pop, and Japanese rock 'n' roll. Artists from Bill Laswell to David Bowie to Sting have all been touched by boogie's enlivening madness.

One might argue that boogie's life story was no different from earlier beat transformations—notably the move from jazz to swing. Yet whereas in swing Black-centered rhythm achieved a pyrrhic victory, its influence coming at the cost of its multiple losses to Black labor, boogie not only launched the rise of rock 'n' roll and rock, it also catalyzed a revolutionary move: Black music would no longer be simply a point of reference but a music performed on its own terms, by Black musicians. By turns, it took the helm of pop. From the mid-1970s, figures such as Ray Charles, Aretha Franklin, and Stevie Wonder joined a new generation of Black celebrities—Whitney Houston, Herbie Hancock, Mariah Carey, Wynton Marsalis, Michael Jackson—as guiding figures in American musical culture. A decade or so later, a cascade of Black innovation overwhelmed popular sound, as hip-hop emerged as the defining force of new sound formations. The broad community of artists encompassing Black music's public presence gained their cultural authority out of their success in the entertainment business. And it was on this authority that free evolved from its initial experiments into a dramatic critical practice: the commercial posture of Black pop set the ground for the efflorescence of a rarefied Black sound, whose critical nature—its musicians (recalling Bechet and Ellington) often rejecting their nominal associations with "jazz"—lent it moral authority in arts circles.

Free's rise as an experimental art form corresponded to the enduring efforts of Black justice movements and the revitalization of a passionate Black intellectualism, their alliances calling attention to the relation of creative expression and radical political thought. The leading figures of the free movement—Ornette Coleman, John Coltrane, Cecil Taylor, Archie Shepp, Albert Ayler, together with those emerging from Chicago's Association for the Advancement of Creative Musicians—were participants in a new musical intervention, generating emancipatory forms performed live and on record that enlisted a way of "listening to black sound beyond the herding effects" of mass culture. This new "black soundwork," as Anthony Reed has called it, exceeded European-centered strictures of Music: it "disturbs the intelligibility of the Western tradition," taking form live and on record, as it asks listeners to consider how "each present—each *now*—produces its own version of the past as part of its self-legitimation." As a creative insurgency in the form of a New Black Music, free joined the fantastic inventions of Chicago, the chitlin' circuit, and R&B in the making of what Reed names a "vernacular avant-garde," a "term . . . [that] captures relays between popular forms and their aesthetic elaboration and imagines them as simultaneous, rather than reinscribing modernism/mass culture binaries."[98]

These spectacular adventures, as actions within the historical present, ignited experiences that were "multiple rather than unitary." The performances opened pathways for experiences of greater temporal complexity, initiating an awareness of what Harry Harootunian has described—to repeat his insight once more—a sense of "the present [as] the crowding of differing historical times, which marks the modern from the presents of prior pasts."[99] Such crowding of multiple pasts in the present initiated the drawing in of past-time into the now. The apotheosis of a New Black Music announced these modes of recovery, enabling ways of hearing and knowing that reasserted the force of a tenacious counterhistory. Black music's surge as counterhistory was enabling broadly, refiguring pop under the guise of hip-hop's formal radicality and inspiring through the incorporation of free's disruption of song—heard not only in Black music but in pop experiments tracing from David Bowie's "Neuköln" to the extraordinary timbral complexity of Sonic Youth—an aesthetic transformation not possible had it not been for the legacy of Black music's curiously enlivened life story.

One way to understand Black music's apotheosis is as a fulfillment of social progress, with Black innovators acknowledged as the central actors in the making of a multiracial public sound. There is certainly credibility to this messaging and to the ways of listening it inspires. Since the 1970s, popular music has been subject to a veritable occupation, its style movements being led by hundreds of influential Black innovators. The likes of Miles Davis and Anthony Braxton would be joined by Wayne Shorter, Roscoe Mitchell, and Wynton Marsalis; Michael Jackson and Grand Master Flash stood with Public Enemy and Afrika Bambaataa. And by the turn of the century, there would be Prince, Jay-Z, Beyoncé, and Kendrick Lamar appearing alongside Anthony Davis, Henry Threadgill, Jason Moran, George E. Lewis, Matana Roberts, Courtney Bryan, and Miguel Zenón. Beyond the inner circle of celebrity, moreover, there has arisen a multitude of artists actively working in multiple genres, from indie to conscious rap; African American composers now represent one part of a larger "Incubator for Afrodiasporic New Music" linking innovators across the Black Atlantic.[100] Observed together, they are evidence of a level of Black achievement unimaginable a hundred years ago. Theirs is a New Black Music whose power and presence has become recognized internationally and has inspired legions of White artists fully aware of their debt to the legacy of African American artistry. It is difficult even to gesture to this turn, its magnitude being so massive.

Yet such portraits of unity-in-diversity are ultimately incomplete, for they miss how the present moment has developed as part of a greater history of value. Such claims often celebrate the phenomenal surfaces of Black successes without comprehending why those surfaces are valued in the first place. As we've witnessed time and again, Black music's aliveness grows from an epistemic radicalism materially bound to production: it arises from the paradox of a once alienable, propertied people owning an inalienable property of their own. This is Black music's primary truth— the engine that has generated its many peculiarly enlivened expressions, its spectacularity so difficult to capture, its "muteness" so challenging to discern. Although African America has long been free, the valuation that is aliveness endures, thriving on the force of racial injustice. A nation's commitment to race is the reason why Black music can still seem racially animated, its alienably inalienable properties the source of a continuing struggle of ownership. Because this crucial contradiction never resolves, the music's illicitness lives on, informing the personae of even the most celebrated performers. Indeed, their star value is often heightened by the illicitness they are assumed to possess and by which they appear to create such fantastic music. Forgetting this history means that we mistake the reasons for the music's ebullient aliveness and why Black music sounds so spectacular. This is how Black music can simultaneously live at the center of public life and also along its margins. It is how and why its scabrous textures resonate, moving in contrary motion, making the past alive in the present.

A different way of listening begins from the contradiction itself. It proceeds by applying pressure to the music's jagged grain, by feeling the syncopations pulsing within a race-obsessed nation to find new insight into its nature and history. From such a posture, one can explore the phenomenon of aliveness, recognizing how its contrary motion offers guidance into Black music's contested history as a means toward the critical activity of double listening, outlined at the end of the previous chapter. Such listening practices bring forward a way of experiencing the sonic presences of the past, of imagining the sensible breakthroughs of the music's initial, spectacular emancipation, and of recognizing how its fleshy powers of "unmuting" overcome capital's encompassing force of abstraction (cf. chapter 8). A critically minded listening, then, offers a way of steadying the inconstancy of a dynamic sound, so full of tragedy and comedy, of swing and groove, of boogified intensity and incorrigible beats. Living with the music this way proposes a strategy that acknowledges a racial legacy still abundantly alive in the present, still informing the way we listen and hear. It provides hope of a newly inspired and inspiring living informed by a music that, while structured in the contradictions of history, guides us, nourishes us, and tells us so much, even as it has nothing inherent to say.

MODERNITY'S

GHOSTS

A coffee mug comes to the table, its arrival impeccable, as if synched to a playlist that at this moment features Drake: "Marvin's Room/Buried Alive Interlude" and "Best I Ever Had." This, a beverage caught up in racial fantasies of addiction, creaturely Africana, and Black bodies; as the shop's sign playfully commands, "Coffee: Drink Your Monkey." The particular setting is neither Drake's Toronto nor, after Hurston, some Harlem "New World Cabaret," but a charming coffee house in Berlin's Charlottenburg neighborhood. Those gathering in the café—judging from my eavesdropping ears, conversing in German, Turkish, English—may or may not know Drake's music. And most likely they are not aware of the vast technological, economic, and legal structures driving Black popular music's global presence, racially embossing living worlds with signs of hipness and cosmopolitanism.

No matter. They can certainly feel the tempos that the artists and producers are laying down, even if they aren't necessarily paying much attention. The heightened state of its commodification is what helps to make Drake's music so satisfying. It gives to the environment a familiar ordering texture, making for this small sample of global humanity a room that seems right, sounds right—a discreet affect of an imagined home, a place. The soundtrack is one indication of the staggering blitz of Black sound overwhelming global metropoles, a creative manifestation of how "the term 'Black' has been generalized." In the new century, it assumes a "new fungibility, [a] solubility, institutionalized as a new norm of existence and expanded to the entire planet." Black sound sustains as an audible sensation what Achille Mbembe calls *"the Becoming Black of the world."*[1]

I'm in Berlin to launch new research on the auditory invention of pre-history: the first recordings of "African music," a vast phonographic archive created by German colonizers amid monumental destruction of indigenous life and culture.[2] This sonic constitution of savagery is where the civilized begins, where Music gains the color of Whiteness against the strange allure of a primal *Negro sound*, thought by its early collectors to be living evidence of humanity's origins. The aurally charged atmosphere of Coffee: Drink Your Monkey shows how Africa's audible past assumes a place in the present. Yet the situation in the café also indicates a departure. Drake's stature among the titans of hip-hop and R&B reflects how the music's metamorphosis has unfolded, realizing the promise of fantastic artistry, which confidently asserts its authority by acoustically inhabiting public spaces. If Black music sustains the mark of difference, if its losses continue to accrue for another's profit—charges famously made against Led Zeppelin, Ed Sheeran, and, among others, Drake himself—it also moves to the forceful presence of artists who've gained greater command of their collective property.[3] Taking control of the music's productive apparatuses—record companies, social media, concert tours, advertising—the new arbiters of creation (among the most prominent, Beyoncé, Sean Combs, Drake, Jay-Z, Kendrick Lamar, Kanye West) claim economic profit as they sustain a sign system that locates value in the worldly pleasure of audibly enlivened difference. This is the tension, the contradiction born of race-capital, that propels Black sound into the world.

In his essay "Black Body," Teju Cole speaks powerfully to Blackness's historical unfolding by way of personal reflection, comparing one of James Baldwin's European encounters in the early 1950s to his own in the present day. Venturing to Leukerbad, Switzerland, where Baldwin holed up with his Bessie Smith records to draft *Go Tell It on the Mountain*, Cole considers how the idea and experience of Blackness have changed after more than half a century. Where Baldwin once felt alienated, estranged—where, as he reported in his essay "Stranger in the Village," "from all available evidence no black man had ever set foot"—Cole found Black references commonplace, in large part through the power of Black music. "Baldwin had to bring his records with him in the fifties, like a secret stash of medicine"; Cole could enjoy Beyoncé, Drake, and Meek Mill as he casually moved about, their music pulsing from clubs at night. "When I sat down to lunch at the Römerhof restaurant one afternoon—that day, all the customers and staff were white—the music playing overhead was Whitney Houston's 'I Wanna Dance with Somebody.' History is now and black America."[4]

The victory of Black music accompanies a victory of the Black body, a new *spectacular revolution* enabling those still burdened by its racial category to nonetheless embrace the world as their own. So successful is this victory it empowers Cole—who, in another instance, celebrates it with an auditory tour he calls "My Black Ears"—to take claim of knowledge beyond the sonic, to embrace traditions that Baldwin had felt himself denied. As did Du Bois in *The Souls of Black Folk*—"I sit with Shakespeare and he winces not"—Cole asserts his right to embrace all that which is aesthetic in the West: "I am not an interloper when I look at a Rembrandt portrait . . . I can oppose white supremacy and still rejoice in Gothic architecture."[5]

The victories, though, do not diminish the constancy of the tragic perpetuated by a legacy of White commitments to race, by which value is routinely extracted from the superfluity of Black being. The extremes depend one on the other. Cole's turn in his essay to the enduring racial and political circumstances in Africa and the United States suggests how the success of Black music's presence draws energy from a counterforce of deepening racial resentment: not only toward Black people but also toward all those who represent the status of difference. The force of resentment generates tragedy as it fuels the production of value. It perpetuates a dynamic of repression that elevates the aesthetic stature of sonic Blackness, by which actors of Black music innovate new forms. The sound of a Black imaginary courses through a contemporary world still burdened by race.

It is through these many turns that Black music comes to be everywhere and absent, making time and texturing the public spaces of global metropoles, yet also seeming audibly invisible, unheard. If the incessant claims on Black music as a powerful commodity affirm its value, the ultimate failure of those claims is what drives new efforts to mask its potency and paradoxically to perpetuate its force. Black music speaks not clear messages but rather establishes structures that haunt the circuits of global entertainment capital: it supplies dialectical energy sustaining what Mbembe names "the ghost of modernity." Black sound is the audible specter occupying the common, the desirable spook, the nightmarish ghoul boogeying down: the source of animated play and fear-generated animus.[6] As it conforms to the motion of capital it disturbs capital's temporal regime, revealing in its ruptures new sensations of aliveness and, with them, both possibility and possibility's negation. Artists who continue to labor within these structures might win fortune and fame, but more often than not they endure pedestrian struggles—unfair practices, bad deals, poverty, artistic theft—living the negative that underlies Black music's animated presences.

Through a vast sonic network stretching worldwide, Black music occupies contemporary spaces, its capacious reach unprecedented. But what do we actually hear, how do we perceive this wash of sound that seems at once present and absent? Music is the engine of aspiration, the means by which the illusory—the fetish character of music—enables us to imagine new heights, to feel in new ways, to *think*, one hopes, positively, progressively, humanely. Yet this is still a one-sided way of listening. Can we find the means of discerning the contradictory nature of racialized sound as it inhabits the twenty-first century—to engage in double listening? For how we choose to interpret the resonances of Black music—so often by turns haphazard, indifferent, uncritical, mythical, delusional—may matter more now than ever before.

INTRODUCTION

Parts of the introduction and chapter 1 appeared as "Black Music Labor and the Animated Properties of Slave Sound," *Boundary 2: An International Journal of Literature and Culture* 43, no. 1 (February 2016): 173–208.

1   Du Bois, *Black Reconstruction*, 124.

2   Du Bois, *Black Reconstruction*, 124.

3   For "singing book," see Baker, *Modernism*, 68. Du Bois writes of the sorrow songs as "the most beautiful expression of human experience born this side the seas." See Du Bois, *Souls of Black Folk*, 186.

4   Du Bois, *Black Reconstruction*, xiii, 580. In this instance, "economic" refers to exchange in capitalist markets. My own use of the term will be broader, involving the multiple systems of productive exchange that realize forms of value.

5   Du Bois, *Black Reconstruction*, 124.

6   Although Marx defines *labor* as a free worker's commodified contribution to the means of production, I am employing the term, as Du Bois does, to describe the kinds of work common among both free and unfree Black workers participating in the social relations of capitalism. The ambiguity of labor within slavery is consistent with slavery's ambiguous relationship to capitalism itself. "Humanly organized sound" is a concept and phrase introduced into music anthropology and ethnomusicology by John Blacking in his book *How Musical Is Man?*

7   I capitalize "Music" throughout this study to identify European-based conceptions of an autonomous art form, recognizing that the distinction between elite forms of "Music" and lower forms called "music" have been contested since at least the 1940s. The term, "music" in "Negro" and then "Black" music remains uncapitalized to underscore how its status always remains suspect.

8   Du Bois, *Black Reconstruction*, 124–25. (The depiction of slaves and Africans as "noisy" was common to the era.) The oppositional relation of negative to positive, Black to White, also forms the key dynamic of labor to capital driving repetition in Du Bois's thought and in this study.

9   Across this study, I avoid the possessive case (as in "Black music's value"), seeking to avoid the implication that Black music possesses an autonomous value.

10   Du Bois, *Black Reconstruction*, 124–25.

11   Du Bois, *Black Reconstruction*, 125.

12   Du Bois, *Black Reconstruction*. For "Can we imagine," 121; "wild truth," 122. For informing literature, see Singh, *Black Is a Country*, 90–96; Hughes, "Can We Imagine," 179–210.

13   For "miracle, of its production," see Johnson and Johnson, *Books of American Negro Spirituals*, 12. For "acoustical shock," see Steinberg, *Listening to Reason*, 86, 88. For "howled the hymn of joy," see Du Bois, *Black Reconstruction*, 126. For Du Bois's interests in Schiller and Beethoven, see Bilbija, "Democracy's New Song," 64–77. See also Bertholf, "Listening."

14   Du Bois, *Gift of Black Folk*. Laviña and Zeuske, *Second Slavery*.

15   Du Bois, *Gift of Black Folk*, 9–10, 19, 105. Du Bois writes, "Music is always back of this gay, Negro spirit and the folk song which the Negro brought to America was developed not simply by White men but by the Negro himself" (105).

16   Marx famously employs the expression "living labor" in Choat, *Marx's Grundrisse*. See, for example, 299. For a genealogy of the concept, see Sáenz, "Living Labor in Marx." For "draft-horse," Du Bois, *Gift of Black Folk*, 9. Performative expressions that we can analytically identify as "Black music" (sound-based performance practices derived from or informed by people of the African continent) reach back before slavery and European contact. I'm proposing, though, that the social recognition of a strange form of musicality, most commonly known at the time among White southerners as "slave music" or "Negro music," did not come into being—was not socially constituted and conceptualized—until the last decades of the antebellum era. I've outlined this position previously in my book *Lying up a Nation*.

17   Hanchard, "Afro-Modernity," 256.

18   I'm making a distinction here at the outset (and over the course of the analysis) between partial truths aligned with meaning and a primary, structural truth located in the contradiction underlying Black music value. The latter conception of truth is informed by Theodor W. Adorno's idea of truth content, as he explores it in his book *Aesthetic Theory*. For elaboration, see Paddison, *Adorno's Aesthetics of Music*; Jarvis, *Adorno*; Pensky, "Natural History," 23–41.

19   Pensky, "Natural History," 37.

20   Okiji, *Jazz as Critique*, 5.

21   Du Bois, *Gift of Black Folk*, chap. 2. On the celebration of Black music as spirit and truth, see Sorett, *Spirit in the Dark*.

22   Du Bois, *Gift of Black Folk*, 9–10. Later, in the same text, Du Bois elaborates: "While the gift of the White laborer made America rich, or at

least made many Americans rich, it will take the psychology of the Black man to make it happy" (19). On socially necessary labor time, see Marx, *Capital*, 129. For a study that brings these historical anomalies of work into the present, see Arzuaga, "Socially Necessary Superfluity," 819–43. For "organized monarchy" and "triumphant industry," see Du Bois, *Black Reconstruction*, 580.

23 Mbembe, *Critique of Black Reason*, 129.

24 Describing slavery as the "peculiar institution" was widespread during the antebellum period. See Stampp, *Peculiar Institution*. Brown, "Reification, Reanimation," 197. Brown is quoting Ernst Jentsch. The term gains traction in psychanalytic theory through its application by Sigmund Freud; see chapter 5 in this volume.

25 Robinson, *Black Marxism*. In the context of Black music, the relation of race to capitalism is formally incommensurable, as discussed ahead. For a series of essays dedicated to Robinson's major work, see Johnson and Kelley, *Forum 1*.

26 Du Bois, *Souls of Black Folk*, 186. The matter of Music's social constructedness was central to debates in musicology in the 1990s. See, for example, the exchange between Lawrence Kramer and Tomlinson that begins with Kramer's "The Musicology of the Future," *Repercussions* (Spring 1992): 5–18, and carries forward in *Current Musicology* 53 (1993). For an elaboration on the "Music" concept in the context of the postcolonial critique, see Radano and Olaniyan, "Hearing Empire—Imperial Listening," in *Audible Empire*, 1–24.

27 Gallope, *Deep Refrains*.

28 My focus here is on Black music as it has been produced and appeared in commercial markets during slavery and in the popular entertainment industry. The participation of African American composers in the history of art music in the United States is another story. Although it is an important one, it has had little impact on the larger question of Black music value. In fact, I would argue that Black music in its commercial forms has had a determining influence on the entirety of music created by African Americans.

29 Perhaps the closest a historian comes to such a material-based reading is Lawrence Levine's magisterial *Black Culture and Black Consciousness*, a book written at a moment when cultural and social historians were vigorously advocating "bottom up" approaches. More recently, slave music has received thoughtful, if passing, discussion in a variety of historical accounts. See, for example, Morgan, *Slave Counterpoint*; Baptist, *Half Has Never Been Told*.

30 A new order of musicological scholarship has pushed hard against this uncritical tendency in American music history. See, for example, Garcia, *Listening for Africa*; Eidsheim, *Race of Sound*.

31 For example, Brooks, *Bodies in Dissent*; Weheliye, *Phonographies*; Lordi, *Meaning of Soul*; and Reed, *Soundworks*. Gilroy, *Black Atlantic*, remains a foundational study.

32 Moten, *In the Break*, 10–11. Moten proposes a comprehension of slave music as a tear or break in the conception of the commodity form resulting from the slave's expressive terror—as a "thing" that actually speaks. This is a rather loose reading of the commodity form, observing it solely in terms of exchange value—an "inspirited materiality" (11)—with little attention to its dual (concrete and abstract) character or to its fundamental basis in labor and production. I'm seeking here a more specific grounding of Black musicality in a racial economy.

33 "Core Values for Jazz"; Wilson, "Black Music," 2. Later in the essay, when analyzing Miles Davis's performance of "Green Dolphin Street," Wilson similarly unites the two terms, suggesting that a "meaningful musical statement . . . is based on an imaginative usage of the values associated with Afro-American music" (21).

34 On this background, see Graeber, "Three Ways." On the attempt to link micro and macro events, see Graeber's discussion of the work of Clyde Kluckhohn. Such a conception was fundamental to nineteenth-century dialectical thought.

35 Porter, *Thing Called Jazz*, 37. The close proximity of meaning to value appears in philosophical studies. See, for example, Metz, "Meaning of Life."

36 For background, see Spitzer, *Metaphor and Musical Thought*; Kramer, *Musical Meaning*. Steven Feld's *Sound and Sentiment* is foundational in the study of music and human communication.

37 Douglass, *Narrative of the Life*, chap. 2; Du Bois, "Of Our Spiritual Strivings," chap. 1 of *Souls of Black Folk*, 79.

38 "Structural causality" was introduced into contemporary criticism by Louis Althusser in his collaborative study with Étienne Balibar, *Reading Capital*. It refers to the way in which structure may be immanent in its concrete manifestations, akin to the relation between abstract labor and concrete labor. In this sense, it is also an "absent cause" since there is no actual structure fully present in concrete forms. Moreover, Jerrold Levinson's analysis of value with respect to European art music offers a contrast to my definition. See "Values in Music," the sixth chapter of his book *Musical Concerns*.

39 "Sonic material" is derived from Adorno's concept of "musical material," which, as Samuel Wilson elaborates—developing an interpretation first proposed by Carl Dahlhaus—"crystallizes aspects found in his thought more generally. . . . Musical material, for Adorno, is all that faces the composer in the present as inherited from the past." I prefer "sonic" to "musical" because "Negro sound" was frequently not understood as "music" by Black and White alike. Moreover, my use of "sonic" extends

what is implied in Adorno's conception of history in its relation to production: a production involving a general musicality, not one specific to the concept of the composer. For Wilson's discussion, see "Notes on Adorno's 'Musical Material,'" 248–49. For Dahlhaus's discussion, see Dahlhaus, "Form." The concept of "musical material" is integral to Paddison's interpretation in *Adorno's Aesthetics of Music*.

40 "Structuring structure" is part of Pierre Bourdieu's formulation of habitus. See Bourdieu, *Outline* and *Distinction*. For a discussion of articulation as a linking of unrelated forms and practices, see Grossberg, "On Postmodernism," especially 141–43; Cook, "Theorizing Musical Meaning," 188.

41 Feld, "Flow Like a Waterfall," 22–47; Shelley, "Holy Ghost Chord"; "Analyzing Gospel," 181–242.

42 Debates over distinctions between meter, beat, and pulse have informed theories of African music since the middle of the twentieth century. I am not seeking to enter those discussions but rather am working from conventional popular notions of musical time as they are commonly conveyed in journalistic writing. To this extent, I'm more interested in phenomenological conceptions of "beat" rather than "pulse," the latter indicating an underlying time marker that may be recognized but is not necessarily consistently expressed. A good place to begin exploring the debates is Agawu, "Structural Analysis," 1–46. For elaborations on these distinctions, see also Cheyne, Hamilton, and Paddison, *Philosophy of Rhythm*.

43 Scholarly studies of the relationship between music and language stretch across European music history, finding a modern beginning in nineteenth-century theories of absolute music and the claims of European music's universal character and transcendental power. They have routinely informed music-theoretical and ethnomusicological thought since the mid-twentieth century, the matter of music communication becoming a point of attention with the turn to semiotics in the 1970s and 1980s. Although the subject has been vigorously debated, there is now a loose, consensus opinion that, as Lawrence Kramer puts it, "Music cannot 'speak' with its own 'voice' until it finds a voice, or voices, among a multiplicity of others that constantly blend with music and chafe against the rest." *Musical Meaning*, 6.

44 Langer, *Philosophy in a New Key*, 240; emphasis in the original. Cumming, *Sonic Self*, 100–101; Moreno, "Review Essay," 286. For Adorno's use of "second hand" mediations, see Paddison, *Adorno's Aesthetics of Music*, 175.

45 Feld, "Communication, Music," 91. In the same essay, Feld offers a valuable elaboration, anticipating views later articulated by Cumming and Moreno, stressing that musical experience cannot be fully specified. Music, as linguistic anthropologists would say, is "a primary modeling system," which means that, in its primacy as a nonverbal grammar, it

is made up of "unique and irreducible symbolic properties. These must be experienced and approached in their own right, . . . freed from any notion that they simply translate or copy the speech mode." What is "primary" and "irreducible"—what in its ambiguity as a sign system does not conform to a precise linguistic analog—is also what enables music's remarkable breadth of meaningfulness (94).

46 Lott, *Love and Theft*, 18. On the idea of racialized investment, see Lipsitz, *Progressive Investment*.

47 Paddison, *Adorno's Aesthetics of Music*, 1. Paddison attributes "condemned to meaning" to Adorno. In fact, it derives from Maurice Merleau-Ponty's *Phenomenology of Perception*. See Ivanova, "Twelve-Tone Identity," 34.

48 Adorno, *Aesthetic Theory*, 228.

49 I borrow the intensive/extensive dynamic from Sewell, "Temporalities of Capitalism."

50 Foucault, *"Society Must Be Defended,"* 70.

51 Foucault, *"Society Must Be Defended,"* 70. More generally informing the theorization I'm mapping out here is Postone, *Time, Labor*.

52 Baraka, *Blues People*, x, 8. Although Baraka doesn't employ the expression "changing same" in print until 1967, *Blues People* is already an elaboration on the concept. "The Negro's music," he writes, "changed as he changed, reflecting shifting attitudes or (and this is equally important) *consistent attitudes within changed contexts*. And it is *why* the music changed that seems most important to me" (153; emphases in the original).

53 Baraka, *Blues People*, 16, 131. For Baraka, Black music's essential Africanity develops not simply from a direct African transmission but from a kind of cultural distillation arising out of Africans' subjugation under slavery. Its original, African basis was already exceptional, being expressive of "some of the most complex and complicated ideas about the world imaginable" (7). At times, he locates this intensified African essence in actual musical practice. Quoting Ernest Borneman, he suggests that in the "African tradition," excellent performance appears in the quality of phrasing, in the improviser's "tendency towards obliquity and ellipsis. . . . No note is attacked straight." Yet he also makes an effort to distinguish the accumulation of meaning from value. Performance strategies of obliquity appear "without ever having committed to a single meaning" (31). For more on value, see Baraka, "Black Value System," 54–60.

54 Baraka introduces his theory of value as "changing same" in "The Changing Same: R&B and New Black Music," which appears as a chapter in his second book, *Black Music*. The concept becomes particularly influential from the 1990s after being revived by Paul Gilroy in his essay "Sounds Authentic" and then in his book *Black Atlantic*. For an example of its application to Black dance—"the *changing-same* of collective movement"—see Hartman, *Wayward Lives*, 306. See also McDowell, *"Changing Same."*

55 I'm elaborating here on a conception of formal development that pushes against widespread mechanistic views of an African musical origin "surviving" despite its mutation and evolution. While such opinions have been largely discredited when discussing culture at large, they still hold considerable currency when discussions turn to music. My disagreements with this position were put forward previously in *Lying up a Nation* and in my exchange with the late Samuel A. Floyd Jr. See Floyd and Radano, "African-American Musical Past," 1–10. Levine proposes a more useful portrait of stylistic evolution, being particularly insightful in recognizing how White practices had become informed by African American ones, suggesting a greater "mulatto" character to American music at the moment when Black styles entered free markets. But he ultimately falls back on a mechanistic argument to explain why subsequent interracial musical exchanges took place. See Levine, *Black Culture*, 195–96.

56 Although Baraka recognizes how Black music developed dialectically, he is ultimately dismissive of those African American forms created outside of the cultures of slavery and the Black poor, and that appear openly indebted to European musical traditions and aesthetics. Yet if "the constant and willful dilutions" of Black music by "mainstream" society and the Black middle class challenged musical "form," they could not disturb the "emotional significance and vitality at its core, [which] remains, to this day, unaltered" (131). It is unclear how one locates undiluted form. Nonetheless, value seems to grow not from interracial musical interaction, but as the result of racial struggle, its "core" intensifying and remaining unchanged.

57 I borrow "mute music" from Adorno's characterization of a unique temporality and truth content embedded in the form of a phonograph record: "It is not the time in which music happens, nor is it the time which music monumentalizes by means of its 'style.' It is time as evanescence, enduring in mute music." See Adorno, "Phonograph Record," 279. I reintroduce and develop the concept in chapter 8.

58 Du Bois, *Black Reconstruction*, 125; *Gift of Black Folk*, 105.

59 It is interesting to note how Du Bois contemplates meaning directly when, in chapter 14 of *Souls of Black Folk*, he asks, "What are these songs, and what do they mean?" (187). He proceeds to write movingly about musical power, revealing the effect of value's production in its relation to meaningful musical imagining. For a discussion of the relationship of Du Bois's dialectics to Hegelian phenomenology, see Shaw, *Du Bois*.

60 Du Bois, *Gift of Black Folk*, 9, 10, 19, 105. Blight, "Du Bois," 49.

61 My conception of phenomenological shifts at once constituted within and outside of capitalism is indebted to Dipesh Chakrabarty's discussion of History 1 and 2. See *Provincializing Europe*, 47–71. I develop this

conception across the study. Also important to my thinking about past-time is Guha, *History at the Limit*.

62 As Massimiliano Tomba explains it, "Formal subsumption is the basis of capitalist production insofar as the production of surplus-value is a process aiming at the production of commodities for sale; real subsumption is presented, instead, as specifically capitalist because it not [sic] longer tolerates the existence of previous social relations, but revolutionises the technical processes of production and social groupings." See Tomba, *Marx's Temporalities*, 148–49.

63 "The Negro as Non-American: Some Backgrounds" is the title of the first chapter of Baraka's *Blues People*.

64 Harootunian, *Marx After Marx*, 26; Liu et al., "Exigency of Time," 25. Earlier, Harootunian states, "One of the major functions of the modern state has been to synchronize the various temporalities of capital, smooth the discordant rhythms of capitalist time" (15). Narrative emplotments contribute to this synchronization.

65 Adorno and Eisler, *Composing for the Films*, 20–21.

66 This corresponds to Harootunian's depiction of capitalism's evening-out and making sense of the order of everyday experience: "One of the major functions of the modern state has been to synchronize the various temporalities of capital, smooth the discordant rhythms of capitalist time." See Liu et al., "Exigency of Time," 15.

67 Gilroy, *Black Atlantic*, 202. Gilroy's conceptualization of the "Black Atlantic" as a temporality rather than as a spatiality mutes somewhat Brent Edwards's critique of Gilroy's study, particularly when we read Gilroy against more recent elaborations by David Scott and Bayo Helsey. See Edwards, "Uses of Diaspora"; Scott, "That Event, This Memory"; Holsey, "Embodying Africa." For a fascinating elaboration on syncopated temporality as a condition of modernity writ large, see Moreno, *Sounding Latin Music*.

68 "For most slaves," Levine observed in his analysis of Christian and African-based folk beliefs, "there was no unbridgeable gulf between [them]." *Black Culture*, 56. References to Africa appear frequently in the WPA narratives. The interviews have been published as part of the digital collections of the Library of Congress as *Born in Slavery*. See also Abrahams, *Singing the Master*; Stuckey, *Slave Culture*; Gomez, *Exchanging Our Country Marks*.

69 Levine's *Black Culture and Black Consciousness* is especially helpful in this regard. See also my book *Lying up the Nation*.

70 Mbembe, "People and Things." For knowledge networks, see Kodesh, *Beyond the Royal Gaze*, 20–26; Schoenbrun, "Pythons Worked," 216–46. Europe's colonization of Africa inspired a flurry of studies of indigenous cultural practices. See, for example, Kingsley, *West African Studies*, and, in German, the works of Karl Weule and Leo Frobenius.

71 As an anthropological concept, "animism" is commonly attributed to E. B. Tylor, who borrowed the term from a seventeenth-century alchemist. See Bird-David, "'Animism' Revisited," S67–S91, and with specific reference to the African diaspora, Johnson, *Spirited Things*. For historical discussions of sound, instruments, and animated forces, see Kodesh, *Beyond the Royal Gaze*, 155; Vansina, *Paths in the Rainforest*, 151; MacGaffey, *Kongo Political Culture*, 88–92; Stoller, *Embodying Colonial Memories*, 34–35; Matory, *Fetish Revisited*, 236–48.

72 For "voices of the dead," see MacGaffey, *Kongo Political Culture*, 88. Soyinka, "Appendix: The Fourth Stage," 144, in *Myth, Literature and the African World*. Soyinka's comment is consistent with MacGaffey's depiction of Kongo political culture at the turn of the twentieth century: "There are no good answers to the question whether the rocks 'represent' or 'contain' the spirits. The 'otherworld' of Kongo thought, the land of the dead (*nsi a bafwa*), is as it were in the next room, around the corner, or even right here, for those who have eyes to see" (57). See also Friedson, *Remains of Ritual*, and Jane I. Guyer's discussion of "real person" in "Wealth in People," 246.

73 Levine, *Black Culture*, 56–61. For "zombi," see Baptist, *Half Has Never Been Told*, 146.

74 Levine gives us particularly strong insight into the conspicuous presence of Africanity in Christian beliefs, writing that "there existed as well a network of beliefs and practices independent of yet strongly related to the slaves' formal religion"; "Africa," one slave reported, "was a land of magic power. . . . The descendants of Africans have the same gift to do unnatural things." Levine, *Black Culture*, 55, 57. I've revised the original text, which appeared in minstrelized dialect.

75 Pietz, "Problem of the Fetish." The second and third installments appeared in subsequent issues of *Res: Anthropology and Aesthetics*. See also Tsing, "Sorting Commodities," 21–43.

76 Mackey, *Bedouin Hornbook*, 20.

77 Paddison, *Adorno's Philosophy of Music*, 1. Jarvis discusses "cognitive character" in chapter 5 of *Adorno*.

78 Baskerville, "Free Jazz," 484–97. In rejecting the term *jazz*, Beaver Harris, in a conversation with Valerie Wilmer, proposes something akin to sonic material: "Jazz itself is only a mixture of all the music before your time. This is the reason why I prefer calling it Black Music" (qtd. on 486). Challenges to the term *jazz* reach back to Ellington's notion of "beyond category" and carry forward to the philosophical views of Anthony Braxton and other experimentalists working today.

79 On James Reese Europe's characterization of *ragtime* as a term invented by the music industry, see chapter 4 in this volume. Du Bois's reference to the songs of the enslaved as "sorrow songs" appeared to be an attempt to revise minstrelized conceptions of them.

80   Davis, *Emancipation Circuit*. I wish I could say more about this remarkable book, which appeared after chapters 2 and 3 of my book were drafted and revised.

81   Hurston, "How It Feels," 215–16.

82   Baraka, *Digging*. Baraka's states in his introduction that his book draws inspiration from Du Bois's *Black Reconstruction*. Simone White offers a compelling critique of Baraka's execution in *Dear Angel of Death*. Du Bois, "Color Line," 30.

CHAPTER 1. SLAVE LABOR AND THE EMERGENCE OF A PECULIAR MUSIC

1   Northup's approach to fiddling was probably informed by British Isle performance traditions, with possible intersections with Africanized intonations and beat organization.

2   Julia Kristeva's theorization of abjection as a repression of ambiguities in subject-object relations carries important implications when thinking about the legal form of the slave body and, particularly, when coupled with notions of the acoustic. One might begin such a pairing with Erlmann, "Acoustic Abject." See also Kristeva, *Powers of Horror*.

3   On the fiddler as precious commodity—"Negro fiddlers were scarce among the plantation hands, except the 'professionals' who were free negroes"—see "Negro Superstition," 329–30.

4   There is an extensive literature on inalienable possessions. For background, see Weiner, *Inalienable Possessions*; Bennett, *Vibrant Matter*; Gordon, *Ghostly Matters*.

5   Hesse, "Symptomatically Black."

6   "Species of property" was commonly employed in primary historical sources. For a modern, secondary reference, see Hahn, *Nation Under Our Feet*, 71. Locke continues, "The Labor of his Body, and the Work of his Hands, we may say, are properly his." Locke, "Property." For "Attached to the soil," see Schweninger, *Black Property Owners*, 146. For "recoordination," see Johnson, *River of Dark Dreams*, 162.

7   Johnson, *Soul by Soul*. Berry, *Their Pound of Flesh*.

8   Patterson, *Slavery and Social Death*. For "natal alienation," see Roberts, *Freedom as Marronage*, 17.

9   "Organized whole" appears in Bastiat, "Social Order." See also Wilentz, *Rise of American Democracy*, 791; Foner, "Meaning of Freedom"; Huston, *Calculating Value*; Einhorn, *American Taxation, American Slavery*.

10   McCord, "Slavery and Political Economy," 435. Hegel, *Philosophy of World History*.

11   Arendt, *Human Condition*; Martin, "Mortgaging Human Property."

12 Baptist, "Toxic Debt." See also Baptist, *Half Has Never Been Told*. The fundamentally racial basis of the southern economy also made Whiteness a critical form of property. See Harris, "Whiteness as Property." See also Stanley, *From Bondage to Contract*; Keysaar, *Right to Vote*.

13 Beckert, *Empire of Cotton*.

14 The quotation appears in Hall, "Race, Articulation," 32. Marx's depiction of plantation owners as capitalists appears in Choat, *Marx's Grundrisse*, 513. For Genovese, see *Roll, Jordan, Roll* and *From Rebellion to Revolution*. For a succinct assessment of Genovese's position, see Johnson, "Pedestal and Veil," and other essays in the same issue.

15 Johnson, *Chattel Principle*, 8–9.

16 Beckert and Rockman, *Slavery's Capitalism*; Clegg, "Capitalism and Slavery."

17 Patterson, *Slavery and Social Death*. For an important critical elaboration, see Brown, "Social Death."

18 Chakrabarty, *Provincializing Europe*, 67.

19 Daina Ramey Berry explores how monetary value of slaves affected social status in "We'm Fus' Rate Bargain."

20 White and White, *Sounds of Slavery*. Long, *Pictures of Slavery*; Campbell, *Negro-Mania*, 192; Castelnau, "Essay on Middle Florida," 243; Olmsted, *Seaboard Slave States*, 394; Criswell, "*Uncle Tom's Cabin*," 69. For more on Black music as noise, see Radano, *Lying up a Nation*.

21 For the mouth-gag description, see "Miscellaneous Department," 4; Grandy, *Narrative of the Life*, 28.

22 Thompson, "Work, Discipline."

23 Ingraham, *Sunny South*, 51; Roper, *Narrative*. For a discussion of bell attachments, see Smith, *Listening*, 73–75; Dresser, *Narrative*, 6–7. For slave coffles, see Bibb, "Plantation Song," 40; Rankin, *Letters on American Slavery*, 45–46; Davies, *American Scenes*, 94; Featherstonhaugh, *Excursion*, 36–37.

24 Best, *Fugitive's Properties*. For prohibitions on singing, see Smith, *Listening*, 79. For "at every turn," see Hall, *Travels in Canada*, 354. For Tom and Cajah, see, respectively, entries for Carter Braxton (July 28, 1768) and Fendall Southernland (September 20, 1783), in Windley, *Runaway Slave Advertisements*, 1:61, 219.

25 For "half starved," see "Levee at New Orleans," 13–14; for rowers in Georgia, Hall, *Travels in Canada*, 216; for porters, Coke, *Subaltern's Furlough*, 236–37. For a depiction of youths hawking sweet potatoes and pears, *Cries of New-York*, 20–22.

26 For stowing cotton, see Harris, *Remarks Made*, 69; *Cries of New-York*. New York formally abolished slavery in 1827. *Cries* was first published in 1809.

27 Smith, *Listening*, 20; Berlin, *Slaves Without Masters*, 236. Van Der Merwe situates Black musical performance within this labor context in *Origins of the Popular Style*, 63–65.

28 That is, a productive force in ways akin to G. A. Cohen's characterization of food in his book *Karl Marx's Theory of History*, 52. Elsewhere, Cohen argues against slave religion as a productive force, in spite of its productive consequence, reaffirming in this instance Marxian orthodoxy: "This result plainly contradicts the intent of Marx's theory" (33). Gang labor was in place across the southern territories west of the coastal Low Country.

29 Tatler, "Management of Negroes," 63. Tatler explains that if the slaves are not "brisk," then they should be beaten. Miles Mark Fisher observes, moreover, "in slavery days, songsters were paid to increase the work upon southern plantations by inducing the laborers to sing. These 'singing bosses,' who had a variety of designations, were usually women; they were also heard in Haiti." Fisher, *Negro Slave Songs*, 21. The source of this rich quotation is unknown; Fisher's citation of Henry Osgood is incorrect.

30 For "allers good singers," see [Olmsted], "Mississippi Home," 1. For "mere sounds," see Smith, *Listening*, 69. Neither were the disciplining capacities of singing lost on the slaves themselves. "A silent slave is not liked by masters or overseers," Frederick Douglass famously wrote. "This may account for the almost constant singing heard in the southern states." Douglass, *My Bondage*, 97.

31 Abdy, *Journal of a Residence*, 3:103. The ballad's lyric appears on 3:104.

32 On performances on the auction block, see Southern, *Music of Black Americans*, 159; and Johnson, *Soul by Soul*. Saidiya V. Hartman provides a fascinating discussion of both slave coffles and the auction block in the first chapter of *Scenes of Subjection*.

33 Brown's comment appears in Hartman, *Scenes of Subjection*, 36–37.

34 Brainerd, "Dinky," 206–12. For de Crévecouer, see Smith, *Listening*, 15. Moten employs this anomaly to suggest the basis of a "freedom drive" and the quality of the "scream" that precedes and is embedded in an otherwise thingly ontology. See "Aunt Hester's Scream," the first chapter of *In the Break*.

35 Hentz, *Planter's Northern Bride*, 409. Although the quotation derives from a novel, it is the author's depiction that is important here. Sobel, *World They Made Together*, 34, 37.

36 Watkins, *Struggles for Freedom*, 12.

37 Stowe, *Uncle Tom's Cabin*, vol. 2, chap. 20, 33. For the story about Lavinia Bell, see Blassingame, *Slave's Testimony*, 341–45.

38 For Cartwright, see Smith, *Listening*, 69.

39 Roger D. Abrahams discusses harvest performances in *Singing the Master*.

40 Paine, *Six Years*, 184. For "The negro is as full of music," see Long, *Pictures of Slavery*, 26; for "none wanted voice," see "Visit to a Negro Cabin," 242.

41 Epstein, "Slave Music," 382.

42   For resorts, see Dunaway, *Slavery*. For carnivals and steamboats, Epstein, "Slave Music," 382. See also Buchanan, *Black Life*; Kleber, *Encyclopedia of Louisville*. On the general practice of slave hiring, see Martin, *Divided Mastery*.

43   Epstein, for example, reports of a free Negro who trained three slaves. "Slave Music," 382. "Surplus" here is not, strictly speaking, surplus value, in the Marxian sense. But it did effectively create capital, profit that could then be invested culturally.

44   For Walker, see Epstein, "Slave Music," 383; Northup, *Twelve Years a Slave*, chaps. 6, 13, 15. On training slaves to hire out for parties, see MacLeod, "Musical Instruments," 45.

45   For Black firemen, see "Negro Music"; Olmsted, *Seaboard Slave States*, 114–15. The references to "temporal vibrations" and "barbarisms" are from G. W. F. Hegel. See Lippman, *Musical Aesthetics*, 117. Creecy, *Scenes in the South*, 20–21; for Seward, see Marsh, *Jubilee Singers*.

46   For "improvisatored," "making tubes," and "Such music," see "Negro Music." Gates, *"Race," Writing, and Difference*, 8; Allen, Ware, and Garrison, *Slave Songs*.

47   Hindemann, "Concert Life," 199–200. For the physician's remark, see Hartman, *Scenes of Subjection*, 44.

48   Stampp, *Peculiar Institution*, 368.

49   On the virtual silence, see Radano, *Lying up a Nation*, chap. 2.

50   Singleton, *Letters*, 101.

51   Voskuhl, *Androids of the Enlightenment*. Missing in this otherwise important study is consideration of the automaton in the context of Atlantic slavery's rapid expansion.

52   Hartman, *Scenes of Subjection*. I discuss the public discourse of "spirituals" in *Lying up a Nation*, chap. 4.

53   Hartman, *Scenes of Subjection*, 74.

54   Erlmann, *Reason and Resonance*, 14–15. Sterne, *Audible Past*, 15.

55   Parrish, *American Curiosity*, 259–60.

56   Tatler, "Management of Negroes."

57   Allewaert, *Ariel's Ecology*. For an introduction to a massive literature on African and African-diasporic supernaturalism, see MacGaffey, *Kongo Political Culture*; Brown, *Reaper's Garden*; Sweet, *Domingos Álvares*; Parks and Sansi, *Sorcery in the Black Atlantic*. On social death, see Brown, "Social Death"; Sweet, "Defying Social Death."

58   Pietz, "Problem of the Fetish," 6–7. See also Pels, "Spirit of Matter"; Morris, "Fetishism"; Matory, *Fetish Revisited*.

59   Richard Leppert, commentary, in Adorno, *Essays on Music*, 88; Paddison, *Adorno's Aesthetics of Music*, 57, 14. Paddison stresses that Adorno's notion of truth is related to the evolution of "musical material" and is historical in character: "For Adorno, truth lies in the particular, which evades the

universalizing tendency of conceptual thought. But the 'truth-content' of musical works is historical and concerns the way in which works, through the particularity of their form, attempt to deal with the antinomies of the handed-down musical material, which are seen as social in origin" (15). See also Jarvis, *Adorno*; Richter, "Aesthetic Theory."

60 Floyd, *Power of Black Music*; Gomez, *Exchanging Our Country Marks*; Durkheim, *Forms of Religious Life*.

61 Among the many, see Matory, *Fetish Revisited*, esp. chap. 8, "Commodities and Gods," and its subsection "The Drums, Too, Are Alive."

62 Hornbostel, "African Negro Music," 59. At the time, Hornbostel was director of the Berlin Phonogram Archive (Das Berliner Phonogrammarchiv).

63 I'm thinking here of Steven Feld's early critique of absolute distinctions between oral and written "cultures" as proposed by Walter Ong and others. See Feld, "Orality and Consciousness."

64 Parrish, *American Curiosity*, 260. Allewaert elaborates on the significance of Parrish's argument in *Ariel's Ecology*, 21. Gates, *Signifying Monkey*. For Marx's comments, see "Chapter 10: The Working Day," *Capital*, 1:342.

65 See, for example, Stampp, *Peculiar Institution*, 67–72; 414–15. Steven Hahn writes: "We may well have underestimated the extent to which slaves in a great many locales—with or without their owners' approval—bought, sold, and bargained with merchants, shop keepers, peddlers, and neighboring Whites." *Nation Under Our Feet*, 27.

66 Penningroth, *Claims of Kinfolk*, 81, 83.

67 Penningroth, *Claims of Kinfolk*, 6, 83–86; for conjure as labor, 101–2.

68 Gilroy, *Black Atlantic*, 37.

69 Anderson, "Letter from a Freedman." He continued, "Surely there will be a day of reckoning for those who defraud the laborer of his hire."

70 For Hicks, see "Local News Items," 3; for Fennell (who died on his way to perform at a party "with his band"), see "Local News," 3; for Abram, and for elaboration on the hiring of slave musicians, see Ping, "Black Musical Activities," 149.

71 Northup, *Twelve Years a Slave*, 216. For Walker, see Epstein, "Slave Music," 383.

72 One report noted how the singing of a "burly-headed negro" driving a wagon drew the attention of the writer, who gave him a bit to explain his gifts in raising vegetables and poultry. "Scenes of the West," 67–69. Whiskey was a recurring theme. Charles Lanman described how a boat captain "treated his negro boatmen to a drink of whiskey, which was a signal for them to march to the bow of the boat for the purpose of singing a song." See Lanman, *Adventures in the Wilds* 2:149. See also Criswell, "Uncle Tom's Cabin," 66–67; Bibb, *Narrative*, 23. For coins, see Kirke, *Among the Pines*, 146.

73 The conception of Negro music as an illicitly retained possession carried a particular significance after political legislation and judicial rulings—notably, the Fugitive Slave Act of 1850 and *Dred Scott v. Sandford* in 1857—reaffirmed the slaves' fundamental legal status as a form of property.

74 Hartman discusses stealing away in *Scenes of Subjection*, 65–70. For nighttime rituals, see Camp, *Closer to Freedom*, chap. 3. It is important to stress, nonetheless, that the claims about "stealing away" have been so overdetermined that it is impossible to know its actual history. That said, Dorothy Scarborough's characterization may be the source for its modern iterations. See *On the Trail of Negro Folksongs*, 22–23.

75 For pinkster, see White, "Pinkster in Albany, 1803," 191–99; for "foolish and ridiculous," see Castelnau, "Essay on Middle Florida," 205. Olmsted, *Seaboard Slave States*, 114–15. Olmsted is quoting a Virginia correspondent to the *New York Times*.

76 Sweet, *Domingos Álvares*, 130–31. For the use of pots as a vocal disguise, see Blench, "Nigeria." For an example of the tub as a muffler of sound—"a big wash-tub full of water in the middle of the floor to catch the sound of our voices when we sung"—see Albert, *House of Bondage*, 12.

77 On "spirited thing," see Matory, *Fetish Revisited*, xix; Johnson, *Spirited Things*.

78 Gilroy, *Black Atlantic*, 197. Gilroy here is noting how "much of the material discussed" in his book conflicts with Euro-modern temporalities as a means of exploring his analysis of Black memory and the slave sublime. I'm indebted to his characterization of racialized memory in his brilliant chapter 6, which he begins strategically (187) with Walter Benjamin's well-known portrayal of the historical past from his "Theses on the Philosophy of History." The past, Benjamin writes, is not "'the way it really was'" but something that "flashes up in a moment of danger." For cognitive character, see Paddison, *Adorno's Aesthetics of Music*, 15. Jarvis discusses cognitive character in *Adorno*, chap. 5.

79 Chakrabarty, *Provincializing Europe*, 64, 68. This different order, as "fleeting glimpse" (69), is what Chakrabarty designates as History 2, an affective, phenomenological realm constituted within and against capitalism, yet existing recognizably prior to and outside of capitalism (History 1), even as capital itself, in its constitution of abstract labor as "living," possesses a parallel, inherent contradiction. Notably, the recognition of History 2 as a realm prior emerges only after and within capitalism. Raymond Williams also considers this sense of possibility attached to performance. See "Base and Superstructure."

80 Castro, "Exchanging Perspectives," 479; Marcuse, "Remarks," cited in Spillers, "Idea of Black Culture," 13.

81 Lewis, *Across the Atlantic*.

82 Marx, *Capital*, 1:152.

83 Trux, "Negro Minstrelsy," 72–79. Allen, Ware, and Garrison, *Slave Songs*, introduction.

84 Marx, *Capital*, 1:166.

CHAPTER 2. SCABROUS SOUNDS OF A VAGRANT PROLETARIAT

1   Abbott and Seroff, "They Cert'ly Sound Good," 413–14. In *Segregating Sound*, Karl Hagstrom Miller writes, "Between about 1910 and 1914, the blues became the new musical marker of Black authenticity" (150). This observation might be place alongside W. C. Handy's comment that he composed *Memphis Blues* in 1909. If we can trust John J. Niles's memory, we do have his recollection of "blues" lyrics performed by Ophelia "Black Alfalfa" Simpson in 1898 that followed an AAB form. Niles, "Shout, Coon, Shout!," 519–20.

2   Brown, "Reification, Reanimation," 182. The term *vaudeville*—likely from the French *voix de ville* (voice of the city)—is usually employed to describe staged variety acts. The acts took place principally in New York City, spreading widely as their popularity grew from the 1880s. According to Karen Sotiropoulous, African American performers entered these venues during this same period, and particularly in the early 1900s, as "vaudeville had replaced minstrelsy as America's favorite form of popular theater." Although the term is now applied loosely to all Black stage theater, including colored minstrelsy, I'm limiting its application to the larger, twentieth-century acts appearing mainly in the urban North. See Sotiropoulous, *Staging Race*, 44.

3   Abbott and Seroff, "They Cert'ly Sound Good," 413. For the use of ventriloquism in blackface minstrelsy, see Lott, *Love and Theft*, 19.

4   Seltzer, *Bodies and Machines*, 3. Horkheimer and Adorno saw the rise of Tin Pan Alley as a cultural "machine which rejects anything untried as a risk." *Dialectic of Enlightenment*, 106.

5   Gaines, *Uplifting the Race*, 21. For background, see Foner, *Reconstruction*; Blackmon, *Slavery by Another Name*; Freehling, *Road to Disunion*.

6   Hungerford, *Old Plantation*, 185.

7   MacLean, *Freedom Is Not Enough*, 6.

8   In his essay "The Plantation Negro," Julian Ralph evokes a sense of the racial picturesque: "To me, the colored folks form the most interesting spectacle in the South. . . . It is delightful to see them. Those open waterways flowing between grassy banks and towards the west end might seem offensive otherwise, but when at every few hundred feet a calm and placid negro man, or a mammy with a brood of moon faced

pickaninnies sprawling beside her, is seen bent over the edges, pole in hand, the scenery becomes 'picturesque'" (38). On the picturesque, see Silber, *Romance of Reunion*, 66–92; Litwack, *Trouble in Mind*, 10–11.

9   Sotiropoulos explores the political force of Black performances when they did not conform to the expectations of White power. See, for example, her analysis of the stage acts of Ernest Hogan, and Williams and Walker, which incited race riots in Manhattan around 1900. *Staging Race*, 42–44. Dvořák's comments appear as part of a lengthy, unsigned article, "Real Value of Negro Melodies," 28.

10   The 1911 compendium *Monarchs of Minstrelsy* by Edward Le Roy Rice makes plain the objective of access: the 360-page work lists over a thousand show musicians, nearly all of them White men, who fashioned stage personas in the image of Sambo, minstrelsy's subject of choice.

11   This would suggest that Black music's cultural ownership could not be adequately understood simply as a use value. Its use, as we will see, occupied a greater range of valuation, informing exchange in ways exceeding the typical relationship of use and exchange. Moreover, the limitations of access to Black music would impact African American reception once it began to flow conspicuously and repeatedly within the distribution mechanisms of reproduction.

12   *Merriam-Webster's Collegiate Dictionary*, 11th ed. (2020), s.v. "scabrous."

13   Notably, Gilroy's discussion of Frederick Douglass in his struggle with Covey, together with his elaborations on "the slave sublime" in chapters 2 and 6 of *Black Atlantic*: "The turn towards death also points to the ways in which black cultural forms have hosted and even cultivated a dynamic rapport with the presence of death and suffering" (198).

14   Sklansky, "Elusive Sovereign," 237. In his compendium *Old Slack's Reminiscence*, Utley lists over one thousand professional stage performers.

15   "The federal census by 1890 reported a total of 1,490 Black 'actors and showmen' in the United States, none in legitimate drama." See Utley, *Old Slack's Reminiscence*, x. By the early 1900s, Black musicians such as the young Eubie Blake were earning as much as fifteen to eighteen dollars per night performing in Baltimore sex houses. Farm laborers were, in contrast, earning seventy-five cents per day. See Gilbert, *Product of Our Souls*, 104.

16   For elaboration on these performance categories, see Odum, "Folk-Song and Folk-Poetry," 258–61.

17   Abbott and Seroff, "They Cert'ly Sound Good," 403. W. C. Handy makes reference to quartet singing in a saloon in *Father of the Blues*, 23. David Robinson describes the career path of a saloon fiddler in *W. C. Handy*, 43.

18   "Negro Love of Music," 9.

19   Moxley quoted in Robertson, *W. C. Handy*, 63. Handy, *Father of the Blues*, 33. On vaudeville, see Gebhardt, *Vaudeville Melodies*; Snyder, *Voice of the City*.

20   Abbott and Seroff, *Out of Sight*, 19, 60–65, 106–7. For more on Hicks, see Southern, *Music of Black Americans*, 232–33.

21   "Negro Love of Music," 9.

22   Gilbert, *Product of Our Souls*, 69. Patrick Joseph O'Connor's account of minstrel and medicine shows at the Whitley Opera House in Emporia, Kansas, during the 1880s lists several colored troupes that performed there. See O'Connor, "Minstrel and Medicine Shows."

23   Stanley, *From Bondage to Contract*, 126.

24   Ike Simond, for example, notes how an otherwise unknown group, Billy Anderson's Minstrels, suddenly disbanded due to mismanagement and lack of funds. See Utley, *Old Slack's Reminiscence*. In his introduction to *Reminiscences*, moreover, Robert Toll notes that such were "problems that plagued so many small minstrel troupes" (xx). Abbott and Seroff identify a touring party based at Memphis's Savoy Theater that didn't receive pay after a performance in Vicksburg, Mississippi, in 1910. "They Cert'ly Sound Good," 431.

25   Odum, "Folk-song and Folk-Poetry," 258. For background on musicians' lives, see Wharton, *Negro in Mississippi*.

26   Miller, *Segregating Sound*, 68. See Adam Gussow's provocative reading of jook violence in *Seems Like Murder There*, 201–11. Tom Fletcher remembers a Black barber growing up in Portsmouth, Ohio, who only accepted White customers. See Fletcher, *100 Years*, 6.

27   Frantz Fanon proposes those of the lumpen, the peasant class—degraded in traditional Marxian analysis for lacking class consciousness—to be potential revolutionaries because they, unlike the urban proletariat, are sufficiently distant from the dominant ideology. He presents this idea in several instances in *Wretched of the Earth*.

28   Fletcher, *100 Years*, 7, 9, 22. He ultimately regretted that obsession, as will be discussed in the next section. On the relationship with Conn, see 21.

29   Handy, *Father of the Blues*, 3.

30   Handy, *Father of the Blues*, 76–77.

31   Handy, *Father of the Blues*, 77.

32   Sotiropoulos, *Staging Race*, 43; Fletcher, *100 Years*, 8–14. See also Hunter, *To 'Joy My Freedom*, 125; Wagner, *Disturbing the Peace*.

33   For wandering musicians, see Hearn, "Black Varieties," 4. "Wandering Minstrels," 60–61; the essay discusses Black vagrant musicians in multiple northern and southern cities. Offenbach, *Orpheus in America*, 136–38.

34   Handy, *Father of the Blues*, 74. For difficulties finding places to sleep, see Fletcher, *100 Years*, 13.

35   Handy, *Father of the Blues*, 11; Stanley, *From Bondage to Contract*, 126.

36   On the pleasurable habit of work, see Rancière, *Nights of Labor*; Quashie, *Sovereignty of Quiet*.

37   Dietz and Steingo, "Experiments in Civility," 44.

38   Both quotations appear in Virno, "Virtuosity and Revolution," 189.

39   On Hegel, see Snead, "Repetition," 63. For more on Black music and repetition, see Radano, *Lying up a Nation*. Noteworthy is the discussion of J. F. Watson (115–17).

40   Peabody, "Notes on Negro Music," 151.

41   "Jubilee Singers," *Dwight's Journal*, 131–32.

42   Tanke, *Rancière*, 25–26. Tanke is paraphrasing Rancière.

43   Graeber, "Value," 450.

44   Virno, "Virtuosity and Revolution," 191–92, 194; Lazzarato, "Immaterial Labor," 137.

45   On the political mobilizations of Black grassroots activists, see Hahn, *Nation Under Our Feet*. Hartman, *Wayward Lives*, 143.

46   Denning, *Noise Uprising*. Denning's analysis focuses on the impact of high-fidelity recording in the making of a new body of global vernacular sound, whose worldwide distribution supports a modern politics of decolonization.

47   Webb, "Notes on Folk-Lore," 290, 292, 296.

48   Webb, "Notes on Folk-Lore," 292. For a brief discussion of "Dallas Blues" and Hart Wand, see Davis, *History of the Blues*, 59. Amid his discussion of the racial characteristics of Negro performance, Peabody describes how workers sang popular tunes, notably "Goo-Goo Eyes" and the virulently racist "The Bully Song." "Notes on Negro Music," 151.

49   Rancière, *Dissensus*, 140–42. See also Panagia, "Partage du sensible," 95–103.

50   Brooks, "Laughing Song."

51   Johnson recorded multiple versions beginning in 1890. See Brooks, *Lost Sounds*, chaps. 2 and 3. Also appearing during this time were the mechanized "Nigger banks" that depicted a Black man recovering a penny. For an analysis of these banks in the wider context of uncanniness, see Brown, "Reification, Reanimation," 175–207.

52   Brooks, *Lost Sounds*; 32; Wagner, *Disturbing the Peace*, 185.

53   Wagner, *Disturbing the Peace*, 186.

54   Brooks, *Lost Sounds*, 17.

55   Brown, *Sense of Things*, 5–6. Brown, "Reification, Reanimation," 181.

56   Wagner, *Disturbing the Peace*, 196.

57   Thanks to Tsitsi Jaji for a valuable exchange about the Africa references in Johnson's lyric.

58   Europe, "Negro Explains 'Jazz,'" 28–29.

59   Bernault, *Colonial Transactions*.

60   Fletcher, *100 Years*, xvii.

61   Fletcher, *100 Years*, xvii.

62   Trotter, *Highly Musical People*; Tanke, *Rancière*, 2.

63   Fletcher, *100 Years*, xvii.

64 Fletcher, *100 Years*, 18.

65 Fletcher, *100 Years*, xvii.

66 Hahn, *Nation Under Our Feet*, 45–46.

67 Levine, *Black Culture*, 57. Levine reprints the original quotations as they appeared in minstrel dialect in the publications of the WPA narratives. I've revised them. The interviews have since been published as part of the digital collections of the Library of Congress as *Born in Slavery: Slave Narratives from the Federal Writers' Project, 1936–1938*.

68 Hahn, *Nation Under Our Feet*, 47.

69 Hahn, *Nation Under Our Feet*, 230. An important new perspective on the nature of political organization in postemancipation churches is Turner, *Soul Liberty*.

70 Spillers, "Moving," 44, 48–49; italics in the original.

71 Hahn, *Nation Under Our Feet*, 185.

72 Lordi, *Meaning of Soul*, 8.

73 Hanchard, "Afro-Modernity." See especially the subsection "Temporality: Racial Time." Hanchard writes, "A key distinction between labor and capital on the one hand and slaves and slave owners on the other is that while the former involved the politics of labor power under capitalism the latter was rooted in *total* labor. Theoretically, no time belonged to the slave. . . . This racial time was a more 'total' imposition of a dominant temporality than an abstract, acultural labor time" (256).

74 Rancière, *Emancipated Spectator*, 103–4. Tanke, *Rancière*, 105.

75 Rancière, *Emancipated Spectator*, 103.

76 Hunter, *To 'Joy My Freedom*, 147–48; Ravenel, "Recollections," 774. Ravenel wrote his essay in February 1876. Heilbut, *Gospel Sound*, xxxii–xxxiii.

77 Harry Harootunian's conception of the everyday as an experience under the suppression of authoritative histories of the nation-state has been influential in my thinking about meaning. See "Shadowing History."

78 Barton, "Hymns of the Slave," 609.

79 "Negro Love of Music," 9. On handkerchiefs worn by women during shouts, see "Magazines for June," 432–33.

80 Ravenel, "Recollections," 774.

81 "No Bodily Resurrection," 7. The "relic of paganism" took the form of a Black funeral where mourners spoke of how "the spirit of the dead might be about the mourners."

CHAPTER 3. MINSTRELSY'S INCREDIBLE CORPOREALITIES

1 For Blind Tom, see "From the Camp," 1; for the Alabama writer, "Negro Love of Music," 9. For banjo players, see Finck, "Mammy's Song," 604–5. For poems, see Wallaschek, *Primitive Music*, 60.

2   Lott, *Love and Theft*, 25.

3   Ellison, "Change the Joke," 53.

4   For Connecticut lawmakers, see "Connecticut"; for Boston rioters, "Mayor of Boston," 1; for segregation, "Color-Phobia," 162; for Van Buren, "Subjoined Toasts," the latter also appearing in other newspapers.

5   Handy, *Father of the Blues*, 33.

6   Printed coon songs appeared as part of a larger commercial initiative to publish popular music in the nineteenth century. For background see Holibaugh and Krummel, "Documentation of Music Publishing." See also Crawford, *America's Musical Life; American Musical Landscape*.

7   The Whigs became known as coons after adopting the coonskin hat—associated with Davy Crockett—to win the White rural vote. See Roediger, *Wages of Whiteness*, 98. Toll, *Blacking Up*; Dormon, "Shaping the Popular Image."

8   David Gilbert suggests that Hogan's own portrayals in the song were not derogatory or intended to be. See Gilbert, *Product of Our Souls*. The vocal score purportedly marks the first published use of the term *rag*.

9   Wiegman, *American Anatomies*, 94. For studies of lynching's symbolism, see Young, *Embodying Black Experience*; Patterson, *Rituals of Blood*.

10   Dennison, *Scandalize My Name*, 388, 394.

11   Dennison, *Scandalize My Name*, 99–100; "Tanned Human Skin," 5.

12   Dennison, *Scandalize My Name*, 255. Like "Negro menace," "Negro problem" was a familiar expression in writing about African Americans, becoming common after the publication of Booker T. Washington's *The Negro Problem* (1903) and W. E. B. Du Bois's reply at the opening to *The Souls of Black Folk*, published the same year: "How does it feel to be a problem?"

13   "Superstitions of Negroes," 330. References to Black people's purportedly superstitious nature showed up repeatedly in the nineteenth century. For example, Ravenel asserted that "the negroes had many superstitions, most of them probably brought over from Africa, and handed down by tradition in the families, besides those which are common wherever ignorance prevails." "Recollections," 775.

14   "Tanned Human Skin," 5. The author tells a related tale of a young man who brings the toe bone of a Negro cadaver into a saloon and places it in a customer's drink.

15   Trux, "Negro Minstrelsy," 72–79. On the detritus of the Civil War, see Blight, *Race and Reunion*, 155; Silber, *Romance of Reunion*, 69, 77, 80, 93; Hilyer, "Relics of Reconciliation," 35–62; Nelson, *Ruin Nation*. On the ritual practice of seeking relics after lynchings, see Patterson, *Rituals of Blood*, 194–97.

16   There is an enormous literature on the concept of the relic. For background relevant to the United States at the turn of the twentieth century, see Brown, *Sense of Things*. See also Geary, "Sacred Commodities."

17   For King Herod, "Relic of Olden Days," 7; for Peter Dudley, a 108-year-old man, see "Quaint Old Negro," 5; for Rebecca Whale, "Last Slave of Kentucky," 13; "Relic Hunters at Corsicana," 1; for relic hunters in Maysville, see "Ashes of Lynched Negro," 5; "He Left a Finger," 1; "Cruelly Tortured," 3; Schomburg, "Lynching a Savage Relic," 8.

18   Trux, "Negro Minstrelsy," 72; Allen, Ware, and Garrison, *Slave Songs*, xiv. "No Bodily Resurrection," 7; Krehbiel, *Afro-American Folksongs*, 38–39. Hearn made his assertions to Krehbiel in a letter, stating that "the blood of the African black has the highest temperature known." Although Krehbiel voiced skepticism, he also chose to publicize Hearn's position, thereby giving validity to it (39). In this light, it is interesting to consider a later report on African "witchcraft" as a "relic of a bygone age." See "Zulu Witch Doctor," 47.

19   Krehbiel, *Afro-American Folksongs*, ix. The book's wide circulation is one indicator of the extent of its reception. Its addition to public libraries was recorded in local newspapers from Tulsa, Oklahoma, to Jackson, Michigan, to Portland, Oregon. See the "New Books" entries in *Daily Tulsa World*, 12; *Jackson Citizen Patriot*, 7; and *Morning Oregonian*, 11. Coleridge Taylor's arrangements of melodies published in Krehbiel's book were performed at a society club meeting in Colorado Springs. They were mentioned in the *Colorado Springs Gazette*, November 1, 1914, 29. A brief review of the book appeared in *The Nation* 98 (March 19, 1914): 311–12.

20   Stadler, "Never Heard Such a Thing," 99.

21   Averill, *Four Parts, No Waiting*, 33.

22   Patterson, *Rituals of Blood*, chap. 2, 201. Patterson's criticism develops from the research of the psychophysicist Trygg Engen, whom he is quoting. Patterson and Engen appear unaware of a legacy of study of how music possesses similar, and perhaps superior, powers of evocation. MacConnell, "Sights and Spectacles," 423. MacConnell is referring to Peirce's example of spectacle in a Shakespearean performance.

23   "Southern States Furnish," 29. The drawings in figure 3.2 depict the struggle over tariff protections in the South. The first illustrates the industrial benefit of protections. In the second, the White man is voting democratic, against his own interests, while the Black Republican exercises his, with ballot in hand.

24   "Chased by Spook Table," 7; "Theatrical Review," *Chicago Defender*, 6. In its June 15, 1918, issue, the *Defender* published a review of "Spooks," "the first ebony comedy to be exhibited in this neighborhood," See "Spooks," 13. A Google Ngram of "spook" and "Negro" documents equivalences dating back to the early 1800s, with a rapid escalation beginning around 1920. W. C. Handy, for example, refers to the "Boogie-house music" of sex workers in *Father of the Blues*, 79.

25   Ramsey, "Cosmopolitan or Provincial?," 11–42. There was copious coverage in Black newspapers of the challenges facing African American classical musicians. For one example—pianist Blind Boone's difficulty finding a hotel after a performance—see "Where is Paola?"

26   Ravenel, "Recollections," 774. Ravenel's essay from 1876 sought to describe "the old life" of plantation slavery, which was still very much in the present among Black southerners. For a discussion of the concept of "wandering melody," see Bohlman, *Study of Folk Music*, 26.

27   Jay, "Music Among the Negroes," 8. *Music Record* reprinted the article first published in the *Sun*.

28   For "rude mouth organ," E. Brainerd, "Plantation Music," 534; for coon skin drum, Jay, "Music Among the Negroes," 8; for vocalist as bagpipe, Peabody, "Notes on Negro Music," 152. Carl Wittke describes a "colored" performer, John Armstrong, who portrayed on stage "the Alabama Slave" and "imitated steam calliopes, planeing [sic] mills and dogs." See Wittke, *Tambo and Bones*, 92. For an elaboration on vocalized imitations, see Abbott and Seroff, *Out of Sight*, 93; for fiddling sounds and guitar slide, Chambers-Ketchum, "Music in the South," part 3, 7–8. Handy describes a Mississippi guitarist employing a knife slide in *Father of the Blues*, 74. For speech effects and train locomotion, see Odum, "Folk-Song and Folk-Poetry," 26. For "a colored man," see Jay, "Music Among the Negroes," 8.

29   "Chin-Music," 347. The illustration appears on 344.

30   "Chin-Music," 347.

31   "Chin-Music," 347.

32   For assertions of African linkages, see, for example, Fortier, "Customs and Superstitions," 136–38; for "ear music," see Chambers-Ketchum, "Music in the South," 7–8.

33   For "syncopated melodies," see Peabody, "Notes on Negro Music," 149; Finck, "Mammy's Song," 604–5; Jay, "Music Among the Negroes," 8.

34   Radano, "Hot Fantasies."

35   Hunter, *To 'Joy My Freedom*, 66.

36   Ralph, "Plantation Negro," 39; For "fetish follies" and imitating immigrants, see Hunter, *To 'Joy My Freedom*, 68, 151.

37   Du Bois, *Gift of Black Folk*, 9.

38   Allen, Ware, and Garrison, *Slave Songs*, iv.

39   Peabody, "Notes on Negro Music," 148–52. For an elaboration of Peabody's dig in relation to blues history, see Gioia, *Delta Blues*, 20–22. "Goo-Goo Eyes" likely referred to Hughie Cannon, comp., and John Queen, lyr., "Just Because She Made Dem Goo-Goo Eyes" (1900). It was recorded by Silas F. Leachman on Victor Records in 1901. "Bully Song" was Charles E. Trevathan's 1896 coon song popularized by the singer May Irwin.

40   Peabody, "Notes on Negro Music," 151.

41   Handy, *Father of the Blues*, 76–77. For background on Bolivar Hall, see
     "Enlightenment of W. C. Handy."

42   On worker hours, see Roediger and Foner, *Our Own Time*, 177–207.
     Foner, *Reconstruction*, 405.

43   Harvey, "Working Day," in *Companion to Marx's "Capital,"* 135–62.
     Harvey's lectures on the book are illuminating. They are available on
     YouTube.

44   Ingersoll, "City of Atlanta." For background, see Blight, *Race and Reunion*.
     For "more of the life," see Foner, *Reconstruction*, 395.

45   Ingersoll, "City of Atlanta," 43.

46   Ingersoll, "City of Atlanta," 43. Tera Hunter notes that Shermantown was
     one of Atlanta's few sites of interracial mixing. See *To 'Joy My Freedom*,
     152–53.

47   Ingersoll, "City of Atlanta," 43.

48   Penningroth, *Claims of Kinfolk*, 6.

49   Weiner, *Inalienable Possessions*, 39.

50   Rancière, *Nights of Labor*; "Chin-Music."

51   Ike Simond makes reference to Lucas's departure from the profes-
     sion without elaboration. See Utley, *Old Slack's Reminiscences*, 9. In this
     context, it is good to bear in mind how blackface could be reconceived
     without regard to White supremacist interpretation. See, for example,
     Cole, *Ghana's Concert Party Theatre*.

52   Interestingly, Bert Williams complained that he could only present one
     side of the stereotype, not that he had to perform the stereotype in the
     first place. See Snyder, *Voice of the City*, 121. Paul Laurence Dunbar sim-
     ilarly bemoaned the appeal of his dialect poetry among White readers,
     which he felt inhibited his artistry. See Gaines, *Uplifting the Race*, 182.

53   Tomba, *Marx's Temporalities*, 136.

54   Tomba, *Marx's Temporalities*, 137; Postone, *Time, Labor*, 288–91; Du Bois,
     Souls of Black Folk, 187; Chakrabarty, *Provincializing Europe*, 251.

55   Chakrabarty, *Provincializing Europe*, 251.

56   As Thomas L. Riis puts it in his review of recent literature, "the general
     state of research pertaining to American popular music in the mid- to
     late nineteenth century is, at best, woefully incomplete." See his untitled
     review, 252.

57   Brooks, *Bodies in Dissent*; Abbott and Seroff, *Out of Sight*, 333–34; Sampson,
     Ghost Walks. Sampson's occasional descriptions of performances—"their
     chants and shouts are very peculiar"—and documentation of groups
     such as the "Couchee Couchee Girls" are nonetheless intriguing (105,
     116). He also records an instance in Titusville, Pennsylvania, in 1876,
     where a "colored person" holding a ticket received as a gift from a White
     man gained admission to a Whites-only theater (27). David Gilbert

presents a valuable list of colored troupes culled from his examination of advertisements in the *Indianapolis Freeman*. See *Product of Our Souls*, 60–61.

58   Utley, *Old Slack's Reminiscence*.

59   Utley, *Old Slack's Reminiscence*, 24–26, 8, 6, 17, respectively.

60   Utley, *Old Slack's Reminiscence*, 25.

61   Locke, *Negro and His Music*, 59.

62   Sotiropolous discusses the secret language but also embraces a characterization of Black creativity as a "push against stereotypes" (*Staging Race*, 46–47, 61).

63   Brooks, *Bodies in Dissent*, 25.

64   Utley, *Old Slack's Reminiscence*, 27; Du Bois, *Gift of Black Folk*, 9.

65   "Black Varieties," 4.

CHAPTER 4. RAGTIME'S DOUBLE-TIME ACCUMULATION

1   "Funeral of Ragtime," 7. It is unclear if the error in misspelling Dvořák's name was Sousa's or the newspaper's.

2   See, for example, "Sousa Says Ragtime Is Dead." Sousa's Band toured Europe in 1900, 1901, 1903, and 1905. From 1910 to 1911, he and his band embarked on a world tour. See Bierley and Hitchcock, "Sousa, John Philip." See also Hitchcock, "Sousa." For background on Sousa as an edifier of taste, see Harris, "John Philip Sousa." Jeffrey H. Jackson discusses how French press reports associated Sousa's performances with African American music. See *Making Jazz French*, 83–84.

3   Sousa's performed arrangements included "Whistling Rufus," "At a Georgia Camp Meeting," "Southern Hospitality." See Hamm, *Music of the New World*, 295. On Sousa's use of ragtime in encores, see "Sousa at the Hippodrome," 9. For reports of ragtime's decline, see Berlin, "Ragtime"; and Berlin, *Ragtime*, 41. For Sousa's international popularization of ragtime, see Hamm, *Music of the New World*, 295; and Magee, "Ragtime and Early Jazz," 392.

4   For "never die," see Berlin, *Ragtime*, 49. Patrick Warfield argues that such calculations were part of Sousa's agenda since his days leading the US Marine Band, when, after practicing acts of piracy himself (orchestrating from piano/vocal scores works by other composers without permission), he became a fierce advocate of composers' ownership rights. Sousa played an instrumental role in the signing of the 1909 Copyright Bill into law. See Warfield, "John Philip Sousa," 455. Sousa's rejection of ragtime was consistent with his efforts to manipulate consumer behavior and legal representation to his own advantage at a time

when sheet-music sales of popular tunes were still booming. See also Suisman, "Selling Properties," chap. 5 of *Selling Sounds*. On sheet music's boom from 1890 to 1905, see Banner, *American Property*, 115–16.

5 Walton, "Is Ragtime Dead?," 6. The size of the group was not indicated. Thanks to Dave Gilbert who called my attention to this article. Reid Badger discusses the same essay in his book *Life in Ragtime*, 50–51.

6 Dvořák's influence was noted by Sylvester Russell, a columnist for the Indianapolis *Freeman*, in 1904. Quoted in Abbott and Seroff, "They Cert'ly Sound Good," 420.

7 Walton, "Is Ragtime Dead?," 6.

8 Walton, "Is Ragtime Dead?," 6. Europe is referring to the third movement, "In Darkest Africa (Nigger in the Woodpile)." See Bierley, *John Philip Sousa*; and Bierley, *Incredible Band*. I'm grateful to Scott W. Schwartz of the Sousa Archives at the University of Illinois for his help in locating the suite and section and to Jame E. Wintle and John Fenn of the Library of Congress for providing a reproduction of Sousa's original score. A film comedy from 1904 was released under the same name. See Stewart, "Introduction," in *Migrating to the Movies*.

9 Walton, "Is Ragtime Dead?"

10 For "ancient," see Trux, "Negro Minstrelsy," 72–79. For "blood thumping," see Moderwell, "Ragtime," 285.

11 Harris, "John Philip Sousa," 218.

12 Rogers, *John Philip Sousa*. According to Scott W. Schwartz of the Sousa Archives, the third movement was first published by Church in 1896. The Sousa Band's cylinder recording was produced as "Three Quotations, No. 3," Edison Amberol 889 (1908). It is available in digitized form: "Three Quotations, No. 3: Nigger in the Woodpile [Quotations]," UCSB Cylinder Audio Archive, http://www.library.ucsb.edu/OBJID/Cylinder9210. In the performance, musicians employ other effects attributable to Black music, such as the cornet's wah-muting in the first repetition of the A theme.

13 Although not formally involved in the exposition, Black performers who would later become known as ragtime musicians—Ben R. Harney, Jesse Pickett, Scott Joplin—purportedly played in nearby locales. See Horowitz, "World's Columbian Exposition."

14 *The Nigger in the Woodpile*, 1860. *Oxford English Dictionary* lists its first appearance in Dan Emmett's "'Twill nebber do to gib it up So!" (1843): "Nigger on de wood-pile barkin like a dog." Its usage continued across the twentieth century. See *Oxford English Dictionary*, 3rd ed. (2003), s.v. "Nigger, Phrases."

15 For "prophecies of doom," see Berlin, *Ragtime*, 41–42. For "passed its zenith" and "anxious to lay," see "War on Ragtime," 4, cited in Berlin, *Ragtime*, 41; for "gradually losing favor," see Hubbs, "What Is Ragtime?," 345, cited in Berlin, *Ragtime*, 41. An advertisement for "Band Concerts" in

the *Evening Star* (Washington, DC) from June 16, 1916, 22, for example, lists "Nigger in the Woodpile" among the works to be performed by the United States Soldiers' Home Band under the direction of John S. M. Zimmermann. For an analysis of decline conceits in debates about African Americans at the time, see the chapters "Vanishing Negro" and "Negro as Beast" in Fredrickson, *Black Image*.

16   For an elaboration on this period, see Snyder, *Voice of the City*. By this time work opportunities for musicians were improving. The 1910 census lists a total of 54,858 musicians and teachers of music in the United States, of which 3,374 were "Negro" and 14,526 "foreign-born white." See Harris, "Occupation of Musician," 299–311.

17   While "Turkey in the Straw" is typically associated with the tradition of Irish fiddling and the musical basis of "Zip Coon," Ralph Ellison asserted in his interview with Hollie West that it was composed by a Black musician. See Singh and Graham, *Conversations with Ralph Ellison*, 245. On the employment of White "recorders" beginning in the 1890s, see "African American Performers." Berlin, *King of Ragtime*, 86.

18   Gilbert, *Product of Our Souls*, 53, 87. On Black composers reframing the African American past, see also 41–46, 67–68.

19   For background on White ragtime composers, see Jasen, *Ragtime*. Among the appendixes in Blesh and Janis, *They All Played Ragtime*, moreover, is a list of ragtime compositions and their publishers. Many of the ragtime works composed by Black musicians were published by John Stark. Edward Berlin provides an outline of group varieties in *Ragtime*, 8, 10.

20   Berlin, *Ragtime*, 123–46.

21   W. C. Handy, who incorrectly credits Hill with composing "After the Ball" (he wrote "At the Ball, That's All"), notes that many White customers were unaware that the publisher Gotham-Attucks, Co. specialized in works by Black composers. See Handy, *Father of the Blues*, 108. Tim Brooks reports that Victor Records did not refer to Europe as an African American musician on the recordings it produced by him. See *Lost Sounds*, 274. Peabody, "Notes on Negro Music," 150–51.

22   White ragtime pianists included Mike Bernard, J. Russel Robinson, Pete Wendling, Clarence Gaskill (composer of the Cab Calloway theme song "Minnie the Moocher"), and others. See pianola.co.nz and Bill Edwards's ragpiano.com.

23   Berlin notes how "Maple Leaf Rag" was a standout for admiration across the races. *Ragtime*, 74–75.

24   Berlin and Dickinson, "Words and Music," 104–5, cited in Berlin, *Ragtime*, 17n12. See also Hamm, *Irving Berlin*, vi. "Maple Leaf Rag" appeared on piano rolls produced by dozens of makers. See Jasen, *Ragtime*, 471.

25   Simmel, "Metropolis and Mental Life" (1902–1903), in *Sociology of Georg Simmel*, 412.

26   For "symbolic of," Berlin, *King of Ragtime*, 88. He is quoting Walter
      Winston Kenilworth. For background on stylistic changes, including
      a succinct analysis of the deracination of ragtime, see Berlin, *Ragtime*,
      123–46; Gilbert explores the rise of ragtime in New York's black Tender-
      loin district in his book *Product of Our Souls*.

27   Suisman, *Selling Sounds*. Berlin offers a generalized model for early rag-
      time form in *Ragtime*, 97–98. Frederick Edward Snyder similarly argues
      that vaudeville established a model for mass production, its productions
      resembling the interchangeable parts of machine structures. See "Amer-
      ican Vaudeville." On the early manufacture of records, with attention to
      labor practices, see Liebersohn, *Music and the New Global Culture*.

28   The comment was quoted in the *Chicago Defender*. See "Mechanism of the
      Player Piano," 8.

29   For musician-labor opportunities arising from 1910, see Badger, *Life
      in Ragtime*, 52–53. On the presence of African American musicians on
      Broadway and, from 1911, in clubs and restaurants, see Berlin, *King of
      Ragtime*, 215. Gilbert, *Product of Our Souls*, supplies a valuable overview in
      its chapters on Black nightclubs and ragtime in Times Square.

30   Europe is quoted in Walton, "Is Ragtime Dead?"; Berlin, *King of Ragtime*,
      89. "What Is American Music?," cited in Berlin, *King of Ragtime*, 89.

31   For "modernized savage," see Farjeon, "Rag-Time," 796, cited in Berlin,
      Ragtime, 40–41.

32   "Down In Jungle Town" was featured on several recordings, including
      Arthur Collins and Byron G. Harlan's release on Victor in 1909.

33   Berlin, "Kerry Mills." On the reference to "Rastus on Parade" as a work of
      ragtime, see Berlin, *Ragtime*, 82. "Rastus on Parade"; "Rastus on Parade:
      A Song of Color." Dunbar, "Colored Band," 44–46. On dialect poetry, see
      Jones, *Strange Talk*. He discusses "The Colored Band" on 191.

34   References to "hot" ragtime reach back to the nineteenth century, as
      in Theodore Metz's "A Hot Time in the Old Town Tonight" (1886). See
      Thacker, "Hot (i)." On the concept of hot rhythm, see my essay "Hot
      Fantasies."

35   According to Rupert Hughes ("Eulogy of Ragtime," 158), for example,
      these included dance-based instrumental practices, largely deriving
      from banjo figurations, percussive interjections of clapping, stomping,
      and shouting, and the infusion of Latin American rhythmic asymme-
      tries showing up in the works of Gottschalk and others.

36   The sentimentality of ragtime grew with the success of the Hollywood
      film *The Sting* (1973), which featured Joplin's "Maple Leaf Rag" and various
      ragtime-inspired renditions composed by Marvin Hamlisch.

37   For Ives, see Berlin *Ragtime*, 49; Moderwell, "Ragtime," 285. Some Black
      ragtime composers sought to demystify the practice of ragging. In his
      contribution to Walton's "Is Ragtime Dead?," for example, J. Tim Brymn

laid out a reasonable definition: "To begin with, ragtime, or syncopated music, is the effacing or shifting the accent of a tone or chord falling on a naturally strong beat by tying it over from the preceding weak beat; a tone or chord thus changed is called 'ragtime.' This we find in the classics as well as the ordinary 'coon songs.'" Brymn goes on to object to calling all of his works "ragtime" since he did not always employ the ragging practice.

38   For a discussion of the evolution of syncopation in ragtime, see Berlin, *Ragtime*, 81–89. Hasse, "J. Russel Robinson," 2. On Bernard, see the comments of W. N. H. Harding in Jasen, *Ragtime*, 117–19.

39   Hyer, "Tonality."

40   Gilbert, *Product of Our Souls*. Europe, "Negro Explains 'Jazz,'" 28–29.

41   On musical training, see Gilbert, *Product of Our Souls*, 4.

42   Johnson and Johnson, *Second Book*, 16.

43   On Tenderloin musicians, see Gilbert, *Product of Our Souls*, 120–21. Davin, "Conversation," 55. The story about Keppard appears in numerous places. See, for example, Shipton, *New History of Jazz*, 98. For vaudevillians—referring to Handy—see Abbott and Seroff, "They Cert'ly Sound Good," 437–38. In *Father of the Blues*, Handy spoke of hearing distinctive rhythms in Cuba, which he "tucked away" (99–100). Weule, *Negerleben in Ostafrika*, 52. As written in the original German—the singer was presumably speaking Swahili—"lebe wohl, meine Stimme!" Berliner, *Soul of Mbira*, 253.

44   For Johnson on White musicians claiming credit, see "Poor White Musician," 4. For Europe, see Brooks, *Lost Sounds*, 276. For "virulent poison," see "Respectively: 'Musical Impurity,'" 16, cited in Berlin, *King of Ragtime*, 88.

45   For Winner (publishing under the pseudonym Alice Hawthorne), see Southern, *Music of Black Americans*, 116; for Hogan, see Gilbert, *Product of Our Souls*, 27–28. (Hogan would later learn to negotiate, earning royalties on his song "All Coons Look Alike to Me.") For Williams and Walker, see "William and Walker Letter." I'm indebted to David Gilbert for sharing a copy of this letter with me. For Handy, see *Father of the Blues*, 116; for Laine and LaRocca—Laine crediting Yellow Nunez and Achille Baquet as its composers—see Parsonage, *Jazz in Britain*, 137–38, and Maskell, "Who Wrote"; for Joplin, see Berlin, *King of Ragtime*, 210, 238.

46   "After ragtime has swept the world and become universally known as American music, there has [sic] been attempts to rob the Negro of the credit of originating it." Johnson, "Poor White Musician," 4. For "taken away from him" see Johnson, *Second Book*, 16. For Still on Handy, see Still, "Negro Music," 92; for Fletcher, see *Tom Fletcher Story*, 316.

47   For George Walker, see Gilbert, *Product of Our Souls*, 58. For "Ragtime . . . ever since," see Walton, "Use of Vulgar Words," 6, cited in Berlin, *King*

of *Ragtime*, 222; for Joplin, "syncopators," see "Theatrical Jottings," 6, cited in Berlin, *King of Ragtime*, 226; for Joplin, "original with colored people," see Walton, "Use of Vulgar Words," 6; for Europe, see Brooks, *Lost Sounds*, 276, and Europe, "Negro Explains 'Jazz,'" 28–29.

48 Johnson, "Negro's Contribution," 26–27. The quotation from 1915 appeared in his essay "Poor White Musician."

49 Through deft maneuvering, Europe secured better-paying jobs for Black musicians at New York parties and restaurants. See Gilbert, *Product of Our Souls*, 132–62; for "laws of nature," 58. Europe resigned from the Clef Club at the end of 1913. See Brooks, *Lost Sounds*, 274.

50 *Religious Folk Songs*. For Moton's second comment, see Foreman, "Jazz and Race Records," 11. Bechet, *Treat It Gentle*, 114; for "a valuable and much-needed gift," see Johnson, "Negro's Contribution," 26–27; for "true American music," see Moderwell, "Ragtime," 286.

51 Sotiropoulos, *Staging Race*, 20; Krasner, "Real Thing," 99–123.

52 In *Product of Our Souls*, David Gilbert underscores the musicians' commitments to racial thinking, particularly in his important sixth chapter, "Rhythm Is Something That Is Born in the Negro." I'm indebted to Dave for many long conversations about this history as he prepared his remarkable book.

53 Johnson, "Negro's Contribution," 27.

54 Moderwell, "Ragtime," 286. The sociologist Robert Levine expands on this notion of characteristic urban tempos. See a discussion of his work in the context of jazz in Dinerstein, *Swinging the Machine*, 33–34.

55 Brooks, *Bodies in Dissent*, 272. Brooks outlines various critical interpretations in her chapter on Williams and Walker while setting aside the matter of whether or not the entertainers were strategic or literal in their claims of racial difference. Kevin K. Gaines discusses how Black elites employed "dark Africa" as a strategy for claiming racial superiority. See *Uplifting the Race*, 38–39. Miller, *Segregating Sound*, 149–50. For "appeal universally," see Johnson, "Negro's Contribution," 27. Writing in the *New York Age* in 1913, Joplin wrote similarly, "The other races throughout the world are learning to write and make use of ragtime melodies. It's the rage in England to-day." Quoted in Berlin, *King of Ragtime*, 222.

56 Du Bois, *Souls of Black Folk*, 186, 40.

57 Ellison, "Richard Wright's Blues," 78.

58 One testament to the perception of Black music as an unsubsumable residue is Nellie Sylvester and William Osborne's song, "Nigger, nigger never die" (1897).

59 Bert Williams, comp., and Alex Rogers, lyr., "Nobody" (1905). Butler's essay, first published in 1911, was reprinted in Scarborough, *Humorous Ghost Stories*, 69–88.

60 My interpretation of Bechet stems from Bryan Wagner's reading. He proposes that Bechet's grandfather becomes Bras-Coupé, as he claims Congo Square and its sound world as cultural property: "It was *his* drums, *his* voice, *his* dancing," Bechet wrote. Wagner, "Disarmed and Dangerous," 138; Odum, "Folk-Song and Folk-Poetry," 255–94. For blues lyrics, Gussow, *Seems Like Murder There*. Waters's account of "Stringbeans and Susie" appears in her autobiography, *His Eye Is on the Sparrow*. Her description is reprinted in Abbott and Seroff, *Original Blues*, 100.

61 For "screaming comedy" and "hot ragtime," see Gushee, *Pioneers of Jazz*, 119, 134. For "solid and groovy," see Davin, "Conversation," 50.

62 Johnson, "Poor White Musician," 4; the *Freeman* quote appears in Abbott and Seroff, "They Cert'ly Sound Good," 425; capitalization in the original.

CHAPTER 5. NEW COALESCENCES OF SPECTACULAR FORM

1 Johnson and Johnson, *Books of American Negro Spirituals*, 12; Du Bois, *Black Reconstruction*, 121.

2 Du Bois, *Black Reconstruction*, 121.

3 Davin, "Conversation," 50.

4 Harlem was already an entertainment destination for racially mixed crowds, particularly after the African American entrepreneur Barron Wilkens opened Barron's Exclusive Club in 1903. Little Africa was the name of an area on the edge of the Lower East Side, including Broome Street. See Flowe, *Uncontrollable Blackness*, 77, 69. Blesh and Janis locate the Jungle between 61st and 63rd, moving west from Tenth and Eleventh Avenues to the Hudson River. See *They All Played Ragtime*, 194. Johnson stated to Davin—when referring to the Black area of Hell's Kitchen—that the Jungle stretched from 60th to 63rd Street, west of Ninth Avenue ("Conversation," 48). Johnson observed that most of those who came to the basement were from South Carolina. Blesh and Janis write, "The area settled around 1900 by the influx of Negroes from Alabama and the so-called Geechees (or Gullahs) from the Charleston area" (*They All Played Ragtime*, 194). They discuss Johnson's childhood on 190.

5 Davin, "Conversation," 49–50. For "hot groove," see Blesh and Janis, *They All Played Ragtime*, 203. The editors of *The Slave Songs of the United States* observed that "in the form here described, the 'shout' is probably confined to South Carolina and the States south of it." Allen, Ware, and Garrison, *Slave Songs*, 15.

6   Johnson's use of the term *groove* is probably anachronistic. I have not observed instances where musicians or critics employed the term during the time prior to jazz.

7   Blesh and Janis, *They All Played Ragtime*, 203–4. On the rhythmic innovations of stride, see Schuller, *Early Jazz*, 214–25.

8   Davin, "Conversation," 48; Blesh and Janis, *They All Played Ragtime*, 194, 188, 148.

9   Johnson remembers first hearing boogie-woogie piano playing in 1914. Davin, "Conversation," 54, 49. Blesh and Janis, moreover, suggest that Texas-born pianists brought boogie-woogie to Chicago around 1908 (*They All Played Ragtime*, 148–49). But "boogie" seemed to refer to a variety of approaches at the time. What Wilbur Sweatman performed on his 1917 Pathé recording, "Boogie Rag," sounds far from what would become the standard practice. (For more on boogie, see chapter 9.) Moreover, although Blesh and Janis argue that piano shouts trace back to early ragtime, this appears to be mere conjecture. Without recorded evidence, we cannot assume that hot ragtime playing from the 1890s resembled stride, which more likely was an invention specific to New York in the 1910s. Henry Martin, finally, provides an informative investigation into Johnson's variation techniques, although he seems to deem them inferior to improvisational approaches later developed in jazz, even as he concludes "we must not thoughtlessly attribute our latter-day understanding of improvisation to early forms of jazz" (296). See "Balancing Composition and Improvisation."

10   Davin, "Conversation," 52. Over the course of the same interview (44–61), which took place in 1953, Johnson details the musical background of several players. For details on Giannini, who was both a vocal and piano instructor, including his work with Johnson and Scott Joplin, see Piras, "Garibaldi to Syncopation." His discussion of Johnson and Giannini appears on 112–15. For further details see Rose, *Eubie Blake*, 12–13; Taylor, "Luckey Roberts"; Dobbins, "Smith, Willie 'The Lion.'"

11   Schuller, *Early Jazz*, 217–18; Davin, "Conversation," 53.

12   "Magazines for June," 432–33.

13   Johnson characteristically varies the call/response practice. Compare his 1918 and 1921 piano rolls to his disc recordings from 1921 and 1944. For the complete transcription, see Scivales, *Harlem Stride Piano Solos*. The transcription is based on Johnson's 1944 recording on LP, Swaggie S 1211. The excerpt in figure 5.1 appears on 36.

14   Variation would have been a principal means by which string players developed form. Such techniques were also likely practiced by piano players from Atlanta to St. Louis to Dallas. For Blake's comment, see Blesh and Janis, *They All Played Ragtime*, 195–96. Seminole, who was

born in 1904 and died in 1932, was playing in the 1920s. For Graham, see Flowe, *Uncontrollable Blackness*, 69.

15   For Ellington, see Gilbert, *Product of Our Souls*, 100. Ellington was referring to the pianist and leader Willie "the Lion" Smith.

16   Hartman, *Wayward Lives*, 4; Davin, "Conversation," 48.

17   On Johnson's presence in the Tenderloin, see Brooks, *Lost Sounds*, 25; Davin, "Conversation," 51–55. He names these and others over the course of the conversation. On Abba Labba, see Blesh and Janis, *They All Played Ragtime*, 194.

18   Hartman, *Wayward Lives*, 4, 8.

19   Tanke, *Rancière*, 2.

20   Locke, *Negro and His Music*, 61.

21   Adorno, *Aesthetic Theory*, 341.

22   Rancière, *Dissensus*, 140–42.

23   Hartman, *Wayward Lives*, 284, 103, 4, 235; emphasis in the original.

24   Schuller, *Early Jazz*, 217, 219.

25   Attali, *Noise*, 91; Steintrager and Chow, *Sound Objects*, 7–8. Pierre Schaeffer introduced the concept of *objet sonore* (sound object) in a 1966 publication that appears in English translation as *Treatise on Musical Objects*.

26   For "Negroes take better," see Brooks, *Lost Sounds*, 30. Carter, "Vox Americana," 31. For "a voice that is uncommonly," see Wagner, *Disturbing the Peace*, 190. On slave-song transcriptions, see Radano, *Lying up a Nation*, chap. 4. Recorded examples of the first Black performances can be accessed via the Library of Congress online source, "African American Performers." For an invaluable forty-four-CD documentation of early recordings by Black performers in Europe, see Green, Lotz, and Rye, *Black Europe*.

27   Taylor, "Commodification of Music," 298–99. For "automatic piano," see Montgomery, Tichenor, and Hasse, "Ragtime on Piano Rolls," 90–91. See also Ord-Hume, "Player Piano."

28   An appendix to the published sheet music provides an optional arrangement of the chorus, "Choice Chorus, with Negro 'Rag' Accompaniment Arr. by Max Hoffman." See Berlin, *Ragtime*, 27.

29   Percy Wenrich, "Memphis Rag" (1908); Tom Turpin, "St. Louis Rag" (1903); Richard Hoffman, "I'm Alabama Bound" (1909); Callis W. Jackson, "Texas Rag" (1905); W. C. Powell, "Missouri Rag" (1907); Albert Gumble, "Georgia Rag" (1910); George L. Lowry, "Florida Rag" (1905). As Berlin observes, William Krell's "Mississippi Rag" (1897) offered yet another domestic geographical reference, it being scored for band. See Berlin, "Ragtime." For documentation on these and other rags, see Jasen, *Ragtime*. On "Louisiana Rag," see Jasen and Tichenor, *Rags and Ragtime*, 70.

30   George Cobb, "The Baboon Bounce" (1913); E. Philip Severin, "Jungle Time" (1905); H. A. Fischler, "Rastus Rag" (1909); Gertrude Cady, "Tar

Baby Rag" (1909); Harry C. Thompson, "Watermelon Trust" (1906); Thomas E. Broady, "Whittling Remus" (1900); H. A. Fischler, "Nigger-Toe Rag" (1910).

31 For ads in the *Freeman* and *Defender*, see "Big Removal Sale"; "Mid-Summer Clearance"; "Blues! Blues! For the Player Piano" (recurring ad); "Latest Hits, Sheet Music"; "Dreazen Grafonola Shop." For a society report describing a Ladies' Club entertained by a hostess "on her beautiful pianola," see "Aurora, Ill." For a joke about the noise of a pianola, see "Between Two Fires"; for a discussion of the piano's design, see "Mechanism of the Player Piano."

32 Berlin, "Scott Joplin." For a list of piano-roll manufacturers producing versions of "Maple Leaf," see the "Ragtime Piano Rollography" in Jasen, *Ragtime.* According to Jasen's list, eight manufacturers produced sixty-five-note rolls, early forms that largely gave way to the eighty-eight-note standard by the end of the first decade of the twentieth century.

33 For a discussion of Joplin's agreement with the publisher of "Maple Leaf Rag," see Berlin, *King of Ragtime*, 54–56. Joplin probably received something for the hand-played piano rolls he made in 1916, a year before his death. They are discussed later in this chapter. On US copyright law and phonographic reproduction, see Banner, *American Property*, 109–29.

34 Jordan, *Machine-Age Ideology.*

35 Jentsch, "On the Psychology of the Uncanny"; Freud, *The Uncanny*; Freud, *Totem and Taboo*, 28–29. (The 1990 translation has a new subtitle.) Thanks to Tony Vidler for alerting me to Freud's early usage of the term in *Totem and Taboo.* Bill Brown restores Jentsch's importance to the history of the uncanny concept in "Reification, Reanimation," 197–99.

36 Sterne, *Audible Past*, 287–334. For Edison, see Attali, *Noise*, 91.

37 Sterne, *Audible Past*, 311–32. Johannes Fabian discusses the use of phonographs in the delirium of early European ethnology in central Africa in *Out of our Minds*, 109–14. See also Shelemay, "Recording, Technology," 277–92; Liebersohn, *Music.*

38 Brown, *Sense of Things*, 27–28; Brown, "Reification, Reanimation," 175–207.

39 Johnson, "Player Piano." Ord-Hume, "Player Piano." On player pianos designed on the model of industrial looms, see Noble, *Forces of Production*, 147–50. Holland, Ord-Hume, and Sitsky, "Reproducing Piano." "History of the Pianola." A useful website contains biographies of several early company-employed pianists and arrangers working in the piano-roll industry. See "Saving the Music of Yesterday," accessed July 26, 2024, http://www.pianola.co.nz/public/.

The website notes that the arranger, Mary Allison, who worked for Vocalstyle, was responsible for introducing a "marimba effect" (rapid tremolos), the effect similarly employed by Alfred Robson Gillham, also for Vocalstyle. Montgomery, Tichenor, and Hasse, moreover, describe a tremolo effect invented by the arranger Mary E. "Mae" Brown, together with a simulation of instrumental strumming heard on many Connorized rolls, the latter achieved by slightly delaying the articulation of pitches in chordal and octave statements. See "Ragtime on Piano Rolls," 95–97. For "machine cut," see Jasen, "Piano Ragtime Rollography," appendix 2 in *Ragtime*. Major manufacturers, such as the Aeolian Company, created their own lending libraries. See McBride, "Roll Lending Libraries."

40   Hasse, "J. Russel Robinson." Robinson was the composer of the popular hit "Cannibal Love" and performed many hand-played rolls manufactured by Imperial and QRS. On Robinson's work for Imperial and QRS, see Jasen, *Ragtime*, 221. Jasen notes that QRS employed Robinson's "colored fingers" tag in its catalog (221).

41   Boone was producing hand-played rolls as early as 1912. See Montgomery, Tichenor, and Hasse, "Ragtime on Piano Rolls," 94.

42   Brown, "Reification, Reanimation," 181. Brown continues, "Our reluctance to think seriously about things may result from a repressed apprehension—the apprehension that within things we will discover the human precisely because our history is one in which humans were reduced to things (however incomplete that reduction)" (207).

43   The piano rolls were recorded on the LP *Scott Joplin—1916*. Francis Bowdery lists "Pleasant Moments" among Joplin's hand-played Connorized rolls from 1916, which is not included on the Biography LP. See Bowdery, "Schools of Ragtime." For "true to the individuality," see Taylor, "Commodification of Music," 298. Jasen's "Rollography" includes rolls produced by Black performers in the 1910s. See Jasen, *Ragtime*.

44   *Scott Joplin—1916*. Even if Joplin could have played the passages it is unlikely that he would have wanted to do so. Despite the tendency among performers to paraphrase and reinvent passages, Joplin frowned on the practice. In his pedagogy book, *School of Ragtime* (1908), Joplin wrote, "We wish to say here, that the 'Joplin ragtime' is destroyed by careless or imperfect rendering." Cited in Berlin, *Ragtime*, 77. Bowdery, "Schools of Ragtime," 60. On Joplin's illness, see Berlin, *King of Ragtime*, 215, 237.

45   See Melton, "Ragtime Compositions." Melton identifies the arranger as "William Axlmann." Other sources name him "Axtmann." Chris Schoenberg's website, pianola.co.nz, notes that during World War I, Connorized anglicized Axtmann's name, calling him "Arlington." See his website for commentary on Axtmann's own playing style.

46   For the canonized reproductions of "Maple Leaf Rag," see Williams, *Smithsonian Collection of Classic Jazz*; Gates and McKay, *Norton Anthology*.

47   Rose, *Eubie Blake*, 150. For a close analysis of Joplin's hand-played rolls, which includes a provocative assessment of the Aeolian release—the

author claiming they sound more plausible when reproduced at a slower tempo—see Bowdery, "Schools of Ragtime."

48   Best, *Fugitive's Properties*, 55–56. See also Brooks, "Puzzling the Intervals."

49   For profiles and discussions of recordings by these artists, see Brooks, *Lost Sounds*. The artists' names appear in the table of contents.

50   The quotation is cited in Foreman, "Jazz and Race Records," 29.

51   Montgomery, liner notes to *Scott Joplin–1916*.

52   Baraka, "Changing Same," 180–211. Sewell, "Temporalities of Capitalism," 517. For "arithmetic," see Simmel, "Metropolis and Mental Life," 1902–1903, in *Sociology of Georg Simmel*, 412.

53   Goble, *Beautiful Circuits*, 158; for "shot out like bullets," see Leonard, *Jazz*, 91; Brown, *Sense of Things*, 5. According to Brown, the anonymous quotation appeared in the *Atlantic Monthly*.

54   Washington, *Negro Problem*. Du Bois famously asks at the outset of *Souls of Black Folk* (1903), "How does it feel to be a problem?" Lukács, "Reification," 83.

55   Lukács, "Reification," 100, 86, 140; Stahl, "György Lukács"; Schiller, "Fifteenth Letter," 76.

56   Du Bois, *Gift of Black Folk*, 10, 19.

57   Du Bois, *Gift of Black Folk*, 9.

58   For "residual ontology," see Brown, "Reification, Reanimation," 182.

59   Martin, "Absolute Artwork," 15–25. For an elaboration on the concept, see ahead, chapter 8.

60   Rancière, "Aesthetic Revolution," 1–2. For more of his commentary on Schiller and play, see Rancière, *Politics of Aesthetics*, 26–28; and *Dissensus*, 123–41.

61   Sewell, "Temporalities of Capitalism." For "ghostly objectivity," see Lukács, "Reification," 100; for "secret," see Marx, *Capital*, 1:152.

CHAPTER 6. COMMODITY CIRCUITS AND THE MAKING OF A JAZZ COUNTERHISTORY

1   Bechet, *Treat It Gentle*, 2.

2   Mohun, "Capital," 68.

3   Bechet, *Treat It Gentle*, 3.

4   Giddens, *Constitution of Society*, 192. Giddens compares the flow of economic circuits to electronic circuits on the same page. Marx develops the concept of the circuit in the second volume of *Capital*. The metaphor of "circulation," moreover, reaches back to Adam Smith's *The Wealth of Nations* (1776); see chapter 2 of the second volume. According to Henry William Spiegel, circulation as an economic concept was introduced by John Law (1671–1729), borrowing the term from physiology. See Spiegel, *Growth of Economic Thought*, 176.

5   The means of production included club dates, concert tours, recording sessions. David Harvey provides a lucid explanation of the three circuits and their relation while also showing how each participates in generating value. See *Limits of Capital*, 68–74.

6   The ODJB was first billed as a "jass band." It would be changed to "jazz" shortly after. See, for example, "Original Dixieland Jass Band," 3, and "Brass Band Gone Crazy!" For a thoughtful discussion of the ODJB, see Schuller, *Early Jazz*, 175–87. As before, though, even the best players at times had to find other employment. In the 1930s, for example, Bechet ran a tailor shop with Tommy Ladnier. See Collier, "Bechet, Sidney (Jazz)."

7   On jazz and mass production, see Lane, *Jazz and Machine Age Imperialism*; Rhodes, *Structures of Jazz Age*; Dinerstein, *Swinging the Machine*. Jeffrey Magee notes that Fletcher Henderson was first known as a recording musician. See *Uncrowned King of Swing*, 34. There were some ragtime hits on record, notably the 1911 Victor recording of Irving Berlin's "Alexander's Ragtime Band" by Byron G. Harlan and Arthur Collins. For background, see Millard, *America on Record*, 99.

8   Ogren, *Jazz Revolution*, 144. In 1919, Ogren notes, Howard Brockway drew a fanciful analogy between jazz and the sounds of wartime, calling the music a re-creation of "the howitzers," "field guns," and "rapid-fire batteries" (144). Vreeland's own militaristic imagery suggested that his fears about jazz were mere farce: the piano's sound, he proposed, "vibrated like a torpedo boat destroyer at high speed." Vreeland, "Jazz, Ragtime," 2.

9   "Livery Stable Blues" was recorded on Victor on February 26, 1917; it was released in May. "Dixieland Jass Band One-Step" appeared on the B side. A test session from January at Columbia Graphophone Company was never released. For background, see Brunn, *Story*. See also Charters, *Trumpet Around the Corner*. The oft-cited claim that "Livery Stable" sold over one million copies is unconfirmed. For more on record sales on the Victor label, see Sanjek and Sanjek, *American Popular Music Business*, 14–15.

10 Kenney, *Recorded Music*, 63. On the ODJB, see Phillips, *Shaping Jazz*, chap. 4.

11 The common opinion that jazz was controversial from the outset probably developed as a conflation of the early period with the widespread disapproval registered in the early 1920s. Morroe Berger's seminal study from 1947 stresses controversies but develops its argument from coverage beginning in 1919. See "Jazz: Resistance," 461–94. Among those initially opposed to jazz were dance instructors who objected to the new shimmies and animal dances. See, for example, Philips, "Shimmy Dances," 5; and "With the Georgia Editors," 6.

12 See, respectively, "Hold Legislative Dance," 4; "Romance of the Redwoods," 2; "Police Band Picnic"; "Theatrical Reviews"; "Whirlwind Dancers," 6. Fred Allen identifies Harry Slatko's Rollickers as a vaudeville group in *Much Ado About Me*, 217.

13   For Zimbalist, "Out to-day," 2. For Zimbalist's recording, see Victor
      64638 in 1922 *Catalogue of Victor Records*. The catalogue includes works
      recorded before 1922. For Handy, see the nationally running ad "Heard
      on the New Handy Orchestra Recordings," 4.
14   "Jazz Music," *Salt Lake Telegram*, 7.
15   Chilton, "Original Dixieland Jazz Band."
16   Pegler, "Jazz Bands Play," 6; "Jazz, the Mysterious Stranger," 1.
17   "'Jazz' Band is Added," 3. See also "Jail Jazz," 22.
18   Phillips, *Shaping Jazz*, 80–81.
19   "What Jazz Music Is," 11; "Jazz, the Mysterious Stranger." What was per-
      haps the first syndicated reference to "three thousand warriors" appeared
      as "Gotham's '15th' Home" 5, image 5. The same text was republished
      in newspapers a month later: for example, the *Citizen Republican* (SD),
      March 6, 1919, image 2. For an early discussion of Kingsley's comments, see
      "Why 'Jazz' Sends Us," 165. See also "Appeal of the Primitive Jazz," 28–29.
20   For an example of the trope of "childlike," see Burlin, "Negro Music at
      Birth," 86–89. Vreeland, "Jazz, Ragtime," 2. Berlin's comment may have
      been a way of affirming his own Whiteness; being Jewish, his racial
      status would have been under question at the time.
21   Such appearances took place in metropolitan settings and in vaudeville
      houses and open-air theaters. For background, see Gebhardt, *Vaudeville
      Melodies*; Gushee, *Pioneers of Jazz*; Miller, *Segregating Sound*.
22   Lukács, "Reification," 83.
23   A compelling case can be made in favor of the fetishized cigarette. See
      Enstad, *Cigarettes, Inc.*
24   "Jazz, the Mysterious Stranger," 1; "Appeal of the Primitive Jazz," 28–29;
      Vreeland, "Jazz, Ragtime," 2.
25   Europe, "Negro Explains 'Jazz,'" 28–29.
26   "Jazzola" was composed by the White songwriters Al M. Kendall, J.
      Russel Robinson, and Theodore Morse. The members of Europe's "Hell-
      fighter's Band," officially the 369th U.S. Infantry Band, were also soldiers
      who fought heroically in France. See Lewis, *Harlem Was in Vogue*; Gilbert,
      Product of Our Souls. "Jazzola" and other works appear on the CD compila-
      tion *James Reese Europe*.
27   Rogers, "Jazz at Home," 216. Rogers was similarly sensitive to matters of
      ownership: "This makes it difficult to say whether jazz is more charac-
      teristic of the Negro or of contemporary America. As was shown, it is
      of Negro origin plus the influence of the American environment. It is
      Negro-American" (219). For a fascinating application of Rogers's paradox
      to the rise of jazz in China, see Jones, "Black Internationale."
28   For "jungle parties," "Why 'Jazz' Sends Us," 165; Jacobson, *Barbarian Vir-
      tues*, 15. One writer, reiterating the fantastic views of Lafcadio Hearn by
      way of Kingsley, stated unequivocally that the word *jazz* "is common on

the Gold Coast of Africa and in the hinterland of Cape Coast Castle." See "Jazz Music Only Negro," 65.

29   "Stale Bread's Sadness," 47–48. The author credits the depiction of a "modern wonder" to an article appearing in the New Orleans *Item*. No date is given.

30   For "snapping delirium," see "Stale Bread's Sadness," 47–48; "Jazz, the Mysterious Stranger."

31   For domestic tastes for the exotic, see Hoganson, *Consumers' Imperium*. "Oriental Jazz" was recorded by the ODJB in 1919. "Burmese Bells" and "Cairo" were recorded by Art Hickman; "Shanghai Lullaby," "Japanese Sandman," "Indian Love Call," and "Song of India" were recorded by the Whiteman Orchestra, the latter being a version of the work by the same title appearing in Rimsky-Korsakov's opera *Sadko*. "Ching-a-Ling's Jazz Bazaar" (1920) is a fox-trot by Ethel Bridges and Howard Johnson, recorded by Joseph C. Smith's Orchestra on Victor in 1919.

32   "Peppery" was a common adjective employed to describe jazz rhythms, implying—in the color of common black pepper—the racial character of a Black person. Employed already during the ragtime era, it was included in in an advertisement for the seminal New York performance of the ODJB at Reisenweber's restaurant. See "Reisenweber's Restaurant," 9. For "dippy" (referring to the ragtime dances around 1914), see Gelatt, *Fabulous Phonograph*, 189. For "retardation and acceleration," see "Why 'Jazz' Sends Us," 165.

33   Vreeland, "Jazz, Ragtime," 2.

34   Cited in Jordan, *Le Jazz*, 75. References to dance rhythms as "swing" were common in foreign metropoles at the time. "The jazz band begins to swing and dancers never stop," observed André Warnod, in his book on popular entertainment, *Les Bals de Paris*, in 1922. See Jackson, *Making Jazz French*, 42–43. In her book *An Englishwoman in the Philippines*, moreover, Mrs. Campbell Dauncey described how in 1905 a Philippine Constabulary band "tootled the first few bars of 'Hiawatha,' which they all struck into with a swing" (282). Thanks go to Fritz Schenker for calling this reference to my attention.

35   "Peppery Pep Artist," 8; "Even Typewriters Jazz," 2.

36   Desmond, "Prussianizing America," 259; Wipplinger, *Jazz Republic*, 4.

37   Bie, "Rhythm," 336, 338. Written in German, the essay was translated by Bie's collaborator, the American musicologist Theodore Baker.

38   Gaines, *Uplifting the Race*, 28.

39   "Jazz Band Parades," 6. There has been over the past couple of decades or so a flourish of historical studies of early jazz in Europe. Titles include: Fry, *Paris Blues*; Parsonage, *Evolution of Jazz in Britain*; Lotz, *Black People*; Pickering, *Blackface Minstrelsy in Britain*.

40   "Superb Dancing," 1755; Jacobson, *Barbaric Virtues*, 25.

41 "Fancy Dress Dance," 1403; "Pierrot Show," 1152. For "snap," see "Christ-mas Season Festivities," 1813. Articles sometimes list programs and repertory. Typically, the dances featured were one-steps, fox-trots, and waltzes.

42 Hershey, "Jazz Latitude," SM5. See also Johnson, *Jazz Diaspora*.

43 "Nigger Serenade," 1098. Among the other programs routinely listed were "Band Programme," 178; "Galle Face Hotel," 1248; "Colombo Garden Club," 1255, all *Ceylon Observer*. Racially ambiguous coon songs circulated on record in China as early as 1905. See Miller, *Segregating Sound*, 164. For background on the Filipino presence in Asian popular music, see Schenker, "Empire of Syncopation."

44 Hershey, "Jazz Latitude." Hershey concluded that the circulation of jazz ultimately exhibited a global condition of "jazz platitude": foreigners preferred a backward music drawn from the ragtime era, which they took for jazz. Musical taste becomes a measure of foreign inferiority as it reaffirms White American ownership.

45 Hershey, "Jazz Latitude."

46 Phillips, *Shaping Jazz*, chap. 4. Whiteman, *Jazz*; photo opposite 206.

47 Whiteman, *Jazz*. Quotations in order of appearance: 9, 265–67, 17, 8, 9, 9, 9, 16, 132, 3. A digital (and searchable) version of the book is available on HathiTrust. At another point, Whiteman locates the essence of jazz not in Negro music but in another kind of conquering, in an imperial re-lation to the magic of "a Brown-skinned, Indian fakir with heavy-lidded, mysterious eyes" who transforms a mango seed into a whole fruit. "America," Whiteman pronounces, "has a magic mango in jazz" (15).

48 Whiteman, *Jazz*, 4, 118, 155, 132, 7, 153–54, 122, 94, respectively.

49 For a critique of the presentism surrounding Whiteman—together with an analysis of his and Grofé's influence on Fletcher Henderson and Don Redman—see Magee, *Uncrowned King of Swing*. Magee's observation of how Black players in mid-1920s Harlem embraced music literacy (29), which he attributes to Henderson's influence, may also be understood as the result of Whiteman's overarching impact. See also Howland, *Ellington Uptown*.

50 A reconstruction of the Aeolian Hall concert on February 12, 1924 (it was repeated on March 7), employing historical recordings, was issued in 1982 as *Paul Whiteman at Aeolian Hall*. Henry O. Osgood affirmed Whiteman's argument in his book *So This Is Jazz*, also published in 1926. The book features Whiteman's music and includes a detailed description of the first Aeolian Hall concert. A photograph of Whiteman appears as its frontispiece.

51 The satellite bands were secondary bands created by Whiteman to per-form his repertoire in multiple places at once. In this way, they mim-icked the effect of mass production. For an elaboration, see Raymo, *Paul*

Whiteman, 46. Raymo makes further reference to them on 48, 50–53, 90, 95, 189.

52   Advertisements for Whiteman's records on Victor routinely appeared in foreign newspapers. See, for example, "Discos Victor," 11; "New Dance Records," 4; "Latest Dance Records," 12; "Latest Victor Record Releases"; "Out Tomorrow! New Victor Records." Kaplan, *Anarchy of Empire*, 12.

53   Early, "Pulp and Circumstance," 393–430. See, especially, 410.

54   Two recordings made for HMV in Calcutta in 1926 by Jimmy Lequime's Grand Hotel Orchestra were strongly influenced by Whiteman's style of symphonic jazz. The titles, "Soho Blues" and "The House Where the Shutters are Green," were rereleased on the Harlequin LP *Jazz and Hot Dance Music in India, 1926–1944*. They are also readily available on You-Tube. For background on the group, see Shope, *American Popular Music*, 73–74. On the presence of local musicians in foreign bands in Asia, see Schenker, "Empire of Syncopation." For the Americas, see two important studies: Putnam, *Radical Moves*; Borge, *Tropical Riffs*.

55   On the uses of *hokum, jazbo, plantation*, and others, see Gushee, *Pioneers of Jazz*, 140–42, and elsewhere. "Novelty"—which shows up in 1909, in the title of Scott Joplin's "Euphonic Sounds: A Syncopated Novelty"—commonly referred to piano works by Zez Confrey and others. However, it also appeared in the name of White bands (e.g., Paul Biese and his Novelty Orchestra) and as a condition affecting dance, as in the "undesirable novelties" of jazz and ethnic melodies. See Roberts, "Novelty Piano." For dance controversy, see "Wave, Trot, Walk," 25.

56   For "the 'downtown' white world" and "better pay," see Tucker, *Duke Ellington: Early Years*, 97.

57   "Hot Lips" was recorded by the Cotton Pickers, an early White studio band, on Brunswick (1922). The same group recorded as The Memphis Five on Columbia. "Hot Lips" was also recorded later in 1922 by Paul Whiteman and His Orchestra. See Weber, "Brunswick." Tucker and Jackson, "Jazz." Collier, "Henderson, Fletcher." For background on symphonic jazz, see Howland, *Ellington Uptown*.

58   The record sold 75,000 copies during its first year of release. See Hadju, "Song That Changed Music." The quotation appears in Brothers, *Louis Armstrong*, 53–54.

59   Dabney, "Bugle Call Blues" (Famous 3120-B, accessed on YouTube). Hegamin was the second blues artist to record, after Mamie Smith. See Kernfeld, "Hegamin [née Nelson], Lucille." For background on Sam Wooding's time in New York, see Gariglio, "Bushell, Garvin."

60   For two recorded examples of Brymn's blues-inflected orchestral performances, see "He's My Man (You'd Better Leave Him Alone") and "I'm Craving for that Kind of Love" (both OKeh, 1921). Both are currently available on YouTube. The *New York Times* advertised Brymn's orchestra

performances at the Casino on Broadway and 39th St. (May 16 and 18, 1919), Hotel Shelburne in Brighton Beach (June 8 and July 1, 1920, and April 27, 1921), and an eight-day series of events at Madison Square Garden (Sept 16, 1920). By 1920, the Black Devil band was reduced to fifty players. In *Duke Ellington: The Early Years*, Tucker states that Brymn performed at the Plantation Café (a cabaret in the Winter Garden building on Broadway) in 1922 (98). There is no citation.

61   On Kansas City, see Rice, "Prelude to Swing"; for Buster Smith, see Pearson, *Goin' to Kansas City*, 39. On Chicago, see Brothers, *Louis Armstrong*; on Oliver, see DeVeaux, *Birth of Bebop*, 124–25; for Williams, see Stearns, *Story of Jazz*, 167–68. Oliver's side of the popular song "I Ain't Gonna Tell Nobody" was among his seminal recordings from 1923. For Sanjek, see Gennari, *Blowin' Hot and Cool*, 100. Sanjek would later become President of the performance rights organization Broadcast Music Incorporated (BMI).

62   Brothers, *Louis Armstrong*, 28. On the Plantation Café, see Tucker, *Duke Ellington: Early Years*, 98. The Cotton Club was in Harlem, the others downtown. Another important catalyst for renewed interest in southern sentimentality was Al Jolson's 1920 hit recording of George Gershwin's song "Swanee."

63   Miley was touring with Mamie Smith when he heard Oliver. See Tucker, *Duke Ellington: Early Years*, 101.

64   Two excellent CDs of these and other "hot" works are: *Hot Notes* and *Happy Rhythm*.

65   Tucker, *Duke Ellington: Early Years*, 79, 83. On Black musicians developing music reading skills, see Magee, *Uncrowned King of Swing*, 29. Hardwick's quote appears in Tucker and Jackson, "Jazz," 9.

66   Hentoff, *Jazz Life*, 34. Ellington grew up middle class in Washington, DC.

67   Many musicians gained musical knowledge as part of their work in town bands, some seeking out coaching from local teachers. Booker Washington, a trumpeter who later played with the Bennie Moten Orchestra, recalls how as a teenager in Missouri he acquired skills from a variety of teachers: "One would take me [for instruction] for intonation, one would . . . write out the scales." Multiple musicians credit the mentoring of high school teachers (often called "professors") who introduced them to the rudiments of harmony, some even gaining experience in improvisation. Orville Minor remembers, for example, how in junior high school he learned to improvise: "Stepping up a little faster. You begin to find out where the rhythm was." See Pearson, *Goin' to Kansas City*, 17, 21. For the biographies of Byrmn, Henderson, Redman, Steele, and Tate, see *Grove Music Online*. For Washington and Dunn, see Pearson, *Goin' to Kansas City*, 17, 21n3. Hsio Wen Shih, "Spread of Jazz," 174; DeVeaux, *Birth of Bebop*, 124.

68   For Barefield, see Pearson, *Goin' to Kansas City*, 37. For Basie, see
      Basie, *Good Morning Blues*, 54; for Bushell, see Gebhardt, *Vaudeville
      Melodies*, 35.

69   For Berresford, see Gebhardt, *Vaudeville Melodies*, 137.

70   For "jazz was a stunt," Gioia, *History of Jazz*, 96; For Ellington and Sweat-
      man, see Tucker, *Duke Ellington: Early Years*, 80–81; for Freddy Crump,
      see Basie, *Good Morning Blues*, 86.

71   For "musical hokum," Gushee, *Pioneers of Jazz*, 142; for performers in the
      touring shows, see their biographical portraits in *Grove Music Online* and
      Pearson, *Goin' to Kansas City*, 6.

72   Gebhardt, *Vaudeville Melodies*, 35, 47, 19, 92.

73   Gushee, *Pioneers of Jazz*, 142.

74   Recordings, respectively, by Mamie Smith and Her Jazz Hounds, the
      Bennie Moten Orchestra, the Fletcher Henderson Orchestra, and the
      Washingtonians. Lemke, *Primitivist Modernism*, 90–91. For Carter and
      Calloway, see Gioia, *History of Jazz*, 95.

75   According to Davarian Baldwin, New York's Black population more than
      tripled from 1910 to 1930, while Chicago's leaped from 44,130 to 233,903
      over the same period. See his introduction to *Escape from New York*. In
      "Our Newcomers to the City," moreover, Baldwin notes that 25% of the
      southern migrants were agricultural workers. Most migrants came
      from towns and cities (175). The authoritative account of labor and labor
      organizing in the North is Cohen, *Making a New Deal*. For an overview of
      changes in musician employment based on the 1910 census, see Harris,
      "Occupation of Musician," 299–311.

76   Among the black and tans were Connie's Inn and Barron's Exclusive
      Club, both in Harlem. Black clubs included Bucket of Blood and Leroy's.
      After-hours sessions took place in Chicago, at the De Luxe, Dreamland,
      Flume, and Sunset cafés; in New York, the Band Box, Bamboo Inn, Her-
      mit's End, and the Rhythm Club. See Kernfeld, "Nightclubs."

77   Kernfeld, "Nightclubs." His coverage includes Kansas City's Lucille's
      Band Box and Lyric Hall; Los Angeles's Cadillac Café; St. Louis's Jazzland
      and Chauffeur's Club; Harlem's Lafayette and Savoy theaters; Chica-
      go's Lincoln Gardens; Philadelphia's Pearl Theater; Detroit's Graystone
      Ballroom; and San Francisco's Percola's Dancing Pavilion. Tucker names
      several performance spots in *Duke Ellington: Early Years*. See also Hobson,
      "New York," 219.

78   Stewart, *Jazz Masters*, 55; Basie, *Good Morning Blues*, 53. For "we welcomed
      them," see Tucker, *Duke Ellington: Early Years*, 97.

79   Tanke, *Rancière*, 75. Tanke is paraphrasing Rancière.

80   Rancière, *Dissensus*, 149.

81   The quotation is from an unpublished manuscript, cited in Magee,
      Uncrowned King of Swing, 134.

82 Magee, *Uncrowned King of Swing*, 62, 40. In the latter item, Magee is quoting Schuller, who referred to Don Redman as the "architect" of the Henderson orchestra.

83 Rancière, *Dissensus*, 149.

84 Casey, "How to Get," 22–27.

85 Magee, *Uncrowned King of Swing*, 35–36, 3–4.

86 Magee, *Uncrowned King of Swing*, 50, 14, 19, 56.

87 Magee, *Uncrowned King of Swing*, 80; Murray, *Stomping the Blues*, chap. 9, which focuses on Kansas City swing.

88 Magee, *Uncrowned King of Swing*, 3, 46–47.

89 Magee, *Uncrowned King of Swing*, 47–50.

90 Magee, *Uncrowned King of Swing*, 60.

91 Du Bois, *Gift of Black Folk*, 53.

92 Lil Hardin Armstrong's "Struttin' with Some Barbecue" was recorded by Louis Armstrong and His Hot Five in 1927. On Ellington's jungle style performed at the Cotton Club, see Cohen, *Duke Ellington's America*, 53–62.

93 On the T.O.B.A., see Abbott and Seroff, *Ragged But Right*, 80. On segregated unions and opportunities to play among Black residents in Chicago, see Smith, "Austin High School Gang," 171. For Hopkins, see Dance, *World of Swing*, 36. For Snowden, see Dance, *World of Swing*, 55. For Dodds, see Brothers, *Louis Armstrong*, 36. The acclaimed Creole Jazz Band led by King Oliver reportedly ended after a dispute over money. For James Reese Europe, see Gilbert, *Product of Our Souls*, 217.

94 Rancière, *Dissensus*, 140–42.

95 Rancière, *Dissensus*, 141, 148; Mackey, *Bedouin Hornbook*, 19.

96 Hartman, *Wayward Lives*, 299.

97 Tomba, *Marx's Temporalities*, 136. For a valuable outline of the various clubs in Harlem, see Vogel, *Scene of Harlem Cabaret*. The quote appears on 118. For an early study of racial interaction in Chicago and Harlem clubs, see Mumford, *Interzones*.

98 Edwards, "Louis Armstrong," 647. Edwards proposes augmentation in contrast to Gary Giddins's critical view that Armstrong's artistry is a transcendence of the buffoonery of his comic roles. Yet we can also think of the "nervous loss of articulacy" not simply as a manifestation of what Nathaniel Mackey calls "unspeakable history" but also relating to double value, which is a historically based, racial-economic structure, not a syntax.

99 Leonard, *Jazz*, 33. Band names appear on 92–93. For "droning, jerky incoherence," see McMahon, "Jazz Path of Degradation," cited in Lemke, *Primitivist Modernism*, 63. For "jungle steps," see "Canon Chase," 12. For "nut bands," see Hobson, "New York," 213.

100 "Decries 'Jazz Thinking,'" 17; "Primitive, Savage Animalism," 13. For "evils" and "danger," see "Dress Extremes," 17. For Rawlings, see Leonard,

Jazz, 33; he is citing an essay from 1922. For the superintendent, see "Wants Legislation to Stop," 1.

101 "Girls on 'Noise' Strike," 19.

102 Leonard, *Jazz*, 39. He cites a newspaper article from January 29, 1922. Wilson, "Jazz Problem," 217–19.

103 In *When Harlem Was in Vogue*, Lewis recorded twenty-five locations where riots occurred, subsequently observing that 1919 was the same year that "the 369th Infantry Regiment marched proudly up Fifth Avenue." See 17–18, 20, 23. See also McWhirter, *Red Summer*; and Tuttle, *Race Riot*. For Georges Duhamel's alignment of jazz and the horror of Chicago stockyards, see Lane, *Jazz and Machine-Age Imperialism*.

104 Roediger and Foner, "Class Conflict, Reform, and War"; "The Working Day from 1907 to 1918," *Our Own Time*, 177–208. See also, among others, Montgomery, *Workers' Control in America*. For "the expression of protest" and "demoralizing effect," see Berger, "Jazz: Resistance," 464.

105 Phillips, *Shaping Jazz*, 179. On the sales of "Crazy Blues," see Dolan, "Extra!," 112. The ruling in *Victor v. Starr* ended Victor and Columbia's monopoly on lateral recording. See Carney, *Cuttin' Up*, 70–71. The ruling itself (Victor Talking Mach. Co. v. Starr Piano Co., Circuit Court of Appeals, Second Circuit, April 4, 1922) is easily accessed on the web. On "Heebie-Jeebies," see Brothers, *Louis Armstrong*, 218. For *Talking Machine World*, see Denning, *Noise Uprising*, 16.

106 Charters and Kunstadt have argued that the Whiteman orchestra's musical success seemed to be the result of "the violent attacks on jazz that had swept the country in 1920 and 1921." See *Jazz*, 134.

107 According to Gennari, "John Hammond was among the first to popularize 'commercial' as an epithet" consistent with "his intense hatred of sweet music" See *Blowin' Hot and Cold*, 36.

108 I'm thinking here of Bourdieu's metaphor of "force field" as outlined in Thomson, "Field," 69–70.

109 For "reversibility," see Sewell, "Temporalities of Capitalism." Kingsley is cited in "Why 'Jazz' Sends Us," 165.

110 "'Spooks' Full of Mystery," 16; Wimberly, "Decline of the Ghost," 240; Scarborough, *Negro Folksongs*, 25, 37–42. See also Scarborough, *Humorous Ghost Stories*, which includes a story by Parker Butler Ellis, "Dey Ain't No Ghosts"; Wimberly, "Spook English," 317–21; Gamble and Kraft, "How I've Got." The author is deft in his racial allusions, making reference on the opening page to "making pygmies of its detractors," "the lies, whether white or black," and an "ape-like ancestor." "Runnin' Wild," 20.

111 Brothers, *Louis Armstrong*, 214, 218–19. On the history of "heebie-jeebies," including its appearances in the comic strip *Barney Google*, see Zimmer, "How Did We Get." See also "Heebie-Jeebies," *Dictionary of American Regional English*. By 1923, the term had become popular in newspaper

sports pages, probably because of its association with the character Spark Plug. See, for example, Gallico, "Jolts Crimson," 22; "Sparky Races," 1.

112   In "Louis Armstrong," Edwards notes the word's appearance in Arna Bontemps and Langston Hughes's *Book of Negro Folklore* (1958) and as the title of a weekly African American review published in Chicago during the 1920s (621).

113   Harker, "Louis Armstrong," 67–121. Edwards, "Louis Armstrong," 647, 622. The acolyte was Mezz Mezzrow. "Jazzmania" was also the name of a revue featuring Armstrong, staged at the Sunshine Café in Chicago in 1926. See Brothers, *Louis Armstrong*, 217–18.

114   Edwards, "Louis Armstrong," 624, 647. In his reference to "telling inarticulacy," Edwards is quoting Mackey.

115   Austin, "Buck and Wing," 476; Johnson, *Black Manhattan*, 214–15.

116   Hornbostel, "African Negro Music," 59. See, for example, Botkin, *Lay My Burden Down*. The collection presented excepts from the Federal Writers' Project's interviews with Black southerners and former slaves. The terms quoted here appear in the table of contents.

117   On "spook nights," see Basie, *Good Morning Blues*, 162. Mingus, *Beneath the Underdog*, 189–90. Krin Gabbard discusses the epithet in *Better Git It*, 165; Ellison, *Invisible Man*, 8; Austin, "Buck and Wing."

118   Rogers, "Jazz at Home," 217–18, 220. Stokowski's quotation appears on 222.

119   For a critique of such "alternative" modernities, including uses of the postcolonial that imagine a stable modern, see Harootunian, "Modernity," 367–82.

120   Burlin, "Negro Music at Birth," 86–89.

121   Hurston, "How It Feels," 215–16; Vogel, *Scene of Harlem Cabaret*, 27–28, 95–97.

122   For Peyton, see Brothers, *Louis Armstrong*, 131.

123   For Coward, see Laubenstein, "Jazz—Debit and Credit," 622. Coward was describing the performance of the Savoy-Orpheans at the Savoy Hotel, London, in 1927. The Conductor of the ensemble replies to Coward in a letter to the editor. See "Jazz Music," *Times*, 8. For background on Coward and his subjection to ridicule in the *Melody Maker* (he was dubbed "Crowhard," a term that was then applied to other opponents of jazz), see Godbolt, *History of Jazz in Britain*, 47.

CHAPTER 7. SWING

1   Dance, *World of Swing*, 13–16.

2   Dance, *World of Swing*, 13. In what was perhaps a more comfortable exchange with the African American critic Albert Murray, Basie was only somewhat more forthcoming: "I think a band can really *swing* when

it swings *easy*, when it can just play along like you are cutting butter."
Basie, *Good Morning Blues*, 370.

3   Dance, *World of Swing*, 22.

4   Dance himself proposed the term. See Dance, "Main-Stream Jazz War," 3.

5   Erenberg, *Swingin' the Dream*; Dinerstein, *Swinging the Machine*. Erenberg
frequently proposes that swing possessed such capacities, for example: "The vogue of crooners, torch singers, and sweet bands expressed
youth's inability in the early 1930s to realize the dreams of the 1920s"
(17–18). Dinerstein's entire argument rests on his claim that the musical
character of swing was consistent with the motion of modern transpor-
tation technologies, mass production, and urban life.

6   On jukeboxes at Black clubs, see Lauterbach, *Chitlin' Circuit*, 44.

7   Postone and Brennan, "Labor," 320. Relevant here is Stuart Hall's characterization of Black popular culture as "a contradictory space. It is a sight
[*sic*] of strategic contestation. But it can never be simplified or explained
in terms of the simple binary oppositions that are still habitually used
to map it out: high and low; resistance versus incorporation; authentic
versus inauthentic." See "What Is This 'Black,'" 470.

8   Chakrabarty, *Provincializing Europe*, 60.

9   DeVeaux, *Birth of Bebop*, 120–21; Erenberg, *Swingin' the Dream*, 12–13.

10 Brooks, "Columbia Corporate History." Basie, *Good Morning Blues*, 144, 218.

11 Victor's retail catalogs are a telling indication of the industry's struggles
and its impact on Black music. In its 1930 catalog, the company featured
hundreds of recordings by seventy-one jazz orchestras (listed under
"Dance Records: Fox Trots"), including a small number of Black ensembles. The following year, it had eliminated the category and printed in
its place an abbreviated selection under the leaders' names. Without
extensive discographic research, knowing how many of these recordings
were released remains uncertain. In its opening statement, "Important
Facts," the company alludes to its new economic challenges, stating
that although "a great number of recordings listed herein are marked
'in preparation' . . . for one or more of a great variety of reasons, [they]
must await their opportune moment" to be recorded, produced, or released. See *Victor Records* (1931), 1. Orchestras identified in the 1930 catalog, finally, included White ensembles led by Ben Pollack, Gus Arnheim,
Paul Whiteman, and others, and Black ensembles led by Ellington's
Orchestra, Charles Johnson Orchestra, Leroy Smith and His Orchestra,
McKinney's Cotton Pickers, Missourians, Morton's Red Hot Peppers,
Moten's Kansas City Orchestra, Fess Williams and His Orchestra.

12 Although the decline in retail sales was offset somewhat by the companies' role as a supplier of commercial jukeboxes—Samuel S. Brylawski
writes that twenty-five thousand coin-operated jukeboxes featuring
popular hits and Black music were in use nationally by 1933—most jazz

musicians still lost out, the mechanical players taking the place of cost-
lier live bands. See Brylawski, "Jukebox."

13   Susan Smulyan maps out this complex history in her chapter "The Rise
     of the Network System," in *Selling Radio*, 37–64. See also Scott, "History
     of Radio Industry"; Brooks, "Columbia Corporate History"; Sanjek and
     Sanjek, *American Popular Music Business*, 29–31.

14   On listenership, see Erenberg, *Swingin' the Dream*; DeVeaux, *Birth of
     Bebop*, 121. CBS continued to carry the Columbia name after an initial
     affiliation with the record company in the late 1920s. From 1927 to 1939,
     however, they were unaffiliated. See Brooks, "Columbia Corporate
     History." RCA bought Victor Records in 1929. See Hull, *Recording Industry*,
     294. The focus on live shows was the way networks sidestepped copy-
     right restrictions on broadcasting commercial recordings.

15   Smulyan, *Selling Radio*, 93–124.

16   Barnes is quoted in Mehnert, "McKinney's Cotton Pickers," 148.

17   DeVeaux, *Birth of Bebop*, 125. Hines played the Grand Terrace until it
     closed in 1937. See "Earl Hines," 2.

18   Mehnert, "McKinney's Cotton Pickers," 147.

19   DeVeaux, *Birth of Bebop*, 122–23. With the help of Irving Mills, Ellington
     devised a market plan in the 1920s that made him an international star.
     See Cohen, *Duke Ellington's America*, chap. 2: "The Marketing Plan."

20   Basie, *Good Morning Blues*, 117; Stewart, *Jazz Masters*, 31–32.

21   Suisman, *Selling Sounds*.

22   Suisman, *Selling Sounds*, 9–10, 280. For "by hand," see Taylor, *Music and
     Capitalism*, 35–36.

23   DeVeaux, *Birth of Bebop*, 123; Stowe, *Swing Changes*, 98–99. For Jonah
     Jones, see Dance, *World of Swing*, 164.

24   Lauterbach, *Chitlin' Circuit*, 36–38, 40, 44–46.

25   For Jonah Jones, see Dance, *World of Swing*, 18. "The Baby Dodds Story"
     excerpt appears in Taylor, Katz, and Grajeda, *Music, Sound*, 91.

26   DeVeaux, *Birth of Bebop*, 62. Schuller, *Swing Era*, 3.

27   DeVeaux, *Birth of Bebop*, 123.

28   Schuller, *Swing Era*, 5.

29   "Dust had been blown from the shotgun, the whip, and the noose," Hil-
     ton Butler wrote in the *Nation*, to make certain "that dead men not only
     tell no tales but create vacancies" (qtd. in Greenberg, *To Ask for*, 25).

30   Dance, *World of Swing*, 164. The "Southwest" was the territory now known
     as the lower Midwest.

31   Although many Black swing musicians were northerners—Tricky Sam
     Nanton, Benny Carter, Count Basie, Chick Webb, Harry Carney, Quinn
     Wilson, and Rex Stewart, to name a few—the southern presence in the
     early orchestras was unmistakable. Jonah Jones (Louisville, Kentucky),
     Andy Kirk (Newport, Kentucky), Budd Johnson (Dallas, Texas), Sandy

Williams (Summerville, South Carolina), Taft Jordan (Florence, South Carolina), Mary Lou Williams (Atlanta, Georgia), and Trummy Young (Savannah, Georgia) were also among the many who brought to swing sounding practices and cultural ways based in the Black southern experience. The foundational study of 1930s and '40s all-girl bands—the gender reference typically appearing without scare quotes during the time of the bands' popularity—is Tucker, *Swing Shift*.

32   On the mobility of jazz and its relation to race, see Berish, *Lonesome Roads*.

33   Louis Armstrong and His Orchestra, "That Rhythm Man" (1929); Jimmie Lunceford Orchestra, "Rhythm Is Our Business" (1934); Fletcher Henderson Orchestra, "I'm Rhythm Crazy Now" (1933).

34   Ellington's comments on jazz and Africa appeared in Bell, "Ellington Orchestra in Cleveland," 53–54.

35   Dance, *World of Swing*, 18.

36   Basie, *Good Morning Blues*, 109. On queer musicians in Black swing ensembles, see Hinton, interview with Johnson. The recordings and transcript are housed at the Institute for Jazz Studies, Rutgers University, Newark, NJ.

37   Dance, *World of Swing*, 18; Basie, *Good Morning Blues*, 141.

38   Bell, "Ellington Orchestra in Cleveland," 53; Dance, *World of Swing*, 19. Panassié is paraphrasing Bigard's comment. See Panassié, "Duke Ellington," 86. Musicians employed the same metaphor of nourishment when discussing their own interactions. Gene Ramey described how Walter Page conceived the bass player's role: "There's a whole lot [you] could do here . . . but what you must do is play a straight line, because that man out there's waiting for food from you. You could run chord changes on every chord that's going on. You've got time to do it. But if you do, you're interfering with that guy [the soloist]. So run a straight line" (qtd. in Tucker, "Count Basie," 54). Basie himself described how during a recording session "I had the band feeding [Coleman Hawkins] like you feed the soloist riffs in a jam session." Basie, *Good Morning Blues*, 247.

39   Basie, *Good Morning Blues*, 126–27, 129, 202.

40   For Ellington, see Gilbert, *Product of Our Souls*, 100; Rogers, "Jazz at Home," 218; Harker, "Louis Armstrong."

41   "Ellington Defends His Music," 80; Panassié, "Duke Ellington," 86.

42   Determeyer, *Rhythm Is Our Business*, 32.

43   On "spooks," see Basie, *Good Morning Blues*, 162. Basie's ironic embrace of racial stereotype is also suggested in his recollection of a vaudeville routine, "Music and Laughter," starring Alice Harris and Garbage Rogers. Basie, playing straight man in the comedy, "put the burnt cork on and everything" (133).

44   Basie, *Good Morning Blues*, 141, 113. On the Henderson band playing baseball, see DeVeaux, *Birth of Bebop*, 163; For Ellington's love of base-

ball, see Bell, "Ellington Orchestra in Cleveland," 53. Basie refers to chopping bands frequently in *Good Morning Blues*. See, for example, 113, 138, 193–94.

45 Dance, *World of Swing*, 115; Basie, *Good Morning Blues*, 161, 197.

46 Ellington, "My Hunt," 88. The musicians' reference to the riff as the "fucking rhythm" was shared with me during a personal conversation with Martin Williams at the Smithsonian Institution around 1987. It is interesting that Schuller, despite his deep personal knowledge of the Black jazz world—and friendship with Williams—seemed to miss the joke. After complaining about Lombardo's "whining, whimpering, effeminate saxophone sound," he writes, "what is really baffling, however, is why so many of the black orchestras which *did* emulate the Lombardo sound and style, felt the need to exaggerate it so. . . . On *Star Dust* . . . it reaches the dimensions of caricature, even though it wasn't meant to at all." See Schuller, *Swing Era*, 170–71.

47 Ellington, "Duke Steps Out," 49.

48 Ellington commented, "I discarded most of the rules I had learned and found greatest success in doing the things that my harmony instructors warned me against" (Bell, "Ellington Orchestra in Cleveland," 53).

49 Dance, *World of Swing*, 19, 23.

50 Schuller, *Swing Era*, 207, 295. Jeremy Hefner, pitching coach of the New York Mets, applied the metaphor to describe good pitching: "Getting on top of the ball—all the things we've been talking about in baseball for a hundred years" (*New York Times*, August 28, 2022).

51 Schuller, *Swing Era*, 273, 275–77.

52 Schuller, *Swing Era*, 205, 302. Austin's quote appears on 302.

53 "Commercially published arrangements were also widely used, but it was the specials (distinctive arrangements owned by individual ensembles and often not circulated) that helped give bands a unique sound." See Tucker and Jackson, "Jazz," 5.

54 Basie, *Good Morning Blues*, 199. Ramey is quoted in Tucker, "Count Basie," 64. For "five saxes," see Dance, *World of Swing*, 102; for "play as one man," see Ellington, "Duke Steps Out," 47.

55 Schuller, *Swing Era*, 47.

56 For "get-off men," see Dance, *World of Swing*, 17. "Few people remember how extensive and beautiful [Henderson's] waltz book was," recalled Rex Stewart. See DeVeaux, *Birth of Bebop*, 125. For "get lips," Basie, *Good Morning Blues*, 121; Schuller, *Swing Era*, 307; Basie, *Good Morning Blues*, 128.

57 DeVeaux, *Birth of Bebop*, 128. On Hammond's use of the "commercial" epithet, see Gennari, *Blowin' Hot and Cold*, 36.

58 Schuller, *Swing Era*, 13, 15.

59 Goodman initially resisted Hammond's suggestion that he incorporate Harlem-styled swing into his repertory. See Schuller, *Swing Era*, 18–20.

60 Notably, Benny Goodman and His Boys' "Shirt Tail Stomp" (1928) and the sessions organized as the Whoopee Makers; other groups, with varying personnel, included the Five Pennies and Irving Mills's Hotsy Totsy Gang. Schuller notes that session work dried up by 1932, with most of the jobs appearing in radio. See *Swing Era*, 18–19.

61 Schuller, *Swing Era*, 13. An example of Goodman's novelty playing is "Shirt Tail Stomp." In *Good Morning Blues*, Basie recalls performing for a football game between Michigan and Ohio State (140).

62 Schuller, *Swing Era*, 17. This overview is indebted to Schuller's assessments, which I considered while listening to and analyzing the recordings, all of which are available on YouTube.

63 Erenberg, *Swingin' the Dream*, 4. As Schuller notes in chapter 1, these shows were heard three hours earlier on the West Coast, drawing a wide listenership and explaining why White dancers recognized the Henderson charts when the Goodman orchestra played them at the Palomar.

64 Dance, *World of Swing*, 22. Benny Goodman later hired Henderson, Cootie Williams, Teddy Wilson, and other Black players. Schuller, *Swing Era*.

65 Armstrong toured Europe in 1932 and 1933; Ellington in 1933. Smith wrote for the *Daily Worker*. Hammond left Yale before graduating and worked in New York as a record producer. Gennari, *Blowin' Hot and Cold*, 34.

66 For example, Earl Hines's Orchestra was broadcasting from the Grand Terrace Ballroom by the mid-1930s. See Taylor, "Hines, Earl." For Hammond and WEVD, see Prial, *Producer*, 35. The station call letters were named after Eugene Victor Debs.

67 See "Benny Goodman," Radio Hall of Fame website, accessed July 26, 2024, https://www.radiohalloffame.com/template-4.

68 Erenberg, *Swingin' the Dream*, 37.

69 Bie, "Rhythm," 336, 338; for "social outlet," see Erenberg, *Swinging' the Dream*, 38; for "American ground," see Dinerstien, *Swinging the Machine*, 18; for "immortal right" and "voice of youth," see Erenberg, 38; for the Lindy Hop, see Giddins and DeVeaux, *Jazz*, 177.

70 Stowe, *Swing Changes*, 99; Gilbert, "Higher Soars," quoted in Stowe, *Swing Changes*, 1–2.

71 For "monotonous" rhythm and "incessant movement," see Laubenstein, "Jazz—Debit and Credit," 606. For Luce, see Dinerstein, *Swinging the Machine*, 5.

72 Braggs, *Jazz Diasporas*, 68–69. For "tempo," see Stowe, *Swing Changes*, 24.

73 Mumford, *Technics and Civilization*, 433.

74 Garcia, *Listening for Africa*. Baker, *Anthropology*; Baker, *From Savage to Negro*.

75 Laubenstein, "Jazz—Debt and Credit," 606; Harootunian, "Some Thoughts on Comparability," 41.

76 Harootunian, "Some Thoughts on Comparability," 41–42. Harootunian is working here from, among other philosophical studies, Henri Lefebvre's *The Production of Space*.

77 For background on Stearns, see Dunkel, "Marshall Winslow Stearns."

78 Mumford, *Technics and Civilization*, 16. Mumford employs the terms "savage" and "savagery" frequently and casually to distinguish the modern West, as in "savage primitive" (335) and "relapses into savagery" (343).

79 Sargeant, *Jazz, Hot and Hybrid*, 65, 81–82.

80 Dodge, "Hot Jazz," 75–83.

81 Dodge, "Hot Jazz," 75–76, 79–80.

82 Dodge, "Hot Jazz," 76–78, 80–81. Emphasis in the original.

83 Quoted in Singer, *Hegel*, 15. Hegel's original statement appears in his *Lectures on the Philosophy of History*. Hegel looms over much of Dodge's essay "Hot Jazz." At one point, Dodge even worries that jazz would remain in the "tradition of undeveloped structural simplicity" (79) characteristic of the "Orient," apparently affirming Hegel's conception of Asian societies as a middling backwardness in the historical pursuit of *Geist*. "For jazz to maintain a vital reason for continuing, it must go ahead—not settle back as did the music of the Orient" (75). He characterizes "Oriental" (i.e., Chinese) musical notation as limited.

84 Thomson, "Swing Music," 29; Thomson, "Swing Again," 34.

85 Panassié, *Hot Jazz*, 2, 4; emphasis in the original.

86 Carter, "Do Critics Really Know," 17, cited in Gennari, *Blowin' Hot and Cold*, 102.

87 Gennari, *Blowin' Hot and Cold*, 43, 51, 102. Davis, "No Secret," 5.

88 "College Band," 1. On swing at Soldier Field, see Erenberg, *Swingin' the Dream*, 35, 37.

89 "Goodman and Webb Will Broadcast."

90 The film is readily available on YouTube.

91 The Gershwins' tune was written for the film.

92 Gennari, *Blowin' Hot and Cold*, 95–96. Brylawski, "Jukebox."

93 For Ulanov and Singleton, see Gennari, *Blowin' Hot and Cold*, 82, 96.

94 Press coverage and Ellington's own writing and speeches give a good indication of this, as documented in Tucker, *Duke Ellington Reader*.

95 For "Origin in Africa," see Bell, "Ellington Orchestra in Cleveland," 53; for "American Soil," see Ellington, "Duke Steps Out," 49; for "the tragedy," "pieced together," and "we as a race," see "Two Early Interviews," 43.

96 Ellington, "We, Too, Sing 'America,'" 147–48.

97 Ellington, "Duke Steps Out," 49.

98 Basie, *Good Morning Blues*, 185, 188.

99 Tanke, *Rancière*, 2.

100 Burke, *Come in and Hear*.

101 Ellington, "Duke Steps Out," 47.

102 Ellington, "Duke Steps Out," 47; Bell, "Ellington Orchestra in Cleveland," 53.

103 Tucker, "Count Basie," 69; Basie, *Good Morning Blues*, 167.

104 Hobson, "Introducing Duke Ellington," 97; Overstreet, "'Secret' of the Ellington Orchestra," 101; Hughes, "Impressions of Ellington in New York," 71.

105 Basie, *Good Morning Blues*, 199, 170.

106 DeVeaux scrupulously details multiple factors—notably, and ironically, how improved civil rights in the North motivated White club owners, fearing the response of White clientele, to hire White bands—that proved fateful for Black bands and musicians. See *Birth of Bebop*, 143–57.

107 Kouwenhoven, "What's American About America," 123–36. The editor's introduction to *The Jazz Cadence of American Culture* is itself expressive of these midcentury sentiments.

CHAPTER 8. LIVING FORMS, IMAGINED TRUTHS

1 Ellison, "Golden Age," 201. In his review of Baraka's *Blues People* published in the same volume, Ellison argues that the blues is "an art form and thus a transcendence of those conditions created within the Negro community by the denial of social justice" (*Shadow and Act*, 257).

2 Ellison, "Golden Age," 208–9.

3 Ellison, "Golden Age," 210. Bechet, *Treat It Gentle*, 2. Minton's opened in 1938.

4 Ellison, "Golden Age"; "On Bird." The quotations appear in succession on 201, 205, 203, 201, 201, 229, 201, 229.

5 Ellison, "Introduction," xix.

6 Ellison, "Golden Age," 201.

7 Ellison, "Golden Age," 210; Lopes, *Jazz Art World*.

8 Ellison, "Golden Age," 210, 201.

9 Ellison, "Golden Age," 209. Monson, *Saying Something*.

10 For Young, see Gitler, *Swing to Bop*, 35. Eldridge and Hawkins appear on 47 and 103, respectively. DeVeaux, *Birth of Bebop*, 103.

11 For Nicholas, see DeVeaux, *Birth of Bebop*, 65; for Gordon and Johnson, see Gitler, *Swing to Bop*, 47 and 36, respectively.

12 Berliner, *Thinking in Jazz*, 348–49. On improvisation and dance, quoting Curtis Fuller, 217.

13 Smith, "Awakening Dead Time," 390. Adorno employs the concept (in contrast to the failure of breakout) throughout his work, from *Minima Moralia* to his book *Mahler: A Musical Physiognomy* (1960). For an elaboration on Adorno's sense of breakthrough, see Buhler, "Breakthrough," 125–43.

14 Adorno, "On the Contemporary Relationship," quoted in Leppert's first commentary in *Essays on Music*, 99.

15 "The nature of this sadness stands out more clearly if one asks with whom the adherents of historicism actually empathize. The answer is inevitable; with the victor." Benjamin, "Theses," 256.

16 These art works are the "cultural treasures" that Benjamin argues have been decontextualized by historicist writing and that dialectical materialism reveals. See Benjamin, "Theses," 256–57.

17 Benjamin, "Convolutes: N," 462. For a penetrating analysis of Benjamin's thought, see Osborne and Charles, "Walter Benjamin," 1–58. Adorno's comment on image appears in *Notes on Literature* and is quoted in Helmling, "Constellation and Critique." For "with the intensity," Tiedman, "Dialectics at a Standstill," 935.

18 For "shadow," see Ellison, "Introduction," xix; for "a summation," see Ellison, "Golden Age," 210; Harootunian, *Marx After Marx*, 26; Liu et al., "Exigency of Time," 25.

19 "Sublation" is the English translation of Hegel's technical use of the German verb *aufheben*. See Maybee, "Hegel's Dialectics." As Simon Choat explains the concept of sublation, "While every state of affairs negates itself, this is a 'determinate negation,' however: the result of negation is not nothing, but a new stage which transcends the old stage while preserving some of its features." Quoting from Hegel's *Science of Logic*, Choat continues, "That which is sublated is thus something at the same time preserved." *Marx's Grundrisse*, 3–4.

20 Berliner, *Thinking in Jazz*. For "licks," 227; "has [something] to say," 170 (the author is quoting Tommy Flanagan); "ebb and flow," 151; "rocks in his blood," 255. Stanley R. Nelson draws a connection between the body's fall (heart failure) and Negro syncopation ("syncope") at the opening of his book, *All About Jazz*, 11.

21 "Flashes of insight" are Berliner's own words. *Thinking in Jazz*, 216–17. For Kenny Barron's comment, see 201.

22 Berliner, *Thinking in Jazz*, 151, 152, 245.

23 For Hill, see Berliner, *Thinking in Jazz*, 353. For Hersch and "different kinds of time," 245.

24 For "tapping," Berliner, *Thinking in Jazz*, 202. Berliner is quoting respectively Emily Remler and Roberta Baum. For Farmer, 485.

25 Berliner, *Thinking in Jazz*, 485.

26 Bjerstedt, "Storytelling in Jazz Improvisation."

27 DeVeaux, *Birth of Bebop*, 268–69. For Ellington, see Porter, *Thing Called Jazz*, 37. Iyer, "Exploding the Narrative," 395. See also Frieler et al., "Telling a Story," 68–82.

28 Ellison, "Man at Chehaw Station," 3. Ellison here is speaking of his jazz transgression from the classical norm "that was demanded in performing the music assigned to me." For Trummy Young, Jimmy Rowles on Parker, Buddy Fleet on Christian, and Eldridge's comment, see Gitler,

Swing to Bop, 40, 154, 42, 47, respectively. On Whetsol, see Elmer Snowden in Dance, *World of Swing*, 53. For Art Blakey, see Lott, "Double V, Double Time," 462. On Hawkins, see Rex Stewart's comments, and for "skillful transpositions," see Buddy Fleet's, both in Gitler, *Swing to Bop*, 48, 69.

29 Cozy Cole notes that the term was used in the 1930s by "western players" (presumably, "Southwest," i.e., Kansas City, Dallas, etc.): "They'd get in a groove," he told Stanley Dance in *World of Swing*, 23. Barry Kernfeld similarly observes that *groove* was a term of choice among 1930s swing players. See his essay "Groove(i)." Geoffrey Whittall, in contrast, argues against groove's African American origin. See Whittall, "Groove." Marc Abel, finally, takes a similar position in his book *Groove*. Abel's is a curious argument that mars an otherwise important investigation of rhythm in its relation to the time of capital. His challenge seems unnecessary as it is historically blind: it reaffirms the racial struggle over property that courses through the history of popular music. A rhythm and blues label, Groove Records, appeared briefly in the 1950s.

30 Keil and Feld, *Music Grooves*; Roholt, *Groove*; Abel, *Groove*.

31 This quality is what Charles Keil famously characterized as "participant discrepancies," or "P.D.s." See Keil and Feld, *Music Grooves*. Matthew Butterfield provides a trenchant analysis of groove character in his essay "Why do Jazz Musicians," 3–25.

32 Ellison, *Invisible Man*, 8.

33 Gitler, *Swing to Bop*, 45; Jones quoted in Dance, *World of Swing*, 30.

34 Adorno, *Aesthetic Theory*, 341; Benjamin, "Theses," 262. See also Buck-Morss, "Walter Benjamin."

35 DeVeaux, *Birth of Bebop*, 70.

36 Niles, "Shout, Coon, Shout," 528.

37 For Ellington, see Porter, *Thing Called Jazz*, 37.

38 Gennari, *Blowin' Hot and Cold*, 74. Gennari combines two instances of Williams's commentaries on the same subject, as he acknowledges. I've restored the quote from Williams, *Jazz Tradition*, 51, while including Williams's reference in the same instance to "flash."

39 Quoted in Lane, *Jazz and Machine-Age Imperialism*, 108.

40 Panassié, *Hot Jazz*, 2, 21. Panassié and the cohort of hot jazz devotees that developed in Paris in the late 1920s formally organized as the Hot Club de France in 1932. It is noteworthy that when Panassié finally got to hear Louis Armstrong perform live in Paris, he was hugely disappointed. Armstrong's minstrel-inspired histrionics were, for Panassié, nothing more than crass commercialism obscuring the recorded realness of "the great creative musician." Panassié, *Hot Jazz*, 62. See also Shack, *Harlem to Montmartre*, xv–xvi, 93–97; Rye, "Hot Club de France."

41 Gennari, *Blowin' Hot and Cold*, 67, 77. Emphasis in the original.

42   Finkelstein, *Jazz*, 15. Gennari, *Blowin' Hot and Cold*, 172, 121, 165. Emphasis is mine.

43   Gennari, *Blowin' Hot and Cold*, 167.

44   Hentoff, "Racial Prejudice in Jazz," 72, 74.

45   Eliot, "Tradition." On Williams and Eliot, see Gennari, *Blowin' Hot and Cold*, 186, 73. The other quotations are Gennari's and appear on 186 and 188. In describing a path to proper jazz criticism, Williams commented, "If I recommend that this training should begin with Plato, Aristotle, and Lucretius and end with Eliot, Tovey and Jung, I would not be saying something academic or pretentious, but merely stating the most ordinary commonplace of Western civilization as it exists." Gennari, *Blowin' Hot and Cold*, 180.

46   Von Eschen, *Satchmo*; Monson, *Freedom Sounds*. Feather's *The Book of Jazz* (1959) is quoted in DeVeaux, *Birth of Bebop*, 19. Feather describes how hearing Armstrong's recording of "West End Blues" in the early 1930s affirmed his conviction that jazz had "elements in common with membership in a resistance movement" (qtd. in Von Eschen, *Satchmo*, 8–9). On the ideology of liberal internationalism that oriented news and culture coverage during the Cold War, see McGarr, *City of Newsmen*.

47   See "Modernism, Race, and Aesthetics," chapter 3 of Monson, *Freedom Sounds*.

48   Feather quoted in DeVeaux, *Birth of Bebop*, 63. For an elaboration on this position, see Hodeir, *Jazz*.

49   Denning, *Noise Uprising*, 137. For a discussion of the Paris conference, see Baldwin, "Princes and Powers," 13–55. PDFs of the original transcripts of *le Congrès des écrivains et artistes noirs* can be readily found on the web, both in French and English.

50   Weheliye, *Phonographies*; Gennari, *Blowin' Hot and Cold*, 204–5.

51   Pleasants, *Agony of Modern Music* and *Serious Music, and All That Jazz!*; Ellison, "Golden Age," 200.

52   Taylor, interview with Max Roach, 106. Feld, *Jazz Cosmopolitanism in Accra*.

53   Adorno was already involving the concept in his references to the "music industry" and "jazz industry" in "On the Social Situation of Music" (1932). The concept was developed formally, with Max Horkheimer, as "The Culture Industry: Enlightenment as Mass Deception." See Horkheimer and Adorno, *Dialectic of Enlightenment*, 94–136. On Adorno's use of the term *jazz*, see Robinson, "Jazz Essays of Adorno," 1–25. Thompson, "Meaning of Fascism."

54   For "under the trademark," see Adorno, "Social Situation of Music," 430; for "perpetual repetition," see Adorno, "On Jazz," 475. Jarvis, *Adorno*, 1–2. James Buhler argues that Adorno's critique of African connections develops from an antiracist position and an insistence that "primitivism" is a European idea, not an African one. See Buhler, "Frankfurt School Blues," 105–6.

55 As Adorno writes in "The Culture Industry Reconsidered," "The culture industry intentionally integrates its consumers from above. To the detriment of both it forces together the spheres of high and low art." Quoted in Buhler, "Frankfurt School Blues," 115. Buhler elaborates: "Both high and low art lose their critical and liberatory potential; art becomes wholly meaningless, nothing but a pleasant diversion evaluated only in terms of the pleasure or social standing it affords its audience. Art reverts to its commodity function: pure entertainment" (116).

56 Buhler, "Frankfurt School Blues," 115, 116.

57 Buhler, "Frankfurt School Blues," 116; Benjamin, "Theses," thesis 9.

58 Richard Leppert provides a detailed overview of the exchange, along with summaries of the two essays, in Adorno, *Essays on Music*, 240–50.

59 Adorno, "Fetish Character of Music," 288, 292. Benjamin, "Work of Art." The essay appears in several edited sources.

60 Adorno, *Aesthetic Theory*, 21.

61 Adorno, *Aesthetic Theory*, 21.

62 Martin, "Absolute Artwork," 18.

63 Martin, "Absolute Artwork," 19.

64 Martin, "Absolute Artwork," 23, 20, 23. Such fragmented "life" is cast as glimmers relating to the role of magic. See Horkheimer and Adorno, *Dialectic of Enlightenment*, chap. 1, "The Concept of Enlightenment," and elsewhere.

65 As Marx famously put it in "The Working Day," chap. 10 of *Capital*, vol. 1, "Capital is dead labour which, vampire-like, lives only by sucking living labor, and lives the more, the more labour it sucks."

66 Adorno, *Aesthetic Theory*, 261.

67 Adorno, "Phonograph," 277, 279.

68 Adorno, "Phonograph Record," 279–80; and "Curves of the Needle," 271–76. Emphasis in the original. Levin, "For the Record," 39.

69 Shellac is produced from the lac bug that inhabits forests in South Asia. It was originally extracted as a raw material by Europeans, eventually forming the basis of early 78-RPM records.

70 Adorno, "On Jazz," 485.

71 Ellison, "Introduction," xix.

CHAPTER 9. APOTHEOSIS OF A NEW BLACK MUSIC

1 Baraka, "Changing Same," 180–82. He discusses Brown on 185–86.

2 Baraka, "Changing Same," 181, 189. The parentheses surrounding "total" appear in the original.

3 Baraka, *Blues People*, 216–20. Baraka introduces the expression "blues impulse" in chapter 10 (142) and develops it with reference to "blues

people" (172) in chapter 11, where he writes, "Jazz demonstrated how the blues impulse and thus Afro-American musical tradition could be retained in a broader [i.e., White-majority] musical tradition" (176). He employs the expression again to begin the essay, "The Changing Same" (180). He may have borrowed it from Ellison, who famously wrote of the impulse in his essay "Richard Wright's Blues." On the weak character of funky and soul approaches, Baraka writes: "The hard boppers sought to revitalize jazz, but they did not go far enough. Somehow they lost sight of the important ideas to be learned from bebop and substituted largess of timbre and quasi-gospel influences for actual, rhythmic and melodic diversity and freshness" (*Blues People*, 217). Baraka's references to "energy" and "spiritual" in "The Changing Same" appear separately and then together on 185.

4   Early, "Leroi Jones/Amiri Baraka," 345

5   Davis, "Honoring and Remembering."

6   Baraka, "Changing Same," 205, 180, 205.

7   Sewell, "Temporalities of Capitalism," 526–27.

8   Reed, *Soundworks*, 10.

9   Benjamin, "Theses," 256. For "mute music," see the discussion in chapter 8.

10 Hall, "Notes on Deconstructing," 230–31. Still valuable is Peterson, "Why 1955?" On the simplification of production, see Dunlavy, *Small, Medium, Large*.

11 Hall, "What Is This 'Black,'" 469–70. West, "Afro-American Popular Music."

12 Gilroy, *Black Atlantic*; Erlmann, *Music, Modernity*; Von Eschen, *Satchmo*; Rollefson, *Flip the Script*. See also the essays in Radano and Olaniyan, *Audible Empire*. Kun is quoted in Hamilton, *Just Around Midnight*, 8.

13 Cohen, *Consumers' Republic*, 54, 13, 83–84.

14 Green, *Selling the Race*, 6–8.

15 Bluebird performers often found work at the West Side establishment Ruby Lee Gatewood's Tavern. Green, *Selling the Race*, 71–72.

16 Green, *Selling the Race*, 69–70, 72, 90.

17 Gennari, *Blowin' Hot and Cold*, 67, 77.

18 The desire to claim racial purity is a version of what Adam Green calls "heroic autonomy." See Green, *Selling the Race*, 72; Collis, *Story of Chess Records*, 10.

19 Gordon, "Muddy Waters." The Bluebird sides were released once Waters became famous. For background, see Collis, *Story of Chess Records*.

20 Green, *Selling the Race*, 74. Robert Palmer discusses the negotiations with Chess and the help of "Evelyn" in *Deep Blues*, 157. A 1989 city document published by the Landmarks Commission names her as Evelyn Aron. See "Chess Records: Preliminary Staff Summary of Information," submitted to the Commission on Chicago Landmarks July 1989, City of Chicago, ac-

cessed July 26, 2024, https://www.chicago.gov/content/dam/city/depts /zlup/Historic_Preservation/Publications/Chess_Records_Office_and _Studio.pdf. Collis, *Story of Chess Records*, 35, 48.

21   Palmer, *Deep Blues*, 3–4.

22   Odum, "Folk-song and Folk-Poetry," 261; Troutman, *Kila*.

23   Doyle, *Echo and Reverb*, 172.

24   Moon, "Strange Voodoo." Recording techniques are described in an advertisement for Reverb's re-recorded drum sounds, "Studio Sampled Sounds: Drum Series Vol. 4, Chess Records Studio." In *Echo and Reverb*, Doyle provides a long quotation from "researcher Robert Campbell" on Chess's studio techniques, taken from a personal correspondence (178n5).

25   Palmer, *Dancing in the Street*, 200–201.

26   Connor, *Dumbstruck*, 38.

27   "Catfish Blues" had been well established in the Delta and Chicago circles. Listen, for example, to Robert Petway's masterful version on Bluebird, recorded in 1941.

28   Thanks to Charlie Dill for an enjoyable debate about how best to notate this seemingly simple riff.

29   Another contemporary version of the raucous guitar sound can be heard on Goree Carter, "Rock Awhile" (1949).

30   Doyle, *Echo and Reverb*, 171.

31   Quoted in Doyle, *Echo and Reverb*, 29.

32   Doyle, *Echo and Reverb*, 169.

33   Lott, "Back Door Man," 701. Palmer describes how this voice was also available live, writing: "He had the hugest voice I have ever heard—it seemed to fill the hall and get right inside your ears, and when he hummed and moaned in falsetto, every hair on your neck crackled with electricity." *Deep Blues*, 233.

34   Robert Palmer, "Church of Sonic Guitar," 656–57. Occasionally, Chess's production methods seemed contrived. Johnny "Guitar" Watson's "Space Guitar" (1955), for example, is a ham-handed attempt to employ echo and reverb to sound "space age."

35   On the residual character of commodities in relation to abstract labor, see Harvey, *Companion to Marx's Capital*, 128.

36   Lauterbach, *Chitlin' Circuit*, 50, 91.

37   Haney's was in Ferriday, Louisiana; the Dew Drop Inn and the Black Diamond were in New Orleans; the Keyhole in San Antonio. Lauterbach, *Chitlin' Circuit*, 132, 143, 166.

38   Lauterbach, *Chitlin' Circuit*, 50. Over the course of his book, the author names many other cities in the circuit.

39   On federal and local laws enforcing licensing restrictions, see the articles appearing under the main title "Demand Permit System Repeal." Lauterbach, *Chitlin' Circuit*, 65.

40 Lauterbach, *Chitlin' Circuit*, 158, 176–77, 185, 193, 197, 223. Among the announcers at WDIA was Riley King, better known as "B. B." Lauterbach's mapping of the expanse of Black-run or Black-owned businesses also includes the Macon City Auditorium, managed by Reese Dupree (149) and the Black-owned Shaw Artists, a Chicago talent agency (164). For further background on radio, see Ward, *Radio and the Struggle*.

41 Lauterbach, *Chitlin' Circuit*, 3, 123, 160. He notes that Walker learned tap dancing and early in his life toured with a medicine show (123). On Howlin' Wolf, see Palmer, *Deep Blues*, 233. Gatemouth Brown, "Atomic Energy"; John Lee Hooker, "Crawling King Snake"; Roy Brown, "Boogie at Midnight."

42 On women fans, see Lauterbach, *Chitlin' Circuit*, 131. On Little Richard, White, *Life and Times*, 36. White is quoting the bandleader and drummer Johnny Otis.

43 Lauterbach, *Chitlin' Circuit*, 131.

44 Simon, *Debt and Redemption*; see also Woods, *Development Arrested*.

45 Keil, *Urban Blues*, 165–67.

46 MacLean, *Freedom Is Not Enough*, 18.

47 Du Bois, *Gift of Black Folk*, 9.

48 Palmer, *Deep Blues*, 276–77.

49 Lauterbach, *Chitlin' Circuit*, 142–43, 159; on Jordan, see Shaw, *Honkers and Shouters*, 68.

50 Palmer, *Deep Blues*. He quotes Hooker on 243. For Waters, see Palmer's prologue. On King, see Lauterbach, *Chitlin' Circuit*, 211–14.

51 Green and Guillory, "Soulful Style," 250–51.

52 Ellison, "Golden Age," 208–9; Adorno, "On the Contemporary Relationship," 99.

53 Quoted in Carr, *Century of Jazz*, 150.

54 Hall, "Problem of Ideology," 27.

55 Lordi, *Meaning of Soul*, 8. Ellison, "Richard Wright's Blues," 78.

56 Ellison, "Introduction," xix.

57 For example: Buddy Johnson, Lucky Millinder, King Kolax, Jay McShann.

58 Lauterbach, *Chitlin' Circuit*, 115.

59 Lauterbach, *Chitlin' Circuit*, 118.

60 Baur, "Backbeat."

61 Nelson, "Haney's Big House," quoted in Lauterbach, *Chitlin' Circuit*, 165. For "blues and electricity," see Waksman, *Instruments of Desire*, 119.

62 "Rocket 88" is credited to Brenston and His Delta Cats, although Turner had organized the band; his Kings of Rhythm included Brenston on sax.

63 Robert Palmer makes note of their friendship in "Church of Sonic Guitar," 654.

64 Palmer, "Church of Sonic Guitar," 652.

65 Gioia, *Delta Blues*, 238.

66   Von Eschen, *Race Against Empire*; Mowitt, *Percussion*.

67   The Wikipedia entry on "Rhythm and Blues" cites two instances: "Night Club Reviews," 12; "Vaudeville Reviews," 28. Wexler was a staff reporter and editor, later a partner at Atlantic Records.

68   "Branding Slaves." See also Wiecek, "Statutory Law of Slavery," 270–74.

69   Ward, *Just My Soul Responding*, 22, 27. There were also a handful of Black-owned initiatives: Class, Dootone, Fortune, Vee Jay, and Robey's Peacock.

70   Ward observes that "there was a relatively buoyant black consumer market" sustaining the proliferation of Black-oriented radio and amassing "particular areas of strength and growth among the teens and young adults [who were] most likely to buy records." See *Just My Soul Responding*, 27. The rare early crossover hits, from R&B to Top 100, included vocal standards sung by Nat King Cole, "Mona Lisa" (1950), and Dinah Washington, "I Wanna Be Loved" (1950). With the Chords' "Sh-boom" (1954), such crossovers became more common.

71   For insights by Ahmet Ertegun on his efforts to launch Atlantic Records, see Bordowitz, "Ahmet Ertegun."

72   For a powerful and insightful overview of the South at this moment, see Daniel, *Lost Revolutions*.

73   McCormick, *America's Half Century*. For a vivid presentation of the formula, see George, *Death of Rhythm and Blues*.

74   Chapple and Garofalo, *Rock 'n' Roll*, 236.

75   Lipsitz, introduction to Otis, *Upside Your Head!*, xxvi.

76   "White Council," 32; "Rock 'n' Roll," 166–68; "Great Rock 'n' Roll Controversy," 40; "Rock and Roll and Riot," 16–17.

77   MacLean, *Freedom Is Not Enough*, prologue and chap. 1.

78   On Thornton, see Mahon, *Black Diamond Queens*. Gendron quoted in Frith, *Performing Rites*, 131. Hamilton, *Just Around Midnight*. After beginning his career imitating Nat Cole, moreover, Ray Charles shifted his approach to involve a deeper, blues-inspired gospel inflected approach. On his recording "It Should Have Been Me" (1954), he reinvents the crooning voice, alternating between a spoken sotto voce whisper and a boisterous chorus where he shouts the song's message.

79   Ramsey, *Race Music*, 4–5.

80   Baraka, *Autobiography*, 44, 80.

81   For Pitts's comment, see *Mean Old World*, 9. Coyle, "Highjacked Hits," 134.

82   Hamilton, *Just Around Midnight*, 7. Jordan, in conversation with Arnold Shaw, quoted in Lauterbach, *Chitlin' Circuit*, 295. Baraka and Baraka, "The Great Music Robbery," in *Music*, 328–32.

83   Cook, *Pricing of Progress*, 237.

84   See, for example, "In Every Family"; "Children's Cute Sayings," 7.

85   "Drama and Music," 13; "Latest Boogie Man," 2; "New Wrinkles," 8; "Beginnings of Pugilists." Yet another reference to boogie appears in a most

unlikely context, a description of the pitching style of the Chicago base-ball player Charles Koenig (a.k.a. "King"): "As an all wool and a yard wide Boogie Man Mr. C. King shines with a fierce, undying luster" ("Wilmot's Now Famous"). For "chin-music," see chapter 3.

86 For a swaggering Black man, see "Boogie." This usage was common in the 1920s.

87 Handy, *Father of the Blues*, 79.

88 "Among the Movies," 5.

89 On the "walking Texas bass," see Davin, "Conversation," 54, 49. On Texas musicians in Chicago, see Blesh and Janis, *They All Played Ragtime*, 148–49. On rent parties and the early precedents of boogie, see Shaw, *Honkers and Shouters*, 52.

90 Shaw, *Honkers and Shouters*, 52; Piras, "Johnson, Pete(r)."

91 Shaw, *Honkers and Shouters*, 52. Oliver, "Smith, Pine Top." The recording was released as "Pine Top" Smith, "Pine Top's Boogie Woogie," Vocalion 1245, Chicago, December 29, 1928.

92 "Boogie-Woogie," 15; Dodge, "Hot Jazz," 75–83.

93 According to the Brian Sisters website, the singers were accompanied by Will Osborne and His Orchestra. See "The Brian Sisters," accessed July 26, 2024, https://www.brian-sisters.org/BoogieWoogie.shtml.

94 Baraka, *Black Music*, 205.

95 Middleton, *Studying Popular Music*, 18–21.

96 Wolf recorded *The Howlin' Wolf London Sessions* in 1971. Waters recorded an album with the Rolling Stones, *Live at the Checkerboard Lounge, Chicago 1981*. Among Moore's notable tracks is "Jenny, Jenny" and "Chained to Your Heart."

97 "Funky Drummer" was reissued on Brown's compilation *In the Jungle Groove* (1986).

98 Reed, *Soundworks*, 3, 7, 9.

99 Harootunian, *Marx After Marx*, 26.

100 *Always, Already There: An Incubator for Afrodiasporic New Music*. Conference program book, Haus der Kulturen der Welt, Berlin, Germany, November 4–10, 2024. The event, organized by George E. Lewis, Harald Kisiedu, and Bonaventure Soh Bejeng Ndikung, showcased performances of works by twenty-two composers. See also Kisiedu and Lewis, *Composing While Black*.

AFTERWORD

1 Mbembe, *Critique of Black Reason*, 6. Italics in the original.

2 Geroulanos, *Invention of Prehistory*.

3   Seabrook, "Case for and Against Ed Sheeran"; Wikipedia, s.v. "Best I Ever Had (Drake Song)," accessed July 13, 2024, https://en.wikipedia.org/wiki/Best_I_Ever_Had_(Drake_song).

4   Cole, *Known and Strange Things*, 5–7. Cole is quoting Baldwin. It is interesting to consider the change in Black music's presence in Switzerland in light of recent scholarship. See, for example, Cox, *Sounds of Black Switzerland*.

5   Cole, "My Black Ears"; Du Bois, *Souls of Black Folk*, 102; Cole, *Known and Strange Things*, 11.

6   Mbembe, *Critique of Black Reason*, 129.

1922 Catalogue of Victor Records. Camden, NJ: Victor Talking Machine Company, 1922.

Abbott, Lynn, and Doug Seroff. *The Original Blues: The Emergence of Blues in African American Vaudeville*. Jackson: University Press of Mississippi, 2017.

Abbott, Lynn, and Doug Seroff. *Out of Sight: The Rise of African American Popular Music, 1889–1895*. Jackson: University Press of Mississippi, 2002.

Abbott, Lynn, and Doug Seroff. *Ragged But Right: Black Traveling Shows, "Coon Songs," and the Dark Pathway to Blues and Jazz*. Jackson: University Press of Mississippi, 2007.

Abbott, Lynn, and Doug Seroff. "'They Cert'ly Sound Good to Me': Sheet Music, Southern Vaudeville, and the Commercial Ascendancy of the Blues." *American Music* 14, no. 4 (Winter 1996): 402–54.

Abdy, E. S. *Journal of a Residence and Tour in the United States of America*. 3 vols. London: John Murray, 1835.

Abel, Mark. *Groove: An Aesthetic of Measured Time*. Chicago: Haymarket Books, 2015.

Abrahams, Roger D. *Singing the Master: The Emergence of African American Culture in the Plantation South*. New York: Penguin, 1993.

Adorno, Theodor W. *Aesthetic Theory*. 1970. Translated by Robert Hullot-Kentor. Edited by Gretel Adorno and Rolf Tiedemann. Minneapolis: University of Minnesota Press, 1997.

Adorno, Theodor W. "The Curves of the Needle." 1927. In *Essays on Music*, 271–76.

Adorno, Theodor W. *Essays on Music*. Introduction, commentary, and notes by Richard Leppert, new translations by Susan H. Gillespie. Berkeley: University of California Press, 2002.

Adorno, Theodor W. "The Fetish Character of Music and the Regression of Listening." 1938. In *Essays on Music*, 288–317.

Adorno, Theodor W. "The Form of the Phonograph Record." 1934. In *Essays on Music*, 277–82.

Adorno, Theodor W. "On Jazz." 1936. In *Essays on Music*, 470–95.

Adorno, Theodor W. "On the Contemporary Relationship of Philosophy and Music." 1953. In *Essays on Music*, 135–61.

Adorno, Theodor W. "On the Social Situation of Music." 1932. In *Essays on Music*, 391–436.

Adorno, Theodor, and Hanns Eisler. *Composing for the Films*. London: Athlone, 1994. Originally published 1947 by Oxford University Press (New York) under Eisler.

"African American Performers on Early Sound Recordings, 1892–1916." Library of Congress. https://www.loc.gov/item/ihas.200038862/.

Agawu, Kofi. "Structural Analysis or Cultural Analysis? Competing Perspectives on the 'Standard Pattern' of West African Rhythm." *Journal of the American Musicological Society* 59, no. 1 (Spring 2006): 1–46.

Albert, Octavia Victoria Rogers. *The House of Bondage; Or, Charlotte Brooks and Other Slaves*. New York: Hunt and Eaton, 1891.

Allen, Fred. *Much Ado About Me*. Boston: Little, Brown, 1956.

Allen, William Francis, Charles Pickard Ware, and Lucy McKim Garrison, comp. *Slave Songs of the United States*. New York: A. Simpson, 1867.

Allewaert, Monique. *Ariel's Ecology: Plantations, Personhood, and Colonialism in the American Tropics*. Minneapolis: University of Minnesota Press, 2013.

Althusser, Louis, and Étienne Balibar. *Reading Capital*. Translated by Ben Brewster. London: Verso, 1997. Abridged translation originally published 1970 by New Left Books (London).

Always, Already There: An Incubator for Afrodiasporic New Music. Conference program book, Haus der Kulturen der Welt, Berlin, November 4–10, 2024.

"Among the Movies." *Chicago Defender*, June 22, 1918, weekend edition, 5.

Anderson, Jourdon. "Letter from a Freedman to His Older Master." Dictated. *New York Daily Tribune*, August 22, 1865.

"The Appeal of the Primitive Jazz." *Literary Digest*, August 25, 1917, 28–29.

Arendt, Hannah. *The Human Condition*. 2nd ed. Chicago: University of Chicago Press, 1998. Originally published 1958 by University of Chicago Press.

Arzuaga, Fabian. "Socially Necessary Superfluity: Adorno and Marx on the crises of labor and the individual." *Philosophy and Social Criticism* 45, no. 7 (2019): 819–43.

"Ashes of Lynched Negro Buried." *New York Times*, December 8, 1899, 5.

Attali, Jacques. *Noise: The Political Economy of Music*. Translated by Brian Massumi. Minneapolis: University of Minnesota Press, 1985.

"Aurora, Ill." *Chicago Defender*, June 21, 1913, 7.

Austin, Mary. "Buck and Wing on Bill Robinson." *Nation*, April 28, 1926, 476.

Averill, Gage. *Four Parts, No Waiting: A Social History of American Barbershop Harmony*. New York: Oxford University Press, 2003.

Badger, Reid. *A Life in Ragtime: A Biography of James Reese Europe*. New York: Oxford University Press, 1995.

Baker, Houston A., Jr. *Modernism and the Harlem Renaissance*. Chicago: University of Chicago Press, 1987.

Baker, Lee D. *Anthropology and the Racial Politics of Culture*. Durham, NC: Duke University Press, 2010.

Baker, Lee D. *From Savage to Negro: Anthropology and the Construction of Race, 1896–1954*. Berkeley: University of California Press, 1998.

Baldwin, Davarian. Introduction to *Escape from New York: The New Negro Renaissance Beyond Harlem*, edited by Davarian Baldwin and Minkah Makalani, 1–28. Minneapolis: University of Minnesota Press, 2013.

Baldwin, Davarian. "Our Newcomers to the City: The Great Migration and the Making of Modern Mass Culture." In *Beyond Blackface: African Americans and the Creation of American Popular Culture, 1890–1930*, edited by W. Fitzhugh Brundage, 159–89. Chapel Hill: University of North Carolina Press, 2011.

Baldwin, James. "Princes and Powers." In *Nobody Knows My Name*, 13–55. New York: Vintage, 1993. Originally published 1961 by Dial Press (New York).

"Band Concerts." *Evening Star* (Washington, DC), June 16, 1916, 22.

"Band Programme." *Ceylon Observer*, February 4, 1920, weekly edition, 178.

Banner, Stuart. *American Property: A History of How, Why, and What We Own*. Cambridge, MA: Harvard University Press, 2011.

Baptist, Edward E. *The Half Has Never Been Told: Slavery and the Making of American Capitalism*. New York: Basic Books, 2014.

Baptist, Edward E. "Toxic Debt, Liar Loans, and Securitized Human Beings." *Commonplace* 10, no. 3 (2010). https://commonplace.online/article/toxic -debt-liar-loans/.

Baraka, Amiri. *The Autobiography of LeRoi Jones*. Chicago: Lawrence Hill Books, 2012. Originally published 1984 by Freundlich Books (New York).

Baraka, Amiri [LeRoi Jones]. *Black Music*. New York: William Morrow, 1967.

Baraka, Amiri [LeRoi Jones]. *Blues People*. New York: William Morrow, 1963.

Baraka, Amiri [LeRoi Jones]. "The Changing Same: R&B and New Black Music." In *Black Music*, 180–211.

Baraka, Amiri [LeRoi Jones]. *Digging: The Afro-American Soul of American Classical Music*. Berkeley: University of California Press, 2009.

Baraka, Amiri, and Amina Baraka. *The Music: Reflections on Jazz and Blues*. New York: William Morrow, 1987.

Baraka, Imamu Ameer. "A Black Value System." *Black Scholar* 1, no. 1, "The Culture of Revolution" (November 1969): 54–60.

Barton, William E. "Hymns of the Slave and the Freedman." *New England Magazine* 19, no. 5 (January 1899): 609–24.

Basie, Count. *Good Morning Blues: The Autobiography of Count Basie*. As told to Albert Murray. Introduction by Dan Morgenstern. Minneapolis: University of Minnesota Press, 2016. Originally published 1985 by Random House (New York).

Baskerville, John D. "Free Jazz: A Reflection of Black Power Ideology." *Journal of Black Studies* 24, no. 4 (June 1994): 484–97.

Bastiat, Frédéric. "Natural and Artificial Social Order." In *Economic Harmonies*, translated by George B. De Huszar, edited by W. Hayden Boyers, chap. 1.

Foundation for Economic Education, 1996. Library of Economics and Liberty. http://www.econlib.org/library/Bastiat/basHar.html. First published in French 1850.

Baur, Steve. "Backbeat." Grove Music Online, 2003.

Bechet, Sidney. *Treat It Gentle: An Autobiography*. 2nd ed. With a new preface by Rudi Blesh. New York: DaCapo, 2002. Originally published 1960 by Hill and Wang (New York).

Beckert, Sven. *Empire of Cotton: A Global History*. New York: Knopf, 2014.

Beckert, Sven, and Seth Rockman, eds. *Slavery's Capitalism: A New History of American Economic Development*. Philadelphia: University of Pennsylvania Press, 2016.

"Beginnings of Pugilists." *Daily Morning Journal and Courier* (New Haven), June 17, 1905.

Bell, Archie. "The Ellington Orchestra in Cleveland." 1931. In Tucker, *Duke Ellington Reader*, 50–54.

Benjamin, Walter. "Convolutes: N, On the Theory of Knowledge, Theory of Progress." In *The Arcades Project*, translated by Howard Eiland and Kevin McLaughlin. Cambridge, MA: Belknap Press of Harvard University Press, 1999.

Benjamin, Walter. "Theses on the Philosophy of History." 1940. In *Illuminations: Essays and Reflections*, edited by Hannah Arendt, 253–64. New York: Schocken Books, 1968.

Benjamin, Walter. "The Work of Art in the Age of Mechanical Reproduction." 1936. In *Illuminations: Essays and Reflections*, edited by Hannah Arendt, 217–52. New York: Schocken Books, 1968.

Bennett, Jane. *Vibrant Matter: A Political Ecology of Things*. Durham, NC: Duke University Press, 2010.

Berger, Morroe. "Jazz: Resistance to the Diffusion of a Culture-Pattern." *Journal of Negro History* 32, no. 4 (October 1947): 461–94.

Berish, Andrew S. *Lonesome Roads and Streets of Dreams: Place, Mobility, and Race in Jazz of the 1930s and '40s*. Chicago: University of Chicago Press, 2012.

Berlin, Edward A. "Kerry Mills." Grove Music Online, 2014.

Berlin, Edward A. *King of Ragtime: Scott Joplin and His Era*. New York: Oxford University Press, 1994.

Berlin, Edward A. "Ragtime." Grove Music Online, 2013.

Berlin, Edward A. *Ragtime: A Musical and Cultural History*. Berkeley: University of California Press, 1980.

Berlin, Edward A. "Scott Joplin." Grove Music Online, 2013.

Berlin, Ira. *Slaves Without Masters: The Free Negro in the Antebellum South*. New York: Pantheon, 1974.

Berlin, Irving, and Justus Dickinson. "Words and Music." *Green Book Magazine*, July 1915, 104–5.

Berliner, Paul F. *The Soul of Mbira: Music and Traditions of the Shona People of Zimbabwe*. Chicago: University of Chicago Press, 1978.

Berliner, Paul F. *Thinking in Jazz: The Infinite Art of Improvisation*. Chicago: University of Chicago Press, 1994.

Bernault, Florence. *Colonial Transactions: Imaginaries, Bodies, and Histories in Gabon*. Durham, NC: Duke University Press, 2019.

Berry, Daina Ramey. *The Price for Their Pound of Flesh: The Value of the Enslaved, from Womb to Grave, in the Building of a Nation*. Boston: Beacon, 2017.

Berry, Daina Ramey. "We'm Fus' Rate Bargain: Value, Labor, and Price in a Georgia Slave Community." In *The Chattel Principle: Internal Slave Trades in the Americas*, edited by Walter Johnson, 55–71. New Haven, CT: Yale University Press, 2005.

Bertholf, Garry. "Listening to Du Bois's 'Black Reconstruction': After James." *South: A Scholarly Journal* 48, no. 1 (Fall 2015): 78–91.

Best, Stephen M. *The Fugitive's Properties: Law and the Poetics of Possession*. Chicago: University of Chicago Press, 2004.

"Between Two Fires." *Chicago Defender*, April 24, 1915, big weekend edition, 5.

Bibb, Henry. *Narrative of the Life and Adventures of Henry Bibb, an American Slave*. New York: published by the author, 5 Spruce Street, 1849.

Bibb, Henry. "The Plantation Song." *National Anti-Slavery Standard* 5, no. 10 (August 8, 1844): 40.

Bie, Oscar. "Rhythm." Translated by Theodore Baker. *Musical Quarterly* 11, no. 3 (July 1925): 331–38.

Bierley, Paul E. *The Incredible Band of John Philip Sousa*. Urbana: University of Illinois Press, 2010.

Bierley, Paul E. *John Philip Sousa: A Descriptive Catalog of His Works*. Urbana: University of Illinois Press, 1973.

Bierley, Paul E., and H. Wiley Hitchcock. "Sousa, John Philip." Grove Music Online, 2014.

"The Big Removal Sale." *Freeman*, February 27, 1909, 4.

Bilbija, Marina. "Democracy's New Song: *Black Reconstruction in America, 1860–1880* and the Melodramatic Imagination." *Annals of the American Academy of Political and Social Science* 637 (September 2011): 64–77.

Bird-David, Nurit. "'Animism' Revisited: Personhood, Environment, and Relational Epistemology." *Current Anthropology* 40, no. S1 (1999): S67–S91.

Bjerstedt, Sven. "Storytelling in Jazz Improvisation: Implications of a Rich Intermedial Metaphor." PhD diss., Lund University, 2014.

Blacking, John. *How Musical Is Man?* Seattle: University of Washington Press, 1973.

Blackmon, Douglas A. *Slavery by Another Name: The Re-Enslavement of Black Americans from the Civil War to World War II*. New York: Anchor Books, 2008.

"Black Varieties: The Minstrels of the Row, Picturesque Scenes Without Scenery—Physiognomical Studies at Pickett's [Tavern]." *Cincinnati Commercial*, April 9, 1876, 4.

Blassingame, John W., ed. *Slave Testimony: Two Centuries of Letters, Speeches, Interviews, and Autobiographies*. Baton Rouge: Louisiana State University Press, 1977.

Blench, Roger. "Nigeria, Federal Republic of: Musical Instruments." Grove Music Online, 2001.

Blesh, Rudi, and Harriet Janis. *They All Played Ragtime: The True Story of an American Music*. Revised edition. New York: Grove, 1959. Originally published 1950 by Grove (New York).

Blight, David W. *Race and Reunion: The Civil War in American Memory*. Cambridge, MA: Harvard University Press, 2002.

Blight, David W. "W. E. B. Du Bois and the Struggle for American Historical Memory." In *History and Memory in African-American Culture*, edited by Geneviève Fabre and Robert G. O'Meally, 45–71. New York: Oxford University Press, 1994.

"Blues! Blues! For the Player Piano." *Chicago Defender*, March 31, 1917, 5.

Bohlman, Philip V. *The Study of Folk Music in the Modern World*. Bloomington: Indiana University Press, 1988.

"Boogie-Woogie." *New Yorker*, December 31, 1938, 15.

Bordowitz, Hank. "Ahmet Ertegun and the History of Atlantic Records." 1991. TeachRock. Accessed October 9, 2024. https://teachrock.org/article/ahmet-ertegun-and-the-history-of-atlantic-records/.

Borge, Jason. *Tropical Riffs: Latin America and the Politics of Jazz*. Durham, NC: Duke University Press, 2018.

Born in Slavery: Slave Narratives from the Federal Writers' Project, 1936–1938. Library of Congress Digital Collections. https://www.loc.gov/collections/slave-narratives-from-the-federal-writers-project-1936-to-1938/about-this-collection/.

Botkin, B. A., ed. *Lay My Burden Down: A Folk History of Slavery*. Chicago: University of Chicago Press, 1945.

Bourdieu, Pierre. *Distinction: A Social Critique of the Judgement of Taste*. Translated by Richard Nice. 1979; Reprint, Cambridge, MA: Harvard University Press, 1984.

Bourdieu, Pierre. *Outline of a Theory of Practice*. Translated by Richard Nice. 1977. Reprint, Cambridge: Cambridge University Press, 2013.

Bowdery, Francis. "Schools of Ragtime: The Piano Rolls of Scott Joplin." *Pianola Journal* 24 (2014): 48–67. https://www.pianola.org/journal/journal_vol23-24.cfm.

Braggs, Rashida. *Jazz Diasporas: Race, Music, and Migration in Post–World War II France*. Berkeley: University of California Press, 2016.

Brainerd, E. "Plantation Music." *Critic*, December 29, 1883, 534.

Brainerd, Mary Beale. "Dinky." *Atlantic Monthly*, August 1884, 206–12.

"Branding Slaves." Encyclopedia.com. Accessed [August 17, 2024]. https://www.encyclopedia.com/humanities/applied-and-social-sciences-magazines/branding-slaves.

"A Brass Band Gone Crazy!" *Evening Star* (Washington, DC), April 18, 1917, 7.

Brooks, Daphne A. *Bodies in Dissent: Spectacular Performances of Race and Freedom, 1850–1910*. Durham, NC: Duke University Press, 2006.

Brooks, Daphne A. "'Puzzling the Intervals': Blind Tom and the Poetics of the Sonic Slave Narrative." *Oxford Handbooks Online*, 2014. https://doi.org/10.1093/oxfordhb/9780199731480.013.023.

Brooks, Tim, ed. "Columbia Corporate History: Market Crash, 1929, and the Early 1930s." In *Electrical Recording and the Late 1920s*, vol. 1 of *Columbia Master Book Discography*. Online edition. Discography of American Historical Recordings (DAHR). https://adp.library.ucsb.edu/index.php/resources/detail/115#HistText_71.

Brooks, Tim. "The Laughing Song." National Registry of the Library of Congress. https://www.loc.gov/static/programs/national-recording-preservation-board/documents/LaughingSong.pdf.

Brooks, Tim. *Lost Sounds: Blacks and the Birth of the Recording Industry, 1890–1919*. Urbana: University of Illinois Press, 2004.

Brothers, Thomas. *Louis Armstrong: Master of Modernism*. New York: W. W. Norton, 2014.

Brown, Bill. "Reification, Reanimation, and the American Uncanny." *Critical Inquiry* 32, no. 2 (Winter 2006): 175–207.

Brown, Bill. *A Sense of Things: The Object Matter of American Literature*. Chicago: University of Chicago Press, 2003.

Brown, Vincent. *The Reaper's Garden: Death and Power in the World of Atlantic Slavery*. Cambridge, MA: Harvard University Press, 2008.

Brown, Vincent. "Social Death and Political Life in the Study of Slavery." *American Historical Review* 114, no. 5 (December 2009): 1231–49.

Brunn, H. O. *The Story of the Original Dixieland Jazz Band*. Baton Rouge: Louisiana State University Press, 1960.

Brylawski, Samuel S. "Jukebox." Grove Music Online, 2001.

Brymn, Lieut. J. Tim. "He's My Man (You'd Better Leave Him Alone)." OKeh, 1921.

Brymn, Lieut. J. Tim. "I'm Craving for that Kind of Love." OKeh, 1921.

Buchanan, Thomas C. *Black Life on the Mississippi*. Chapel Hill: University of North Carolina Press, 2004.

Buck-Morss, Susan. "Walter Benjamin—Revolutionary Writer (I)." *New Left Review* 1, no. 128 (July–August 1981): 50–75.

Buhler, James. "'Breakthrough' as Critique of Form: The Finale of Mahler's First Symphony." *Nineteenth Century Music* 20, no. 2 (1996): 125–43.

Buhler, James. "Frankfurt School Blues: Rethinking Adorno's Critique of Jazz." In *Apparitions: New Perspectives on Adorno and Twentieth-Century Music*, edited by Berthold Hoeckner, 103–30. New York: Routledge, 2006.

Burke, Patrick. *Come in and Hear the Truth: Jazz and Race on 52nd Street*. Chicago: University of Chicago Press, 2008.

Burlin, Natalie Curtis. "Negro Music at Birth." *Musical Quarterly* 5, no. 1 (January 1919): 86–89.

Butterfield, Matthew. "Why Do Jazz Musicians Swing Their Eighth Notes?" *Music Theory Spectrum* 33, no. 1 (March 2011): 3–25.

Camp, Stephanie M. H. *Closer to Freedom: Enslaved Women and Everyday Resistance in the Plantation South.* Chapel Hill: University of North Carolina Press, 2004.

Campbell, John. *Negro-Mania: Being an Examination of the Falsely Assumed Equality of the Various Races of Man.* Philadelphia: Campbell and Power, 1851.

"Canon Chase Seeks to Bar Jazz and Put Taboo on Jungles Steps." *New York Times*, February 24, 1922, 12.

Carney, Court. *Cuttin' Up: How Early Jazz Got America's Ear.* Lawrence: University Press of Kansas, 2009.

Carr, Roy. *A Century of Jazz.* New York: Da Capo, 1997.

Carter, Benny. "Do Critics Really Know What It's All About?" *Metronome*, May 1937, 17.

Carter, Scott. "Vox Americana: Voice, Race, and Nation in U.S. Music, 1880–1924." PhD diss., University of Wisconsin–Madison, 2014.

Casey, Edward S. "How to Get from Space to Place in a Fairly Short Stretch of Time: Phenomenological Prolegomena." In *Senses of Place*, edited by Steven Feld and Keith H. Basso, 13–52. Santa Fe: School of American Research Press, 1996.

Castelnau, Comte de. "Essay on Middle Florida, 1837–1839." *Florida Historical Quarterly* 26, no. 3 (January 1948): 300–324.

Castro, Eduardo Viveiros de. "Exchanging Perspectives: The Transformation of Objects into Subjects in Amerindian Ontologies." *Common Knowledge* 10, no. 3 (2004): 463–84.

Chakrabarty, Dipesh. *Provincializing Europe.* Princeton, NJ: Princeton University Press, 2007. First published 2000.

Chambers-Ketchum, Annie. "Music in the South, Part 3." *American Musician* 19 (December 6, 1890): 7–8.

Chapple, Steve, and Reebee Garofalo. *Rock 'n' Roll Is Here to Pay: The History and Politics of the Music Industry.* Chicago: Nelson-Hall, 1977.

Charters, Samuel. *A Trumpet Around the Corner: The Story of New Orleans Jazz.* Jackson: University Press of Mississippi, 2008.

Charters, Samuel, and Leonard Kunstadt. *Jazz: History of the New York Scene.* 1962; New York: Da Capo Press, 1981.

"Chased by Spook Table." *Washington Bee*, June 15, 1907, 7.

Cheyne, Peter, Andy Hamilton, and Max Paddison. *The Philosophy of Rhythm: Aesthetics, Music, Poetics.* Oxford: Oxford University Press, 2019.

"Children's Cute Sayings." *Weekly Rocky Mountain News* (Denver), June 16, 1898, 7.

Chilton, John. "Original Dixieland Jazz [Jass] Band [ODJB]." Grove Music Online, 2001.

"Chin-Music." *Frank Leslie's Illustrated Newspaper*, August 5, 1871, 344, 347.

Choat, Simon. *Marx's Grundrisse*. London: Bloomsbury Academic, 2016.

"Christmas Season Festivities." *Ceylon Observer*, December 3, 1919, weekly edition, 1813.

Clegg, John J. "Capitalism and Slavery." *Critical Historical Studies* 2, no. 2 (Fall 2015): 281–304.

Cohen, G. A. *Karl Marx's Theory of History: A Defence*. Expanded edition. Princeton, NJ: Princeton University Press, 2000. First published 1978.

Cohen, Harvey G. *Duke Ellington's America*. Chicago: University of Chicago Press, 2010.

Cohen, Lizabeth. *A Consumers' Republic: The Politics of Mass Consumption in Postwar America*. New York: Vintage, 2004.

Cohen, Lizabeth. *Making a New Deal: Industrial Workers in Chicago, 1919–1939*. Cambridge: Cambridge University Press, 1990.

Coke, Edward Thomas. *A Subaltern's Furlough*. London: Saunders and Otley, 1833.

Cole, Catherine M. *Ghana's Concert Party Theatre*. Bloomington: Indiana University Press, 2001.

Cole, Teju. *Known and Strange Things*. New York: Random House, 2016.

Cole, Teju. "My Black Ears." Keynote lecture to the conference, Pleasure and the Pleasurable in Africa and the African Diaspora, Department of African Cultural Studies, University of Wisconsin–Madison, April 13–15, 2017.

"College Band Even Swings Waltzes as Campus Rhythm Concert Draws 3000—Faculty Attends and Taps Feet, Too." *Down Beat*, January 1937, 1.

Collier, James Lincoln. "Bechet, Sidney (Jazz)." Grove Music Online, 2003.

Collier, James Lincoln. "Henderson, Fletcher." Grove Music Online, 2001.

Collis, John. *The Story of Chess Records*. London: Bloomsbury, 1998.

"Colombo Garden Club: Pierrot Entertainment." *Ceylon Observer*, August 18, 1920, weekly edition, 1255.

"The Color-Phobia as It Is." *Liberator*, October 11, 1839, 162.

"Connecticut." *United States Telegraph*, June 13, 1833.

Connor, Steven. *Dumbstruck: A Cultural History of Ventriloquism*. Oxford: Oxford University Press, 2001.

Cook, Eli. *The Pricing of Progress: Economic Indicators and the Pricing of American Life*. Cambridge, MA: Harvard University Press, 2017.

Cook, Nicholas. "Theorizing Musical Meaning." *Music Theory Spectrum* 23, no. 2 (Fall 2001): 170–95.

"Core Values for Jazz." Public Radio Program Directors Association. Accessed February 4, 2024. https://prpd.org/resources/core-values/format/jazz.

Cox, Jessie. *Sounds of Black Switzerland: Blackness, Music, and Unthought Voices*. Durham, NC: Duke University Press, 2025.

Coyle, Michael. "Highjacked Hits and Antic Authenticity: Cover Songs, Race, and Postwar Marketing." In *Rock over the Edge*, edited by Roger Beebee,

Denise Fulbrook, and Ben Saunders, 133–60. Durham, NC: Duke University Press, 2002.

Crawford, Richard. *America's Musical Life: A History*. New York: W. W. Norton, 2001.

Crawford, Richard. *The American Musical Landscape: The Business of Musicianship from Billings to Gershwin*. Berkeley: University of California Press, 2000.

Creecy, James R. *Scenes in the South, and Other Miscellaneous Pieces*. Washington, DC: Thomas McGill, 1860.

The Cries of New-York, with Fifteen Illustrations Drawn from the Life by a Distinguished Artist. New York: Printed and sold by Samuel Wood, 1822. First published 1809.

Criswell, Robert. *"Uncle Tom's Cabin" Contrasted with Buckingham Hall, the Planter's Home; Or, A Fair View of Both Sides of the Slavery Question*. New York: D. Fanshaw, 1852; Reprint, New York: AMS Press, 1973.

"Cruelly Tortured: A Relic of the Inquisition." *Morning Oregonian*, May 25, 1892, 3.

Cumming, Naomi. *The Sonic Self: Musical Subjectivity and Signification*. Bloomington: Indiana University Press, 2000.

Dabney, Ford. "Bugle Call Blues." 1922. Famous 3120-B, accessed on YouTube. https://www.youtube.com/watch?v=L5J2dGqR_vU.

Dahlhaus, Carl. "Form" (translated by Stephen Hinton). In *Schoenberg and the New Music: Essays by Carl Dahlhaus*, translated by Derrick Puffet and Alfred Clayton, 248–64. Cambridge: Cambridge University Press, 1987.

Dance, Stanley. "The Main-Stream Jazz War." *Melody Maker*, April 16, 1955, 3.

Dance, Stanley. *The World of Swing: An Oral History of Big Band Jazz*. 1974. Reprint, New York: Da Capo, 2001.

Daniel, Pete. *Lost Revolutions: The South in the 1950s*. Chapel Hill: University of North Carolina Press, 2000.

Dauncey, Mrs. Campbell. *An Englishwoman in the Philippines*. New York: E. P. Dutton, 1906.

Davies, Ebenezer. *American Scenes, and Christian Slavery: A Recent Tour of Four Thousand Miles in the United States*. 1849. New York, 1973.

Davin, Tom. "Conversation with James P. Johnson." In *Jazz Panorama*, edited by Martin Williams, 44–61. New York: Collier Books, 1964. First published 1958.

Davis, Francis. *The History of the Blues: The Music, the People from Charley Patton to Robert Cray*. New York: Hyperion, 1995.

Davis, Frank Marshall. "No Secret—Best White Bands Copy Negroes." *Down Beat*, June 1938, 5.

Davis, Thulani. *The Emancipation Circuit: Black Activism Forging a Culture of Freedom*. Durham, NC: Duke University Press, 2022.

Davis, Thulani. "Honoring and Remembering Singer Aretha Franklin and Her Voice." Interview by Audie Cornish. *All Things Considered*, NPR, August 16, 2018.

"Decries 'Jazz Thinking.'" *New York Times*, February 15, 1925, 17.

"Demand Permit System Repeal." Multiple articles from *Billboard*, April 8, 1944, 65.

Denning, Michael. *Noise Uprising: The Audiopolitics of a World Musical Revolution.* London: Verso, 2015.

Dennison, Sam. *Scandalize My Name: Black Imagery in American Popular Music.* New York: Garland, 1982.

Desmond, Shaw. "Prussianizing America." *North American Review* 223, no. 831 (June–August 1926): 259.

Determeyer, Eddy. *Rhythm Is Our Business: Jimmie Lunceford and the Harlem Express.* Ann Arbor: University of Michigan Press, 2006.

DeVeaux, Scott. *The Birth of Bebop.* Berkeley: University of California Press, 1997.

Dietz, Bill, and Gavin Steingo. "Experiments in Civility." *Boundary 2* 43, no. 1 (February 2016): 43–74.

Dinerstein, Joel. *Swinging the Machine: Modernity, Technology, and African American Culture Between the World Wars.* Amherst: University of Massachusetts Press, 2003.

"Discos Victor." *La Nacion* (Buenos Aires), August 23, 1922, 11.

Dobbins, Bill. "Smith, Willie 'The Lion.'" Grove Music Online, 2015.

Dodge, Roger Pryor. "Hot Jazz: Notes on the Future." HRS *Society Rag* (1941). In *Hot Jazz and Jazz Dance: Roger Pryor Dodge Collected Writings, 1929–1964*, selected and edited by Pryor Dodge, 75–83. New York: Oxford University Press, 1995.

Dolan, Mark K. "Extra! Chicago Defender Race Record Ads Show South from Afar." *Southern Cultures* 13, no. 3 (Fall 2007): 106–24.

Dormon, James. "Shaping the Popular Image of Post-Reconstruction American Blacks: The 'Coon Song' Phenomenon of the Gilded Age." *American Quarterly* 40, no. 4 (December 1988): 450–71.

Douglass, Frederick. *My Bondage and My Freedom.* Auburn, NY: Miller, Orton, and Mulligan, 1855.

Douglass, Frederick. *Narrative of the Life of Frederick Douglass, An American Slave.* Boston: Anti-Slavery Society, 1845.

Doyle, Peter. *Echo and Reverb: Fabricating Space in Popular Music Recording, 1900–1960.* Middletown, CT: Wesleyan University Press, 2005.

"The Drama and Music." *Milwaukee Sentinel*, October 16, 1892, 13.

"Dreazen Grafonola Shop." *Chicago Defender*, May 4, 1918, 2.

Dresser, Amos. *The Narrative of Amos Dresser, with Stone's Letters from Natchez—An Obituary Notice of the Writer, and Two Letters from Tallahassee, Relating to the Treatment of Slaves.* New York: Anti-Slavery Society, 1836.

"Dress Extremes of Chicago School Girls." *New York Times*, January 26, 1922, 17.

Du Bois, W. E. B. *Black Reconstruction in America, 1860–1880.* 1935. Introduction by David Levering Lewis. New York: Atheneum, 1992.

Du Bois, W. E. B. "The Color Line Belts the World." *Collier's* 28, no. 4 (October 20, 1906): 30.

Du Bois, W. E. B. *The Gift of Black Folk: The Negroes in the Making of America*. 1924. With an introduction by Glenda Carpio. New York: Oxford University Press, 2007.

Du Bois, W. E. B. *The Souls of Black Folk*. Edited with an introduction by David W. Blight and Robert Gooding-Williams. Boston: Bedford Books, 1997.

Dunaway, Wilma. *Slavery in the American Mountain South*. Cambridge: Cambridge University Press, 2003.

Dunbar, Paul Laurence. "The Colored Band." In *Lyrics of Love and Laughter*, 44–46. New York: Dodd, Mead, 1903.

Dunkel, Mario. "Marshall Winslow Stearns and the Politics of Jazz Historiography." *American Music* 30, no. 4 (Winter 2012): 468–504.

Dunlavy, Colleen A. *Small, Medium, Large: How Government Made the U.S. into a Manufacturing Powerhouse*. London: Polity, 2024.

Durkheim, Émile. *The Elementary Forms of Religious Life*. Translated by Carol Cosman. Abridged with an introduction and notes by Mark S. Cladis. Oxford: Oxford University Press, 2001. Originally published 1912 in French.

Dvořák, Antonin. "Real Value of Negro Melodies." *New York Herald*, May 21, 1893, 28.

"Earl Hines and Grand Terrace Close Forever." *Down Beat*, February 1937, 2.

Early, Gerald. "The Case of Leroi Jones/Amiri Baraka." *Salmagundi* 70/71 (Spring–Summer 1986): 343–52.

Early, Gerald. "Pulp and Circumstance: The Story of Jazz in High Places." In *The Jazz Cadence of American Culture*, edited by Robert G. O'Meally, 393–430. New York: Columbia University Press, 1998.

Edwards, Brent Hayes. "Louis Armstrong and the Syntax of Scat." *Critical Inquiry* 28, no. 3 (Spring 2002): 618–49.

Edwards, Brent Hayes. "The Uses of Diaspora." *Social Text* 19, no. 1 (Spring 2001): 45–73.

Eidsheim, Nina. *The Race of Sound: Listening, Timbre and Vocality in African American Music*. Durham, NC: Duke University Press, 2019.

Einhorn, Robin L. *American Taxation, American Slavery*. Chicago: University of Chicago Press, 2006.

Ellington, Duke. "The Duke Steps Out." 1931. In Tucker, *Duke Ellington Reader*, 46–50.

Ellington, Duke. "My Hunt for Song Titles." 1933. In Tucker, *Duke Ellington Reader*, 87–90.

Ellington, Duke. "We, Too, Sing 'America.'" 1941. In Tucker, *Duke Ellington Reader*, 146–48.

"Ellington Defends His Music." 1933. In Tucker, *Duke Ellington Reader*, 80.

Eliot, T. S. "Tradition and the Individual Talent." *Poetry* magazine, October 13, 2009. https://www.poetryfoundation.org/articles/69400/tradition-and-the-individual-talent. Originally published 1919 in the *Egoist* (London).

Ellison, Ralph. *Invisible Man*. 1952. New York: Vintage, 1972.

Ellison, Ralph. "Change the Joke and Slip the Yoke." 1958. In *Shadow and Act*, 45–59.

Ellison, Ralph. "The Golden Age, Time Past." 1959. In *Shadow and Act*, 199–212.

Ellison, Ralph. "Introduction." 1964. In *Shadow and Act*, xi–xxiii.

Ellison, Ralph. "The Little Man at Chehaw Station." 1977. In *Going to the Territory*, 3–38. New York: Vintage, 1986.

Ellison, Ralph. "On Bird, Bird-Watching, and Jazz." 1962. In *Shadow and Act*, 221–32.

Ellison, Ralph. "Richard Wright's Blues." 1945. In *Shadow and Act*, 77–94.

Ellison, Ralph. *Shadow and Act*. New York: Vintage, 1972.

"Enlightenment of W. C. Handy, Cleveland, Bolivar County, Mississippi." *Mississippi Blues Travellers*. Accessed February 8, 2024. https://www .mississippibluestravellers.com/enlightenment-of-wc-handy-cleveland -mississippi/.

Enstad, Nan. *Cigarettes, Inc.: An Intimate History of Corporate Imperialism*. Chicago: University of Chicago Press, 2018.

Epstein, Dena. "Slave Music in the United States before 1860: A Survey of Sources (Part 2)." *Notes: The Quarterly Journal of the Music Library Association*, 2nd ser., 20, no. 3 (Summer 1963): 377–90.

Erenberg, Lewis A. *Swingin' the Dream: Big Band Jazz and the Rebirth of American Culture*. Chicago: University of Chicago Press, 1998.

Erlmann, Veit. "The Acoustic Abject: Sound and the Legal Imagination." In *Sound Objects*, edited by James A. Steintrager and Rey Chow, 151–66. Durham, NC: Duke University Press, 2019.

Erlmann, Veit. *Music, Modernity, and the Global Imagination: South Africa and the West*. Oxford: Oxford University Press, 1999.

Erlmann, Veit. *Reason and Resonance: A History of Modern Aurality*. London: Zone Books, 2010.

Europe, James Reese. "A Negro Explains 'Jazz.'" *Literary Digest*, April 26, 1919, 28–29.

"Even Typewriters Jazz." *Miami Herald*, April 2, 1920, 2.

Fabian, Johannes. *Out of Our Minds: Reason and Madness in the Exploration of Central Africa*. Berkeley: University of California Press, 2000.

"Fancy Dress Dance at Nuwara Eliya." *Ceylon Observer*, September 18, 1919, weekly edition, 1403.

Fanon, Frantz. *The Wretched of the Earth*. Translated by Richard Philcox with a preface by Jean-Paul Sartre and foreword by Homi K. Bhabha. New York: Grove, 2005.

Farjeon, Harry. "Rag-Time." *Musical Times* 65 (September 1, 1924): 796.

Featherstonhaugh, G. W. *Excursion Through the Slave States*. New York: Harper and Brothers, 1844.

Feld, Steven. "Communication, Music, and Speech about Music." 1984. Revised version. In Charles Keil and Steven Feld, *Music Grooves*, 77–95. Chicago: University of Chicago Press, 1994.

Feld, Steven. "'Flow Like a Waterfall': The Metaphors of Kaluli Musical Theory."
    Yearbook for Traditional Music 13 (1981): 22–47.

Feld, Steven. *Jazz Cosmopolitanism in Accra: Five Musical Years in Ghana*. Durham,
    NC: Duke University Press, 2012.

Feld, Steven. "Orality and Consciousness." In *The Oral and the Literate in Music*,
    edited by Tokumaru Yosihiko and Yamaguti Osamu, 18–28. Tokyo:
    Academia Music, 1986.

Feld, Steven. *Sound and Sentiment: Birds, Weeping, Poetics, and Song in Kaluli Expres-
    sion*. 3rd ed. Durham, NC: Duke University Press, 2012. First published
    1982.

Finck, Julia Neeley. "Mammy's Song: A Negro Melody." *Music* (Chicago) 13,
    March 1898, 604–5.

Finkelstein, Sidney. *Jazz: A People's Music*. With a foreword by Geoffrey Jacques.
    New York: International Publishers, 1988. Originally published 1948.

Fisher, Miles Mark. *Negro Slave Songs in the United States*. Ithaca, NY: Cornell Uni-
    versity Press, 1953.

Fletcher, Tom. *100 Years of the Negro in Show Business: The Tom Fletcher Story*.
    New York: Burdge, 1954.

Flowe, Douglas J. *Uncontrollable Blackness: African American Men and Criminality in
    Jim Crow New York*. Chapel Hill: University of North Carolina Press, 2020.

Floyd, Samuel A., Jr. *The Power of Black Music: Interpreting Its History From Africa to the
    United States*. New York: Oxford University Press, 1995.

Floyd, Samuel A., Jr., and Ronald Radano. "Interpreting the African-American
    Musical Past: A Dialogue." *Black Music Research Journal* 29, no. 1 (Spring
    2009): 1–10.

Foner, Eric. "The Meaning of Freedom in the Age of Emancipation." *Journal of Amer-
    ican History* 81, no. 2 (September 1994): 435–60.

Foner, Eric. *Reconstruction: America's Unfinished Revolution, 1863–1877*. Updated
    edition. New York: Harper Perennial Modern Classics, 2014. Originally
    published 1988.

Foreman, Ronald C., Jr. "Jazz and Race Records, 1920–1932: Their Origins and
    Their Significance for the Record Industry and Society." PhD diss., Uni-
    versity of Illinois, 1968.

Fortier, Alcée. "Customs and Superstitions in Louisiana." *Journal of American Folk-
    lore* 1, no. 2 (July–September 1888): 136–38.

Foucault, Michel. *"Society Must Be Defended." Lectures at the Collège de France, 1975–76*.
    Edited by Mauro Bertani and Alessandro Fontana. Translated by David
    Macey. New York: Picador, 2003.

Fredrickson, George. *The Black Image in the White Mind: The Debate on Afro-American
    Character and Destiny, 1817–1914*. Middletown, CT: Wesleyan University
    Press, 1971.

Freehling, William W. *The Road to Disunion, Volume II: Secessionists Triumphant,
    1854–1861*. New York: Oxford University Press, 2007.

Freud, Sigmund. *Totem and Taboo: Some Points of Agreement between the Mental Lives of Savages and Neurotics*. 1913. Translated and edited by James Strachey, with a biographical introduction by Peter Gay. New York: W. W. Norton, 1990.

Freud, Sigmund. *The Uncanny*. 1919. Translated by David McLintock, with an introduction by Hugh Haughton. New York: Penguin, 2003.

Friedson, Steven M. *Remains of Ritual: Northern Gods in a Southern Land*. Chicago: University of Chicago Press, 2009.

Frieler, Klaus, Martin Pfleiderer, Jakob Abe, and Wolf-Georg Zaddach. "'Telling a Story': On the Dramaturgy of Monophonic Jazz Solos." *Empirical Musicology Review* 11, no. 1 (2016): 68–82.

Frith, Simon. *Performing Rites: On the Value of Popular Music*. Cambridge, MA: Harvard University Press, 1998.

"From the Camp: Correspondence of the Observer." *Fayetteville Observer* (NC) 43, May 19, 1862, 1.

Fry, Andy. *Paris Blues: African American Music and French Popular Culture, 1920–1960*. Chicago: University of Chicago Press, 2014.

"The Funeral of Ragtime." *Pinehurst Outlook* (NC), March 13, 1909, 7.

Gabbard, Krin. *Better Git It in Your Soul: An Interpretive Biography of Charles Mingus*. Berkeley: University of California Press, 2016.

Gaines, Kevin K. *Uplifting the Race: Black Leadership, Politics, and Culture in the Twentieth Century*. Chapel Hill: University of North Carolina Press, 1996.

"Galle Face Hotel Fancy Dress Dance." *Ceylon Observer*, August 18, 1920, weekly edition, 1248.

Gallico, Paul. "Jolts Crimson." *Daily News* (New York), November 19, 1923, 22.

Gallope, Michael. *Deep Refrains: Music, Philosophy, and the Ineffable*. Chicago: University of Chicago Press, 2017.

Gamble, E. L., and Karl C. Kraft. "How I've Got the Ku Klux Klan Blues." In *Gamble's Minstrel Song Book*. East Liverpool, OH: E. L. Gamble, 1925.

Garcia, David F. *Listening for Africa: Freedom, Modernity, and the Logic of Black Music's African Origins*. Durham, NC: Duke University Press, 2017.

Gariglio, Raymond J. "Bushell, Garvin." Grove Music Online, 2003.

Gates, Henry Louis, Jr. *"Race," Writing, and Difference*. Chicago: University of Chicago Press, 1986.

Gates, Henry Louis, Jr. *The Signifying Monkey: A Theory of African-American Literary Criticism*. New York: Oxford University Press, 1988.

Gates, Henry Louis, Jr., and Nellie McKay, eds., *The Norton Anthology of African American Literature*, with Robert G. O'Meally, contributor. New York: W. W. Norton, 1996.

Geary, Patrick. "Sacred Commodities: The Circulation of Medieval Relics." In *The Social Life of Things: Commodities in Cultural Perspective*, edited by Arjun Appadurai, 169–92. Cambridge: Cambridge University Press, 1986.

Gebhardt, Nicholas. *Vaudeville Melodies: Popular Musicians and Mass Entertainment in American Culture, 1870–1929*. Chicago: University of Chicago Press, 2017.

Gelatt, Roland. *The Fabulous Phonograph, 1877–1977*. 2nd revised edition. New York: Collier Books, 1977.

Gennari, John. *Blowin' Hot and Cool: Jazz and Its Critics*. Chicago: University of Chicago Press, 2006.

Genovese, Eugene D. *From Rebellion to Revolution: Afro-American Slave Revolts in the Making of the Modern World*. Baton Rouge: Louisiana State University Press, 1979.

Genovese, Eugene D. *Roll, Jordan, Roll: The World the Slaves Made*. New York: Pantheon, 1974.

George, Nelson. *The Death of Rhythm and Blues*. New York: Pantheon, 1988.

Geroulanos, Stefanos. *The Invention of Prehistory: Empire, Violence, and Our Obsession with Human Origins*. New York: Liveright, 2024.

Giddens, Anthony. *The Constitution of Society: Outline of the Theory of Structuration*. Berkeley: University of California Press, 1984.

Gilbert, David. *The Product of Our Souls: Ragtime, Race, and the Birth of the Manhattan Musical Marketplace*. Chapel Hill: University of North Carolina Press, 2015.

Gilbert, Gama. "Higher Soars the Swing Fever." *New York Times Magazine*, August 14, 1938, 6.

Gilroy, Paul. *The Black Atlantic: Modernity and Double Consciousness*. Cambridge, MA: Harvard University Press, 1993.

Gilroy, Paul. "Sounds Authentic: Black Music, Ethnicity, and the Challenges of a 'Changing Same.'" *Black Music Research Journal* 11, no. 2 (Autumn 1991): 111–36.

Gioia, Ted. *Delta Blues*. New York: W. W. Norton, 2008.

Gioia, Ted. *The History of Jazz*. New York: Oxford University Press, 1997.

"Girls on 'Noise' Strike; Inmates of Bedford Reformatory Jangle Cell Doors and Scream." *New York Times*, January 25, 1920, 19.

Gitler, Ira. *Swing to Bop: An Oral History of the Transition in Jazz in the 1940s*. New York: Oxford University Press, 1985.

Goble, Mark. *Beautiful Circuits: Modernism and the Mediated Life*. New York: Columbia University Press, 2010.

Godbolt, Jim. *A History of Jazz in Britain 1919–50*. London: Quartet Books, 1984.

Gomez, Michael A. *Exchanging Our Country Marks: The Transformations of African Identities in the Colonial and Antebellum South*. Chapel Hill: University of North Carolina Press, 1998.

"Goodman and Webb Will Broadcast to England—Boswell to Make Movie." *Down Beat*, January 1937, 1–2.

Gordon, Avery F. *Ghostly Matters: Haunting and the Sociological Imagination*. Minneapolis: University of Minnesota Press, 1997.

Gordon, Robert. "Muddy Waters: Can't Be Satisfied." American Masters website, PBS, May 24, 2006. https://www.pbs.org/wnet/americanmasters/muddy -waters-cant-be-satisfied/730/.

"Gotham's '15th' Home." *Evening Capital News* (Boise, ID), February 17, 1919, 5, image 5.

Graeber, David. "Three Ways of Talking about Value." In *Toward an Anthropological Theory of Value: The False Coin of Our Own Dreams*, 1–22. New York: Palgrave, 2001.

Grandy, Moses. *Narrative of the Life of Moses Grandy, Formerly a Slave in the United States of America*. Boston: Oliver Johnson, 1844.

"The Great Rock 'n' Roll Controversy." *Look!*, June 26, 1956, 40.

Green, Adam. *Selling the Race: Culture, Community and Black Chicago, 1940–1955*. Chicago: University of Chicago Press, 2007.

Green, Jeffrey, Rainer E. Lotz, and Howard Rye, eds. *Black Europe: The Sounds and Images of Black People in Europe—Pre 1927*. With contributions by Horst Bergmeier, Konrad Nowakowski, and Susanne Ziegler. 2 vols. Holste-Oldendorf, Germany: Bear Family, 2013.

Green, Richard C., and Monique Guillory. "Question of a 'Soulful Style': Interview with Paul Gilroy." In *Soul: Power, Politics, and Pleasure*, edited by Richard Green and Monique Guillory, 250–66. New York: New York University Press, 1996.

Greenberg, Cheryl Lynn. *To Ask for an Equal Chance: African Americans in the Great Depression*. Lanham, MD: Rowman and Littlefield, 2009.

Grossberg, Lawrence. "On Postmodernism and Articulation: An Interview with Stuart Hall." In Morley and Chen, *Stuart Hall: Critical Dialogues in Cultural Studies*, 131–50.

Grove Music Online. Oxford University Press. https://oxfordmusiconline.com/grovemusic/.

Guha, Ranajit. *History at the Limit of World-History*. New York: Columbia University Press, 2002.

Gushee, Lawrence. *Pioneers of Jazz: The Story of the Creole Band*. New York: Oxford University Press, 2005.

Gussow, Adam. *Seems Like Murder There: Southern Violence and the Blues Tradition*. Chicago: University of Chicago Press, 2002.

Guyer, Jane I. "Wealth in People and Self-Realization in Equatorial Africa." *Man* 28, no. 2 (June 1993): 243–65.

Hadju, David. "A Song That Changed Music Forever." *New York Times*, August 8, 2020.

Hahn, Steven. *A Nation Under Our Feet: Black Political Struggles in the Rural South from Slavery to the Great Migration*. Cambridge, MA: Belknap Press of Harvard University Press, 2005.

Hall, Francis. *Travels in Canada and the United States in 1816 and 1817*. London: Printed for Longman, Hurst, Rees, Orme, and Brown, 1818.

Hall, Stuart. "Notes on Deconstructing 'the Popular.'" In *People's History and Socialist Theory*, edited by Raphael Samuel, 227–40. London: Routledge and Kegan Paul, 1981.

Hall, Stuart. "The Problem of Ideology: Marxism Without Guarantees." 1986. In Morley and Chen, *Stuart Hall: Critical Dialogues in Cultural Studies*, 25–46.

Hall, Stuart. "Race, Articulation, and Societies Structured in Dominance." 1980. In *Black British Cultural Studies: A Reader*, edited by Houston A. Baker Jr., Manthia Diawara, and Ruth Lindeborg, 16–60. Chicago: University of Chicago Press, 1996.

Hall, Stuart. "What Is This 'Black' in Black Popular Culture?" 1992. In Morley and Chen, *Stuart Hall: Critical Dialogues in Cultural Studies*, 465–75.

Hamilton, Jack. *Just Around Midnight: Rock and Roll and the Racial Imagination.* Cambridge, MA: Harvard University Press, 2016.

Hamm, Charles. *Irving Berlin: Songs From the Melting Pot, the Formative Years, 1907–1914.* New York: Oxford University Press, 1997.

Hamm, Charles. *Music of the New World.* New York: W. W. Norton, 1983.

Hanchard, Michael. "Afro-Modernity: Temporality, Politics, and the African Diaspora." *Public Culture* 11, no. 1 (1999): 245–68.

Handy, W. C. *Father of the Blues.* Edited by Arna Bontemps, with a foreword by Abbe Niles. New York: Macmillan, 1944.

Happy Rhythm: New York Columbia Recordings, Volume 1. CD. Frog DGF32.

Harker, Brian. "Louis Armstrong, Eccentric Dance, and the Evolution of Jazz on the Eve of Swing." *Journal of the American Musicological Society* 61, no. 1 (Spring 2008): 67–121.

Harootunian, Harry. *Marx After Marx: History and Time in the Expansion of Capitalism.* New York: Columbia University Press, 2015.

Harootunian, Harry. "'Modernity' and the Claims of Untimeliness." *Postcolonial Studies* 13, no. 4 (2010): 367–82.

Harootunian, Harry. "Shadowing History: National Narratives and the Persistence of Everyday." *Cultural Studies* 18, nos. 2/3 (2004): 181–200.

Harootunian, Harry. "Some Thoughts on Comparability and the Space-Time Problem." *Boundary* 2 32, no. 2 (2005): 23–52.

Harris, Cheryl. "Whiteness as Property." *Harvard Law Review* 106, no. 8 (June 1993): 1710–91.

Harris, Henry J. "The Occupation of Musician in the United States." *Musical Quarterly* 1, no. 2 (April 1915): 299–311.

Harris, Neil. "John Philip Sousa and the Culture of Reassurance." In *Cultural Excursions: Marketing Appetites and Cultural Tastes in Modern America*, 198–222. Chicago: University of Chicago Press, 1990.

Harris, William Tell. *Remarks Made During a Tour Through the United States of America.* London: Sherwood, Neely, and Jones, 1821.

Hartman, Saidiya. *Scenes of Subjection: Terror, Slavery, and Self-Making in Nineteenth-Century America.* New York: Oxford University Press, 1997.

Hartman, Saidiya. *Wayward Lives, Beautiful Experiments: Intimate Histories of Social Upheaval.* New York: W. W. Norton, 2019.

Harvey, David. *A Companion to Marx's "Capital."* London: Verso, 2010.

Harvey, David. *The Limits of Capital*. London: Verso, 2018. First published 1982.

Hasse, John Edward. "J. Russel Robinson, 'The White Man with Colored Fingers.'" *Resound: A Quarterly of the Archives of Traditional Music* 4, no. 2 (April 1985): 2. scholarworks.iu.edu.

"Heard on the New Handy Orchestra Recordings on Columbia." *Grand Rapids Press*, January 2, 1918, 4.

Hearn, Lafcadio. "Black Varieties/The Minstrels of the Row." *Cincinnati Commercial*, April 9, 1876, 4.

"Heebie-Jeebies." *Dictionary of American Regional English*, edited by Frederic G. Cassidy and Joan Houston Hall. Cambridge, MA: Harvard University Press, 2013.

Hegel, Georg Wilhelm Friedrich. *Lectures on the Philosophy of World History*. Translated by Hugh Barr Nisbet, with an introduction by Duncan Forbes. Cambridge: Cambridge University Press, 2021. Originally published 1837 in German.

Heilbut, Anthony. *The Gospel Sound: Good News and Bad Times*. 1971. Revised and updated, New York: Limelight Editions, 1992.

"He Left a Finger." *Evening Press*, July 16, 1907, 1.

Helmling, Steven. "Constellation and Critique: Adorno's Constellation, Benjamin's Dialectical Image." *Postmodern Culture* 14, no. 1 (September 2003). https://www.pomoculture.org/2013/09/18/constellation-and-critique-adornos-constellation-benjamins-dialectical-image/.

Hentoff, Nat. *The Jazz Life*. New York: Da Capo Press, 1975. Originally published 1961 by Dial (New York).

Hentoff, Nat. "Racial Prejudice in Jazz: It Works Both Ways." *Harper's*, June 1959, 72–79.

Hentz, Caroline Lee. *The Planter's Northern Bride*. 1854. Introduction by Rhoda Coleman Ellison. Chapel Hill: University of North Carolina Press, 1970.

Hershey, Burnet. "Jazz Latitude." *New York Times*, June 25, 1922, SM5.

Hesse, Barnor. "Symptomatically Black: A Creolization of the Political." In *The Creolization of Theory*, edited by Shu-mei Shih and Françoise Lionett, 37–61. Durham, NC: Duke University Press, 2011.

Hilyer, Reiko. "Relics of Reconciliation: The Confederate Museum and Civil War Memory in the New South." *Public Historian* 33, no. 4 (November 2011): 35–62.

Hindemann, John Joseph. "Concert Life in Ante Bellum Charleston." PhD diss., University of North Carolina, 1971.

Hinton, Milt. Interview with Albert "Budd" Johnson. Washington, DC: Smithsonian Institution, March 1975. Archive of the Institute of Jazz Studies, Rutgers University, Newark.

"History of the Pianola—Music Roll Manufacturers." The Pianola Institute website. Accessed February 3, 2024. https://pianola.org/history/history_rolls.cfm.

Hitchcock, H. Wiley. "Sousa, John Philip." Grove Music Online, 2014.

Hobson, Wilder. "'Introducing Duke Ellington." 1933. In Tucker, *Duke Ellington Reader*, 93–97.

Hobson, Wilder. "New York Turns up the Heat." In *Jazzmen*, edited by Frederic Ramsey Jr. and Charles Edward Smith, 213–20. New York: Harcourt, Brace, Jovanovich, 1967. *Jazzmen* originally published 1939 by Harcourt, Brace (New York).

Hodeir, Andre. *Jazz: Its Evolution and Essence*. Translated by David Noakes. New York: Grove, 1956.

Hoganson, Kristin L. *Consumers' Imperium: The Global Production of American Domesticity, 1865–1920*. Chapel Hill: University of North Carolina Press, 2007.

"Hold Legislative Dance, February 5." *Olympia Daily Recorder*, January 28, 1919, 4.

Holibaugh, Ralph W., and D. W. Krummel. "Documentation of Music Publishing in the U.S.A. in the 19th Century." *Fontes Artis Musicae* 28, nos. 1–2 (January–June 1981): 94–97.

Holland, Frank, Arthur W. J. G. Ord-Hume, and Larry Sitsky. "Reproducing Piano." Grove Music Online, 2001.

Holsey, Bayo. "Embodying Africa: Roots-Seekers and the Politics of Blackness." In *The Trouble with Post-Blackness*, edited by Houston A. Baker Jr. and K. Merinda Simmons, 144–61. New York: Columbia University Press, 2015.

Horkheimer, Max, and Theodor W. Adorno. *Dialectic of Enlightenment: Philosophical Fragments*. Edited by Gunzelin Schmid Noerr, translated by Edmund Jephcott. Stanford, CA: Stanford University Press, 2002. Originally published 1947 in German.

Hornbostel, E. M. "African Negro Music." *Africa: Journal of the International Institute* 1, no. 1 (January 1928): 30–62.

Horowitz, Joseph. "World's Columbian Exposition." Grove Music Online, 2014.

Hot Notes: New York—Volume 1. CD. Frog DGF8.

Howland, John. *Ellington Uptown: Duke Ellington, James P. Johnson, and the Birth of Concert Jazz*. Ann Arbor: University of Michigan Press, 2009.

Hsio Wen Shih. "The Spread of Jazz and the Big Bands." In *Jazz: New Perspectives on the History of Jazz by Twelve of the World's Foremost Jazz Critics and Scholars*, edited by Nat Hentoff and Albert J. McCarthy, 171–87. New York: Holt, Rinehart, and Winston, 1959.

Hubbs, Harold. "What Is Ragtime?" *Outlook* 118 (February 27, 1918): 345.

Hughes, Rupert. "A Eulogy of Rag-Time." *Musical Record* 447 (April 1, 1899): 158.

Hughes, Spike. "Impressions of Ellington in New York." 1933. In Tucker, *Duke Ellington Reader*, 69–71.

Hughes, Tomos. "'Can We Imagine this Spectacular Revolution?': Counterfactual Narrative and the 'New World Peasantry' in W. E. B. Du Bois's *Scorn* and *Black Reconstruction*." *ELH* 87, no. 1 (Spring 2020): 179–210.

Hull, Geoffrey P. *The Recording Industry*. 2nd ed. New York: Routledge, 2004.

Hungerford, James. *The Old Plantation, and What I Gathered There in an Autumn Month*. New York: Harper and Brothers, 1859.

Hunter, Tera. *To 'Joy My Freedom: Southern Black Women's Lives and Labors After the Civil War*. Cambridge, MA: Harvard University Press, 1998.

Hurston, Zora Neale. "How It Feels To Be Colored Me." *World Tomorrow* 11 (May 1928): 215–16.

Huston, James L. *Calculating the Value of the Union: Slavery, Property Rights, and the Economic Origins of the Civil War*. Chapel Hill: University of North Carolina Press, 2003.

Hyer, Brian. "Tonality." In *Cambridge History of Western Music Theory*, edited by Thomas Christensen, 726–52. Cambridge: Cambridge University Press, 2006.

"In Every Family There Is a Boogie Man to Frighten the Children." *Atchison Daily Globe* (KS), May 3, 1892.

Ingersoll, Ernest. "The City of Atlanta." *Harper's New Monthly Magazine* 60 (December 1879): 30–43.

Ingraham, Joseph Holt [Kate Conyngham]. *The Sunny South; or, The Southerner at Home, Embracing Five Years' Experience of a Northern Governess in the Land of Sugar and Cotton*. Philadelphia: G. Evans, 1860.

Ivanova, Velia. "Twelve-Tone Identity: Adorno Reading Schoenberg through Kant." MA thesis, University of Ottawa, 2013.

Iyer, Vijay. "Exploding the Narrative in Jazz Improvisation." In *Uptown Conversation: The New Jazz Studies*, edited by Robert G. O'Meally, Brent Hayes Edwards, and Farah Jasmine Griffin, 393–403. New York: Columbia University Press, 2004.

Jackson, Jeffrey H. *Making Jazz French: Music and Modern Life in Interwar Paris*. Durham, NC: Duke University Press, 2003.

Jacobson, Matthew Frye. *Barbarian Virtues: The United States Encounters Foreign People at Home and Abroad, 1876–1917*. New York: Hill and Wang, 2000.

"Jail Jazz." *Kansas City Times*, February 6, 1920, 22.

James Reese Europe and the 369th U.S. Infantry 'Hell Fighters' Band, Featuring Noble Sissle, The Complete Pathé Recordings—1919. IAJRC CD 1012.

Jarvis, Simon. *Adorno: A Critical Introduction*. Cambridge: Polity, 1998.

Jasen, David A. *Ragtime: An Encyclopedia, Discography, and Sheetography*. New York: Routledge, 2007.

Jasen, David A., and Trevor Jay Tichenor. *Rags and Ragtime: A Musical History*. 1978. Reprint, New York: Dover, 2012.

Jay, Hamilton. "Music Among the Negroes." *Musical Record*, December 1883, 8.

"'Jazz' Band Is Added to Jail Cabaret Hits." *Tucson Citizen*, August 17, 1917, 3.

"Jazz Band Parades to King's Palace." *Montgomery Advertiser* (AL), November 18, 1918, 6.

"Jazz Music." *Salt Lake Telegram*, October 23, 1917, 7.

"Jazz Music." *Times* (London), September 26, 1927, 8.

"Jazz Music Only Negro Folk Music." *Cleveland Plain Dealer*, September 15, 1918, 65.

"Jazz, the Mysterious Stranger of the Musical World." *Kansas City Star*, June 17, 1917, 1.

Jentsch, Ernst. "On the Psychology of the Uncanny." 1906. Translated by Roy Sellars. *Angelaki* 2, no. 1 (1997): 7–16.

Jimmy Lequime's Grand Hotel Orchestra. "Soho Blues" / "The House Where the Shutters are Green." LP. Harlequin, *Jazz and Hot Dance Music in India, 1926–1944*.

Johnson, Bruce. *Jazz Diaspora: Music and Globalisation*. London: Routledge, 2020.

Johnson, Edmond T. "Player Piano." Grove Music Online, 2013.

Johnson, James Weldon. *Black Manhattan*. 1930. New York: Da Capo Press, 1991.

Johnson, James Weldon. "The Negro's Contribution to American Art." *Literary Digest*, October 20, 1917, 26–27.

Johnson, James Weldon. "The Poor White Musician." *New York Age*, September 23, 1915, 4.

Johnson, James Weldon, and J. Rosamond Johnson, eds. *The Books of American Negro Spirituals*. New York: Da Capo, 1977. Originally published as *The Book of American Negro Spirituals* (1925) and *The Second Book of American Negro Spirituals* (1926), both by Viking (New York).

Johnson, James Weldon, and J. Rosamond Johnson, eds. *The Second Book of American Negro Spirituals*. New York: Viking, 1926.

Johnson, Paul Christopher, ed. *Spirited Things: The Work of 'Possession' in Afro-Atlantic Religions*. Chicago: University of Chicago Press, 2014.

Johnson, Walter, ed. *The Chattel Principle: Internal Slave Trades in the Americas*. New Haven, CT: Yale University Press, 2005.

Johnson, Walter. "The Pedestal and the Veil: Rethinking the Capitalism/Slavery Question." *Journal of the Early Republic* 24, no. 2 (Summer 2004): 299–308.

Johnson, Walter. *River of Dark Dreams: Slavery and Empire in the Cotton Kingdom*. Cambridge, MA: Harvard University Press, 2013.

Johnson, Walter. *Soul by Soul: Life Inside the Antebellum Slave Market*. Cambridge, MA: Harvard University Press, 2001.

Johnson, Walter, and Robin D. G. Kelley, eds. *Forum 1: Race, Capitalism, Justice*. Boston: Boston Review, 2017.

Jones, Andrew F. "Black Internationale: Notes on the Chinese Jazz Age." In *Jazz Planet*, edited by E. Taylor Atkins, 225–55. Jackson: University Press of Mississippi, 2003.

Jones, Gavin. *Strange Talk: The Politics of Dialect in Gilded Age America*. Berkeley: University of California Press, 1999.

Joplin, Scott. *Scott Joplin—1916. Classic Solos Played by the King of Ragtime Writers and Others from Rare Piano Rolls*. Notes by Michael Montgomery with Trevor Tichenor. LP. Biograph BLP-1006Q, 1971.

Jordan, John M. *Machine-Age Ideology: Social Engineering and American Liberalism, 1911–1939*. Chapel Hill: University of North Carolina Press, 1994.

Jordan, Matthew F. *Le Jazz: Jazz and French Cultural Identity*. Urbana: University of Illinois Press, 2010.

"The Jubilee Singers." *Dwight's Journal of Music* 33, no. 17 (November 29, 1873): 131–32.

Kaplan, Amy. *The Anarchy of Empire in the Making of U.S. Culture*. Cambridge, MA: Harvard University Press, 2002.

Keil, Charles. *Urban Blues*. Chicago: University of Chicago Press, 1966.

Keil, Charles, and Steven Feld. *Music Grooves*. Chicago: University of Chicago Press, 1994.

Kenney, William Howland. *Recorded Music in American Life: The Phonograph and Popular Memory, 1890–1945*. New York: Oxford University Press, 1999.

Kernfeld, Barry. "Groove (i)." Grove Music Online, 2003.

Kernfeld, Barry. "Hegamin [née Nelson], Lucille." Grove Music Online, 2003.

Kernfeld, Barry. "Nightclubs and Other Venues." Grove Music Online, 2003.

Keysaar, Alexander. *The Right to Vote: The Contested History of Property in the United States*. New York: Basic Books, 2000.

Kingsley, Mary. *West African Studies*. London: Macmillan, 1899.

Kirke, Edmund [James Robert Gilmore]. *Among the Pines; Or, South in Secession*. New York: J. R. Gilmore, 1862.

Kisiedu, Harald, and George E. Lewis, eds. *Composing While Black: Afrodiasporische Neue Musik Heute / Afrodiasporic New Music Today*. Frankfurt: Wolke Verlag, 2023.

Kleber, John E., ed. *The Encyclopedia of Louisville*. Louisville: University Press of Kentucky, 2000.

Kodesh, Neil. *Beyond the Royal Gaze: Clanship and Public Healing in Buganda*. Charlottesville: University of Virginia Press, 2010.

Kouwenhoven, John. "What's American About America." 1955. In *The Jazz Cadence of American Culture*, edited by Robert G. O'Meally, 133–36. New York: Columbia University Press, 1998.

Kramer, Lawrence. *Musical Meaning: Toward a Critical History*. Berkeley: University of California Press, 2002.

Kramer, Lawrence. "The Musicology of the Future." *Repercussions* 1, no. 1 (Spring 1992): 5–18.

Krasner, David. "The Real Thing." In *Beyond Blackface: African Americans and the Creation of American Popular Culture, 1890–1930*, edited by W. Fitzhugh Brundage, 99–123. Chapel Hill: University of North Carolina Press, 2011.

Krehbiel, Henry Edward. *Afro-American Folksongs: A Study in Racial and National Music*. 1914; New York: Frederick Ungar Publishing Co., 1962.

Kristeva, Julia. *Powers of Horror: An Essay on Abjection*. Translated by Leon S. Roudiez. New York: Columbia University Press, 1982.

Lane, Jeremy F. *Jazz and Machine-Age Imperialism: Music, "Race," and Intellectuals in France, 1918–1945*. Ann Arbor: University of Michigan Press, 2013.

Langer, Susanne K. *Philosophy in a New Key: A Study in the Symbolism of Reason, Rite, and Art*. 3rd ed. Cambridge, MA: Harvard University Press, 1972. First published 1942.

Lanman, Charles. *Adventures in the Wilds of the United States and British American Provinces.* 2 vols. Philadelphia: John W. Moore, 1856.

"The Last Slave of Kentucky." *New York Herald-Tribune*, June 26, 1869, 13.

"The Latest Boogie Man." *Atchison Daily Globe*, February 29, 1896, 2.

"Latest Dance Records." *Times of India* (Bombay), January 13, 1922, 12.

"Latest Hits, Sheet Music, Player Rolls, Records." *Chicago Defender*, March 23, 1918, 12.

"The Latest Victor Record Releases." *Manila Times*, 1922.

Laubenstein, Paul Fritz. "Jazz—Debit and Credit." *Musical Quarterly* 15, no. 4 (October 1929): 606–24.

Lauterbach, Preston. *The Chitlin' Circuit and the Road to Rock 'n' Roll.* New York: W. W. Norton, 2011.

Laviña, Javier, and Michael Zeuske, eds. *The Second Slavery: Mass Slaveries and Modernity in the Americas and in the Atlantic Basin.* Vienna: Lit Verlag, 2014.

Lazzarato, Maurizio. "Immaterial Labor." In *Radical Thought in Italy: A Potential Politics*, edited by Paolo Virno and Michael Hardt, 133–48. Minneapolis: University of Minnesota Press, 1996.

Lemke, Sieglinde. *Primitivist Modernism: Black Culture and the Origins of Transatlantic Modernism.* New York: Oxford University Press, 1998.

Leonard, Neil. *Jazz and the White Americans: The Acceptance of a New Art Form.* Chicago: University of Chicago Press, 1962.

"The Levee at New Orleans." *Illustrated London Times* 32 (June 5, 1858): 13–14.

Levin, Thomas Y. "For the Record: Adorno on Music in the Age of Its Technological Reproducibility." *October* 55 (Winter 1990): 23–47.

Levine, Lawrence. *Black Culture and Black Consciousness: Afro-American Folk Thought from Slavery to Freedom.* New York: Oxford University Press, 1977.

Levinson, Jerrold. *Musical Concerns: Essays in Philosophy of Music.* New York: Oxford University Press, 2015.

Lewis, David Levering. *When Harlem Was in Vogue.* 1981. New York: Oxford University Press, 1989.

Lewis, John Delaware. *Across the Atlantic.* London: George Earle, 1851.

Liebersohn, Harry. *Music and the New Global Culture: From the Great Exhibitions to the Jazz Age.* Chicago: University of Chicago Press, 2019.

Lippman, Edward A. *Musical Aesthetics: A Historical Reader.* New York: Pendragon, 1985.

Lipsitz, George. *The Progressive Investment in Whiteness.* Philadelphia: Temple University Press, 1998.

Litwack, Leon. *Trouble in Mind: Black Southerners in the Age of Jim Crow.* New York: Vintage, 1999.

Liu, Joyce C. H., Viren Murthy, Chih-ming Wang, and Ming Hung Tu. "Exigency of Time: A Conversation with Harry Harootunian and Moishe Postone." *Concentric: Literary and Cultural Studies* 38, no. 2 (September 2012): 7–43.

"Local News." *Memphis Daily Avalanche*, March 6, 1867, 3.

"Local News Items." *Columbus Ledger Enquirer* (Columbus, GA), September 2, 1861, 3.

Locke, Alain. *The Negro and His Music*. Washington, DC: Associates in Negro Folk Education, 1936.

Locke, John. "Property." *Second Treatise on Civil Government*, §§ 25–51, 123–26, 1689. *The Founder's Constitution*, edited by Philip B. Kurland and Ralph Lerner, web edition, University of Chicago Press. https://press-pubs.uchicago .edu/founders/documents/v1ch16s3.html.

Long, John Dixon. *Pictures of Slavery in Church and State, Including Personal Reminiscences, Biographical Sketches, Anecdotes, etc. etc.* 3rd ed. Philadelphia: published by author, 1857.

Lopes, Paul. *The Rise of the Jazz Art World*. Cambridge: Cambridge University Press, 2002.

Lordi, Emily J. *The Meaning of Soul: Black Music and Resilience since the 1960s*. Durham, NC: Duke University Press, 2020.

Lott, Eric. "Back Door Man: Howlin' Wolf and the Sound of Jim Crow." *American Quarterly* 63, no. 3 (September 2011): 697–710.

Lott, Eric. "Double V, Double Time." In *The Jazz Cadence of American Culture*, edited by Robert G. O'Meally, 457–68. New York: Columbia University Press, 1998.

Lott, Eric. *Love and Theft: Blackface Minstrelsy and the American Working Class*. New York: Oxford University Press, 1993.

Lotz, Rainer. *Black People: Entertainers of African Descent in Europe, and Germany*. Bonn: Birgit Lotz Verlag, 1997.

Lukács, Georg. "Reification and the Consciousness of the Proletariat." 1923. In *Georg Lukács: History and Class Consciousness, Studies in Marxist Dialectics*, translated by Rodney Livingstone, 83–222. Cambridge, MA: MIT Press, 1971.

MacConnell, Dean. "Sights and Spectacles." In *Iconicity: Essays on the Nature of Culture: Festschrift in Honor of Thomas A. Sebeok on his 65th birthday*, edited by Paul Bouissac and Michael Herzfeld, 421–36. Tübingen: Stauffenburg Verlag, 1986.

MacGaffey, Wyatt. *Kongo Political Culture: The Conceptual Challenge of the Particular*. Bloomington: Indiana University Press, 2000.

Mackey, Nathaniel. *Bedouin Hornbook*. Lexington: University of Kentucky, 1986.

MacLean, Nancy. *Freedom Is Not Enough: The Opening of the American Workplace*. Cambridge, MA: Harvard University Press, 2008.

MacLeod, Bruce A. "The Musical Instruments of North American Slaves." *Mississippi Folklore Register* 11, no. 1 (Spring 1977): 34–49.

McBride, Jerry. "Roll Lending Libraries in the Early Twentieth Century." 2nd Global Piano Roll Meeting, Bern, June 17–20, 2022. https://www.hkb -interpretation.ch/fileadmin/user_upload/documents/Veranstaltungen /2206_GPRM.pdf.

McCord, Louisa. "Slavery and Political Economy." In *Louisa McCord: Political and Social Essays*, edited by Richard C. Lounsbury, 422–69. Charlottesville: University Press of Virginia, 1995.

McCormick, Thomas J. *America's Half Century: United States Foreign Policy in the Cold War and After*. 2nd ed. Baltimore: Johns Hopkins University Press, 1995. First published 1989.

McDowell, Deborah. *"The Changing Same": Black Women's Literature, Criticism, and Theory*. Bloomington: Indiana University Press, 1995.

McGarr, Kathryn J. *City of Newsmen: Public Lies and Professional Secrets in Cold War Washington*. Chicago: University of Chicago Press, 2022.

McMahon, John R. "The Jazz Path of Degradation." *Ladies' Home Journal* 26 (January 1922): 71.

McWhirter, Cameron. *Red Summer: The Summer of 1919 and the Awakening of Black America*. New York: Henry Holt, 2011.

"The Magazines for June." Review of Thomas Wentworth Higginson's *Atlantic Monthly* essay, "Negro Spirituals." *Nation* 4, no. 100 (May 30, 1867): 432–33.

Magee, Jeffrey. "Ragtime and Early Jazz." *Cambridge History of American Music*, edited by David Nicholls, 388–417. Cambridge: Cambridge University Press, 1998.

Magee, Jeffrey. *The Uncrowned King of Swing: Fletcher Henderson and Big Band Jazz*. New York: Oxford University Press, 2005.

Mahon, Maureen. *Black Diamond Queens: African American Women and Rock and Roll*. Durham, NC: Duke University Press, 2020.

Marcuse, Herbert. "Remarks on a Redefinition of Culture." *Daedalus* 94, no. 1 (1965): 190–207.

Marsh, J. B. T. *The Story of the Jubilee Singers, with their Songs*. Preface to the music by Theo. F. Seward, 7th ed. London: Hodder and Stoughton, 1877.

Martin, Bonnie. "Mortgaging Human Property." *Journal of Southern History* 76, no. 4 (2010): 817–66.

Martin, Henry. "Balancing Composition and Improvisation in James P. Johnson's 'Carolina Shout.'" *Journal of Music Theory* 49, no. 2 (2008): 277–99.

Martin, Jonathan D. *Divided Mastery: Slave Hiring in the American South*. Cambridge, MA: Harvard University Press, 2004.

Martin, Stewart. "The Absolute Artwork Meets the Absolute Commodity." *Radical Philosophy* 146 (November/December 2007): 15–25.

Marx, Karl. *Capital*. 1867. Vol. 1, translated by Ben Fowkes. London: Penguin, 1990.

Marx, Karl. *Grundrisse: Foundations of the Critique of Political Economy*. 1939. Translated with a foreword by Martin Nicolaus. London: Penguin, 1973.

Maskell, Katherine Murphy. "Who Wrote Those 'Livery Stable Blues'? Authorship Rights in Jazz and Law as Evidenced in *Hart et al. v. Graham*." MA thesis, Ohio State University, 2012.

Matory, J. Lorand. *The Fetish Revisited: Marx, Freud, and the Gods Black People Make*. Durham, NC: Duke University Press, 2018.

Maybee, Julie E. "Hegel's Dialectics." In *The Stanford Encyclopedia of Philosophy*, Winter 2020 edition, edited by Edward N. Zalta. https://plato.stanford.edu/archives/win2020/entries/hegel-dialectics/.

"The Mayor of Boston." *Liberator*, December 12, 1835, 1.

Mbembe, Achille. *Critique of Black Reason*. Translated with an introduction by Laurent Dubois. Durham, NC: Duke University Press, 2017.

Mbembe, Achille. "People and Things in African Systems of Thought." Wits Institute for Social and Economic Research, lecture 2, March 13, 2019. Internet Archive, https://archive.org/details/MbembeOnTheRestitutionOfAfricanArtObjects.

Mean Old World: The Blues from 1940 to 1994. 4 CDs. Notes by Lawrence Hoffman. Washington, DC: Smithsonian Collection of Recordings, 1996.

"Mechanism of the Player Piano." *Chicago Defender*, May 15, 1915, big weekend edition, 8.

Mehnert, Alyssa. "McKinney's Cotton Pickers and the 'Unseen Audience': Constructing Blackness on the Radio." *American Music* 37, no. 2 (Summer 2019): 146–71.

Melton, Larry C. "Ragtime Compositions on Piano Rolls—Scott Joplin (1900s)." National Recording Preservation Board, Library of Congress. https://www.loc.gov/static/programs/national-recording-preservation-board/documents/RagtimeScottJoplin.pdf.

Metz, Thaddeus. "The Meaning of Life." In *The Stanford Encyclopedia of Philosophy*, Summer 2013 edition, edited by Edward N. Zalta. https://plato.stanford.edu/archives/sum2013/entries/life-meaning.

Middleton, Richard. *Studying Popular Music*. Milton Keynes, UK: Open University Press, 1990.

"Mid-Summer Clearance." *Freeman*, August 3, 1912, 8.

Millard, Andre. *America on Record: A History of Recorded Sound*. Cambridge: Cambridge University Press, 1995.

Miller, Karl Hagstrom. *Segregating Sound: Inventing Folk and Pop in the Age of Jim Crow*. Durham, NC: Duke University Press, 2010.

Mingus, Charles. *Beneath the Underdog: His World Composed by Charles Mingus*. New York: Vintage, 1991. First published 1971 by Alfred A. Knopf (New York).

"Miscellaneous Department: An Inside View of Slavery." Review of Charles Parsons, *An Inside View of Slavery*. *National Anti-Slavery Standard* 16 (January 26, 1856): 4.

Moderwell, Hiram K. "Ragtime." *New Republic*, October 16, 1915, 284–86.

Mohun, Simon. "Capital." In *A Dictionary of Marxist Thought*, 2nd ed., edited by Tom Bottomore, 68–71. Oxford: Blackwell, 1991.

Monson, Ingrid. *Freedom Sounds: Civil Rights Call Out to Jazz and Africa*. New York: Oxford University Press, 2010.

Monson, Ingrid. *Saying Something: Jazz Improvisation and Interaction*. Chicago: University of Chicago Press, 1996.

Montgomery, David. *Workers' Control in America: Studies in the History of Work, Technology, and Labor Struggles*. Cambridge: Cambridge University Press, 1980.

Montgomery, Michael, Trebor Jay Tichenor, and John Edward Hasse. "Ragtime on Piano Rolls." In *Ragtime: Its History, Composers, and Music*, edited by John Edward Hasse, 90–101. New York: Schirmer Books, 1985.

Moon, D. Thomas. "Strange Voodoo: Inside the Vaults of Chess Studios." *Blues Access*, no. 36 (Winter 1999). http://www.bluesaccess.com/No_36/chess .html.

Moreno, Jairo. "Review Essay." *Music Theory Spectrum* 27, no. 2 (Fall 2005): 283–307.

Moreno, Jairo. *Sounding Latin Music, Hearing the Americas*. Chicago: University of Chicago Press, 2023.

Morgan, Philip. *Slave Counterpoint: Black Culture in the Eighteenth-Century Chesapeake and Low Country*. Chapel Hill: University of North Carolina Press, 1998.

Morley, David, and Kuan-Hsing Chen, eds. *Stuart Hall: Critical Dialogues in Cultural Studies*. London: Routledge, 1996.

Morris, Rosalind. "Fetishism: Overview." In *New Dictionary of the History of Ideas*, 6 vols., edited by Maryanne Cline Horowitz, 2:822–26. Detroit: Charles Scribner's Sons, 2005.

Moten, Fred. *In the Break: The Aesthetics of the Black Radical Tradition*. Minneapolis: University of Minnesota Press, 2003.

Mowitt, John. *Percussion: Drumming, Beating, Striking*. Durham, NC: Duke University Press, 2002.

Mumford, Kevin J. *Interzones: Black/White Sex Districts in Chicago and New York in the Early Twentieth Century*. New York: Columbia University Press, 1997.

Mumford, Lewis. *Technics and Civilization*. New York: Harcourt, Brace, 1934.

Murray, Albert. *Stomping the Blues*. New York: McGraw-Hill, 1976.

"Negro Love of Music." *Musical Record*, July 1885, 9.

"Negro Music." *Daily Herald and Gazette* (Cleveland), no. 293, August 14, 1838, col. A.

"Negro Superstition Concerning the Violin." *Journal of American Folklore* 5, no. 19 (October–December 1892): 329–30.

Nelson, Megan Kate. *Ruin Nation: Destruction and the American Civil War*. Athens: University of Georgia Press, 2012.

Nelson, Stanley. "Haney's Big House." *Concordia Sentinel*, November 26, 2007.

Nelson, Stanley R. *All About Jazz*. London: Heath, Cranton, 1934.

"New Books at the Public Library." *Jackson Citizen Patriot*, May 16, 1914, 7

"New Books at the Public Library." *Morning Oregonian*, May 10, 1914, 11.

"New Books at the Public Library." *Daily Tulsa World*, April 11, 1915, 12.

"New Dance Records." *Nyasaland Times*, May 4, 1922, 4.

"New Wrinkles at Boxing Shows." *Sun* (New York), January 17, 1904, 8.

The Nigger in the Woodpile. Lithograph. New York: Currier and Ives, 1860.

"A Nigger Serenade." *Ceylon Observer*, July 22, 1919, weekly edition, 1098.

"Night Club Reviews." *Billboard*, February 27, 1943, 12.

Niles, John J. "Shout, Coon, Shout!" *Musical Quarterly* 16, no. 4 (October 1930): 516–30.

Noble, David F. *Forces of Production: A Social History of Industrial Automation*. New York: Routledge, 2011. First published 1984.

"No Bodily Resurrection." *New York Times*, January 17, 1898, 7.

Northup, Solomon. *Twelve Years a Slave: Narrative of Solomon Northup*. Buffalo: Derby, Orton, and Mulligan, 1853.

O'Connor, Patrick Joseph. "Minstrel and Medicine Shows—Creating a Market for the Blues." *Overland Review* 32, no. 1–2 (2005). http://www.kansashistory.us/oconnorminstrel.html.

Odum, Howard W. "Folk-Song and Folk-Poetry as Found in the Secular Songs of Southern Negroes." *Journal of American Folklore* 24, no. 93 (July–September 1911): 255–94.

Offenbach, Jacques. *Orpheus in America: Offenbach's Diary of His Journey to the New World*. 1877. Translated by Lander MacClintock. Bloomington: Indiana University Press, 1957.

Ogren, Kathy J. *The Jazz Revolution: Twenties America and the Meaning of Jazz*. New York: Oxford University Press, 1989.

Okiji, Fumi. *Jazz as Critique: Adorno and Black Expression Revisited*. Stanford, CA: Stanford University Press, 2018.

Oliver, Paul. "Smith, Pine Top [Clarence]." Grove Music Online, 2001.

Olmsted, Frederick. *A Journey in the Seaboard Slave States, with Remarks on Their Economy*. New York: Mason Brothers, 1859.

[Olmsted, Frederick]. "Mississippi Home." *National Anti-Slavery Standard* 21, no. 1052 (August 4, 1860): 1.

Ord-Hume, Arthur W. J. G. "Player Piano." Grove Music Online, 2001.

"Original Dixieland Jass Band." Victor Records advertisement. *Chicago Daily Tribune*, April 28, 1917, 3.

Osborne, Peter, and Matthew Charles. "Walter Benjamin." In *Stanford Encyclopedia of Philosophy*, Winter 2020 edition, edited by Edward N. Zalta. https://plato.stanford.edu/archives/win2020/entries/benjamin/.

Osgood, Henry O. *So This Is Jazz*. Boston: Little, Brown, 1926.

Otis, Johnny. *Upside Your Head! Rhythm and Blues on Central Avenue*. Introduction by George Lipsitz. Hanover, NH: Wesleyan University Press and University Press of New England, 1993.

"Out To-day, New Victor Records for August." *Anaconda Standard* (Anaconda, MT), August 1, 1917, 2.

"Out Tomorrow! New Victor Records." *Manila Times*, 1922.

Overstreet, H. A. "The 'Secret' of the Ellington Orchestra." 1933. In Tucker, *Duke Ellington Reader*, 98–101.

Paddison, Max. *Adorno's Aesthetics of Music*. Cambridge: Cambridge University Press, 1993.

Paine, Lewis W. *Six Years in a Georgia Prison: Narrative of Lewis W. Paine*. Boston: Bela Marsh, 1852.

Palmer, Robert. "The Church of the Sonic Guitar." *South Atlantic Quarterly* 90, no. 4 (Fall 1991): 649–73.

Palmer, Robert. *Dancing in the Street: A Rock and Roll History*. London: BBC Books, 1996.

Palmer, Robert. *Deep Blues: A Musical and Cultural History from the Mississippi Delta to Chicago's Southside*. New York: Penguin, 1981.

Panagia, Davide. "Partage du sensible: the distribution of the sensible." In *Jacques Rancière: Key Concepts*, edited by Jean-Phillippe Deranty, 95–103. Durham, UK: Acumen, 2010.

Panassié, Hugues. "Duke Ellington at the Salle Pleyel." 1946. In Tucker, *Duke Ellington Reader*, 81–86.

Panassié, Hugues. *Hot Jazz*. Translated by Lyle and Eleanor Dowling. Revised edition. Westport, CT: Greenwood and Negro Universities Press, 1970.

Parks, Luis Nicolau, and Roger Sansi, eds. *Sorcery in the Black Atlantic*. Chicago: University of Chicago Press, 2011.

Parrish, Susan Scott. *American Curiosity: Cultures of Natural History in the Colonial British Atlantic World*. Chapel Hill: University of North Carolina Press, 2006.

Parry, Harry, and His Radio Rhythm Club Sextet. "Boogi." Parlophone R2860, 1943.

Parsonage, Catherine. *The Evolution of Jazz in Britain, 1880–1935*. London: Routledge, 2005.

Patterson, Orlando. *Rituals of Blood: Consequences of Slavery in Two American Centuries*. New York: Basic Books, 1998.

Patterson, Orlando. *Slavery and Social Death: A Comparative Study*. Cambridge, MA: Harvard University Press, 1982.

Paul Whiteman at Aeolian Hall. Smithsonian Collection of Recordings, RO28, 1982.

Peabody, Charles. "Notes on Negro Music." *Journal of American Folklore* 16, no. 62 (July–September 1903): 148–52.

Pearson, Nathan W. *Goin' to Kansas City*. Urbana: University of Illinois Press, 1987.

Pegler, J. W. "Jazz Bands Play and Society Lolls While Guns Roar." *Wilkes Barre Times Leader* (PA), March 26, 1918, 6.

Pels, Peter. "The Spirit of Matter: On Fetish, Rarity, Fact, and Fancy." *Border Fetishisms: Material Objects in Unstable Spaces*, edited by Patricia Spyer, 91–121. New York: Routledge, 1998.

Penningroth, Dylan. *The Claims of Kinfolk: African American Property and Community in the Nineteenth-Century South*. Chapel Hill: University of North Carolina Press, 2003.

Pensky, Max. "Natural History and Aesthetic Truth in *Aesthetic Theory*." In "Adorno's Aesthetic Theory at Fifty," edited by Peter E. Gordon. Special issue, *New German Critique* 48, no. 2 (August 2021): 23–41.

"Peppery Pep Artist Here to Start Jazz." *Evening Herald* (Klamath Falls, OR), August 14, 1919, 8.

Peterson, Richard A. "Why 1955? Explaining the Advent of Rock Music." *Popular Music* 9, no. 1 (1990): 97–116.

Philips, Harold K. "Shimmy Dances and Jazz Music Must Go." *Baltimore American*, September 2, 1919, 5.

Phillips, Damon J. *Shaping Jazz: Cities, Labels, and the Global Emergence of an Art Form.* Princeton, NJ: Princeton University Press, 2013.

Pickering, Michael. *Blackface Minstrelsy in Britain.* London: Routledge, 2008.

"The Pierrot Show at the Garden Club." *Ceylon Observer*, July 28, 1920, weekly edition, 1152.

Pietz, William. "The Problem of the Fetish, I." *Res: Anthropology and Aesthetics* 9 (Spring 1985): 5–17.

Ping, Nancy R. "Black Musical Activities in Antebellum Wilmington, North Carolina." *Black Perspective in Music* 8, no. 2 (Autumn 1980): 139–60.

Piras, Marcello. "Garibaldi to Syncopation: Bruto Giannini and the Curious Case of Scott Joplin's *Magnetic Rag.*" *Journal of Jazz Studies* 9, no. 2 (Winter 2013): 107–77.

Piras, Marcello. "Johnson, Pete(r)" [Holden, Kermit]. Grove Music Online, 2013.

Pleasants, Henry. *The Agony of Modern Music.* New York: Simon and Schuster, 1955.

Pleasants, Henry. *Serious Music, and All That Jazz! An Adventure in Music Criticism.* New York: Simon and Schuster, 1969.

"Police Band Picnic Held Large Crowd Witnesses Lively Programme and Contributes to Fund." *Oregonian*, August 6, 1917.

Porter, Eric. *What Is This Thing Called Jazz? African American Musicians as Artists, Critics, and Activists.* Berkeley: University of California Press, 2002.

Postone, Moishe. *Time, Labor, and Social Domination: A Reinterpretation of Marx's Critical Theory.* Cambridge: Cambridge University Press, 1993.

Postone, Moishe, with Timothy Brennan. "Labor and the Logic of Abstraction: An Interview." *South Atlantic Quarterly* 108, no. 2 (Spring 2009): 305–30.

Prial, Dunston. *The Producer: John Hammond and the Soul of America.* New York: Farrar, Straus, Giroux, 2006.

"Primitive, Savage Animalism, Preacher's Analysis of Jazz." *New York Times*, March 3, 1922, 13.

Putnam, Lara. *Radical Moves: Caribbean Migrants and the Politics of Race in the Jazz Age.* Chapel Hill: University of North Carolina Press, 2013.

"Quaint Old Negro, Remarkable Centenarian, a Relic of Slavery Days." *Daily Inter-Ocean* (Chicago), July 13, 1896, 5.

Quashie, Kevin. *The Sovereignty of Quiet: Beyond Resistance in Black Culture.* New Brunswick, NJ: Rutgers University Press, 2012.

Radano, Ronald. "Black Music Labor and the Animated Properties of Slave Sound." *Boundary 2* 43, no. 1 (2016): 173–208.

Radano, Ronald. "Hot Fantasies: American Modernism and the Idea of Black Rhythm." In *Music and the Racial Imagination*, edited by Ronald Radano and Philip V. Bohlman, 459–80. Chicago: University of Chicago Press, 2000.

Radano, Ronald. *Lying up a Nation: Race and Black Music*. Chicago: University of Chicago Press, 2003.

Radano, Ronald. "On Ownership and Value." *Black Music Research Journal* 30, no. 2 (2010): 363–69.

Radano, Ronald, and Tejumola Olaniyan, eds. *Audible Empire: Music, Global Politics, Critique*. Durham, NC: Duke University Press, 2016.

Ralph, Julian. "The Plantation Negro." *Harper's Weekly* 37 (January 14, 1893): 38–39.

Ramsey, Guthrie. "Cosmopolitan or Provincial?: Ideology in Early Black Music Historiography, 1867–1940." *Black Music Research Journal* 16, no. 1 (1996): 11–42.

Ramsey, Guthrie. *Race Music: Black Cultures from Bebop to Hip-Hop*. Berkeley: University of California Press; Chicago: Center for Black Music Research, 2003.

Rancière, Jacques. "The Aesthetic Revolution and Its Outcomes." *New Left Review* 14 (March/April 2002): 133–51.

Rancière, Jacques. *Dissensus: On Politics and Aesthetics*. Edited and translated by Steven Corcoran. London: Continuum, 2010.

Rancière, Jacques. *The Emancipated Spectator*. Translated by Gregory Elliott. London: Verso, 2009.

Rancière, Jacques. *The Nights of Labor: The Workers' Dream in Nineteenth-Century France*. Translated by Donald Reid. Philadelphia: Temple University Press, 1989. First French publication 1981 by Fayard.

Rancière, Jacques. *Politics of Aesthetics: The Distribution of the Sensible*. Translated by Gabriel Rockhill. London: Continuum, 2004.

Rankin, John. *Letters on American Slavery, Addressed to Mr. Thomas Rankin, Merchant at Middlebrook, August County Virginia*. 5th ed. Boston, 1838.

"Rastus on Parade." Words by Kerry Mills. New York: F. A. Mills, 1895. Sheldon Harris Collection, Archives and Special Collections, University of Mississippi Libraries. https://egrove.olemiss.edu/sharris_a/24/.

"Rastus on Parade: A Song of Color." Words by George F. Marion, Music by Kerry Mills. New York: F. A. Mills, 1896. Lester S. Levy Sheet Music Collection, Sheridan Libraries of University Museums, Johns Hopkins University. https://levysheetmusic.mse.jhu.edu/collection/143/104.

Ravenel, Henry William. "Recollections of Southern Plantation Life." *Yale Review* 25 (1936): 748–77.

Raymo, Don. *Paul Whiteman: Pioneer in American Music*. Vol. 1, *1890–1930*. Studies in Jazz 43. Lanham, MD: Scarecrow Press, 2003.

Reed, Anthony. *Soundworks: Race, Sound, and Poetry in Production*. Durham, NC: Duke University Press, 2020.

"Reisenweber's Restaurant." Advertisement for the Original Dixieland Jass Band. *New York Times*, March 16, 1917, 9.

"Relic Hunters at Corsicana." *Columbus Enquirer-Sun* (GA), March 15, 1901, 1.

"A Relic of Olden Days." *Kansas City Star*, October 30, 1893, 7.

Religious Folk Songs of the Negro, as Sung on the Plantations. New edition. Arranged by the musical directors of the Hampton Normal and Agricultural Institute from the original edition by Thomas P. Fenner, 1874. Hampton, VA: Institute Press, 1909.

"Respectively: 'Musical Impurity.'" *Etude* 18 (January 1900): 16.

Review of *Afro-American Folk-Songs* by Henry Edward Krehbiel. *Nation* 98 (March 19, 1914): 311–12.

Rhodes, Chip. *Structures of the Jazz Age: Mass Culture, Progressive Education, and Racial Discourse in American Modernism*. London: Verso, 1998.

Rice, Edward Le Roy. *Monarchs of Minstrelsy*. New York: Kenny, 1911.

Rice, Marc. "Prelude to Swing: The 1920s Recordings of the Bennie Moten Orchestra." *American Music*, 25, no. 3 (Fall 2007): 259–81.

Richter, Gerhard. "Aesthetic Theory and Nonpropositional Truth Content in Adorno." *New German Critique*, no. 97 (Winter 2006): 119–35.

Riis, Thomas L. Untitled review. *Journal of the American Musicological Society* 62, no. 1 (Spring 2009): 252–60.

Roberts, David Thomas. "Novelty Piano." Grove Music Online, 2001.

Roberts, Neil. *Freedom as Marronage*. Chicago: University of Chicago Press, 2015.

Robinson, Cedric. *Black Marxism: The Making of Black Radical Thought*. 2nd ed. Chapel Hill: University of North Carolina Press, 2000. First published 1983 by Zed Books.

Robinson, David. *W. C. Handy: The Life and Times of the Man Who Made the Blues*. Tuscaloosa: University of Alabama Press, 2009.

Robinson, J. Bradford. "The Jazz Essays of Theodore Adorno: Some Thoughts on Jazz Reception in Weimar Germany." *Popular Music* 13, no. 1 (January 1994): 1–25.

"Rock and Roll and Riot." *Senior Scholastic*, October 4, 1956, 16–17.

"Rock 'n' Roll." *Life*, April 18, 1955, 166–68.

Roediger, David R. *The Wages of Whiteness: Race and the Making of the American Working Class*. London: Verso, 1991.

Roediger, David R., and Philip S. Foner. *Our Own Time: A History of American Labor and the Working Day*. London: Verso, 1989.

Rogers, J. A. "Jazz at Home." In *The New Negro*, edited by Alain Locke, with a new preface by Robert Hayden, 216–24. New York: Atheneum, 1968. First published 1925 by Albert and Charles Boni (New York).

Rogers, R. Mark, ed. *John Philip Sousa: Three Quotations, Suite for Band*. 1895. San Antonio, TX: Southern Music Company, n.d.

Roholt, Tiger C. *Groove: A Phenomenology of Rhythmic Nuance*. New York: Bloomsbury, 2014.

Rollefson, J. Griffith. *Flip the Script: European Hip Hop and the Politics of Postcoloniality*. Chicago: University of Chicago Press, 2017.

"Romance of the Redwoods at the Rialto Theater." *Anaconda Standard*, August 8, 1917, 2.

Roper, Moses. *Narrative of the Adventures and Escape of Moses Roper, from American Slavery*. 4th ed. London: Harvery and Darton, 1843.

Rose, Al. *Eubie Blake*. New York: Schirmer Books, 1979.

"Runnin' Wild." *Variety* 72, no. 11 (November 1, 1923): 20.

Rye, Howard. "Hot Club de France." Grove Music Online, 2003.

Sáenz, Mario. "Living Labor in Marx." *Radical Philosophy Review* 10, no. 1 (2007): 1–31.

Sampson, Henry T. *The Ghost Walks: A Chronological History of Blacks in Show Business, 1865–1910*. Metuchen, NJ: Scarecrow Press, 1988.

Sanjek, Russell, and David Sanjek. *American Popular Music Business in the 20th Century*. New York: Oxford University Press, 1991.

Sargeant, Winthrop. *Jazz, Hot and Hybrid*. 3rd ed. New York: Da Capo, 1975. Originally published 1946 by E. P. Dutton.

Scarborough, Dorothy, ed. *Humorous Ghost Stories*. New York: G. P. Putnam and Sons; Knickerbocker Press, 1921.

Scarborough, Dorothy. *On the Trail of Negro Folksongs*. Cambridge, MA: Harvard University Press, 1926.

"Scenes of the West—No. 1, Culture of Poor Sandy Souls in Kentucky." *American Agriculturalist* 2, no. 2 (May 1843): 67–69.

Schaeffer, Pierre. *Treatise on Musical Objects: An Essay Across Disciplines*. Translated by Christine North and John Dack. Berkeley: University of California Press, 2017.

Schenker, Frederick. "Empire of Syncopation: Music, Race, and Labor in Colonial Asia's Jazz Age." PhD diss., University of Wisconsin–Madison, 2016.

Schiller, Friedrich. "Fifteenth Letter." 1795. In *On the Aesthetic Education of Man*, translated by Reginald Snell. Mineola, NY: Dover, 2004.

Schoenbrun, David. "Pythons Worked: Constellating Communities of Practice with Conceptual Metaphor in Northern Lake Victoria, ca. A.D. 800 to 1200." In *Knowledge in Motion: Constellations of Learning Across Time and Space*, edited by Andrew Roddick and Ann Brower, 216–46. Tucson: University of Arizona Press, 2016.

Schomburg, Arthur A. "Lynching a Savage Relic." *New York Times*, June 28, 1903, 8.

Schuller, Gunther. *Early Jazz: Its Roots and Musical Development*. New York: Oxford University Press, 1968.

Schuller, Gunther. *The Swing Era: The Development of Jazz, 1930–1945*. New York: Oxford University Press, 1989.

Schweninger, Loren. *Black Property Owners in the South, 1790–1915*. Urbana: University of Illinois Press, 1990.

Scivales, Riccardo. *Harlem Stride Piano Solos: 26 Classic Solos by The Greatest Jazz Pianists of the Swing Era*. Bedford Hills, NY: Ekay Music, n.d.

Scott, Carole E. "The History of the Radio Industry in the United States to 1940." *EH.Net Encyclopedia*. https://eh.net/encyclopedia/the-history-of-the-radio-industry-in-the-united-states-to-1940/.

Scott, David. "That Event, This Memory: Notes on the Anthropology of African Diasporas in the New World." *Diaspora* 1, no. 3 (1991): 261–84.

Seabrook, John. "The Case for and Against Ed Sheeran." *New Yorker*, June 5, 2023.

Seltzer, Mark. *Bodies and Machines*. New York: Routledge, 1992.

Sewell, William H., Jr., "The Temporalities of Capitalism." *Socio-Economic Review* 6, no. 3 (2008): 517–37.

Shack, William A. *Harlem to Montmartre*. Berkeley: University of California Press, 2001.

Shaw, Arnold. *Honkers and Shouters: The Golden Age of Rhythm and Blues*. New York: Macmillan, 1986.

Shaw, Stephanie J. *W.E.B. Du Bois and "The Souls of Black Folk."* Chapel Hill: University of North Carolina Press, 2013.

Shelemay, Kay Kaufman. "Recording, Technology, the Record Industry, and Ethnomusicological Scholarship." In *Comparative Musicology and Anthropology: Essays on the History of Ethnomusicology*, edited by Bruno Nettl and Philip V. Bohman, 277–92. Chicago: University of Chicago Press, 1990.

Shelley, Braxton D. "Analyzing Gospel." *Journal of the American Musicological Society* 72, no. 1 (Spring 2019): 181–242.

Shelley, Braxton D. "'I Love It When You Play the Holy Ghost Chord': Sounding Sacramentality in the Black Gospel Tradition." *Religions* 11, no. 9 (Summer 2020). https://www.mdpi.com/2077-1444/11/9/452.

Shipton, Alyn. *A New History of Jazz*. London: Continuum, 2001.

Shope, Bradley. *American Popular Music in Britain's Raj*. Rochester, NY: University of Rochester Press, 2016.

Silber, Nina. *The Romance of Reunion: Northerners and the South, 1865–1900*. Chapel Hill: University of North Carolina Press, 1993.

Simmel, Georg. *The Sociology of Georg Simmel*. Translated, edited, with an introduction by Kurt H. Wolff. 1950; Glencoe, IL: Free Press, 1964.

Simon, Julia. *Debt and Redemption in the Blues: The Call for Justice*. University Park: Pennsylvania State University Press, 2023.

Singer, Peter. *Hegel: A Very Short Introduction*. 1983; rev. ed. New York: Oxford University Press, 2001.

Singh, Amritjit, and Maryemma Graham, eds. *Conversations with Ralph Ellison*. Jackson: University Press of Mississippi, 1995.

Singh, Nikhil Pal. *Black Is a Country: Race and the Unfinished Struggle for Democracy*. Cambridge, MA: Harvard University Press, 2004.

Singleton, Arthur [Henry Cogswell Knight]. *Letters from the South and West*. Boston: Richardson and Lord, 1824.

Sklansky, Jeffrey. "The Elusive Sovereign: New Social and Intellectual Histories of Capitalism." *Modern Intellectual History* 9, no. 1 (2012): 233–48.

Smith, Charles Edward. "The Austin High School Gang." In *Jazzmen*, edited by Frederic Ramsey Jr. and Charles Edward Smith, 161–82. New York: Harcourt, Brace, Jovanovich, 1967. *Jazzmen* originally published 1939 by Harcourt, Brace (New York).

Smith, Mark M. *Listening to Nineteenth-Century America*. Chapel Hill: University of North Carolina Press, 2001.

Smith, Stephen Decatur. "Awakening Dead Time: Adorno on Husserl, Benjamin, and the Temporality of Music." *Contemporary Music Review* 31, nos. 5–6 (October–December 2012): 389–409.

Smulyan, Susan. *Selling Radio: The Commercialization of American Broadcasting, 1920–1934*. Washington, DC: Smithsonian Institution Press, 1994.

Snead, James A. "Repetition as a Figure of Black Culture." In *Black Literature and Literary Theory*, edited by Henry Louis Gates Jr., 146–54. New York: Routledge, 1990.

Snyder, Frederick Edward. "American Vaudeville—Theatre in a Package: The Origins of Mass Entertainment." PhD diss., Yale University, 1970.

Snyder, Robert. *Voice of the City: Vaudeville and Popular Culture in New York*. New York: Oxford University Press, 1989.

Sobel, Mechal. *The World They Made Together: Black and White Values in Eighteenth-Century Virginia*. Princeton, NJ: Princeton University Press, 1987.

Sorett, Josef. *Spirit in the Dark: A Religious History of Racial Aesthetics*. New York: Oxford University Press, 2016.

Sotiropoulous, Karen. *Staging Race: Black Performers in Turn of the Century America*. Cambridge, MA: Harvard University Press, 2008.

"Sousa at the Hippodrome." *New York Times*, January 15, 1906, 9.

"Sousa Says Ragtime Is Dead from Imitations." *Los Angeles Herald* 36, no. 166 (March 16, 1909).

Southern, Eileen. *The Music of Black Americans*. 3rd ed. New York: W. W. Norton, 1997.

"The Southern States Furnish a Curious Example of Political Perversity." Illustration, with captions. *American Economist* 27–28 (January 18, 1901): 29.

Soyinka, Wole. "Appendix: The Fourth Stage." In *Myth, Literature and the African World*, canto edition, 140–60. Cambridge: Cambridge University Press, 1990.

"Sparky Races into Kansas City in the Lead; Barney Misses Diploma Mill Degree." *Casper Daily Tribune* (WY), December 15, 1923, 1.

Spiegel, Henry William. *The Growth of Economic Thought*. Revised and expanded edition. Durham, NC: Duke University Press, 1983.

Spillers, Hortense J. "Idea of Black Culture." *New Centennial Review* 6, no. 3 (Winter 2006): 7–28.

Spillers, Hortense J. "Moving on Down the Line: Variations on the 'African-American Sermon.'" *The Bounds of Race: Perspectives on Hegemony and Resistance*, edited by Dominick LaCapra, 39–71. Ithaca, NY: Cornell University Press, 1991.

Spitzer, Michael. *Metaphor and Musical Thought*. Chicago: University of Chicago Press, 2004.

"Spooks" (theatrical review). *Chicago Defender*, June 15, 1918, 13.

"'Spooks' Full of Mystery." *New York Times*, June 2, 1925, 16.

Stadler, Gustavus. "Never Heard Such a Thing: Lynching and Phonographic Modernity." *Social Text* 28, no. 1 (Spring 2010): 87–105.

Stahl, Titus. "György Lukács." In *The Stanford Encyclopedia of Philosophy*, Winter 2013 edition, edited by Edward N. Zalta. https://plato.stanford.edu/archives /win2013/entries/lukacs/.

"Stale Bread's Sadness Gave 'Jazz' to the World." *Literary Digest*, April 26, 1919, 47–48.

Stampp, Kenneth M. *The Peculiar Institution: Slavery in the Ante-Bellum South*. New York: Knopf, 1956.

Stanley, Amy Dru. *From Bondage to Contract: Wage, Labor, Marriage, and the Market in the Age of Slave Emancipation*. Cambridge: Cambridge University Press, 1998.

Stearns, Marshall. *The Story of Jazz*. New York: Oxford University Press, 1956.

Steinberg, Michael. *Listening to Reason: Culture, Subjectivity, and Nineteenth-Century Music*. Princeton, NJ: Princeton University Press, 2004.

Steintrager, James A., and Rey Chow, eds. *Sound Objects*. Durham, NC: Duke University Press, 2019.

Sterne, Jonathan. *The Audible Past: Cultural Origins of Sound Reproduction*. Durham, NC: Duke University Press, 2002.

Stewart, Jacqueline Najuma. "Introduction: A Nigger in the Woodpile or Black (In) Visibility in Film History." In *Migrating to the Movies: Cinema and Black Urban Modernity*, 1–20. Berkeley: University of California Press, 2005.

Stewart, Rex. *Jazz Masters in the '30s*. New York: Macmillan, 1972.

Still, William Grant. "Negro Music in the Americas." 1938. In *William Grant Still Reader: Essays on American Music*, edited by Jon Michael Spencer, 91–94. Durham, NC: Duke University Press, 1992.

Stoller, Paul. *Embodying Colonial Memories: Spirit Possession, Power, and the Hauka in West Africa*. New York: Routledge, 1995.

Stowe, David. *Swing Changes: Big-Band Jazz in New Deal America*. Cambridge, MA: Harvard University Press, 1994.

Stowe, Harriet Beecher. *Uncle Tom's Cabin, Or, Life Among the Lowly*. Vol. 2. Boston: John P. Jewett, 1852.

Stuckey, Sterling. *Slave Culture: Nationalist Theory and the Foundations of Black America*. New York: Oxford University Press, 1987.

"The Subjoined Toasts." *Raleigh Register* and *North-Carolina Gazette*, July 23, 1833.

Suisman, David. *Selling Sounds: The Commercial Revolution in American Music*. Cambridge, MA: Harvard University Press, 2009.

"Superb Dancing at the Public Hall." *Ceylon Observer*, November 26, 1919, weekly edition, 1755.

"Superstitions of Negroes in New Orleans." *Journal of American Folklore* 5, no. 19 (October–December 1892): 330–32.

Sweet, James H. "Defying Social Death: The Multiple Configurations of African Slave Family in the Atlantic Word." *William and Mary Quarterly* 70, no. 2 (April 2013): 251–72.

Sweet, James H. *Domingos Álvares, African Healing, and the Intellectual History of the Atlantic World*. Chapel Hill: University of North Carolina Press, 2013.

Tanke, Joseph J. *Jacques Rancière: An Introduction; Philosophy, Politics, Aesthetics*. London: Continuum, 2011.

"Tanned Human Skin. Something About a Bit of a Negro's Hide—a Curious Relic." *Macon Weekly Telegraph*, June 7, 1887, 5.

Tatler. "Management of Negroes." *Southern Cultivator* 8, no. 11 (November 1850): 63.

Taylor, Arthur. Interview with Max Roach. In *Notes and Tones: Musician-to-Musician Interviews*, 106–21. New York: Da Capo Press, 1993. First published 1982 by Perigree (New York).

Taylor, J. R. "Hines, Earl (Kenneth) [Fatha]." Grove Music Online, 2022.

Taylor, Jeffrey. "Luckey Roberts [Charles Luckeyth]." Grove Music Online, 2015.

Taylor, Timothy D. "The Commodification of Music and the Dawn of the Era of 'Mechanical Music.'" *Ethnomusicology* 51, no. 2 (Spring/Summer 2007): 281–305.

Taylor, Timothy D. *Music and Capitalism: A History of the Present*. Chicago: University of Chicago Press, 2016.

Taylor, Timothy D., Mark Katz, and Tony Grajeda, eds. *Music, Sound, and Technology in America*. Durham, NC: Duke University Press, 2012.

Thacker, Eric. "Hot (i)." Grove Music Online, 2003.

"Theatrical Jottings." *New York Age*, August 14, 1913, 6.

"Theatrical Review." *Chicago Defender*, July 11, 1914, 6.

"Theatrical Reviews: Hippodrome." *Salt Lake Herald Republican Telegram*, April 8, 1918.

Thompson, E. P. "Work, Discipline, and Industrial Capitalism." *Past and Present* 38 (December 1967): 56–97.

Thompson, Mark Christian. "The Meaning of Fascism: Adorno on Jazz." In *Anti-Music: Jazz and Racial Blackness in German Thought Between the Wars*, 89–112. Albany: State University of New York Press, 2018.

Thomson, Patricia. "Field." In *Pierre Bourdieu: Key Concepts*, edited by Michael James Grenfell, 65–80. London: Routledge, 2014.

Thomson, Virgil. "Swing Again." 1938. In *A Virgil Thomson Reader*, 33–37. Introduction by John Rockwell. Boston: Houghton Mifflin, 1981.

Thomson, Virgil. "Swing Music." 1936. In *A Virgil Thomson Reader*, 28–32. Introduction by John Rockwell. Boston: Houghton Mifflin, 1981.

Tiedman, Rolf. "Dialectics at a Standstill." In Walter Benjamin, *The Arcades Project*, translated by Howard Eiland and Kevin McLaughlin, 929–45. Cambridge, MA: Belknap Press of Harvard University Press, 1999.

Toll, Robert. *Blacking Up: The Minstrel Show in Nineteenth-Century America*. New York: Oxford University Press, 1977.

Tomba, Massimiliano. *Marx's Temporalities*. Translated by Peter D. Thomas and Sara R. Farris. Chicago: Haymarket Books, 2013.

Trotter, James M. *Music and Some Highly Musical People*. Boston: Lee and Shepard; New York: C. T. Dillingham, 1878.

Troutman, John W. *Kīlā: How the Hawaiian Steel Guitar Changed the Sound of Modern Music*. Chapel Hill: University of North Carolina Press, 2016.

Trux, J. J. "Negro Minstrelsy—Ancient and Modern." *Putnam's Monthly* 5 (January 1855): 72–79.

Tsing, Anna. "Sorting Commodities: How Capitalist Value Is Made Through Gifts." HAU: *Journal of Ethnographic Theory* 3, no. 1 (2013): 21–43.

Tucker, Mark. "Count Basie and the Piano That Swings the Band." *Popular Music* 5 (1985): 45–79.

Tucker, Mark, ed. *The Duke Ellington Reader*. New York: Oxford University Press, 1993.

Tucker, Mark. *Duke Ellington: The Early Years*. Urbana: University of Illinois Press, 1991.

Tucker, Mark, and Travis A. Jackson. "Jazz." Grove Music Online, 2020.

Tucker, Sherrie. *Swing Shift: "All-Girl" Bands of the 1940s*. Durham, NC: Duke University Press, 2000.

Turner, Nicole Myers. *Soul Liberty: The Evolution of Black Religious Politics in Postemancipation Virginia*. Chapel Hill: University of North Carolina Press, 2020.

Tuttle, William M., Jr. *Race Riot: Chicago in the Red Summer of 1919*. Urbana: University of Illinois Press, 1970.

"Two Early Interviews." 1930. In Tucker, *Duke Ellington Reader*, 41–45.

Utley, Francis Lee, ed. *Old Slack's Reminiscence and Pocket History of the Colored Profession from 1865 to 1891*. Introduction by Robert Toll. Bowling Green, KY: Popular Press, 1974. Originally published 1891.

Van Der Merwe, Peter. *Origins of the Popular Style: The Antecedents of Twentieth-Century Popular Music*. Oxford: Oxford University Press, 1989.

Vansina, Jan. *Paths in the Rainforest: Toward a History of Political Tradition in Equatorial Africa*. Madison: University of Wisconsin Press, 1990.

"Vaudeville Reviews." *Billboard*, March 4, 1944, 28.

Victor Records: The New Complete Catalog. Camden, NJ: RCA Victor, 1930.

Victor Records: The New Complete Catalog. Camden, NJ: RCA Victor, 1931.

Virno, Paolo. "Virtuosity and Revolution: The Political Theory of Exodus." In *Radical Thought in Italy: A Potential Politics*, edited by Paolo Virno and Michael Hardt, 189–212. Minneapolis: University of Minnesota Press, 1996.

"Visit to a Negro Cabin in Virginia." *Family Magazine* (New York) 3 (December 1835).

Vogel, Shane. *The Scene of Harlem Cabaret: Race, Sexuality, Performance*. Chicago: University of Chicago Press, 2009.

Von Eschen, Penny M. *Race Against Empire: Black Americans and Anticolonialism, 1937–1957*. Ithaca, NY: Cornell University Press, 1997.

Von Eschen, Penny M. *Satchmo Blows up the World: Jazz Ambassadors Play the Cold War*. Cambridge, MA: Harvard University Press, 2006.

Voskuhl, Adelheid. *Androids of the Enlightenment: Mechanics, Artisans, and Cultures of the Self*. Chicago: University of Chicago Press, 2013.

Vreeland, F. T. "Jazz, Ragtime, By-Product, Revives a Lost Art of Rhythm." *Sun* (New York), November 4, 1917, 2.

Wagner, Bryan. "Disarmed and Dangerous: The Strange Career of Bras-Coupé." *Representations* 92, no. 1 (Fall 2005): 117–51.

Wagner, Bryan. *Disturbing the Peace: Black Culture and the Police Power After Slavery.* Cambridge, MA: Harvard University Press, 2009.

Waksman, Steve. *Instruments of Desire: The Electric Guitar and the Shaping of Musical Experience.* Cambridge, MA: Harvard University Press, 1999.

Wallaschek, Richard. *Primitive Music: An Inquiry into the Origin and Development of Music, Songs, Instruments, Dances, and Pantomimes of Savage Races.* London: Longmans, Green, 1893.

Walton, Lester A. "Is Ragtime Dead?" Music and the Stage. *New York Age*, April 8, 1909, 6.

Walton, Lester A. "Use of Vulgar Words a Detriment to Ragtime." *New York Age*, April 3, 1913, 6.

"Wandering Minstrels on Harlem Lane." *Frank Leslie's Illustrated Newspaper* 34, no. 862 (April 6, 1872): 60–61.

"Wants Legislation to Stop." *New York Times*, February 12, 1922, 1.

Ward, Brian. *Just My Soul Responding: Rhythm and Blues, Black Consciousness, and Race Relations.* Berkeley: University of California Press, 1998.

Ward, Brian. *Radio and the Struggle for Civil Rights in the South.* Gainesville: University Press of Florida, 2004.

Warfield, Patrick. "John Philip Sousa and 'The Menace of Mechanical Music.'" *Journal of the Society for American Music* 3, no. 4 (2009): 431–63.

"War on Ragtime." *American Musician* 5 (July 1901): 4.

Washington, Booker T., ed. *The Negro Problem.* New York: James Pott, 1903.

Watkins, James. *Struggles for Freedom; or the Life of James Watkins, Formerly a Slave in Maryland, U.S.* 19th ed. Manchester: Printed for James Watkins, 1860.

"Wave, Trot, Walk, the Winter Steps: Dancing Masters Urge Censorship to Prevent Undesirable Novelties." *New York Times*, August 14, 1921, 25.

Webb, H. Brook. "The Slang of Jazz." *American Speech* 12, no. 3 (October 1937): 179–84.

Webb, W. Prescott. "Notes on Folk-Lore in Texas." *Journal of American Folklore* 28, no. 109 (July–September 1915): 290–99.

Weber, Jerome F. "Brunswick." Grove Music Online, 2013.

Weheliye, Alexander G. *Phonographies: Grooves in Sonic Afro-Modernity.* Durham, NC: Duke University Press, 2005.

Weiner, Annette B. *Inalienable Possessions: The Paradox of Keeping-While-Giving.* Berkeley: University of California Press, 1992.

West, Cornel. "On Afro-American Popular Music: From Bebop to Rap." In *Prophetic Fragments: Illuminations of the Crisis in American Religion and Culture*, 177–87. Grand Rapids, MI: William B. Eerdmans; Trenton, NJ: Africa World Press, 1988.

Weule, Karl. *Negerleben in Ostafrika: Ergebnisse einer Ethnologischen Forschungreise*. Leipzig: F. U. Brodhaus, 1908.

Wharton, Vernon Lane. *The Negro in Mississippi, 1865–1890*. Chapel Hill: University of North Carolina Press, 1947.

"What Is American Music?" *Musical America*, February 24, 1906, 8.

"What Jazz Music Is." *Dallas Morning News*, September 2, 1917, 11.

"Where is Paola?" *Topeka Plaindealer*, December 4, 1903.

"Whirlwind Dancers of the Globe." *Philadelphia Inquirer*, August 14, 1917, 6.

White, Richard. *The Life and Times of Little Richard: The Authorised Biography*. London: Omnibus, 1984.

White, Shane. "Pinkster in Albany, 1803: A Contemporary Description." *New York History* 70, no. 2 (April 1989): 191–99.

White, Shane, and Graham White. *The Sounds of Slavery: Discovering African American History through Songs, Sermons, and Speech*. Boston: Beacon, 2005.

White, Simone. *Dear Angel of Death*. New York: Ugly Duckling, 2019.

"White Council vs. Rock and Roll." *Newsweek*, April 23, 1956, 32.

Whiteman, Paul. *Jazz*. New York: J. H. Sears, 1926.

Whittall, Geoffrey. "Groove." Grove Music Online, 2003.

"Why 'Jazz' Sends Us Back to the Jungle: A Broadway Ethnologist Tells of the Savage Origin of This 'Delirium Tremens of Syncopation.'" *Current Opinion* 65 (September 1918): 165.

Wiecek, William M. "The Statutory Law of Slavery and Race in the Thirteen Mainland Colonies of British America." *The William and Mary Quarterly* 34, no. 2 (April 1977): 258–80.

Wiegman, Robyn. *American Anatomies: Theorizing Race and Gender*. Durham, NC: Duke University Press, 1995.

Wilentz, Sean. *The Rise of American Democracy: Jefferson to Lincoln*. New York: W. W. Norton, 2005.

"William and Walker Letter, April 20, 1904." Booker T. Washington Papers, reel 251, Library of Congress.

Williams, Martin. *The Jazz Tradition*. New and revised edition. New York: Oxford University Press, 1983. First published 1970.

Williams, Martin, comp. and ed. *The Smithsonian Collection of Classic Jazz*. Washington, DC: Smithsonian Collection of Recordings, 1973.

Williams, Raymond. "Base and Superstructure in Marxist Cultural Theory." 1973. In *Culture and Materialism*, 31–49. London: Verso, 2005.

"Wilmot's Now Famous." *Daily Inter Ocean* (Chicago), July 1, 1891.

Wilson, Edmund. "The Jazz Problem." *New Republic*, January 13, 1926, 217–19.

Wilson, Olly. "Black Music as an Art Form." *Black Music Research Journal* 3 (1983): 1–22.

Wilson, Samuel. "Notes on Adorno's 'Musical Material' During the New Materialisms." *Music and Letters* 99, no. 2 (2018): 260–75.

Wimberly, Lowry Charles. "The Decline of the Ghost." *Prairie Schooner* 1, no. 4 (October 1927): 240–45.

Wimberly, Lowry Charles. "Spook English." *American Speech* 1, no. 6 (March 1926): 317–21.

Windley, Lathan W., comp. *Runaway Slave Advertisements: A Documentary History from the 1730s to 1790.* 4 vols. Vol. 1, *Virginia and North Carolina.* Westport, CT: Greenwood, 1983.

Wipplinger, Jonathan O. *The Jazz Republic: Music, Race, and American Culture in Weimar Germany.* Ann Arbor: University of Michigan Press, 2017.

"With the Georgia Editors: Dance Reform." *Macon Telegraph*, September 6, 1919, 6.

Wittke, Carl. *Tambo and Bones.* Durham, NC: Duke University Press, 1930.

Woods, Clyde. *Development Arrested: The Blues and Plantation Power in the Mississippi Delta.* London: Verso, 2017.

Young, Harvey. *Embodying Black Experience: Stillness, Critical Memory, and the Black Body.* Ann Arbor: University of Michigan Press, 2010.

Zimmer, Ben. "How Did We Get the Heebie-Jeebies?" Vocabulary.com, July 29, 2015. https://www.vocabulary.com/articles/wordroutes/how-did-we-get -the-heebie-jeebies/.

"Zulu Witch Doctor Real African Ruler." *New York Times*, July 8, 1928, 47.

INDEX

Page references in *italics* indicate illustrations.

becoming, 18, 25, 34

Beethoven, Ludwig van: "Ode to Joy," 6

Beiderbecke, Bix, 248

being(s)-in-labor, 8, 14, 34, 41, 42, 45, 74, 98, 112, 117, 147, 345

Bell, Lavinia, 71

Below, Fred, 394

Benjamin, Walter, 337, 338, 346, 348, 358–59, 443n78, 482n16

Bennie Moten Orchestra, 251, 290, 296, 470n67

Benson, Al, 374

Berigan, Bunny, 308

Berlin, Edward A., 169, 181, 456n27, 461n29, 466n20

Berlin, Irving, 171, 231

Berliner, Paul, 339, 340

Bernard, Mike, 176, 455n22

Bernault, Florence, 108

Berresford, Mark, 252

Berry, Chuck, 375, 385, 397, 400, 419

Berry, Daina Ramey, 45, 439n19

Best, Stephen A., 49, 215

Betty Boop (cartoon character), 273, 274

Beyoncé (musician), 422

Bie, Oscar, 237

Bigard, Barney, 296, 299, 300, 477n38

bigness in playing, 335

Billboard (magazine), 399

Bitches Brew (Davis), 409

Bjerstedt, Sven, 341

Black Atlantic, 254, 422, 436n67; temporality of, 29

Black body: alienation and, 218; blackface and, 186; Black music and, 117; colonialism and, 60–61, 62; jazz and, 233, 258; minstrelsy and, 127; nature and, 202; Negro music and, 60, 69, 215; reification and, 190, 218; repetition and, 133, 323; scabrousness of, 353; singing and, 122, 125; sound and, 218, 369; spectrality of, 417; swing and, 293; syncopation and, 204; voice and, 202–3; White perceptions of, 119; White performance and, 180; White reception of, 224

Black Devil orchestras, 246

Black Diamond (venue), 384

blackface, 154; African Americans in, 148–49, 152; aliveness and, 120, 150, 154–55; allusions to, 165; animation and, 121–22; Black body and, 76–77, 186; objectification and, 122; popularity of, 126; representations of, 416; scholarship on, 119; sensation and, 127; tragedy and, 126, 127, 413; truth and, 126; White people and, 32, 85, 121–22, 143, 149. *See also* minstrelsy

Black labor (nonmusician), 1; capital and, 15, 26, 46–47, 234, 285; collective, 43; Du Bois on, 1, 5,

6–8, 10, 26; as enslaved property, 44; "laziness" charges and, 11, 23, 137, 265, 388; past-time and, 26; reification and, 321; repetition and, 165, 197; sacrificing remunerative labor for music worship, 136; slaves' reinvention of, 27; as special, 42; superfluity and, 2, 11, 83, 94, 95, 231, 234, 413, 427; task system and enslaved, 68–69; temporality and, 29; violence and, 268, 270; White capital and, 137, 238. *See also* being(s)-in-labor; Black music labor; labor

Black life, 200; challenges of, 294; consciousness, 186; the everyday and, 404–5; interiorities, 163; phonography recordings in, 404; ragtime allusions to, 205; recordings in, 404–5, 408; southern, 27; in Southern United States, 82–84, 87, 92, 93–94, 96, 98, 100–101, 103, 377, 391, 402–3; struggles of, 197; subjugation of, 373

Black men: struggles for, 197

Black music: defined, double character, 4–5; aesthetics and, 355; affect and, ix, 3, 151; affect for non-Black listeners, ix, 3; aliveness and, 12, 13, 20, 22, 25, 33, 74, 86, 137, 143, 155, 201, 225, 257–58, 261–62, 346, 350, 353, 369, 391, 405, 406–7, 422, 423; American experience and, 339, 363; animation and, 126, 338, 370, 422–23; antebellum era and, 14, 29, 54, 73; authenticity and, 217; back-leaning tendency of, 112; becoming and, 18; Black body and, 117; Black labor and, 2; Blackness and, x; capital and, xiii, 3–4, 24, 25, 148, 227, 275–76, 362, 364; capitalism and, 67, 155, 199; as commodity, x–xi, 6, 14, 22, 23, 33, 106, 142–43, 159, 167, 178, 182, 184, 199, 200, 204–5, 212, 217, 218–19, 221, 222, 224–25, 226, 266, 275, 346, 367–68, 371, 400; in contrast to European music, 13–16; cultural context for, 13–15, 22–23; Du Bois on, 4, 5–6, 9, 11, 12, 26, 161, 186, 429n3, 430n15, 435n59; embodiment and, ix, 9–10, 29, 196, 216; epistemology and, 112; history and, 35–36, 73, 81, 87; labor and, 78, 388; loss and, 190–91, 234, 237; metamorphoses of, 37; modernity and, 81, 185; as natural resource, 85, 127, 133, 167, 179, 231, 241; negation and, 76, 363; New, 409–10, 421, 422; noise and, 101; ontology and, 38, 66, 103–4, 121, 128, 221, 333, 346–47, 363; vs. other music, 13, 16, 21, 33, 34, 76, 85, 117, 126, 218–19, 253, 370; vs. other Music, 184, 276; ownership over, 6–7, 18, 23, 24–25, 84, 85, 109, 167, 198, 226, 233, 264, 334, 367, 410, 445n11; peculiarities of, 95; performance and, 84, 88–91, 92–93, 94–95; performativity and, 15; physicality and, ix; political form of, 75; popularity of, 334–35; popular music (as dominant value in), 121, 176, 212, 222; popular music

double character: defined in relation to Black
music, xi, xiii, 4–5; alienable/inalienable
tension and, 44, 77, 86; aliveness and, 7, 13,
22; blackface and, 119; boogie and, 410; in bop,
346; counterhistory and, 65, 224; as distinctive
pattern of music circulation, 11, 34, 65, 222,
224, 410; double listening and, 364, 423, 428;
Ellington and, 324; enslaved sound and, 43; less
than/greater than pattern of, 9, 14, 121; Lukács
and, 218–19; negative dimensions and, 36, 221;
in Negro jazz, 264; Negro problem/commodity
problem and, 218–19, 221; New Black music and,
369; past-time and, 33, 187; profit-from-loss
and, 216; race-capital and, 23, 285; ragtime and,
159–88; returns into Black worlds via commercial circuits, 244; soul and, 403, 407; swing
and, 285, 296; temporal incongruity in ragtime,
164–65, 174; tragedy and, 7, 17; as truth, 10, 187;
the uncanny, 207; value dominance and, 121, 190,
296, 353, 370; vaudeville circuit, 251, 252
Douglass, Frederick, 17, 440n30, 445n13
"Down in Jungle Town" (Morse, Madden), 174,
456n32
"Down in the Jungle" (song), 239
Doyle, Peter, 378, 381
Drake (musician), xi, 425
dreams, 338
drumming, 252
Du Bois, W. E. B., 390, 449n12; on apocalypse/
revelation, 1–2, 27; on Black music, 4, 5–6, 9, 11,
12, 26, 161, 186, 429n3, 430n15, 435n59; on Black
people, 151, 191; on the color line, 38; critiques
by, 254; on labor, 3, 5, 7, 8, 25, 26, 97, 220–21,
265, 388, 430n22; musical imagery, 1–2; "Negro
problem" and, 218; reception of thought, 46; on
sensation, 262; spectacular revolution for, 18,
190, 221; on spirit, 35
Dunbar, Paul Laurence, 170, 174–75, 452n52
Dunn, Johnny, 250, 251
Durham, Eddie, 253, 296, 306
Durkheim, Émile, 65
DuSable Lounge (venue), 374
Dvořák, Antonín, 85, 160, 161, 262, 453n1
"Dynamite!" (Sly [Stone] and the Family Stone), 409

Early, Gerald, 242, 366
"East St. Louis Toodle-oo" (Ellington), 262, 302
Ebony Sax-Horn Band, 58
echo, 381
ecocriticism, 62
economies: collapse in 1929, 287, 288; enslaved
people and, 68; extensive, 139, 143; intensive,
24, 139, 143; musicians and, 90–92, 93, 95–96,
108–9, 112, 118; relational, 146; temporalities
and, 143; value and, 146
Edison, Thomas Alva, 208
EDM (electronic dance music), 420
Edmonds, Elga, 381–82
Edwards, Brent Hayes, 266, 273–74
Eisler, Hanns, 28
Eldridge, Roy, 335, 336, 344
electricity (metaphor), 225
electronic dance music (EDM), 420
Eliot, T. S., 352
Ellington, Duke, 196, 198, 248, 249, 250, 252, 253,
261, 263, 278, 289, 296, 300, 301, 302–3, 304,
305–6, 319, 323–24, 327, 328–29, 341, 348, 404,
476n19, 478n48, 479n65; "Creole Rhapsody,"
262; "Daybreak Express," 260; "East St. Louis
Toodle-oo," 262, 302; "It Don't Mean a Thing
(If It Ain't Got That Swing)," 293
Ellington Orchestra, 259, 289, 296, 326, 327, 475n11
Ellison, Ralph, 26, 119–20, 275, 331, 332, 333, 337–38,
344, 374, 391, 392–93, 481n1, 482n28, 486n3
Emancipation, 231; Black music after, xi
Emancipation Circuit (Davis), 37
embodiment: Black music and, ix, 9–10, 29, 196,
216; Blackness and, 165; dancing and, 299; history and, 29; Negro music and, 179; repetition
and, 197; sound and, 3; swing music and, 342
Emmett, Dan, 122
Engen, Trygg, 450n22
enslaved people: the body and, 45, 50, 51–52, 53,
59, 60; as commodities, 52; descriptions of,
47–50, 52–53, 54, 56–57, 58; economies and,
68; health of, 45; humanity of, 57, 59, 63; as
musicians, 2–3, 41, 42–43, 47, 53, 55–58, 59–60,
64–65, 71, 72; noise of, 47, 48, 61; ontology and,
62, 63, 66, 218; as property, 44–45; property of,
68, 69, 71, 72, 109, 387–88; religion among, 110;
rituals and routines of, 65; singing of, 69, 70;
sound and, 47, 48, 191, 218; truth among, 64
entertainment capital, 270
epistemology, 61–62, 66, 112, 343
Epstein, Dena, 55
Erenberg, Lewis A., 294, 475n5
Erlmann, Veit, 372
Ertegun, Ahmet, 375
eschatology, 1–2, 5, 27
essentialism, racial, 183–84
Eurocentrism, 4, 13, 47, 326
Europe, James Reese, 107, 161–62, 163, 164, 165,
169, 173, 174, 177, 178, 181, 182, 183, 187, 203, 215,
231, 233, 241, 249, 263, 437n79, 458n49

Hughes, Rupert, 456n35

Hugo, Victor: *Les Misérables*, 131

humanity: jazz music and, 233–34; of recordings, 217

humming, 114, 115

Hungerford, James E., 84

Hunter, Alberta, 246

Hunter, Tera W., 136, 452n46

Hurston, Zora Neale, 38, 277, 278, 279, 285, 313, 355

Hy-Tone Records, 374

"I Be's Troubled," 377, 378

Ibrahim, Abdullah, 420

"I Can't Be Satisfied" (Waters), 377–78, 379, 380

icon/iconicity, 50, 126–27, 130

ideology, 392, 398

"I Got a Woman" (Charles), 391

"I Got Rhythm" (Gershwin, Gershwin), 296

"I'll Be Glad," 273

imaginary: race and, 201, 323, 325; White people and, 155

"I'm Gonna See You," 260, 261

immaterial labor, 100

Imperial Player Roll Company, 216

improvisation, 19, 57, 107, 113, 138, 192, 230; groove and, 344; jazz and, 192, 230, 248, 257, 335–36; storytelling and, 336, 340, 341, 342; swing music and, 284, 306, 338, 342–43, 347

inalienable/inalienability: absolute commodity and (Adorno), 359–60; alienable vs., x, xiii, 4, 5, 6, 9, 20, 36, 43, 44, 77–78, 342, 398, 422, 423; blackface and, 120, 123, 127; Black music labor and, 18, 22, 212; Black music property, xi, 3, 4, 5, 7, 18, 24, 36, 37, 56, 60, 74, 167, 170, 183, 346, 350, 422; boogie and, 417; breakthrough and, 346; commodity exchange and, 106, 143, 199, 275–76, 342, 350; contradiction of commodity fetishism, 199; double character and, 44; enlivened sound, 120, 123, 188, 191, 199, 226, 369; inalienable possessions, 24, 35, 37, 146; irreducible materiality and (Pietz), 63; Negro jazz and, 226, 264, 269, 275; New Black music and, 369, 398; past-time and, 33, 60, 127, 339; piano rolls and, 212; race/racism and, 76, 86, 191; ragtime and, 167, 170; scabrous sound and, 86, 106; spectrality and, 270; swing and, 286, 314; temporality and, 286, 314; tragedy and, 73; truth and, 25, 73; value and, 86, 169–70, 269–70, 353, 369. *See also* aliveness

incorrigible/incorrigibility, 7, 190; commodity form, 201, 212, 218, 219, 221, 222, 224, 364; groove and, 345; modern jazz and, 347, 363; Negro jazz and, 224, 226, 264; New Black music

and, 369; past-time and, 381; short-circuit and, 270; swing and, 286, 294, 313, 314, 323; temporalities (Black music) and, 408, 423

In Dahomey (Cook, Shipp), 170

"Indian Love Call," 235

Industrial Revolution, 290

Ingersoll, Ernest, 143, 144, 145, 147, 148, 150

instruments, 88, 93, 116, 131, 206

intensive economies: of the past, 148; race and, 179; of swing music, 301, 314. *See also* intensive-extensive relation

intensive-extensive relation, 24, 139, 143, 222

International Sweethearts of Rhythm (musical group), 296

interregnum period, 32

"In the Groove" (Kirk), 344

"In the Morning by the Bright Light" (Bland), 413

intimacy, 335, 344, 386

Invisible Man (Ellison), 275

Ipana Troubadours (musical group), 267

irreducible quality in Black music: commodity fetish and, 209; fetish and, 124; irreducible materiality (Pietz), 32, 63, 77, 105, 106; in music generally (Steven Feld), 433n45; sound of Negro problem and, 269

Irwin, Cecil, 304

Irwin, May, 451n39

Islam, 357

"It Don't Mean a Thing (If It Ain't Got That Swing)" (Ellington), 293

"It Must Be Jesus," 391–92

"I've Got to Cool My Puppies Now" (Sam Wooding Orchestra), 246

Ives, Charles, 175

"I Wonder Who's Boogiein' My Woogie Now," 417

Iyer, Vijay, 342

Jack Pettis and His Orchestra, 309

Jackson, Mahalia, 373; "Since the Fire Started Burning in My Soul," 391

Jackson, Michael, 422

Jackson, Milt, 392

Jacobson, Matthew Frye, 239

Jagger, Mick, 403

James, Elmore, 397

"Japanese Sandman," 235

Jay, Hamilton, 130–31, 135

Jay-Z (musician), 422

jazz: use of term, 231, 241–42, 243, 245, 336, 370, 437n78; abstraction and, 270; affect and, 226, 256, 346; aliveness and, 232, 240, 244, 263, 278, 335, 340, 350–51; authenticity and, 248;

jazz (continued)

    Black body and, 233, 258; Black labor and, 241; Blackness and, 241, 243, 263; capital and, 235–36, 275–76, 357; as commodity, 225, 227–39, 240, 243, 244, 263–64, 265, 266, 269, 276, 288, 342, 357; commodity circuits and, 223–79; criticism on, 257, 316–17, 348–53, 355, 357; dancing and, 239, 240, 251; descriptions of, 236; experience and, 237–38; fetishism and, 227; as form, 238; history, 33, 216, 224, 227, 232–33, 237, 240–41, 316–17, 352–53, 465n11; hot playing, 245–46, 248–49, 277, 278, 309, 310, 362, 483n40; humanity and, 233–34; improvisation and, 192, 230, 248, 257, 335–36; innovation in, 257–58, 264–65; labor and, 250–52, 257, 264, 278–79; memory and, 223, 224, 226, 228; metamorphosis of, 226, 243, 245; metaphysics and, 275; modernity and, 228, 237, 248–49, 256, 292; musicality and, 262–63; ontology and, 340, 351; in other countries, 238–40; vs. other Music, 262, 266, 269, 276; place and, 258; popularity of, 244, 256, 267–69, 355, 367; race and, 17, 223, 226, 228, 229, 230–32, 233, 244–45, 249–50, 254; recordings, 228–29, 231, 233, 235, 243, 246, 247, 249, 250, 259–60, 268, 326–28, 348–50, 352–53, 355, 356, 357; repetition and, 234, 237; representations of, 277–78; rhythm and, 276, 292; sensation and, 235; sound formations and, 256; sounding practices and, 342–43; space and, 258; spectrality and, 277, 278; spectrality of, 353–54; storytelling and, 336, 340, 341, 342; temporality and, 228, 236, 245, 248–49, 275, 277, 278, 339, 407–8; truth and, 226, 358; value and, 224, 232, 242, 249, 262, 264, 332; vaudeville and, 254, 256–57; venues, 265; vernacularity and, 262; White people and, 17, 223, 226, 228, 229, 231, 232, 233, 235, 236, 240, 241, 242–44, 245–46, 248, 249, 264–65, 266–67, 270, 351; White power and, 257, 266, 269, 276; White supremacy and, 238, 240, 242. *See also* Whiteman, Paul

"Jazzola" (tune), 233

Jentsch, Ernst, 207, 462n35

Jim Crow era, 29, 76, 85, 103, 120, 121, 122, 125, 163–64, 184, 197, 206, 208, 214, 215, 230, 297; life during, 254–55

John, Big, 297

"Johnny B. Goode," 419

Johnson, Bunk, 414

Johnson, Charles I.: "Dill Pickles Rag," 204

Johnson, George W., 104–7, 169, 186, 198, 203; other references to, xi

Johnson, James P., 191–92, 194, 197, 212, 213, 261, 343, 414; "Carolina Shout," 195, *195*

Johnson, James Weldon, 137, 178–79, 180, 182–83, 184, 188, 274

Johnson, J. Rosamond, 170

Johnson, Keg, 336

Johnson, Pete, 414, 415

Johnson, Walter, 46–47

Jones, Dave, 257

Jones, Elvin, 409

Jones, Jonah, 284, 291, 292, 298, 303, 344–45

Joplin, Janis, 403

Joplin, Scott, xi, 182, 205–6, 212, 213, 216, 463n44; as reified body, 212–22; tragedy and, 214–15; "Maple Leaf Rag," 171, 205, 206, 212, 213–15, 456n36, 462n32

Jordan, John M., 206

Jordan, Louis, 373, 394, 404, 406, 417

"Juke," 381–82

jukeboxes, 475n12

Jungles Casino (New York), 191

Kahn, Roger Wolfe, 296

Kaluli gisalo singing, 19

Kansas (United States), 89, 90, 247, 297–98, 299, 414, 446n22

Kansas City Orchestra, 283

Kant, Immanuel, 319

Kari, Sax, 386

Keil, Charles, 392, 483n31

Kentucky (United States), 92, 124

Kentucky Club (venue), 248, 263

Keppard, Freddie, 180

Kernfeld, Barry, 255

"Ketchup Rag" (Giblin), 204

key changes, 195

Keyhole Club (venue), 384

Kildare, Dan, 215

King, B. B., 384, 390, 397

"King of the Zulus," 254

King Oliver, 247, 248, 263, 292, 472n93

Kingsley, Walter, 231, 270

Kirk, Andy: "In the Groove," 344

Kizart, Willie, 395

Knuckles, Frankie, 419

"Ko-Ko," 326

Krasner, David, 184

Krehbiel, Henry Edward, 125, 450n18; *Afro-American Folksongs*, 125–26

Krell, William: "Mississippi Rag," 461n29

Kristeva, Julia, 438n2

Krupa, Gene, 416

Kun, Josh, 372

labor: use of term, 145, 429n6; abstract, 76, 360, 432n38; animated, 76, 222; being-in-, 8, 14, 34, 41, 74, 112, 117, 147, 345; Black music and, 78, 264, 291, 324, 388; Black people in the South and, 84, 87–88, 95, 96–97, 98, 100–101, 112; the body and, 105; vs. capital, 448n73; capitalized, 137; concrete, 100, 432n38; Du Bois on, 3, 5, 7, 8, 25, 26, 97, 220–21, 265, 388, 430n22; entertainment industry and, 169; Filipino music and, 239; immaterial, 100; jazz and, 250–52, 257, 264, 278–79; living, 8, 101, 147, 220, 286, 360, 361, 388, 430n16, 485n65; micro-labor practices, 68–69; musicians and, 250–53, 287, 291, 389, 455n16; nights of labor (Rancière), 147, 221, 256; performance and, 100; productive, 74–75, 407; propertied, 109; race and, 286; reification, 218, 219; repetition and, 97, 133, 165; singing during, 69, 114–15, 140; songs and singing and, 442n72; sounding practices and, 136; surplus, 142, 143; swing and, 285; temporalities and, 11, 49, 51, 136, 137, 142, 147; total, 8, 112, 448n73; work vs. leisure, 144. *See also* Black labor
Lafayette Theater, 252
Laine, Papa Jack, 181
Lamar, Kendrick, 422
Lang, Eddie, 308
Langer, Susanne, 20
Langford, William, 238
Lanman, Charles, 442n72
"La Pas Ma La" (Hogan), 181
LaRocca, Pete, 181
Laubenstein, Paul Fritz, 314
"Laughing Song," 104–7, 186
laziness, 7, 51, 54, 58, 69, 74, 97, 137
Lazzarato, Maurizio, 100, 392
Leachman, Silas F., 451n39
Leadbelly, 414
leisure time, 144
Lemke, Sieglinde, 254
Lemonier, Thomas, 161
Leonard, Neil, 267
Le Roy Rice, Edward, 445n10
Levin, Theodor, 362
Levine, Lawrence, 29, 431n29, 435n55, 436n68, 437n74, 448n67
Levine, Robert, 458n54
Levinson, Jerrold, 432n38
Lewis, David Levering, 2, 268
Lewis, George E., 422
Lewis, Mead Lux, 317, 415
Lincoln Center, 283
Lindy Hop (dance), 298, 312
"Linger Awhile," 259

Lion, Alfred, 375
Lipsitz, George, 401
"Listening to the Mockingbird" (Winner), 181
Little Richard, 384, 386, 387, 394, 400, 403, 406, 418–19
Little Walter, 375, 381–82
Litwack, Leon, 85
"Livery Stable Blues" (Yellow Nuñez, Baquet), 181, 229, 465n9
living labor, 8, 101, 147, 220, 360, 361, 388, 430n16; abstract, 286. *See also* Black labor; Black music labor; labor
Locke, Alain, 154, 254
Locke, John, 44
Lockwood, Robert, 375
Lomax, Alan, 377
Lombardo, Guy, 247, 289, 478n46
London (United Kingdom), 420
"Long Tall Sally," 419
Lordi, Emily J., 112, 391, 392
loss, 185–86, 190–91, 234, 237, 238, 266
Lott, Eric, 22, 119, 321–22
"Louisiana Rag" (Northrup), 205
Louisville (United States), 295
lovemaking, 335
Lucas, Sam, 149
Luce, Henry, 312
Lukács, Georg, 218, 219, 220
lumpenproletariat, 92
Lunceford, Jimmie, 289, 291, 315, 325
Lunceford Orchestra, 300, 305
luxury, 84
lynching, 124, 125, 126, 268, 270–71, 295

MacConnell, Dean, 127
MacIntyre, Arthur, 192
Mackey, Nathaniel, 34, 264, 273–74
MacLean, Nancy, 84, 388
Madden, Edward, 174
Magee, Jeffrey, 260, 261, 465n7, 468n49
Maggot Brain (Funkadelic), 409
"Magnetic Rag," 212
mandolins, 88, 94, 140
Manone, Wingy, 308
"Maple Leaf Rag" (Joplin), 171, 205, 206, 212, 213–15, 456n36, 462n32
march music, 160, 174, 176–77
Marcuse, Herbert, 76
Marion, George F., 175
Marsalis, Wynton, 422
Martin, Henry, 460n9
Martin, Sara, 252

Moten, Fred, 16, 52, 432n32
Moton, Robert R., 183
mouths, 105
Mowitt, John, 397–98
Moxley, George, 90
Muddy Waters, 373, 375, 376–78, 381–82, 390; "I Can't Be Satisfied," 377–78, 379, 380; "Rollin' Stone," 379–81, 380
"Mule Train Boogie" (Taylor), 418
"Mule Walk" (tune), 194
Mumford, Lewis, 313, 480n78
Mundy, Jimmy, 284, 304, 306
Murray, Albert, 260, 297, 474n2
Murray, Sunny, 409
Music: defined (as European concept), 13, 429n7; Black music vs., 13–14, 16, 21, 33, 54, 76, 78, 85, 117, 126, 145, 173, 184, 218–19, 253; language and, 433n43; musicological debates in 1990s, 431n26; Negro jazz vs., 262, 266, 269, 276; signification and, 20–21, 26, 96, 127; sound of the enslaved vs., 56. *See also* temporalities; tonality; truth; value
musical imagery (Du Bois), 1–2
musicality: aliveness (sensations of) and, 257–58; Black, 204, 254, 300, 302; the body and, 42, 69–70; jazz and, 262–63; past-time and, 148; private/public life and, 98; racism and, 42, 62, 69–70; swing and, 291
musicianers, 87
musicians: Black vs. White, 352; children, 131–33; economies and, 90–92, 93, 95–96, 108–9, 112, 118; enslaved people as, 2–3, 41, 42–43, 47, 53, 55–58, 59–60, 64–65, 71, 72; imitation of living by, 259; labor and, 250–53, 287, 291, 389, 455n16; life for, 339, 344; sensory order of, 301; skill levels, 308; White, 308–9
mute music (Adorno, as applied in Black music), 9, 25, 188, 221, 231, 297, 357–64, 368, 390, 391, 393, 422, 423, 435n57
"My Kind of Love" (Pollack), 309
"Mystery Train," 419

National Broadcasting Company (NBC), 288
nature, 55; Black body and, 202
Nazism, 313, 354
negation: Black music and, 363
negativity, 64, 199, 359, 370; Blackness and, 294, 411
Negro, use of term, 149, 163, 169, 240, 268
Negro jazz. *See* Black music
Negro music: as historical term and its use, 3, 430n16; aliveness and, 77, 185–86, 188; antebellum era and, 63; authenticity of, 203; the body and, 60, 69, 77, 215; as category, 56;

as commodity, 133, 152–53; descriptions of, 76; embodiment and, 179; "excesses" of, 210; fleshiness and, 179; historical context, 44, 47, 60, 73; late antebellum South and, 63; "Negro problem" of, 135–36, 270; vs. other Music, 78, 145, 173, 184; ownership over, 278; performance and, 74; political form of, 75; popular music and, 163; as possession, 69, 443n73; profit and, 70; recordings, 187; repetition and, 164; rhythm of, 115; the sensible and, 70; signification and, 61; suffering and, 57; symbolism and, 56; tempo, 199; temporality and, 134, 187; truth in, 64; value and, 67, 72, 74, 75, 88, 98, 135–36, 143, 163, 170, 172–73, 218; White ownership over, 101, 178, 179, 180–81; White perceptions of, 76, 118–19; White power and, 186–87, 188; White reception of, 57–58, 67–68, 175
"Negro Problem" as problem of commodity, 212–22
Nelson, Stanley R., 482n20
Nesbitt, John, 295, 305
"New King Porter Stomp," 261
New Orleans (United States), 187, 192, 223, 227, 234, 241, 247, 248, 257, 271
New York (United States), 178, 180, 191–93, 197, 199–200, 245, 249–50, 252, 254, 255–56, 257, 287; life for musicians in, 339; Lincoln Center, 283; playing styles of musicians, 341; skill of musicians, 308; venues, 262
New York Clipper (newspaper), 152
New York Syncopated Orchestra, 227–28
Nicholas, Big Nick, 335
Nicholas, Red, 308
Nigeria, 420
Nigger in the Woodpile, The (lithograph and work by Sousa), 165, 167–68, 168, 218
"Nigger Serenade, A" (minstrel act, probably), 239
"Nobody" (Williams), 186
"Nobody Knows the Trouble I've Seen" (song), 170
noise, 366; Black music and, 101; of enslaved people, 47, 48, 61; vs. Music, 54
North Carolina (United States), 159
Northrup, Theodore: "Louisiana Rag," 205
Northup, Solomon, 41, 42–43, 53, 60, 71, 438n1
nostalgia, 223, 226

objectification: blackface and, 122
objectivity: ghostly, 222
objects: sound, 202; talismans, 350, 375
O'Connor, Patrick Joseph, 446n22
octave displacements, 213, 214
"Ode to Joy" (Beethoven), 6
Odum, Howard W., 91, 187
Offenbach, Jacques, 94

replacement of musician labor, 204; uncanniness of, 207–8

"Pleasant Moments," 212

Pleasants, Henry, 356

pleasure: Black popular music and, 385; minstrelsy and, 120–21; in music, 96

policing, 198

Pollack, Ben: "My Kind of Love," 309

popular music, 163, 245, 347–48, 356, 367, 369–71, 402, 409, 420; Black music's dominance of, 121, 176, 212, 222, 225, 245; Negro jazz and, 244–79; Negro music and, 163; racial intensity as key factor in, 243; ragtime's double movement and, 163; swing and, 416

Postone, Moishe, 150, 286, 434n51

postwar culture, 370–71, 372, 376, 377, 389, 391, 393, 401, 407

potentiality of music, 363

poverty, 69, 148, 191, 198, 220, 388, 415

Presley, Elvis, 403, 406, 419

"primitive," as notion, 141, 174, 484n54

primitivism, 274

Prince (musician), 422

private life, 98, 154

productive capital, 225

productive labor, 74–75

profit-from-loss, 18, 25, 34, 38, 70, 112, 163, 178–88, 236, 323, 353, 367, 368, 406, 407, 426

progressivism, 324

propertied labor, 109

property: abstraction of, 407; agonistic (breakthrough), 335, 338; animated, 43, 58–67, 98, 146, 182, 286, 333, 350; audible, 5, 14, 28, 48–58; Black congregations' claims on, 200; Black musicians' protection of, 160–63, 263, 370, 397, 408, 417, 426; Black piano music and, 198; boogie as, 416; collective, 342; commercial, 160; contested ownership of music, 11, 12, 114, 224, 321, 356; counterhistory and, 154; enslaved, 25; fugitive, 103; illegal ownership of (among enslaved), 18; illicit, x, 191; inalienable, 35, 37, 94, 179; land owned by African Americans, 93; living, 6; lost musical (White attempted reclamation of), 75–76, 120, 167, 191; music, 83; -of-property, 4, 22, 34, 35, 43, 48, 67, 343, 363; past-time and, 398; propertied labor and, 47, 109; R&B's property rites, 399–407; sonic descent of enslaved, 82, 218, 227, 278, 367; swing as animated form of, 293, 294; swing-time and, 315; truth and, 422; White debt to Black forms of musical, 284; White protection of, 181, 238. See also chin-music

prostitution, 413

protest, 100, 269

Pryor, Arthur, 246

Public Enemy (musical group), 422

public life, 98, 99, 100, 170, 200, 371; Black music and, 21–22

Quashie, Kevin, 96

raccoons, 131. See also coon (slur)

race: Black sound and, 258; -capital, 23, 24, 25, 26, 34, 139, 164, 369; difference and, 76, 130; essentialism, 183–84; fascination with, 217; hierarchy of, 17; imaginary and, 201, 323, 325; intensity and, 179; jazz and, 17, 223, 226, 228, 229, 230–32, 233, 244–45, 249–50, 254; labor and, 286; ontology and, 218; purity, 486n18; racial capitalism, 12–13, 73; racial time (Hanchard), 8; ragtime and, 181, 182, 185, 205, 206, 207–8, 211–12, 246; vs. reason, 244; segregation, 120, 289, 366–67; social construction of, ix; swing and, 286, 318, 329; temporalities and, 151, 313; the uncanny and, 208–10; violence against, 268

race-capital. See capital

racism: codes of, 396–97; fantasy and, 118–21; historical formations, 53–54; mechanical reproduction and, 214–15; minstrelsy and, 148; musicality (assumptions of) and, 42, 62, 254, 300; music and, 174; past-time and, 150, 151; in political theory, 45–46; rhythm and, 184; sayings and slurs, 154 (see also coon [slur]); segregation, 215, 366–67; stereotypes, 262; superiority, 140; White power and, 301

radio, 288, 289, 308, 349, 358–59, 385, 390, 401

Radio Corporation of America (RCA), 288

ragtime, 139, 457n37; use of term, 204, 370, 437n79; aliveness and, 164; Black life (allusions to) and, 205; Blackness and, 172, 174, 209–10; Black practices within, 163, 164, 174; capital advancement of, 163, 164, 165, 212; commercialism and, 202; commodity fetishism and, 172; deracinated child of capital, 172; double character of, 163, 164; end of, 159–62; inalienable qualities of, 174; metamorphosis of, 163, 176; ontology and, 207, 211; piano rolls, 190; popularity of, 162–64, 165, 168–69, 170–72, 176–77, 189, 201, 227, 228, 455n19, 457n46; the primitive (associations with), 174, 185; race and, 181, 182, 185, 205, 206, 207–8, 211–12, 246; rags, 204–5, 212; recordings, 202, 212, 214; repetition in, 163; rhythm and, 162, 164–65, 169, 292; sheet music, 205; slave songs and, 170; Sousa and, 453n4; vs. stride piano, 192, 195–96; structure of, 195;

Sanjek, Russell, 247

Sargeant, Winthrop, 316

satire, 136

"Saturday Night Fish Fry," 394

savage, notion of, 231, 234, 273, 314, 323, 480n78

Savoy Ballroom, 262, 299

Savoy Bearcats (musical group), 249, 259

saxophone playing, 301–2, 326, 327, 348, 395

scabrousness, 85–86, 87, 103; Black and White
people (between), 113; of Black body, 353; Black
music and, 107, 116, 117; Blackness and, 107–8;
the body and, 345; circulation and, 86; labor
and, 106, 150, 388; minstrelsy and, 123–24,
153–54; resonance and, 106

Scarborough, Dorothy, 270–71

scat (music), 266, 271, 273

Schaap, Walter, 311

Schaeffer, Pierre, 202

Schiller, Friedrich von, 219, 221–22; "An die
Freude," 5–6, 221, 222

Schomburg, Arthur, 125

Schuller, Gunther, 194, 201, 244, 292, 294–95,
303–4, 306, 308, 472n82, 478n46, 479n63

Schwartz, Scott W., 454n12

Scott, James, 205

secrecy, 71

secular songs, 181

seigneurialism, 46, 47

Seldes, Gilbert, 228, 241

self-: assuredness, 242; awareness, 184; legitima-
tion, 421; making, 112; mockery, 154; mutila-
tions, 123; possession, 316

Seltzer, Mark, 83

Seminole, Paul, 196

sensation: aliveness and, 18, 26, 257, 278; blackface
and, 127; Black music and, ix–x, 103–4, 265;
capital and capitalism and, 337; jazz and, 235;
minstrelsy and, 127, 143; past-time and, 27–28,
29, 32; swing and, 409; the uncanny and, 207

sermons, 111

Seroff, Doug, 81, 152

Seward, Theodore F., 57

Sewell, William, 217, 222, 367

sex work, 413

"Shake Your Feet," 260

Shall We Dance (film), 320–22, 322, 323

"Shanghai Lullaby," 235

sheet music, 102, 160, 161, 178, 204, 205, 250

Shepp, Archie, 409, 421

Shih, Hsio Wen, 250

Shipp, Jesse A., 170

"Shirt Tail Stomp," 479nn60–61

short-circuit (Black music's ability to), 221, 226,
227, 232, 264, 265, 270, 275, 277

Shorter, Wayne, 422

shouting, 72, 194–95, 196, 459n5

signification: Black music and, 21, 22, 33, 35, 216;
listening and, 16–17, 21; minstrelsy and, 149,
150; music and, 20–21, 26, 96, 127; Negro music
and, 61

Simmel, Georg, 220

Simon, Julia, 387

Simond, Ike, 153, 155–56, 253, 413, 446n24, 452n51

Sims, Willie, 395

"Since the Fire Started Burning in My Soul"
(Jackson), 391

Singleton, Zutty, 323

Sissle, Noble, 215, 233

"Skeleton in the Closet," 273

"Skeleton Jangle" (ODJB), 271

Skelly, Joseph P.: "The Boogie Man," 411–413, 412

"Slap That Bass," 320

slavery: as term, 45; being sold into, 41, 45,
55; capitalism and, 7, 46–47, 49, 59; chattel,
41–42; music as byproduct of labor, 2; ontology and, 106, 212; political economy of, 47;
recordings (echoes in), 215; songs and singing
and, 50–52, 220, 440n29; temporality and,
29, 31, 134; tragedy and, 42, 61, 62, 64; tragic
afterlife of, 17, 35

Sly Stone and the Family Stone: "Dynamite!,"
409

Small, Paul, 310

Small's Paradise (venue), 262

Smith, Bessie, 252

Smith, Buster, 247, 301–2

Smith, Charles Edward, 311

Smith, Cricket, 253

Smith, Joe, 253

Smith, Leo, 389

Smith, Mamie, 246, 251, 471n74

Smith, Mark M., 50

Smith, Pine Top, 415

Smith, Stephen Decatur, 337

Smith, Willie "the Lion," 193, 196, 198, 305

Snowden, Elmer, 249, 263

Snyder, Frederick Edward, 456n27

social class, 83–84, 96–97, 371

social construction, 183–84

social death, 48, 62

sociality, 69, 71, 74, 77, 336, 404; music and, 96

society music, 249

"Somebody Stole My Gal," 259, 261

"Something Doing," 212, 213

songs and singing: ballads, 52, 102; Black body and, 122, 125; call-response, 242; chitlin'-circuit and, 394; congregational, 19, 193; coon songs, 121, 122, 123, 128, 135, 139, 154, 165, 239, 468n43; descriptions of, 54–55, 66; groups, 137–38, 215; harmonizing, 194; improvisation, 113–14; joyful (Du Bois), 6; Kaluli gisalo, 19; during labor, 69; labor and, 69, 114–15, 140, 442n72; "Nobody Knows the Trouble I've Seen" (song), 170; recordings, 169, 170, 215–16; responsorial singing, 57, 71, 98, 135; slavery and, 50–52, 220, 440n29; sorrow, 2, 70, 161, 220, 429n3, 437n79; in Southern United States, 89, 98; spontaneous, 113–14; White reception of, 101–2, 113, 114, 137–38

"Songs of India," 235

sonic material: defined, xi, 18, 432n39, 437n78; as accumulated sounding practices in jazz, 342–43; archaic and, 151; as Black modern, 328, 333, 334; Black ownership of, 224; Black reclaiming, 294; breakthrough and, 338, 339, 343; changes in, 19, 193; coherences and coalescences of, 86, 257; devaluation and revaluation of, 187; as disruption conjuring past, 33, 73, 104, 190, 284–85, 293, 336, 343; expansion and accumulation of, 23, 24, 25, 37, 60, 83, 96, 114, 148, 244, 258, 314, 393, 408; history and, 324, 325; reiterating and innovating, 65, 66, 97, 194, 226, 232, 406; value among the enslaved, 64

sorrow, 17; Black music and, 21, 33; songs and singing, 2, 70, 161, 220, 429n3, 437n79

Sotiropolous, Karen, 184, 444n2, 445n9, 453n62

soul: use of term, 109, 390–91; Black people associated with, 124; suffering and, 112; value and, 390–91

soul (music), 370, 391, 392, 398, 403

Soul Brothers (Charles, Jackson), 392

"Soul Eyes" (Waldron), 392

sound: authenticity and, 203; Black body and, 218, 369; Black labor and, 3–4, 26, 44, 47, 48, 53, 74, 99; Blackness and, 404; embodiment and, 3; enslaved people and, 47, 48, 191, 218; as exceeding Music, 381; mystification of, 146; object, 202; ontology and, 260; ownership over, 60; personhood and, 62; of public life, 200; as scabrous, 85–86; sonic material, 37; sounding practices, 37

sound formations: accumulation and, 227; aliveness as modern in, 188, 383; Black piano rolls and, 188, 190; Black vaudeville and, 253; boogie as, 411, 416; bop and, 333; capital advancement of, 103, 165, 383; chin-music as, 131–32; concept of, 37, 78, 96; double character of, 226; as "fiction," 256; as form of life, 300; hip-hop as,

420; history and, 346; moaning as, 114; Negro jazz and, 223, 242; New Black music and, 398; ontological ambiguity of, 87, 227; past-time and, 165, 324, 393; as "phantom-like," 278; profit-from-loss and, 112; scabrous, 78, 86, 95, 101, 115, 117; stride piano and, 188, 190, 193

sounding practices: aliveness and, 8, 10, 17, 43, 75, 221, 258, 263; anomalous capitalized behavior and, 9–10, 47, 109, 172, 202, 263; Black swing and, 284, 302, 328, 342–43; blues in seminal form and, 82, 83, 140; conceived as "Negro music," 56–57, 60, 67, 119; concept of, x, 30, 37, 324; congregational, 111–12; disaggregated from Black labor, 231, 286–87; double character of, 215, 253, 403; of the enslaved, 6, 26, 32, 42, 48, 65; as genre basis, 242; hot, 249; inalienable character of, xi, 9, 10, 44, 88, 215; innovation inspired by European music, 193–94; innovation of, 67, 74, 97–98, 104, 130–31, 140–41, 177, 193–95, 253, 284, 286, 333, 342–43; as knowledge, 32; labor and, 50, 52, 136; meaning variability and, 10; modern jazz and, 342–43; Negro jazz and, 258; New Black music and, 398, 405, 409; pastime and, 174; past-time and, 27, 29, 31, 33, 63, 109, 174, 276–77, 324; profit-from-loss and, 368; as property, 4, 64, 85; repetition and, 107; scabrous, 85, 95, 104; slavery political economy and, 48; spectrality and, 275; "spirited things" and, 30; truth and, 99; value accumulation and, 11, 18, 75, 104, 190, 347; as White loss, 70, 177, 188; White musicians' use of, 115, 177; White reports about, 3, 54–55, 58–59, 63, 86, 140, 174

Sousa, John Philip, 159–62, 163, 165–68, 166, 179, 190, 218, 246, 453nn2–4

South Carolina (United States), 194–95

Southern Tones (musical group), 391–92

Southern United States: Black life in, 27, 82–84, 87, 92, 93–94, 96, 98, 100–101, 103, 377, 391, 402–3; Black popular music and, 384; Emancipation Circuit (Davis), 37; musical practices (Black), 43–44; slave ownership in, 46

sovereignty, 112

Soyinka, Wole, 30, 437n72

spectrality: abstraction and, 238, 276; appearances of body in capital, 238, 240; blackface minstrelsy and, 128, 130, 151, 152; Black vaudeville and, 82, 187; fetish and, 11, 87; ghost of modernity, 12; global circuits and, 276; Hurston and, 277–78; located in Black music, 5; as modern intervention, 38; past-time and, 28, 36; piano rolls and, 203, 206–10; primary truth and, 64; profit-from-loss and, 236; ragtime and, 179; reification/